Folklore and Society

*Series Editors*

Roger Abrahams
Bruce Jackson
Marta Weigle

*A list of books in this series appears at the end of this book.*

Publications of the American Folklore Society

New Series

*General Editor*, Patrick B. Mullen

Wobblies, Pile Butts, and Other Heroes

# Wobblies, Pile Butts, and Other Heroes

## Laborlore Explorations

Archie Green

UNIVERSITY OF ILLINOIS PRESS
Urbana and Chicago

Manufactured in the United States of America
C 5 4 3 2 1

*This book is printed on acid-free paper.*

Library of Congress Cataloging-in-Publication Data

Green, Archie.
Wobblies, pile butts, and other heroes : laborlore explorations / Archie Green.
p. cm.
Includes bibliographical references and index.
ISBN 0-252-01963-6 (acid-free)
1. United States—Occupations—Folklore. 2. Folklore—United States.
GR105.G74 1993
398'.0973–dc20 92-20168
CIP

*For Louanne*
*who lived within this book*
*before it found form*

# Contents

# Acknowledgments

In my book's explorations, I have shared trails with friends in and out of libraries, archives, museums, classrooms, union halls, and work sites. I have named many individuals and institutions directly in the book's three parts and concluding reference list. The list below serves as a "thank you" note to the stalwarts who have long preserved and presented work traditions.

For many insights, I have fallen back on memories of conversations—formal or informal—on the job and in the academy. Here I name friends whose thoughts echo through the book: Roger Abrahams, Tom Adler, the late Jimmy Allan, Barry Ancelet, Henry Anderson, June Anderson, Jane Archer, Julie Ardery, Nancy Balz, Dick Bauman, Marty Blatt, Laurel Blaydes, Joe Dan Boyd, Dick Boyden, Joey Brackner, Beverly Brannan, Maria Brooks, Hal Cannon, Bob Cantwell, Sandra Cate, Paul Clemens, Gerry Cohen, Norm Cohen, Ron Cohen, John Cowley, Rodger Cunningham, Harlan Daniel, Joanne Delaplaine, Doug DeNatale, Barbara Dennis, Gil Donahue, Joe Doyle, John Durham, Doris Dyen, Gene Earle, Lisa Feldman, Carl Fleischhauer, Ronald Foreman, Bill Friedland, the late Phil Garman, Joe Glazer, Ken Goldstein, Goddard Graves, Jim Green, the late John Greenway, the late Sarah Gunning, Diane Hamilton, the late Wayland Hand, Phyllis Harrison, Bess Hawes, the late George Hayward, Mike Heisley, Jack Henning, Joe Hickerson, Fred Hoehler, Fred Hoeptner, Maggie Holtzberg-Call, Dick Hulan, Sandy Ives, Alan Jabbour, Miriam Johnson, Paula Johnson, Walter Johnson, Rosemary Joyce, Morry Kadish, Ed Kahn, Bernie Karsh, Debora Kodish, Joyce Kornbluh, the late George Korson, Michio Kunitani, the late MacEdward Leach, Jim Leary, Tim Lloyd, Guy Logsdon, Eleanor Long, Richard March, Ottilie Markholt, Ellie Matus, the late Brenda McCallum, Paul McKenna, Doyle Moore, Mike Munoz, the late Joe Murphy, Bill Myers, the late John Neuhaus, Tom Nicolopulos, Bruce Nelson, Nancy Noennig, Barry O'Connell, Glenn Ohrlin, Gerry Parsons, Oscar Paskal, Dan Patterson, Manuel Peña, the late Norm Pierce, Bob Pinson, Agnes Pritchard, Mary Quinn, the late Anne Rand, Roger Renwick, the late Dick Reuss, Ralph Rinzler, Dave Roediger, Shelly Romalis, Franklin Rosemont, Neil Rosenberg, Al Rosenstein, Sal Salerno, Dave Samuelson, Jack Santino, Bob Sayers, Saul Schniderman, Paul Schroeder, Ted Schuchat, Frank Scott, Mike Seeger, Gary Smith, Nick Spitzer, Dick Spottswood, Ron Stanford, Ellen Stekert, Chris Strachwitz, Shiro Takahisa, Frances Tamburro, the late Peter Tamony, David Taylor, Lori Taylor, the late Fred Thompson, Judith Tick, the late Merle Travis, Joe Uehlein, Dell Upton, Dick Vlach, John Vlach, Martin Wagner, Tom Walker, Don Watson, Stan Weir, Dave Whisnant, the late D. K. Wilgus, Brett Williams, Joe Wilson, Doug Wixson.

In the progression from manuscript to book, Bruce Jackson, Michael Kazin, Bob McCarl, Yvonne Lockwood, and Pat Mullen reviewed the initial drafts. I benefited from all their suggestions. Bruce Bethell and Patricia Hollahan handled copyediting chores with equanimity. Finally, Judy McCulloh at the University of Illinois Press guided this book in all its steps.

Part One

# Keywords

"Sunday on the Waterfront"

# A Shipwright's Journey

Upon entering the shipwright's trade, I found myself navigating between shoals of mechanical secret, union custom, and verbal art. Job literacy consisted of reading blueprints or handling print-derived templates. Blueprints seemed related to books, for they literally held white lines and symbols on blue paper sheets. By contrast, templates fashioned out of sweet-smelling spruce battens appeared as mysterious as rune stones or cuneiform tablets.

Formal knowledge, sanctioned by the paper and pattern of engineer or architect, coexisted with abundant lore: wordplay, arcane nomenclature, raw jests, admonitory tales, outlandish boasts, bawdy humor. Journeymen took apprentices and helpers in hand by cautioning them to listen to elders: "Don't play the fool; use your mouth for more than a flycatcher."

I gauged my growth on the launching ways and on the hull under construction by learning to work, look, and talk like a shipwright. In time, these combined traits led to "hitting the deck" at union meetings, to wrestling with matters of concept and cause. Ultimately, such verbal experience carried over to new scenes in college classroom and legislative lobby.

Fifty years have elapsed since my introduction to adze and maul, to mold loft and ship ways. While writing this laborlore book, I have talked to students and workers, wanting to bring them together within joined audiences. San Pedro pile drivers and Tacoma longshoremen as well as Santa Cruz undergraduates and Chapel Hill graduates have shared daily experience and cultural exploration with me. At some sessions, discourse has tailored itself to the current work site; at others, metaphor has colored recall of past toil.

For auditors in the union hall and the college seminar, I have questioned those rhetorical conventions that divide toilers from thinkers. Pragmatic workers do not live immune from language's charm or legend's hold. Present-day construction "stiffs" relish explanation of such nicknames as *pile butt, rod buster, rust eater, tin knocker,* and *wood butcher,* as well as tales about what these "hands" do. I have chosen to treat not only the etymology of *pile butt* but also pile-driving rituals. I have called up ancient stories of Roman bridge builders as ceremonial pontiffs engaged in sacred rites at the Tiber, anecdotes about Glaswegian stevedores practicing sabotage at the Clyde, and tales of San Francisco electricians honoring their old-timers with memorable retirement ceremonies.

This book can be seen simultaneously as a mosaic of traditional anecdotes, a lament for antique skills, an invocation to the search for workplace dignity, and a picture of inventive playfulness on the job. These complementary elements converge in a series of case studies encompassing time-tested laborlore forms. Eight chapters treat single texts and their variants, their connections and enactments; two chapters bring disparate texts together. In brief, the ten studies cover a pair of heroes, two words, two tales, two ballads, a ritual grabbag, and an obscure trade in which patterned material of great value surfaces and mingles.

Other students have arranged similar data by chronology, geography, theoretical construct, or theme. One approach does not automatically establish itself as superior to the others. Training in folklore, language, and literature has inclined me to detailed studies of particular texts: When do workers create songs and stories, ballads and blues? How do words jump boundaries? Why do some tales live beyond others? How does expressive learning shape notions of identity and reality? What communities retain or reject traditional gifts?

Here I sketch something of one individual's journey leading to a concern for occupational culture. After my undergraduate years, I turned to San Francisco's waterfront and construction trades; Paul Bunyan and John L. Lewis then contended for my loyalties. I could envision no greater good than blue-collar status, no gift more rewarding than fabricating a buoyant vessel—frame by frame, plate by plate. Leaving California for Illinois in 1960, I looked back at shipwrights, pile drivers, longshoremen, and building tradesmen as members of a folk society; their expressive culture fit the rubric *occupational folklife.*

My sense of skilled workers forming an enclaved community owed much to Robert Redfield's studies of Yucatan peasantry. Before encountering his categorical term *folk society,* reading labor history by Louis Adamic and Samuel Yellen had prepared me for ethnographic views of work sites. I especially enjoyed descriptions such as Katherine Archibald's *Wartime Shipyard* and Joseph Mitchell's "Mohawks in High Steel." I had worked at Moore's Drydock, described by Archibald; she had labored there (on the Oakland Estuary) in a steamfitters' gang. Her book provided a model: This is the way to represent a work scene—objectively, boldly! Similarly, Mitchell signaled with great flair: You, too, can honor fellow workers!

I began writing to members of the American Folklore Society, sharing experiences with collectors who had delved into the culture of miners, railroaders, seafarers, and oil-field hands. George Korson and Wayland Hand offered the proverbial sesame—seed, oil, fragrance. In the late 1950s, I coined the term *laborlore* for use in letters and workers' classes. It appeared in print first in my tribute to John Neuhaus (1960) and subsequently in an article title for *Industrial Relations* (1965). The coinage originally distinguished union material from its parent industrial body, but in recent years I have blurred the distinction between "pure and simple" union lore and workers' traditions in their totality (1989).

Writing from Copenhagen, Flemming Hemmersam offered "Workers' Folklore and Worker Culture," a careful exposition in which he examined European definitions of central terms, including *laborlore,* without skirting controversy or matters of dogma. Previously, Martin Bulmer and John Clarke had each edited useful essay collections on British working-class culture. Hemmersam, Bulmer, Clarke, and their associates offer impressive reading leads, but these do not apply to our own country. We still lack a comprehensive bibliography of American laborlore.

During 1977 in Washington, D.C., I had occasion to meet the medievalist and historian Bronislaw Geremek. We exchanged views about our specialties—Polish gypsies on his part, Wobbly songs on mine. In 1980, Geremek helped Lech Walesa forge bonds between Gdansk shipyard workers and Poland's intellectuals. The historian and the electrician, along with many friends in Solidarity, brought together two internal camps in joint resistance to a repressive regime.

No one knows whether American workers and intellectuals will forge similar alliances. We have lived for decades with dichotomies of Archie Bunkers and philosopher kings. In the glow of television comedy, workers and intellectuals dwell in procrustean beds doomed to continued isolation. No single book holds the power to break stereotypes or build coalitions, yet I would like my effort here to reach laborers and academicians alike, to add sinew to their dialogue.

What compelling barriers divide workers from observers? I have welcomed conversations between folk artists and museum curators, lumber-pile storytellers and modern novelists. Life experience has tilted me toward a pluralistic philosophy, away from seductive paradigms of singularity. I am unimpressed by teleological arguments for working-class destiny, for victory's inevitability. Laborlore messages can be oracular as well as irrational, tawdry, bizarre, paradoxical, platitudinous, or cosmic. To touch this prism questions the Sphinx.

Clearly, reading and experience merge as roads into laborlore. The route of practice, of "doing it," seems effortless to workers who express themselves and comment on creativity: to linger at a water cooler when a crony gossips; to observe a cabinetmaker hide a pitch pocket with an insert "dutchman"; to ask how this ethnic tag became a sign of skill; to treasure an old-timer's hand tools; to display ship models at a hiring hall; to join in a picket-line chant; to carry a parade banner.

Folklorists who examine talk and its meanings cross trade and disciplinary boundaries, but I must offer readers a caveat about the range of my book. It does not survey all work scenes, the entire skill rainbow, the myriad languages, or every tag used by American workers in self-identification. The roster of roads I have not walked is full. Other scholars have approached some of these varied work areas: prisons, sports, health, gambling, high tech—the list stretches to the horizon.

Nor does my span of chapters connect every included item of lore to all its variants found in our land or overseas. Within *Only a Miner* and a series of articles on graphics for the *JEMF Quarterly,* I pursued the talismanic term *folk,* a keyword that wears a thousand masks. These efforts, along with those of colleagues, only begin to reveal the provocative nature of cultural discourse.

Some books can be seen as political platforms hammered out of convenient planks. Radicals will prefer the symbolic soapbox, which is also a stage for creed and polemic. Conscious of my book's planks, I have named a few (pluralism, syndicalism), but I have left it to readers to voice the rest.

I have tested laborlore research with attention to two areas, public folklife's growth and Appalachian regionalism. In tracing the move of civic agencies into folkloric areas, I have drawn upon works such as Debora Kodish's biography of Robert Winslow Gordon, who gathered ballads from shellbacks and hoggers, "met" many hundreds of workers via the pulp magazine *Adventure,* and initiated the Library of Congress's folk archive. In 1979, writing about Sarah Ogan Gunning, I paid respect to a Kentucky woman who tied militant coal-union songs to mountain balladry and hymnody. Robert Cantwell, Rodger Cunningham, and David Whisnant have enriched my efforts in limning Sarah and in seeing the multiple clouds under which she and her neighbors lived.

The case studies that follow expand my initial treatment of the term *laborlore;* in them I ease open the gates that separate jobsite from union-hall culture. In short, I am more concerned with similarities in workers' traditions than with distinctions based on organizational affiliation. For this book, *laborlore,* broadly conceived, covers expressivity by workers themselves and their allies: utterance, representation, symbol, code, artifact, belief, ritual. Such expansiveness cuts through conventional schemes that layer culture as well as divide it ideologically.

At this juncture, I identify the core subjects within the chapters to follow. Part 1, "Keywords," comprises three sections. "A Shipwright's Journey" is my prefatory statement. "Putting Laborlore to Work" takes up definitions, techniques, and unresolved problems and credits sister disciplines. "Tiffany Touch and Talking Back" treats recorded music, film, and art as they carry work's meaning beyond specific jobs.

Part 2 presents ten case studies:

1. John Henry remains the major American folk hero, known in ballad, work song, and traditional narrative. I focus on the visual John Henry, commenting on pictorial representations of the legendary steel-driving tunnel stiff.

2. Joe Hill, martyred songwriter of the Industrial Workers of the World, can be seen as a folk hero if we accept his union as constituting a folk society, enclaved by ideological conviction. I touch his significance with a close analysis of the popular song (by Alfred Hayes and Earl Robinson) memorializing the IWW bard. Juxtaposed narratives about the twin demigods Joe Hill and John Henry help us measure work culture's place in society at large.

3. The word *Wobbly* has long intrigued historians and lexicographers. I treat this IWW nickname as a social text holding intrinsic value and as a building block in the construction of many labor narratives. Matters of origin, extension, and meaning intersect in tracing this word's travels.

4. "Fink: Streets, Docks, Factories" dissects a word both pejorative and playful. It has moved through student, criminal, and unionist ranks, from Germany to the United States. *Fink* carries as much dynamite as any labor shibboleth.

5. Harry "Haywire Mac" McClintock relates a Butte, Montana, copper tale, "Marcus Daly Enters Heaven," with roots in a thousand-year-old Norse tradition. Mining magnate Daly stands in contrast to John Henry and Joe Hill. We enjoy Mac's story for its overt oppositional content and its abundant allusion: survival by wits, inversion of status, power in narrative.

6. No workers escape job anecdotes of cuckoldry and sexual impotence. "Home-Front Harassment," a compensatory tale with many variants, reveals difficulties in treating feminist concerns within trades so long dominated by men.

7. The Homestead, Pennsylvania, steel strike (1892) precipitated a number of ballads and poems. John J. Kelly's Tin Pan Alley piece had appeal within occupational communities far beyond the Monongahela River. Today, Kelly's ballad belongs to labor-union educators and folksong "revivalists."

8. A North Carolina textile rhyme of 1900 penned by a Piedmont "linthead" made its way variously to a hillbilly phonograph

record, a communist journal, a Broadway stage play, a university archive, and folksong "revival" performers. My focus on one song's path calls attention to complex strands in cultural analysis.

9. In a study of work rituals, sacred and profane, I treat diverse events: Labor Day parades, charivari, retirement customs, and acts of sabotage. Explosive sabotage has been talked about more often than practiced. A set of linked anecdotes about shovel blades illustrates how rhetoric blankets ritual.

10. Naming each other *pile butt* and *pile buck*, members of pile-driving crews have hoisted figurative pennants over their rigs on land and at the water's edge. This closing case study delineates a trade setting in which various folkloric genres function. Today, pile-driving speech touches on concern for land development and ecology. How will tomorrow's builders use yesterday's lore in protecting the earth itself?

Part 3, the Afterword, turns to a memory of Spokane Tom, an Irish pile butt and shipwright. In rescuing him from anonymity, my recollections raise questions about limits within laborlore exploration. Can folklore, a humanistic discipline, touch labor economics or industrial relations? Will American workers accept *folk* as a viable term in self-definition? How do we best recycle job tradition?

These case studies, keywords, and afterword compose a dwelling of fourteen rooms. I have not built each room to the same width or length; nevertheless, I have attempted a sound structure. Readers will bring their own metaphors to my book: manse, vessel, maze. Regardless of the chosen image, I have utilized building materials of varied bulk and hue: empirical research, personal experience, reflexive values. Questions resound in all my dwelling's corners: How do scholars conjure persuasive queries and match their curiosity to needs in subject realms? How do workers unearth their relics and erect their monuments?

Throughout my studies I send a persistent message: young workers should decode job mysteries, articulate craft lore, and write their own histories. Those who undertake such tasks will find librarians, museum curators, and audiovisual archivists to be indispensable friends. By way of example, I suggest a few "tools" found within documentary centers. A journal article or sound recording can literally open laborlore vistas.

Edward "Sandy" Ives has written widely on Maine woodsmen. In "The Teamster on Jack MacDonald's Crew," he discusses a local ballad touching a teamster's death near Mount Katahdin in 1908. Earl Stubbs rated no obituary, only a song recalled by Joseph Walsh at his Prince Edward Island home. I shall not reveal Ives's findings, but I commend his exemplary essay. Greatly removed in time and place, in 1952 the Sterling Jubilees of Bessemer, Alabama, offered a soul-stirring piece entitled "The Spirit of Phil Murray." Honoring the head of the CIO and its steel union, the Jubilees harmonized, "God has called Mr. Murray home."

The woods ballad and the gospel song hold ten score contrasts in style and setting, yet they touch hands as elegies composed by rank-and-file workers to respect companions, whether in a lumber camp or a union suite. Fortunately, both compositions can be heard on *Songs of Labor & Livelihood*, edited by Richard Spottswood for the Library of Congress. The Murray memorial appears on two other LPs: Joe Glazer's *Songs of Steel & Struggle;* Doug Seroff's *Birmingham Quartet Anthology.* Brenda McCallum adds substantially to our sense of the intersection between work and worship in songs such as the Murray farewell.

I have offered these representative references to articles and recordings as travel signs and puzzle clues. Sherlock Holmes has looked over my shoulder as I searched for this book's details. Figuratively, laborlore bibliography/discography lives on Baker Street. Apprentices in occupational folklife will mount future investigations and discover distant galaxies of meaning as they convert findings into exhibit, monograph, sound recording, or film. Tasks in demystifying workers' tropes, antique or emergent, will never cease, for work itself never ends.

A work-inspired metaphor closes my prefatory remarks. Within a waterfront scene, a superannuated docker, perhaps injured, receives a pension and serves as a watchman. He sits, guarding a pier and its towering container crane with a red warning flag. Out of sight, an unseen computer technician has prepared a printout directing the operator to stow the numbered boxes. The watchman cannot peer into the containers to comment upon sealing wax or fragrant spice, nor can he chat with the operator overhead. Unable to master computer or crane, the old-timer knocks together a flower box from scrap lumber. He plants geraniums.

My book asks why a flower box, why geraniums, why any gesture to mark pier or crane. Observing the box, a young longshoreman may laughingly dismiss the watchman's pastime, while a nearby shipwright explains the flowers: earth's fertility defies computer and crane.

Questions about the meaning of metaphor continue to surround the rubric *laborlore* and its parallels. Problems posed in my studies will not vanish. Union membership rises and falls; individuals veer from emotional support to indifference to hostility; work sites appear and disappear; old techniques linger as new ones spring into being; worldwide competitors move into local factories and shopping malls; and work's role in signifying status surges with each tide.

New workers transcend their daily experience by seeking rewards beyond the horizon. Others are overwhelmed by toxins, ethnic clash, work's pace, or work's lack. Some resist, some endure, and others fall under the juggernaut. Together they invoke ballad, blues, yarn, prank, and rite to define identity. Not all toilers find comfort in the fold of self or community. Not all build flower boxes, literally or imaginatively. Nevertheless, job wisdom persists that touches geraniums—in all their guises. Explorers who seek and guard the lore of the artisan and the activist will not run out of themes and tasks for the century to come.

Ironworkers on the Mall

# Putting Laborlore to Work

Work, whether pleasant or painful, helps define individual identity. Strangers ask, "What do you do?" We reply to casual or ideological queries by naming skills or places of employment. We relate occupation to race, ethnicity, gender, region, and religion in struggling to comprehend the essential reality of self or community. Our daily tasks give lives coherence; by contrast, the lack of work denies our basic humanity. Workers uncomfortable with abstract discourse assert, "I'm a workaholic" or "Hard work's my middle name." Philosophers may translate such vernacular lines into "I work, therefore I am."

Working people range widely in naming and evaluating their conditions. Some see toil only as degrading and life defeating. Others see work as central to life's meaning, as a precondition for creation or worship. Frequently, workers judge their own labor by comparing it to that of others and by asking, are their jobs more or less rewarding than mine? To comprehend esoteric skills, we talk with acquaintances and probe the nature of their respective livelihoods. In addition to listening to anecdotal descriptions, we read about work in the press or periodicals and view films touching on craft and calling.

Although only a few mariners serve on modern whaling vessels, some continue to read Melville's *Moby Dick*. Voyaging vicariously on the *Pequod* helps us understand Ahab's quest and his harpooners' tasks. Similarly, Twain's *Life on the Mississippi* reveals secret traditions of river pilots. In recent decades, *The Grapes of Wrath*, *On the Waterfront*, *Norma Rae*, and *Matewan* have enlarged visually our sense of the lives of the field hand, the dockwalloper, the linthead, and the coal digger.

Film and prose fiction can strengthen our appreciation of the work of others. We accept external imaginative forms as complementary to the lore generated and circulated within our respective occupational communities. A worker laughs at a buddy's nickname, sends an apprentice after a bucket of volts, buries a silver coin in mortar, curses a callous boss, covers for a mate's mistake, or leaves for home early after a skyscraper's topping-out ceremony. Such acts occur without any articulation of academic terms.

Using many rubrics, men and women at work share story, song, brag, jest, prank, custom, belief, artifact, and ritual. I describe such laborlore in case-study chapters, moving from particular words to patterned words, to words gathered in tale, ballad, or rite, to clustered words explaining art and music. Novelists, playwrights, historians, ethnographers, sociologists, and economists also pull job lore to the surface. My belief in working people linked with a commitment to occupational-culture studies lets me bring analytic concepts to bear on techniques and on-the-job expression.

This book brings together definition, documentation, and attention to unresolved problems. Readers may ask whether laborlore's past and present is seamless, whether its themes hold future promise. How does the word *labor* combine with *heritage, tradition,* or *lore?* Do such combinations produce a panacea or a grail? Do these links conjure pictures of brawny workers in sweaty toil, defeated workers at rusting mill gates, cool workers at gleaming display terminal screens, exuberant workers at strike demonstrations, or somber workers at memorial services?

Standing alone, *heritage* implies transmission, legacy, and gift; it encompasses privilege and exploitation, as well as egalitarian promise. An individual's inheritance derives from family and friends. The collective heritage of workers resides in a congeries of intangibles—belief in solidarity, respect for skill, shared vocabulary, idealized vision. Unionists are not immune to disputes over heritage or disagreements about its largesse.

*Tradition,* which is itself a prismatic term, turns constantly, like a sun-seeking poppy. I rely on a triadic application of the concept: oral transmission and craft imitation as social process, a corpus of expressive forms, a norm that interweaves pejorative and ameliorative elements. These abstractions can be voiced: for example, I heard shipwrights' traditions on launching day; traditionally, we marched on Labor Day; Local 1149's tool auctions for deceased members touched a deeper vein of tradition than did subsequent impersonal welfare payments.

Delving into laborlore necessitates attention to chronology, whether of a millennium or a decade. When did a worker first log esoteric trade nomenclature in a diary? When did a unionist, sensing a charter's emblematic role, carry it home after a local disbanded? When did a public library gather "labor question" ephemera for a special collection? Which museum first prepared formal exhibitions of work processes? Which folklorists pioneered in presenting job skills as public display events? Who bounded occupational folklife as a discrete "field"?

I have no ready answers but advance such questions to probe matters of institutional consciousness and to satisfy the historical record. More than a century ago, Jane Addams visited Toynbee Hall, a London settlement house founded by students of Tolstoy and Ruskin. In 1889, she established a similar mission in Chicago, Hull-House, to help immigrants assimilate and working people cope with raw brutality. By 1900, Addams added a Labor Museum to Hull-House—not to hold union artifacts, but rather to heal rifts between "foreign" parents and their American-born children. The trauma of transatlantic passage and the trapping of whole families in slum sweatshops often resulted in the children's failure to share their parents' traditional wisdom.

The Labor Museum opened with textile-craft demonstrations (spinning, weaving, carding, dyeing) and objects (for example, Navajo looms on loan from the Field Museum). Parents from European lands displayed their family treasures; children offered folksongs. Visiting lecturers expounded on Roman slave labor and other topics of the day. Addams carefully bound strands from two movements, arts and crafts and social reform. In so doing, she anticipated the rise of community and neighborhood museums. As we honor Jane Addams as reformist, feminist, and peace advocate, we need also to laud her imaginative turning of an old gymnasium into America's first labor museum (Cushman).

Jane Addams avoided neither debate over immigration nor the interminable fights between radicals and laborites coupled to sectarian tension within parties on the left. Such conflict has long fascinated participants and historians. From one such dispute, I cull an early view of laborlore.

During 1894, Daniel DeLeon's Socialist Labor party members had joined Knights of Labor New York District Assembly 49, thereby breaking Grand Master Workman Terence V. Powderly's grip on the Knights. Buoyed by temporary victory, the DeLeonites divided on the matter of building an industrial union or "converting" AFL craft unions to their cause. In July, Charles Sotheran, a dissident SLP member and inveterate bibliophile, challenged DeLeon's right to membership in the Knights; the latter unceremoniously expelled the former. Alluding to Sotheran's "encyclopedic knowledge of the early socialist movement," DeLeon trumpeted that the SLP had no room for "this 250 pound perambulating scrap book and historic junk shop" (Quint, 155).

Sotheran was neither the first nor the last big man to collect labor/radical esoterica, whether mental oddment or artifactual treasure. Further, DeLeon was not the first hardhead—pragmatic or principled—to scorn antiquarians, romantics, junkers, curiosity-shop proprietors, and keepers of the tribal flame. Ideally, Charles Sotheran should have added his compulsion to Jane Addams's patient vision at Hull-House. I salute both for their passions.

This flashback to the 1890s, to labor within museum walls and a quarrel on the left, isolates just two kinds of attention to the culture of work. By the era of Addams and Sotheran, trade-union editors had assimilated evangelistic fervor in their journal pages. Well before Labor Day or May Day became formal holidays, Fourth of July speakers—echoing the self-evident truths of 1776—urged working people to re-declare independence: republicanism, mutual endeavor, abolition of wage slavery. In short, toilers had already internalized much spirited rhetoric, political or poetic, and had learned to use it in economic arenas.

Today, we may find early union language to be flowery or inflated. At times, it becomes easier to accept high rhetoric in visual form than to attempt its aural reconstruction. For example, from the inception of colonial guilds and friendly societies, workers marched under heraldic banners and mounted printed charters in elaborately carved cases in labor temples. Such dramatic artifacts give solidity to our present understanding of labor's past. When anarchists, socialists, and syndicalists soapboxed on urban corners, their rebellious language energized traditional acts. It is now equally difficult to recapture radical and republican speech, whether from editorial page or soapbox. Hence, in looking back at pioneers, we tend to stress their contradiction in action, tension in belief, or failure in cause above their substantial contributions.

Working people in our own century's last decade "hear" resonant voices by turning back to Jane Addams and Charles Sotheran. A third figure from their era who helps us recapture the past, William James, lives as an exponent of American pragmatism, pluralism, and radical empiricism. One of his illuminating passages addresses the outsider's discovery of work's dimensionality. During an 1892 public lecture, "What Makes Life Significant," the philosopher James described a train trip to Buffalo:

> The sight of a workman doing something on the dizzy edge of a sky-scaling iron construction brought me to my senses very suddenly. And now I perceived, by a flash of insight, that I had been steeping myself in pure ancestral blindness, and looking at life with the eyes of a remote spectator. . . . Heroism . . . was before me in the daily lives of the laboring classes . . . on every railway bridge and fire-proof building that is going up to-day. On freight-trains, on the decks of vessels, in cattle-yards and mines, on lumber-rafts, among the firemen and the policemen, the demand for courage is incessant; and the supply never fails. . . . As I awoke to all this unidealized heroic life around me, the scales seemed to fall from my eyes; and a wave of sympathy greater than anything I had ever before felt with the common life of common men began to fill my soul. (274)

Listing such exemplars as James, Sotheran, and Addams does not do justice to their respective roles in helping us penetrate laborlore thickets. New students who plunge ahead will fashion their own chaps and name their own guides. Here, I pause to elaborate the work of Benjamin A. Botkin, who popularized *industrial folklore* as a discrete rubric, thus raising questions that still trouble today's specialist in occupational folklife.

As a young teacher of English in Oklahoma, Botkin gravitated to folklore, regional studies, and local-color literature. In Depression years he added to these subjects a restless need to utilize knowledge beyond the classroom. Becoming the folklore editor for the WPA Federal Writers Project in 1938, he faced a world of guidebooks, experimental theater, "living lore," and "folk-say." He also encountered urban and industrial material, at times championed by Marxist activists with beliefs in art as a class weapon.

Botkin, favoring New Deal norms, met WPA field collectors who had gathered the lore of seamen, sandhogs, hackies, and garment cutters. We do not know who first joined *industrial* and *folklore* as a generic category. Levi C. Hubert used the new label to cover an interview with members of the Brotherhood of Sleeping Car Porters in their Manhattan hall (January 3, 1939). The novel term caught on in Chicago, where Jack Conroy, Nelson Algren, and other Writers Project writers extended its use from collection to literary adaptation (Green 1978a).

WPA editors in New York and Chicago planned (but never published) two work anthologies: *Chase the White Horse* and *A Real Chance to Work*. These books were never published. However, Ann Banks made such material available to new audiences in *First Person America;* a selection of Conroy's work pieces had appeared previously in Botkin's first popular anthology, *A Treasury of American Folklore*. In 1949, Botkin moved beyond presentational forms to a succinct entry on "industrial lore" for the influential *Standard Dictionary of Folklore, Mythology, and Legend*. His statement anticipated present theoretical concerns (Hirsch; Widner).

Jack Conroy has poked fun at his apprenticeship as a "toad" (car builder and repairer) in Moberly, Missouri: "Any boy who was big enough and looked bright enough to come in out of the rain could go to work at the Wabash Railroad shops and remain there, with interludes of strikes and layoffs, until he retired at sixty" (1985, ix). Conroy's irreverence and Botkin's universality gave industrial folklore a lift into public consciousness.

Botkin's and Conroy's contributions paralleled efforts by Zora Neale Hurston, J. Frank Dobie, Langston Hughes, Meridel Le Sueur, and their peers who veered from the unadorned representation of folkloric bits and pieces to the elaborate refashioning of such findings in short stories, plays, and novels (Wixson 1993). In looking back at these authors, we can respect their creativity without compromising current efforts to preserve and present work culture as it actually emerges at countless job sites.

I am aware that a few academicians have been distressed by literary treatments of Paul Bunyan, Joe Magarac, and other colorful work giants. This negative view occasionally has spilled over into criticism of labor's goals. To treat workers' culture in all its aspects, we ought not to be deflected by questions of where particular heroes originated. Rather, we need to understand the complex relationship of folklore to popular culture. Who expanded the Paul Bunyan narratives—and why? Most workers I know are able to distinguish their lore from that offered externally in their name. After surviving job pranks and comic exaggeration of work loads, they learn to handle hokum in all its guises.

Essentially, collectors and commentators attracted to work's culture assemble forms, analyze findings, and remark on ideas embedded in song or story, artifact or ritual. Together, students reveal the constant alteration in each job's expressive form and advance explanations for change, whether it be generation, retention, erosion, reconstruction, dissemination, or regeneration.

Collectors do not present their findings in isolation. Preservation leads to presentation; acquisition circles back to statements of theory. Individuals concerned with laborlore are not immune from ideological dispute. Each observer selects a baseline from a variety of analytic positions. Some see work culture as substance—monolithic or fragmented, granitic or sandy. Others focus on given perspectives—empirical, structural, Marxian, Freudian. Still others put aside issues of substance in favor of process—creolization, creation of a counterhegemony, image manipulation, consensus building, class formation, identity shifts.

No savant in any particular ivory tower holds a monopoly on work-culture study. We probe a ballad's mystery with the same tools whether its plot turns on ethereal romance or grinding toil, whether its characters are shining knights or grimy miners. Laborlore researchers pay little attention to the affiliations of specialized students, for they welcome alternate insight. We come to our exploration from Cockaigne's lands and the Monongahela's banks.

Enthusiasts reach folklore from academy or job site and try various cloaks for size: *workers' culture, anthropology of work, labor's heritage, occupational folklife.* For example, Robert McCarl speaks out of an apprenticeship as a sheet metal "tin knocker" (1974). Experience heightens his concern that carriers of work tradition have some control over the use of their bounty. Maggie Holtzberg-Call, having engaged in printing fine books, turns to a study of displaced typographers. Interest in object and artistry propels her to the human dimension of technological change. She reports on workers formerly called the "aristocrats of labor."

Paula Johnson documents the lives of women at the "bottom" of the labor force, Maryland's Patuxent River oyster shuckers: black, rural, seasonally employed, untouched by innovative technology or media attention. Patricia Cooper limns cigar makers using a feminist perspective to frame the intersection of class and gender within a competitive industry. She is sensitive to union exclusivity as a destructive social force. Hal Rammel joins vernacular to popular-culture modes while explicating work's utopian impulses. Unafraid of the irrational, he enlarges our feeling for those spells and charms that decorate the work scene.

The similarities between these five explorers balance their differences. Essentially, folklorists, historians, and their peers "read" work's ontological chronicle to make sense of human existence. No single shibboleth reveals all of work's mysteries, for laborlore encompasses job technique, customary practice, verbal art, and ideological cause. Some investigators view an item of lore as a template to modify work or to reduce its burden. Others see this same item as pointing to new structures, new relationships of power.

Generally, social historians find economic and political codes of dominance and opposition within traditional societies. Looking at these same groups, many folklorists find cultural layering resembling upended and metamorphosed strata in road cuts. For example, when a worker uses vulgar or satiric language to ward off the boss, a historian may place such speech in categories of class struggle; studying this same language, a folklorist may comment on its traditionality, variation, or relationship to other expression across cultural boundaries.

Fortunately, students have the luxury of splicing ideas from sister disciplines, of combining conceptual formulas. At the heart of differences, stated and overcome, lies one's sense of the constant interplay of two ancient words, *labor* and *lore.*

Articulating norms, we face choices in describing work sites: rural craft versus urban industry, handicraft versus factory production, skilled human versus Chaplinesque robot. Too often the physical setting projects binary figures jousting in tournaments. Crafty artisans battle factory hands, while professional scholars sit at their raised dais awarding ribbons to winners. At times, this horizontal playing field transforms itself into a ladder of struggle: hunting, gathering, agriculture, feudal shop, satanic mill, advanced capitalism, socialism—evolutionary rungs leading to empyrean spheres.

Ladder climbers, by definition, carry the positive tag *progressive.* Those on bottom rungs suffer other labels—*backwards, marginal, peripheral.* Approaching the ladder, we accept an excruciating dilemma: some identify with nonclimbers; others favor only those who advance. Curiously, left and right ideologues may join in championing "progress." Radicals may view technical prowess as evolution's goal, whereas conservatives see profits and technology joined as nature's reward.

Despite mechanical advances that rival the fantasies of science-fiction dreamers, America's work force today is not entirely engaged in data processing, computer programming, desktop publishing, or "ladder climbing." Some workers retain antique skills in the metal and building trades. Others eke out a hand-to-mouth existence in entombed communities from which industry has fled. Still others, simultaneously urban and rural, work two jobs (on the farm and in the factory). Affluent citizens don denim garb to build second homes in cut-over regions and master old techniques for weekend tasks. Meanwhile, homeless workers squat in high-rise doorways watching job habits dissipate. Ghetto children grow up without observing sustaining crafts, without getting their hands on either antiquity's or modernity's tools.

Beyond differences in workplace position, level of competence, degree of political sophistication, or material comfort, many workers still base their beliefs in consensual images: old-fashioned, enclaved, close to the soil, inner directed, parochial. Toilers holding such "natural" views may be militant without voicing revolutionary goals. I blanch when I hear campus pundits explain "backwardness" by notions of false consciousness. I am dismayed by those who assign medals only to vanguardists who articulate a flaming sense of class. Who decrees that workers are confused or cheated by Sylvester Stallone or Dolly Parton?

Conceptual speech—whether abstract or concrete, descriptive or prescriptive—does not surface every day in archival filing manuals or school budgetary schedules. Yet I know of no facile way for scholar or activist to put the term *laborlore* to work without invoking the most compelling language that addresses minute changes on everyday jobs and tidal shifts in global economy.

The very phrase "putting laborlore to work" asks us to decode verbal messages, to stand commonsense speech on its head, to sense both utility and irony in wordplay. The word *labor* equates with *work; lore,* with *play.* How do these join? When do they clash? Some workers view their jobs as the ultimate negation of play—does one not work to buy playtime? We play or watch TV to soften work's burden. We also "dog it" or "goof off" on the job "to make it through the day."

Workers symbolically "buy back" dignity or identity with prank, jest, and other folkloric forms. Among the contradictions they face is that of sorting out horseplay from wordplay. The former endangers life on the shop floor; the latter eases time's toll. In short, neither union member nor campus-based scholar remains immune from the tension built into linguistic expression.

Labor historians, whether disciples of John Commons or of E. P. Thompson, view their discipline as contested terrain—a battlefield for capital and labor to which calm professors return as park rangers pointing out ruins and monuments. Commons's followers see trenches and gun mounts in the marketplace, dug or erected by institutional unionists. Thompson's students see flags of class formation or collective practice flying above barricades. Folklorists have learned to excavate trenches, conserve pennants, and link both by commentary.

Curators attracted to a quilt's design devote attention to the quilter's circumstance so that audiences can interpret the quilt's entire appeal. Folklorists who comment on workers' traditions must be familiar with job techniques (for example, how frontier plows or surgeons' scalpels are fashioned from the same metal).

Knowledge of working skill leads back to locale and to ideological cause. Did the blacksmith who crafted a plow favor Mother Jones, Sam Gompers, Gene Debs, Bill Haywood, or none of these public figures? Did the metalsmith who crafted a scalpel leave a diary, a bundle of letters, a sketchbook, or none of these source materials?

Even the most rudimentary reading of labor history or industrial sociology reveals a great variety of positions and concomitant figurative language: *business, uplift, revolutionary,* and *predatory unionism;* labor (the entity) as *bourgeois apologist, industry lackey, historical agent, transformational forge, imprisoned genie, sleeping giant*. I find it important to restate that unionists in all types of organizations, as well as nonunion workers, create and carry lore. Young performers of labor songs, and their cousins working with drama, storytelling, and graphic design, often prod blue-collar Gullivers to awaken. Union educators urge sisters and brothers to make their own history, to call on teachers for help in salvaging golden eras.

Some activists, clinging to pyrotechnic formulas, assert that radicals alone shaped workers' tradition and that Red children by themselves can be trusted to play out proletarian promise. Indeed, it comes as a surprise to many partisans to learn that workers across the rainbow of belief have treasured lore. Cultural historians continue to sort out disputes over "ownership" of our heritage. The view that creativity belongs to an elect few—patrician or plebeian—can be traced back several centuries.

We lack a comprehensive study focused on radical attention to workers' culture. Among folklorists, Richard Reuss made the best start. In 1990, Mari Jo Buhle and colleagues included brief essays touching aspects of laborlore in the *Encyclopedia of the American Left*. Here I pick up the thread in the early 1930s when Charles Seeger, composer and musicologist, encountered Marxism (Dunaway 1980; Green 1979c; Reuss 1979).

Writing for the *Daily Worker,* Seeger sought to introduce avant-garde music to labor audiences (who largely ignored his call). Accepting a New Deal assignment in 1935, he shifted attention from discordant sound to a second esoteric area, folksong. In 1941, his son Peter helped form the Almanac Singers, a group of young radicals who embraced traditional folksong as they composed new topical pieces such as "Talkin' Union." The Almanacs used music as a Popular Front political weapon and named themselves "progressives" or "antifascists." Caught up by twists in Communist party position and early Cold War winds, the Almanacs disbanded.

The present disarray on the left requires attention to debate on Popular Front culture and an evaluation of luminaries such as Earl Robinson, Jack Howard Lawson, Howard Fast, Clifford Odets, William Gropper, and Paul Robeson. However, Woody Guthrie remains the Popular Front star with the greatest hold on union educators. Despite considerable attention to Guthrie, we lack criticism of his contradictory roles: proponent of free thought and chauvinsim in life-style, promulgator of protest and affirmation in song content, partisan of Franklin Roosevelt and Joseph Stalin in politics. Some fans equate Woody with Joe Hill, ignoring vital differences between the Wobbly bard's syndicalism and Guthrie's Stalinism.

During 1986, historian Jesse Lemisch harshly criticized several of Woody's "children." The critic's polemical tone detracted from the challenging substance in his position. Unionists, he asserted, need to understand pop-culture modes, discard dated paradigms, and open their eyes and ears to the myriad voices with which Americans actually express their hopes and fears. Lemisch offered bitter medicine to those still within the Popular Front fold, as he reopened questions about Red responses to workers' living traditions.

I find it useful to contrast Lemisch's attraction to pop culture with Alan Wald's stance on Popular Front realities in "Remembering the Answers." When Communist party arbiters touted "democratic" arts, workers and their intellectual allies often abandoned vanguard tasks in favor of commercial dross. Succumbing to political amnesia, some Reds buried their troubled political history alongside their faith in both vernacular and avant-garde artistry.

In the first years of *glasnost,* Soviet Union newscasts and journalistic reports described provocative new films, dramas, novels, and art exhibits. Moscow critics then adjusted their lines to treat nonrepresentational art, postmodern fiction, formalist poetry, gloom-drenched cinema, and other Western "sins." Fortunately, Russian artists forged ahead of critics. The spirit of *glasnost,* however, did not reach back to the United States with critical eye and ear to touch Popular Front mandarins. The price of such revisionism, if it comes, may well be the devaluation of sacrosanct texts and tunes favored by guardians on the left.

To evade responsibility in detailing the Communist party's political culture sets back our exploration. To give way to euphoric discourse by overlooking crime and corruption, or gulag and party-state, in the name of building socialism burdens the carriers of leftist belief. Some partisans seek paths between recrimination and cliché; still others avoid any criticism of Red causes. I have felt it a disservice to working people to mask retrograde idols in crimson and to excoriate conservatives, liberals, anarchists, or syndicalists while elevating communists to "progressive" heights. Can we not touch radical lore without mythologizing a solitary party's "leading role" as judge for workers' culture?

An entry point for debate on the thorny cultural relationship between communists and workers opens when we turn to "proletarian" experience in the 1930s. We remove aural and visual screens in rehearing and reseeing the reverential representation of "the workers" as "de Voykaz"—the symbolic elevation of an exploited class destined to glory (Cowley, 42). We hear this accolade, this honorific, echoing lament and worship mingled with parody in the needle-trades ditty:

Oh, the right-wing cloak makers
And the Socialist fakers,
Are making by de Voykaz
Doublecrosses.

We need also to turn to expression that renders lip service to workers' culture in other parts of the world. How have radicals elsewhere reconciled tradition's innate conservatism with their belief in liberation and emancipation? Has our history paralleled theirs? Although the answers lie beyond my case studies, I note a single book addressing these concerns. Lynn Mally's *Culture of the Future* describes revolutionary Russia's *Proletkult* movement. She reports caustic debates on the heterogeneous nature of workers' expression, the incompatibility between cultural and political agents of change, and the price of defeat when proletarian-culture enthusiasts conflicted with Lenin's belief in Bolshevik supremacy. Perhaps the best symbol of hope and failure in the revolution's aftermath is an architectural maquette of a transparent building designed in 1924 for *Pravda*. The Vesnin brothers, constructivist artists, wanted the workings of the Soviet press to be fully open. Needless to say, this glass newspaper plant was never erected (Strigalev).

In drawing comparisons between our work culture and that of other lands, we learn that considerable radical expression in America, from proletarian literature to socialist realism in art, mired itself in lard, while some consisted of cotton candy. Students strengthen themselves by rejecting insubstantial junk food. We need nourishment equal to the complexity of vision demanded in pluralistic society. This reach stretches from union educators who commission poster artists, to convention planners who order souvenirs, to archivists who mount photo exhibits, to folklorists who view factories as "fields."

Learners benefit from divergent postures, whether established or innovative. In stressing vernacularity and traditionality, we must not assume that experimental strategies or modes of ambiguity and allegory lie beyond the threshold of all workers' experience. In holding open modern avenues, cultural arbiters should not sanitize, trivialize, or homogenize their wares. To suggest that plebeians cannot enjoy Faulkner, Picasso, or Schoenberg forces much of humanity into the prison house of philistinism. To respect the homespun does not demand rejection of the avant-garde. Clearly, cultural equity means appreciation for Yoknapatawpha County as a mansion for imaginative literature as well as a soil for deeply rooted folklore.

Detroit's auto workers deserve the freedom to enjoy Diego Rivera's murals touching their industry as they fashion vernacular art: Sunday paintings of factory scenes; personally decorated clothing or safety gear; ornaments fashioned from "surplus" or "scrap" paint, metal, or plastic. This rank-and-file artistry should not be judged against Rivera's aesthetic. Rather, it should be understood internally within shop-floor, ethnic, and neighborhood codes.

To place Faulkner's novels or Rivera's murals in our domain may offend purists who set workers in cages. Trade unionism did not touch Faulkner's America, but the author left an indelible portrait of the sharecroppers and mechanics he knew. Some Yoknapatawphans migrated to northern factories carrying along Mississippi folkways. Rivera, a dedicated revolutionary, identified with labor, yet many Detroit auto workers found his murals troubling. Here, writer and artist do not stand as guides into laborlore's manse; rather, they serve to suggest our open rooms and wondrous inhabitants.

Whether we reach out to innovative or oral literature, fine or folk art, we seek balance between authenticity and appeal. Who best pulls us to work's window? Among many workers who turned the kaleidoscope of experience and reflection, Gilbert Mers and Jim Garland have given us the gift of fine rank-and-file autobiographies. Such books have been neglected by critics. We need a checklist of these accounts, rich in vernacular expression and reports on everyday happenings. Until a bibliographer assumes the task of searching out such autobiographies, the following two books will represent this vein.

In 1988, the University of Texas Press issued *Working the Waterfront* by Gilbert Mers, "a fair-to-middlin' cotton cutter" (a longshoreman on the Texas coast). Mers ranges widely from traditional humor to reflections on Wobbly strategies. In 1983, the University Press of Kentucky published *Welcome the Traveler Home* by Jim Garland, a mountain coal miner and folksong composer ("The Death of Harry Simms"). Julia Ardery enhanced Jim's memoir with a model introduction, sensitive in detailing the relationship of editor to self-educated worker.

Laborlore champions unlock antique gates and peer into blooming gardens. In the chapters that follow, I note varied roles for folklorists who approach the assembly line or office tower: guide, documentarian, analyst, critic. One caution: not all work tradition lives alongside the legendary heroism of Joe Hill or John Henry. Only some outsiders experience William James's sense of epiphany on seeing climbers on sky-scaling iron. Many toilers feel the imperative of cultural pluralism without having read Horace Kallen. Not all viewers share Ben Shahn's vision of anarchists Sacco and Vanzetti as labor martyrs.

Folklorists do not confine themselves to the mythic, epic, or sacred. We encounter discriminatory, bizarre, tawdry, and scatological material. Work tools invoke sexual imagery; job practices call up analogs of bodily function; sheer boredom in repetitive tasks or in work's loss leads to escape with erotic fantasy or self-abasement. Job tales help surface fears of impotence and cuckoldry as well as boasts of conquest and power.

Laborlore travelers do stumble into tannic pits and tenement cellars as they find netherworlds from the Bowery to the Styx. In tradition, bosses may metamorphose into monsters as workers transform themselves into tricksters. Some lore holds oppositional or contestational content; some runs in quixotic channels. Activists who prod proletarians to seek their class destiny often decry lore as aimless or, worse, as "holding workers back." Scholars face tension in bridging cultural diversity or contradictory messages and in "paying dues" to those from whom they derive professional strength.

I recall personal work experience, and, as a folklorist, I have also observed and read about the tasks of others. The chapters ahead combine these job and library experiences—reading, listening, remembering. For apprentices in the academy, I stress the widest use of history and ethnography, whether spread out in monograph or in film.

The American work scene that emerges from reading or viewing is a bubbling cauldron into which hands pour immigrant muscle, ethnic clash, racial subjugation, segmented work roles, management strategies for efficiency and loyalty, governmental intrusion, radical cults, union achievement, and union ossification. At times, Macbeth's witches stir this mixture. We taste their malevolent brew on learning that Detroiters killed a Chinese student out of hostility to Japanese auto-making competition.

We name this national cauldron our *melting pot,* knowing that it produced bodies for Model T Fords, plate for battleships, and tin for red-white-and-blue convention medallions. The pot also served as matrix for the doleful anthracite ballad "The Avondale Mine Disaster," collected by George Korson (1938) and for the IWW's near-surrealistic "Kitten in the Wheat" (Green 1965). Above all, iron and steel giants cast out considerable physical slag for industrial dumps, ballasted railway tracks, and polluted streams. We are reluctant to describe workers as slag, yet while some prospered, others wasted away in charity wards, county farms, and skid-road missions.

A few observers, seeing melting pot and slag, have taken up museum tasks. During 1971, the Smithsonian Institution in its

Festival of American Folklife presented contemporary ironworkers erecting a two-story structure on the National Mall. Previously, festival planners had favored preindustrial tradition. During 1971, we noted continuities from handicrafts to modern labor on a living stage for young "hard hats." To mark the event, *The Ironworker*, the journal of the International Association of Bridge, Structural and Ornamental Iron Workers, pictured the proud "performers." Festival visitors saw erectors, with the Washington Monument behind them, bolting up columns and girders. Mall "sidewalk supers" asked inevitable questions about dangerous work.

For two decades this "Working Americans" format has proved successful in regional and local folk festivals. Essentially, audiences serve as students while skilled men and women teach by enacting their job techniques and "talking up" trade customs. Robert McCarl's essay "Occupational Folklife in the Public Sector" describes tool and die makers (members of the International Association of Machinists) on the Mall. He does not avoid discussion of differences, resolved or unresolved, between festival staff and participating machinists.

Some of the best reports on occupational presentation appear in public-agency ephemeral publications. Funded in 1988 by the North Carolina Arts Council, Michael and Debbie Luster brought together at Beaufort a group of menhaden fishermen, retired mariners who had retained the last functional sea shanties in the United States. In *NC Arts*, the Lusters noted their assistance to the men in regrouping and staging music at concerts and festivals. Folklorists do not turn back technology's clock to the era of traditional work songs; they do help former crew members present their expressive life with dignity.

After industrial dislocation, workers face not only economic hardship but also the traumatic loss of heritage. Although folklorists cannot restore livelihood, they can achieve a sensible blend of memory and respect in re-presentations of past customs and in descriptions of emerging traditions. In citing attention at festivals to fishermen and ironworkers, I touch several unresolved matters. Do we favor certain crafts out of a sense of danger, struggle, or romance? Do we validate special forms of performance, such as shantying over net mending? How do we influence funding agencies in selecting definitions of work culture? Shall we go back only to preindustrial work in documentary and presentational assignments?

I suspect that most Americans who hear the rubric *occupational group* will visualize cowboys. At one level we know that these productive workers function in the food chain—cousins to old butchers and new supermarket stackers or baggers. Yet wranglers, more than any other workers, engage in myth making as they guard their traditional status. Folkloric attention to this culture began with Jack Thorp and John Lomax. The number of novels and films about buckaroo experience overshadows depictions of other toilers. Collecting from cowboys and commentary on their lore continues. Three important contemporary interpreters are Glenn Ohrlin, working cowboy, who presents song lore from within his community; Guy Logsdon, librarian, who offers long-bowdlerized puncher balladry; and Hal Cannon, public folklorist, who sparks cowboy poetry gatherings.

In recent years, professionals in several fields have helped develop innovative forms in displaying work lore not only by concert and festival but also within museum walls. The Botto House at Haledon, New Jersey, dates to 1908. This immigrant's home played a role in the Paterson silk strike of 1913. Botto House—now an intimate museum with grape arbor, bocci court, and wine cellar—presents the experience of families in the textile and clothing industries. By contrast, the Sloss Furnace in Birmingham, Alabama, represents a huge outdoor muesum in which retired steelworkers and a technical staff offer year-round educational programs. The smokestack and casting shed become backdrops for historical and cultural exhibits.

I have visited the Botto House and Sloss Furnace; other sites I know only through catalogs. Richard Hill's *Skywalkers* documents a 1987 exhibit at the Woodland Indian Cultural Centre, Brantford, Ontario. With formal and oral history, photos and graphics, guest curator Hill negates the "myth" that Mohawk and other native ironworkers possess "genetic equilibrium." This "myth is shattered each time an Indian falls from the lifeless steel" (11). *Skywalkers* abounds in job wisdom; Norton Lickers, a champion riveter, speaks for buddies in many trades beyond the Six Nations Reserve: "If you're going to go up on the iron, you might as well go all the way up. That's where the work is, on top" (52).

The Smithsonian Institution's National Museum of American History has mounted "Symbols and Images of American Labor," an exhibit of guild-decorated pitchers, trade cards, dinner pails, hard hats, framed charters, apprentice certificates, convention ribbons, political cartoons, and movie posters. Curator Harry Rubenstein describes these and other artifacts in an illustrated article for *Labor's Heritage*. Fortunately, this exhibit has traveled to other museums, providing a broad audience for labor memorabilia.

Friends have helped me formulate riddles that come with scholarly territory. Have I broadened *laborlore* beyond precision? Should I expand its meaning to include elite art, soap opera, punk music, cult fashion? What should I exclude? Rather than erecting "final" standards here, I suggest that readers turn to the case studies ahead. For the present, we can leave open such questions of category. Folkloric training pointed me to tradition's core, to occupational expression patterned over time. Others will seek artistry in drama, novel, and film, or in television's nightly fare. Ultimately, the rubric *laborlore* will be tested in use.

We can put this key term to work with close analysis of particular texts and acts, as well as comprehensive overviews. My chapters lean primarily on work I know by experience or by observation—textures marked by saw and hammer. Through site visits and library or museum resources, I treat occupations in copper mines and textile mills—scenes known to me indirectly. I have encouraged others to look at lore of anchor women, burger flippers, data-entry clerks, hospital orderlies, lapel stitchers, market checkers, spin doctors, teflon scratchers, and zookeepers.

To explore such trades a student will have to open a bibliographic path: my case studies offer leads but not a comprehensive list. A full laborlore bibliography must reveal disciplinary breadth as it goes beyond formal folkloric study. A few citations suggest needed range: Mary Van Kleek, in 1913, combined ethnography and empathy to describe young women in the artificial flower and bookbinding trades. Elton Mayo, in 1924, linked setting, fatigue, and productivity at Western Electric's Hawthorne (Chicago) plant. This human-relations-in-industry approach led to the attention business schools presently give to "corporate culture." Today, social scientists join reformers and personnel technicians in labor studies. Kai Erikson, June Nash, and John Calagione, among others, offer leads to current research in the sociology and anthropology of work.

Welcome to old waterfronts and new silicon valleys, to a work force of men and women, native and foreign born. I trust that my book points to a lifetime of trails for those interested in working people's culture. Because the term *laborlore* includes substance as well as study, it is broad enough to touch work process, institutions, and traditional wisdom. It serves well in addressing queries inherent in expressive life about origin, structure, function, meaning. Whether or not my tag will persist or be replaced remains to be seen. However, *labor, work, craft, industry, heritage, tradition,* and *lore* will continue to combine in everyday job speech, union office, and academy.

Gnomes emerge from caves to caution our impending journey into their realm of story, song, and speech. Sister and brother sibyls and elves—themselves longtime underground workers—join to whisper that those who would link *labor* to *lore* must go cannily, for the latter usage carries centuries of controversy surrounding its governing concept, *culture*.

Matthew Arnold in Victorian England contrasted culture with anarchy as E. B. Tylor explored the culture of primitive (anarchic) people. Tylor turned to neglected life—"the uncivilized"—whereas Arnold remained with the cultivated and privileged. Anthropologists have diverged further both on explanations for diversity and on assaying its value. Do we cherish pluralism as intrinsically appropriate to the human condition, or do we smother it with a veneer of shining ideology?

There are other differences beyond those between the followers of Arnold and of Tylor; social anthropologists and labor historians also divide among themselves on matters of self-definition: humanist/structuralist, idealist/materialist, empiricist/determinist, Thompsonian/Althusserian. Such dualities concern scholars who identify with labor. Review essays in *Labour/Le Travailleur* by Bryan Palmer and Ian McKay offer Marxist critiques of those who put culture over class. Controversy swirls around their key phrase, *working-class culture*. Many radicals use this in an overarching sense, as an equivalent of *political economy*. Others limit it to expressive material and process. Those who take up laborlore quests can refine the notion to suit their needs. We can anticipate constant disagreement between Marxists and empiricists on the connection of both *folk* and *class* to *lore*.

However antiquated or problematic the term *folk* remains, and however great our wish to relegate it to history's dustbin, we still invoke *folk* to restate the power in homespun and the pleasure in handicraft. Why do workers decorate personal-computer keyboards or space-center control panels with comfortable decals and off-color jests? Our very ability to work with new tools hinges on familiarizing their aura. Essentially, we use traditional material as building blocks in constructing fresh realities.

Working people buffeted by world-market changes, and by struggle against disaster, strive to comprehend the generative processes that bring their lore into consciousness. The rubric *laborlore* helps citizens demystify and articulate work's meaning. Song, story, custom, costume, jest, and rite combine to shore up identity. Each of our two keys—*labor* and *lore*—holds a long and honorable lineage.

From onion field to packing shed

# Tiffany Touch and Talking Back

Ships rise on launching ways; docks stand on piles; pier sheds sit on sills; cargo rests on decks. Working on such structures raises consciousness of footings and fastenings. In gathering lore from diverse trades across the continent, I have not sought mechanical connections from story to song or jest to rite. However, I have observed that verbal art and customary practice require their own nails and rivets.

Figuratively, certain labor terms or slogans have emerged as thematic glue to bind individuals into movements: *solidarity, organize the unorganized, an injury to one is an injury to all.* Teaching concepts that are often cast as frozen polarities can also serve to weave together a book's units. In this prefatory sketch of work lore represented in and conveyed by sound recording, film, and visual art, I suggest the device of abstract oppositions to link disparate material: fact/fiction, direct experience/vicarious perception.

Fact and fiction blur even on technically demanding jobs. I have heard fragments of exaggerated tales usually after a construction accident, such as a fall into an elevator shaft or a crane's boom touching a high-voltage line. Each person in a circle of talk would describe previous harrowing personal injuries. It hardly mattered whether the narrator had seen the accident described, heard about it, or indulged in imaginative projection. Those of us absorbed in the session used fantasy to dissolve fears in a mate's tragedy or to borrow courage from a heroic fellow worker.

Historians and ethnographers decry the welding of fiction to fact, yet they employ poetic imagery in their "scientific" writing. The most objective labor historian may animate findings with class-destiny belief or barricade rhetoric. In the realm of film and disc, we confront make-believe representations as we sort notions of reality. I have never met any workers who did not incorporate some visions from the media into their trick-and-treat bags.

We experience occupational lore directly at particular sites and firm our individual reports by asserting fact—the whole truth, nothing but the truth. We perceive the lore of others vicariously by hearing, reading, or seeing their experience compressed into artistic form. A rainbow of fictive modes hovers over every workplace. At the tool crib, loafers swap amatory jokes. In the saloon on check-cashing Friday, cowboys ride jukebox trails. At home, the tube enchants. Where is the line between the lore enacted at work and the imagery conveyed by satellite beam?

In reviewing V. S. Naipaul's book *A Turn in the South,* Roger Shattuck penned a few lines in which recorded music echoes: "All day mechanics and construction workers across America keep a radio twanging next to the socket wrenches or hooked onto bare studs." At night, "ghost armies" of service workers carry transistor sets into high-rise office towers. Shattuck, like other teachers working late, may well have heard country music in campus corridors. He calls it "our samizdat," a tag not often voiced in Nashville.

Some years ago a Santa Barbara Channel pilot shared a job incident with me. After transporting roustabouts and supplies to an offshore drilling platform, he stayed on the rig long enough to return men and gear to shore. One evening the tool pusher asked the boatman to join the gang for a movie rerun, Clark Gable in *Boomtown.* The pilot recalled that the oil hands chattered over the soundtrack, snorting at anomalies, howling at Gable's errors in simulating work.

Professor Shattuck notes the ubiquity of recorded and broadcast country music. It reverberates in the truck cab carting lumber to the tract and runs between fir and pine framed against the horizon. It rolls from studio to honky-tonk to family room. We know its presence. We know, too, the critical blast: country music is banal, tawdry, enervating; it induces passivity among listeners. Our harbor pilot paints a different picture. In memory his drillers talk back to the screen as they match self-esteem and skill against Hollywood make-believe.

Some critics invoke the password *hegemony* to mark the authority of screen and disc, of media power over the masses. Workers who attempt resistance engage in *counterhegemonic* practice. Does the term also apply to Santa Barbara's roustabouts in mocking Clark Gable? This matter deserves a tome; I raise it here as one of several approaches to occupational lore mediated through commercial channels.

Radicals find it easy to criticize commodified culture (mind control, brain washing) as they ask workers to resist. Activists urge unionists to use their own cameras or microphones as struggle instruments. Actually, rank-and-file citizens do "take charge" of such tools, but not always with leftist sentiments. Helen Lewis speaks of "self-documentation" in Appalachia. At a black Pentecostal church in McRoberts, Kentucky, she asked politely if she might record some music. "Oh, don't worry," the minister replied, "I've got a videotape set up over here. We're going to videotape the whole thing. We'll send you a copy" (Patterson, 9).

Readers going beyond firsthand experience for cultural commentary will notice disproportion in laborlore studies. We know much more about union songs than about union tales; we find more books on Woody Guthrie than on composers who record occupational "singles" or cassettes in local studios. In recent decades, Joe Glazer, Utah Phillips, and Pete Seeger have issued dozens of recordings holding union and industrial items. They have also performed on the concert/festival circuit. (I treat a few of their songs in chapters ahead.) At this juncture I note only the need for broad receptivity to work's many voices.

Peter Tamony coined the term *vocumentary* to encompass a recording's textual and melodic content, as well as the performing style of the singer or instrumentalist. Perhaps the best way for a listener to talk back to playback machines is to decode the aural messages in each recorded vocument, to array songs by traditional norms. For example, the Library of Congress has issued two recordings of anthracite and bituminous ballads collected by George Korson. Place these albums next to coal items by "revivalists." Listen for differences; ask for explanations.

In 1983, Richard Reuss compiled a labor discography listing 150 LP albums and 800 song titles. He noted slow advances in developing this corpus and identified problem areas for additional study. Reuss's list, now out of print, needs updating. Each educator, each collector, sets private agendas for research. Among neglected areas, I suggest concentrated attention to "foreign language" material. Basque shepherds, Belgian glass blowers, Chinese sewing women, and Chicana cannery hands remind us that America is an immigrant nation.

I propose an available entry into work cultures that are distant in speech and style. From our century's first decade, pioneer recording firms (Victor, Columbia, Edison) included "foreign" songs in their catalogs. Pekka Gronow and others have described such items in *Ethnic Recordings in America* (American Folklife Center, Library of Congress). Richard Spottswood, extending this research, compiled a magnificent seven-volume discography entitled *Ethnic Music on Records*. In the material that follows, I select two songs that simultaneously illustrate bicultural elements within the work scene and comment on the poles of fiction and fact.

Chaim Tauber (the "Pagliacci of Yiddish Poetry") composed a ballad of great appeal to New York garment workers during the Depression years. Metro Music published his "Motel" in sheet music in 1934. "Motel" also formed a stage play's theme. In 1939, Tauber starred in a melodramatic film titled *Motel the Operator.* About 1947, he recorded "Motl der Operator" with pianist Hary Lubin (Asch 6018, a 78-rpm disc). The song gave Tauber a strong needle-trades identity; for many years he hosted a radio series at Manhattan's WEVD as Motel the Operator.

Tauber's ballad centered on a sewing-machine operator who joins fellow strikers on a New York picket line. A gangster with a bottle kills Motl. His wife and children weep. How can they accept his sacrifice? In the film, Motl survives the brutal attack but lives thereafter in a valley of family grief. The song, standing alone outside of play or film, does not reveal whether employer, radical leader, or cloakmakers' union official hires the "gorilla."

In 1981, Henry Sapoznik and friends in a klezmer band recorded "Motl" on *Kapelye: Future & Past*. Motl returned to life, 1982–87, in the off-Broadway musical *The Golden Land* (Mlotek). Most recently, Sapoznik again recorded the ballad on a Workmen's Circle audio-cassette. We can reflect on the poignant appeal in an innocent's death from gangsterism—a wound hidden by labor-song enthusiasts. Further, Tauber caught the New World fusion of Yiddish and English, an unending process of linguistic borrowing and blending. Wherever immigrant speakers met at mine mouth or shop floor, their speech coalesced.

During 1967, Willie Lopez, a resident of McAllen, Texas, composed the corrido "Rinches de Texas," a ballad marking a melon pickers' strike in which Texas Rangers assaulted farm workers. One stanza revealed that Governor John Connally guarded the interest of ranchers: "Esos rinches maldecidos / Los mandó el gobernador / A proteger los melones / De un rico conservador" (Those hated rangers / Were sent by the governor / To protect the melons / Of a conservative rancher). Lopez fell back on the corrido's essential narrative function as he touched an emotional nerve: many Texans of Mexican birth or ancestry do not share Anglo faith in ranger justice.

Lopez worked as a radio announcer at XEOR, Reynosa, Mexico, across the Rio Grande from McAllen, and independently in his garage recording studio. At the melon strike's end, he recorded El Dueto Reynosa singing "Rinches de Texas" and released it on a 45-rpm disc (Oro 230). Subsequently, Lopez gave "Rinches" air play on XEOR. Two terms help situate "Rinches": *norteno* (northern), *conjunto* (group or band). They denominate the Mexican-American border music favored by the working people of Texas (Heisley; Peña). Like thousands of similar topical and regional recordings, "Rinches" might have been forgotten had not Chris Strachwitz and Les Blank "rescued" it for their 1976 film *Chulas Fronteras* and for a subsequent soundtrack recording. This film has carried Rio Grande border music from Berkeley to Stockholm to Tokyo.

Brochures with Yiddish/English and Spanish/English texts hold translations for "Motl der Operator" and "Rinches de Texas." These songs represent hundreds of "foreign language" compositions that go to the heart of labor problems faced by "strangers."

Americans concerned with the state of our polity and economy cannot escape the fact that immigrant and refugee workers will continue to tote water and haul ashes, as well as to compress core feelings in song and story.

That laborlore partisans should treat many musics (art, pop, folk) seems self-evident. By seeking "foreign" recordings, in labor's aural chambers, we encounter the stylistic patchwork marking American expression. A listener can contrast tone and tempo in setting a fictive lament about sewing-machine Motl alongside a factual ballad about melon pickers and Texas Rangers. Our response to stylistic nuance intersects with and colors our comprehension of text. Is Tauber's operator less authentic than Lopez's pickers? Should our evaluation of this song pair hinge on familiarity with the musical idioms or on narrative truth? How do norms of truth in story and in style intersect?

We shall never run out of queries about recorded sound, from cylinders to CDs. Curiosity also serves well when we challenge cinema at drive-in, theater, home parlor, or union hall. As a folklorist, I view films differently than do labor historians or union educators. My perceptions are not superior to theirs, however; essentially, I seek some respect for tradition by movie moguls.

Archivists have issued extensive film and video catalogs; we supplement such lists (for example, Henry Giroux on *Norma Rae*, or Peter Biskind on *On the Waterfront*) and interviews (Paul Schrader on *Blue Collar*). Some critics fault such films for denigrating labor, ignoring leftist causes, or promising easy solutions. Other activists assert that workers need to make their own movies, to practice "self-documentation," "to take charge of their own lives."

The historian Stephen Brier looked unkindly at *Matewan* for what he saw as plot weakness and distortion in detail. Meanwhile, West Virginia miners have praised its truth and power. The historian's interpretation of events conflicts with folk memory. Grandchildren of coal-war veterans find in *Matewan* certification of their loyalties. Did not their grandfathers fight for justice? Laborlore students must look in two directions: objective records and rank-and-file evaluations.

*Matewan* pictures a tornado of violence—sadistic strikebreakers, double agents, resolute organizers. Composer Mason Daring adds bold music to coal's inherent drama. For three sets of miners—Appalachian, African-American, and Italian immigrant—he replicates the sounds of fiddle, harmonica, mandolin. These instruments speak editorially in establishing mood, as does folksinger Hazel Dickens with hymn and ballad. Sound both underscores the rivalry among workers and, through harmony, reflects the rise in solidarity within stigmatized groups. *Matewan* and an explanatory book by John Sayles reinforce our notion that exploration belongs to coal miner, filmmaker, historian, folklorist, and critic.

Another coal film, the documentary *Out of Darkness,* uses traditional and popular music with great effect. The United Mine Workers of America commissioned it for the union's centennial convention in 1990. Its editors fashioned a 100-minute visual collage out of miles of footage, from grainy newsreels to recent TV clips of the Pittston strike. Tom Juravich and fellow musicians joined Appalachian and rock material. In a cassette album drawn from the soundtrack, Tom deliberately fit selections to "today's miners who grew up on rock-and-roll." In correspondence with me, he noted the need to bring bedrock songs "forward without being either patronizing or flippant."

I applaud Juravich's efforts and results—a fresh blend that invokes 1970s Austin music ("cosmic cowboy," "outlaw," "progressive country"). Here, I touch the Tar Baby matter of taste in film and fiction, art and music. Clearly, many miners respond to musicians as diverse as Jimmie Rodgers, Bob Wills, Hank Williams, Merle Travis, Merle Haggard, Willie Nelson, and Ricky Skaggs. The stylistic thread that binds the music of these stars often serves to denominate blue-collar sensibility.

No single form—musical comedy, modern jazz, blues, heavy metal, folksong revival, world beat—touches the experience of all American workers. Even the most popular hit does not cut through regional, linguistic, and communal associations. Thus, film musicians and other artists geared to labor education must be sensitive to roots as well as to foliage, to non-English tongues, and to the merry-go-round we designate "American style."

Many workers will view *Out of Darkness* as a stirring documentary and say that if *Matewan* is historical fiction, the UMWA film is fact. Partisans also see the latter as factual, chronicling unrelenting force directed against toilers by state and capital combined. I suggest that we use both films with their exciting visual and aural juxtapositions as cultural sermons questioning anew the balance we seek between tradition and innovation, experience and perception, authenticity and accessibility.

Movies often resemble keening at a wake: shrill and emotion drenched. By contrast, ethnographic films remain calm and understated. We see them mainly on public television broadcasts or at academic meetings. To my knowledge, no one has compiled a checklist of visual occupational ethnographies: bread baking, wood graining, tie hacking, gold beating, saddle making. I cite a representative title, *Billy Moore, Chesapeake Boatbuilder,* on crafting a deadrise oyster boat with a firm hand, keen eye, and tradition's chart. The films that anthropologists, sociologists, and folklorists produce detailing work processes clearly touch issues of large purpose. When laborlore exploration combines with cultural criticism, students will find the lines that tie Captain Ahab to Billy Moore.

Long before Hollywood, Nashville, and Motown packaged labor's skill or cause, gifted individuals harnessed their energies into artistry on the job site and off. Here I look at occupational art and suggest the hidden relationship of artists to ethnographers. We see the closeness of shop lithographer to studio printmaker, but not of steel erector to ballet dancer. Why do some tasks call for art in work itself, whereas other toil directs creative impulses elsewhere?

Many scholars have long separated their own work from that of creative sisters and brothers. Nor have scholars agreed either to separate art about work from art inherent in work, or, conversely, to bead these enactments on a single string. Early travelers with brush and palette offered rich pictures of work techniques from fur trapping to tepee building. William Sidney Mount and George Caleb Bingham, in easel paintings, firmed Jacksonian haymakers and raftsmen, while Richard Henry Dana and Herman Melville, in classic prose, etched jack tars' duties.

Novelists or artists with their tools and technicians with chart, graph, and formula at times replace or reject "homegrown" occupational categories, feeling that outsiders find them inexplicable. Yet men and women who accept job routines or follow work rules do not lose the power to describe their artistry to one another. A tinner "eyeballs" a welded joint, trusting sight over touch. A trim carpenter quickly "splits the difference" in a faulty mitred joint. Mechanics laud accurate work as "on the button," "plumb to the world," "straight as a frozen rope."

I recall a jeweled metaphor from apprenticeship days. A ship joiner hangs a cabin door. After setting metal butt plates (hinges) to connect door to jamb, he may take an extra minute to vertically line up a dozen slotted screw heads. The act of twisting wood screws to present a pleasant visual appearance does not add strength to the door's jamb connection. Not one passenger in scores cares about the position of wood screws. The joiner's gesture becomes a token of artisanal pride overlooked by those who daily open and shut cabin doors. The mechanic acts not for boss, not for passenger, but for himself and his predecessors. A sense of self-worth tells him that an extra minute adds pleasure to a finished job. Mates compliment the joiner's act and name it the "Tiffany touch."

Whether we turn to folklorist, diarist, novelist, or social scientist, we find abundant material on workers' aesthetic norms (or their destruction by the alienation structured into modern life). Sadly, we lack a synoptic view of work-process as art that relates it to art about work. Michael Owen Jones and four colleagues discuss this matter in *Western Folklore,* suggesting new and problematic paths of inquiry. In the past two decades, several public folklorists have experimented with festival and museum presentations of work techniques and job-inspired art without condescension or apology.

Marsha MacDowell and Kurt Dewhurst call attention to the inherent worth of workers' art in *Cast in Clay,* a catalog/monograph treating Michigan's Grand Ledge pottery industry. These authors do not picture sylvan potters turning earthenware but describe blue-collar workers who produced drain tile, sewer pipe, and telephone-wire conduit. About 1900, Grand Ledge factory hands began to use their "free time" to mold and fire little sphinxlike lions for home use as doorstops or family ornaments. Made on "company time" and carried home, the miniature lions grew into highly complex symbols—competence, overalls-clad creativity, the "purchase" of on-the-job esteem.

Each lion also asserted that a worker's time belonged to the crew. Clock-reading differences go to industrial tension's heart. Does "company time" merge into "free time?" Does either include lunch and coffee breaks, pick-up time (when mechanics gather tools before the quitting whistle), and portal-to-portal travel as miners ride to the coal or ore face? One who owns job time shapes personal identity.

In "The Joy of Labor," Yvonne Lockwood uses *homers* and *government jobs* as defining terms for pleasurable objects produced secretly at work, such as chess sets, belt buckles, hash pipes, children's toys, plastic sculptures, or jewelry. She notes that Rebecca Harding Davis described such goods as early as 1861 in her short story "The Korl Woman." Davis's hero, an iron mill slave, sculpts a life-size figure from the porous refuse remaining after pig metal runs. I know of no museum that has shown the great variety in such take-home gifts.

"The Korl Woman" and *Cast in Clay* reopen nettlesome questions on the twin terms *worker art* and *labor art*. Among other observers, Marsha MacDowell asks whether the first rubric should be restricted to "inside" art by working people. Should the second be expanded to touch all "outside" art about work? Over the years these labels have covered indigenous crafts, nineteenth-century wood engravings, popular lithography, labor-press cartoons, trade-union ephemera, realistic photography, union-hall murals, and oil paintings of social significance. Below, I suggest leads to analysis of work depicted in fine, popular, and folk art.

Rosemary Joyce and John Michael Vlach offer, respectively, sensitive biographies of Dwight Stump, an Ohio basketmaker, and Philip Simmons, a South Carolina blacksmith. Simmons, a proud contributor to Charleston's character, knows that his hands and eyes helped fashion his city's emblematic iron gates and grills. Stump labored in the Hocking Hills as a timber cutter, well digger, field tiler (drainage), and paper factory hand. Yet his most memorable achievement has been that of crafting white-oak, round-rod baskets. Although the two men are model workers, critics divorce their handicraft from "labor," understood ideologically.

Two other folk artists, a continent apart, speak to work's overt messages. Before his death in 1969, Ronald Debs Ginther, Seattle cook and Wobbly, painted eighty-five watercolors of skid road misery. Ginther confronted viewers with souls for whom the American dream had failed, as he pushed spectators to enter the swamp of "dehorns"—those who drank poisonous alcohol derived from Sterno and lived in Hooverville shacks.

Ralph Fasanella, born in 1914 in Greenwich Village (then a blue-collar enclave), paints the factories and tenements of his childhood. His poignant "Iceman Crucified" limns his father as a sacred icon crowned with his trade's tools, giant tongs. American folk artists live under varied descriptive tags: *visionary, naive, obsessive, self-taught*. Fasanella adds to such qualifiers a conscious political role as union organizer, Spanish Civil War volunteer, and tireless campaigner for communist causes.

In moving from Stump and Simmons to Ginther and Fasanella, we are free to construct a conceptual array after considering wrought-iron scroll and sweat-shop scene. I suggest that we begin well before Stump and Simmons "discovered" their biographers. In the era of Richard Henry Dana and Herman Melville, anonymous mariners carved whale bone into elegant and utilitarian scrimshaw. Among the countless examples of this art, belaying pins to make rigging lines fast and jagging wheels to crimp pie crusts seem especially exotic. Beyond receiving sheer aesthetic pleasure in the objects, we can appreciate the layers of meaning in their use—pins to aid work at sea, wheels to aid work at home.

Our array opens on the *Pequod* and closes at Detroit's Ford plant (River Rouge), the subject of paintings by Charles Sheeler between 1927 and 1931. As a Precisionist, he favored functional grids and pure geometric forms devoid of working people. In its solitude, the factory became a cathedral untouched by blood, sweat, and tears. We need to ask whether Sheeler ever saw assembly liners or whether his neglect called attention to them (Troyen).

Whaling-crew members created folk art out of impulses similar to those of Grand Ledge potters shaping clay lions. Do lions and "ivory" bric-a-brac—clearly workers' products—rule out industrial moonscapes as examples of labor art? How do Sheeler's paintings, evoking technological triumph, relate to the gifts carried home to wives and sweethearts from pottery shed or whale ship? A catalog by Mary Jane Jacob treats the Detroit imagery of Diego Rivera and Charles Sheeler. Another catalog by Robert Schwendinger documents maritime folk art. Fine articles on Ginther by

Marilyn Ziebarth and on Fasanella by Nick Salvatore add to our appreciation of workers' art.

Within my own exploratory book, I do not restrict our course either to folk scrimshanders or modernists interpreting industrial might. Rather, I suggest that in crossing boundaries we inaugurate a forum including folk art collectors and critics, material culture specialists, and labor historians. Today, film opens all eyes to the artistry of others, complementing painter's easel and lithographer's stone. Art historians, in museum catalogs and monographs, anticipate and supplement Hollywood's visual offerings. Let us imagine an anthology or exhibit geared to work's changing faces and select representations.

Thomas Hart Benton, a regionalist and populist from Missouri, consciously used folk music and legend in his lithographs, paintings, and murals. He saw plow-line patterns and guitar runs as structured entities projecting an autochthonous citizenry's values. His depictions of sharecroppers, hill farmers, hymn singers, and country dancers still telegraph democratic messages. Within this corpus, Benton also sketched riverboat roustabouts, railroad-tie spikers, steel-mill furnacemen, and striking coal miners.

In 1921, Benton turned to a tool destined to become as emblematic as the log cabin or coonskin cap, as the bald eagle or spotted owl. For much of this century, the jackhammer—whether at quarry, mine, building foundation, or city street—symbolized American expansiveness. Benton's *Drillers,* an oil painting, holds two idealized jackhammer men seemingly sculpted from the stone they shape. Arched backs, rounded torsos, swirling wall, and sinewy air hose carry viewers beyond a particular work site to platonic labor (Hyland).

A decade later, the artist placed a single black jackhammer man in the *City Building* panel (in the mural set *America Today*) at Manhattan's New School for Social Research. Benton's angular construction stiff, bone weary, seems to work ten thousand miles away from the gleaming skyscraper behind him. This laborer holds a highly detailed air drill at chin height rather than at his hips. The tool that cuts rock and stops talk becomes a proletarian sceptre (Braun).

Ben Shahn began an apprenticeship at Hessenberg's lithography shop on Beekman Street, Manhattan, at age fifteen (1913). Four years later, he possessed a journeyman's card in the Amalgamated Lithographers Union. Turning from commercial printing to easel and mural painting, print making, calligraphy, and photography, he never forgot his trade-union roots. In the 1930s, Shahn tempered didactic norms of Social Realism with meditation and mystery, giving long life to his works.

Shahn's art, widely spread in books and museums, includes many labor pieces: CIO wartime posters, gouache paintings about Tom Mooney and Sacco and Vanzetti, magazine graphics on Centralia's coal-mine tragedy, photographs of Depression victims, a serigraph entitled *Silent Music*. Technically, the last-named print shows a semiabstract platform holding empty chairs and music stands. Shahn joked that its real title, *Local 802 on Strike*, commented on the New York unit of the American Federation of Musicians (Pohl; Prescott).

Rather than elaborate on Shahn's cornucopia or extend the list of artists who have wandered from textile alley to picket line, I suggest two catalogs: Patricia Hills, *The Working American*, and Marianne Dozema, *American Realism and the Industrial Age*. Readers can voice their own queries. Have union officers ever discarded an artist's poster because it depicted workers as "too ugly"? How do union educators define their role in pulling workers to avant-garde or cosmopolitan art norms? Have labor leaders defaced murals bearing subversive lines? How do working people connect their vernacular artistry to labor's cause? Do folklorists respect connections of ballad or blues to basket, gate, cartoon, or mural?

In "Keywords," this collection of introductory statements, I have opened an initiation into folkloric exploration, suggested strategies for using occupational traditions, and treated forms that communicate workers' expression across boundaries. Sound recordings, films, and visual art join to bridge the diverse experiences and perceptions of working people. In this manner, sea shanty or elegiac ballad, fictive or ethnographic film, and scrimshaw pin or union mural can serve as nails and rivets in laborlore structures.

No matter the level of individual or group consciousness, we rely on book, beam, disc, tube, or screen to comprehend the experience of others, to penetrate their facts and fictions. The honky-tonk jukebox blares gossip; the TV set paints in scarlet; the museum gallery whispers questions. These magic tools help lore seep and surge into everyday life. In the chapter case studies ahead, I urge readers to acquire their own Tiffany touches and to talk back.

Part Two

# Case Studies

"John Henry Building a Railroad"

# 1

# The Visual John Henry

No siren song, no beguiling tale, no isolated artifact can claim to represent all American workers. There are, of course, widespread symbols. Some unionists have elevated Mother Jones and Joe Hill to legendary status, and many activists consider "Solidarity Forever" as their hymn. In past decades, cartoonists seized on a printer's folded paper hat as a symbolic marker. Today, some union members wear billed caps stamped with a local's number or a pictorical logo geared to craft. However, such "feed-store" or "gimmie" caps are accepted far too widely to evoke work itself. Ultimately, a diverse work force and its fluid cultures preclude one expressive construct from signifying labor as a class or institutional monolith.

In past years, socialists and communists used the arm and hammer or the hammer and sickle as emblems; these have not become points of light for most working people in the United States. From time to time, a popular culture figure emerges from the television screen to address blue-collar stereotypes. The fictive Archie Bunker and the factual Roseanne Arnold fit this role. Nonetheless, I suggest that more workers have denied examplary status to Arnold and Bunker than have accepted them as universals.

Seemingly, working people are left without a particular mark, mascot, or myth that states grandly, "I am labor." Despite such reality, we cast about for representative signs. Our quest raises questions: Do we constitute a social movement? Can any solitary emblem touch a rainbow of skills, histories, and values? Has a figure of overarching spirit spoken to the aspirations of all workers?

## Tunnel Face to Drawing Board

John Henry in ballad, rhythmic chant, children's story, and pictorial form comes closer than any other folk hero to personifying our work experience. Despite birth in a minority community, he emerges from the tunnel face to tower above other workers. The hammerman does not pound his way to the top, nor does his hammer carry him to fortune. Skill, strength, and endurance, although virtues, lead to a pyrrhic victory. Ultimately, he signifies an individual defeated by industrial might rather than one buoyed by modernity. Does John Henry become un-American because of failure to master his employer's machine?

I assume that most of my book's readers are familiar with John Henry—swinging hammer, defying steam drill, dying tragically—either through sound recording, folksong anthology, or children's tale. It is true that John Henry shares honors with such ballad figures as Barbara Allen, Brave Wolfe, Jesse James, Stagolee, and Captain Kidd, but with these we invoke love, war, outlawry, gambling, and piracy rather than work. Essentially, John Henry stands in the company of Gene Debs, Mother Jones, Joe Hill, Paul Bunyan, Casey Jones, Joe Magarac, and similar work giants, mythic or historic.

Here, I trace John Henry's appearance in graphic form, indicating movement from ballad and legend to sketch pad, studio easel, drawing board, or lithographer's stone. I do not raise the kinds of questions we ask for steel-strike songs from the Homestead and textile songs from the Piedmont. I note only the distinction between John Henry as the subject of a sequential ballad and as a fleeting figure within a rhythmic work chant. One narrative stanza conveys essential information on the tunnel man's superiority to the machine:

> The man that invented the steam drill
> Thought he was mighty fine;
> John Henry sunk fourteen feet,
> The steam drill only made nine.

One chanted couplet punctuates drilling/spiking as it challenges fate: "Nine-pound hammer—kill John Henry— / But 't won't kill me, babe—'t won't kill me."

Neither ballad nor work song specifies John Henry's chronology. Hence, folklorists have begun with railway construction along West Virginia's Greenbriar River after the Civil War. In the years 1870–72, Chesapeake & Ohio crews completed the Great Bend Tunnel, popularly called Big Bend, through a spur of the Allegheny Mountains in Summers County. No one has demonstrated with ironclad certainty that the C&O's contractors hired a particular black worker named John Henry. No one has documented the actual competition at Big Bend between a hand driller and a Burleigh steam drill. Regardless, by the turn of the century, a ballad emerged centering on a worker's defiance of and loss to a then-modern machine.

Louise Rand Bascom became the first collector to submit a John Henry fragment (from North Carolina) to the *Journal of American Folklore.* Subsequently, E. C. Perrow and others offered bits and pieces. Josiah Combs encountered a full ballad text in Kentucky in 1909. W. C. Handy published "John Henry Blues" in 1922, setting it at Muscle Shoals Dam, Alabama. Handy's sheet music included a commentary by Phil H. Brown, the first printed explanation of the hero's meaning intended for the general public (Green 1983). Fiddlin' John Carson recorded an eleven-stanza "John Henry" in Atlanta for the Okeh label during 1924.

Norm Cohen and Brett Williams, in their respective books and in talks with me, have filled in accounts of John Henry's journey from steel driller to national icon. In this transition, hundreds of performers moved work tradition into commercial recording and publishing channels. Paralleling the efforts of Carson, Handy, and other musicians, a few laborers also extended their legend from tunnel face to journal pages and archive cabinets.

Leon Harris, secretary of the Rock Island Railway Colored Employees Club, submitted a John Henry short story, "The Steel Driving Man," to the *Messenger,* the Brotherhood of Sleeping Car Porters' periodical. Harris identified himself as a "rambler," a "folksong fiend," and a "grader" (from grading or leveling a railroad right-of-way). He also submitted a full ballad text to Guy Johnson at the University of North Carolina. Harris represents kindred enthusiasts who internalized or embellished job traditions and who freely contributed songs or stories to academic collectors and editors.

Howard W. Odum and Guy B. Johnson, Chapel Hill sociologists and regionalists, presented their account of John Henry in *Negro Workaday Songs*. Previously, Louis Watson Chappell, a young teacher of English at the University of West Virginia, had undertaken fieldwork to establish the ballad's historicity. However, his findings did not appear in print until 1933.

Of all those drawn to the John Henry legend, Guy Johnson first called attention to the hero's leap from oral to visual artistry by publishing a Tar Heel workman's anecdote: "Dey buried [John Henry] dere in de tunnel, an' now dey got his statue carved in solid rock at de mouth o' de Big Ben' tunnel on de C&O—das right over dere close to Asheville somewhere. No, I ain't never been dere, but dere he stan', carved in great big solid rock wid de hammer in his han' " (Odum, 240).

No one has identified the first folksinger or tale teller imaginative enough to project a legendary worker into a monument guarding his own tunnel or memorializing his own death. Guy Johnson's encounter with a Carolina workman indicates that belief in a statue dates at least to the early 1920s. In 1927, Johnson returned to John Henry in a synoptic article for *Ebony and Topaz*, a collection issued by the National Urban League. The sociologist restated his prescient anecdote: "I marvel that some poet . . . does not sing John Henry's praises, that some playwright does not dramatize him, that some painter does not picture him as he battles with the steam drill, or that some sculptor does not fulfil the wishful phantasy of that Negro pick-and-shovel man who said to me, 'Cap'n, they tells me that they got John Henry's statue carved out o' solid rock at the head o' Big Ben' Tunnel. Yes, sir, there he stan' with the hammer in his han' " (51).

In the more than six decades since Johnson penned these anticipatory words, John Henry has been given visual life: he has appeared on the Broadway stage, has been a subject in educational films, has served in classical music settings, and now stands in sculpture above the tunnel portal. Writers and artists from the realms of elite and popular culture have joined to shape a folk hero's journey.

Focusing on the visual John Henry, I open with his first-known portrait, one by Eben Given for Frank Shay's *Here's Audacity* (1930), a book that included separate chapter-length accounts for nine American heroes, traditional or newly minted. Given contributed sixteen illustrations; curiously, he placed John Henry against a factory background, possibly a steel mill. I like this dignified portrait, but I am baffled by seeing a tunnel stiff so far from his mountain setting and railway construction job. Despite Given's questionable choice of background, he initiated John Henry's pictorial adventures.

To appreciate the role of Given and those artists who followed him, I ask what circumstance shaped the transformation of John Henry from verbal to visual hero. Itinerant workers carried Big Bend lore east to the Carolina lowlands and west to the Texas plains, a geographic spread documented by the recovery of songs in scattered locales. Until the mid-1920s, John Henry "belonged" both to the folk and to a tiny band of academic collectors. By noting the effort of Leon Harris, a grading-camp rambler, we have met a worker who walked both sides of the track that separated construction camp from campus.

When Carl Sandburg placed a John Henry text and tune in *The American Songbag,* the ballad began to move to concert singers removed from folk society. It is not a coincidence that Johnson's Urban League article on John Henry appeared close to the publication of Sandburg's popular collection. The poet and the professor, assisted by men and women in the ranks, were part of a strong intellectual current in the 1920s calling attention to African-American folk culture.

In the years of Calvin Coolidge prosperity and Henry Ford marvels, a few Americans placed celebratory value on expression denominated *bygone, old-time,* or *folk.* Urbanization and industrialization made necessary the nostalgic stories of pioneers in leather stockings and workers in denim. In the contradictory enterprises of honoring John Henry for railroad building and mourning his untimely death, Guy Johnson, Carl Sandburg, and Frank Shay joined hands.

Shay edited a fine collection of sea shanties in 1924. Following that, he compiled three anthologies of drinking songs. As a member of the Texas Folklore Society and a friend of J. Frank Dobie, he was conversant with academic controversy in ballad and tale study. The title of Shay's collection, *Here's Audacity,* captured perfectly the spirit in which folklorists and popularizers could treat disparate heroes such as Stormalong, Hiawatha, and John Henry.

Guy Johnson, a southern regionalist versed in folklore studies, projected symbolic analysis of John Henry into popular consciousness. In 1929, Johnson expanded findings into a full-length book, *John Henry: Tracking Down a Negro Legend.* Louis Chappell, in *John Henry: A Folk-Lore Study,* offered interpretations similar to those of Johnson but criticized him for using a preliminary Chappell report without credit. Nevertheless, to this day, all popularizers of the driller's story have turned back to these two scholars.

Seemingly, before Given's portrait of John Henry as a factory or steel-mill hand, no visual artist (whether of allegory, narrative, landscape, or genre) staked out a claim to the tunnel stiff. I touch here the complex issue of choice of traditional subjects by those outside folk society. Similarly, few studio painters dealt with industrialization's scars or with the tension generated in labor conflict during two centuries of nationhood. Given, following Shay's lead in treating John Henry, bridged local color nostalgia and social commentary on work's cause.

John Henry did not spring to life on the minstrel circuit or Tin Pan Alley's stages. The legendary steel driver came from the rich imagination and rhetorical skill of two sets of creators: former slaves new to industry; Appalachian balladeers involved in subsistence farming, logging, coal mining, and railroading. Accordingly, John Henry did not jump directly from folk tradition into the nets of fine or commercial artists but reached visual art's realm only after appearing in folksong anthology and popular fiction.

Only one black artist, Palmer Hayden (true name, Peyton Cole Hedgeman), turned to the John Henry legend. Hayden was born at Wide Water, Virginia, on July 15, 1890. Beginning in 1944, Hayden, working at his New York studio, spread the driller's story in fourteen oil paintings. Although Hayden had retained a vague childhood memory of the ballad, he benefited mainly from two decades of popular attention to the hero.

I offer an additional word on Eben Given to prepare for viewing those fine artists who subsequently portrayed John Henry. In 1924, brother and sister Bill and Katy Smith took a summer cottage at

Provincetown on Cape Cod, staying for years. They attracted a group of intellectuals to their home, Smooley Hall; it became a creative center. John Dos Passos married Katy; her friend Edith Foley married Frank Shay. Another Smooley regular, Eben Given, shared adventures with Dos Passos and provided illustrations for Shay's books. Thus, I suggest that Given saw John Henry initially through the prose sketch in *Here's Audacity.* In time, other illustrators climbed stairs similar to those from Cape Cod to the Big Bend Tunnel.

A few months after the appearance of Shay's book, *Hearst's International-Cosmopolitan* serialized a condensed version of Roark Bradford's *John Henry.* The four installments ran between December 1930 and April 1931. One of the last white writers to contrive fiction from black folklore, Bradford exploited dialect as he burlesqued experience. Occasionally, he crafted a sparkling vignette, but in the main he burdened John Henry with caricature.

*Cosmopolitan* selected Rose O'Neill to illustrate the Bradford stories with eleven drawings—cute babies, glistening stevedores, a seductive Julie Anne. In retrospect, O'Neill's drawings for John Henry's magazine debut seem absurd; in the Depression's pit, *Cosmopolitan* editors had employed light fiction and lush illustrations as an antidote to national gloom. It is a testimony to the inherent strength within the John Henry legend that the hero overcame all portraiture, demeaning or comic.

When Harper & Brothers issued Bradford's *John Henry* in 1931, the publisher wisely chose Julius J. Lankes, a distinguished woodcut artist, to embellish the book. The Literary Guild widely distributed Bradford's episodic novel, thus helping to popularize John Henry lore. For many years, Americans saw the hammerman as a figure in a Lankes woodcut—for example, a grimacing John Henry toting a huge bale of cotton down a sidewheeler's gangplank; a diapered baby, stevedore hook in hand, bursting out of a cradle. Lankes also represented Henry realistically in cotton-picking and track maintenance work.

In 1939, Bradford adapted the novel for a Broadway play with music by Jacques Wolfe. Paul Robeson took the lead, Ruby Elzy played Julie Anne, and Josh White cavorted as a banjo-picking roustabout. Unfortunately, the Broadway fantasy failed to capture the folk narrative's vitality. Anticipating success, Harper & Brothers published the play in an attractive book holding photographs of five stage sets.

Today, in looking back to the initial depictions of John Henry by Eben Given, Rose O'Neill, and J. J. Lankes, we see a great arc of ambivalence with which readers of popular fiction and popularized folklore met a legendary black exemplar. O'Neill, creator of the Kewpie Doll, saw burly workers and pudgy sweethearts as cloying figures. Lankes, too, veered from accurate work settings to ludicrous portraits. Only Given avoided the temptation of seeing John Henry as hustler, trickster, or clown.

In the past half-century, publishers of children's books have expanded the John Henry canon. I call special attention to James Daugherty's handsome anthology, *Their Weight in Wildcats: Tales of the Frontier.* Daugherty, born on an Indiana farm, had enjoyed his grandfather's memories of Daniel Boone. The artist drew pioneers in Boone's image—tall men moving in rhythm with forest and stream, earth and sky. For the frontier tales, Daugherty included three fine drawings of John Henry, going beyond previous items by Given and Lankes.

During World War II, Daugherty contributed drawings to Irwin Shapiro's *John Henry and the Double Jointed Steam Drill.* The artist transcended the writer's syrupy text, for Daugherty sensed Henry as a tragic hero. The topical frontispiece placed the driller in a then-relevant political frame. John Henry, in 1945, had become a bold defense worker flanked by a black GI soldier and mother and child. Below the hammerman, a frieze of real-life personalities (Joe Louis, George Washington Carver, Paul Robeson, Marian Anderson, Booker T. Washington, Richard Wright) spoke to the quest for wartime national unity.

In contrast to Daugherty, who depicted near-mythic figures, a number of illustrators presented John Henry as a friendly tot who might live in a suburban tract. In such books, the black worker emerges as bland rather than vital, as neighborly rather than olympian. Avoiding the perils of sanitization, Ezra Jack Keats, in *John Henry: An American Legend,* filled his book with multicolored, highly imaginative lithographs, catching the worker's strength without reducing him to cardboard.

Artists approaching the John Henry narrative have been puzzled by differences between hand drills, steam drills, electric drills, and pneumatic (jack) hammers. Also, they have not distinguished tunnel construction from railroad track laying, longshoring, and other occupations. Despite such technological mysteries, most John Henry offerings have had the virtue of bringing to children appreciation of hand labor and machine power.

Juvenile books on John Henry parade endlessly. In 1986, David Godine published Steve Sanfield's *Natural Man: The True Story of John Henry* with eighteen delicate black-and-white drawings by Peter Thornton. Choosing among young John's many skills, Thornton depicts him playing the piano so vigorously that keys jump into the air. In 1988, the Kipling Press issued *John Henry,* retold and illustrated by Gary Gianni. This handsome oversized book holds more than a dozen colored illustrations showing John's progression from a child picking cotton to a hammerman applauded by friends, one of whom salutes him with a banjo song.

Not all the art devoted to John Henry appeared in children's books. Other categories included commercial advertisements; art for films and recordings; animated cartoons within films; tourist souvenirs; postcards; postage stamps; sheet-music covers; ceramic ware; statuettes; medallions; T-shirts; posters; and magazine illustrations. Between 1978 and 1983, I touched on such material in a series of articles for the *JEMF Quarterly.* Here, I note two examples, a John Henry china decanter issued by the James Beam Distilling Company in 1972 and a series of posters for the John Henry Folk Festival at Princeton, West Virginia, beginning in 1973.

## Palmer Hayden and Fred Becker

Palmer Hayden and Fred Becker, from dual perspectives, represent fine artists attracted to John Henry. Previously, I noted Hayden's birth in rural Virginia and his ambitious project to complete a set of linked canvases covering the hero's exploits. After serving in World War I, Hayden located in Greenwich Village, where he worked as a janitor while studying art at Cooper Union. In 1925, he continued formal study at the Boothbay Art Colony in Maine. Two years later, a patron helped him travel to France for five years of exposure to avant-garde art.

Back in New York, during the Depression years, he turned to realistic canvases on the waterfront, as well as to satiric Harlem street scenes and depictions of everyday ritual in African-American life. Occasionally, he reached back into personal memory for southern folk themes. Some critics responded with hostility to Hayden's search for roots. One naysayer charged the artist with tasteless talent gone astray by the emulation of blackface minstrel show billboards. Others, participants in the "New Negro" movement of completing emancipation, found it difficult to read, see, or hear expressions that connoted "primitive" origins or echoed the habits of peonage and slavery.

Despite this criticism, Hayden pushed deeply into black experience, undertaking an ambitious John Henry narrative set. Beyond seeking factual content for individual paintings, he moved consciously from academic to "folk art" style: vivid colors, flat surfaces, distorted perspectives, incongruous juxtapositions, time-tested decorative patterns, earthy themes, bucolic emblems.

The need to depict a ballad with a paintbrush stimulated Hayden as he found himself in a position similar to that of Mark Twain embellishing folk speech or William Faulkner transforming folk anecdotes into troublesome metaphors on the human condition. By the end of 1946, Hayden had completed eleven John Henry paintings. The Argent Galleries in Manhattan exhibited the set between January 20 and February 1, 1947, using the artist's descriptive group title, *The Ballad of John Henry in Paintings.*

For the Argent show, Hayden prepared a brief brochure statement treating the hero's symbolism and the artist's sources in boyhood listening and adult reading. He wrote:

> The song of John Henry, the steel-driving man, I first heard when a boy in my early teens at home in Virginia. At that age whenever I heard the ballad sung by older boys or men at work, it appealed to me chiefly because it told in sober words and tune the life and tragic death of a powerful working man who belonged to my section of the country and to my own race.
>
> As I grew older, I came to realize the deeper significance of the story and the literary significance of the ballad. To the Negroes in our country at the time of the building of

> the Big Bend Tunnel, their physical strength and ability and willingness to use it was their chief asset in the struggle for economic survival. Hence, to them John Henry became a symbol of greatness and so popular a folk hero that during his day and for several generations following many Negro babies in the Southern states where christened for him.

Following the Argent debut, the John Henry paintings traveled to Pittsburgh, Nashville, Washington, D.C., and other cities. Pleased with the public response at the Smithsonian, Hayden arranged to place his set on loan at the National Collection of Fine Arts in 1972. A decade later, Mrs. Miriam Hayden transferred the canvases to the Museum of African American Art, Los Angeles.

In the mid-1970s, I viewed the John Henry series at the Smithsonian. In correspondence, Mrs. Hayden shared an explanation of her late husband's thoughtful preparation for the series. She wrote:

> It was shortly after our marriage in 1940 that my husband and I began talking about what he had been thinking of for a long time. He was fascinated by the story and wanted to be the one to immortalize it in paintings. As neither of us knew where the "Big Bend Tunnel" was, I researched the legend in the Art and Drama department of the New York Public Library. There I was fortunate to find a copy of a carefully written, scholarly study of the legend written by a professor of English at West Virginia University, Louis W. Chappell. After delightedly reading the book, Palmer wrote to the author who responded with an encouraging letter and a gift of a copy of the book, which was titled *John Henry: A Folk-Lore Study.* A little later Palmer traveled to Morgantown for an interview with Professor Chappell.
>
> Then we decided to visit the John Henry country. . . . We drove around the countryside staying at Hinton, fascinated to see the local people: Indians, blacks, and what looked like red-haired Scotch Irish—as Professor Chappell had described them—walking down the country road on which we were driving. Our several days in that vicinity gave the artist time to absorb the atmosphere, do any sketching he wished, and prepare for putting his impressions on canvas. The twelve

> John Henry paintings that you saw in Washington on the loan to the Smithsonian were the result. There is one other which Palmer did not include in the series although it belongs, as it pictures the tunnel in a collage of events that were told of the construction.

In further correspondence, Mrs. Hayden presented me with a glossy print of the *Big Bend Tunnel.* Assuming that this collage closed the narrative set, I was surprised to note an additional painting in Allan Gordon's catalog for the Hayden exhibit in Los Angeles, 1988. Gordon included *It's Wrote on the Rock,* an undated oil-on-canvas in which a grave tender or observer points out a monument inscription to a man and woman. The stone reads, "John Henry . . . Virginia," the artist's birthplace rather than the West Virginia site of the steel driller's exploits.

In this final painting closing the John Henry ballad series, a smoke-belching train in the distance moves toward a tunnel portal. I view the canvas imaginatively as depicting Palmer Hayden himself describing John Henry's importance to a well-dressed black couple, perhaps removed from folk society. With such a reading, the fine artist becomes the interpreter of meaning for a folk narrative. I do not know whether Hayden had heard any stories envisioning a stone memorial for John Henry before he painted *It's Wrote on the Rock.*

The following list includes eleven titles first noted in the Argent catalog and adds three others. The Los Angeles catalog reproduces all fourteen paintings in full color.

1. *When John Henry Was a Baby*
2. *He Laid Down His Hammer and Cried*
3. *The Dress She Wore Was Blue*
4. *John Henry Was the Best in the Land*
5. *Where'd You Git Them High-top Shoes*
6. *My Hammer in the Wind*
7. *A Man Ain't Nothin' but a Man*
8. *John Henry on the Right. Steam Drill on the Left*
9. *Died wid His Hammer in His Hand*
10. *Goin' Where Her Man Fell Dead*
11. *There Lies That Steel-drivin' Man*
    (completed after Argent exhibit)

12. *John Henry*
13. *Big Bend Tunnel*
14. *It's Wrote on the Rock*

Palmer Hayden died in Manhattan's Veterans Administration Hospital on February 18, 1973. Galleries and museums continue to display his oil paintings; writers on African-American life comment on his role. Some liken his art to Langston Hughes's poetry, for each turned to vernacular expression, to the speech and sights of street corner gin mill and storefront church. Other critics place Hayden in a Harlem Renaissance frame, finding parallels in his art to the achievements of Aaron Douglas, Zora Neale Hurston, and James Van Der Zee.

Like other workers climbing from poverty, Hayden walked a constricted trail. After he won a Harmon first prize for painting in 1927, the *New York Times* described him as a cleaning man who liked to dabble in oil colors. When Hayden left for Paris, another paper headed its story, "Negro, 33, Quits Scrub Bucket to Paint Abroad" (Reynolds, 107). In commenting on Hayden's shift from menial labor to art, Mary Campbell also touched on his apparent willingness to employ distorted symbols of Negro life (33).

Campbell noted that in 1939 Hayden had completed an autobiographical oil, *The Janitor Who Paints.* Some observers then viewed it as a self-effacing caricature, an Uncle Tom janitor. Internalizing such response, Hayden repainted this piece in the 1950s to stress charm and domesticity. Interestingly, critics of the original *Janitor Who Paints* did not see it as marking a worker's aspiration but rather as commenting on racial stereotype.

During his expatriate days in France, Hayden incorporated geometric imagery and expressionist technique into his paintings. In WPA days, he added elements of moral engagement to craft. Happily, oppositional elements of abstraction and social movement fused in his exploration of African-American folk themes. Hayden's John Henry remains neither surrealistically limp, triangularly frozen, or photographically stark. The hammerman does not pose at the barricades as a militant polemicist; rather, he stands bravely in a frieze of humorous fantasy graced by a banjo-picking siren and concerned fellow workers. Hayden's gentle mules, black and white, are wise; they know, as do the birds singing at John's birth, that the tunnel will be completed despite nature's obstacles and workers' deaths.

We face the interweaving of fact and fancy among the many meanings in John Henry lore. Black workers died in the construction of the Big Bend Tunnel, but Henry came to life in folk imagination. Palmer Hayden, working for decades as a professional artist, consciously selected historical and expressive elements in the driller's story. I view Hayden's achievement as balancing Paris and Harlem, high and folk art. His John Henry series touches energy generated at many work sites as it decorates lore springing from labor.

We know that folk expression is not mere raw ore to be refined in the crucible of fine art. Creators within folk communities need to be lauded for their skills before they climb ladders. Palmer Hayden had heard fragments of the John Henry ballad in boyhood. Curiosity led him to the Big Bend Tunnel and to Professor Chappell, a teacher whose personal path had turned rocky after following John Henry's trail. Both Chappell and Hayden, in their special ways, stimulated appreciation of a black tunnel worker's humanity. In our complex society, occupational creativity should not be walled off from its prime carriers. Palmer Hayden, bringing a tunnel stiff into fine art's domain, employed techniques that helped working people carry on John Henry's tasks.

A decade before Palmer Hayden painted his first John Henry canvas, the steel driver's epic had challenged Fred Becker, a Manhattan woodcut engraver and printmaker. While employed on the WPA Federal Art Project, Becker produced a number of vignettes of jazz musicians, as well as nine John Henry cuts. The jazz pieces (with titles such as *Piano Player, Clambake,* and *Jam Session*) focused on single performers or small combos of the swing band years. By contrast, his John Henry set served a narrative function.

I first encountered Becker's woodcuts in Washington, D.C., during the Bicentennial Celebration, when the National Collection of Fine Arts presented a major exhibition entitled "America as Art." Joshua Taylor, the NCFA director, then edited an extensive catalog also titled *America as Art;* it held four of Becker's John Henry engravings (230). The show and catalog prompted me to reach the artist by telephone and to request that he make his full series available to a new audience. He consented graciously to my appeal.

The following list gives Becker's John Henry pieces in a sequence that seems appropriate to me; it does not represent the artist's chronology or a sense of order inherent in the material. Comments in parentheses are my own.

1. *John Henry Carryings On,* undated. (Designed either to serve as a publication title page or as an opener in a gallery exhibition.)
2. *Black River Country,* undated. (Imaginative setting of swamp at sunset far removed from West Virginia's Big Bend Tunnel. Does the sword encased in stone suggest a link to King Arthur?)
3. *Birth of John Henry,* 1938. (Hero emerges full grown from river; steamboat is link to Roark Bradford's novel.)
4. *John Henry Building a Railroad,* 1936. (Baby John drives spikes; closest scene to traditional ballad.)
5. *John Henry and the Witch Woman,* undated. (Sorcery and sex point to doom.)
6. *John Henry Picking Cotton,* undated. (This work typifies progression from agriculture to industry.)
7. *John Henry Loading Cotton,* 1938. (Theme straight out of Bradford.)
8. *John Henry's Hand,* 1936. (Most abstract within series; railroad tracks become palm lifelines.)
9. *John Henry's Death,* 1937. (A female devil prods Henry to hell. Does the hero hold up or uproot urban civilization with his strength?)

The five dated items completed during 1936–38 are wood engravings, each about six inches by four inches. *Black River Country* and *Witch Woman* are also true wood engravings. However, *John Henry Carryings On* and *John Henry Picking Cotton* result from scratchboard prints. Fred Becker informed me that the Vienna scratchboard he used in the late 1930s had been made of a chalk gesso coating on heavy paper. Because of the heavy stock, he could engrave it with burin tools in the same way that he cut endgrain boxwood. Technically, these last two items are not woodcuts but rather prints (or rubbings) from scratchboard blocks.

In 1979, I reproduced Becker's full John Henry set in the *JEMF Quarterly.* In our conversations, Becker recalled the first public showing of his "folk" cuts. On April 14, 1936, Orson Welles produced for the WPA Theatre Project an all-black production of *Macbeth* at Harlem's Lafayette Theatre. A staff member obtained *John Henry Building a Railroad* for foyer display, making an unusual connection between the black hero and Shakespeare. At the end of 1936, the Museum of Modern Art in Manhattan presented a groundbreaking exhibition entitled "Fantastic Art, Dada, Surrealism." For this show, curators selected two of Becker's WPA engravings, *The Monster* and *John Henry's Hand.* I believe that the latter items represented the first appearance of John Henry in an American museum.

In July 1979, Amherst professor Barry O'Connell met Fred Becker, subsequently providing me with biographical details. Born in 1913 in Oakland, California, Becker first studied art at the Otis Institute, Los Angeles. Moving to New York during the Depression, Becker listened to jazz, drawing caricatures (black chalk on newspaper stock) of musicians in nightclubs for sale on the premises. On 48th Street, he heard stars such as Adrian Rollini, Fats Waller, Teddy Wilson, Wingy Manone, Red Norvo, and John Kirby.

Becker recalls Kirby as the first performer he had heard singing "John Henry." In the mid-1930s, Becker—still sketching jazz musicians on the spot—followed new friends uptown to after-hours clubs in Harlem. In this setting, he sorted out the jazz scene's multiple sights before delving into this music's folk roots. Like many fans, he equated jazz with modern experience. A question Becker posed but did not resolve touched the matter of which art best fits jazz.

Following his WPA years, Becker worked for the Office of War Information. In 1946, he turned to teaching art in Philadelphia; subsequently, he taught for two decades at Washington University in St. Louis. In 1968, he joined the faculty at the University of Massachusetts at Amherst. Beginning his career during the realistic 1930s, Becker, against the grain, pursued an abstractionist bent. He credited Eugene Steinhoff, a Viennese artist-craftsman, for opening his eyes to new currents in architecture, music, and psychiatry.

I have noted how Palmer Hayden reached out to Louis Chappell's academic study to fill out the knowledge of John Henry he had derived from rural Virginia tradition. Fred Becker inverted this path. Prior to hearing the ballad in a Manhattan nightclub, he had read Roark Bradford's popular novel, noting the woodcuts by J. J. Lankes. Hearing John Kirby's jazzy "John Henry," Becker undertook his own illustrations roughly geared to the novel's episodes. Becker sought a manner distinct from the serene realism of Lankes.

For his initial WPA assignment, Becker asked his teacher, the wood engraver Lynn Ward, if he might begin with the spike-driving baby, a railroad track spiraling overhead. In this manner, Bradford, Lankes, Kirby, Ward, and Becker forged an unlikely chain in moving John Henry into fine art's domain. Of all the depictions of the hammerman, Becker's prints travel the greatest distance from pure representation. His imaginative hero remains innocent and decadent, naive and wise, youthful and ancient.

We can draw various lessons from seeing John Henry through the eyes of Palmer Hayden and Fred Becker. The former sought a warm, recognizable style and a sequential narrative. The latter encompassed abstraction without attention to story line. Hayden benefited from an academic study; Becker, from a popular novel. The painter grounded his imagery in ballads and work chants heard in childhood; the wood engraver, in adult jazz artistry. More important than such contrasts, though, is our awareness that Becker and Hayden, together, displayed the amazing breadth in John Henry's appeal.

## Roadside Statue and Folk Carving

Travelers using automobiles can speed across the United States in less than a week. Those who choose interstate highways see few natural or man-made wonders. Others who favor back roads can find scattered monuments to workers, famed or anonymous. In Bangor, we stand before a marble block holding three rugged woodsmen with ax and peaveys frozen in bronze. On the

San Francisco Embarcadero, our eyes follow the swirling lines of a stainless steel abstraction dedicated to longshoreman-writer Eric Hofer.

Between Bangor and the Embarcadero, a continent apart in space and spirit, we encounter memorials to Sam Gompers, Frank Little, and Mother Jones, as well as to the victims of the Ludlow Massacre and the Sunshine Mine Disaster. Ludlow's granite cenotaph speaks to a coal strike broken by troops and thugs. Sunshine's silver miner, sculpted in welded steel, stands with a jack-leg drill pointing to the sky, away from underground danger and death. Many years ago, a fellow shipwright told me that we needed no fine statues, in that our achievements dwelled in the ships we had crafted and launched. I have long reflected on his thoughts while visiting cemeteries to identify workers' graves and while searching for statues that honor the toil and skill, the dreams and devotion of working people.

Near Talcott, West Virginia, an eight-foot, bronze John Henry rests in a quiet roadside park some 400 feet above the old Great Bend Tunnel. The steel driller, standing on a pedestal of native-cut stone, invites Route 3 tourists to linger and question him about past deeds in the tunnel below. The park also holds a plaque to Louis Watson Chappell, who established the factual basis of the John Henry legend. Does any other such marker recognize a scholar who explored work traditions? The John Henry statue has been photographed frequently, sold in miniatures, and distributed in postcard form. Sadly, it has also been vandalized, whether by mindless hoodlums or by race-hate zealots we do not know.

Those who have enjoyed the John Henry ballad and legend are not surprised at the driller's dual roles as a humble laborer and a mysterious hero. Commissioned to create the Talcott John Henry, the sculptor Charles Cooper, in my eyes, failed to invest the hero with power, either natural or supernatural. To compensate, the roadside park, its mountain foliage, and the railroad tracks below combine to form an appropriate setting. Viewers in the park can readily imagine ringing hammers and clanging steel.

No bronze figure wills itself into being. Behind each labor landmark stands a group of dreamers and activists. After seeing John Henry at Talcott, I learned something of the park's story from John Faulconer, one of the statue's "fathers." For years, members of the Talcott-Hilldale Ruritan Club had wanted to make tangible their interest in Big Bend lore. Ross Evans, a retired C&O dining-car porter, did considerable research that combined his personal interests in railroad unionism and Negro history.

No plans seemed to jell until Johnny Cash presented a railroad program on his national TV show in the summer of 1969. Prefacing his ballad rendition by locating the hammerman's death at Beckley, West Virginia, Cash touched a raw nerve, for Hinton had long rivaled Beckley in school athletics. After the broadcast, John Faulconer used his July 16 "Hinton Around" column to editorialize on the Cash gaffe. Soon, the singer sent a handwritten apology to the *Hinton Daily News* with a $500.00 check enclosed for the monument drive.

With this outside spur to action, Summers County residents took up the challenge. William Halstead, a Pence Springs dairyman, did much of the spade work for the Ruritans in building the John Henry Memorial Park. Ted O'Meara, former editor of *Track*, the C&O's company magazine, helped locate sculptor Cooper in Williamston, Michigan. He in turn selected Fred Petrucci, at nearby Clarkston, for the foundry work. The statue reached Hinton on Christmas Day, 1972, pulled in a rented trailer by Cooper's car. On December 28, a C&O crew guided the bronze on a "Chessie" flatbed car through the (new) Big Bend Tunnel to Talcott. Local truckers carried John Henry, "wrapped in a white cloth shawl like an old lady," to the overlook park, where riggers bolted it to the stone pedestal. Ross Evans, Bill Halstead, and their friends had triumphed (Steele, Faulconer).

No one has listed all the outdoor landmarks that signify work in the United States. Behind each monument we find railroad porters, dairymen, stonemasons, foundry hands, journalists, secretaries, and librarians. In saluting those individuals who placed a bronze John Henry above his tunnel, I recall the half-century span in which some workers dreamed of a monument to the "natural man." In 1925, a Tar Heel workman had made the imaginative leap from oral to visual artistry: "Dere he stan', carved in great big solid rock."

Whether anyone has carved John Henry in solid rock, I do not know. However, in 1972, Shields Landon Jones, a retired C&O railroader, did carve the steel driller in wood. I never met Jones;

for the facts I depend on an excellent article by Charles Rosenak in *Goldenseal.* Born in 1901 in Franklin County, Virginia, Jones arrived in Summers County when his sharecropper father sought a better life for his family. S. L. Jones himself worked for the C&O from 1918 until 1967. As a youth, he had hunted, whittled, and played the banjo. As a railroader, he played the fiddle in a rural string band.

After the death of his first wife in 1969, Jones remarried, settling at Pine Hill, a few miles from the Big Bend Tunnel. In retirement, he fell back on woodcarving. Rosenak reports that "heads and figures began to emerge from logs of yellow poplar, walnut, and maple, gathered from the woods behind Pine Hill." After Jones began showing his folk art in county fairs in the early 1970s, gallery owners and museum curators discovered his craftsmanship. Fame came to this modest senior citizen, who remarked sagely on his destiny: "A person has to have some work to do, so I carved some and play the fiddle."

In August 1972, at the West Virginia State Fair, Jones exhibited a carving of John Henry, offering it for fifty dollars. It won first prize in its category. The hammerman stands on a polished wood block mounted on a replica of the tunnel portal. To allay any problem of identity, Jones provides a little white sign inscribed BIG-BEND TUNNEL. The positioning of John Henry over the portal suggests both the actual setting for the hero's exploits and Jones's likely knowledge that a statue was to be erected in Memorial Park.

The carving's bas-relief trees flanking the tunnel may signify the forest over the portal, as well as the Pine Hill timber from which the artist secured his raw material. A rail handcar carrying a water barrel exits the tunnel. I see this barrel as containing the life-giving force that sustained Big Bend's laborers. However, I am baffled by the birdlike gadget at the head of the tool leaning against the portal face. Does this object represent a railroaders' tool with which Jones worked, or is it something he attributed to the period of tunnel construction?

Some viewers, unsympathetic to folk art, may see the Jones carving as inartistic. I find it to be as attractive and provocative as the ballad's most memorable recordings. Living close to Big Bend, Jones may have been familiar with the oldest local narratives about John Henry—those living for a century in oral tradition. In this case, the wood carving gave physical shape to a set of songs and stories.

I suggest that S. L. Jones may have been influenced by illustrated books for children or popular souvenirs, as well as by traditional legendry. Recall that Roark Bradford's *John Henry* circulated widely beginning in 1931. Wherever readers encountered it, they saw J. J. Lankes's woodcuts. Hence, visible commercial and popular models of John Henry could have filtered back to Jones in the years before his retirement.

Many woodcarvers and other folk artists remain hidden as their gifts grace private homes and museum cases. Ideally, we should know something of the physical and conceptual models that Jones used in crafting John Henry. I see railroader Jones, fiddler and carver, in a long procession of workers and singers who created the earliest chants and narratives about America's premier work hero.

## Reflections

Explorers of occupational tradition sail between reefs. Shall we seek a panoramic overview or favor particular cases? Do *work* and *labor* equate to each other, or does the latter term restrict itself to institutional unionism? Is legendary John Henry less significant than flesh-and-blood Joe Hill? Shall I stress Hill's ideology at the expense of Henry's humanity, or look for meaningful links in their deaths by firing squad and by steam drill?

I have not sought in these pages to catalog all visual depictions of John Henry or to describe more than a handful of available illustrations. Given, O'Neill, Lankes, Daugherty, Hayden, Becker, Cooper, and Jones represent the universe of artists attracted to the Big Bend Tunnel's hero. Additional pictures of him can be found in media ranging from collector's lithograph to huckster's T-shirt, from film poster to LP jacket cover. Readers will take pleasure in their discoveries.

Two key books serve as guides for reading, listening, and viewing: Norm Cohen, in *Long Steel Rail,* treated railroad ballads and blues with special attention to early race and hillbilly recordings. In case studies of the John Henry ballad and work chants, he summarized previous research and added full discographies. Brett Williams, in *John Henry: A Bio-Bibliography,* offered a superb treatment of the steel driller as an exemplar in popular culture.

Professor Williams, an anthropologist in Washington, D.C., combined bibliography, discography, interviews, and critical analysis of American culture. Noting that John Henry had been treated by scholars using formulas of craft, class, region, race, and erotic impulse, Williams tied his life in popular imagination to a notion of ambiguity. Her John Henry, no matter how bright on stage or screen, continued to live in tunnel shadows. Uncertainty about the hero stems partially from the circumstance that we know him from song rather than through the pages of formal history.

Because John Henry dwells in folk and popular realms, those who follow his trail find many anomalies. I have previously noted that illustrators of juvenile books dressed the tunnel stiff in varied robes. Depicting him with assorted tools—cotton-picker's sack, roustabout's hook, carpenter's clawhammer, metalsmith's ballpeen hammer, mallet, sledgehammer, spiking mall, railroad-tie tamping bar, steel drill bit, pneumatic jackhammer, steam drill—symbolizes his status as a folk figure. Within history books, John Henry would properly use a tool identified by type, brand, and date.

Folklorists often assert that pop culture sanitizes and softens vernacular expression, yet Brett Williams indicates that popularizers have neither flattened nor weakened John Henry. In song, the machine defeats him; in imagination, he remains powerful as he continues to hammer not only at mountain rock but at American concepts. Many listeners use his narratives, songs, and visual depictions to hammer out their own realities about work and community.

We ask whether any black laborer ever imposed his will on a white inventor's machine. Did John Henry die only because he was black, or because all workers are doomed who defy modernity? How do losers function in a society caught up by worship of competitive sports and entrepreneurial spirit? Ideally, the C&O contractor or capitalist who brought the steam drill to Big Bend should have been honored by song, canvas, and bronze. Are we perverse in having elevated a defeated driller to Olympus?

On listening to a John Henry ballad or seeing him in art, we ponder the meaning of his versatile roles. Over the years, he has lived within frames of black society, white country music, the political New South, railroad romance, juvenile fiction, and Freudian imagery. To encompass such diversity, we fall back on empathy for the driller's tragic destiny. The ballad's phrase "A man ain't nothin' but a man" speaks to universality, as well as to our resolution of uncertainty while facing Henry's role shifting. John's courage reaffirms human worth. When we use the hammerman's narratives and art to resolve matters of identity and community, the hero has succeeded in his blows.

I close these reflections on John Henry by returning to the earliest academic interest in his legend. In 1924, Howard Odum founded the Institute for Research in Social Science at the University of North Carolina. When staff members took up problems of race relations, farm tenancy, prison reform, and industrial labor, the institute plunged into controversy. Within this setting of large concern, Odum and his young researchers also explored folklore—"the soul of the people."

About 1925, H. L. Mencken, immersed in American speech and esoterica, suggested to Odum that he investigate John Henry, real or fictitious (Singal, 320). Guy Johnson took up the quest. In 1980, he and his wife, Guion Griffis, looked back at their initial attention to folk culture. The Johnsons and Odum, all southerners, had encountered Negro material in childhood and during their travels. At Chapel Hill, they could also collect songs and stories literally within sight of their campus office. The Johnsons wrote:

> In the mid-1920s, the University was entering into a period of construction of new buildings and renovations of the old original buildings. In that preautomation era, large gangs of pick-and-shovel men and other hand-laborers were needed, and black laborers from several Deep South states came to Chapel Hill to work. Many a student and professor listened, spellbound, as a group of diggers sang a work song, with picks whirling in unison on the upstroke and a mighty "hunh" of exhalation at the end of the downstroke. At twilight and dawn, plaintive calls and "hollers" could be heard in the barracks area where the workmen lived, only a hundred yards across the Pittsborough Highway from the residences. (134)

I interpret Guy Johnson's collecting in campus shadows as a metaphor for working people and their allies interested in laborlore. Not all of us can travel to the roadside park at the Big Bend Tunnel—or, for that matter, to Mt. Olive, Illinois, where Mother Jones is memorialized, or to Sugarhouse Park in Salt Lake City, where Joe Hill was executed. We experience some lore directly on our particular jobs. However, for the work expressions of others we depend on library, archive, and museum; we use the tools of tape, disc, and screen.

Workers build traditionalizing arenas of speech and memory in every corner of our land, at every busy airport and shopping mall, in high-rise towers and entertainment domes. Such talking circles carry their own markers: "shooting the breeze," "clowning," "taking five," "coffee break," "goofing-off time." Metaphorically, John Henry stands in these rings as his children continue to drive steel and instruct shakers. In short, his hammer rings on present-day assembly lines and at computer terminals. We need to feel the tunnel stiff's spirit wherever we toil, for he comes closer than any American hero, mythic or historic, to make both the pleasure and the pain in work palpable.

"To Fan the Flames"

# 2

# Singing Joe Hill

By any definition of the accolade, John Henry is a folk hero. Americans have learned to pin this ribbon on bank embezzlers, rock stars, porn queens, and superspies. Do we also find virtue in naming the IWW martyr Joe Hill a folk hero? I pair the legendary tunnel stiff and Wobbly bard not to elevate the latter to a folk Valhalla but to reveal elusive shadings within laborlore categories.

Hill worked with a pen; Henry, with a hammer. Joe Hill did labor as a seaman and stevedore, but his status accrues from his cause, not his toil. Today, Hill is a union hero; to link him to Henry is to suggest that the labor movement constitutes a folk community analogous to a group walled off from mainstream society by language, region, or ethnicity. Few workers engage this matter, although it does puzzle scholars. In part 1, I asked whether the rubric *laborlore* should apply only to traditional groups and their enactments. Readers will respond from their special perspectives.

Although I have no need to anoint Joe Hill with folk glamour, I consider it appropriate to place him in a book exploring the expressive culture of working people. This seeming paradox flows out of multiple meanings arising from splicing the terms *folk* and *lore* to *labor.* Not only do we shrink from stretching speech beyond familiar meanings, but Joe Hill himself poses substantial problems for folklorists and labor historians. A few of his compositions entered tradition, thus becoming folksongs, and the popular piece that begins with the line "I dreamed I saw Joe Hill last night" is often said to be a folksong.

The title of this chapter, "Singing Joe Hill," can be read either as a biographical introduction to a major labor song composer or as our action in singing a particular piece about him. Here, I underplay both these concerns in favor of attention to the genesis of the song about Joe Hill. I assume that readers know Hill's story: Swedish immigrant, IWW itinerant, executed in Utah in 1915, Industrial Workers of the World exemplar. Gibbs Smith fills in details in a challenging biography, although mystery continues to trail Hill's legacy.

I turn to "Joe Hill," the memorial by Alfred Hayes and Earl Robinson, as well as to its ideological cradle. The ballad comments on the ambiguous role of leftists in extending trade unionism's legacy. It also helps illustrate how radical groups cannibalize each other's heroes. The song that now carries Hill's memory has become a building block in labor's manse of tradition, thereby drawing to itself the pervasive ambivalence many Americans feel in treasuring lore. In short, my analysis of workers' culture leads into swamps of controversy over uncertain words and controversial deeds.

I approach the Hayes-Robinson ballad indirectly by invoking the spirit of another song, one known to the poet and the musician before they collaborated on "Joe Hill." For more than a century, "L'Internationale" echoed final conflict and ultimate triumph. In beat and belief this revolutionary march stands far from "Joe Hill," a pensive elegy. Juxtaposing these two songs helps readers and listeners explicate each, for the contrast between them opens a path to the understanding of laborlore's complexities.

## Assaying Ore

In 1871, with the French army crushing a revolt in Paris, Eugene Pottier wrote a poem entitled "L'Internationale." Pottier could not have known that it would become a transnational radical hymn, as well as the Soviet Union's anthem. Pierre Degeyter, a Belgian woodturner, set the poem to music in 1888; the new offering appealed broadly to socialists, anarchists, and syndicalists. In June 1989, TV newscasters sent this song around the globe from China's Tiananmen Square, where young people sang it defiantly and fearfully. "L'Internationale" did not ring from Moscow, when, in August 1991, barricade builders defended their parliamentary building from Red Army tanks.

Pottier, like many rebels juggling past and future, stated in his poem, "Du passé faisons table rase." Some singers understood *table rase* literally, as the French echo of the Latin *tabula rasa,* a tablet from which writing had been erased. Pottier used the line figuratively, however, to suggest, "of the past, let us make a broken tablet," or "level rules." Metaphorically, he called to rebels to make a fresh start with an open mind, an idyllic mind unmarred by external sensation.

Translators in Great Britain freely rendered Pottier's line as "Now, away with all superstitions," whereas Americans sang "No more tradition's chains shall bind us." In *Carry It On!* Seeger and Reiser present "L'Internationale" in French and in ten translations. The current IWW songbook holds an American English variant credited to an adaptation by Charles H. Kerr. Over the years, Pottier's statement on superstition/tradition has resonated among radicals who have pictured themselves denouncing sacred tablets, wiping slates clean, defying superstitious beliefs, and breaking tradition's chains.

Within an enclave of the dominant society they abhorred, IWW rebels created and treasured a particular corpus of tradition. This Wobbly cornucopia (idea, action, expression) can be likened to ore dug from earth. Some adventurers encounter pure gold nuggets; others, iron pyrites. Some assay ore; others refine metal before transforming it into a structural beam or a surgeon's scalpel. I suggest that, in the firming of IWW tradition, members wrested ore from earth, turning to blacksmithing in forging anchor chains or ankle links. Thus, we see Wobblies variously as chain makers, as metaphoric chain breakers, and as creators of tradition's chains. I use this seeming contradiction of divergent roles to highlight the ambiguity built into Joe Hill legendry.

At this juncture, I shall not catalog any Wobbly lore. Joyce Kornbluh's *Rebel Voices,* a treasury of IWW tradition, has been available since 1964, and my next chapter reveals the etymological journey of the nickname *Wobbly.* Regardless of their entrance into the labyrinth, readers will encounter Joe Hill. Among many others, Elizabeth Gurley Flynn, Ralph Chaplin, Wallace Stegner, Barrie Stavis, Joe Glazer, Joan Baez, and Bo Widerberg have reinforced Hill's hold on our imagination. His beatification process is not fully understood, although abundant raw material spreads out from little red songbooks to Gibbs Smith's biography, *Joe Hill.*

Here, I assert that Hill himself paved the path for his ascension to a proletarian heaven. Many Wobblies intensely dislike words such as *ascension* or *beatification,* for they connote the sacred belief system that bound workers in chains. Rebels declared that workers were "dehorned" when under the influence of "sky pilots" (priests and preachers), bourgeois journalists, saloonkeepers, and brothel madames. Just as a ranch hand dehorned cattle with a saw, boss agents from the pulpit, newspaper office, and bordello emasculated workers with sermons, editorials, and joie de vivre.

We can debate whether religion is the opiate of the masses, but we can be certain that the IWW did not want Joe Hill to be remembered as a religious icon, a sanctified or mythological figure. I favor the terms *legend* and *legendry* to indicate that Hill lived in history and that traditional narratives continue to cluster around his memory. In this sense, he is more a companion of Buffalo Bill and Annie Oakley than of Zeus and Hera.

The historian William Preston, who spoke for many in his field, as well as for IWW members coping with their ambiguous place in tradition, observed the following:

> History that popularizes and makes myths of the men and movements the country once feared and destroyed is a traitor to its past. Utah killed Joe Hill in 1915. Fifty years later the Salt Lake City Public Library gave a folk song concert-lecture to a great folk hero. But Americans don't take their folk heroes seriously, the proof being that no one confronts the realities Hill's martyrdom challenged (the whole question of equal justice in America). Hill then became a legend, exaggerated, Bunyanesque, and anaesthetic rather than a threat. And wearing a Joe Hill sweatshirt does not make anyone a radical.
>
> The I.W.W. and other radical movements can be rescued from the historical cycle of myth and counter-myth only if Americans comprehend fully why large segments of the population have been "born to lose" in an equalitarian-libertarian society with a uniquely affluent material base. (1971, 436)

Anyone who has thought seriously about Joe Hill has encountered Preston's litany in multiple forms. Reality (fact/truth) contends with romance, illusion, fiction, myth, and lore. Good workers and their academic comrades in arms battle with purveyors of the arcane, bizarre, and jejune. A critical comment in the IWW press marks such tension.

In January 1990, California members of AFL-CIO unions presented a Labor Heritage Festival (San Francisco) in which Earl Robinson discoursed on Joe Hill and Pete Seeger sang IWW songs. Jess Grant wrote about the event in the *Bay Branch Bulletin,* as well as in the *Industrial Worker:* "Joe Hill Is Dead! Long Live the IWW!" Grant asserted that fellow workers needed "to counteract the grave-robbing antics of those who would mythologize Joe Hill without ever acknowledging the radical context in which he wrote his songs, or admit that the ideas of the IWW are more relevant today than they were in 1910." Grant spoke for Wobs in questioning the motives of "progressive" trade unionists who have long coveted Wobbly imagery.

We cannot deny the differences between young Wobblies and their sisters and brothers in "official" unions. We also know that individuals distant from IWW principles helped decorate Joe Hill's story. In the years between 1915 and 1925, IWW members primarily carried the burden of Hill's martyrdom. However, in the mid-1920s—years of agitation to free Sacco and Vanzetti—several liberal authors (for example, Edna St. Vincent Millay and John Dos Passos) took up the cause of the anarchist prisoners.

Dos Passos reveals how one free-thinking intellectual sympathetic to the IWW came to identify with Joe Hill. During his freshman year at Harvard (1912), Dos Passos followed the murder trial of three IWWs—Arturo Giovannitti, Joe Ettor, Joe Caruso. Before and after the trial, textile workers marched and sang in the streets of Lawrence. Years later, Dos Passos recalled this action for "Camera Eye 25" in *The 42nd Parallel,* the opening novel in his trilogy *U.S.A.*

In 1924, Upton Sinclair wrote a four-act tract, *Singing Jailbirds,* based on a San Pedro maritime strike. Red Adams, the play's Wobbly hero, resembled Joe Hill; waterfront strikers in prison sang Hill's songs. In December 1928, Eugene O'Neill and John Dos Passos helped stage the play for a diverse audience at Greenwich Village in the Provincetown Playhouse. In *U.S.A.*, Dos Passos introduced a working-stiff hero, a young IWW typesetter named Fenian McCreary. Mac continues to live as one of many finely etched Wobblies in fiction. *U.S.A.* also held a memorable prose portrait of Joe Hill with a closing line, "The first of May they scattered his ashes to the wind."

In *Mid-century* (1961), Dos Passos returned to the experimental techniques of *U.S.A.*, as well as to a "mature" labor movement. Reports from the United States Senate McClellan Committee highlighted corruption in union office and alienation in workers' ranks. Parallel to his sketches of Jimmy Hoffa, Harry Bridges, and Walter Reuther, Dos Passos reserved his most vital portrait for Blackie Bowman, a garrulous old Wob dying in a Veterans Administration hospital. Blackie invoked Joe Hill's "last and final will" to touch on the loss of memory by an old vet of many wars. Also, Bowman felt himself "hanging like Mohamet's coffin between heaven and hell" (148). It is not Blackie alone who hangs suspended but all old Wobblies buffeted by their inability to halt the flow of lore out of their unions and by indifference to their sacrifice.

While poets, novelists, and playwrights linked hands to turn Hill into a demigod, American communists also joined the procession. With the 1917 Russian Revolution hailed as a "Red Dawn," some IWW members (such as Elizabeth Gurley Flynn and Harrison George) abandoned anarcho-syndicalism in favor of Leninism. Weakened by such defections, as well as by governmental persecution, the Wobblies experienced a terrible split in 1924. Characteristically, rivals named themselves "Four Trey" (from their headquarters at 3333 W. Belmont, Chicago) and "EP" (from an Emergency Program). No partisans won this internal fight; rank-and-filers peeled away from both sides.

In a setting of conflict over centralized/decentralized authority and over allegiance to Moscow, Joe Hill's songs and lore moved into many channels, including Communist party units. Three items mark such lateral dissemination. In the Depression's depth, proletarian writers emerged—some from intellectual circles, others from factory aisle and hobo jungle. H. L. Lewis, a Missouri plowboy poet, then embraced the distant Soviet experiment. When his *Thinking of Russia* appeared, an anonymous *New Republic* critic hailed Lewis: If he "would set himself to the task of fitting new words to old tunes, he might become the red-starred laureate, the Joe Hill of the Communist movement" (Wixson 1993).

H. L. Lewis remains obscure; his reviewer in April 1932 anticipated the desire by communists to appropriate Wobbly treasures. For years, Mike Gold had pontificated on cultural matters in a *Daily Worker* column entitled "Change the World." On October 19, 1933, he described a meeting of New York City's Irish Workers Club wherein the discussion period ended with a "sing-song." Gold wrote, "One comrade [sang] an old ballad in Gaelic, haunting and soulful with its ancient sorrow of a persecuted race. . . . Labor songs of Ireland and England were sung, too. . . . Why don't American workers sing, the Wobblies knew how, but we have still to find the Communist Joe Hill."

Without a history focused on Communist party cultural decisions, we do not know which Red first reached enviously to Hill's legacy. As late as 1927, Anthony Bimba, in *The History of the American Working Class,* had not mentioned Hill. Bimba knew that Wobblies did not flinch in struggle, but he branded them as ideologically bankrupt. I do not doubt that Bimba, a communist, had heard Hill's songs, but the former's politics prevented him from appreciating the IWW bard's contribution.

We credit Mike Gold as the first Party spokesman to elevate Hill as a musical exemplar rather than as a miscreant libertarian spreading false consciousness. It is difficult today to convey the intensity of antagonism among radicals of different stripes. One measure of Joe Hill's legacy is found in his acceptance by enemies of the IWW, past and present.

A year after Mike Gold's call for a communist Joe Hill, Alan Calmer wrote "The Wobbly in American Literature" for the *New Masses.* The article has not worn well over the years. Calmer undercut his thesis by a belief that "the Wobbly literary movement was buried long ago. Its revolutionary heritage has passed on to the Communist men of letters." I cite the following lines (1934), not for their blatant grab at IWW glory but rather for the first printing of "I Dreamed I Saw Joe Hill Again" and for Calmer's assertion that a "young Communist poet [Alfred Hayes] salutes his predecessor." The Hayes poem reads:

> And standing there as big as life,
> And smiling with his eyes,

Joe says, "What they forgot to kill
Went on to organize."

"Joe Hill ain't dead," he says to me,
"Joe Hill ain't never died,
Where workingmen are out on strike,
Joe Hill is at their side."

"From San Diego up to Maine,
In every mine and mill,
Where workers fight and organize,"
Says he, "You'll find Joe Hill."

Neither Calmer nor Hayes possessed a crystal ball capable of revealing that these three stanzas would be expanded to seven, set to music, and enter tradition to become a sign of labor values.

Within this chapter, I touch on but a few details in the ballad's travels. In the summer of 1936, Al Hayes met Earl Robinson at Camp Unity, a Communist party retreat near Wingdale, New York, where as staff members they prepared musical and theatrical entertainments, as well as campfire skits and sings. One afternoon Hayes gave Robinson his brief Joe Hill poem; the latter recalls, "I simply went into a tent with my guitar and in about 45 minutes had a song . . . I sang it that evening." The next morning, a few campers "came around" to request the poignant text and tune (1986c).

The casual circumstances of composition and the need to prepare an instant song joined to light a beacon. Composing in 1936, Robinson did not select a tune firmed in Anglo-American or African-American folk tradition. Most of the Unity campers had come from New York City, many of Eastern European and Jewish origin. All had been exposed to then-current Tin Pan Alley melodies. The "folksong revival" had not yet elevated Delta blues or Appalachian laments as the appropriate mode for labor song.

We can measure the instant appeal of "Joe Hill" by its appearance as a printed song shortly after Camp Unity participants returned to Manhattan. The *Daily Worker* carried lyrics and melody (for voice and piano) on September 4, 1936. Apparently, neither Hayes nor Robinson sensed potential profits in their Hill piece until they gave it to Bob Miller in 1938 for copyright purposes. Hayes had not sent his poem to the Copyright Office at time of writing or when the *New Masses* printed it.

No one has unearthed an appearance of the text earlier than Calmer's 1934 article, or of the tune earlier than the 1936 *Daily Worker.* These two dates hold importance in that the ballad's phrase "ten years dead" has led many commentators to date the poem back to 1925—literally a decade after Hill's death. For many years, the folklorist Richard Reuss and I shared a running dialogue over the birthday for Hayes's poem. In 1966, Rondo Anderson contributed a note to *Western Folklore* stating, among other matters, that mourners had chanted "Joe Hill" at the time of his execution in 1915. In 1967, Reuss sent the journal a follow-up note: the Hayes-Robinson piece could not have been sung in 1915; it had been composed in 1925 ("ten years dead"). It took me more than a decade to convince Reuss to advance the time of composition to about 1932. Our differences—1925 or 1932—signified much more than a shift in calendar. By delving into chronology, I sought to fill out an ideological picture.

## Al Hayes

I based my date estimate for the memorial ballad on the fact that Alfred Hayes was born in London on April 17, 1911. The Hayes family emigrated from England in 1913, joining other workers in New York's then-Jewish Harlem neighborhood. It seems unlikely that a fourteen-year-old with no known connection to the IWW would have penned a nostalgic poem about Joe Hill. A young Wobbly, of course, might have done so. Hence, in seeking to date Hayes's poem, I turned to a consideration of his political beliefs.

Dr. Nathan Adler, Al's childhood friend, has helped me glimpse his companion's literary/political growth. In the fifth grade at New York City Public School 84, Al entertained assembled classmates with a ringing recitation of Poe's poem "The Bells." At Commerce High, Al submitted poetry to the school paper; his first published efforts derived from Swinburne and other romantics. After reading Ben Hecht's fiction, he experimented with realistic writing. As an early "dropout," he did copyboy work and crime reporting on Hearst's *American* and *Daily Mirror.* In 1928, he joined the Young Communist League; with a focused worldview, he began sending radical poetry to little magazines.

In a 1934 report to *New Masses* readers, Orrick Johns noted Hayes's status in communist circles: "There was Alfred Hayes, dark, Dantean, witty, conscious to imperiousness that he personifies a new sort of 'young generation,' the lyric poet of the New York working class, the strike front, the writer of sketches that bite into memory." Hayes served in the army in Italy during World War II. Two novels marked these years, *All Thy Conquests* and *The Girl on the Via Flaminia.*

In 1947, Hayes completed *Shadow of Heaven,* a novel about Harry Oberon, a forty-year-old union organizer in the runaway garment shops of Pennsylvania's anthracite region. This novel appears as the mirror opposite to John Steinbeck's *In Dubious Battle,* with its disciplined California apple strike organizer and its idealized neophyte. In *Shadow of Heaven,* Oberon, disillusioned and unfulfilled, leaves Marxism behind. Reflecting on his youth, he recalls that when he was nineteen, his choices had seemed simple; his energy and passion, inexhaustible. In a revery he sees mounted police smashing a demonstration: "The placards fell, the captains scattered, the speeches ended . . . leaving only the photographers . . . as though it were done for the photographers" (151).

Hayes, like his fictional character Oberon, abandoned radical dogma. I do not know the precise years of Hayes's move from the YCL into and out of the Communist party. Did he react to the Moscow trials? Did he meet comrades in Italy who challenged his beliefs? Did Hollywood turn Red visions to dust? In a 1982 interview with Judith Spiegelman, he made no reference to a political past. Until his death on August 14, 1985, he wrote poetry, novels, and screenplays for TV and cinema. We continue to see *Paisan, Bicycle Thief,* and other films in which Hayes worked alongside Fellini, Amidei, Pagliero, Rossellini, and De Sica.

To date, no one commenting on "Joe Hill" has delved into Hayes's crucial role in extending the Wobbly songster's appeal. Had Hayes not met Robinson at Camp Unity, there would have been no "Joe Hill" for Paul Robeson and Joan Baez to sing to worldwide audiences, no key line—" 'I never died,' says he"—to cite in retrospects touching on IWW glory. Surely a student turning back to the radical culture of the 1930s will find some challenge in Hayes's contribution.

Commentators frequently equate the Hayes-Robinson ballad with the totality of IWW tradition. My studies have convinced me that "Joe Hill" is as widely known as any labor song in the United States and retains strong affective power. Many listeners assume that Joe Hill himself wrote it; others cannot believe that it came from the hands of a writer and musician outside the Wobbly camp. By demystifying mind-sets of borrowers and travelers, we can gain clarity in viewing the path along which Joe Hill lore moved away from the IWW.

In the early 1930s, when Alfred Hayes assimilated labor history, the Communist party mired itself in sectarian politics and Stalinist exegesis. During those apocalyptic years, often labeled the Third Period, only a few comrades such as Margaret Larkin had the vision to embrace Anglo-American folksong. I have already indicated that Earl Robinson did not select a traditional tune for the Hayes poem. Yet the simplicity of poem and song suggested to many that "Joe Hill" had begun life as a folksong. Margaret Boni "certified" such status by including "Joe Hill" in her well-received *Fireside Book of Folk Songs.*

We can gauge something of the public's receptivity to Hayes's "Joe Hill" and Robinson's melody by contrasting the song with another Hayes poem, "Into the Streets May First," set to music by Aaron Copland. In 1931, several musicians in or close to the Communist party had formed the Pierre Degeyter Club and the Composers Collective of New York. When, in 1934, the *New Masses* announced a competition for a new "mass song," the editors sent Hayes's poem to the collective. Aaron Copland won the prize with his musical setting.

On May 1, the *New Masses* printed the strident text and vigorous tune. Ashley Pettis, anticipating that comrades would have difficulties with Copland's score, tied its "experimental nature" to the "awakening consciousness and growing power" of American workers. Charles Seeger, active in the collective and a *Daily Worker* critic, had helped award the prize. Decades later, in interviews, Seeger cited it to mark flaws in revolutionary music—freak modulations, big skips of sevenths, dissonances, numerous key changes. In 1934, Seeger had questioned Copland rhetorically about "Into the Streets May First": "Do you think it will ever be sung on the picket line?" (Copland, 225).

I do not know whether such musical criticism affected Hayes. As a communist poet in the mid-1930s, he did not escape harsh polemics about proletarian literature. Immediately after the Russian Revolution, some writers had embraced avant-garde forms with considerable freedom to experiment. By 1932, marching under the banner of Socialist Realism, Soviet commissars mandated formulaic literature: optimistic, accessible to the masses, party-minded (*partijnost*). These calls reverberated throughout America's John Reed Clubs. Hayes served on the editorial board of the New York club's *Partisan Review* in its initial years, contributing poetry and criticism.

I need not reopen old wounds in Red literary wars; I want only to suggest that the Hayes-Robinson ballad poses questions about the intersection of culture and politics on the left. "Joe Hill" does not resemble Hayes's own didactic political poetry. Two examples illustrate the latter form: "In a Coffee Pot" ("We shall not sit forever here and wait / We shall not sit forever here and rot"); "To Otto Bauer" ("For you / History prepares a shameful grave").

"Into the Streets May First" opens windows to a period and reinforces our sense of "Joe Hill's" elegiac quality. Hayes's "marching poem" reads as follows:

Into the streets May First!
Into the roaring Square!
Shake the midtown towers!
Shatter the downtown air!
Come with a storm of banners,
Come with an earthquake tread,
Bells, hurl out of your belfries,
Red flag, leap out your red!
Out of the shops and factories,
Up with the sickle and hammer,
Comrades, these are our tools,
A song and a banner!
Roll song, from the sea of our hearts,
Banner, leap and be free;

Song and banner together,
Down with the bourgeoisie!
Sweep the big city, march forward,
The day is a barricade;
We hurl the bright bomb of the sun,
The moon like a hand grenade.
Pour forth like a second flood!
Thunder the alps of the air!
Subways are roaring our millions—
Comrades, into the Square!

At the time that Hayes met Robinson at Camp Unity, many communists felt comfortable in supporting Franklin Roosevelt in his 1936 reelection bid. Four years previously, they had reviled FDR as a "social fascist." In the few years between Hayes's writing of "Joe Hill" and its Camp Unity musical debut, American communists made a dramatic turn from sectarian to liberal lines. This switch to Popular Front positions facilitated an acceptance of song styles—both rhetorical and musical—that softened previously overt messages. We can "hear" shifting political gears by listening to Copland's setting for "Into the Streets May First" and Robinson's for "Joe Hill."

In the Depression era, communists felt no pangs in rejecting the Wobblies philosophy while adopting their martyrs and song lore. It has proved impossible over the years to elevate William Z. Foster, Earl Browder, and other Red luminaries to any pantheon. Thus, Joe Hill became fair game for pundits like Mike Gold. One can say, tongue-in-cheek, that communists who absorbed IWW lore took it for a ride on history's train.

I report with regret my failure to reach Al Hayes and to learn his views on "Joe Hill." In several letters to him, 1972–84, I introduced myself as a folklorist interested in work culture. He chose not to reply. Caught between my respect for his privacy and my feeling that we needed his recollection of the ballad, I telephoned him at his San Fernando Valley home in Encino (February 12, 1984). Ascertaining my purpose, he terminated the conversation. I state these facts in sorrow and with sympathy. Clearly, Hayes did not want to dredge his poem, or its nativity, out of memory.

On Hayes's death, the *New York Times* cited not only his contributions to film and fiction but also "Joe Hill": "It became a rallying cry on the picket lines of the post-Depression labor movement and is still heard in folk music programs" (Mitgang). Would Hayes have relished being memorialized mainly as the author of a union elegy?

On Earl Robinson's death in Seattle on July 20, 1991, many newspapers noted the importance of his "Joe Hill." Writing in the *Los Angeles Times,* Burt Folkart suggested that this piece had become "an unofficial anthem for the Flower Children of the '60s and '70s as it had been for their working-class mothers and fathers." I call attention to the *Times'* obituary for its transgenerational insight, as well as to reiterate that we necessarily judge a song's place in tradition long after its early trail may have been obliterated.

On May 30, 1982, Gwen Gunderson interviewed Al Hayes and Earl Robinson in Culver City while gathering data for the latter's biography. She found Hayes to be casual about his poem and its circumstance of origin and ambivalent concerning its meaning. As Hayes remembered, he wrote "Joe Hill" while living with his parents on East Fremont Avenue in the Bronx, possibly as early as age nineteen. "It was not pre-meditated—not conscious," he said. Hayes described a little room overlooking an airshaft, a narrow single bed, and a table. "I got up in the morning and wrote it right then; in about a half-hour, and it just came like that—and there it was."

Talking to Gunderson, Hayes could not or would not name any specific political or trade union event that called up the poem. He did not tell her how or when Joe Hill slid into his consciousness, nor did he provide clues on how the poem might have reached the *New Masses* in 1934. Key details on the writing of "Joe Hill" may never come to light. Mrs. Gertrude Hayes, in a letter to me, suggests that her husband wrote the poem as late as 1934—four years after the "age nineteen" he had recalled for Gunderson.

At Camp Unity, Hayes had liked Robinson's "simple, very catchy" tune, but he had not thought the song would last. Thus, he was surprised and pleased to receive handsome royalties after Joan Baez sang "Joe Hill" at the Woodstock Festival in 1969. Cotillion Records widely distributed the festival soundtracks on an LP set that included "Joe Hill." Baez also recorded it with Nashville sidemen for a Vanguard album. Did these country musicians know the Wobbly bard's story?

Gwen Gunderson attempted to elicit from Hayes his sense of the song's importance by noting that previously she had asked novelist Albert Maltz to comment on the Baez recordings. Maltz tied the popularity of Baez's "Joe Hill" to 1960s audiences "receptive to necessary change in the country." Hayes dismissed such blatant "sociological interpretation" by returning to the notion that he had just dashed off a folklike ballad in half an hour. Clearly, "Joe Hill" did not and could not rank in Hayes's mind with his serious poetry.

Reflecting on the interview, I have speculated that, in 1982, Hayes not only rejected Maltz's analysis but, beyond that, relegated to a cave the doctrines of past associates on the *Daily Worker* and the *New Masses*. Perhaps a scholar turning to Hayes's fine novels and poetry will take a fresh look at "Joe Hill" and bring to the surface a comparative reading of this poem set in 1930s literary radicalism.

While still living in the Bronx, Hayes had joined the John Reed Club in Manhattan. In the club's active years, he shared dreams with Kenneth Fearing, Sol Funaroff, Kenneth Patchen, Edwin Rolfe, and other "Red Poets." Patchen's "Joe Hill Listens to the Praying" appeared in the *New Masses* just two months after Alan Calmer had used Hayes's "Joe Hill" stanzas. Patchen's long poem carries readers to Salt Lake City's prison yard on the eve of Hill's execution. The chaplain drones; the riflemen finger their weapons; an unseen narrator declaims Hill's songs. The poem ends by noting that creative art itself is a redemptive activity (Nelson, 147).

In 1990, Joe Glazer recited Patchen's verses for a Smithsonian recording. This 1934 poem presently appeals only to a small audience, yet its closing message holds relevance: why does Hill's cultural role as songwriter elevate him above fellow labor organizers and socioeconomic analysts? Could Hayes and Patchen have talked about this matter? I believe that they knew each other's Hill elegies, so different in form and tone. The two poets had walked early roads together; the divergent paths of their poems memorializing Hill speak volumes to those who decipher laborlore tablets.

## Continuities

Without question, today's Joe Hill belongs to workers both in and out of IWW ranks and beyond national borders. A few examples support these points. The Hayes-Robinson ballad is the best-known American labor song in Great Britain (Richards). It was Walter Reuther's favorite song; friends sang it at the UAW leader's funeral. I need not underscore Reuther's social democratic politics in contrast to both Wobbly and Communist party positions. Earl Robinson sang "Joe Hill" to his own pinao accompaniment at a University of California memorial for Reuther (May 1970).

On Labor Day, 1990, to mark the seventy-fifth anniversary of Hill's death, a Salt Lake City committee of AFL-CIO and IWW activists sponsored a concert in Sugarhouse Park, the site of Hill's execution at the Utah State Prison. Pete Seeger, Joe Glazer, Earl Robinson, Utah Phillips, and others performed. This physical setting, now a verdant meadow, proved more powerful than the individual songs.

In November, the committee followed with an academic conference on the University of Utah campus. Many of the participants questioned the fairness of the state's 1915 trial and returned to the matter of Hill's innocence or guilt. Others focused on "reclaiming the myth"—essentially, touching on the relevance of laborlore for present-day workers. Portions of the anniversary concert and conference in print, tape, and film have been archived at the Folk Arts Program of the Utah Arts Council.

We shall continue to hear Joe Hill's own compositions, as well as songs about him, in many settings. In 1991, Chicago filmmaker Eric Scholl produced *The Return of Joe Hill*, a one-hour videotape including interviews with the IWW artist Carlos Cortez, the author Joyce Kornbluh, and others. The film concludes with a scene of Wobblies scattering the last bit of Joe Hill's ashes among the tombstones of coal miners killed in a 1927 strike at the Columbine Mine in Colorado. This video production, literally a labor of love, reveals again how images of the Wobbly bard determine the general representation of workers' traditions.

Another tribute comes in the form of a sound recording titled *Don't Mourn—Organize! Songs of Labor Songwriter Joe Hill.* Lori Elaine Taylor edited this CD/LP/cassette for the Smithsonian

Institution (released in June 1990). She gathered fifteen recordings from 1941 though 1990—new issues and reissues—stressing variety in performing styles. Taylor noted that "learning and perpetuating stories and songs of Joe Hill is a rite of passage." A Joe Hill recording sponsored by America's national museum reinforces our sense of the long road traveled by Wobbly spirit, as well as the difficulty in confining Hill's life narrative narrowly to industrial union partisans or widely to labor idealists.

Not all IWW stalwarts welcome university conferences on Joe Hill or Smithsonian recordings of his music. Nor were partisans pleased in 1936 when a Camp Unity song about Joe Hill circulated in communist ranks. Not all present-day Wobblies accept the reality that their values frequently filter through AFL-CIO education departments, liberal arts classes, public folklife programs, or folksong revival festivals. In opening this chapter, I noted Jess Grant's wry response to Earl Robinson and Pete Seeger at a labor festival. Similar IWW blasts greeted Bo Widerberg's 1971 film *Joe Hill* and Wallace Stegner's 1950 novel *The Preacher and the Slave.*

Wobblies will continue to criticize film, fiction, song, and graphic art that "distort" IWW history and "deflect" the organization's purposes. I shall neither extend the list of Wobbly polemics nor rebut them, but I note again the metaphor of an assayer testing ore for metal destined to forge tradition's chains. At the organization's inception in 1905, IWW members willed a *tabula rasa*—a slate wiped clean of exploitation, discrimination, and superstition. On egalitarian and libertarian roads to the commonwealth of toil, Wobblies created a vibrant body of tradition. Both Joe Hill the working-stiff songwriter and Joe Hill a hero within a ballad remain emblematic of this heritage.

Alfred Hayes and Earl Robinson found it easy in 1936 to invoke Joe Hill's spirit, to move Wobbly elan across sectarian lines. In their creative acts, they broadened the audience for all IWW lore. Their ballad has outgrown both its Third Period and Popular Front cradles. More than any other song, it has conferred a folk hero accolade on Hill. We remain indebted to Hayes for melding "ain't never died" and dream themes. Consciously or not, he placed himself as the dreamer/narrator and Hill as the archetypal death-and-resurrection figure. Visionary poety dissolve time; reborn heroes affirm humanity. Wobbly artists before Hayes had also invoked mythic imagery for Joe Hill, but their drawings and poetry did not move far beyond IWW circles, as did the Hayes-Robinson composition.

The Joe Hill ballad continues to help young workers and their allies touch complex issues. To a large degree, all working Americans live within popular culture's palace and share its fare. Some workers seek consciously to define themselves in oppositional terms as outsiders and to use *counterculture* as a marker. All working people, on their respective jobs, share specific occupational lore. A few activists value folkloric expression as it buttresses their identity. Songs and stories lead individuals to conceptual questions about themselves and their institutions. "I Dreamed I Saw Joe Hill Again," the original poem, and "Joe Hill," the Camp Unity contribution, help all who toil sense the conjunction of truth and myth, manifesto and tale, chain maker and chain breaker.

" 'Wobbly': 80 Years of Rebel Art"

# 3

# The Name *Wobbly* Holds Steady

"I knew he was a Wobbly by the button that he wore." With this assertive statement, a singer/narrator identifies a special individual within the American labor and radical movements. Further, the declamation stands on the threshold but does not enter the mansion of large meaning. To cross the threshold we look back in time and turn the confident declaration into a set of questions: Who wore the button? When? Where? How did a little stamped-tin emblem, picturing the entire globe, come to signify large causes? When did other Wobbly expressions—song, story, sketch—emerge to trumpet dramatic messages, calls unlike those of previous unionists?

Our stark opening line never appeared alone but rather came to life by inclusion within a ballad text that gave its component stanzas reverberating overtones of event, agency, and ideology. Appearing during 1914 within the new song "Overalls and Snuff" (set to the tune of "Wearing of the Green"), the tag *Wobbly* to the present day has denominated a member of the Industrial Workers of the World. Before "Overalls and Snuff," most speakers of English understood the words *wobble* and *wobbly* in commonsense frames sanctioned by long usage: waver, quaver, tremble, hobble, vacillate, deviate, stagger, shake, rock about, move irregularly.

## Nickname

After 1914, *Wobbly* embedded itself in American speech as the main nickname for IWW members. Revolutionary industrial unionists then wore their new name proudly, while left and right opponents sounded it pejoratively. Many unionists, unaffiliated with the IWW, used it to shape a sense of position by placing themselves outside the industrial union's orbit. Regardless of nuance in the label's meaning, *Wobbly* has served working people as a benchmark for eighty years and will probably continue to function in this manner for decades to come.

As their nickname took hold, Wobblies fashioned fresh anecdotes or reclaimed traditional stereotypes to explain the term's origin. Some of these brief explanatory stories have been enjoyed and accepted by historians and lexicographers; others have been scorned and rejected. Together, these shared minitales have become part of the labor movement's treasure house of expressive culture. In this chapter, I note various anecdotes touching *Wobbly* and assay its meaning, past and present.

By way of opening, I assume that readers know something of the IWW's history or have access to the wide body of commentary this movement has generated (Miles). Hence, I need only indicate that a band of proletarians from the ranks and from office—socialists, syndicalists, anarchists, pragmatic trade unionists—met in Chicago during 1905 to form a challenging industrial union. Initially, IWW members had no special name, addressing each other as *brother* or *comrade*. Casting about for distinguishing signs, they adopted *industrial unionist, rebel, slave,* or *fellow worker*. These terms gave way to the vivid *Wobbly*.

Over the years, some members of the IWW, as well as outside observers, have seen attention to its vernacular name (and clustered lore) as peripheral to the union's enunciated purpose. These critics have asserted that a cadre formally dedicated to educate, organize, and emancipate wage earners ought not to be deflected by a nickname's odd tales. Further, class-conscious workers have much more to do than to delve into crannies of American esoterica.

Despite such strictures, I have not separated lore from mission or anecdote from philosophy. Rather, I have searched for connections between expressive form and social structure, believing that single words illuminate complex issues. In this sense, *Wobbly* not only serves as the smallest constituent unit in the related literary and historical narratives but stands tall as a self-contained social text demanding critical analysis.

My study opens with a flashback to the group's formative years. Even before the IWW's formal chartering in 1905, great controversy had surfaced between craft unionists in the American Federation of Labor and leftist opponents. Partisans in both camps used speech as sticks and stones, wounding each other with verbal blows. The Socialist Labor party leader Daniel DeLeon constantly altered the craft title to read American "Fakeration" or "Separation" of Labor; he and his cohorts branded the AFL "Organized Scabbery."

In March 1905, AFL President Samuel Gompers denounced DeLeon and comrades as "the socialist trade-union smashers and rammers from without, and the borers from within," as well as the " 'Pirates' and 'Kangaroos' hugging each other in glee over their prospective prey" (140). Leaders such as DeLeon and Gompers have long managed to share uneasy rooms in the house of labor, at times amplifying invective levels, at times muting voices in common cause.

I leave to other students the explication of vocal spears hurled in internal battle—*impossibilist, fakir, scab, misleader, coffin society, bummery*—and turn directly to early attempts to characterize the IWW with pejorative phrases. Writing in the summer of 1913, Paul Brissenden, an economist-historian, found "I Won't Works," "I Want Whiskey Brigade," and "Irresponsible Wholesale Wreckers." Such constructions, based on supercharged rhetoric, wordplay involving initials, or both, proliferated as editorialist and orator entered the fray.

Two examples suffice. In the first, the *San Diego Evening Tribune* (March 4, 1912), in a piece concerning an IWW free-speech fight, brayed, "If there was the slightest possibility of inflicting upon these worthless creatures the full penalty provided for treason, there would be no objection to giving them the benefit of the rope. Hanging is none too good for them, they would be much better dead; for they are absolutely useless in the human economy; they are the waste material of creation and should be drained off into the sewer of oblivion there to rot in cold obstruction like any other excrement."

A decade later, playwright Eugene O'Neill brought together a similar string in *The Hairy Ape* (scene 6). When police jail Yank (the ship's coal stoker), a prisoner counsels him to "get back" by joining the Wobblies. Because Yank has never encountered any IWWs, his cell mate identifies the "tough gang" by reading from a *Sunday Times* speech by Senator Queen: "There is a menace existing in this country today which threatens the vitals of our fair Republic—as foul a menace against the very life-blood of the American Eagle as was the foul conspiracy of Catiline against the eagles of Ancient Rome! . . . I refer to that devil's brew of rascals, jailbirds, murderers and cutthroats who libel all honest working men by calling themselves the Industrial Workers of the World; but in the light of their nefarious plots, I call them the Industrious *Wreckers* of the World!"

O'Neill used this senatorial prose satirically, yet we know that it echoed considerable political rhetoric of the day. Neither patriotic polemic nor turning the IWW's initials into clever phrases filled needs of rank-and-file members for a memorable signifier. Vital groups require clipped names, pet tags, acronyms, logos, or emblems to mark covenant and scripture. Metaphorically, a pungent label can either rush or ooze into a vacuum to fill linguistic space. *Christian, Marxist, Yankee, royalist, carpetbagger, New Dealer, commrat, freedom fighter, WASP, mandarin, hippy,* and *yuppie* name social formations of great appeal or terrifying threat.

After *Wobbly* caught on beyond IWW ranks in 1914, novelists and historians extended it back in time to cover the organization's first decade. For example, John Dos Passos, in the opening of *U.S.A.*, treated the IWW sympathetically, both in biographical/historical "portraits" and in fictive characters. Dos Passos placed Fenian McCreary, a young typesetter, in San Francisco during the earthquake and fire year of 1906. Meeting a freighter donkey-engine man who has joined the revolutionary IWW, Mac decides to go to Goldfield, Nevada, to help striking hardrock miners, He neglects to tell his sweetheart, Maisie, about his new affection for "the wobblies." Dos Passos crafted a compelling character in

McCreary, but neither Mac nor anyone else applied *Wobbly* to the IWW in 1906.

The IWW's historian Fred Thompson noted the "zeal with which the Wobblies battled for textile workers in Lawrence, steelworkers in McKees Rocks" (1988). Thompson hit the target in zeal, but missed the mark in assigning *Wobbly* as a rubric in the years through Lawrence. He knew, of course, when the nickname first circulated, but he felt comfortable in applying it broadly and retroactively. The proponents of One Big Union and direct action (who met in Chicago in 1905), as well as Goldfield miners (1906), McKess Rocks steelworkers (1909), Lawrence wool mill strikers (1912), and Paterson silk workers (1913), raised many banners but none embroidered with the singular thread *Wobbly*.

## Wheatland

Paterson's strike culminated in a dramatic pageant at Madison Square Garden on June 7, 1913. We lack evidence of *Wobbly* (as an organizational nickname) surfacing in New York even as late as Paterson. That summer, however, a continent removed, a short tragic hop field strike in California's Sacramento Valley propelled the name *Wobbly* from esoteric IWW speech to its continuing presence in the American language. Wheatland has not been forgotten (see, e.g., Downing, Pollock, Bell, Whitten, Daniel, Coe, DiGirolamo).

A few details establish background. With a large hop crop ripening on 641 acres, the Durst Ranch (in Yuba County) advertised for itinerant pickers. Nearly 3,000 men, women, and children gathered in tents without basic sanitary facilities. Dysentery plagued the work force. With an excess of labor far beyond actual need, the Durst brothers depressed wages, while fierce heat aggravated intolerable conditions. Two dozen national groups thrown together made it difficult to articulate discontent.

Alert to trouble and appealing across the barriers of language and ethnicity, Richard "Blackie" Ford and Herman "Hook-nose" Suhr, IWW activists, called for a strike; the Dursts called for an armed sheriff's posse. In the ensuing confrontation on Sunday, August 3, 1913, district attorney Edward Manwell, deputy sheriff

Eugene Reardon, and two pickers—a Puerto Rican and an English lad—fell. Did the battle gods determine full names for the dead lawmen and namelessness for the dead migrants?

Governor Hiram Johnson called out the National Guard as workers fled Wheatland. On August 7, a coroner's jury attributed the four deaths to murderous anger by IWW agitators, not to the social pathology in baronial agriculture. Yuba County authorities hired Burns Agency detectives to track down and intimidate strike "ringleaders." In January 1914, a Marysville jury convicted Ford and Suhr of murder; after their appeals failed both received life sentences. Ford went to San Quentin, Suhr to Folsom; each served until 1926. The state retried Ford and found him innocent; the court paroled Suhr.

Attention to Wheatland's meaning resurfaces in California decade after decade. John Steinbeck's *In Dubious Battle* and Dorothy Lange and Paul Taylor's *American Exodus* transcend locale and event. Boycotts and pilgrimages led by Cesar Chavez and the long strike by Mexican-American women in Watsonville's canneries during 1986–87 replayed issues noted in 1913.

Within the Wheatland setting of ripe crop, strike, death, trial, and prison, I seek a single locution's nativity. At dawn on August 3, Ford and Suhr had trekked down to the Southern Pacific depot, where station agent R. V. Moore doubled as both Wells-Fargo agent and Western Union telegraph operator. Suhr gave Moore a message for the Stockton IWW local: "Strike on at Durst Bros. twenty five hundred out. Send literature at once. Notify Sacramento." Two hours later, Suhr sent a second telegram to Sacramento asking for "books and due stamps and delegate if possible at once." These two messages can be seen as requests for organizational tools at a spontaneous strike's start.

That afternoon, as Durst Ranch passions boiled over, Suhr returned to send telegrams to locals in San Francisco, Sacramento, Los Angeles, Oakland, Stockton, and Fresno: "Strike on in full, demands turned down, I.W.W. ordered off the grounds but are here to stay. Send all speakers and wobbles possible. Money needed, lots of families destitute, boycott all employment sharks. Answer." The ninth message, to the *San Francisco Bulletin,* did not mention "wobbles" but called for a "reporter to take news"—

for someone outside labor's ranks to bear witness to a social volcano in eruption.

Looking back from today's perspective, these telegrams held a message more important than their stated text. They reveal that in the summer of 1913, California members had previously voiced the word *wobbles* (or a related noun) in reference to themselves. Paul Brissenden did not use the term in his 1913 monograph on the IWW's launching. No one has uncovered the nickname at the Paterson silk strike in 1913. Hence, I assume a short period of oral circulation for the nickname before Wheatland.

Apparently, the fist recognition of the telegrams' key role came in the late summer of 1913, as Yuba County district attorney Edward Stanwood and special prosecutor J. J. Carlin—a former Durst Ranch lawyer—prepared their case against the IWW. Unable to prove that the organizers possessed or used murder weapons, the attorneys shaped a conspiracy case, giving the word *wobbles* a sinister meaning. By contrast, the IWW downplayed the Western Union messages.

The IWW publicist Mortimer Downing served in the Ford-Suhr defense. Reporting to the *International Socialist Review* (1913), he wrote, "Just before the shooting some of the strikers had telegraphed to various IWW locals for organizers and assistance." Matters rested there until the Marysville trial, January 12–31, 1914, when special prosecutor Carlin and defense attorneys R. M. Royce and Austin Lewis, respectively, tried to elaborate or neutralize *wobbles*. Initially, Royce objected to the admission of the telegrams as "incompetent, immaterial and irrelevant" to the case. After Judge McDaniel accepted the Western Union "originals," Carlin asked telegrapher Moore about the unusual *wobbles*. Moore responded that he did not know the word and had sent it out on the wire as it was "plainly written" on the appropriate blank.

Royce then questioned witness Edwin Goetz, an AFL Barbers union member, asking him, "Do you know the meaning of the word *wobbles* or *wabbley?*" Goetz responded, "*Wobbley* is supposed to be a corruption of the word *wobbles*." Royce asked, "Have you heard that word used in trades union circles?" Goetz responded, "Some, yes." Carlin objected that the "word in the telegrams is *Wobbles*," not *Wobbley*. Royce and Carlin, with separate strategies, turned to Mortimer Downing. With attention back to *Wobbles*, Downing offered that *Wobbley* was "used generally in the working class . . . to designate . . . I.W.W."

Despite some interchange or confusion between the linked terms *wobbles, wabbley,* and *wobbley,* the prosecution did characterize the neologism—at least to the judge and jury's satisfaction—found in six of the telegrams: incendiary, threatening, demogogic, conspiratorial. Sensing deep trouble, the defense discounted any novelty or secrecy surrounding the coinage. Ultimately, the government lawyers proved more adept at philology than the IWW defenders.

I have summarized the details above from newspaper accounts and the Yuba County Superior Court's massive trial transcript, *California v. Ford* (itself incomplete). Because Wheatland became a cause célèbre, it merited considerable coverage—reports that echoed or summarized official court proceedings. The Edward Stanwood family gathered many clippings into a valuable scrapbook, now deposited in the University of California's Bancroft Library. Three entries provide illustrative citations.

The *Marysville Appeal* (January 22, 1914) used a subhead that drew attention to the prosecutors' reliance on the Western Union messages: "Telegrams Sent by H. D. Suhr Calling for Assistance from I.W.W. Still Guns of the Defense." On January 8, a *San Francisco Examiner* lead writer used *Wobblies* descriptively in a context wider than a call for help: "Hop Trial Jurors Hear IWW Songs / Selection from the 'Wobblies' Collection / Is Read." The *Marysville Democrat* (January 30) reported that in explaining the telegrams, Carlin had contradicted the genial Downing by revealing that *Wobles* meant "gun men" called to "combat scissorbills" and "minions of the law."

At the trial's end, Judge McDaniel remained puzzled over the full meaning of the revealed colloquialism. In summation, special prosecutor Carlin invoked jury laughter by scathing reference to "psychology"—used by the defense to situate concern over the plight of hop pickers. Employing his own psychological weapon, Carlin asserted, "We have a right to mistrust any body of people that speaks a language not understood by civilized folks" (Barry,

February 4). He spoke shrewdly for those who guarded state power with linguistic propriety. Carlin touched the mandarinate's fear of barbarians who use foreign or wild tongues, thus stigmatizing themselves by vulgar discourse or deviant code.

Early in 1914, the IWW, joined by AFL and Socialist party forces, carried the superior court decision to the California Court of Appeals, but to no avail. Meanwhile, the California Commission on Immigration and Housing had hired economist Carleton Parker to report on agricultural conditions leading to the hop strike. Parker's findings circulated widely and reappeared in his popular book, *The Casual Laborer.*

As Wheatland accounts proliferated, *Harper's Weekly* carried a long feature on "The Marysville Trial" by Inez Haynes Gillmore. Editor Norman Hapgood enhanced the article with a watercolor cover by illustrator Everett Shinn showing a heroic Puerto Rican migrant, the "gigantic brown negro" killed in battle. Gillmore noted that the most important evidence against Ford and Suhr had been the telegrams, requesting "organizers, literature, dues-stamps and 'wobblies.' " She changed spelling of the word in question from *wobbles* to *wobblies.* With the latter printed in a national journal geared to liberal and mainstream audiences, there could be no turning back for the nickname's recognition.

During the summer of 1914, an unnamed bard had composed the defiant "Overalls and Snuff," identifying the man with a Wobbly button as "an old-time hop picker" with "his blankets on his back." With Ford and Suhr "in the pen," the old-timer asserted that "we'll pick no more damned hops for them, for overalls and snuff" (Kornbluh, 238). This song may have been modeled after "We Won't Build No More Railroads for Overalls and Snuff," a probable Joe Hill piece. Louis "Frenchy" Moreau, a camp delegate in British Columbia during the 1912 Canadian Northern Strike, recalled Hill using the tune of "Wearing of the Green" to ridicule the CNs "gunnysack contractors" (Gibbs Smith, 26).

Wheatland's "Overalls and Snuff" (without tune specified) appeared on August 1 in Cleveland's IWW newspaper, *Solidarity,* and San Francisco's AFL building trades paper, *Organized Labor.* The two periodicals printed identical texts, except that Cleveland's

Ben Williams favored *wobbley* whereas San Francisco's Olaf Tveitmoe used *Wobley.* Possibley one editor copied the song from the other without credit; the coincidence in date seems strange. Alternatively, the author may have mailed it to both papers requesting that the song be held until August 1 to spark a hop-picking boycott in the campaign to free Ford and Suhr.

As is the case with some folksongs, "Overalls and Snuff" lent itself to a discursive statement. Tveitmoe printed it with a commentary, "The Wobley's Warning," in which he linked the IWW's creativity and name. I paraphrase a portion: During the last year the Wandering Workers of California have become known to each other as "Wobley." Most of the names we revere today were once terms of ridicule and shame. The song "Overalls and Snuff" is straight "Wobley." They create their own creed and hymns. Beware of a movement that makes its own song.

Just as the song's narrator had warned the hop barons, Tveitmoe warned the public—and fellow AFL craft unionists—that neither jail nor nostrum would settle California's migratory labor problems. In retrospect, his editorial on brutality, bastilles, hymns, and a year-old nickname remains refreshing. What insight led him to appreciate the utility of "Overalls and Snuff" in making sense of the IWW challenge?

Tveitmoe, a Norwegian immigrant and craft-conscious syndicalist, had taught school in Minnesota and worked as a cement mason in California (Hustved). Convicted of transporting dynamite after the bombing of the *Los Angeles Times,* he served briefly in Leavenworth Penitentiary. Unwilling to accept labor's subordinate role, he reached out both to union "barons" and to rank-and-file "spittoon philosophers." Tveitmoe's effusive "Wobley's Warning" coupled with the debut printing of "Overalls and Snuff" in *Organized Labor*—a paper not geared to IWW readers—pointed to semantic wisdom: today's fine labels may connote yesterday's shame.

By recapitulating 1913–14 events we see *Wobbly*'s spread from its initial base:

A *wobbles* in telegram, August 3;
B telegrams read in court, January 21;

C *wobblies* in *Harper's Weekly,* April 4;
D *Wobley* and *wobbley* in IWW song, August 1.

In December 1914, the IWW published the "Joe Hill Edition" of its little red songbook; it included "Overalls and Snuff." During the 1915 harvest season, Richard Brazier extended the imagery and shortened the moniker to *Wob:* "I met him in Dakota when the harvesting was o'er / A 'Wob' he was, I saw by the button that he wore" ("When You Wear That Button," in Kornbluh, 240). Similarly, in 1915, Ralph Chaplin ended the poem "Harvest Song" by coupling the then-new name to the IWW button/emblem and to the image of job sabotage: "The earth is on the button that we Wobblies wear, / We'll turn the sab cat loose or get our share" (Salerno, 113).

## Tamony's Cradle

With *Wob* and *Wobbly* alive in IWW usage, members sought attributive stories or speculated about their nickname's birth. As the colloquialism spread across jurisdictional lines, outsiders added their explanations. In an appendix following this chapter, I list two dozen natal representations in chronological order as they reached print. Readers who consult the list will find familiar and unfamiliar elucidations that blend fact and fancy.

One tale, oft told, hinges on a Chinese railroad construction camp cook who mispronounced IWW as "I Wobble Wobble" (sounded or spelled variously), thus "inventing" *Wobbly.* The other account, less frequently circulated, suggests that a class enemy—right or left—named the industrial rebels *Wobblies.* Harrison Gray Otis, *Los Angeles Times* editor, and Daniel DeLeon, Socialist Labor party leader, poles apart, have both been named as baptismal fathers.

No one in or close to the IWW, no student of labor history, has escaped hearing or reading these anecdotes, told jocularly or seriously. Essentially, the naming tales display alternate concepts of word origin geared either to priorities of sound or sense.

Alfred Holt has dealt with difficulties in pronouncing two successive Ws. Over the years, IWW soapboxers had voiced their union's name as "the eye-double-double-you" or "the eyedoubleyou-doubleyou." Such soundings likely predated the Wheatland telegrans, and, over time, led to phonetic considerations in tracking *Wobbly*. Ultimately, those who could accept the "All loo eye wobble wobble" fancy fell back on notions of onomatopoeia and echoism—word formation by sound imitation (for example: *buzz, hiss, arf, pow, zap*).

Students who scout new words look to joined building blocks: phonemes, the smallest meaningful units of sound; morphemes, the smallest meaningful linguistic units. Comic strip readers feel such definitions as they enjoy the structuring of explosive sound with inventive sense. Wordsmiths coin acronyms (such as *snafu* or *WASP*) by sounding the initials of strung-together terms. Although IWW soapboxers and pamphleteers treasured bright locutions, I submit that they did not transform the union's initials into an acronymic or echoic word.

Franklin Rosemont, a student of surrealism and popular culture and an IWW member, has noted in correspondence with me that the odd "dialectic of sight and sound is somehow at the root" of *Wobbly*. He hears "eye-double-double-you" as "almost a magical invocation, reminiscent of witches chanting in *Macbeth:* 'Double, double, toil and trouble.' " Influenced by attention within modern poetics to conjunctions of visual and auditory elements, Rosemont suggests that the sight of the IWW's initials opened a path to the nickname's acceptance.

Despite the highly developed Wobbly gift for wordplay—a declaration of independence from absolutism (grammatical, economic, political)—sound alone, however humorous, does not stand as a sufficient cause for the extension of *wobbly* (waver, fluctuate, deviate) to the IWW's distinguishing tag. Recognizing that *wobble* has been circled by rings of meaning for centuries before everyday speech to the rebel organization's domain, the pleasurable voicings of "eye-double-double-you" reinforced the new nickname's utility.

Words do not march in resolute ranks through the decades from speaker to writer to speaker. Scholars are not always skilled in sifting evidence or reaching conclusions; they do not invariably avoid the temptation to judge "correct" usage. Peter Tamony, my mentor in etymology, taught patience in search, pleasure in discovery, and pluralism in philosophy (Green 1976; McLain).

On Peter's death in 1985, his sister Kathleen contributed his word files to the Western Historical Manuscript Collection, University of Missouri, Columbia (Roberts). For four decades Tamony gathered examples of *Wobbly* in speech and print, summing up findings for *Western Folklore* (1971). He never accepted the explanation of Chinese "lingual difficulty." Instead, he heard the nickname as a nom de guerre of labor struggle—not only workers against bosses, but also, alas, workers against each other. An internal tradition of "persistent backsliding in radical thought and philosophy" undergirded the IWW's colloquialism.

Knowing that we more often extend words from old to new settings than "invent" new ones, Tamony hypothesized that factional polemicists rather than class-war enemies gifted the IWW with its hypocorism. Seeking verifiable cites in the years before Wheatland's telegrams, he turned to thunder on the left. I picture Tamony placing *Wobbly* in an ideological cradle, wobbling from side to side, vacillating in line.

A British political usage illustrates Tamony's exploration: "Victory or defeat in most English constituencies hangs on the inclinations of a few hundred wobblers, men without any very definite sympathies, who vote Liberal one year and Conservative the next" (52). This 1900 example dealt with uncertain parliamentarians, opportunistic and shallow in loyalty, weak in rhetoric. By contrast, Samuel Gompers, Max Hayes, Daniel DeLeon, and William Haywood (who debated craft-industrial unionism and socialism-syndicalism before and after the IWW's chartering) were grand masters of cutting prose. Each reveled in charging others with wavering line, confusion in purpose, or unhealthy deviationism.

English-language speakers know that the verb *to wobble* (and its derivatives) has inhabited many domains: personal, political, technical, recreational. Accordingly, Tamony moved past *wobbler*, used politically, to note other associations. This reach to wide linkages helps ground philological tracing in realms beyond an "origin" imagined by a singular nativity scene or with a lightning-flash naming metaphor. To the extent that we can recall the banter of those California IWW members who received the hop strike telegrams, we believe that they had known *wobble* to carry plural meanings long before they narrowed it to their moniker.

Tamony noted that toilers who worked by hand (hefters, haulers, lifters, and diggers) or who fought the elements could literally feel or see themselves wobble in their gait. Each demanding physical task carried its correlative sense of motion, whether tense or relaxed. Circus roustabouts, teamster lumpers, spike drivers, slate pickers, and riverboat deckhands learned balletlike routines, although they might have been offended by terpsichorean comparisons. Outsiders perceive wobbly walk best in viewing sailors home from the sea. College enthusiasts who savor sea shanties often enact rolling, pitching, and wobbling motions to authenticate their staged singing sessions. Ironworkers, particularly, have long reached for metaphoric language to describe proper ways of moving about on high steel.

Tom West and Bob Tipton, on a Chicago Loop high-rise in 1971, explained to reporter Fred Klein: "When the metal comes up, [the connector] can't be on the Arkansas (wrong) side. He's got to be set so he can swing that piece the way it ought to go. If he can't swing the piece right, that piece will swing him." These two raising-gang men elaborated: "Cooning"—"putting one foot on each side of the bottom flange of an 'I' beam, one hand on each side of the top flange, and then scurrying along on all fours, like a raccoon"—is a safe way to walk steel, but "to be a real ironworker, you've got to get off your ass and onto your feet." One doesn't seek safety alone; one doesn't inch along; to be esteemed, and ironworker must walk with a "businesslike clump, his hands swinging normally at his sides instead of stretched out tightrope walker style."

I have elaborated on swinging, Arkansawing, cooning, and clumping to suggest distinctions in the identification of proper stance on just a single job. At least a few Wobs have guessed that words for posture at work might carry over to "free-time" activity. Some critics have asserted that the IWW acquired its nickname from members too intoxicated to "navigate" except by wobbling (Brissenden 1960). I extend this alcoholic association to sexual humor, commonplace at most work scenes.

We continue to hear near-erotic allusions in present rap or rock and roll and in past African-American dance or blues phrases such as in Barbecue Bob's (Robert Hicks) "Doin' the Scraunch"

("You wiggle and you wobble, you move it around"). Lillian Glinn's "Wobble It a Little Daddy" is fully explicit. The provocative shimmy dance has a long association with the words *wiggle/wabble/wobble* (Stearns, 104). During the summer of the Wheatland troubles, George Turner warned *McClure's* readers of the dangers to white youth in "nigger" dances—stemming from "crude and heathen sexual customs of middle Africa" (108).

No one has claimed that a blues singer or jazz dancer alone gifted the IWW with its familiar name. I suggest that some members, hearing *wobble* or *wobbly* voiced pejoratively against their union, reacted not defensively but with quickened pulse and hidden pleasure. In my mind's eye, I see a connection between the Shimme-Sha-Wabble dance at San Francisco's Barbary Coast, mainstream antipathy to supposed black sexuality, and the California IWW's quick acceptance of the special nickname *Wobbly*. In short, industrial unionists enjoyed the well-worn word for its multiple associations, ideological to bawdy.

Working stiffs who literally saw dockwallopers wobble under too-heavy loads, who lingered in tenderloin joints to savor wabbling hips, or who wobbled on leaving closed saloons found themselves prepared to decorate a new tag with a bouquet of felt sensation. Peter Tamony, conscious of electrically charged language, observed workers toting words from job and joint to union hall and labor press office. IWW editors seemed especially open to linguistic novelty. Unable to escape their organization's wobbly trajectory—a few dramatic victories, many painful defeats—they embraced humor, both subtle and slapstick, to mitigate loss.

Not all American radicals could cope with membership decline and disillusionment. Some tried to stave off reality with the shibboleth "false consciousness"; others guided themselves by a belief in rational behavior; still others equated "inevitable progress" with their mastery of "the science of society." Although some Wobblies shared such dogma, others, marked by brutal job experience and libertarian belief, saw humanity as irrational. Paths to the commonwealth of toil could be both thorny and comedic.

A drawing in the *Industrial Pioneer* (April 1926) speaks volumes: A worker—heavy boots, lumberjack's plaid shirt, printer's folded-paper hat—jabs an editorial pen at the corporate devil

"GLOOM." The penetrating weapon literally skews the letters composing "WOBBLES" as the illustration heads the union magazine's humor page. I see the drawing's lancer as both a Wob dispelling gloom and a light-bearer illuminating *Wobbly*.

Various metaphors provide naming guides. Perhaps in visualizing penmen lancers we can also see blacksmiths in action. A rusty bar can be reheated and rehammered on the anvil to shape a new tool or toy. We allow many words to rust away, as simultaneously we alter and extend the life of others. IWW members heated *wobbly* in struggle's forge and tempered it in humor's vat.

These thoughts on a given term's multiple resonances, its constant slipping in and out of tradition, amplify an early connection: *Wobbly* as a "corruption of wallaby" (Holbrook). At the turn of the century, Farmer and Henley had cited the Australian phrase *on the wallaby track* as denoting "tramping the country on foot looking for work" or water and dated it back to 1869. Itinerants who had followed (small kangaroo) tracks into the bush or scrub also called each other sundowners.

The Australian colloquialism *sundowners* reached the American West, where prospectors and ten-day-stiffs (metal miners) wandered by day and bedded down in lonely camps by night. We can read the phonological *wallaby-wobbly* tie as a disgression from sequential study or hear these near-sound-alikes as part of trampdom's identity—sundowner, bindle stiff, boomer, junglehound, maggotory laborer, wobbly. Many Americans understood *Wobbly* to represent a hobo without reference to ideology.

During a 1959 visit, IWW songwriter Richard Brazier assured me with great certainty that his union had "adopted" its nickname from *wallaby*. I countered that, more likely, after members became comfortable with their informal name, someone with Austrialian experience recalled wallaby adventures to reinforce the acceptance of *Wobbly*. Rebutting, Brazier cited caricaturist David Low—"Colonel Blimp's" creator—to confirm the link. Perhaps Low did actually pen a cartoon of a wobbly wallaby; I have not found such a drawing. I use this belief to penetrate the linguistic maze, to observe that speakers become their own etymologists. Peter Tamony never tired of turning lexical exploration back to "native speakers" such as Richard Brazier.

Visiting Eugene Barnett in Spokane in 1961, I learned a "native" naming anecdote that hinged on wobbling walk. Barnett had been imprisoned at Walla Walla following the American Legion attack on the Centralia IWW hall on Armistice Day 1919. Previously, he had heard of an old-timer jailed during a farm strike. The authorities had kept the worker on bread and water "til they starved him down." A newsman, possibly from Fremont Older's California paper, covered the release story at the prison gate. He observed the emaciated striker's wobbly walk to freedom and, in his report, gave the IWWs their nickname. Barnett, incarcerated for years, certified this oral tale's "truth" out of personal experience, bolstered by a sense that he, too, had built a wall in tradition's manse.

## Bubka and Marcus Ring True

During 1965, Tony Bubka, a member of Local 6 of the International Longshoremen's and Warehousemen's Union, wrote to Peter Tamony and to me for help in tracing *Wobbly*. Previously, he had enlisted similar help from Fred Thompson. During the 1960s, Bubka had worked in industrial Oakland and lived in Berkeley near the University of California library. He researched labor history and literature with special attention to Jack London. I met Tony only once; we shared a day at a campus folk festival, recognizing kinship on our bent to walk back roads.

Bubka put long hours and much candlelight into searching for a solid christening claim or single birth certificate to firm the IWW nickname. Tamony suggested to the warehousemen a challenging counterquest—the need for pre-Wheatland labor press citations for the old verb *to wobble*. Tony pressed ahead with this search and, in 1968, presented findings to *American West* as part of an article on Wobbly stickers (silent agitators). Unfortunately, the editor cut Bubka's lexical discoveries in favor of colorful stickers.

Bubka, a bachelor, died in Oakland on May 14, 1983. I do not know whether someone carelessly discarded his files, including draft submissions to journals and voluminous references citations. Fortunately, not all his papers vanished, for after each search for

*Wobbly* he shared findings with Tamony. At this juncture, I expand Bubka's quest.

William C. Owen (1854–1929), born in India and educated in England, served as a translator for anarchist Peter Kropotkin (Poole, 40). Arriving in California during the 1890s, Owen espoused Edward Bellamy's utopian views. From 1910 to 1916, he edited the English-language section of *Regeneracion*, published in Los Angeles by Ricardo and Enrique Magon. I shall not comment on Owen's anarcho-syndicalist belief, or detail nuances in the Magonistas' left-libertarian position, but note that on April 27, 1912, Owen penned a short criticism of Eugene Debs's failure to stand by the Mexican Revolution. The stark editorial ended: "Debs wobbles and the man or movement that wobbles has only hysteria, not strength."

This *Regeneracion* statement carried no heading, but it caught the sympathetic eye of the editor of the Spokane IWW's *Industrial Worker* (May 9, 1912). He captioned it "WOBBLY GENE." Today, Owen's piece serves as a general reminder of deep philosophical disputes, endless left-doctrinal quarrels, and as a specific example of an IWW newspaper's usage of *wobbly* as a straight political pejorative directed at a rival wobbler. Owen, presumably secure in his beliefs, found it appropriate to diminish Debs's standing.

In 1913, the *Los Angeles Citizen*, a labor paper with Socialist party ties and staff, criticized IWW organizer Joe Ettor for failure (lack of courage implied) to attend a San Diego meeting. The writer, Patrick Ignatious "Patsy" O'Bang (most likely the editor Stanley Wilson), may have selected his nom de plume to signal Irish strength in the building trades—nail bangers, tin knockers, paint slappers, rod busters. On April 11, O'Bang offered a satiric, anti-IWW, anti-"Rip, Roaring Revolution" message: "The capitalist system will be abolished if only the workers would place some molasses in Nellie's switch [hairpiece], smear some arsenic in Tillie's powder puff and puncture the tire of Rockefeller's machine."

Again, we need not pause to spin out all the internal differences (over job action, sabotage, and working by the rule) among AFL, SLP, SP, and IWW unionists or to track the deep tension generated by the bombing of the *Los Angeles Times* and the imprisonment of the McNamara brothers, ironworker union leaders. The *Citizen* addressed readers loyal both to Debs and to the McNamaras but critical of the cantankerous IWWs. O'Bang, who disliked "General" Ettor's style, as well as his substantive values, fulminated: "Sabotist, Syndicalist and fearless I.W.W. with a red, flowing tie, with fire in his eye and fight in his backbone, the I Wobbily-Wobbily organizer and chief candle bearer for the Put-Flies-in-the Raisins cause, travels the country."

On April 24, *Miners' Magazine*, the journal of the militant Western Federation of Miners headquartered in Denver, reprinted O'Bang's "tribute" to Ettor. (This well-edited magazine circulated widely; Vernon Jensen, among others, has traced the WFM's turbulent path.) I return to O'Bang's sarcasm. Regardless of whether he had heard *I Wobbily-Wobbily* from a previous speaker or had composed it at his typewriter, we can now properly credit O'Bang, a literate socialist editor—surely a member of the International Typographical Union—with our first documented usage (April 11, 1913) within a humorous frame of one variant of the IWW nickname.

Technically, O'Bang's I Wobbily-Wobbily intensified humor by sound reduplication and helped speakers turn the standard word *wobbly* into a self-contained joke independent of constructions based on initials such as Illustrious Wonder Workers. Perhaps a Chinese cook in the Canadian Rockies had mispronounced the letter *W*, sending *Wobbly* on a long journey to O'Bang's typewriter in April 1913 and to a Wheatland telegrapher's office in August. Perhaps the cook (if indeed he existed) had been an IWW member, for the industrialists set exemplary standards for other unionists in opening membership across the fences of language, ethnicity, and gender.

Regardless of endless elaboration for the camp cook tale, it stretches credulity to accept this journey down the Pacific Coast from British Columbia once we know about the contributions of Owen and O'Bang, both of whom lived in Los Angeles. IWW members read anarchist and socialist newspapers along with the bourgeois press. One of the hop strike telegrams had gone to Los Angeles—a sure sign that before the Wheatland strike flared, IWW members in California had been familiar conversationally with their nickname. We can well believe that a core of IWW activists used *Wobbly* internally before O'Bang seized it to demean rivals.

Our word's Pacific Coast travel detours to Ohio. During 1963, Joyce Kornbluh, while gathering material for *Rebel Voices,* visited Ben and Rose Williams in Lorain, Ohio. Ben Williams (1877–1964), a typesetter, early organizer in California's redwood region, and influential editor of the IWW's *Solidarity,* lived out his declining years in poverty. Eager to share memories, he gave Kornbluh an autobiographical manuscript and an antique purple-ink hectograph, itself a veteran of agitational years. She deposited both in the University of Michigan library's Labadie Collection.

The Williams manuscript provided several promising leads. According to Williams, when the Socialist party debater and *Cleveland Citizen* editor Max Hayes "referred to the IWWs as the 'I Wiggly Wobblies,' the men to the west instead of showing resentment immediately adopted the name." Williams likened this acceptance to the previous response to a favorite song: "When called bums [members] sang 'Hallelujah, I'm a Bum' in the teeth of their would-be traducers."

By letter, I pressed Williams for collaborative details. He replied that he had been unaware of any mystery about the name *Wobbly.* Because his information about Hayes seemed logical, he "could not conceive of such a nickname coming from any other source than an intended insult from an outside enemy." Williams elaborated that western IWWs were conditioned rebels without illusions as to social recognition from respectable citizens. The IWW gave its outcast members a new inspiration Hence, they met epithets with "deep-bellied horselaughs. They could not be insulted by name-callers."

The Wobbly editor Williams knew the Socialist party editor Hayes personally. As a perennial debater with Gompers at AFL conventions, and as an International Typographical Union official, Hayes made known to one and all his long hostility to the dual IWW. Although Williams believed that he had read the socialist's insult in the *Cleveland Citizen,* he could not recall its exact appearance. I doubt that "Wiggly Wobblies" will be found in Cleveland print. Regardless, Williams offered a plausible explanation despite raising lingering questions about the word's journey from Ohio to California.

On October 4, 1963, the Wayne State University Labor History Archives presented "A Night with the Wobblies," featuring songs and stories. Fred Thompson and Carl Keller reminisced; I offered folkloric background. At the evening's close, Charles G. Marcus casually shared with me a memory of *Wobbly*'s origin. Librarian Patricia Wilson and I arranged for a tape session; I draw here on her summary of Marcus's remarks.

Born in Canada, 1886, Marcus worked as a farm hand, river driver (Spokane), galena ore miner, railroad construction laborer (north bank Columbia River), longshoreman (San Francisco), and Santa Fe Railway telephone wire lineman. He recalled hanging around the Los Angeles IWW hall in 1911, where he enjoyed the enthusiasm of new members attracted like snowbirds to the Southland. He also remembered the bitter encounters between the Socialist Labor party and the Industrial Workers of the World. In 1910, in an early IWW split, DeLeonites had established a Detroit IWW unit to rival the "official" Chicago-based IWW. Marcus explained:

> They called us bummery because we were just migratory labor. One SLP that could write a bit came into our hall to hear the guys talk, and went back and wrote a derogatory article—a tract or handbill—about the foolish ideas that the IWW had about what the workers should do to take over. He named it I Wibbly Wobbly. The name seemed to stick with the people who didn't like the IWW and was taken over by the IWW themselves. As long as I can remember, I first heard the word Wobbly in Los Angeles. The guy had a cigar store on Seventh.

Marcus may have been off a year in chronology, but his unadorned story rings true. His use of experience held in memory parallels the academic use of social science formula, linguistic rule, or narrative theory. I stress that within his story, *Wobbly* did not come from the class-enemy capitalist editor Otis of the *Times*. Instead, it stemmed from a local disputant who had actually attended IWW meetings. Today, Marcus helps us picture an SLP member—perhaps a cigar maker and AFL trade unionist—circulating his locally printed tract and engaging in running debate with rivals on the left.

I met Marcus only briefly and to my regret did not correspond with him. Nor have I found a confirming SLP tract or handbill from the years 1911–13. Thousands of crevices in laborlore's cliffs remain unexplored. Nevertheless, Marcus's account complements Williams's memory of Max Hayes, with the added virtue of bringing this explanation from Cleveland to Los Angeles, the territory for *Regeneracion* and the *Citizen*.

Marcus offered an oral history vignette recalling an SLP "guy who could write a bit," perhaps an imaginative DeLeonite versed in the "Socialist Pope's" polemical epithets. Newspaper editors Owen and O'Bang left printed cites. Owen penned "Debs wobbles" as a serious charge in 1912. O'Bang tendered "I Wobbily-Wobbily" as a phonological jest in 1913. Although anarchist and socialist editors opposed each other constantly, they found common cause in branding IWW members as critically flawed radicals—wobbling in commitment to revolution.

My meeting with Charles Marcus in 1963 helped him pull a persuasive account from memory, uncluttered by diverting references in history books or dictionaries. Further, he knew nothing of the hop strike telegrams but fell back on direct experience in the Los Angeles IWW hall. Close reading of local Socialist party and Socialist Labor party publications may yet bring to light printed citations to complement or confirm Marcus's recollection.

The need to read the radical press in search of cultural detail cannot be overstated. In 1989, Franklin Rosemont found an overlooked "Wabbly" cite—central to this chapter's thrust. On June 12, 1913, the *Industrial Worker* printed Phineas Eastman's report from Rosepine, Louisiana, commenting upon the May 19 Alexandria convention of the Brotherhood of Timber Workers (affiliated with the IWW's National Industrial Union of Timber and Lumber Workers). He noted lively floor debate, working-stiff talk bristling with humorous logic, and regret at Arthur L. Emerson's resignation as BTW president.

Eastman also reported that "Fellow Worker Filigno was on hand, and his long experience as a 'Wabbly' was often drawn upon by the convention, and proved of value to the green but militant representatives." I read two interpretations into *Wabbly* set by Eastman in quotation marks: (1) The nickname, then unfamiliar to Louisiana workers, has to be placed apart from accepted speech; (2) Filigno had articulated it in self-definition, perhaps explaining its unusual meaning to "green" rebels at the Alexandria convention. Presently, I note *Wabbly*'s internal placement in an ameliorative rather than pejorative position several months before the Wheatland hop strike.

A background sketch situates Phineas Eastman's report. In 1912, the independent, impoverished BTW had turned to the IWW out of southern populist and socialist conviction and in response to employer "Iron-Heel" terror. Despite its roots in the Texas-Louisiana piney woods and cypress swamps, as well as the loyalty of white, black, Cajun, and Tejano (Texas-Mexican) woodsmen, the union faced bone-crushing opposition from the "Sawdust Ring" and its civic allies. (The *International Socialist Review* carried reports on the BTW by Covington Hall and Bill Haywood; articles by J. Fickle, J. Green, and M. Reed provide retrospective analysis; Jeff Ferrell's thesis surveys this union's travail and heroism. Together, these writers remind us to deal with records of unions that have vanished.)

When a strike at Grabow, Louisiana, led to death for workers and company guards on July 7, 1912, Calcasieu Parish officials charged more than sixty BTW members with murder, jailing them pending trial. Prisoners tagged their cells "The Black Hole of Calcasieu." The Southern Lumber Operators Association hired the influential Lake Charles congressman A. P. Pujo to direct the prosecution. To assist the defense, seasoned IWW organizers traveled to Lake Charles, among them C. L. Filigno from San Francisco, E. F. Doree from Seattle, and Clarence Edwards (origin unknown).

The Grabow trial dragged on from October 1 to November 2, ending in the unionists' acquittal, a "victory" that left the BTW exhausted and penniless. Within the various accounts of an organization, judged by some historians as a "failure," I have been interested in Filigno's Louisiana sojourn, in that he carried the name *Wabbly* east from California. Building on Charles Marcus's memory of the nickname's appearance in Los Angeles about 1911, I picture Filigno and his active fellow workers moving *Wobbly/ Wobble/Wabbly* across the continent to job site, courthouse, and agitational arena.

The historian Earl White has gathered relevant material on Phineas Eastman (1871–1937): born in Clinton, Mississippi; held various "genteel" clerical jobs; turned to Louisiana saw mill towns after 1902; active in BTW; moved to Kansas in 1917 to assist in IWW oilfield organization; jailed with other Wobblies at Leavenworth, 1919; paroled, 1923. No historian has similarly summed up Filigno's experience.

To amplify Filigno's usage of *Wabbly,* I note a few mileposts. He appeared in 1909 in the IWW press and the *International Socialist Review* within reports of free-speech fights at Missoula and Spokane. After his arrest with Elizabeth Gurley Flynn (November 3, 1909), the Spokane jury freed her and jailed him. Years later, attorney Ben Kizer recalled Filigno as a "young Italian" defendant (112). By December 1910, Filigno had been jailed in California during Fresno's free-speech agitation (Foner 1981).

On October 10, 1912, the *Industrial Worker* carried a brief notice from Eureka's IWW redwood local: "C. L. Filigno has accepted a position with the B.T.W. as organizer and is on his way south." Two weeks later, the *Lake Charles American Press* reported that Calcasieu Parish Sheriff Henry Reid had jailed Filigno, Doree, and Edwards on charges of bribing and intimidating Grabow trial witnesses. A month later, with the three organizers still imprisoned, the *Industrial Worker* (November 28) carried a biting narrative, probably by Covington Hall, entitled "Louisiana—A Rival to Despotic Russia," Hall charged that the Burns Detective Agency and assorted degenerate hirelings, pimps, gunmen, and Lumber Trust rurales were railroading three fearless class champions to the levee (convict labor).

On release from jail, Filigno returned to organizing woodsmen. Phineas Eastman's dispatch to the *Industrial Worker* (January 23, 1913) picked up the story thread: "Rosepine Rebels in Action." At their meeting, BTW-IWW members sang the "Red Flag" to "an accompaniment played by Mrs. Filigno. (Please pass the rice.)" Did Eastman imply Filigno's recent marriage in Louisiana, or did the rice signify a good meal following the music?

Leaving Rosepine, Filigno appeared in New Orleans bringing the IWW appeal to river longshoremen and merchant seamen. His *Industrial Worker* message began "May Day As It May Be." (I have already noted Wabbly Filigno at the Brotherhood of Timber Workers convention.) By October, Filigno had journeyed from Louisiana to New York, accepting the challenging position of secretary-treasurer of the Marine Transport Workers Industrial Union, IWW. There, I lose his trail.

Writing to his friend Covington Hall in New Orleans, Filigno described activity among coal yard lighter-ship crews in Philadelphia. At an MTW meeting, "a rough-neck of workingman told the boss that he would take his friendly feelings in the shape of three dollars more per week." Hall ran Filigno's dispatch in the *Voice of the People* (October 16, 1913). The organizer continued, "Kelly (who is an old veteran in the wobblers from Aberdeen and San Diavolo, or Diego . . .) was serving on the [MTW] committee."

I place great significance in the usage *wobblers* to describe West Coast veteran Kelly. The Wheatland telegrams had been sent in August 1913, but the trial bringing the provocative wire messages to the surface had not yet occurred when Filigno reached Philadelphia's coal docks. Hence, *wobblers*—voiced or written positively by a rebel who had been active in California from December 1910 (Fresno) through October 1912 (Eureka)—helps reconstruct the path of the old words *wobble/wobbler/wobbly* to the new nickname for IWW members.

I would like to believe that Filigno on his cross-continental hegira—Missoula, Spokane, Fresno, Eureka, Rosepine, New Orleans, New York, Philadelphia—had occasion to explain *wobblers* and *Wabbly*. Unfortunately, like many IWWs, he remains in the shadows. I do not know the dates or places of his birth and death or what work he followed as a young man. In January 1913, Covington Hall began to edit the *Lumberjack* for the BTW in Alexandria, Louisiana. In July, he moved the newspaper to New Orleans, changing its name to the *Voice of the People*. I have seen a few copies of the *Voice* carrying Filigno's reports. It seems reasonable to assume that he also wrote for the *Lumberjack*, although I have not seen any copies.

Who can add to Filigno's story? Can we elucidate fully the setting in which Charles Marcus heard an SLPer brand IWWs as *wobblers*, or that in which C. L. Filigno cheerfully picked up the brand? What impelled Tony Bubka to search microfilmed journals for *Wobbly* citations? I raise such questions in sketching limited biographies and partial etymologies with material at hand. For the present, Louisiana stands as our first documented site outside California for the new nickname *Wabbly*, and Pennsylvania confirms the extension of *wobblers* within the IWW.

## John D. Barry

Grain winnowers leave chaff; do hop pickers leave cone-shaped flowers in their fields? In my reading about the Wheatland maelstrom, did I harvest a full crop? Hops give malt liquor its bitter flavor. Could one of Wheatland's migrants have left a gift to sweeten a student's journey?

I have noted previously that a few months had elapsed between the hop strike telegrams (August 3, 1913) and the IWW's compelling need to rationalize its nickname at the subsequent trial. Although the IWW publicist Downing initially ignored the telegrams' importance, his ostrichlike stance could not continue after the Western Union messages became courtroom ammunition in January. Downing and his fellow workers, then, had no choice but to deflect the inflammatory neologism.

Recall that Suhr had sent one message specifically to the *San Francisco Bulletin* asking for a "reporter to take news." This liberal newspaper not only covered the August events but in January dispatched John D. Barry to the Marysville trial. For several years Barry had graced the *Bulletin*'s editorial page each week with five long features entitled "Ways of the World," which ranged widely from literary and dramatic criticism to social reportage.

At the hop trial's end, Barry filed six still-fresh commentaries on the IWW cause. He met IWW members in their temporary defense headquarters, "The Jungle"; visited the county jail to talk to imprisoned pickers; noted the IWW's popular song "Mr. Block"; reported on prosecutor Carlin's speech to the jury; and found areas of agreement and disagreement between the AFL and the IWW.

When Barry probed for the meaning of the word *Wobblies,* a member asserted:

> We like to take names that other people call us by. For instance, we're often called hoboes and bums and blanket-stiffs. We don't mind. . . . All we care about is what we call our dope . . . to organize the workers of the world from the bottom up and make labor solid. [A second friend specified that our name] grew out of a satirical reference to the organization, made by Harrison Gray Otis, "I wiggelly wobbelly." The members were so pleased that they snatched at the phrase. Now, in their slang, a member would refer to himself as a "Wobbly." When, in a critical situation, a group of workers was wanted to stand by and make a showing an order would be sent out for "Wobblies." [A third friend] spoke up to offer another version. "Some of the men say the word comes from the Chinese in Oregon who couldn't say 'I.W.W.' and said 'Wobblies' instead." Here [Barry] thought was a problem sure to be of some interest to the dictionary makers of the future.

I trust that readers will share my excitement in discovering Barry's prescient column of February 3, 1914. He demonstrated that both the Otis and Chinese natal anecdotes had circulated at the trial's end. Were these "origins" made up consciously to negate the telegrams' impact? He also anticipated decades of interest in the nickname. Barry proved right in his wise guess that the name would move outside IWW "slang." Futher, he left an excellent clue as to the eventual popularity of the Chinese ascription over that of Otis. Barry wrote:

> If the name "Wobblies," now established in the slang of the I.W.W. and pretty certain to make its way into our everyday vocabulary, could be definitely traced to the Chinese it would be seen to be related to the most attractive of the organization's qualities. The members cultivate a spirit that strives

> for a solidarity reaching even beyond the prejudices of race. In this regard it is remarkable. Only too often in the past has labor, crushed by capital, shown a similar cruelty to the labor of an alien people and a bitter and determined hostility.

Before and during this century's opening decades, much of American society accepted the "yellow peril" shibboleth as received truth. Barry, to his deep credit, spoke against such conventional "wisdom." Mortimer Downing and Fred Thompson, IWW stalwarts, helped circulate the Chinese cook anecdote out of their sense of justice rather than with a real belief that they actually might have established its historicity or linguistic veracity.

We shall find no evidence for the Chinese lingual tale, nor shall scholars drive it out of circulation. It remains too vivid a story, has circulated widely, and carries "the truth" of folktales long believed. Yet in recent years this anecdote has come under renewed scrutiny within the IWW as the cultural consciousness of labor activists has altered.

During February 1981, Utah Phillips, an IWW singer, appeared at the Vancouver Folk Music Festival. Aural Tradition in Canada and Philo in the United States released an LP recording of his songs and stories from the festival. In brochure notes for Joe Hill's "Where the Frasier River Flows," Phillips reported that the song stemmed from a 1912 strike during the construction of the Canadian Northern Railroad. "That's where the term 'Wobbly' was coined. . . . The Chinese camp cook, who couldn't say IWW, would say 'wobbly wobbly.' . . . It's a story that we're not particularly proud of, because it's a racist perception."

Henry Anderson, while gathering material on the IWW's Vincent St. John, reinforced criticism of the restaurateur story, noting its "transparent falsity." It "does not bespeak solidarity"; rather, it indicates "a sniggering condescension at best, ridicule at worst." Anderson speaks for enlightened friends who acknowledge the tale but make clear its meretricious nature.

In 1914, John Barry talked to Wobblies who heard the Oriental-in-Oregon anecdote as one affirming friendship across divisive lines in race. In 1981 and 1991, Philips and Anderson found this IWW explanation to hold intrinsic racist implications. Perhaps their viewpoint will drive the story from labor texts and dictionaries. More than a problem in word choice confronts us. Our continued acceptance or rejection of the nickname *Wobbly* speaks to the use of tradition in defining the identities of working people.

## Tradition's Maze

In 1986, the *Oxford English Dictionary* issued volume 4 of its *Supplement*, nothing "origin uncertain" for *Wobbly* as an IWW member. In 1989, the *OED* second edition repeated this entry. However, with access to Peter Tamony's article, the editors cited the *Miners' Magazine* for *Wobbily-Wobbily*'s appearance. We can now backdate the Colorado printing to "Patsy" O'Bang in the *Los Angeles Citizen*, April 11, 1913. Also, we can flesh out the circumstance surrounding the original Wheatland telegrams and the nickname's surfacing based on details within the Yuba County Superior Court transcript. (The *OED* cited only the California Court of Appeals' abbreviated report.)

Lexicographers seek dated usages in print for challenging words; labor historians and economists seek quite different proofs, quantitative or conceptual: expansion in labor markets, rise of institutional unionism, shifts in job techniques, manifestations of struggle, snapshots of barricades. For a penetrating study, the work of historians and linguists need be complementary.

Here, I note that Paul Brissenden's 1919 reference to Otis christening the Wobblies in the *Los Angeles Times* has sent students on a fruitless search through library files. Otis detested the IWW. Ideally, we should locate his *Times* editorial blast, a rhetorical thunderbolt hurled at enemies. If such a printing exists, it has never been sighted. Ironically, present evidence points to someone far removed from Otis's office—a Socialist party or Socialist Labor party activist residing in Los Angeles.

I am convinced that some IWW members (masters of sardonic narrative and satiric song) knew from the very beginning at Wheatland that they had turned a radical's rhetoric—not Otis's—into a boomerang. I suspect that Wobblies, first involved in the defense of Ford and Suhr, "invented" the Chinese mispronunciation jest to enhance the nickname's solidarity appeal. When the hop field case prosecutors chose to mystify *wobbles* as a conspiratorial code word, IWW members brilliantly promulgated two key alternatives (class-enemy Otis; friendly Chinese cook). These contradictory and diversionary explanations have intersected over the years, puzzled dictionary editors, and delighted Wobblies.

Folklorists seek to prove traditionality for varied and conflicting speculations on word origin. In a 1926 *American Mercury* dispute, Stewart Holbrook attributed the Otis coinage to rumor and the Chinese tale to IWW tradition. In their own "wars," General Otis and the unionist in Los Angeles both drew on demonology's time-tested vocabulary. California workers had heard dialect songs and cruel jokes about the Chinese at least as far back as the Gold Rush. Hence, IWW members could dip into a reservoir of stereotypes as a vital need developed to neutralize their nickname.

At Wheatland, defenseless migrants faced drunken armed deputies; the court trial moved hop field terror into legal channels with state agents determined to jail strike leaders. Only in retrospect do we focus on a creative aspect of the trial—a void filled by a fresh locution, an anvil on which IWW members shaped a powerful tool, a traditional compass boxed by questing workers. Despite their rejection of feudal and clerical customs, industrial unionists enclaved the new IWW sodality with recycled ore, fresh lore. With spirit, hop pickers and rank-and-file organizers enacted rites as their group's new moniker emerged.

The word combination *Old Wobbly* illuminates the path of one of the labor movement's most durable tags. Before 1913, IWW members heard variants of *wobble* as familiar verbs and nouns. During 1913, some IWWs—among them C. L. Filigno and Phineas Eastman—wrote out *wobblers* and *Wabbly* as their organization's distinguishing name. At its inception in 1905, the IWW had gathered young and old workers. Courageous and vigorous, these activists gave the industrial union an especially youthful glow. However, at some point in the 1920s, a few members began to see themselves as old-timers—ancient in years, veterans of struggle, seasoned passengers on history's train.

William "Big Bill" Haywood had been sentenced to federal

prison after the 1917 antiradical drive. Fleeing to Moscow, the IWW leader's energy flagged and his influence waned. Well before his death in 1928, Haywood, confiding in Walter Duranty, philosophized, "The trouble with us old Wobblies is that we all know how to sock scabs and mine-guards and policemen or make tough fighting speeches to a crowd of strikers but we aren't so long on this *ideelogical* theory stuff as the Russians" (169). To my knowledge, Haywood's reflective statement marks the earliest formulation of the category "old Wobblies."

During 1954, following a split in the Socialist Workers party, Bert Cochran likened Old Guard/Trotskyists to Old Wobblies "who could not comprehend the new world that had emerged from the first world war." At the time of anti–Vietnam War demonstrations in Berkeley, the *San Francisco Examiner* pictured Al Plummer, 70, and Ben Baker, 84, as Old Wobblies who had joined students at the campus edge.

Fred Thompson, in many conversations with me and other "youngsters," took umbrage at the designation *Old Wobbly.* In his heart, the union had never aged; the IWW deserved recognition beyond the ranks of antiquarian, curator, or etymologist. In a letter (May 23, 1960), Thompson expressed irritation at "omniscient" scholars, often superficial and smug in their treatment of the IWW. He objected strongly to "their calling the Wobs a bunch of old men living on memories of their more turbulent past." Thompson, ever-helpful to young historians, did not take kindly to those "shoving us into the scrapcan."

I trust that my formulations on *Wobbly* will honor old-timers Fred Thompson, Peter Tamony, Tony Bubka, and Charles Marcus, as well as touch the imagination of new unionists. Conjecture and speculation on language, whether ancient or innovative, is endless. Nevertheless, a broad-shouldered name that has held steady for decades can well carry a heavy load.

Word sleuths suffer their own occupational disorders—immune systems unable to reject additional citations. Just one more find may carry us back a step; another lead may spice our story. A literary memoir by Alfred Kazin holds a Depression flashback to 1935 in Manhattan's Union Square: "There were the usual 'wobblies,' as they called themselves, tramps glumly parked at the base of the equestrian statue with their heads down on their chests" (33). Surely, Kazin also knew Wobblies, proud and erect.

Colleagues with whom I have shared questions about *Wobbly* remind me that I, too, have felt glum at laborlore's amorphous mass and have waffled/wabbled over metaphysical matters. Not all wobblers carry IWW cards. Without my commenting on them, a few clippings from the *San Francisco Chronicle* attest to an old word's utility: "Why the Earth Wobbles Like a Clothes Washer"; "Choreographers: Ballet's Wobbly Future"; "Hubble's Wobble Stops."

Among the most interesting IWW spinoffs is the use of *wobble* to designate a wildcat or quickie strike by unorganized workers. Upton Sinclair, in *Singing Jailbirds,* had used the phrase "We'll wobble on the job!" During the 1980s Cecil Jordan, an electrician, worked for Brown & Root, the notorious open-shop Texas contractor. In correspondence, he indicated that he had first heard *wobble* as a work-connected word in November 1980 at Corsicana, when he and a group of buddies pulled a quickie. His mates had not joined the International Brotherhood of Electrical Workers and lacked knowledge about the IWW. Cecil guessed that their strike term described the act of wobbling management's foundations. Covington Hall, in 1923, had explained the IWW's name analogically as wobbling society's foundations.

In an unpublished short story, "The Agony and the Ecstasy," Jordan elaborated that a wobble also helped restless workers in mobility—their constant search for a job in the "Big Rock Candy Mountains." He recalled a particular wobble on a cold, wet day. The crew made its point but "could have picked a better time weather wise to turn self-righteous." Jordan quipped that "construction men are the only people I know who will show up in sleet and snow just to quit a job."

Bennie Graves, a former Texas pipeliner, has described *wobble* as a term going back to the days when teams of horses hauled pipes. Graves assumed that crews learned it from IWWs, perhaps during early organizational drives in southwestern oil and gas fields. However, he has been unable to trace the precise place or time of its shift into his trade's argot. We have yet to learn how *wobble* moved from pipeliners to building-trades electricians. Do other workers unaffiliated with the IWW also use this term to describe a quickie strike?

These never-ending word citations languish in files, overflow storage cartons, and, put to work, stimulate thought. In their collective range of meanings, lexical examples illustrate again the need within laborlore commentary for careful reading and analysis. We ask: which cryptic usage best decodes *Wobbly*'s history or adds substance to our explication?

## Circle Back

I circle back to the simultaneous printing of "Overalls and Snuff" on August 1, 1914 (San Francisco for the AFL building-trades paper; Cleveland for the IWW paper), and repeat its key declamation, "I knew he was a Wobbly by the button that he wore." One had only to see a tiny stamped-tin emblem to know its wearer's essential being. IWW members have understood the conjunction of seeing and knowing better than other unionists have. From 1905 until today, Wobbly artists have offered thousands of visual messages in the form of stickers, cartoons, and posters. Franklin Rosemont has commented perceptively on such art (1988).

At this juncture, I share a puzzle with readers. In 1924, Upton Sinclair took the IWW's favorite naming anecdote and placed it within a stage drama, helping theatergoers see wordplay enacted. Did a cartoonist feel similarly impelled to depict the encounter of Chinese cook and construction camp striker? For that matter, where are the drawings of Harrison Gray Otis in his act of "christening" Wobblies? At the Wheatland trial's end, John Barry alerted San Franciscans to appropriate questions surrounding the IWW's nickname. Surely someone in the labor or radical press saw artistic possibilities in the exuberant stories generated to explain the cognomen.

Although we lack drawings interpreting the genesis of *Wobbly,* the nickname appeared as a picture caption in June 1915, in E. F. Doree's "Gathering the Grain." Detailing the Agricultural Workers Organization drive, Doree summed up AWO activity with an aphorism: "Don't . . . harvest the wheat in the summer and starve in breadlines in the winter" (743). His article included a photo of two standing "straw cats" (harvest hands), one shaving the other. The caption "A WOBBLY SHAVE," blended description and humor.

Similarly, in 1919, *Wobbly* appeared in a cartoon caption. On January 13, the *California Defense Bulletin* ran a drawing depicting class-war prisoners (Kornbluh, 341). Following wartime raids and mass conspiracy trials at Chicago, Omaha, Wichita, and Sacramento, federal courts had jailed the IWW leadership. One cartoonist responded, "Have You a Little Wobbly Service Flag in Your Local?" IWW members, of course, understood the reference to their prisoners as honored warriors in a different cause.

It took decades after 1919 before anyone moved beyond caption to link nickname to one of the IWW's most persistent symbols—a crouching worker rises from and transcends a set of low-lying factories. Stage designer Robert Edmund Jones first placed this heroic figure on the poster and booklet announcing the Paterson (Silk) Strike Pageant at Madison Square Garden, June 17, 1913.

Long after the Paterson dispute ended, Jones's drawing continued to circulate. It received wide attention during the 1980s in the film *Reds* when John Reed (Warren Beatty)—writing a poem—picked up the flyer showing the crouching worker. In 1913, Jones had lettered the identifying initials IWW behind his silk striker's head, for neither Jones, Reed, nor any of the pageant's planners then knew the defiant nickname *Wobbly*.

During 1985, IWW artist and poet Carlos Cortez gathered cartoons for a traveling exhibit entitled "Wobbly: 80 Years of Rebel Art." For his catalog cover, he reproduced Arturo Machia's "The Shovel Stiff" from the *International Socialist Review* (October, 1913). Machia's stern laborer personified work itself. When the exhibit reached San Francisco State University in 1987, IWW typesetter Richard Ellington redesigned the Cortez catalog, changing contents and cover. Working with the advantage of time, Ellington replaced the shovel stiff with Jones's crouching worker. The latter hero appeared under the rubric "Wobbly."

It would have pleased me to reveal a *Wobbly* nativity scene visualized by an artist. Noting this lack, I return to verbal images embedded in the nickname's source explanations, phonological or semiotic. Fred Thompson found the aural formula "lingual difficulty" useful to negate charges of IWW vacillation. Peter Tamony advanced the notion of speech wars altering meanings—IWWs hurling back missiles on the left—and likened *Wobbly* to *Yankee*. Britons had used *Yankee* as a slur; Revolutionary troops accepted the new name proudly.

We are free to believe either that a Chinese camp cook or a left critic "coined" *Wobbly*. The historian David Roediger shared his views on such actors and enactments during my 1989 visit to Columbia, Missouri. Reflecting on the central question of why IWWs would extend and cherish an old term rather than project a new sound symbol, he observed the following:

> How do we account for a group of radicals adopting a label which implied uncertain movement, even slipping and sliding? In general, the twentieth-century left has considered itself the very embodiment of the inevitable forward motion of humanity. Can we imagine—taking groups contemporary with the IWW—the Socialist Party calling itself the "Slightly Unstable Party" or the Bolsheviks billing themselves as the "Party of Rather Uncertain Balance"?
>
> Part of this riddle's answer lies in the industrial union's readiness to embrace the swaggering and rambling aspects of the word *wobbly*. In their name, IWW members also accepted notions of uncertainty, indeterminance, and, even, the craziness of the modern world in a manner abhorrent to "scientific socialists." As the IWW approved the nickname, members faced uncertain times. Unionists experienced great elation in the mass strike at Lawrence, but harsh gloom as Paterson's loss plummeted spirits.
>
> To be a Wobbly involved tremendous uncertainty—state-sponsored victimization and vigilante-based repression. Other left organizations experienced fluctuating fortunes, but consoled themselves as having mastered the laws of societal evolution and the science of revolution. Such groups could not "own up" to their internal wobbles. Instead, as weaknesses became apparent, they intensified serious self-characterization and grand theory.

> Wobblies understood their heritage of direct action rooted in anarchist and syndicalist postures. No polemical line could rival everyday deeds against injustice. Pragmatic IWWs enjoyed victory, but also lived with defeat. T-Bone Slim's song "The Popular Wobbly" (They go wild, simply wild, over me) is the perfect example of the importance of defiant laughter amidst disaster.
>
> IWW members—more libertarian than authoritarian—felt that belief in necessary struggle superseded visions of inevitable victory. Workers who wrote and performed "Nuthouse News" skits could direct black humor and sardonic wit against society's lunacy, as well as against socialist rationality. Enjoying their name, Wobblies flaunted it at jungle campfire, in jailhouse play, and on the job. Accepted in 1913, *Wobbly* continues to ring proudly, the sole effervescent self-referential name on the left.

David Roediger, like Peter Tamony, used song and skit as semiotic devices to frame the extension of *wobbly* from everyday speech to a revolutionary industrial union's marker. Roediger's analysis leads back to the song "Overalls and Snuff" and its dominant images, circular union button and wearer. With blankets on his back, an old-time hop picker (not yet an Old Wobbly) agitated to free Wheatland's prisoners, informing the world that he'd "pick no more damned hops . . . for overalls and snuff" (snuff sold for 5¢ a can in 1914).

The song's statement of pure economic struggle continues to resonate because of its placement within a social text. It remains appealing and is still sung at IWW gatherings; its subject matter recalls fact and belief. The 1914–26 fight to free Ford and Suhr began with their jailing and involved appeals to courts, to legislative bodies, to a governor's office, and, beyond Sacramento, to a coast-to-coast and overseas public.

The Wheatland case moved inexorably from ranch field to civic arena. In this enlarged compass, and with the principals incarcerated for life, could Ford or Suhr have sensed the emblematic role hidden in their telegraphed cry for help? Could fellow workers Charles Marcus or C. L. Filigno, in the immediate years before

Wheatland, have foreseen the longevity of their then-now coded badge of identity?

Although Wobblies today pride themselves on their nonpolitical roots and belief in direct economic action, we look back with wonder at their many successful forays into civic and cultural forums. Not only did rebels and slaves defy their ever-present exploiters at the point of production, but they confounded biographers and historians as IWW members donned rainbow robes: idealist, zealot, pragmatist, puritan, harvester, builder, artist, teacher, trailblazer.

IWW loyalists in their many incarnations richly earned a memorable nickname, one overcoming any hints of vacillation, instability, stumbling, or ambivalence. With great aplomb, rebel unionists wobbled society's foundations. Muscle and laughter inverted a commonsense term sanctioned by centuries of usage. Essentially, Wobblies turned language on its head as they twisted epithet into cockade.

## Appendix: Natal Explanations

Available evidence reveals that *Wobbly*, in variant forms, circulated orally within California before the Wheatland hop strike of August 1913. We do not know when anecdotal explanations for the nickname arose. However, John Barry heard such accounts at the Ford-Suhr trial in January 1914. His report on *Wobbly* (*San Francisco Bullletin*), seemmingly, did not reach historians or lexicographers.

My list below begins with Brissenden's history of the IWW (1919) and closes with Flexner's popular book on American speech (1982). I have selected representative citations; readers will find others.

1. In 1919, the Columbia University Press published Paul Brissenden's seminal history of the IWW, a substantial expansion of his 1913 monograph. He added "Imperial Wilhelm's Warrior" to the play-on-initials list, assigning it to Arizona Senator Ashurst (57). Brissenden also noted that Harrison Gray Otis, the editor of the *Los Angeles Times,* "christened" the "Wobblies," an attribution that has persisted for decades. (In correspondence with me, 1960, Brissenden could not recall his source for the Otis story.)

2. Waldo Browne (1921), in the first major dictionary of labor terms, restated the Otis origin and added *wobblyism* for IWW philosophy.

3. The *Industrial Worker* (March 21, 1923), in a feature by Covami (Covington Hall) entitled "Why Is a Wobblie?" explained: "Wobblies, who get their name from the fact that they are forever wobbling the immutable foundations of society. . . ."

4. The *Nation* (September 5, 1923) printed a letter by Richard Hogue on political prisoners at Leavenworth. In closing, he quoted a letter from inmate Mortimer Downing on the word's birth. This attribution has come to dominate all others:

> How "Wobbly" Originated
> Up in Vancouver, in 1911, we had a number of Chinese members, and one restaurant keeper would trust any member for meals. He could not pronounce the letter "w," but called it "wobble," and would ask: "You I. Wobble Wobble?" and when the card was shown credit was unlimited. Thereafter the laughing term among us was "I. Wobbly Wobbly," and when Herman Suhr, during the Wheatland strike, wired for all foot-loose "Wobblies" to hurry there, of course the prosecution made a mountain of mystery out of it, and the term has stuck to us ever since. Considering its origin, I rather like the nickname. It hints of a fine, practical internationalism, a human brotherhood based on a community of interests and of understanding.

5. On May Day 1923, the IWW called a maritime strike at Los Angeles harbor. Two weeks later, police arrested Upton Sinclair for reading the Bill of Rights at a Liberty Hill rally in San Pedro. Subsequently, he turned to this strike in *Singing Jailbirds* (1924), a four-act didactic play. Erwin Piscator staged it elaborately in Berlin; in December 1928, John Dos Passos and Eugene O'Neill helped present it at the Provincetown Playhouse in Greenwich Village. Sinclair used act 2, scene 2, to dramatize the naming tale set in a harbor cafe. A few key lines follow, in which One Lung feeds a crew of strikers (38–39):

| | |
|---|---|
| Jake: | One Lung, I'm busted. You trust me? |
| One Lung: | Su', plenty tlust! |
| J: | Why you trust me? |
| OL: | You wobble-wobble! |
| J: | How you say I.W.W.? |
| OL: | I-Wobble-Wobble. (they all laugh) |
| J: | Say, boys, you know that old Chink made a new word in the language. He made the name "wobblies." |
| Matt: | Come off! |

J: Sure thing! You hear him—he can't say the letter W. [Jake details telegram episode in which he and the 'cutor discussed secret codes. Was a wobbly a dynamiter; did he cause bank safes or the government to wobble?]

Joe: Hurrah for the wobblies!

Jerry: We'll wobble on the job!

In correspondence with me in 1959, Sinclair indicated his source for the tale as "what the Wobblies told me," not Mortimer Downing.

6. James Stevens (1925, 138) reported that "the 'Wobblies'—they themselves, not a California editor, invented this name. . . ." In 1926, Stevens expanded his declaration: "It is true that Otis (or the *Los Angeles Times*) was the first to use the word *wobbly* in print, but it is doubtful if he was its originator. I have an idea that one of his editorial writers got it from a police reporter, who got it from the wobblies themselves."

7. Stewart Holbrook (1926a, 62) offered a colorful account for *American Mercury* readers. Elaborating on the Chinese eatery legend, he set it in the far wastes of Saskatchewan, twelve years previously (ca. 1914) on the Canadian Northern Line. "The Chink, being a go-getter and a believer in Service, lined-up [joined] with the gang. In a laudable effort to cash in on his affiliation, he would show his card to all potential customers telling them that he was a member of the I.W.W. But the heathen tongue was not equal to the letter *w*. 'Me likee I Wobbly Wobbly,' was the best it could do. It proved enough." Holbrook added a "theory" he felt to be unsound, in that it "lacks the support of a specific legend": "The word came over from Australia, and is a corrupton of *wallaby*."

8. James Lance (1926), a Portland Wob, differed with Holbrook: "Harrison Gray Otis, former owner of the *Los Angeles Times* and rabid labor-hater, was the first to christen members of the I.W.W. *wobblies*. He coined the name long before the C.N.R. had began building to the coast . . . and before the I.W.W. had any membership worth speaking of in Canada." Holbrook responded to Lance by attributing the Otis coinage to rumor, as well as to a Spokane police magistrate. "But the rank and file of the I.W.W., . . . will tell you about the Chinaman. . . . Of course, there is no etymological proof; all of it is tradition."

9. George Milburn (1930) reiterated the anecdote about Chinese mispronunciation, identifying the IWW as the International Workers of the World. (I shall not allude further to this common error in substituting *international* for *industrial*.)

10. *Webster's* (1934) cited the Chinese "distortion," safely qualifying it with "said to be" and "slang."

11. H. L. Mencken (1936, 190) quoted Downing's tale but found it unlikely. Mencken listed *wobbly* with other terms that had vexed American lexicographers.

12. Alfred Holt (1936, 323) returned to the "distressing result of a Chinese attempt to pronounce two successive 'double-yous,' " but added several slim possibilities: *wobbler* for infantryman; *nobbler* for pickpocket or thimble-rigger. Uncertain about these fanciful alternates, Holt stated sagely that " 'wobbly' does not describe the characteristic 'Industrial Worker of the World,' who is considered rather stubborn than otherwise."

13. Rose Pesotta (1944, 143) also mentioned Otis, but she qualified the attribution: "Spoken of as 'Wobblies' by their enemies, supposedly to indicate instability, they ignored the derisive implication and adopted that term as a convenient handle." She must be credited for applying the concept of inversion in language formation to the IWW nickname.

14. Ray Ginger, in a 1949 biography of Eugene Victor Debs, added Daniel DeLeon's name to the coiner's list, but without evidence (332).

15. Mitford Mathews (1951) entered the IWW nickname in *A Dictionary of Americanisms,* noting that the account of Chinese distortion lacked confirmation. (In my conversations and correspondence with Mathews, 1959, he stressed that no one had confirmed this popular ascription.)

16. Fred Thompson was a California criminal-syndicalism prisoner who knew Ford, Suhr, and Downing. Reflecting on the nickname in the IWW's "official" history, Thompson accepted the fact of uncertain origin but returned to the notion that "legend assigns it to the lingual difficulties of a Chinese restaurant keeper" (1955, 66). In place of Downing's site and date (Vancouver, 1911), Thompson suggested British Columbia, 1912, during the construction of both the Canadian Northern and Grand Trunk railway lines.

Acknowledging Mencken's skepticism, Thompson stuck to the Chinese anecodote, claiming that the alternative sense of a wobbler as a vacillator "fits no accusation ever made against IWW." (In short, Thompson could not place the union to which he had dedicated a life of high principle and pure energy as wobbling on any issues.)

With doubt lurking in the background, Thompson casually added that *wobble saw*—cutting a groove wider than its own thickness—might have fit the IWW. (In many conversations and much correspondence with him over the years, I suggested that his wobble saw might serve as an imaginative metaphor for a small band of idealists cutting a wide swath through grainy American timber. However, to the very end of his life [March 9, 1987], Thompson adhered to the "lingual difficulty" notion in that it came closest to an expression of workers' solidarity across barriers of ethnicity and language.)

17. In a memorial to Wobbly folklorist John Neuhaus (1960), I summed up then-available details on the nickname's chief attributions. In his appreciation of Neuhaus's efforts, Thompson (1960), asked, "Could Wobbly have come from someone trying to combine the initials IWW-OBU into the readily pronounceable syllable 'Wob'?" (OBU has long signified One Big Union.)

18. Raven McDavid (1963, 235) cast doubt on Downing's problematic Chinese tale: "Respectable lexicographers still cite this etymology for want of a better, but none really accepts it."

19. Philip Foner (1965, 128) referred *Wobbly* appropriately to Suhr's telegram. However, Foner erred in citing the message's printing in *Solidarity* (November 1, 1913).

20. Patrick Renshaw (1967, 21) cited Otis's hostility to labor after the dynamiting of the *Los Angeles Times* in 1910. Renshaw also mentioned Downing's "All loo eye wobble wobble" tale and credited Joyce Kornbluh with an additional source: "When Max Hayes, the American socialist, first used the word 'wobbly' he meant simply 'unstable.' "

21. Kenneth Allsop (1967, 304) generously offered five explanations: (1) A Chinese restaurant owner in 1911 near Kamloops (British Columbia) on the Grand Trunk Railroad job could not pronounce *W.* (2) The nickname "Wibbly-Wobblies" was sneeringly used of the IWW about 1909 by the socialist editor of the *Cleveland Citizen* (Hayes). (3) Wobblies "took their tag from the wobbling motion of the boxcars which were their transportation." (4) "Saying IWW out in full must quickly have palled. . . . Wobbly was a natural onomatopoeic comic contraction." (5) Wobbly was first used "as a term of disapprobation which was scornfully taken over and proudly worn as a cockade in the hat."

22. With Allsop's multiple explanations at hand, seemingly nothing new could be advanced, but old ground might be replowed. For example, Jack Scott, in *Plunderbund and Proletariat* (1975), a history of the IWW in British Columbia, returned to Downing's "authoritative" letter in the *Nation* (1923). Significantly, Scott found nothing in Canadian experience to document the tale.

23. In a 1980 novel honoring martyr Wesley Everest, Thomas Churchill recycled the wobble-saw guess: Seattle's IWW logger and boilermaker Herb Edwards asserted that "the nickname . . . wasn't a derogatory tag laid on by hostile people; we gave it to ourselves from a machine called the 'wobble-saw,' because it cut in both directions" (7). Edwards may have heard this in tradition or, very likely, read it in Fred Thompson's history of the industrial union.

24. Stuart Berg Flexner, in *Listen to America* (1982, 522), hit on an entertaining mix: "Any I.W.W. member was soon called a *wobbly* or, in parts of the U.S. and in Canada, a *wobbie* or *wobby.* Though this is often said to be from the West Coast Chinese pronunciation of I.W.W. as 'I Wobb(l)y Wobb(l)y,' it is most probably from the pronunciation of the union's less frequently used abbreviation *W.O.W.* (Workers of the World) as *wow* + b(l)y."

JULY 1912

The

INTERNATIONAL SOCIALIST REVIEW

PRICE TEN CENTS

THE FIGHTING MAGAZINE OF THE WORKING CLASS

FIVE "COPS" GUARDING ONE "FINK."

The Newspaper War in Chicago

"Five 'Cops' Guarding One Fink"

# 4

## Fink: Streets, Docks, Factories

For a century throughout the United States, Americans have used *fink* pejoratively to denominate a contemptible person. Within three speech communities, this word has accumulated extra meaning: criminals voiced it to brand informers; students, to put down both conformist and nonconformist peers; labor unionists, to isolate strikebreakers. *Fink* has served equally as noun and verb. Two 1960s examples, widely circulated in the *New York Times* and *Rolling Stone,* respectively, indicate the range: "A serious young man observed, 'the values of the college are such that if you study too hard, you're a fink' " (Boroff, 149). "Then the gang tries to sell their smack to a black hippie pusher who finks on them."

Students and druggies in the 1960s did not exhaust *fink*. San Francisco's veteran columnist Herb Caen calls on it frequently, at times nostalgically: "A tired Sam Spade sank onto a counter stool and said to Rosie the waitress, 'Gimme a cuppa java, sweetheart, black as a fink's heart.' Two stools away Harry Bridges gave him an approving nod." Caen's 1986 reference to Sam and Harry carried knowing readers back half a century by merging private detective fiction and labor history—two areas key to unraveling *fink*'s yarn.

Just as Peter Tamony helped me trace *Wobbly*'s travels, he reached into his cornucopia to stimulate my curiosity about *fink*'s multiple meanings. Like other San Franciscans in the 1930s, he had heard *fink* as a near-expletive among waterfront speakers.

Encountering this word in a George Ade fable (1903), Tamony queried the Chicago humorist about his source. In 1937, Ade replied that he had "heard it used once in a while by the lads who were addicted to the fly idion. . . . [It] meant about the same as a slob or no-good or rummy" (Tamony 1948, 29).

During March 1948, *American Notes & Queries* received a question on the labor term *fink*. Responding, Tamony submitted Ade's usage: " 'Does the Faculty permit you to be guilty of Disorderly Conduct?' asked the parent. 'Any one who goes against the Faculty single-handed is a Fink.' " In the light of this collegiate setting, Tamony observed that *fink* could not be assigned solely to trade union discourse. Thus, he included three passages from noncampus sources in his *AN&Q* response and formulated a contextual problem: Who carried *fink* from the repertoire of varsity lads to that of picket line militants?

When Gerald Cohen during 1979 offered an etymology based on a joke about Fink, a crafty tailor, Tamony—reacting to this singular exposition—sent his extensive clippings on *fink* to Cohen. The latter arranged this material for *Comments on Etymology* (1980). Thus, the tailor joke stimulated additional contributions to *CoE* by the Benjamins, Cassidy, Cohen, Gold, and Maher, as well as my lengthy report in 1988. David Shulman returned attention to a George Ade sketch, " 'Stumpy' and Other Interesting People," first printed in the *Chicago Record* on March 17, 1894.

Ade had depicted Stumpy Carroll, a West 12th Street lout. In court, as a witness in an assault and battery case, Stumpy described a bandaged plaintiff: "Everybody that's on to him says he's a fink." The justice of the peace needed elaboration; Stumpy obliged, "He's a stiff, a skate. He drinks and never comes up. He's always layin' to make a touch." On further questioning, Stumpy added for good measure that "his rabs" (plaintiff) is both a "gazabo" and "nutty," whose "lamps is out" and whose "trolley's off." Within this string of pejoratives, I focus on Ade's usage of *fink*—the first in print in the United States to denominate a contemptible person, but not yet an informer or strikebreaker.

Over the years, some lexicographers and popularizers have stayed close to George Ade's sense of *fink*, whereas others have contributed various definitions setting it within diverse frames: American rivers, whaling ships, labor strikes, jails, brothels, carnivals, German fraternities. In an appendix following this chapter, I summarize a baker's dozen of such applications.

## Origins and Ear Grabbers

Fink, unlike *Wobbly,* does not fall into a neat pattern either of chronological advance or lateral borrowing. The extension of *Wobbly* to the IWW occurred in a few year's time; *fink* served as a pejorative in Germany for centuries. IWW members accepted their nickname in humorous self-reference; no one has taken similar pride in being called a *fink.* In tracing the latter's path, we learn that words jump time hurdles to reach new eras and slip under hedgerows to enter adjacent pastures.

*Fink* and *finkenschaft* had been used in German academies during the eighteenth century—these words conveying images of excrement-eating birds. Mariners on whaling ships associated *fenks* with scum, the refuse in blubber rendering. How long, and on what oceans, did whalers sound *fenks* prior to its lexicographical capture in 1820? Mike Fink, at the Yellowstone River's mouth, may have murdered his protégé in 1822. Allegedly, Mike and companion took turns shooting cups of whiskey off each other's heads before the foul deed. We ask: did a Jena student, a *Pequod* sailor, or a western frontiersman initiate the long march that led to the naming of labor spies and strikebreakers as *finks?*

*Fink*'s calendric steps and institutional meandering intrigue language buffs. Further search leads to speakers who brighten their lives by projecting creative meanings for special words. Explanations often follow the circumstance of hearing and claiming. Although other extensions, folk or learned, may yet surface for *fink,* it seems unlikely that a single explication will emerge dominant. Most likely, a number of "origins" will converge to cover fresh discoveries. The *Random House Dictionary* (1987) observes wisely that the transmission of *fink* from German to English and the word's "range of meanings have not been clarified fully."

In attending to occupational locutions, I have drawn widely on labor historians, dialectologists, and folklorists. Receptive to workers' words, I have sought those mapping boundaries between unionists and others. Labor cardholders employ many harsh terms to identify "outsiders" but few to mark internal values such as desired militance or devotion to cause.

By scanning pejoratives similar to *fink,* we see the American labor movement as mainly reacting to society's large forces. Unionists close ranks by hurling verbal sticks and stones at those who do not join them in solidarity. Among the put-downs we find *ape, blackleg, brownnose, crimp, dehorn, fakir, freerider, goon, gypo, homeguard, hog, hooker, moonlighter, pacesetter, piecard, popsickleman, porkchopper, rat, redapple, runner, salmonbelly, scab, scissorbill, seagull, sellout, shorttail, skate, spotter, suck, yellowdog, whiterat.*

Some of these "ear grabbers" reached me during my early employment as a shipwright's helper in San Francisco. All the waterfront mechanics who took me in hand knew and used *fink, fink hall,* and *fink book.* Many of the journeymen teachers had been to sea, some on windjammers, some on tramp steamers. Hence, I did not separate *fink* from the hundreds of then-new-to-me nautical terms. More concerned with learning job secrets, technical nomenclature, and union ritual than with academic research, I absorbed words without probing for the genesis and genre of specific expressions.

In retrospect, had I asked my teachers about their understanding of *fink,* they might have revealed cogent ties. *Whale shit* became the earliest explanatory analog I heard for *fink,* but, as it happens, I had no opportunity to talk to any whaleman until I met Stan Hugill. Coming as a shantyman to San Francisco's Hyde Street Pier to present maritime lore at a 1985 sea festival, he knew *finks* as designating try-pot scum thrown overboard. Associating this word with whalers who had sailed from Aberdeen, Scotland, in the 1930s, Hugill seemed unaware of any link between whaling talk and labor turmoil.

I dwell on Hugill's remarks because they represented for me the once-in-a-lifetime hearing of a whaling word in living speech. Taking advantage of his presence, I offered a figure learned during waterfront days: "You're lower than whale shit that sinks to the bottom of the sea." It seemed logical that a whaler could have employed *fenks/finks* to describe a prostitute, a strikebreaker prostituting himself, or any other wretch destined for the sea's floor. Hugill laughed at my conjecture but could not confirm it.

In a popular history of San Francisco's harbor, William Camp advanced an analog: "Nothing is lower than a fink—not even a whale's belly, and that's at the bottom of the sea" (450). Can anyone date this simile's antiquity? The Chicago jazz musician "Mezz" Mezzrow, about 1915, had been jailed in a "reformatory." When he identified himself as a musician, "that deputy warden made [musician] sound like it was lower than whaleshit, and that's at the bottom of the ocean" (35).

Barbara Raskin demonstrates this speech figure's persistence. After her 1987 novel *Hot Flashes* became a best-seller with strong appeal to mobile urbanites, Raskin recalled previous "poverty" by noting that she had been " 'lower than whale droppings,' taking boarders into her brick town house to make ends meet" (Cuniberti).

In 1933, the *OED* picked up a 1928 citation for *fink* as a strikebreaker and, in 1972, glossed it widely, beginning with George Ade's 1903 example. The 1989 *OED* did not add to the 1972 record. Hence, I advance additional usages and comment on labor settings for dissemination, leaving to others the needed study of *fink* in criminal haunts. Conventional and sequential lexical practices serve to describe a particular word's movement into trade union speech. In the organized labor community, key words act out meanings during confrontational strikes and tedious bargaining sessions, at hiring halls and skid road saloons. Thus, I view *fink* (like *Wobbly*) as a discrete social text—a solitary word showing expository and evocative faces. *Fink* also serves as a building block in large texts: union narratives, ideological guidons.

Stewart Holbrook's colorful naming anecdote collapses the wall between the words *fink* and *pink*. Unionists have enjoyed his account, which moves smoothly from a single word to an embellished tale. Holbrook's story appears in this chapter's appendix; here, I sketch background facts for his belief that Pinkerton guards and gun thugs gave birth to *fink* during the Homestead strike. Although neither contemporaneous accounts from 1892 nor subsequent reports by historians support Holbrook, his rendering persists, if only because it holds tragedy's tension dissolved in humor.

For decades, working people had very good cause to fear Pinkerton detectives and agent provocateurs. Labor partisans, observing their action after the Civil War, tagged them Hessian hirelings of plutocracy—anarchical and lawless (Flower, 513). When a dispute arose early in 1886 at Chicago's McCormick Harvester factory, the owner shut it down and locked out employees. Next, McCormick hired Pinkerton agents to guard scabs and reopen the plant. Unionists, socialists, and anarchists staged a series of protest meetings culminating in the May 4 Haymarket Square tragedy—workers and police killed; the trial and hanging of anarchists.

Paul Averich, in a superb history, and David Roediger and Franklin Rosemont, in a fascinating scrapbook, cover Haymarket. I report only that some Chicago radicals labeled Pinkerton detectives as *pinks* during 1886. On March 2, Albert Parsons and Michael Schwab protested McCormick's use of police, "Pinks," and "scabs" (David, 187). This seems to be the first reporting of *pink* as a labor pejorative, and, as such, it carries Holbrook's anecdote to Haymarket rather than Homestead. Perhaps after the formation of the IWW in Chicago, 1905, a few members continued to clip *Pinkerton* to *pink*.

Apparently, *pink* never became widespread in labor or left circles although hostility to the Pinkertons persisted for decades and carried over to several hundred other private agencies that herded scabs and spied on workers. In 1910, the *Industrial Worker* included a letter from Oscar Rengo on his search for work in an Arizona gold camp. Sent by an employment office to the Theil Detective Agency, which "wanted a man without conscience or scruples," Rengo refused the dishonor. Theil sought miners, regardless of their skill, who would report fellow workers' concerns. The IWW editor headed Rengo's letter, "Hiring a Pink."

In July 1912, Joe Hill's topical "John Golden and the Lawrence Strike" appeared in the IWW's little red songbook. Hill (in commenting on action by woolen mill workers) noted that preachers, cops, money kings, and boys in blue opposed the strikers but "that weaving cloth with bayonets is hard to do." Further, "John Golden pulled a bogus strike with all his 'pinks and stools' " (Gibbs Smith, 245). Hill or his editor placed *pinks* and *stools* in quotation marks, suggesting that IWWs found these words either colloquial or archaic.

Despite a considerable search, I have found no evidence that

Wobblies conflated *pink* and *fink* because of sound shift or an inability to distinguish word meanings. On the contrary, IWW soapboxers and correspondents enjoyed a magnificent command of language, reveling in wordplay and coining neologisms. Better than other creators in labor's ranks, they used comedy, poetry, job report, and manifesto to imagine a new world, to harness metaphor to the power of hammer and drill.

In *Rebel Voices*, Joyce Kornbluh provides a fascinating look at IWW lore. She helps us understand that these masters of rhetoric saw *pink*'s debt to the Pinkertons but heard *fink* as a discrete locution. George Ade did not invent *fink* in 1894. Rather, he learned it from speakers he characterized as "fly idiom" lads—perhaps as early as his Purdue University years, 1883–87, or after graduation during Chicago newspaper days. I suggest that some Wobblies, like Ade, had also heard *fink* in their learning years in mine and mill, on the road, and in the jungle.

During 1910, the *Industrial Worker* ran a twelve-stanza poem, "The Workin' Stiff," by Lionel C. Moise. With Robert Service rhetoric and Walt Whitman vision, Moise described the life of a casual laborer—track worker, granite splitter, wheat harvester. A few lines from his poem reveal handles known to itinerants in this century's first decade:

> On the road he's a cat, and a bloody fink.
> And a scissor-bill to boot;
> And bindle-stiff is a gentle link
> In the names that he must bruit.
>
> And truth of it is that he's neither a tramp,
> Nor a fink, nor a Johnny Yegg,
> Nor a fly-by-night, nor a vagrant scamp,
> Nor much of a fellow to beg.

Moise's travels, literary experience, and fate have eluded me. I do not doubt his authorship, though he may have enlarged a recitation already in tradition. During 1931, the sociologist Nels Anderson included in a hobo handbook eight lines from the poem, without credit to an author (31). Matters of provenance and tradition aside, Moise's offering marks the earliest printed example known to me of *fink* in reading matter about or for tramping workers. In short, Moise's fink did not scab or break strikes, nor was he a pink. Rather, he built railroads but rode the rods and harvested wheat but often went hungry.

Louis Jackson, a Portland, Oregon, police detective, first noted *fink* in a 1914 lexical compilation: current chiefly among eastern criminals as an "unreliable confederate or incompetent sympathizer." By placing citations from Ade, Moise, and Jackson in sequence, we encompass hoodlum, student, tramp, and criminal realms. Where and when did one such speaker extend *fink* to a labor union scene?

## Strikebreaking: Chicago, Akron

I search for a specific strike during which *fink* caught a journalist's ear or, possibly, made its way into correspondence or a minutes book. In 1935, an inquisitive reporter on the *New York Post,* Edward Levinson, came closer than any historian or philologist in tracking the word. *I Break Strikes!* reads like a Ring Lardner sketch or an A. J. Liebling profile. The book's title boast came from Pearl L. Bergoff, the self-proclaimed "King of the Strikebreakers"—a king with cynical pride in extortion and violence.

Beyond keenly observing finks in action, Levinson dipped into past newspaper stories, early muckraking accounts in popular magazines (McQuiston, Craigie), and labor spy exposes (Friedman, Howard, Spielman). He commented on agencies such as Baldwin-Felts, Railway Audit & Inspection Company, Waddell-Mahon, William J. Burns, Sherman Service, Mooney & Boland, and George H. Theil. Like other top reporters, Levinson heeded vernacular expression. To explain *fink,* he wrote,

> Casting about for a word to express adequately their loathing of the professional strikebreakers, the Industrial Workers of the World and, soon after, other trade unionists, selected "fink" as the proper description. The term was borrowed from the criminal world where fink, as a verb, means to turn informer, to betray, to squeal. A second interpretation defines a fink as "a criminal who is dissatisfied with his loot." The inspiration of the I.W.W. came from the verb, and gave to it a new meaning—one who betrays his fellow workers by scabbing for money. . . . When the passions of strikes run

> high there are more vigorous expressions [for *fink*], most of them suggestive of excrement of supposedly less worthy parts of the anatomy. (53)

Levinson's 1935 explanation continues to make sense: "Professional strikebreakers have accepted the designation of finks with little concern for its implications. They have kept the word alive" (54). I assume, then, that underworld speakers carried *fink* as a general pejorative into scenes of labor conflict and carried it out as a specific marker for strikebreakers. I seek the time and place of this word's shift.

Levinson asserted that Wobblies initially applied *fink* during "Potato Face" Jim Farley's reign (29). Within the strikebreaking profession, he ruled as the pathbreaker, the subject of considerable legend. Farley took the first streetcar through a mob of strikers; he held battle scars on every inch of his tall body; he paid underlings generously; he refused to hire out as a strikebreaker where workers were underpaid. Starting in the ranks, he opened his agency in New York in 1902 and rose to glory in San Francisco's violent transit strike of 1907 (Fredericks, Meloney, Scott). Contracting tuberculosis, Farley died in 1913 at age forty-three, having spent his final years as a horse race aficionado.

The precise disturbance in which Farley, or rival detectives and their hired guns, earned the tag *fink* has yet to be found. One possible setting among many is Chicago. Following an unusual newspaper lockout/strike, Phillips Russell wrote a lead article for the *International Socialist Review* (July 1912). To call special attention to their city's newspaper war, *ISR* editors ran a magazine cover photo: five policemen protecting a scab newsboy, a disconsolate striking newsy in the background. This picture's caption read, "FIVE 'COPS' GUARDING ONE 'FINK.' "

History books accord no space to obscure strikes; however, Philip Taft described the Chicago dispute—its complex unfolding, leadership rivalries, and ultimate failure. I touch on this event to document early printed references to strikebreakers as finks. A few facts help situate the word's spread in a then-popular socialist periodical.

Disunity marked the strike's opening on May Day, 1912. While printers in the typographers' union Local 16 observed their contract by working on Chicago's major papers, other crafts—pressmen in Local 7, stereotypers in Local 4—pulled out. To slow scab-sheet distribution, teamsters/drivers, newsboys, and home delivery circulators joined in sympathy with the strikers. Faced by militance in "bottom" ranks, Hearst's local chief, W. A. "Andy" Lawrence, and Mayor Carter Harrison deployed city policemen and private strong-arm men to protect the scab vendors.

Russell's prose fit the comic-pathetic scene: "Negroes, old women, and small girls were put out to fill the places of the newsboys. . . . It was not unusual to see three or four cops, both in uniform and plain clothes, guarding one trembling little fink. . . . The days work done, many cops forced the 'finks' to hand over half of their receipts."

Behind the assault on union newsies and the exploitation of scab "replacements" hovered the memory of Chicago's previous "circulation wars" between the respectable *Tribune*, the yellow *Examiner*, and their lesser rivals. Hired sluggers had raided competing newsstands; stockyard thugs, in that day's parlance, "put the screws to the newsboys" or "the arm on each kid." During 1908, newsboys had organized their own independent local in response to beatings by circulation warriors. Newsboys also sought to alter their pariahlike status in the eyes of skilled printing tradesmen and white-collar reporters.

An *ISR* writer (probably Phillips Russell, who signed himself "Union Man"), commenting on the newspaper strike, called up one of labor's most cherished nicknames to describe a foot soldier in the class war: "It is a long way that stretches between the music room of the Hotel La Salle, where President Lynch [of the International Typographical Union] sits signing contracts with the masters of lying [the Publishers' Association], and the corner outside, where Jimmy Higgins stands selling Socialist papers in the hard-falling rain" (13).

Russell's idealized Higgins (the rank-and-filer who accepts drudgery) occupies the sacred corner; a fink, the profane corner. In this war, to say the least, enemies stood up in their respective trenches. Our imagination lets us see finks openly guarded by gunmen. Can we locate the scene where undercover spies and secret informers first acquired their infamous name *fink?*

Akron, which dominated American rubber production, could have served as a setting. Early in this century, industrialists Firestone, Goodrich, Sieberling, and Goodyear welded their talents to Taylorism (scientific management) and Bull-Moose progressivism (the gospel of efficiency). Despite such "enlightenment," these owners treated their workers as serfs. Responding to pay cuts, speed ups, and job hazards, the IWW in 1912 organized the Rubber Workers Industrial Union Number 470.

Radical unionists preached: "You don't have to die to get to hell. Just come to Akron, Ohio, and get a pass to enter any one of the many rubber shops." On February 11, 1913, a handful of Firestone tire builders walked off the job. Their spontaneous example inspired others as thousands of workers flocked to the IWW banner. Nonetheless, in the face of employer resistance, ALF craft union rivalry, and waning enthusiasm among new unionists, the strike failed before the end of March (Roberts; Wortman).

Subsequently, John W. Reid, a Diamond Rubber Company worker and secretary-treasurer of Local 470, confessed that since 1908 he had been a secret operative for the rubber bosses' agent, the Corporations Auxiliary Company. Within the plant he gathered "dope" on troublemakers; at meetings he copied vital correspondence. Finally, he balked at absconding with Local 470's treasury, for Reid "would not be a thief." His revelation appeared in the IWW's Cleveland newspaper *Solidarity* (January 17, 1914).

Reid underscored the impotence of workers facing hidden enemies. Having sold himself to the bosses, he agonized over his Judas role. Many years later, IWW leader "Big Bill" Haywood wrote that "the companies learned that a strike was possible in spite of the finks and detectives that they employed" (1929, 266). In fact, Reid had noted that most of the IWW's leading officers in Akron were spies.

At this juncture, I pause for speculation. Reid, the corporate lackey, commanded sufficient guile to be elected to a key position in Akron's IWW rubber union. For more than five years, he played dual parts—a fink with a forked tongue. It does not stretch imagination to "replay" conversations between Reid and his Cleveland superiors, or among Wobblies after Reid's confession. Surely, by 1914, the word *fink* had reached Akron. When did

Haywood first brand rubber spies as finks? No sound recording preserves IWW speech from its formative years. Hence, I look to the press for strike-born colloquialism.

## Streetcar Strikes: Wilkes-Barre, Kansas City

In the two decades between 1900 and 1920, American streetcar men engaged in hundreds of bitter strikes—clashes that carried labor banners from urban centers to village crossroads. One of the longest of such disputes took place in Wilkes-Barre, an anthracite coal union stronghold. In January 1915, the Wilkes-Barre Street Railway Company and the Amalgamated Association of Street and Electric Railway Employees, Division 164, could not agree on wages.

An April strike led to protracted arbitration and stalemate. The strike resumed in October as the traction company contracted with Pearl Bergoff for strikebreakers; Luzerne County unionists, rightfully fearful of the King, fought for jobs and lives. With the paralysis of regional transportation, "tin lizzie" entrepreneurs turned their autos into "jitneys." Wild and reckless driving caused fatal accidents; three passengers murdered a "jitney chauffeur" on March 12, 1916 (McCarthy).

The editors of *Outlook* (December 8, 1915), responding to strikers and jitney drivers, thundered anarchy, decried the weakness of local police in quelling riots, and lauded the state constabulary as peace bringers. This Pennsylvania mounted police force, established in 1905, had broken many strikes, at times in tandem with the industrial "Coal and Iron Police." Labor partisans, lumping together private and public bluecoats as "Cossacks," found it especially galling when peace officers aided underworld thugs.

On Saturday evening, March 25, 1916, a crowd gathered in Wilkes-Barre's Public Square to hear round-by-round megaphone returns (telegraphed from New York) of the Jess Willard–Frank Moran championship boxing match. As strikebreakers drove trolley cars through the sqaure, young sports fans and strike sympathizers attacked scab crews. The *Wilkes-Barre Record* reported the "frenzy of the unruly mobs," painting youths as lawless toughs and vicious ruffians. When city police proved unable to stem rioting, the state police "restored order."

Irving Crump, a popular writer of books for teenage boys, commented on the mêlée: the streetcar strikers had left their cars "in the hands of a number of strike breaking 'finks' " (98). Where did Crump, who was unsympathetic to labor, learn the then-new strike term *fink?* He could have heard it voiced by police or by Bergoff's hirelings or read it in a spy's secret report. Surely, other commentators must also have heard the daily banter of the strikebreakers. Stretching out for two years, the dispute may well have stimulated familiarity with *fink.*

The strike proved extremely profitable to Bergoff. Some of his fink "captains" retailed prostitutes to their charges. Others took cuts from crap game concessions. "Noble" Eddie Dineen murdered the fink George Haskins in a carbarn. "Beef Stew" Murphy had his skull fractured after feeding finks a steady diet of liver stew. At the strike's end, Bergoff tried to cheat his finks out of their sordid earnings by promising to pay them on return to the New York headquarters. The finks themselves staged a ministrike, refusing to clear the carbarns until the Pennsylvania Labor Bureau ensured their pay (Levinson, 68, 140, 226).

One could write a thriller on fink lore—anecdotes about theft, graft, and assault veneered with macabre humor. However, I return to Irving Crump's usage in *The Boy's Book of Mounted Police* and his 1916 setting in Wilkes-Barre. Previously, in 1912, a socialist writer had extended *fink* to Chicago strikebreakers. A patriot and a conservative, Crump found this pejorative term appropriate in a book directed at American boys. Through the summer of 1916, the *Independent* carried many articles and photographs on striking traction workers in New York City. On September 25, this widely circulated magazine's news-pictorial section included a photo captioned "Sleeping fink." I have not found any earlier photo or cartoon using *fink* as part of a caption. Do such illustrations exist?

*Fink* reached mainline journalists again during a 1917 strike by Kansas City carmen. That summer, Pearl Bergoff's brother Leo recruited several thousand finks and secured their railroad journey from New York and Chicago. On August 10, the strikers, falling back on a frontier anti-horse-thief tradition, greeted Leo's foot soldiers as they debouched to their carbarn posts. The *Kansas City Star* reported a "general rout of the 'finks' " as trolley workers and fellow citizens laid siege to the riff-raff.

Police Chief Flahive, reversing the customary civic support to paid strikebreakers, called for a committee of streetcar men to arrange the finks' departure. Escorting the outsiders to the train station, a well-wisher jeered, "Back to Sing Sing." One reporter asked, "Why do they call you finks?" His quarry replied, "Dunno, I'm an Easterner, not a fink." Finally, the angry marchers went after Bergoff at the Hotel Biltmore, but he eluded the unionists. The *Kansas City Times* closed out commentary by noting that "forty cowed 'fink' captains" left town under the cover of night.

Ed Levinson featured this Kansas City rout because it reported one of labor's few victories over professional strikebreakers. The reporter also invoked community memory—the Anti-Horse-Thieves Association from frontier-vigilante days. Indeed, it was unusual for new vigilantes to aid unionists. In retrospect, we can trace 1916–17 usages by Irving Crump, the *Independent*, and Kansas City reporters as *fink* moved from criminal speech to popular print.

Two visual markers help bound the half-decade within which *fink* gained currency as a labor term. In August 1915, Art Young contributed a savage cartoon to the *Masses* entitled "A Strike-Breaking Crew." Young named his six uglies but did not tag any of them as *finks*. Had he heard this word in 1915? In April 1919, the *One Big Union Monthly* used a drawing by "Dust" Wallin of a pigeon on a stool; he labeled it "Species: Finkus Scaborium." Significantly, Waldo Browne issued a major labor dictionary with encyclopedic references during 1921. He defined *fink* as an undercover man: "Of the printable names given them by those upon whom they spy, 'stool pigeons,' 'stools,' 'gumshoes,' and 'finks' are perhaps commonest." Ideally, Browne would have dated these tags and related them to specific strikebreaking acts.

## Puget Sound Dockers

Opening this chapter, I noted that both Peter Tamony and I knew *fink* as a waterfront expression. Pursuing the connection, in 1961, I shared interest with Ottilie Markholt in Tacoma, where she had read widely in minute books and news reports while researching Pacific maritime labor. Markholt's studies alerted me to the background of animosity toward fink halls, fink cards, fink books, fink herders, and fink rackets (Goldberg, Nelson, Schwartz).

Throughout the nineteenth century, many American bucko mates drove seamen cruelly, while unscrupulous boardinghouse masters and bloody crimps hounded them in port. As early as 1732, British mariners designated those who entrapped or seduced them into service as *crimps* (Rediker, 224). By 1795, English journals carried descriptions of unsavory *crimping houses;* in America, *crimping den* emerged to categorize harbor employment office and labor exchange. After the California Gold Rush, San Franciscans added the verb *shanghai* to the crimping scene (Tamony 1966). *Shanghai* also points to early efforts by American seamen to organize independent unions, in part, to curb practices of "sailor stealing."

Fink halls, in substance but not in name, go back at least to 1892, when San Francisco shipowners established an office run by Captain "Scantling Bill" Roberts to offset both union hiring halls and private boardinghouses. The *Coast Seamen's Journal* blasted the employers' new hall as a "scab office" competing for "cumshaw" with deep-water crimps and shanghaiers. Sailors made no fine distinctions between "runners" who pushed and pulled victims into crimping dens and the "solicitors" (pimps) and "confidence men" who assisted Scantling Bill in recruiting duties.

Peter Gill, born in Norway in 1863, took to the sea as a youth. While in California in 1885, he joined the Coast Seamen's Union and participated in its subsequent transformation into the Sailors' Union of the Pacific. He served for many years as SUP port agent in Seattle, gathering material for an unpublished history. Gill helps us step figuratively from crimping den to scab office to fink hall. Also, he details the CSU 1886 strike after shipowners demanded that seamen surrender their union books in favor of "grade books." These devices nominally listed qualifications and employment history. They also enabled captains and shipping masters to "grade" crew members as if they were schoolboys.

In the same year that Kansas City streetcar unionists repelled strikebreaking finks, Puget Sound longshoremen verbalized their own opposition to finks, fink halls, and fink cards. Without dwelling on the rich occupational culture of "men-along-the-shore," I note only that workers who loaded and unloaded ships named themselves and their craft variously: *stevedore, ship laborer, rigger, winch driver, timber stower, grain handler, coal loader, wharf rat, wharfie, dockwalloper.* Longshore literature is extensive (e.g.: Barnes, Larrowe, Magden, Pilcher, Rubens); hence, I turn directly to the apparent site where dockmen incorporated *fink* into waterfront speech.

The 1915 opening of the Panama Canal brought good times to Pacific ports, as well as renewed tension between International Longshoremen's Association members and their employers. The issue of closed shop/open shop then lay like an earthquake fault between worker and boss. Seeking their share of prosperity, forty-three ILA locals from Prince Rupert to San Diego voted to cease work on June 1, 1916.

Unable to maintain coastwide unity, the longshoremen faltered in their strike. While internal differences heightened, scabs murdered ILA men in several Pacific ports. Meanwhile, the Milwaukee Railroad filled Tacoma terminal jobs with black strikebreakers guarded by gun thugs imported from Chicago. In some ports, employers housed scabs on "prison" vessels moored at dockside to prevent strikers' attacks on job takers. The Seattle ILA strike ended on October 4, 1916; the Tacoma strike, on October 18.

Puget Sound stevedore bosses pressed victory by transferring their new men from "ship hotels" to "normal" quarters and by initiating regular dispatching through waterfront employers' hiring halls. To tame their workers, Tacoma bosses hired Harvey Wells, who had previously broken lumber strikes in the Northwest. For a few months, Wells resorted to the old shape-up, or line-up—literally hiring men who gathered on the docks each morning. Early in 1917, Wells set up a new Tacoma hiring hall at the corner of Eleventh and A streets: "A derby hat and a sawed-off shotgun were [his] badges of office" (Magden 1982, 37).

Wells introduced a special dispatch card coded to distinguish loyal ILA members from recent scabs. This emblem of defeat resembled a cafeteria punch card with numbered squares along the edge. As Wells tried to punch unionists into oblivion, some longshoremen dubbed his device a *rustling card,* a term previously used by metal miners in the West (Larrowe, 89). Employers found neutral euphemisms for their industrial passports or work permits; workers chose strong language for these blacklisting artifacts. I touch on the practice of job rustling and the term *rustling card* in chapter 5. Here, I note only that the latter word combination did not survive on Puget Sound docks, losing out to the pungent *fink card*.

Labor unions do not disappear after single failures, or from novel cards. Actually, a cadre of loyalists remained in Tacoma, devising informal techniques to temper fink hall rules. Unable to drive activists away, employers sought to limit the number of union stalwarts (from ILA Local 38–3) hired for each job. Tom Green, in a 1980 interview, recalled his father's stories of the checkerboard policy:

> The strikebreakers lined up on one side of the hall . . . union men lined up on the other side and [the dispatcher] took two for one, two strikebreakers' gangs, one union gang. But these men, they were great union men and they very soon convinced the employer that the strikebreaker was the wrong kind of labor. They just went out and busted their tails and outworked them. They kind of fiddled along and fiddled along and these strikebreakers kept leaving, going elsewhere. There's an awful lot of pressure comes on a strikebreaker once a strike is over. One that stays, nobody ever forgets him; he's not adopted into the clan. So ultimately they got to the point that [it] got to be a two for one advantage—two union for one scab going. (Magden 1982, 37)

Tom Green's recollection marks the ingenuity of rank-and-filers in setting their own conditions by subverting employers' procedures during wartime and postwar years. His phrase "the wrong kind of labor" holds considerable meaning. Repugnant scabs and finks deserved to be shunned in that they violated the work community's unity. Additionally, they lacked skill, thus posing danger on the job. Green's picture of dockers who "busted their tails" contradicts the notion that unionists know only how to shirk. Who mandates that bosses alone hold the wisdom to set work's tempo?

Tacoma longshoremen not only established local rules, formal and informal, but they also reached across the continent to the nation's capital. In April 1917, America entered World War I. Previously, in war preparation, the government established the United States Shipping Board to build and staff an enlarged merchant fleet. Throughout the 1920s, employers and their federal patrons used Sea Service Bureaus and Marine Service Bureaus to handle maritime labor. These agencies assumed fink-recruiting duties.

The historian Ron Magden describes the wartime cat-and-mouse steps taken by Tacoma longshoremen in regaining hall control from Harvey Wells. Their fight ranged beyond Puget Sound, for, to deflect dock trouble, the government had established the National Adjustment Board. Thus, Jack Bjorklund—ILA activist, Mason, Democrat—traveled to Washington, D.C., to persuade NAC officials that Tacoma unionists could manage job distribution more efficiently and equitably than employers. The government then took control of the Tacoma hall, terminating rustling cards and ceding actual dispatching to Bjorklund (Magden 1991, 92).

During World War I, longshoremen relished their ingenuity in turning the tables on Wells and his strikebreaking finks. Present-day dockers in Tacoma—affiliated with the International Longshoremen's and Warehousemen's Union—have lived for decades with artifacts marking resistance and victory. Early in 1917, Wells had commissioned the Defiance Sawmill to build backless wooden benches for his hall. When the ILA reclaimed control, the unionists appropriated the benches, moving them in following years to new dispatching halls.

On a visit to Tacoma ILWU Local 23 (April 11, 1991), I had the pleasure of sitting on a scarred 1917 bench and swapping stories with old-timers. They chuckled in describing the act of "liberating" fink hall furniture and keeping it in use. Clearly, the task of explicating metaphor does not belong exclusively to teachers of language and literature. Tacoma stevedores, who traditionalize accounts of inverting boss power, understand the meaning of turned tables and scarred benches.

At this point, I ask when Tacoma or Seattle longshoremen first voiced *fink hall* and when *rustling card* gave way to *fink card. Fink*, denominating a strikebreaker, must have reached Puget Sound during the 1916 strike. Over the years, it spread down the coast. Ottilie Markholt has generously supplied initial documentation:

1. *Seattle Union Record* (October 14, 1916), report of the Seattle Central Labor Council meeting: the Riggers and Stevedores Auxiliary requested that F. W. Becker's (waterfront employers) "employment office" be placed on the unfair list for his failure to "keep the compact" and for introducing a " 'card' system similar to that of the Metal Trades Association."
2. Riggers and Stevedores (ILA 38–12) delegates' report to Seattle Central Labor Council (Minutes of August 29, 1917): "On the job and intend to stay in spite of the fink hall."
3. Similar minutes (October 3): "Voted unanimously to refuse to use Fink card."
4. Similar minutes (October 19): "Fink hall creating much bitterness of feeling."
5. *Tacoma Labor Advocate* (February 22, 1918), report on meeting of all waterfront workers: "For some time past the 'fink' hall [has led to] serious conflictions with the workers and this meeting will devise some means of doing away with the hall."
6. *Seattle Union Record* (May 30, 1918, letter by F. G.: "A Fink is the remains of what once was a human being, but who, through ignorance is a menace to himself and society."
7. Twelfth Annual Convention, Pacific Coast District ILA, Seattle (May 5–10, 1919), report in *Proceedings*, by S. R. Lines (Bellingham, ILA 38–25): accept government's proposal "provided union gangs are not mixed with Finks."

These seven passages demonstrate continuous opposition by Puget Sound longshoremen to finkery in all its permutations but leave open to speculation the actual natal circumstance for *fink hall* and *fink card*. Several possibilities exist: Puget Sound dockers in 1916 either heard imported gun thugs with criminal connections use *finks* among themselves, heard imaginative Wobblies voice *fink* to brand their enemies, or previously had read *fink* either in the labor/radical press, or in dime novel/pulp fiction accounts of criminal doings.

We have already found *fink* during 1912 in the *International*

*Socialist Review* but lack references from pulp journalism prior to the 1920s. Hence, I turn back to Levinson's notion that Wobblies borrowed *fink* from underworld speech. We need not assume a single time and place for such transmission. We also need to be open to the chance that AFL members preceded IWW activists in applying *fink* during labor actions. Craft and industrial unionists interacted variously with hostility and solidarity, depending on the circumstances of association.

In Puget Sound's longshore strike of 1916, ILA members favored written agreements, whereas Wobs opposed formal contracts. ILA officers generally viewed IWWs as cantankerous rebels and dual unionists. Wobblies, in turn, soapboxed that ILA leaders were fakirs, grafters, or union scabs. Despite such supercharged rhetoric and occasional fisticuffs, ILA book members and IWW casuals did share dock work when jobs became plentiful.

Living circumstance helped pragmatists shelve differences in dogma. Many longshoremen, sailors, lumberjacks, and sawmill hands moved circularly from woods camp to waterside sawmill to loading dock to schooner deck. Some Wobs, self-designated "double headers," paid simultaneous dues to their respective craft and industrial locals. This doubling in affiliation linked to lateral moves in job skill created a fluid setting for lexical borrowing.

Word study advances by patient reading and listening and is set back by diversionary anecdotes. I return again to Holbrook's tale of *fink* emerging out of the Homestead battle between Pinkertons and Carnegie strikers. In Seattle, during the 1920s, Holbrook enjoyed the confidence of Northwest timberbeasts, shingle weavers, and dockers who were present when the very first Puget Sound fink halls opened their doors. Perhaps a Wobbly, tongue-in-cheek, told Holbrook about pinks at Homestead without relating *fink* to then-current waterfront practices.

Despite the passage of time, it may be possible to find an overlooked account of Seattle-Tacoma fink cards and halls. Between 1913 and 1923, the Marine Transport Workers Industrial Union 510 (IWW affiliate) included in its ranks many gifted worker correspondents, among them C. L. Filigno (introduced previously for his role in spreading *Wobbly* east from California). A "Five-Ten" member may have reported on Puget Sound conditions when the employers' hiring hall opened. The MTWIU itself formed a rhetorical rainbow—Hispanic engine room (black gang) crewmen in the Atlantic, African-American dockers in Philadelphia, Scandinavian seamen in the Pacific. Some of these Wobblies, knowing English only as a challenging second language, became marvelous teachers in matters of tradition and principle.

We continue to wonder how *fink* reached Puget Sound ports. I have no trouble in "hearing" a Tacoma worker call Harvey Wells, with his derby hat and shotgun, a dirty fink. Such an attribution could have been made in Seattle or at any of its satellite work sites. Seemingly, the then-novel tag for a corporate janissary caught on in union speech. Throughout the 1920s, waterfront workers voiced *fink*. It served in a major waterfront strike in Portland, Oregon, in 1922. A year later *fink* surfaced in a San Pedro strike with consequences dramatized by Upton Sinclair (Van Valen, Zanger).

## Carthaginian Peace

During the immediate postwar years, 1919–22, ILA-AFL longshoremen had lost strikes in San Francisco, Seattle, and Portland. Defeat led to internal secession on the Pacific Coast and the formation by ILA dissidents of the Marine Transport Workers Federation. In turn, the ILA and the IWW Marine Transport Workers Industrial Union criticized the new independent union. San Pedro dockmen then splintered: unorganized individuals, MTWF Local 1, ILA Local 38-18, MTWIU 510.

Andrew Furuseth, leader of the Sailors' Union of the Pacific, exhorted his loyalists to champion the mariners' craft. He urged them to steer clear of dockers in both the old ILA and new MTWF and especially to shun "Five-Ten" sailors in the IWW. Furuseth distrusted longshoremen as jurisdictional rivals and Wobblies as polemical enemies. On May Day, 1923, the MTWIU-IWW called a nationwide maritime strike—aboard ship and on the dock—with a "political demand" for the release of those arrested under criminal syndicalism laws. Los Angeles, undergoing an unprecedented building boom, depended solely on shipping to its San Pedro port for hundreds of millions of board feet of lumber. The lack of a stick of wood threatened the new prosperity.

The *Los Angeles Times* alternately excoriated the strikers and denied that they had shut down the harbor. In the three weeks after May Day, the Hammond Lumber Company, moguls in the Merchants' and Manufacturers' Association, and municipal police joined hands to smash the harbor strike. I note these background matters—union factional rivalry, mercantile strength, political arrests, police intervention—to illustrate the complex of forces framing our knowledge of labor tradition's ebb and flow.

Linguists enjoy noting the movement of a word from a nurturing group to the consciousness of large society. In this task, writers help scholars by conveying to general readers occupational lore from discrete associations. A *New Republic* sketch by Alvin Johnson in 1916, and two postwar *Survey* articles by George West about SUP leader Furuseth, carried labor concerns to professionals and intellectuals far from keel and mast. West's second report introduced readers to the hated fink hall through the words of an "Old Testament prophet" (Old Andy): "Everybody must go through 'Fink Hall.' The strike at San Pedro has only riveted the chains" (1923, 88).

Upton Sinclair brought additional attention to the maritime cause. Arrested on suspicion of criminal syndicalism for reading the Bill of Rights at a San Pedro rally on May 15, 1923, Sinclair placed his Liberty Hill adventures in *Singing Jailbirds*. This four-act tract gave viewers a taste of IWW song and spirit, as well as an enactment of the nickname *Wobbly*'s presumed nativity (treated previously). Radicals hailed the play as "expressionist drama"; in 1928, the New Playwrights Theatre, including John Dos Passos and Eugene O'Neill, presented *Singing Jailbirds* in Greenwich Village.

Students of dialect properly note the vernacular's "upward" movement into belles lettres. To the best of my knowledge, Sinclair was the first to present *fink* as a labor term in any "literary work." In *Singing Jailbirds*, the district attorney (Mr. 'Cutor) attempts to bribe Red Adams, an IWW militant and San Pedro strike leader. In turn, Red taunts the DA to "get these finks that run the employment business for the Shipowners" instead of the workers "herded in the slavemarket, showing our muscles to the dealers, trampling each other to get a job" (7).

In 1923, a young sailor from Norway came ashore at Seattle to join the Sailors' Union of the Pacific. In time, Harry Lundeberg, a direct action advocate influenced by Norwegian syndicalism, succeeded Furuseth as SUP secretary. Those who had viewed Sinclair's Red Adams defying Mr. 'Cutor on stage could sense life mimicking art in Lundeberg. He relished presenting rank-and-file imagery. Appearing at formal hearings without tie but with a white cotton cap, he reminded politicians that he had once sailed in a three-masted bark out of New York to Buenos Aires to England—one of the last union crew voyages before the failed seamen's strike of 1921 (Congressional testimony, 1955).

After that strike, shipowners rejected skilled seamen and loyal unionists in favor of fink crew "stumblebums, Harvard stiffs, college boys." Lundeberg, ever direct in speech, equated open-shop slave markets with fink halls. "On most ships you could not get a job when [employers] had what was called the Fink book, or grade book. . . . If you came aboard a ship with a union button in your lapel, you were fired" (443, 463). In 1955, Lundeberg referred back to 1921 for the transition from grade to fink books. I assume that sailors and stevedores voicing *fink card* simply extended the name to *fink book* as soon as employers introduced the pocket-size identification books.

In the dismal 1920s, some workers switched identities to beat fink hall rules; others obtained multiple fink books to juggle jobs; still others avoided hall and book to eke out a living ashore. Despite resistance, a Carthaginian peace smothered Pacific Coast maritime hiring from 1921 to 1934. Lundeberg recalled the devastating "peace" for its filthy hiring halls "with a big loudspeaker going." Halls were "filled with all kinds of stiffs, hop heads, dope-peddlers, floaters. . . . Sure, you got a ship if you patronized the blind pig run by the [boss'] clerks" (Gill, 649). Distant bosses pontificated about industrial calm while their clerks handled petty graft. Seamen used the phrase "to piece off" on paying dispatchers blood money for jobs.

The blaring loudspeaker in Lundeberg's memory may have been wired electrically, and, as such, it served as an innovative dispatching aid. It also served as an emblem for the "loud speakers" who controlled the hall. These distant speakers—cynical, strident, pompous, persuasive—spoke out for Harvard stiffs and hop heads over men who walked and talked like seafarers, men who internalized centuries-old maritime traditions.

Well before the 1929 stock market crash, maritime workers had reached bottom—whale scum on the sea's floor. Nevertheless, a few activists who were job or class conscious maintained their belief in a union turnaround. The 1934 Big Strike of longshoremen, seamen, teamsters, and their allies marked the rebirth of Pacific Coast labor. This conflict also signaled the rise of the longshoreman Harry Bridges and drew national attention to waterfront mores. At the strike's end, the old viking Andrew Furuseth, nearing his long journey home, joined his "boys" in a San Francisco bonfire of Marine Service Bureau fink books. While seafarers voiced *fink books*, stevedores termed these same badges of oppression *blue books* (ILA books displayed maroon covers). The symbolic act on the Embarcadero of turning hated fink and blue books into ashes anticipated a new freedom and vision. Today, memory of the fink book bonfire is amplified to recall labor's vital past. Often, the phrase "We ended the shape-up and closed the fink hall" compresses 1934's glory.

A Big Strike vignette offers a glimpse into the oft-hidden route of pejorative language from enclaved speaker to mainstream leader. After the 1934 strike's end, the U.S. National Longshoremen's Labor Board held hearings prior to its arbitration award. Board deliberations filled thirteen volumes; one reported detail on fink halls by its chairman, Archbishop Edward J. Hanna, remains priceless: "I can understand what a 'scab' is, a sore infesting a healthy body. But, 'fink,' that is a term I do not understand" (Resner, 116).

The archbishop, of course, was on target for *scab*. It had been extended in England, at least as early as 1777, from a wound's crust or sore's infection to a craven cordwainer (shoemaker) working during a Bristol strike. After 1934, perhaps Hanna, in all his dignity, helped explain the "new" word *fink* to the clergy. I suspect that a number of San Francisco priests from working families could have explicated waterfront talk for the archbishop.

Fink book issues continued to plague maritime industrial relations until World War II. In 1936, when Senator Royal S. Copeland, seeking "stability" at sea and an end to quickie strikes, called for new federal continuous discharge books, radicals dubbed them *Copeland fink books*. Protestors asked why seamen should willingly carry blacklists in their own hip pockets.

Incredibly, one deck-and-dock debate spoke to this period's convoluted politics. As Communist party lines changed in the mid-1930s to embrace New Deal reform, loyal members opted for stable maritime labor practices and mainstream political action. Left anticommunists—embracing either revolutionary or direct action creeds—then attacked Kremlin weathervanes for fudging response to the hated Copeland books. Some sea-going anti-Stalinists asserted that CPers had caved in to the federal government by accepting "progressive fink books," a sardonic oxymoron (Schwartz, 118).

An incident in September 1937 illustrates the underlying tension within New Deal labor relations. When the crew of the SS *Algic* refused to handle "scab" cargo in Montevideo, Uruguay, the U.S. Maritime Commission ordered the vessel's captain to place his National Maritime Union rebels in irons. Instantly, maritime workers named the *Algic* a *fink ship*.

In *Maritime*, Frederick Lang offered a Socialist Workers party historical sketch and militant program. Looking back at a plan by the U.S. Maritime Commission to establish training ships, he called them "factories where a shoddy substitute for the skill and experience of union men would be turned out on a mass production basis" (103). Lang reported a joint meeting at Mobile, Alabama, in December 1938 of members of the Seafarers' International Union and the National Maritime Union. The chairman excoriated the government for a "hellfire plan" formulated with the shipowners' "conniving lobbyists" that linked "the Maritime Commission Fink Hall and the Training Ship Schemes" (102).

Four decades later, the usage *factories* reemerged in a nautical setting. Nancy Quam-Wickham shipped out on Atlantic-Richfield tankers in the 1980s. During a Pacific run on the *Arco Fairbanks*, she heard shipmates describe federal and state maritime academies as "fink factories." In conversations with me she contrasted academy graduates with officers who had "come up through the hawse pipes"—sailors advancing by dint of hard work and acceptance of rank-and-file traditions. Her vernacular phrase served to distinguish real salts from imitations, those seasoned at sea from those trained in "fink factories." Quam-Wickham touched on the longstanding distinctions internalized by working people familiar with the labels *old-hand/greenhorn*, or *real McCoy/phony*.

Polar markers seemed particularly strong in the 1930s. Then, mariners had divided bitterly into rival camps: craft/industrial, casual stiff/palace guard, direct action/political program. During a brief three-year span (1939–41), waterfront workers argued very large issues—Nazi-Soviet pact, "Yanks Are Not Coming," the invasion of Finland, Pearl Harbor. Much of the antagonistic debate dissolved temporarily during World War II but resumed after the war ceased, for divisive impulses etch the American grain.

It may be difficult for contemporary readers to recapture both the fear and hatred directed by unionists against those who exploited them. Regardless of whether they chose reformist or revolutionary path, workers who rallied to the union cause despised finks. From the Gay Nineties through the eve of World War II, major cities in the United States had informal street corner exchanges where detective agencies recruited strike mercenaries to be used at factory gate, mine mouth, pier head.

Where tenderloin and skid road touched, casual laborers—migrating from job to job—constantly rubbed shoulders with derelicts at employment halls and gospel missions. Bergoff and other fink herders sought pimp, pickpocket, swindler, slugger, yegg, fence, fugitive, footpad, gambler, gunsel, briber, userer, con, extortionist, wino, rapist, madman, murderer. Such unfortunates formed a latter-day savage fraternity scorned by loyal unionists. In contrast, robber barons, and their genteel apologists, denigrated workers by giving *labor union* itself a pejorative tone.

I have looked to Chicago, Akron, Wilkes-Barre, Kansas City, Seattle, Tacoma, San Pedro, and San Francisco as a few of the sites where labor spies penetrated unions, thugs broke pickets' heads, or employer and government clerks conspired against unionists seeking some control over their conditions. I have made examples of newsstands, rubber factories, trolley barns, harbor docks, and ships' decks to point to the convergence in labor usage for *fink* as agent provocateur, spy, or strikebreaker.

## Rogues in Phynkia

By stressing *fink*'s labor connections, I have downplayed other associations: criminal, collegiate, political, literary. If, indeed, criminal strikebreakers taught *fink* to unionists, the latter helped convey the word to friendly commentators. During the 1930s, radicals, caught up by internal sectarian divisions, constantly used *fink*. It dwelled in a charnel house of invective. Malcolm Cowley recalls that some Red language "took the form of revulsion . . . expressed by the incantatory use of such terms as 'bloated,' 'cancerous,' 'chancres,' 'diseased,' 'distended belly,' 'fistula,' 'gorged with,' 'maggots,' 'naked,' . . . 'nauseating,' 'pus,' 'putrefying,' 'retching,' 'rotted flesh,' 'spew forth,' 'syphilis,' and 'vomit' " (249).

*Fink* eventually made its way to mainstream reporting. A few examples mark its transition from picket line to civic corridor. The novelist Albert Halper recalled a John Reed Club meeting in Manhattan with Diego Rivera and his wife Frieda Kahlo (93). The Mexican muralist spoke in French on revolutionary art. Bill Dunne, a *Daily Worker* editor, attacked Rivera for using effete intellectual language and for painting a Trotskyite mural in Rockefeller Center. A comrade joined the onslaught against the guest: "He knows goddam well he's guilty! Renegade, fink" (96).

Benjamin Stolberg, in an early book on the CIO (1938), criticized Communist party polemicists for their baiting of left rivals, their slandering of other Reds with slurs such as "moral degenerate, rat, fink, stool-pigeon, 'Trotskyist' spy, fascist agent, British agent, Japanese stooge" (144). A. B. Magil, in the *New Masses*, offered these pearls in defending a Soviet line: "Trotsky Admits It / The master fink unwittingly reveals his 'program' for the Ukraine. It's the same as Hitler's. . . . But a fink, even a clever, skillful, 'Marxist' fink, can hardly be dignified with the title 'ally' " (15). Magil's rhetorical overkill anticipated the brutal Stalinist assassination of Trotsky.

During the Watergate days of "plumbers," "deep throats," and "bag men," Special Prosecutor Archibald Cox and Attorney General Elliot Richardson battled President Nixon over his secret tapes. The columnist Joseph Kraft urged Richardson to support the Cox claim. Kraft opined that giving in to presidential pressure would make Richardson "a complete White House fink."

From vituperative Marxists to the Watergate-era White House I move to China's trial of the century, the alleged plot to assassinate Chairman Mao. The first defendant, Chinese air force chief Wu Faxian, age 65, had camped with Mao on the Long March and served as a loyal ally. In the trial dock, Wu "freely confessed," implicating his co-defendants in treason. A *San Francisco Chronicle* head writer summed up Wu's testimony as "A Fink in the Gang of Four" (November 25, 1980).

In 1988, *Chicago Tribune* columnist Mike Royko blasted presidential "flunky" Larry Speakes for his "finking" on Ronald Reagan in the former's "fink book," *Speaking Out*. Essentially, the flack tattled that he had made up several banal Reagan quotes. When Merrill Lynch "dumped" Speakes from his $250,000-a-year job, Royko gleefully advised the "sacked" aide to take out an ad: "Position wanted. Top-level experience as congressional aide, White House press officer and corporate spokesman. Advanced training in finkery, back-stabbing and ingratitude."

Magil, a communist Pooh-Bah, intended his invective to be taken seriously; surely, the *Chronicle* treated Wu's "confession" with skepticism. H. L. Mencken would have enjoyed Speakes's folly and Royko's flurry. Here, I turn back to an Akron anecdote that notes a humorous stage in labor's broadening of *fink*. The CIO campaign to build a new union in rubber enjoyed the help of John L. Lewis, Rose Pesotta, and other gifted organizers. While Goodyear workers struck in February 1936, Akron's erstwhile mayor Sparks established the vigilante Law & Order League. Behind the scenes, Pearl Bergoff aided the civic authorities.

Sensing the irony of the criminal Bergoff keeping order, the United Rubber Workers paid $500 to "buy" a radio station for the whole night of March 17. Their publicist, McAlister Coleman, improvised a running skit in which he impersonated Fanny Fink, the daughter of a blundering strikebreaker. Frank Grillo, the URW secretary, played Papa Fink Bergoff.

The all-night drama parodied Fanny Brice's popular radio feature "Baby Snooks." Coleman bombarded Grillo with infantile questions as Akron's West Virginia tire builders, direct from picket duty shacks, spelled the "actors" by singing "I Like Mountain Music," "Nobody's Darling," and other hillbilly favorites (Coleman, 165; McKenney, 363; Pesotta, 221). The Akron radio juxtaposition of Coleman (a socialist intellectual from Columbia University), Grillo (an up-from-the-ranks URW official from an immigrant family), and down-home Appalachian musicians represented the cultural ferment frequently generated during New Deal days by industrial unionism's partisans.

Every good fighting word deserves a few guffaws. We are entitled to view Akron's Fanny Fink as a grandchild of Mike Fink, America's ripsnorting, braggadocious keelboatman. In spirit, Fanny had many siblings, one of whom, George Mink, appeared on Philadelphia's docks in 1926. Whether George drifted to the waterfront or Communist party functionaries planted him there, I do not know.

In time, some of Mink's disgruntled comrades came to view him as a gunman, whore-hound, pornographer, and Soviet GPU agent. While he ran a Red "stewpot" (the International Seamen's Club in New York—a combined lunch counter, flop house, and propaganda mill), Mink's detractors alleged that he skimmed such meager profits as penniless seamen could bring to the club. For other assaults on decency, he eventually earned the moniker, "Mink the Fink" (Nelson, 91, 192; Richmond, 175; Schwartz, 70).

We have come full circle from Mike Fink, folk hero, to Mink the Fink, antihero. The latter's nickname signifies that, although Reds of every stripe—anarchist, syndicalist, socialist, communist—feared and despised finkery, rank-and-filers had no trouble in identifying a platonic fink. This ability of workers to put down one of their own "leaders" displays the semantic elasticity built into *fink*—a word useful to students, hoboes, addicts, squealers, thugs, spys, reformers, and red-hots.

Clearly, I have not entered all the lairs in which finks resided or dealt with the word's circulation in general speech. During the Barry Goldwater campaign of 1964, some Republicans assailed "the rat-fink Eastern press" (Rovere, 201). Who combined these opprobrious words? The Albany, New York, Typographical Society had circulated a rat list as early as 1816. Does an aural thread stretch from New York's hand compositors to Senator Goldwater's "New Right" partisans? In 1986, San Francisco humorist Arthur Hoppe, while commenting on the Philippines' Ferdinand Marcos, invented a potentate named "The Ratt of Phynkia." I suspect that rat finks, regardless of spelling, will continue to thrive in arenas of political tension.

I turn now to a 1983 labor usage. Paul McKenna, a staff researcher for the San Francisco Hospital Workers Local 250 of the Service Employees International Union, composed "The Union Buster," set to the tune of "Oh, Susanna." McKenna's latter-day fink is Jack Shyster, a management consultant in a three-piece suit; finkery has come a very long way from Bergoff's stable of uglies. Sophisticated Jack states that "In the old days we used gun thugs, we used ginks and finks and goons. / Nowadays we use fancy words, but sing the same old tune." In connecting *gink*, *fink*, and *goon*, McKenna drew on a linkage previously made by Woody Guthrie in his 1941 song "Union Maid" (Seeger and Reiser).

## Journey's End

The knowledge that new words dress up in fancy duds but sing old tunes closes our journey. Language marauders, of course, look to the old and the new, early examples reporting a word's history and fresh citations marking a word's unfolding meaning. Readers will stumble on choice usages; several follow.

During July 1989, *fink* surfaced in flexible form. Michael Herz, an avid sailor and environmentalist, undertook a self-appointed task of protecting the San Francisco Bay against polluters. Skimming across the water in his Olympic outboard, *Bay Keeper*, he sought oil tanker spills, dredger droppings, and industrial toxic waste. The *San Francisco Chronicle* reporter Jon Stewart quoted "Enforcer" Herz as saying, "Of course, I can't do it alone. . . . I'll need . . . a set of finks . . . whistle-blowers. . . . We'll protect their anonymity." In *fink*'s many guises, seldom had the word appeared in such positive light. Armed with camera, tape recorder, and knowledge of environmental law, Herz required a squad of waterborn finks to save the bay.

Miles away from "Enforcer" Herz in both distance and spirit, an anonymous "Jack" served as a modern "Fink for Hire," an undercover agent with the Minneapolis–St. Paul Applied Confidential Services. "With a tie-dyed shirt, blue jeans, long hair, and a beard, Jack blends into the blue-collar workplace"—not to spy on unionists but to ferret out drug dealers/users. As his co-workers smoked marijuana or snorted cocaine, Jack finked (D'Addesa).

From San Francisco marine inlets to Twin City factory parking lots and restrooms, *fink* lives in everyday speech. During the 1987 professional football strike, sportswriters penned *scab Sunday, scab ball,* and *scab sub,* while fans voiced *fink.* Dan Rather of CBS News explained carefully that *scab* served as an especially derogatory labor term. Surely, he also knew *fink*'s applicability in the athletic arena.

Responding to these autumn sports newscasts, William Safire in the *New York Times* turned to *scab,* tying it to similar labor pejoratives. Seeking "origins," he favored the Pinkertons at Homestead story for *fink* over the German excrement-eating bird analysis. Safire suggested that the shift from a dirty bird to an undesirable person made "a less likely etymon than the mispronounced *Pinkerton.*"

My studies have led away from phonological explanation to semiotic exploration. As words cross social boundaries they acquire fresh meaning. We have observed that George Ade, in 1894, used *fink* as part of a street hoodlum's speech. Eight years later, he placed the word in a campus context, echoing the German terms *fink* and *finkenschaft.* Students in Ade's "fable" knew *fink* as a "slob or no-good or rummy" before the term reached unionists.

In 1910, Lionel Moise called up *fink* in a poem about casual laborers. His IWW readers had no reason to confuse *fink* with *pink.* Ed Levinson asserted that, in the decade before World War I, IWW and AFL members heard strikebreakers and spies with criminal ties voice *fink.* Between 1912 and 1917, many labor activists, adding *fink* to their vocabularies, had combined it with other terms such as *hall* and *card.* Picket lines at industrial battlefields functioned to amplify combatants' language by hoisting words over factory fences.

To delve further into *fink*'s movement; we must peel back a complex of social scenes and enactments: German speakers who transmitted their contemptible *fink* to Americans ready for additional deprecatory ammunition; whalers who knew this word to mean try-pot scum; mariners ready to label whores. Before scholars can rest with assurance on *fink*'s travels from Europe to North America, they will need to unearth the word's wide appeal both on campus and in the underworld.

Students, unionists, and criminals together have accounted for *fink*'s semantic shifts. Focusing on only a corner within this word's broad domain, I have treated *fink* largely as a laborlore text, an actor on the industrial stage. I anticipate that workers, on and off their jobs, will continue to use it as a near expletive. Better than other terms, *fink* denigrates outside enemies as it reinforces internal identity and affirms labor's large claim to status in society.

## Appendix: *Fink*'s Applications

The following citations range widely in chronology and geography, yet I have not exhausted all examples offered in print. In their searches, students may wish to focus particularly on usages linking German and American speech.

1. Mike Fink: the Ohio-Mississippi River boatman and the legends about his treacherously shooting his protègé/son (Tamony 1980; Botkin, 47). Possibly, Fink's name became a colloquial synonym for treachery, but we lack supporting linguistic and folkloric evidence. Finche, Finc, and Vinck (spelled variously) have served as English-language surnames or placenames since the eleventh century (Reaney). Some may have acquired pejorative tones—for example, simpleton—long before Mike Fink's birth. In recent times, a few writers have switched the name facetiously to Phynque. Mike Fink tales no doubt will continue to be invoked to explain *fink*'s origin.
2. Pink: backclipped from *Pinkerton detective* in the setting of assaults on steel workers during the Homestead strike of 1892. Stewart Holbrook (1926) suggested a Wobbly etymology: when armed Pinkerton guards and strikebreakers approached Carnegie Steel's Homestead plant, upriver from Pittsburgh, an ensuing battle left a dozen dead and scores of wounded. Foreign-born workers picked up the battle cry "Th' goddam Pinks are comin'." Mispronunciation led to "goddam finks." Holbrook's hypothesis, unlikely phonologically, is not supported by labor histories, nor can we mark *pink*'s progression from Pennsylvania mill hands to the IWW.
3. Finn: pronounced fink in some immigrant speech. During 1915, Charles Gilliam worked in a munitions plant with several thousand foreign-born workers. He heard Greeks and Turks sound Finn with a terminal *k* (Tamony 1980). Gilliam's notion that ethnic prejudice reinforced pronunciation difficulty has not been confirmed by others.
4. Fenks/Finks: fibrous parts of whale's blubber; refuse of rendered blubber (*OED* citations 1820, 1836, 1876). Sailors working the try-pots (blubber boilers) may have applied *fink* directly to an offensive shipmate

or, indirectly, associated sinking offal with waterfront prostitutes and equated *fink* with *whore* and *fink house* with *whore house* (Camp, 450). The earliest such linkage in print, to my knowledge, dates to the 1934 San Francisco waterfront strike: " 'Fink' is an old seafaring men's term for prostitute" (Resner, 116).

5. Strikebreaker: in 1936, the Senate Committee on Education and Labor (La Follette) hearings brought wide attention to industrial espionage and violations of workers' rights. Resulting public documents, newspaper stories, a history (Auerbach), several popular books, and a novel (Appel) ranked the strikebreaker's caste system: noble, fink, missionary, street operator, shadower, roundsman, hooker, roper, slugger—all distinct from run-of-the-mill scabs. Clinch Calkins asserted that strikebreakers took over *fink* and *hooker* "from the vocabulary of prostitution" (132).

6. Funk: thinning of *funk* led to *fink* (Partridge 1949). What process does "thinning" describe?

7. Finger: to point a finger, to squeal, to inform. Mitford Mathews (1951) suggested the possible source of *fink* in *finger* as in one who informed. White it is difficult to account for the sound shift from *g* to *k*, attestations exist for finks who finger: detective, plainclothesman, prison guard, screw, secret agent, gumshoe, fly mug, dick, squealer, snitch, stool pigeon, canary.

8. Fink: in tramp/hobo usage, one who "depends entirely on backdoor bumming." Oliver sets such activity in the 1932 Depression of high unemployment, jungle talk, and fink sign language on trees and fences (341). See also Monteleone for begging hobo.

9. Fink: a nonspending customer who shops merely to kill time or to come in out of uncomfortable weather. D. W. Bolinger conveyed this Nebraska explanation to Tamony in 1939. It surfaced again in 1950 carnival talk, "One who comes not to spend but to find cause for complaint to police"; a complainer "not patronizing the game, as a nonspending busybody" (Golden).

10. Fink: a circus word meaning a broken novelty or torn balloon (Milburn 1931). See also Wentworth and Flexner (1960) for the use of the word to mean any defective, worthless, or small article of merchandise, a souvenir, or a larry.

11. Fink: an anti-Semitic joke. I supplement Gerald Cohn's contribution with a related explanation from Tristram Potter Coffin, the University of Pennsylvania ballad scholar (1965). During his childhood in Providence, Rhode Island, neighborhood boys equated *fink* with "dirty Jew." Herbert Resner, interviewing participants in the 1934 San Francisco waterfront strike, heard this "source" for *fink hall:* "A gentleman

by the name of Finklestein operated the first hall of this kind" (116). In 1942, a Philadelphia Navy Yard worker heard a similar interpretation shorn of ethnic cast: *Fink* meant a "strikebreaker, after a shipping master on the West Coast, in the 1920's, who sold seamen their jobs" (Arbolino).

12. Fink: the German word for a student who does not belong to a club; originally from *finch* (one of a large group of singing birds). The *Random House Dictionary* (1966) first offered this connection to the American pejorative *fink*. Subsequently, the Benjamins, Gold, Cassidy, and Maher in *Comments on Etymology* elaborated various Germanic transmission lines. *Webster's* (1988) also tied *fink* to *finch*, dating the linkage to about 1740 by Jena students to designate nonfraternity individuals.

The German-language *fink* led to *finkenschaft*, the totality of "barbarian" students. Behind such usages lay several meanings for *finch:* a bird pecking in horse manure (*dreckfink, dreckvogel*); a bird wallowing in mud; wild birds contrasted with caged birds. Speakers formed compounds of *fink* with *dreck* (excrement), *mist* (manure), and *schmutz* (dirt)—for example: *schmutzfink*, pig, filthy creature, grubby little urchin; *schmierfink*, sloppy writer, dauber; *dreckfink*, dirty little beggar (Duden).

Such terms may have reinforced the notion of a "barbaric" student as unkempt and slovenly or, alternatively, as hopping about, unregulated, or unwilling to conform. We need German, Pennsylvania Dutch, or Yiddish citations from intermediaries to document the movement of *fink* into American speech. Gold discounted Yiddish channels in that few of its speakers used *fink* in a "slangy sense." However, he added a Yiddish colloquial meaning as jail (clink or slammer); this may have helped tie *fink* into American speech. As a freshman at Rochester in 1951, Maher heard *city fink* for day students and *house-fink* for boarders. Hence, he associated *fink* with student life well before he learned its criminal and labor applications.

13. To pull a finch: metaphoric usages back to Chaucer related *finch* to the act of cheating or swindling. Frederic Cassidy (1983) lengthened *fink*'s time line by noting that birds easily caught or victimized (a gull, booby, or noddy) led to speech figures such as *to pull a finch, to gull, to pluck a pigeon*. Further, pigeons attached to stools or perches served as decoys. To squeal and sing like birds also had long criminal/informer connotations in several European languages.

The emblematic finch needs exploration parallel to that for the metaphoric finch. On seeing a Pennsylvania Dutch distelfink (thistle finch) pictured, Peter Tamony made a cryptic note (now in his word files,

Western Historical Manuscript Collection, University of Missouri, Columbia): "mother love, bird pecking own breast, similar symbols on Catholic altars." Where and when could Chaucer's finch, figuratively, have been caught in flight, clipped of its wing, or caged on an altar to live in campus/underworld/trade union infamy?

**Marcus Daly**

# 5

# Copper Bards

No matter what our birthplace or station, we hear stories during childhood. To entertain and instruct youngsters, parents fall back on familiar tales. Similarly, librarians recite or read fairy tales and other household classics during story hours. Parents and librarians alike use folk narratives to enhance cultural continuity within their communities.

A child listens to Sinbad's adventures before comprehending fully this crafty mariner's path. We may reach adulthood before sensing Sinbad's grasp of work rules stemming from his respect for wind and wave. Another young listener marvels at the exploits of Daniel Boone, national pathfinder, and Davy Crockett, frontier trickster. With but a few imaginative steps from the Cumberland Gap and the Alamo, we elevate John Henry, tunnel stiff, and Paul Bunyan, lumberjack, to America's pantheon.

Labor partisans seek to place Mother Jones and Joe Hill into legendary company. Essentially, unionists, conscious of their traditions, wish the Wobbly bard and coal miners' "mother" to march in the parade of folk exemplars—Hiawatha, Coyote, Bre'r Rabbit, Anansi, Stagolee, Gregorio Cortez, Cinderella, Snow White, Jack-the-Giant-Killer. Some laborlore guardians will be distressed to find Joe Hill and Mother Jones likened to heroes or heroines in the realm east of the sun, west of the moon. It is not my purpose in this chapter to detract from the status of any exalted workers or to add lustre to unionism's champions. Rather, I offer a tale about an industrialist, a figure of immense power.

Marcus Daly's name no longer echoes in our land. While he

lived in Butte, Montana, the scene of his triumph, many copper miners lauded him; only a few faulted him. After his death, miners and their children contributed to erect a bronze statue in his honor. A few unionists who held socialist or syndicalist conviction demeaned his memory. The tale "Marcus Daly Enters Heaven" not only ridicules the mogul but, today, represents the recall by some workers of their traditions.

A few milestones on Daly's earthly span can establish background for understanding his heavenly journey. Born in County Cavan, Ireland, on December 5, 1841, Daly survived the famine, emigrating to New York at age fifteen. Casual work on the Brooklyn docks and an ambitious spirit led him to California's Grass Valley gold mines. Earning his living with singlejack (hammer) and steel (hand drill), Marcus moved on to become a foreman in Virginia City's silver mines. In 1872, he married Margaret Evans in Salt Lake City. Four years later, he turned to Butte as a venturesome silver mine manager.

In 1882, miners working Butte's great Anaconda silver vein ran into copper ore, then undervalued. A continent away, Thomas Alva Edison and his fellows had ushered in the age of electricity—generators, motors, transmission lines, arc lights, incandescent lamps, street railways. These wonders demanded copper. Daly's peers believed that "he could see farther into the ground than any mining man." This talent, combined with his presence on the "richest hill on earth," propelled the Anaconda Copper Mining Company and its interlocked firms to world power in nonferrous metal mining, production, and fabrication.

Historians attracted to Butte have documented the war of the copper kings, as well as the dominant role of Daly's company in Montana politics. During the 1980s, Michael Malone, David Emmons, and Jerry Calvert treated varied aspects of Butte history; their books frame Daly's role as they open doors to additional interpretation. Daly died in New York City on September 12, 1900; his influence lingered for decades. A tribute in 1950 by the Anaconda's W. H. Hoover typifies corporate America's memory of Marcus Daly:

> Of his capacity as an organizer of men, a director of their activities, of his inspiration as a leader, it is difficult to find

> words of adequate expression. He brought furnace men and metallurgists from Wales, mill men from Michigan, and miners and superintendents from the gold and silver mines of the Southwest. He paid his miners, workmen, and supervisory staff well, but personal loyalty to Marcus Daly was in large measure responsible for his close-knit aggressive organization. He helped and trained young men for the specialties of copper mining and metallurgy. . . .
>
> Daly knew his miners by name. He hired most of them himself. Applicants for work applied to him personally. He knew their families; he looked after their needs; he seldom refused a request for help. His philanthropy was personal, and it was unlimited. He expected personal loyalty from his people and his friends, and he was accorded that loyalty to a marked and unusual degree. (17)

Marcus Daly commanded the loyalty of a work force largely composed of Irish immigrants. As he attracted "spalpeens" (migratory laborers) to Montana, the miners and the magnate made Butte the most Irish of American centers. Unlike many raw camps in the Rockies, it became an industrial city—more like Pittsburgh than Cripple Creek. Irish workers in the United States have long struggled to balance the forces of Catholicism, Fenianism, populism, and trade unionism. Some workers joined the revoutionary Clan-na-Gael to free Eire from England; others joined the revolutionary Industrial Workers of the World to free themselves from wage slavery; still others embraced both causes.

David Emmons offers a telling metaphor to explain the tension stemming from the intersection of class and ethnicity within Butte (50). Irish miners, he said, possessed a generous but "fanatic and divided heart," showing itself as a visible seam along which partisans of political and economic freedom camped, prayed, declaimed, and fought. At times, presenting a seamless front, rivals reconciled their differences; at times, the seam turned into a yawning chasm.

Emmons's striking figure serves particularly well for Butte, where men worked copper seams below ground and they faced above-ground rifts engendered by emotional and ideological cause. We know that many Butte miners accepted Daly's benevolence out of a sense of Irish brotherhood. We assume that radical workers had cause to reject his rule. Who can explain why so few Irish miners did so?

## Paddy Burke

We find the best example of a worker's unwillingness to accept Daly's paternalism in a folktale told by Harry ("Haywire Mac") McClintock to Sam Eskin in San Pedro, California. On November 17, 1952, Eskin taped "Marcus Daly Enters Heaven," along with a variety of Wobbly songs and occupational ballads. The collector deposited the tapes in the New York State Historical Association, with copies to the Library of Congress and Moses Asch of Folkways Records. In 1972, Asch released a selection of Haywire Mac's songs and stories on an LP recording (Folkways 5272). My transcription of the Daly tale follows:

> Well, there used to be an old fellow around the western mining camps by the name of Paddy Burke. Paddy was a strappin' big Irishman, and he had a handlebar mustache. It looked something like the horns of a belligerent bull. Paddy was a great storyteller. In fact, he got so that he wouldn't work. He would tell stories around the barrooms, and so forth. And, he was well-known in the Coeur d'Alene country, and, also, in the Nevada mining country. But, he got—those were all gold and silver camps, and the boys were pretty generous with shellin' out money for Paddy's entertainment.
>
> But he wandered into Butte, and he fell upon hard circumstances. The boys didn't shower down very good, and he had to go to work. So he hustled himself a job muckin' in a mine called the Neversweat. It was one of Marcus Daly's properties, and Marcus was, as you well know, the king of Butte at the time, or thought he was.
>
> Paddy was workin' in the Neversweat on the night shift. And old Marcus wandered into the place one time. It was a habit of Daly's to visit his properties every once in a while in the middle of the night. He'd put on diggin' clothes and an old hat all covered with candle grease, just like any miner, and he would prowl around. And it was understood that if

Marcus caught you with your back straightened up, you was fired.

Well, this time Marcus stepped onto the cage, told the hoistman to drop him off at the 1,300-foot level. The cage drops down, Marcus steps out, the cage ascends again, and Marcus is left alone in the darkness with his candle, and he listens. He doesn't hear the sound of a drill or a shovel on the whole level, no sounds of activity whatever. So he starts prowlin'. Well, it's time for lunch anyway, so, he finally locates the gang. They're all in a big stope, and they've got their candles stuck into the stones around and about.

Enthroned on a muck pile in the middle of the assemblage is Paddy Burke. He's telling them a story, which is a darn sight easier than workin'. And, when this stranger joins the group, there's a chill sweeps over the boys: Uhh. Paddy—being, he had his audience well in hand—he felt this sudden chill. He didn't know just what caused it, but he suspected. So he finished that story, and the gang got up. He said, "Well," Paddy says, " Well, boys," he says, "wait a minute." He says, "I'll tell you another one." So the gang—they were fired anyway, which they figured—[remained in the stope].

Paddy says: "I had a dream the other night. I dreamed that I died and went to heaven. And for miles upon countless thousands of miles, I climbed the stairs until I stood before the great pearly gates. I drew back my fist and I hit the door a rap, and an old gentleman with long white whiskers sticks his head out, and he says, 'And who may you be?'

I says, 'I'm Paddy Burke.'

'Oh, you are, are you?' he says. 'Where are you from?'

I says, 'I'm from Butte, Montana,'

'Huh,' he says, 'I've had nobody from there for a long time, I'll tell ya that." He says, 'I'll look you up in the book. Burke, is it?'

'Yes,' I says, 'Paddy Burke, if you please.' So after a few minutes he sticks his head out again, and he says, 'You can come in, Paddy, but you'll have to behave yourself.' I says, 'I'll do that.'

"So he opens the gate a crack, and I stepped in. And old Saint Peter—for it was no less—he pressed a button, and here comes an angel. And he says, 'Angel,' he says, 'take my friend Paddy down to the storeroom and fit him out.' He says, 'Give him a good pair of wings, and given 'im a golden crown, size 7½. And give 'im a harp and be sure it's in tune.' So with that we went away to the storeroom to get me equipment.

"After I was rigged out in the heavenly style, I was turned over to another angel, who took me out to show me the sights of heaven. And, 'twas the most magnificent place that the mind of man can conceive of. The sidewalks were of solid gold. The doorknobs was of great jewels. And the hosts of heaven were flitting about with their wings outspread, and sitting on clouds and strummin' their harps, and singing, oh, the most glorious tunes that you ever heard.

"The angel said, 'Well, we'll hurry or we'll be late for the great banquet.' So we went to the hall where the hosts of heaven were assembled. When we entered the hall, it took me breath away. It stretched away on evey side for miles, and miles, and miles, as far as the eye could carry in every direction. And here were the tables fairly groanin' with the most rare and delicate viands. We sat down to a meal of nightingales' tongues, and all manner of quaint and foreign delicacies. We drank the most rare and delicate wines, and the goblets that we drank from were hollowed out of great emeralds, and rubies, and diamonds. And they had waitresses flittin' about servin' everybody. They were on roller skates that were jeweled like a railroader's watch.

"And of a sudden, all of a sudden, there was a hell of a commotion in heaven. The word was passed around that Marcus Daly had died. And no sooner had the word been passed around until there was a great fanfare of trumpets at the door, and a voice was heard saying, 'Marcus Daly is here!' And from the other end of the hall, where the great golden throne was, came another voice, 'Marcus Daly, welcome to heaven. Advance to the foot of the throne.' So the hosts of heaven parted like the Red Sea when the Israelites passed over. And Marcus Daly, all alone, walked down the aisle to the foot of the great golden throne. Almighty God arose, and He says, 'Marcus, I bid you welcome.' And turnin' to his right hand, He says, 'Come, Jesus, get up and give Marcus your seat.' "

Harry McClintock died in San Francisco on April 24, 1957, without knowledge that any of his San Pedro material would eventually appear on a Folkways album. I regret that I never met him to hear directly his copper-mining tale. Rather, in 1968, I listened to a Sam Eskin dub of some of Mac's song's and stories, including "Marcus Daly Enters Heaven." Previously, I had known something of Haywire Mac's adventures as railroad boomer, Wobbly musician, radio entertainer, recording artist, pulp fiction writer, and hobo raconteur.

On my first hearing of Mac's story about Daly, it sounded familiar, yet I could neither place it in published form nor recall hearing any close analogues. Mac's Irish brogue and superb depiction of Paddy Burke's traditional role spurred my curiosity. Burke refused to disappear in memory. Invited during 1982 to a Butte conference on "The Urban Frontier," I transcribed Mac's text, bringing it "home" to Montana.

Knowing that Eskin had recorded McClintock in San Pedro and that Asch had issued his album in Manhattan, I felt obligated to return a story about Marcus Daly to Butte. Following the conference, I submitted preliminary findings to a Butte magazine, *The Speculator* (1984). This represented only a beginning, for I revisited scenes within Mac's tale for the Archer Taylor lecture series at UCLA and in a subsequent article for *Western Folklore* (1987). Additionally, I treated the conjunction of craft and celebration by hard rock drillers, singlejackers and doublejackers, for the anthology *By Land and by Sea* (1985).

Scholars seek to explain riddle and rhyme, ballad and blues. They work by talking; Paddy Burke, in the Neversweat Mine, talked when he should have worked. In talking or writing about Burke, I wish to extend the life of McClintock's tale as I address its meaning. In this task, I use overlapping strategies by combining academic analysis with the re-presentation of traditional narrative.

## A String in the Labyrinth

Among the many persistent motifs running through fairy tale and myth, we find one of escape—the string in the labyrinth, the bread crumbs in the forest. We enjoy entering tortuous chambers when armed with the means of release. Figuratively, we construct a trail into a tale's thicket and pray that no bird takes up the crumbs for sustenance or the string for its nest. Scholars feel rewarded in conducting narrative analysis when they find their way out of such thickets. The act of returning stories to old audiences, as well as presenting them to new auditors, "tops out" our sense of worth in our chosen tasks.

Sam Eskin (1898–1974) died at Woodstock, New York, mourned mainly by friends on the "folksong circuit" (Hinton). To the best of my knowledge, he never commented on "Marcus Daly Enters Heaven." Eskin, the son of a railroad engineer, maintained a lifelong affection for working people and their lore. It is our loss that he left no clue to help us appreciate Mac's tale but only made it available to Moses Asch for album release.

In explicating McClintock's copper-mining story, I imagine myself at Sam's side asking Mac endless questions. Did the latter create Paddy Burke to situate a traditional tale? Where and when did the story reach Mac? Did he sense its antiquity? Who cast Paddy's exploit in tale form rather than as a ballad or jest? How did it serve miners? What does this story mean today to listeners unfamiliar with Daly and unable to visualize a mine stope's interior? I run such queries together formulaically—origin, form, use, meaning—and pray that my analysis holds a bit of the wisdom inherent in folktale.

Each line of formal examination has the potential of shaping itself as an enchanted string or trail of bread crumbs to mark paths in and out of a labyrinth or forest. No matter how one enters the study of tales, Haywire Mac's gem beckons in vinyl groove and on magnetic tape. The transcribed text displays its own rhetorical strategies, but Mac's recorded telling jumps out of physical disc or tape to help listeners experience his living artistry.

I urge my book's readers to seek McClintock's Folkways recording, to listen to it, and to reflect on his tale's meaning. A Rounder LP reissue album, *Hallelujah! I'm a Bum,* carries listeners back to Mac's earliest 78-rpm selections. Beyond these two sound recordings, which let us hear McClintock at early and late sessions, *Haywire Mac and the Big Rock Candy Mountain,* a booklet written by Henry Young, locomotive engineer, also opens the door to Mac's world of adventures.

Within "Marcus Daly Enters Heaven," plot action, textual subtlety, and stylistic expression transport hearers to a Butte copper mine, specifically, to a deep stope—the steplike chamber where miners extract ore from earth by breaking rock and muckers shovel ore into wheelbarrows or cars destined for the smelter. However, Mac's particular stope also functions as a storyteller's circle. Daly's hard rock miners, stealing leisure, enthrone a gifted spinner on a muck pile. Miners from coast to coast know the all-purpose work *muck* as ore to be lifted to the surface or rock and waste (gob) to be discarded.

Figuratively, as Mac's album spins on turntable, I stand at the muck pile's edge, straining to absorb Paddy's details, to catch his inflections. Reflexively, I take possession of the tale to the extent that I can test it against my knowledge of mining craft and miners' aspirations. I am conscious of listening at home, not in the stope. Nevertheless, I can play and replay Mac's recording until every nuance of text and tone becomes clear.

Listening blends with commentary; I reflect on Mac's formal opening: the introduction of Paddy Burke, who prefers barroom sessions to hard work. With his luck played out elsewhere, he finds employment at Daly's Neversweat Mine. Like Harun al-Rashid, the mine owner disguises himself for night prowling. Unlike an Arabian Night caliph, however, Daly does not reward deserving subjects; rather, he punishes lazy workers. Daly hears Burke yarning and fires the whole gang. Here, the storyteller discards an outer shell to reveal an inner kernel.

Mac uses a normal voice in recounting Paddy's wanderings. When Daly catches the shirkers, a chill sweeps the stope. Responding, Mac shifts his voice to accent Paddy's brogue. Mac had told a story about Paddy; now Paddy places Daly within a story. Skillfully, the linked accounts integrate dual journeys—Burke travels from Nevada to Coeur d'Alene to Butte; Daly, from Butte to heaven. These follow each other in sequence, but they are not exactly parallel. Although the boss bests his miners by dismissal, one worker imaginatively employs verbal art to best the big boss. Mac realistically presents Paddy's wandering as a "ten-day-stiff," whereas the latter dreams Daly's path to judgment.

Mac's tale holds several messages, among them ideological and eschatological commentary. Ultimately, the proletarian holds the capitalist to a moral code—a startling inversion within American society. This tale's Butte listeners would have known that Daly came to the Rockies as a poor Irish immigrant, later amassing a fortune on the world's richest hill. Some Butteans hailed him as a hero; others, as a despot. Montana residents have told many Daly stories centered on the magnate's cocksure ways and aggressive bent.

Without engaging in polemical tirade, Haywire Mac reveals "which side he's on" by a shocking ending to Daly's journey. "Come, Jesus, get up and give Marcus your seat" shouts blasphemy. We can appreciate such daring by recognizing that Burke's listeners were largely Catholic. Paddy, of course, uses an Irish sacred belief system to bring an empire builder down from heaven itself. Here, in a seemingly simple tale, Daly's fall from grace occurs 1,300 feet below ground in a Dantean stope, an earthly hell.

Mac balances his story units evenly: Paddy avoids work; Paddy relates a dream. When joined, these self-contained halves of realism and fantasy gain power. One and one make three! We use the analytic term *structure* variously: to denote oppositional elements, to reveal beams or pillars, or to search for glue or mortar. As Mac talks about Burke and Burke talks about Daly, I see a form resembling a walnut: outer shell, inner morsel. One can also see discrete elements converging as Paddy journeys to Butte and Marcus to heaven. These opposite paths merge as workers assert their moral worth over their oppressors.

Listeners to Haywire Mac's sound recording hear him shift verbal gears to signal a story within a story, a symbolic change of scenes upon a verbal stage. Audiences at home in traditional communities develop sensitivity to a tale teller's manipulation of sound. We deal here with elements well captured by sound-recording technology.

Normally, copper miners at work—even prior to mechanization—make considerable noise. Daly, prowling in the mine, hears no hammer, drill, shovel, or car wheel. Well before he catches his men, his ears report their dereliction. Silence, indeed, can make great sound. The quiet stope signals trouble for Daly and pleasure for his crew.

We hear further a manipulation of sound as Mac shifts the tale's dual settings from Neversweat Mine to heaven, where Paddy hears glorious singing and magical harps. A trumpet fanfare announces Daly's arrival on high. The Lord's magnificent voice closes the story. But even with this dramatic ending, hearers anticipate that on Daly's fall, he will be reduced to mining sulphur, not his beloved copper. How loudly will Marcus's hammer ring in the fiery pit below?

Tale analysis itself shifts about in raising questions. Did Harry McClintock receive "Marcus Daly Enters Heaven" as a self-contained story, or did he fashion it from fragments overheard during his wanderings? Did Mac really encounter Paddy Burke? Did the former create the latter to personify all casual workers? Could Mac have heard a discrete dream-of-heaven narrative, splicing it to a preexisting brag about a tricky miner? Such questions remain open, for neither McClintock nor Eskin left clues to the origin of the Burke/Daly tale.

Two internal details suggest age, near and distant: Daly, in his midnight prowl, disguises himself with mining clothes and an old felt hat covered with candle grease. The men entertained by Paddy stick their candles into the stope's stone face. Hence, these lights reveal that Mac placed Paddy's adventures back to Butte's early decades, before miners used carbon or battery lamps. In heaven, Paddy feasts on nightingales' tongues. Surely, this delicacy did not spring to life in Butte during Daly's reign, 1880–1900. To invoke the sweet-singing nightingale's name calls up the voice of a courtly minstrel, not a strapping hardrocker. Waving a verbal wand, Mac collapsed time more quickly than Daly's men descended their mine shaft.

Curious about the genesis of "Marcus Daly Enters Heaven," I speculated that McClintock might well have heard a story about a Celtic chief who ascended to heavenly realms only to be rebuked by the gods. I searched for, but did not find, an Irish fairy tale structured similarly to Mac's narrative. Happily, folklorists generously share findings. At UCLA, on April 24, 1987, Donald Ward heard me suggest an Irish background for Mac's humor. Previously, in 1972, Professor Ward had elaborated on the motif (god orders son to surrender seat to villain) in a setting remote from Butte.

The *Lokasenna* (Loki's Flyting or Wrangling—a running dialogue of vituperation), an Icelandic Eddic poem, occupies a spicy position in Norse mythology. Within the poem, Loki, the god of mischief intent on violence, enters the heavenly hall. Odin, chief of all gods, notices Loki and turns to his son Vidar with an order: "Get up, Vidar / tell the father of the wolf [Loki] to take a seat" (Ward, 118). We glimpse this command's original strength in a modern translation by Lee Hollander:

Othin said:
"Arise, then, Vithar, let the Wolf's father
be benched at our banquet;
lest that Loki fling lewd words at us
in Aegir's ale hall."

The *Lokasenna* dates to A.D. 800–1050. We do not know precisely when Odin's command to Vidar first appeared in mythic form. We do know that the motif reappeared in Kiel, Germany, during this century in anecdotal form. The story concerned a wealthy shipbuilder and city father, August Anton Heinrich Sartori, who lived from 1837 to 1903 wielding great economic and political power (Hensen; HFR). Folklorist Kurt Ranke, in a study of jokes, reported that when Sartori ascended to heaven, "God turned to his son, Jesus, and said: 'Get up, so Sartori can sit down' " (Ward, 119). Ranke's punchline reads, "Steh auf, Christus, lass Sartori sitzen!" (53).

The connection surfaces once more between the heavenly arrival of magnates from Keil and Butte. God, by words and deeds, reminds mine owner Daly and shipbuilder Sartori that worldly power must be shed in the afterworld. Placing the Loki poem, the Sartori joke, and the Daly tale side by side, we wonder at the thousand-year transition in time and place. Kurt Ranke, commenting on the Kiel anecdote, felt reluctant to assume a direct link from Norse mythology to twentieth-century jokes about earthly lords. However, Donald Ward, going beyond Ranke's analysis, did posit a genetic relationships within the several give-up-your-seat jests—a linked sense of irony.

Professor Ward's fine analysis shifts emphasis from the matter of origin for Mac's narrative to its core meaning. Loki, scolding the gods, seeks to destroy them. Odin knows Loki's evil purpose, yet he cannot refrain from ordering his son Vidar to surrender his seat. Human logic today demands that Odin reject Loki, but the Viking's supreme being had no choice but to bow to intractable fate. Essentially, Vidar gave up his place within a scene of cosmic tragedy.

In Harry McClintock's Butte story, humor overtakes fate; God need not accept Daly, for only nominally does Jesus leave his seat. We who listen know that Mac's tale closes with ironic play. Jesus is not displaced; instead, God cloaks Daly in ridicule. In pre-Christian Scandinavia, Loki punished Norse gods. In copper camp Butte, some miners wanted God to punish mine bosses. Somewhere, in the many steps from the *Lokasenna* to Paddy Burke's dream about Daly, comedy's smile replaced tragedy's scowl.

If we had no links from Loki to Sartori and Daly, we would have to ask about the motif's movement over the span of a thousand years. Fortunately, an epitaph and a tale fill in part of the gap. In 1777, Christoph Frederich Nicolai related the following incident: "The Spanish musician, Gutierez, reportedly had this inscription on his tombstone: 'When he entered heaven, God stood up and told his angels, "Shut up and let Don Emanuel Gutierez, court musician and choir-director for God, sing" ' " (Ranke, 53).

The German magazine *Niedersachsen* (October 1908) carried an elaborate dream story, "Sin Droom," from Lower Saxony:

> The wealthy von Kloppenburg dreams he died. Archangel Gabriel comes and takes him to heaven; at the gates he is greeted by St. Peter, who requests him to step forth. Gabriel floats down a hallway, followed by Peter and von Kloppenburg, and all three enter a magnificently lighted hall. Straight ahead is a splendid throne of pure gold on which God sits. Von Kloppenburg tries to make himself inconspicuous by retiring to a corner, but God sees him, and calls out to his Son: "Jesus, get up and let Herr von Kloppenburg have your chair; Herr von Kloppenburg come, please, and sit down!" God then notices that von Kloppenburg is cold from his journey, and has a mug of hot grog brought to him. . . . At this point, Frau von Kloppenburg wakes up her husband,

telling him it is time to get up, to which our dreamer responds, "The least you could have done was let me finish my grog!" (German précis by Ranke [53]; translation by Ward [letter, 1987])

We can now place the traditional uses of this ironic jest or tale from Loki to Gutierez to von Kloppenburg to Sartori to Daly. This chronological sequence helps reveal similarities and dissimilarities in these accounts. We can search for additional variants involving God's command to his son to surrender his place. Despite the appeal of such missions, I return to our tale's setting at Butte and its spotlight on the Anaconda's Marcus Daly.

## Matty Kiely

In raising a set of interrelated questions about "Marcus Daly Enters Heaven," I have likened folktale study to a labyrinth's path. As my act of analysis becomes a figurative path, the copper mine becomes a maze. Butte's Neversweat Mine—with seven smokestack fingers poking the sky and miles of shafts, drifts, and chambers below—has lived in my imagination since first hearing Mac's tale during 1968. Where Paddy and his fellows broke rock to extract copper, I sought a tale's inner essence. Optimistically, I believed that with enough luck I would find a parallel to McClintock's story set either in Butte or in another section of the Rocky Mountain West.

Hard rock miners throughout the United States have generated a considerable body of lore, some of which has reached local color fiction, poetry, and regional history, as well as ephemeral and academic mine technology studies. Professor Wayland Hand's annotated articles about nonferrous mining folklore remain our best source for these miners' songs and stories, their customs and beliefs. In 1982, I shared Mac's story with Hand. He enjoyed it but had not encountered it in print or in the field.

Continuing the search, I turned to locally published booklets by three authors who had observed everyday life in Butte: Walt ("Rags") Holliday, *Mining Camp Melodies* and *Mining Camp Yarns;* Joseph Duffy, *Poems* and *Butte Was Like That;* and William Allen Burke, *Rhymes of the Mines.* Although I failed to find Mac's story, I came to appreciate the immense body of vernacular culture displayed in a single occupational community.

Bill Burke (1893–1969) knew Butte as a city of a million stories (Vancouver *Columbian*). Having worked as a "nipper" (mine tool boy), newsman, and publicist, he brought considerable talent to bear in editing *Copper Camp*. This colorful grab bag for the WPA Writers Program remains in print and serves as one testimony to the New Deal's commitment to cultural democracy. Although Burke did not include Mac's tale in *Copper Camp*, the editor led me to a gifted Butte bard.

I turn to miner-minstrel Matty Kiely, identified by Burke as a "Paul Bunyan of the camp" (202). Did the editor intend the allusion to mark the miner's physical size or his reputation as Butte's folk hero? Like Paddy Burke, Kiely pleasured his fellow workers on the gob pile below ground and the gallows frame high at the mine shaft's head.

While singing Butte's favorite folksong, "I rustled at the Diamond / I rustled at the Bell," Matty added the sound of a "widow maker" (air drill)—B-r-r-r-r-r-r-r-r-r—to his rendition (202). Calling to the bartender to "Fill 'em up, this buzzy can't run without plenty of ile," Kiely indulged in comic wordplay: machines run on oil; miners, on whiskey—both proper lubricants. In the largest sense, Kiely's "ile," his Irish blarney, lubricated everyday life in Butte.

Two Kiely anecdotes reported by Bill Burke complement "Marcus Daly Enters Heaven." Before his death, Matty summed up decades of Montana politics: "She's a free town now, and no man need wear a copper collar but for the eight hours he's down in the hole" (54). Rich in ambiguity, this aphorism requires a contextual backdrop. Today, police in action-packed movies collar criminals. During 1894, an Idaho coroner's jury investigating a fatal cave-in at the Bunker Hill & Sullivan Mine called on the state inspector to visit the tragic site. The jury urged the inspector to assert his freedom from company politics by demonstrating that "he wears not the collar of any individual or corporation" (Wyman, 192). In 1923, Arthur Fisher contributed a muckraking report to the *Nation* entitled "Montana: Land of the Copper Collar."

Kiely's *copper collar* relates to other metal bands, leg irons, and handcuffs marking imprisonment or servitude. This image picked up polish, if not tarnish, from the terms *brass collar* and *brass check*. Connoting an immoral or illicit payment, the latter usage denominated tokens used in western brothels. Copper miners were familiar with such brass checks; some Butte readers also knew Upton Sinclair's *The Brass Check* (1920), an exposé of the "kept press."

Etymological detail returns attention to the substance of Kiely's saying that Butte is "a free town now, and no man need wear a copper collar but for the eight hours he's down in the hole." He looked back at the past as one of constant toil but divided his present night and day (perhaps the years when he was too old to work) into sixteen hours of freedom and eight hours of slavery.

Kiely seems utterly realistic, if not fatalistic, in accepting the copper collar as a necessary condition of work in the mines. Clearly, Paddy Burke, who preferred yarning to mucking, would have rejected Kiely's acceptance of the copper collar at any time. In Wobbly parlance, Paddy might have called Matty a *scissorbill* or *dehorn* (a worker who believed the company line).

Kiely, born in 1871, arrived in Butte directly from Waterford, Ireland, at age seventeen. Daly gave the lad his first job when the big Anaconda Mine reached the 400-foot level. Matty never forgot his patron. On Daly's death in 1900, Butte citizens contributed more than $5,000, including many children's copper pennies, toward a bronze statue to be designed by Augustus Saint-Gaudens. On Labor Day, 1907, Anaconda officials and city fathers joined to erect the bronze in front of the North Main Street post office. Surely, this unveiling marks one of the few Labor Day celebrations honoring a capitalist.

Kiely visited the monument weekly to keep Daly's spirit informed about local events. We can judge Matty "strange" for talking to a statue or "wise" in his reach beyond the grave. Despite Kiely's constant visits to the post office site, he remained deeply troubled that the statue had been placed with its backside to the copper hill. Summing up his anxiety, he intoned, " 'Tis no luck will ever come of it. In life Marcus Daly never turned his arse on the mines of Butte or the miners who dug them" (204).

Not only did Kiely express the view of many Irish miners who saw Daly as friend rather than oppressor but the mucker tapped into a vein of folk anecdotes about statues of heroes. While living in Washington, D.C., I heard southern-born cab drivers circling Scott Circle say that although the mounted Union army general faced the White House, he had the good sense to turn his ass to the north. This expression dates at least to the turn of the century, when Washingtonians erected a statue of General Sherman at the Treasury Building's south entrance. The Treasury Secretary asked a southern correspondent his opinion of the unveiling. The newsman replied, "From the north side, where we stand, you see General Sherman as a soldier and gentleman, but from the south side all you can see is a horse's hind end" (Kiplinger, 431).

An additional anecdote from Utah reaffirms the traditionality of Kiely's expression. William Wilson heard fellow Mormons make fun of Brigham Young's "overly materialistic emphasis in the church by joking about [his] statue in downtown Salt Lake City which has Brigham's back to the temple and his hand extended towards Zion's First National Bank" (325). A folk verse sums up feeling:

> Here stands Brigham
> Like a bird on a perch,
> With his hand to the bank
> And his back to the church.

The jingle about Young's statue hinges on moral concern over churchly materialism. The jokes about the placement of monuments for Scott and Sherman remind Americans of sectional conflict and contested beliefs in national sovereignty. Matty Kiely's anxiety about Daly's statue touches superstitious fear of bad luck flowing from a community's disregard for the source of its patron's largesse. The contrast is obvious between Paddy Burke's wry treatment of the plutocrat Marcus Daly and Matty Kiely's respect for the same man.

Many cities hold monuments around which lore clusters. I stress Kiely's relationship to the Daly statue in that it marks a worker's respect for his boss. Paddy and Matty may well represent poles of tension felt within workers' ranks across the lines of craft skill, industry, region, religion, or ethnicity. In short, laborlore in its fullest dimension ranges from Kiely's identification with his employer to Burke's dissension.

I have already indicated my inability to document Paddy Burke's existence. He lives in Harry McClintock's tale without a supporting birth certificate or a death notice. I know Matty Kiely through Bill Burke's eyes: "Many's the ton of first class ore [Matty] broke for the company in the saloons of Butte" (207). This tribute is traditional: George Korson encountered anthracite barroom ballads in which drinking coal miners boasted of prodigious underground output.

Burke's *Copper Camp* offers a tantalizing clue to Kiely's bardic role by mentioning a lengthy article in the *San Francisco Leader* on Matty's witticisms (205). Father Peter Yorke, an early labor priest and modernist in church dogma, edited the *Leader.* I have not found the article on Kiely but have found his obituary in the *Montana Standard* (September 15, 1936): "Old-time Butte Man Succumbs." The obit spells his name as Matt Kiley.

I close my account on Kiely with a cautionary note to readers. Folklorists, historians, dramatists, and novelists dip into story streams to select tales that fit authorial purpose. By stressing Paddy Burke and Matty Kiely's paradigmatic roles along the divide of loyalty/disloyalty to miner owner, I have narrowed their real complexity. Only a few workers avoid the compromises forced by each day's task or guard the passion needed to hold a pure ideological line.

Joseph Duffy's *Butte Was Like That* overflows with copper and Celtic lore. In a Kiely anecdote, Duffy reveals that the former's respect for his benefactor did not extend to other owners and their lackeys. The arrival of Slavic immigrants in Butte found the city unable to provide housing for new workers. "The Slav invasion was the cue for several of the mine bosses on the hill, to buy or build a number of cabins and by furnishing employment to the new arrivals, they had a monopoly on the rent situation" (343).

Duffy details Matty's response to mine bosses becoming landlords:

> Matty Kiley, an old-time miner of Butte, who has since passed on to his reward, was the man—so it has been said—that killed the goose that laid the golden eggs, for these Get-rich-quick Wallingfords of the hill.
>
> Matty—so the story goes—went up the hill one morning

to rustle. Taking his place in the waiting line, Matty was finally facing the foreman of the mine. Ignoring that worthy completely, Matty turned and addressing his remarks to a structure of steel that surmounted the shaft, he said: "Good morning, Mister Gallows-Frame, have you any cabins for rent this morning?"

What the mine foreman had to say about the incident has never been recorded, but suffice it to say that the real estate holdings of the bosses from that day forward, took on a sudden slump and the rent game went into a decline.

I would like to believe that Kiely could singlehandedly break boss exploitation of Slavic immigrant miners, although such victories came more readily in a raconteur's tale than on Butte's copper hill. We can appreciate Matty's command of storytelling in his mock address to the mine head structure as "Mister Gallows-Frame." Irish and Slavic miners, as well as their fellow workers from all the corners of the earth, knew sudden death by fire and flood in Butte. Slow death by constant accidents and tuberculosis hovered daily in the community.

Even the hardrockers most loyal to their employers had need to allay anxiety with gallows humor. Workers in Butte's mines, like their brothers and sisters throughout the United States—and the world—used lore to pace and lighten the burden of work, to soothe job-generated tension, and to assert purpose in life beyond daily tasks. Matty did not need diplomas in functional psychology or literary criticism to decode narrative, to sublimate everyday grinding toil, or to externalize fear. By traditionalizing everyday experience, workers empowered their lives, at least to some degree. Matty Kiely, with jest and wordplay, left a marvelous gift for brother and sister toilers leagues removed from Butte.

## Olympus to Hades

In bidding farewell to the bards Kiely and Burke, I note two neglected areas in this chapter: nonferrous mining technology and folktale history. Beyond suggesting that children, even in modern society, continue to hear traditional stories, I have not alluded to the Brothers Grimm, Charles Perrault, Andrew Land, Antti Aarne, and their many colleagues in collection and analysis. Nor have I cited present-day references to accessible scholarship.

One notion of a folktale serves my purpose: a narrative shaped within an enclaved society and commenting on the experience and reveries of its members. Contemporary tale scholars, of course, have altered or expanded this definition. Readers who enjoy "Marcus Daly Enters Heaven" or "Mister Gallows-Frame" will begin their own course of analysis.

I have not cited the extensive body of technical monographs and historical studies indispensable in understanding and measuring the actual labor of Kiely and Burke. Butte workers distinguished strongly between subcrafts. Nominally, all who worked in and around the mines could be termed *miners;* actually, the work force separated itself by degree of skill and payment. Wayland Hand illustrated the point by noting the horror of a chambermaid in the fabled Hazel Block Hotel when she discovered "a mucker in a miner's bed" (1946, 160). Readers can ferret out other hard rock roles in useful books by Ronald Brown, Richard Lingenfelter, Mark Wyman, and Otis Young.

Of the many questions folklorists ask, those of meaning are most appropriate to contemporary audiences. When we hear Harry McClintock describe Paddy Burke in the Neversweat Mine, we have a choice of identifying with Marcus Daly, betrayed by his bemused employees, or conversely, with Paddy, who steals a bit of freedom from Marcus. Clearly, this tale's largest meaning derives from its current audience's understanding of the differences signaled by the word pairings *worker/boss* or *exploiter/victim.*

"Marcus Daly Enters Heaven" builds on the assumption that hearers—initially miners, but today any workers—accept some notion of class. Yet Mac's tale does not hold any specific agitational or polemical content, nor does it touch on formal issues of unionism or radicalism. We cannot connect it to early independent unions, the dominant Butte Mine Workers Union, the Western Federation of Miners, or the Industrial Workers of the World.

Listeners and readers cannot establish the historicity of Mac's tale by reference to the dynamiting of a hall or the initiation of a rustling (hiring) practice. McClintock was well acquainted with Joe Hill's death by firing squad in Salt Lake City and Frank Little's lynching by a company mob in Butte. Mac's tale held no echo of the ringing rhetoric suitable to prose and poetry memorials for Little, Hill, or other Wobbly martyrs.

Mac's story compares in strength to the best in labor legendary, although he spins it out elusively rather than with direct class portraiture. He wastes no time in Dickensian descriptions of mine horrors. Instead, he turns to an appealing description of heaven; listeners, then and now, can enjoy his goblets of emeralds, sidewalks of gold, and angels on skates as fine as railroaders' watches. We know these images to be literary—the gossamer from children's fairy tales. Metaphorically, the heavenly furnishings serve to expose Butte's biggest boss as both sneaky and greedy, unfit to sip from bejeweled goblets. The tale's rich embroidery envelops the Anaconda empire builder, bringing him down from Olympus to Hades.

Readers in the 1990s will know that Paddy Burke and Matty Kiely, despite the differences in their values, filled their barrows and mine cars against a backdrop of a seemingly inexhaustible supply of ore. Today, copper goods come to Butte from ore mined in Chile, the Congo, and the East Indies. Paddy Burke believed in freedom from wage slavery. How do Americans who share his values define the right to work and job freedom when Butte's copper veins run out or become unprofitable in world markets?

Parallel questions concern the matter of workers' status after coal, oil, timber, water, or soil vanish. Even when these precious resources are conserved, workers may face a toxic cauldron, a devil's brew on many jobs. We have long accepted the fact that mine camps were destined to become ghost towns, settings for TV dramas. But what of giant Pittsburgh and Detroit when workers no longer find employment in machining piston rings, weaving wire nets, or winding copper wire?

I have elevated Burke and Kiely as emblematic figures not only for copper miners but for American labor at large. Further, I have assumed that their tales hold relevance for modern workers' audiences. I do not feel it presumptutous to suggest that these two Celtic bards represent others, from hog butcher to flight attendant.

Surely, some contemporary employees feel the need to bring their employers down from Olympus, to speak up against corporate power. Such workers will identify with Paddy Burke, but they may be puzzled by my linking him with Matty for honor over other copper miners. Do these two muckers form a pair? Yes; essentially, they filled trickster roles in turning their backs on the Protestant work ethic.

Despite Kiely's once-a-week sojourn at Daly's statue, he did not linger at the post office site. Rather, he turned to Butte's many saloons. Both he and Paddy preferred the brass footrail to the shovel handle, for their blarney gifts far outweighed the rock in their barrows. Burke and Kiely articulated the pain and passion of their peers, who were less verbal, less able to transform everyday experience into expressive form and formula.

Radical activists might argue that Burke and Kiely should be judged apart, each by the norm of class consciousness. The latter seemingly disqualified himself by his respect for Daly, whereas the former diminished his credentialed stance by masking his protest with arcane humor. Syndicalists and socialists in Butte must have roasted Daly before and after his death. Haywire Mac, an early member of the IWW, probably heard such accounts. However, in his encounter with Sam Eskin, he avoided a direct blast at Daly. Instead, he offered a crafty folktale.

We can underscore both the traditionality and artistry of "Marcus Daly Enters Heaven" by comparing it to a few lines from a Butte workers' poem, "Cornelius Kelly." In examining a rare booklet entitled *New Songs for Butte Mining Camp,* Page Stegner noted that Cornelius Francis "Con" Kelly, a Daly successor at the Anaconda Company, had defied a 1918 strike call by the Metal Mine Workers Industrial Union Number 800. When the Wobblies spoke of halting production, Kelly threatened to let grass grow on the muck heaps before the company would deal with the IWW (1967, 162).

Scottie, a Wobbly poet, picked up on the hallowed grass threat and consigned Kelly from the sixth floor (company headquarters) to eternal hell. Paddy Burke had used dream and fantasy to undermine Daly. Scottie used burlesque patter to send Kelly below. The Butte poem reads:

> "The grass would grow," so says this plute,
> "In Anaconda and in Butte,
> Before I meet the men's demands,
> And this is final as it stands."

Now, look here, Con, just take a tip,
It's going round on every lip,
A job you will be rustling soon
I hope you get it in the moon,
Or in a hot-box, where the sweat
Drips off your hair and burns your neck,
Or where the dust and powder smoke
Would make a guy like you just croak.

Scottie's class relationship to Con Kelly matched that of Paddy Burke to Marcus Daly, yet the rhetorical texture of their respective offerings reveals great distance. I do not fault Scottie by judging him against the aesthetic norm of John Keats. Much of the workers' verse printed in the United States lacks the lyric grace and linguistic elegance we build into poetry's very defintion. The best workers' poems compensate by using job-familiar symbols, sequential narration, and direct polemics. Regardless of the artistic merit in Scottie's poem, it presents a moral judgment of a boss by a worker.

Miners loyal to Daly and Kelly disputed union terrain with rebels as they agreed on the cause of freedom for Ireland. It became difficult for many Irish copper miners to break with employers to whom they were bound culturally. Although some miners joined with Scottie in wishing Kelly to "croak," others accepted Con's authority because it derived from Daly's. While Kelly presided on the sixth floor, his power seemed automatic to many. Yet those who could not accept Anaconda's dominance in Montana found the means to spurn the company,

Many miners "on the hill" viewed Daly as a Horatio Alger hero, fighting his way from poverty to riches, as well as a generous patron in the Irish "patriot's game." Clearly, Kiely, who identified with Butte's father figure, and Burke, who denigrated Daly, both described the very same man. Each mucker, responding to a compelling vision, drew on discrete perspectives long sanctioned by American workers in their fundamental internal differences over class identity.

Historians and economists drawn to Butte as a site of American struggle have commented on rustling cards as marking class division. Readers will have noted that when Paddy Burke reached

Butte, "the boys didn't shower down very good . . . so he hustled himself a job." Similarly, when Matty Kiely dealt with rent-gouging foremen, he "went up the hill one morning to rustle." Scottie, in his poem "Cornelius Kelly," challenged the "plute": "A job you will be rustling soon."

The ancient word *rustle* to signify sounds made by falcons' wings or by royal banners passed into occupational speech in the 1870s, if not before, to note vigorous movement and strenuous action. In many situations, job seekers needed to push their way ahead, to show a little hustle. We do not know why hard rock miners favored *rustle* over *hustle.*

Idaho's silver mine owners at Coeur d'Alene had required written job permits as early as 1899 (Jensen, 82). The Anaconda Copper Company installed a card system at its Montana smelters in 1903. A Butte fraternal organization, the Hibernians, heard a good report in 1908, "Get . . . rustling clothes on; the mines are back at work" (Emmons, 272). On December 1, 1912, Anaconda formalized employment requirements by issuing mandatory cards for workers. Men had to deposit these cards in the office while on the payroll. If a miner quit or were discharged, Anaconda might refuse to "return" his card, thus turning the card into a blacklisting tool (Brissenden, 1920).

Antipathy to rustling cards and the rustling office fueled labor disputes from 1912 until the late 1930s, when miners rebuilt their union (the International Union of Mine, Mill, & Smelter Workers) within the CIO. Despite this advance, the term *rustle* never died in Butte. Wayland Hand found many references to the locution in Butte's favorite folksong (1950, 20–27). Two examples follow:

Well now, I've rustled the High Ore,
I've rustled the Bell;
I've rustled the Diamond,
I've rustled like Hell;
I've rustled the Mountain Con,
Mountain View, too;
And I've landed a job,
In the Ellermerloo [Ormolu].

I rustled the High Ore,
I rustled the Sweat [Neversweat],

The winter is over,
And I'm rustling yet.
The big burly Dutchman,
Come over the Rhine,
To go slinging muck
In the Big Diamond Mine.

My study of *fink* revealed that *rustling* had reached Tacoma's docks by 1917. Here, I note the latter term's wide circulation throughout the West. In 1942, Duncan Emrich collected rustling songs in Virginia City, Nevada, and Grass Valley, California. He reported that some tramp miners preferred to recite such songs in the bar "to the accompaniment of accentual fist thumpings or glass rappings" (226). This rhythmic effect returns us to Butte's Moonlight Saloon, where Matty Kiely had imitated the buzzy air drill in his rustling song. Ultimately, Matty and his fellows who "took five" on the job or rapped tumblers on the bar sought to assert a direction within their lives.

My concern with laborlore has led me to analyze Burke's tale and Kiely's jests. Beyond detailing the specific adventures of this pair, I have asked why workers gather in traditionalizing circles at the stope, watercooler, or loading dock. In asking such questions touching on past behavior on the job, I have related hoary traditions to present-day conditions. Reconstructing the road from Loki to Daly leads to the most significant question about "Marcus Daly Enters Heaven"—does this tale live? Is it meaningful only to a handful of nostalgic Butte citizens, or does it serve American workers across the rainbow of age, gender, color, place, and craft?

Many workers come to grips daily with dead-end jobs in our economy's real tombs—shuttered factories and stagnant shops. Some individuals continue to claw their way out of the grave, to defy the gallows-frame present at all work sites. Other workers are deskilled and dehumanized by the very forces with which they make a living. In past years, America's laborers have relied heavily on economic and political organization to advance their aims. Without formally attending to the discipline of folklore, workers have also used bonnie tunes, sly jests, and vernacular speech to demystify experience and redress loss.

Paddy Burke and Matty Kiely in the Neversweat's and Anaconda's depths, as well as in Butte bars, spoke to fellow workers from San Francisco's piers to the Potomac's corridors. Each used his Celtic gift of wordplay and his strong sense of personal autonomy to help fellow miners lift their copper collars. In summation, both called on verbal art and traditional wit to speak against the subordination of one human to another.

## Inquiry

Robert McCarl, in commenting to me on this study, noted multiple contrasts embedded in linking Burke's tale to Kiely's jests. Each marks value oscillations as currents flow from anger to respect for Daly. However, pairing two miners and showing their commonality rather than conflict also poses broad questions about oppositions between folkloric and popular forms. Why does Arnold Schwarzenegger merit a hundred-million-dollar film while Paddy and Matty live only in an obscure LP album and WPA guide? Who accepts responsibility to bring work's culture out of the mine's shadows?

Questions about copper bards spin endlessly as they turn on themselves, revealing new facets of inquiry. We can look far back to son Vidar personifying the chief motif that stands behind Paddy's tale of Daly's heavenly journey. We can look ahead from Matty's conversations with Daly's statue to the continuous rearticulation and re-presentation of workers' lore. Listeners who hear Harry McClintock on disc or tape enjoy his signifying brogue. Readers who chase Matty Kiely through *Copper Camp*'s pages relish his wordplay. Together, those who fall under Butte's spell can go beyond the enjoyment of a sound recording and a book to specific probes—to particular formulations for occupational narrative and trickster peregrination.

In looking back at two of Butte's many hardrock miners, we do well in amplifying an aspect of judgment above. Clearly, some radicals will invoke the Leninist formula of "false consciousness" (mental sluggishness, ideological backwardness, lumpen belief) to describe both Burke and Kiely. Under this rubric, Paddy weakened his tale's effect by avoiding an overt contestational message, whereas Matty "sold out" his class interests by worshipping a capitalist.

These pronouncements come easily to left mandarins who watch over brothers and sisters, alert to false steps or deviation from dogma. Having known workers who talked like Haywire Mac and who acted like Paddy Burke and Matty Kiely, I have had no trouble in accepting the authenticity of Mac's stylized presentation and the reality of Paddy's and Matty's expressions.

It is tempting, of course, to criticize Kiely's homage to Daly from the perspective that elevates the term *class*. This analytic construct has served alternately to illuminate social reality and to mesmerize its users. If Matty's respect for his employer becomes an emblem of class betrayal, then what moral does "Mister Gallows-Frame" offer? In repeating Joseph Duffy's account of mine bosses becoming landlords, I have suggested that Matty spoke against the exploitation of Slavic immigrants. Did he not represent class interests in resisting a form of economic domination?

Bill Burke's *Copper Camp* peels back Kiely's bold act. In "The Bohunk Scare," Burke reprints a long report from the *Butte Evening News* (July 24, 1910) that pits "white man" against "bohunk." The latter "buys his job from the foreman . . . pays him for keeping it . . . lives in a cabin . . . never adapts himself to American life any more than does a Chinaman" (134). The journalistic equation of immigrants from the Balkans and from China serve as an inflammatory curse.

Bill Burke identifies the High Ore Mine as the site of Matty's mock address at the shaft's head when Butte's labor force faced another wave of newcomers. In its full span of "settlers," Butte assimilated Yankee, "Cousin Jack" (Cornish), Irish, Slav, Finn, Joplin Missourian, Mexican, and Dust Bowl "Okie." Burke pinpoints Matty's escapade at the High Ore to the Monday morning following the *Evening News* blast, "The Story of the Butte Bohunk." Kiely exposed the cabin-renting foreman who fired him; ultimately, Matty's pithy oration became a camp classic.

Kiely's gallows-frame jest pits worker against boss in a setting of inter-ethnic hostility. In effect, Matty strained class conflict through ethnicity's sieve. By enacting Irish ("white") values, did the mucker prove himself false to class? To deny ethnic conflict within the work force distorts history. To simplify the analysis of a folk anecdote compounds such distortion as it robs occupational lore of its complexity.

We can enjoy "Marcus Daly Enters Heaven" because of its

radical message revealed in layers of meaning. Kiely helps us penetrate a problematic area for labor's goals—the continuing tension generated by linguistic, religious, and national difference. In short, from today's perspective, I like his "put down" of the slumlord foreman, but I am distressed by his chauvinism.

In screening "Mister Gallows-Frame" for its mix of class and ethnic subtexts, I have treated lightly another vital strand. For many years, labor activists discussed exploitation in the mines in terms of toil in dark and danger, cost to life and limb. In recent years, we have added ecological damage to mining's toll. To rip ore from earth violates Mother Nature—destruction paid for in fire, flood, disease, and death.

Paddy Burke defied Marcus Daly from a syndicalist platform hidden within a traditional narrative. Can we anticipate Burke's children striking back at all the demon Dalys who despoil the earth? If Haywire Mac's story continues to reach new audiences, its members will have to sort out economic and ecological messages. Essentially, future auditors will have to bring Paddy's and Matty's respective stories out of the copper mine and into the next century's consciousness.

Finally, I return to another pairing of truth and falsity in laborlore explication. Paddy Burke may have lived only in Harry McClintock's imagination. Matty Kiely lived in Butte. Do we reject the former as a fairy tale figure of no substance in pragmatic labor studies? Rather than contrasting Matty and Paddy as polar figures, I feature their commonality, their shared role in our construction of and reflection on copper mine experience.

Within Bill Burke's description of Matty Kiely, we can see and hear Haywire Mac's portrait of Paddy Burke: "Red-faced Matty with his homely Irish grin and his ready wit . . . worked in every mine, large or small, on the hill, but he never tarried long at any one mine. His irrepressible spirits and too glib tongue took care of that. As he sang himself in rhyme: 'I've been hired and fired tin thousand times, / 'Tis Matty Kiely who dug their mines!' "

Matty did little work below ground. Bill Burke notes that "he was a past master at finding ways and means of avoiding any exertion. This would not have been so bad from the bosses' point of view, but while Matty was on a mine level he kept everyone else from work while he sat around telling tall stories of his exploits" (204). We have come full circle to Paddy Burke yarning in the stope as Marcus Daly spies on his enchanted miners.

Matty and Paddy both valued talk over work, turning their underground chambers into forums. Clearly, their brothers and sisters had to work, literally filling in the continent from coast to caost. Leprechauns did not break copper-bearing rock, smelt ore, fabricate it, heat and hammer copper into high-pressure steam ducts, or strand wire on poles along endless miles of transcontinental tracks. Do we demean our twin bards for their laziness or honor them for their verbal artistry? Did not their wit disclose the core values of Butte's workers?

Conscious that complete answers to such questions about hard rock storytellers are beyond our ken, I put aside the various aids that have helped me both descend into Butte's rocky stopes and escape from Matty and Paddy's narrative labyrinths. The maze is not totally mysterious; the worker who talks is not entirely doomed to false steps; the laborlore explorer is not always lost in the realm of fantasy.

Within "Marcus Daly Enters Heaven," Paddy Burke revealed that St. Peter had not received many ten-day stiffs (itinerant miners) from Butte. Neither miner or mucker has joined the tunnel stiff John Henry or the songsmith-organizer Joe Hill in the parade of folk exemplars. Nevertheless, I hope that Burke and Kiely have met in a workers' Valhalla—perhaps the fairest copper mine in the sky. Their ideological differences ought not to prevent them from swapping stories wherever they rest. On a silent day, with the buzzy drills down and the gallows-frame sheave wheels still, we should hear Paddy and Matty chortling as they tarry together within sight of the throne.

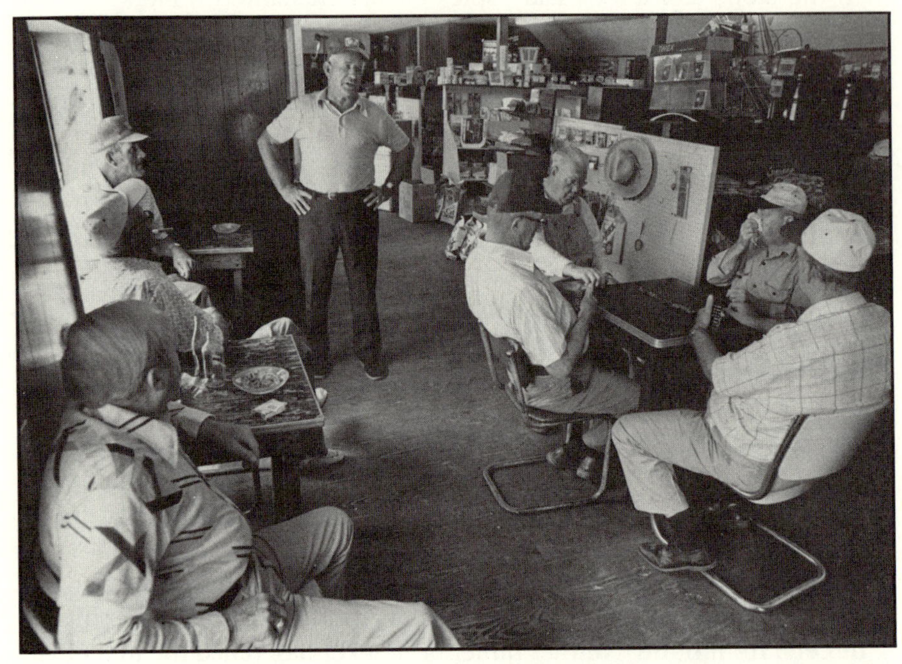

Yarning and playing dominoes

# 6

# Home-Front Harassment

In recent years, feminists have called attention to on-the-job sexual harassment, generally within the white-collar or professional sector. In addition women entering the blue-collar trades have been burdened by a heavy load of macho mores and have responded with various techniques to educate job toughs. Contemporary artists working in graphics, film, and fiction have also commented on such degrading practices, whether at office, factory, or construction site. Together, these activists and artists point to needed change.

Given the constant rise throughout the United States in women's numbers within the work force, their deployment throughout industry, and their battles for job equality, I turn my attention to gender-based occupational tradition. Presumably, jokes told by men about home-front harassment have been and will be inverted to suit women's needs. Such lore, captured in print and film, may reveal both continuity in the response to unresolved tension and discontinuity in the perception of problems across gender's fence.

In eras past, families in blue-collar occupations faced harassment at home—among other things, in the form of bosses imposing themselves on workers' wives. Unable always to respond directly, some aggrieved husbands channeled their concerns into song, jest, or acecdote. Individuals who shared such lore moved imaginatively from the mine mouth or factory gate to the parlor and bedroom. Stories told largely by men to men revealed particular work patterns and assumed that the auditors knew something about the actual time and place for each narrative.

American union members absorbed a few harassment yarns and used them didactically to demonstrate the need for organization. Whether told as "straight" work jokes or as part of labor's soapbox oratory, these jests held ancient notions of seigniorage or seignorial rights. Starkly put, some feudal lords had asserted—beyond their claims to land, manor, or coinage—the power to intrude on their subjects before or during the bridal night. I shall not trace the history of *droit de seigneur,* or "first night," lore; rather, I turn directly to a baker's dozen of narratives—twelve brief stories and a single blues text. Within this group, all thirteen items touch sex at home; eleven hold together by an ironic punchline, rationalizing guilt and impotence.

Karl Kortum, chief curator of San Francisco's National Maritime Museum, has conducted a long series of interviews with Pacific Coast seamen as part of an "Annals" project. During 1977, he talked with Art Matson, a "crusty old Finn" and a veteran of California's steam schooner lumber trade. Matson had broken in when "old salts" made the transition from sail to steam. Hundreds of schooners—two, three, and four masters—carried timber from the north coast to San Francisco. The proverbial saying "wooden ships and iron men" made sense in the redwood country's exposed anchorages (dog-hole ports) where sailors used chutes from cliffs and dangerous aerial tramways to take lumber aboard (Kemble; Olmsted).

Sandwiched in Matson's account, we find a self-contained anecdote, "Sailors with a Hook in Their Pocket":

> You could tell them walking around on the wharves. They were all bent over from packing those heavy redwood ties. Some of them were married and some would brag about how they could trust their wives—the wife would be down on the dock giving the breadwinner a big send-off.
>
> The stream schooner would put out to sea. The engine was just a coffee grinder in the small ones. They get outside bucking into those northwesterly summer trade winds and they couldn't get anywhere; the vessel would have to put back. So sometimes a fellow would be suddenly home again. And he would find that the wife that gave him the big send-off was not to be trusted. She was in bed with someone else.

> A big row follows. One of my shipmates got the worst of it. The visitor got insulted by the remarks that were made and ran the steam schooner sailor out of his own house.

Art Matson's matter-of-fact account parallels other stories, brief or extended, heard on thousands of jobs. It represents a class of narratives accepted as descriptive of marital infidelity. Note that the intruder goes unnamed. Is he another mariner, a neighbor, or the wife's steady lover? Whatever his status, the "visitor" not only breaks family codes but adds insult to injury by running the steam schooner man out of his own home.

In some circumstances, storytellers at work name their bosses as "love stealers," thus merging job and home advantages. One song example makes the point. During May 1969, Mike Leadbitter, an English discographer, visited Lake Charles, Louisiana, where he recorded Sidney Semien ("Rockin' Sidney") singing "Keep on Pushin'." Born in St. Landry Parish in 1938, Rockin' Sidney performed "swamp pop" music in dives, roadhouses, and bars catering mainly to blue-collar workers on the Louisiana-Texas Gulf Coast (Broven). Over the years, Rockin' Sidney boxed a regional compass (rock, soul, cajun, zydeco), achieving a massive hit in 1985 with "Don't Mess with My Toot Toot."

I have transcribed "Keep on Pushin' " from Leadbitter's *Nothing but the Blues* (CBS-UK 66278), a two-disc album released in 1971 as a companion to an anthology drawn from the magazine *Blues Unlimited*:

> While I'm out here workin',
> My fingers to the bone,
> My boss havin' coffee
> With my woman at home.
>
> Got to keep on pushin',
> Lord have mercy,
> 'Cause I'm just a workin' man, yes, I am.
> You see, I got a house full of children,
> And a hard-headed woman,
> Who just don't understand.
> It's so hard on me,
> I cough and sweat.

The more I work,
The harder it gets.

(Chorus)

Play it one more time (instrument break).

While I'm out here workin'
My fingers to the bone,
My boss's drinkin' coffee
With my woman at home.

(Final Chorus)

Folklorist Gary Smith, in Austin, Texas, called "Keep on Pushin' " to my attention, suggesting that similar songs might have been sung by Gulf Coast rockers. Particularly, he had heard T-Bone Walker, the influential Texas bluesman, voice a similar complaint. Following Gary's correspondence, I queried folklorist Barry Jean Ancelet of Lafayette, Louisiana, who, in turn interviewed Semien on December 2, 1990.

Twenty-one years elapsed between Mike Leadbitter's visit to Lake Charles and Ancelet's questions. Initially, Semien's recollection was vague. As the phrase "workin' my fingers to the bone" came to mind, he reported that the song commented on the offshore oil system of working seven days on the marine-drilling platform with seven days off at home. In short, Rockin' Sidney had described a local situation concerning oil workers without naming their industry. He knew that Gulf Coast roustabouts would make the right association for "out here workin' " (oil) and "havin' coffee" (sex). The latter euphemism has long circulated in blues songs: "Coffee Blues," " 'Bout a Spoonful," "All I Want Is a Spoonful."

In searching his memory for his song's setting, Semien also commented on a musician's occupational concern. He believed that he had given a copy of "Keep on Pushin' " to entrepreneur Eddie Shuler for publication, but he had never received a royalty payment from Shuler, Leadbitter, or anyone connected with CBS in England. No one had sent him *Nothing but the Blues*, the first "foreign" LP album to hold one of his songs.

My intitial interest in home-front harassment tales stemmed from the way they blend themes of sexual and economic exploitation. When Semien confided to Ancelet that he had never seen or heard his song on *Nothing but the Blues,* he jumped from a comment on an oil-drilling boss "drinkin' coffee" at a roughneck's home to the matter of recording bosses depriving musicians of their due.

I suspect that blues like "Keep on Pushin' " will yet be found in forms more elaborate than Semien's sparse text. Essentially, Rockin' Sidney repeated a gripe heard on many work sites: an exhausted worker pushes himself on the job; his boss, presumably relaxed and vigorous, pushes coffee and himself at the worker's home. Sidney's lament is so elemental as to defy rhetorical elaboration or moral summation.

A key difference between Matson's anecdote and Semien's blues lies in the intruder: in the former, he is an unnamed stranger; in the latter, the worker's boss. Although Rockin' Sidney's narrator knows his exploiter and the steam schooner sailor does not identify his wife's visitor, both workers are humiliated. At some point, men who heard tales similar to this song and this story took such accounts of betrayal and tacked on a moral either to assuage pain, to rationalize their low status, or to characterize employers.

More than a century ago, immigrant hard rock miners from Cornwall acquired the nickname "Cousin Jacks." Fanning out from Michigan across the Rockies to California's Sierras, they carried Old World lore West, refashioning elements to fit their new circumstances. Among their stock of occupational humor, they relished stories of buddies going home from work to find amatory adventurers in their bedrooms.

At times, Cousin Jacks keyed such accounts to long-held superstitious beliefs: if a miner's candle goes out three times, or falls off the underground chamber's rock face, he had better run home to catch a love intruder. Similarly, when the mine blacksmith's apron strings came untied, the loosening augured that someone was home making love to his wife.

Miners with skill in storytelling honed such candle beliefs through transatlantic passage and generational span. Over the decades, some anecdotes dropped their superstitious elements on moving away from mining country. In the shift of hard rock lore across boundaries of craft, particular items acquired new regional, rhetorical, ethnic, and ethical overtones. Readers will note that, regardless of other altered elements, editors often bowdlerized cuckold tales. A sexually explicit story may be cleansed when told to an outside collector or toned down by the latter for publication.

The following narrative cluster comprising home-front harassment episodes touches on varied occupations and chronologies. I note that workers have used many different terms to name their tales—among them, *story, yarn, joke, windy, lie.* In my sequence, the collectors have named three items (# 4, # 9, and # 10). I supply the remaining eight titles. The list opens arbitrarily with the oldest joke defined by trade and time rather than with the first in print.

## In Sequence

*1. Perfic Stranger*

In California in the early days [of gold mining, Judge William C. Matthews worked] in a mine with a Cousin Jack—J. W.—when his companion's candle fell out of the wall three times. "Somebody 'ome with ole woman," J. W. remarked, laying down his tools and leaving the drift. Much to Judge Matthews's surprise, in about half an hour, J. W. was back to work. Judge Matthews inquired about his visit home, imagining that all was well. But J. W. confessed that the candle was right. "What did you do?" asked Matthews, startled. "Nuthin'," was the answer. " 'Ee was a perfic stranger to me." (*Source:* Caroline Bancroft, "Folklore of the Central City District, Colorado," *California Folklore Quarterly* 4 [1945]: 332.)

*2. Jacky 'arris 'ad a Wife*

"A chap from 'ome called Jacky 'arris 'ad a wife," Tabey would recount. "She got keepin' company on the sly with a chap called Sammy Scadden. She tried to 'ide what she was carrying on but folks soon found out about it and took 'er to task. Told 'er she was doin' 'arm to 'erself and 'er 'usband. She up an told 'em to go to 'ell! Finally Jacky 'erd 'bout it. Jacky was some tearin' 'ostile. When 'e failed to act in the matter, some of 'is friends says to 'im—What are thee going do 'bout it, Jacky? Why don't thee tell this Scadden chap to lay off?"

" 'Ow in 'ell can I do that,' says Jacky—'th' bloomin' blighter is a perfect stranger to me'!" (*Source:* Joseph Duffy, *Butte Was Like That* [1941], 96.)

3. *Going to the Ball Game*

A very docile male office wage slave developed a yen to have the afternoon off. He had noticed others getting time off by saying they were fairly well caught up with their work and wanted to go to the ball game. He made the same pitch, and it worked. However, he was not interested in ball games and soon went home. He opened the front door quietly and saw his boss making love to his wife on the davenport. Quietly and quickly he closed the door and went to the ball game, feeling lucky his boss had not caught him in a lie. (*Source:* told by Fred Thompson to Archie Green in Chicago, November 22, 1959.)

4. *Six Twelves*

Oh, this is an old ethnic joke. When they used to have—at one time, years and years ago—the foreman on the job, the line foreman, could hire and fire people.

So Toivo and Waino—and this is supposed to be a true story—Toivo and Waino and all them guys are working underground. And they worked like six twelves, that's six days a week, twelve hours a day. And on Saturday night, they'd close the mine. Saturday afternoon shift was the last one and at midnight they'd close the mine until Monday at six. So them guys had a part of a day off.

Well Toivo was going to leave early on Saturday night. And this is true. Or supposed to be true. This is passed on. And Toivo left at ten o'clock. And he went to his house, which is an Oliver house that U.S. Steel had built and all of this shit. And he went home, and he walked in the door quietly. He was going to surprise his wife. And there was this foreman banging his old lady.

He looked in. "Oh my god." He ran back to the job. He told the guys on the job, he says: "Kot tammit, I come close. I almost got caught leaving early."

And that's supposed to be true. Now whether it is, I don't know or not, but that's one of them that tells how scared they were. These were line foremen, not superintendents or anything. These were just your foremen on the job that you were working on.

That's getting back in the olden days, but that's the stories that we hear, and we catch onto, and we love. (*Source:* James Leary, *Midwestern Folk Humor* [1991], 170; collected from Frank Strukel at Hoyt Lakes, Minnesota, August 4, 1978.)

5. *Anudder Stunt*

Ole and Lars worked on a construction crew. One day Lars noticed that the foreman always left the project about an hour early. "Say Ole," suggested Lars. "Why don't WE take off a little early too . . . yust like da foreman." So they agreed to try it. As soon as Ole got home, he looked all over for Lena. Finally he opened the bedroom door . . . and there she was in bed with the foreman. Ole silently closed the door and tiptoed out of the house. The next day he confronted Lars. "Ve better not try anudder stunt like ve did yesterday. I almost got caught." (*Source:* E. C. "Red" Stangland, *Grandson of Norwegian Jokes* [1982], 10.)

6. *Afraid of His Boss*

Ole was terribly afraid of his boss, so one day when he felt sick, and a fellow worker suggested he go home, he said, "Oh, I couldn't do dat. Da boss vould fire me." "Don't be silly," said Ole's friend. "He'll never know. He's not even in the office today."

So Ole went home. When he got to his house, he looked in the window, and there was his boss, passionately kissing his wife, Lena.

Racing back to the office, he rushed up to his friend. "A fine friend yew are, giving me dat advice!!" he shouted, "I nearly got caught!" (*Source:* Charlene Powers, *The New Uff-Da* [1978], 51.)

7. *Office Fool*

The office fool sneaks home during working hours for a short nap, having been out gambling the night before. He comes back unexpectedly soon and confides to an office-mate, "Boy, did I just have a narrow escape! When I walked in the house, there was the boss screwing my wife. But I tiptoed out without him noticing I wasn't on the job." (*Source:* Gershon Legman, *Rationale of the Dirty Joke* [1968], 736; heard in New York, 1940.)

*8. Punching Out*

This goes back before there was a union at Dodge Main [Hamtramck, Michigan]. The first part is serious, and no exaggeration. Auto workers suffered great indignities at the hands of bosses. Some workers brought wine and fruit baskets to the plant. They'd do favors to hold jobs. Some would paint a foreman's house or cut the grass. Some foremen at Ford sold cars to their workers. Some bosses would ask favors of a worker's wife. That leads to a story.

Some of you may have heard of Dick Frankensteen, the big guy, our organizer at Chrysler. He headed the independent union at the Dodge Main Plant. Dick told this story while organizing:

The Dodge Main Plant was massive—at least half a mile long. In those days, lot a people lived in the neighborhood and could punch in and out for lunch. One day, a worker from the neighborhod wanted to slip away early. He asked his buddy to punch him out, and said he'd get back to punch in before the end of lunchtime. The buddy agreed, and this guy slipped away, easing down and through the gate. He walked home and found the house quiet. Going upstairs, he found his wife in bed with the superintendent. He didn't say a word. Instead, he snuck down the stairs quietly, returned to the plant and punched in.

Next day, his buddy asked: "Do you want me to punch you out again?" The worker replied, "Hell, No! I almost got caught yesterday." (*Source:* told by Douglas Fraser, former president of the United Automobile Workers of America, at the fiftieth anniversary of UAW Local 72, Kenosha, Wisconsin, May 11, 1985; transcribed by Archie Green from a cassette tape recorded by Joe Glazer.)

*9. The Men Who Went Back*

Down on the 1400 East, a crew of copper miners and muckers in Butte take five on their shift boss's departure. They talk about the war in Europe, President Wilson's engagement, and town happenings. The genial Malone lights a cigarette from a candle and opens his story with a night shift stunt of some years ago.

A couple of yaps—Smith, married, and boarder Brown, single—work in a very small mine, the old Clark Fraction. Their foreman, a night rider, dates the frisky Mrs. Smith. Feeling that he has put the Indian sign on his men by laying out more work than the partners can handle each night, the foreman leaves the Fraction for hijinks at the Smith cottage.

Storyteller Malone, absorbed in his narrative, lets his dream punk go out. Fellow miner Barney passes his candle to Malone, who relights his cigarette and picks up the tale's thread.

With no one present to keep tab on their work, the partners take up lunch buckets and candlesticks, climb the ladder, and make a quiet dive for home. Nearing Smith's house, they hear laughter and see a parlor light. Stepping softly on the porch, they peek into the window, viewing their Old Romeo foreman in his ardent moves.

Barney interrupts to ask, "Did Smith and Brown break in on the family buster and finish him off?" Malone retorts, "No, they ran for it." Barney, incredulous, asks again, "Did they go back for powder [dynamite] to blow up the love birds?" Malone ends sarcastically, "Like hell they went for powder." They returned to finish out the shift and not get caught quitting before tally! (*Source:* Joseph Duffy, *Butte Was Like That* [1941], 308–13; paraphrased by Archie Green from Duffy's short story.)

*10. Fooling the Captain*

The iron miners used to use lard-oil lamps—medium thick oil made a big flame in the wick. The superstition was that if the miner's lamp went out, trouble was brewing and he'd better get out and go home. Alfred Penpraze's lamp went out so he climbed up to the surface and went home. He noticed a light in the kitchen and the bedroom, peeked in the window, and saw his wife had company—the captain of the mine. Alfred immediately returned to work, and reported to the boys. "Well, I fooled Captain Dick tonight. He doesn't know that I saw 'im 'ome there with my missus." (*Source:* Richard Dorson, "Dialect Stories of the Upper Peninsula," *Journal of American Folklore* 61 [1948]: 137; collected from Walter Gries, Ishpeming, Michigan, May 17, 1946.)

*11. How the Union Came to Aliquippa*

During the Blue Eagle period (1934–35), the old Amalgamated (Association of Iron, Steel & Tin Workers) came to life in western Pennsylvania. Former AA members rejoined their old lodges, and new members began to sign up. However, the Jones & Laughlin plant at Aliquippa was very tough. Its bosses scared most of the workers by threatening them if they joined the union.

One day, Pete, an Italian puddler, felt rough and went home early. When he got to his house and opened the door, he found it very quiet. Looking around, Pete found the mill boss in the bedroom humping his wife. This enraged Pete; after he beat up the boss and tossed him out of the house, he walked down to the Amalgamated and signed up.

The next day, he organized his gang. These men soon spread the good word through the whole J & L plant. And that's how the union came to Aliquippa! (*Source:* told by Emory Bacon, United Steelworkers of America educational department, to Archie Green at Madison, Wisconsin, November 18, 1959; written from memory by Green, October 26, 1986.)

## Spiderweb of Complexity

During my years in the maritime and building trades, nearly all crews in which I worked included a joker, though I never met a job clown who arranged jokes in any particular sequence or labeled them by numbers. A few gifted individuals knew more stories than Scheherazade, telling them constantly to amuse their mates or to comment on their work's flow. Many jobs also included a "sourpuss" hostile to humor or a "dimwit" who asked plaintively, "What's the joke?" This latter query helped the tellers amplify their meaning by explanation and stimulated the listeners to offer their variants.

With a harvest of harassment jokes at hand, I faced the necessity of placing them in some kind of order. Two chronological schemata arose: placement by date of collection/publication and by internal reference to time setting. I shared this problem of arrangement with Roger Renwick at the University of Texas, who suggested a logic geared to the human relationships revealed within the narratives.

In these jokes and minitales, workers (husbands) and bosses (lovers) are unequal, not only by virtue of economic function, but also by cultural judgment. Bosses force husbands to rationalize cuckoldry, thus distorting or displacing the self-esteem of the losers. In contemporary parlance, workers became wimps. To open: a Cousin Jack gold miner calls on a social imperative to mask his passivity—one does not speak to strangers without a proper introduction.

Professor Renwick suggests that many of the joke's various carriers had moved away from rules of etiquette to transitional forms of rationalizing unequal status. The condition of not liking baseball games—a type of American deviance—renders powerless the "docile slave" within Fred Thompson's soapbox story. Other "wage slaves" became equally incapacitated by virtue of their stupidity, which at times correlates to ethnicity. The immigrant's cultural impotence reinforces his economic weakness. Together, both lacks lead of sexual misfortune.

At some point in the harassment joke's circulation, a Pennsylvania narrator rejected his unequal status by refusing to accept his inadequacy. This storyteller turned to an overt ideological statement combining masculine and economic pride. Steel puddler Pete, my final tale's hero, negates cuckoldry by thrashing his boss and helping to organize an Aliquippa union. Such a march from docility to direct action under CIO banners made sense to those auditors who believed that steps to collective behavior held inherent value.

No particular ordering of narratives is intrinsically superior to others. Roger Renwick and I offer a progression from powerlessness to empowerment. The initial character, the gold miner named J. W., appeals to conventional manners to cover his loss of honor. Heroic Pete, in the last tale, reverses this role to assert his identity as a husband and member of a labor community. Of course, readers will freely develop alternate sequences for these eleven items. I illustrate contrasting possibilities of arrangement by time, place, or craft in table 1.

My chart reveals the difficulties in any sequences established by scholars. Obviously, chronology breaks down when raconteurs place their anecdotes in the distant past without specifying dates. For example, Frank Strukel (who told "Six Twelves" to the collector Jim Leary) established his story's time setting as "years and years ago." He might have specified the period before the strike of 1908 or 1912 on the Mesabi Range.

Listeners in Strukel's occupational and regional communities

Table 1

| Story | Time | Place | Job Site |
|---|---|---|---|
| 1. Perfic | pre-1900 | California | gold mine |
| 2. Jacky 'arris | unknown | Montana | copper mine |
| 3. Ball Game | pre-1934 | unknown | office |
| 4. Six Twelves | pre-1912 | Minnesota | iron mine |
| 5. Stunt | unknown | South Dakota | building project |
| 6. Afraid | unknown | North Dakota | office |
| 7. Fool | 1940 | New York | office |
| 8. Punching Out | 1935 | Michigan | auto plant |
| 9. Went Back | pre-1917 | Montana | copper mine |
| 10. Fooling | unknown | Michigan | iron mine |
| 11. Aliquippa | 1935 | Pennsylvania | steel mill |

gained their time clue from two references: his claims that foremen had been free to fire people at will and that miners worked "six twelves," or seventy-two hours a week. Strukel, a union loyalist conversant with labor history, felt a greater need to mark exploitation by the United States Steel Corporation than to specify a date already part of the consciousness of his peers.

Arrangement by geographic distribution holds its own snares. Joe Duffy mentioned particular Butte mines as the settings for the copper tales he related. Richard Dorson presented "Fooling the Captain" within a collection of Upper Peninsula lore. By contrast, the construction and office items from the Dakotas appeared in Norwegian joke collections. In short, "Anudder Stunt" and "Afraid of His Boss" functioned in an ethnic context with little stress on job site or craft. Further, we can assume that Norwegian dialect acecdotes moved readily across state boundaries in the Midwest.

Table 1 offers a quick overview of certain relationships in these eleven jests; at the same time, it masks problems in theme, motif, and setting. Five jokes come from mining and three from office work. Despite the latters' white-collar association and the far greater number of women working at such sites, the office items have moved away from the extractive industries without reference to working women. Where do we find evidence that women inverted home-front harassment anecdotes to fit their perspective?

Some readers will be especially interested in the joke's tie to the superstitious belief involving the snuffing out of a miner's candle. Three of the eleven tales touch on this belief; it has dropped out of the other variants. Wayland Hand, in reference to "Perfic Stranger," noted that American miners throughout the West knew the candle superstition. Hand also felt that it had been carried to the United States from Cornwall, but he could not document its actual transatlantic passage (1942, 135; 1946, 18). Without such evidence, we can also posit origin in the United States for this particular belief.

Professor Hand noted that candles "went out" because of "poor air" (life-threatening gas). A miner's maxim made the point: "If your candle goes out, you go out too." In some instances, safety inspectors closed mines after detecting gas. This combination of danger and pay loss signaled by the warning omen constituted bad luck. Somehow, at a time beyond recall, job disaster merged with domestic anxiety. By extension, the candle augury came to mark trouble in the bedroom.

Perhaps the connection of a lifeless candle to sexual loss can be traced elsewhere than to a Cornish tin mine. Various metaphoric usages offer leads. "The Barnyards of Delgaty," a Scottish bothy ballad, reports a farmworker's exploits. After boasting of his many lusty capacities, he concludes, "My candle it is burned out" (Ord). This parallels the wastrel's confession, "I've burned my candle at both ends." The child's riddle ("Little Miss Etticote / In her white petticoat / And a red nose / The longer she glows / The shorter she grows") can be tied to fear of vitality's extinction (Taylor, 221). Renwick adds a note from his McGill student days in Canada: *wick* was a vernacular term for penis. We can only guess that such ballads, riddles, or speech stood behind the Cousin Jack superstition linking a guttered candle to polyandric passion or sexual exploitation.

With or without the candle motif, the gathered harassment anecdotes (except Aliquippa) all hinge on a worker sighting an intruder and retreating ignominiously. No matter how the husband rationalizes his weakness, he seeks cover, a pseudovictory. He can grovel to save his job at any cost, he can don a fig leaf of manners, or he can seek a bit of status by implying that he fooled the boss.

With all these ploys, however, the cuckold does not escape his fate.

Gershon Legman's "Office Fool" focuses on the weak husband, a nincompoop who seemingly connives at his wife's adultery. Legman hears the joke as a vehicle formalizing the fool's withdrawal in the boss's favor (736). Joe Duffy's "Jacky 'arris" reinforces the notion of open cuckoldry. When Mrs. 'arris's neighbors take her to task for an affair with Sammy Scadden, she retorts, "go to 'ell." Her defiance of conventional mores emphasizes her husband's impotence.

Some listeners hear anecdotal humor within singular frames. For them, each joke has but one message. Other auditors revel in a spiderweb of complexity, interweaving analysis suggested by Freud, Marx, and Lévi-Strauss. However, workers need not fall back on academic savants to extract significance from their occupational lore. At this juncture, I note that four of these raconteurs (Frank Strukel, Fred Thompson, Douglas Fraser, and Emory Bacon) were labor activists who by direction or implication used the joke to contrast harassment/weakness with unionism/strength.

Fred Thompson's "Going to the Ball Game" holds special merit in that he identified it as a Wobbly soapbox story. I first heard him spin it during a 1959 visit at his home in Chicago. In a Bastille Day letter (1984), he supplied contextual details. Fred had adapted the baseball story from fellow worker Frank Cedervall's enactment at the American Stove Company's main gate in Cleveland, 1934.

Interestingly, neither Fred nor Frank located the narrative within the factory they sought to organize for the Industrial Workers of the World. Rather, they set it in an office—perhaps to suggest that white-collar clerks were even more docile than blue-collar metal fabricators. In this way, the soapboxers may have tried to deflect the sense of weakness held by the stove company's "wage slaves."

Wobbly stories combined hortatory messages with flamboyant rhetoric. The soapboxer expanded or contracted his account to hold the attention of street casuals or busy workers entering the plant. In turn, each narrative became a prelude to a class conscious appeal. We can be certain that Cedervall and Thompson, in telling

"Going to the Ball Game," subordinated the matter of domestic dalliance to that of their ultimate cause: One Big Union. It is our loss that we lack tape recordings of IWW soapbox oratory. However, a Swedish film, Bo Widerberg's *Joe Hill,* depicts such a street-corner happening.

We can visualize soapboxing with literal imagery—stout wooden box, solitary orator, eager crowd. Nonetheless, I caution readers that articulate workers also harangued their mates in factory aisles, on loading docks, at watercoolers, and during hatch cover and tarpaulin muster meetings—in essence, wherever an opinionated soul commanded an audience. A cynical auto worker (during a brief Illinois gab fest) called such talkers *Calhouns,* after the loquacious "sea lawyer" in radio's *Amos and Andy.*

Douglas Fraser made labor cause soapboxing explicit in attributing "Punching Out" to Dick Frankensteen, who had organized the Dodge Main Plant at Hamtramck prior to the UAW's affiliation with the CIO. Because the UAW has encouraged its members to preserve their past, we can reconstruct the setting for Fraser's anecdote. When Kenosha auto workers celebrated their anniversary, John Drew edited an attractive thirty-six-page illustrated booklet entitled *UAW Local 72: The First 50 Years.*

Drew outlined shifts from early Nash cars to the Nash-Kelvinator merger, to the American Motors Corporation, and finally, to AMC's merger with Renault. UAW history is available; here, I note only one Kenosha detail: in December 1944, a few workers asked union permission to collect funds for a foreman's Christmas present. Local officer George Molinaro reminisced: "A request like this recalls the old basket brigade of 10 years ago before the union was formed. Those were the days when you had to bring a gallon of wine, a goose, a turkey, or a quart of whiskey to your boss in order to hold your job. Those days are gone forever" (23).

Under many names, the basket brigade remains embedded in UAW tradition: the old days of currying favor balanced against the union days of personal dignity. Opening his story at Kenosha with workers carrying baskets to the Dodge factory, Fraser concluded with a superintendent's amatory privilege. Dick Frankensteen had used this harassment narrative of inequality to organize Dodge in the mid-1930s. At the same time, Aliquippa steel mill hands refashioned the tale to favor a battler fighting for honor on the job and at home. Three decades after hearing this steel story, I corresponded with its teller, Emory Bacon. As a young man he had lived in Duquesne, a Carnegie-Illinois mill town. Joining the SWOC staff (Steel Workers Organizing Committee) in 1936, he heard Aliquippa workers describe the coercive power of their "American" bosses.

I return to iron miner Frank Strukel, having previously noted that he placed his story in the bad "olden days." Beyond establishing this time setting, Frank related that Toivo and Waino went home to an "Oliver house that U.S. Steel had built and all of this shit." Readers distant from the Mesabi Range may catch the reference to company housing in Oliver but be puzzled by the expletive. Oliver housing was notorious for lacking insulation, a particularly significant deprivation in the cold Minnesota winters. Collector Leary suggests multiple purposes within Strukel's tale. Without naming his own union, the United Steelworkers of America, or mentioning previous labor organizations on the Mesabi Range, Strukel described dismal working conditions as he vented his anger against powerful line foremen.

In addition, Strukel, a Slovenian-American, touched on the problem of internal differences within the work force by making "kot tammit" Finns the butt of his joke. Leary elaborates that Toivo and Waino, like the Irish clods Pat and Mike, were stock characters in Finnish-American humor. The Iron Range work force represented a totem pole of ethnicity—Finns, Italians, and Slavs at the bottom, Cousin Jacks from Cornwall at the top.

In reading Strukel's "Six Twelves," we cannot overlook the fact that many unionists though committed to economic solidarity and participatory politics, do not blanch at ethnic or dialect humor. In short, a joke accepted by some listeners in psychological terms, and by some with reference to matters of social justice, reaches others by appeal to feelings of ethnic separation. It is likely that on-the-job humor will persist in interweaving these strands.

Jim Leary has cautioned me that ethnic on-the-job jokes hold considerable ambiguity, veering from rank discrimination to egalitarian camaraderie. Who has not heard "dumb bohunk," "stupid kraut," "egg-sucking frog," "bloody limey," or similar pejoratives exchanged at work? With our present-day sensitivity, we take offense. Over the years, such handles accompanied the give-and-take of immigrant adjustment within industry and urban community. Some newcomers groped for solidarity in trade unionism; others, rejected and excluded, found no home in the labor movement.

I turn again to the implicit questions raised on many jobs when workers joke about sneaking home, nearly getting caught, or fooling the boss. Do we hear such home harassment narratives only as reporting the weakness of husbands? Alternatively, do we view such tales in a spiderweb of meaning—one that reveals intertwined sexual and economic exploitation, as well as coping mechanisms developed over the centuries by working people?

## To Slay the Dragon

The readers of this book remain free to pose their own questions and to draw their own conclusions as they encounter apocryphal harassment anecdotes. Depending on our personal stance, we assign rival meanings to given jokes within psychological, social, aesthetic, and ethical bounds. Besides performing many other functions, joking serves to cope with the worker's worry about the stability of family life or anger at the authority of bosses. In part, our baker's dozen of minitales excite the imagination precisely because love and work intersect to shape identity.

Here, I interject a job aphorism I heard while learning the shipwright's trade. Many of Local 1149's members, despite their belief in solidarity, felt superior to surrounding craft mechanics. To explain the conditions of the less fortunate (fitter, flanger, chipper, welder, burner, painter, rigger—the list stretches endlessly), my journeymen teachers asserted that other craftsment lacked competence both in bed and on the job. We labled these bumblers "Joe McGees."

When I objected to such a broad generalization, noting that boilermakers and loftsmen matched our skills, my mentors dismissed these protestations. Without invoking the names of these seers, they integrated the essentials of Marx and Freud. My shipwright teachers, drawing on experiential wisdom, offered this advice: to avoid disorder, you have to function equally well in the realms of affection and toil.

By this standard, the two workers introduced in the opening

Louisiana blues lyrics and the California waterfront anecdote do not pass muster. Rockin' Sidney's hero in "Keep on Pushin' " loses status and bliss, for he cannot go beyond verbal job complaint to take action at home. Similarly, Art Matson's steam schooner sailor fails when a rival runs him out of his own domicile. In short, working your fingers to the bone or walking bent over from packing redwood ties cannot ensure job prestige in the face of disaster at home.

Somehow, the first storytellers who crafted home harassment jokes holding an ironic punchline brought bedroom anxiety into conjunction with everyday work tension. Because such humor bridged a gulf of feeling, listeners could simultaneously scorn and be sympathetic with "the husband who nearly got caught." Although those who observed the wretch could laugh at his predicament, he had very little room in which to maneuver. By rationalizing his powerlessness, the cuckold participated in his own unmanning. Put bluntly, he erected a personal guillotine.

At this juncture, we need a feminist reading or recasting of the harassment anecdotes. In the present variants, nearly all the wives are inanimate, except Mrs. Smith, who enjoys her fling with the Fraction's shift boss, and Mrs. Jacky 'arris, who guards her pleasure by rebuking copper camp gossips. The other wives serve as story props rather than developed subjects who might enact dreams, indulge in fantasy, or struggle to hold families intact despite proletarian indignities.

Another element in these gathered jokes calls for elaboration on the matter of provenance. I have already noted Wayland Hand's assumption of their movement from Britain to America and my inability to confirm his hypothesis. In 1986, C. Banc and Alan Dundes collaborated in a collection of political jokes from Romania. One gag—not a developed narrative—follows:

> Popescu talks with his friend.
>
> "You know what happened to me last night? I came home and found my wife in bed with a Russian officer."
>
> "What did you do?"
>
> "I tiptoed out, of course. I was lucky. He didn't see me." (107)

Wherever the Red Army ruled, such political jokes have lived underground. Banc and Dundes cite several parallels from East Germany and Czechoslovakia published between 1965 and 1980. I leave to others the intriguing question of dissemination's path. Did the joke travel east and west from Cornwall, or did it originate in the United States and fly to Europe, perhaps as late as World War II?

Another matter open to exploration is that of structure. Popescu's sparse joke makes its point with but forty-two words. By contrast, Joe Duffy stretches "The Men Who Went Back" into a short story of more than 2,000 words. He employs an excellent framing device in telling about a crew of miners and muckers "down on the 1400 East, where the heat was intense and the air was foul and almost suffocating." As narrator Duffy pictures the crew "goofing off," miner Malone horns in on the conversation. This genial Celt then launches into the "not getting caught" adventure. Duffy retires, Malone performs, and we learn the cuckold's fate.

Previously, in my chapter on copper bards, I noted this story-within-a-story technique. Harry McClintock had described Paddy Burke's adventures in a Butte stope before Burke himself took up his tale about Marcus Daly. Douglas Fraser, a union president and skilled public speaker, also calls on this time-tested form. He warms his Kenosha audience by recalling basket brigadeers currying favor. "Some bosses would ask favors of a worker's wife. That leads to a story." At this point, Fraser discards the shell for the kernel—Frankensteen's organizational narrative from Hamtramck.

Good jokes and wandering yarns attract varied interpretations: comparativist, structuralist, feminist, psychological, socioeconomic. I return to Fred Thompson's worldview categorizing workers as "rebels" or "slaves." In reality, many individuals balanced these attributes. The meekest "slave" can deflect pain with humor to face each workday as it dawns. The job militant externalizes feeling by direct action and by advocacy of solidarity with sisters and brothers. Ultimately, each bit of joke lore helps workers sort their bedrock attitudes on questions of job power, as well as on the potent role of work in shaping family mores.

Most present-day work sites include storytellers of some skill. Such everyday entertainers—at the photocopier or the watercooler—hear old tales circulate and take pleasure in recycling them to fit new situations. Who can add variants to this chapter's home-front harassment examples?

In a 1991 letter, Robert McCarl alerted me to a variant involving a job mate rather than worker and boss. Fire fighters tell of an off-duty stud who sends his own company out on a false alarm. This ploy gives the perpetrator time for an uninterrupted visit with an on-duty man's wife. Behind the tale, we hear tones of twined rule breaking—false alarm, cuckoldry. Who knows other stories of up-to-date encounters that move from computer room to tract condo rather than from fire station to bungalow or from metal mine to company shack?

Essentially, working people create and cherish a cornucopia of lore: ballad, blues, belief, custom, corrido, gesture, yarn, rap, button, banner. Within its multiple forms, a well-wrought jest serves as a bargaining ploy and survival instrument. Workers diminish their power to shape institutions and lives by allowing lore to fall into hidden corners. Some expressive material must be lost as cultural norms change. To discard folkloric items merely because of age or fashion robs working people of their tools and weapons.

Many workers have learned, at times at great cost, that we strengthen ourselves by clinging to imaginative aids created in times past. Trade unionists, as well as their unorganized allies, possess a bountiful heritage in memory, anthology, sound and film vault, archive file, or museum case. Their treasures are abundant. Within the body of lore at hand, these acecdotes touching on home-front harassment in the past can function again to slay the dragon of exploitation.

**"Stand by the Workmen at Homestead"**

# 7

# Homestead's Strike Songs

Across our land, memorable names mark trade union cataclysms: Homestead, Gastonia, Ludlow, Lawrence, Calumet, Paterson, Pullman, Flint. At times, we subordinate place to event—Memorial Day Massacre, Triangle Shirtwaist Fire—and invoke views of a meadow at South Chicago's edge or a loft in Manhattan's vertical canyons. Working people especially interested in institutional history string geographic sites into chronicles of courage and despair. A partisan reverently fingers place-name beads in a necklace of valor; another turns landmarks into a litany to cloak sorrow.

For many citizens, the word *homestead* conjures warmth and friendship in that it pictures an ancestral home, a pioneer farm, or a time of beginning. For some, the same word is cold and grim. It names the steel mill borough where Andrew Carnegie's hired Pinkertons murdered strikers, destroying their union in 1892. For a century, Pittsburgh's close neighbors in the Allegheny and Monongahela valleys functioned as America's most vital industrial center. Homestead's craftsmen and laborers fashioned plates to clad battleships and rails to span continents. Homestead's girders continue to support the Empire State Building and the Verazzano Narrows Bridge.

After 1892, Homestead epitomized big steel's muscle and labor's agony—inhumane hours, serfdom's wages, wretched housing, staggering tolls in injury and death. In 1919, when Mother Jones arrived to help "her boys," constables jailed her. Frances Perkins, Franklin Roosevelt's Secretary of Labor, addressed Homesteaders in 1933 from the steps of their post office after local authorities denied her access to the borough building for a town meeting. Not until formation of the CIO's Steel Workers Organizing Committee (SWOC) in 1936 did a band of courageous unionists establish a New Deal beachhead in "Mon Valley."

In 1986, the United States Steel Corporation changed its name to USX Corporation and, among other cutbacks, closed the Homestead works. During recent years, many satellite towns near Pittsburgh have become an industrial wasteland of rust and neglect. *Lightning over Braddock* documents the chilling regional scenes of weeds in deserted plants, boarded store fronts, and disbelieving workers at "fight-back" rallies. A few Homesteaders have campaigned to preserve their elegant Carnegie Library and to restore the Bost Building, the original 1892 strike headquarters. Today, no one can predict whether Pittsburgh steel will return to prosperity, which of the area's mill towns will live, or whether the preservationist strategies will meet with success.

A continent removed from the Monongahela, I unravel the story of Homestead's strike songs. It is not unusual for a dramatic strike to spark a journalistic ballad of limited circulation; however, such pieces infrequently become folksongs. Reconstructing the adventures of one topical number, I puzzle over the relationship of song lore study to efforts in historical preservation, and indeed, to the task of maintaining occupational communities.

## The Strike

As American colonists found iron ore deposits from Virginia to Massachusetts, they undertook metal manufacturing in primitive furnaces and forges. Hardwood-fired charcoal provided heat; water power drove hammers. In 1840, Lehigh Valley blast furnaces used anthracite coal successfully. The Civil War decade, with its insatiable demand for metal, served to expand tremendously the iron trades work force—puddlers, boilers, heaters, hookers, catchers, roughers, rollers. Even before the war, unorganized Pittsburgh puddlers, who converted pig into wrought iron, had engaged in brief strikes and secret meetings. In 1858, Pittsburgh iron makers formed their first stable local union, the Iron City Forge of the Sons of Vulcan. This group emerged during 1862 as a national organization, the Grand Forge of the United States, United Sons of Vulcan.

By 1876, the Vulcans and other craft groups combined into the strong Amalgamated Association of Iron and Steel Workers (Robinson). The AA grew steadily for but a decade before it roiled Andrew Carnegie, America's dominant industrialist, who had entered the iron business as a bridge builder in 1862. The Carnegie Steel Company, Limited, a vertical and integrated trust—ore mines, limestone deposits, coal fields, coke plants, steel mills, railroads, lake steamship lines—put aside its personal name in 1901 to become the United States Steel Corporation. Carnegie's growth had occurred when Bessemer steel making crowded iron maufacture into a background position because of advances in technology. Steel production first surpassed that of iron in 1892—the year of Homestead's bloody conflict.

Labor's defeat caught the imagination of outsiders who placed their findings in history books, academic theses, biographies, poetry, music, fiction, graphic art, and court cases. Homestead inspired immediate newspaper reporting and woodcut engravings in Gilded Age magazines. Reams of contemporary opinion by partisans of all hues and congressional reports added to the record. Arthur Burgoyne and Myron Stowell each published eye-witness histories in 1893. Two years later, the strike's first novel appeared, James Martin's *Which Way, Sirs, the Better? A Story of Our Toilers*. Haniel Long's *Pittsburgh Memoranda*, a 1935 book-length poem, in part reflected on Homestead. An educational film entitled *The Masses and the Millionaires: The Homestead Strike* (1974) reenacted the events; a TV documentary entitled *Turnaround* (1976) probed the strike's meaning.

An unintended monument had been "erected" in 1909 by the publication of Paul Kellogg's prefatory article, "The Pittsburgh Survey," in *Charities and the Commons*. With Pittsburgh's transition from Iron City to Steel City, the area's Calvinistic steelmasters had proved unable to make their city as "rational" as their mills. Thus, a group of social investigators "blue printed" Pittsburgh, seeking its "organic truth." The Russell Sage Foundation published findings (of Kellogg, John Fitch, Margaret Byington, Crystal Eastman, and Elizabeth Butler) in six volumes with complementary maps, charts, diagrams, tables, and superb photographs and drawings by, respectively, Lewis Hine and Joseph Stella. Today, some critics look back at *The Pittsburgh Survey* and fault its authors' optimism and reformism. However, no one can discount the trauma revealed by the text and illustrations in the study's many pages (McClymer).

John Bernard Hogg completed a University of Chicago thesis entitled "The Homestead Strike of 1892" (1943) which supplemented predecessor accounts by including his own interviews with strike veterans. Historian Henry David prepared concise reports (1952, 1964); Leon Wolfe followed with a popular overview (1965). Over the years, local newspapermen added rank-and-file memories to the record (Banik). Edward Bemis offered early academic analysis in 1894, setting a course for subsequent scholars (Brody, Cohen, Couvares, Demarest, Krause, Montgomery, Schneider).

Scholars touching on issues of class and culture see Homestead as both the quintessential labor-capital struggle in the United States and as a parade of tension. This latter figure implies marchers flaunting polar banners: skill/unskill, native/immigrant, despotism/dignity, plutocracy/republicanism. In this sense, some paraders broke ranks and altered their colors through the years, while others never abandoned their original visions.

During 1892, the strike's immediacy made exciting news far beyond Pittsburgh as the ordeal thrust itself on the consciousness of many commentators, including songwriters. No one knows how many stike songs reached print; I can cite twelve. We remember two: "Father Was Killed by the Pinkerton Men" and "A Fight for Home and Honor at Homestead, Pa." To place this pair in perspective, I summarize the event's highlights.

The Homestead Steel Works, nine miles upstream from Pittsburgh on the Monongahela River, had been organized by the Amalgamated Association. Although this set of artisans helped stabilize a competitive industry, steelmasters viewed the AA as a constant deterrent to improved technology, efficient production, and high profits. In 1889, the combined AA lodges (locals) had won a strike at the Homestead Works. Early in 1892, a corporate reorganization of various units into the Carnegie Steel Company brought Henry Clay Frick to the helm as the firm's new manager.

Some years previously, Frick had demonstrated his antilabor position by breaking a long coke strike of Connellsville miners. During March 1892, Carnegie decided to let his contract with eight Homestead lodges expire, and, on April 4, he drafted a notice to employees: "the firm cannot run Union and Non-Union. It must be either one or the other." Anticipating resistance, he ordered superintendent Potter to "roll a large lot of plates ahead . . . should the works be stopped for a time" (Bridge, 204). In the spring, Carnegie crossed the Atlantic for his annual vacation in Scotland, and Frick prepared for a showdown by having carpenters ring the mill with a stout timber fence.

Frick's military fence made visible the rumors about his secret arrangement with the Pinkerton National Detective Agency to hire 300 armed guards to protect the mill (at five dollars per head per day). On July 2, someone submitted a bit of doggerel, "The Fort That Frick Built," to the *Homestead Local News:*

Twix Homestead and Munhall
If you'll believe my word at all
Where once a Steel Work's noisy roar
A thousand blessings did out-pour
There stands today with great pretense
Enclosed within a white-washed fence
O wondrous change of great import
The mill transformed into a fort. (Demarest 1992, 49)

Labor economists have detailed Homestead's complicated pattern in collective bargaining. It based pay for iron workers on sliding scales that followed the market price of the muck bar, the product of the puddling furnace, and pay for steel workers on sliding scales that followed the price of the steel billet, the product of the converter. In retrospect, negotiations were futile, for the firm had determined to end bargaining with its men. The last actual sessions between Frick and the AA took place on June 23; on the evening of June 29 the great mill shut down; technically, a lockout began. Frick challenged the union to total surrender as he prepared to break the organization. Carnegie backed Frick in this rigid posture, although previously the magnate had written sanctimoniously on the sacred rights of workingmen to combine and to strike.

By 1892, the AA had organized eight hundred of the mill's skilled men, but in the face of Frick's layoffs, nearly three thousand helpers, day laborers, and ordinary mechanics joined hands with the craftsmen. Overnight, Frick forged a proto–industrial union and turned the lockout into a strike. Unwittingly, he also helped Welsh, Irish, and Slavic nationals—Protestant, Catholic, Orthodox—put aside their differences. Pickets ringed the fence that ringed the mill; the unionists deployed their side-wheeler *Edna* downstream to scout for hated "blacksheep" (scabs).

Before dawn, July 6, the tugboats *Little Bill* and *Tide* had towed the barges *Iron Mountain* (fitted out as a dormitory) and *Monongahela* (as a dining hall) upstream to the plant's edge. Each barge contained blue-clad, armed Pinkerton guards—a mix of regular hired guns and temporary strikebreaking riffraff. The battle commenced with barge landings. Homesteaders used small arms, stones, scrap iron, dynamite, burning oil, and an antique cannon; the guards used new Winchesters. By nightfall observers found ten dead combatants; no one counted the many wounded. (Reporters could not agree on total casualties from bullets, beatings, drownings, and suicide.) By nightfall, the workers possessed Carnegie's mill. Knowing its passages intimately, they had no trouble ensuring its safety. Homesteaders had long been accustomed to political office in the borough, maintaining law and order, and protecting their homes. Guarding the mill proved an exciting challenge.

Hugh O'Donnell, the young Irish heaterman who led the strike advisory committee, arranged a surrender by the Pinkerton guards. Decades later, workers retained brass "P" buttons and Winchester rifles as grim souvenirs of the river landing's battle. Trade unionism's memorabilia reduces violence to curious artifacts. Strikers burned the Pinkerton's barges with oil and ritualistic passion, but sad music marked the initial victory: "Dead March" at American funerals, strange dirges at Slavic funerals.

The workers' advisory committee governed the community for a few days, until Governor Robert Pattison sent in the Pennsylvania militia on July 12. Homestead's skilled crafsmen, subscribing to republican principles, felt free to defy industrial barons but ambivalent in the face of state power. A few unionists understood the militia's threat, while others could not believe that the government would turn against its own citizens. In effect, the strike ended with Pattison's decision, but the erosion of union power dragged on for more than four months. Incredibly, Pennsylvania prosecutors charged the disciplined and conservative craft leaders with riot, murder, conspiracy, and treason. While the unionists languished in jail, their funds ebbed away in costly legal defense.

On July 23, a tragic footnote underscored the strike's passion. Alexander Berkman, a young anarchist, attempted but failed to murder Henry Clay Frick in his Pittsburgh office. Berkman had identified with the workers; his action intensified pressure on strikers. While soldiers guarded the plant and the government upheld Carnegie's private rights against social rights for workers, Frick gradually recruited a new labor force. On July 22, scabs first appeared; on October 17, four union members broke ranks and returned to work. By November 18, the day laborers voted to return; two days later, the remnants of the once-powerful AA lodges gave up the strike. Needless to say, Charles Schwab, the new manager, blacklisted active unionists. The twelve-hour day, seven-days-per-week load and the unrelenting open shop became basic to steel's work pattern for decades to come.

Carnegie crushed unionism at Homestead, thereby setting unilateral standards throughout the industry until the mid-1930s, when John L. Lewis's voice and spirit boomed into Monongahela Valley company towns. On Independence Day, 1936, four thousand CIO-SWOC members celebrated the first open union meeting at Homestead since 1892. On Labor Day, 1941, Local 1397 dedicated a stone shaft showing a furnace charger at his task. A handful of Monongahela veterans who had repelled Pinkertons a half century before participated in the dedication. Beyond the obvious symbolism of unionism's rebirth in Carnegie country, this commenorative shaft fulfilled an idealistic promise in 1892 for a proposed monument to Homestead's heroes (Burgoyne 1979, 299).

## Plebeian Culture

Pinkerton buttons hidden in chests and inscribed statuary hold memory physically; another carrier of emotion, more volatile than brass or stone, is folksong. Historians find it easy to marshal a strike's drama into orderly sequences that reveal rhythms of cause and effect. Ballad scholars find it difficult to arrange subjects into neat chronologies or causal currents. Thus, I am challenged to place Homestead songs in their time setting and travel routes. With few exceptions, labor historians have neither encountered nor commented on steel's song lore.

From its beginning, Pittsburgh served as a frontier crossroads and emerging urban center. When backwoodsmen carried then-forming modes of Anglo-American folk balladry, hymody, and instrumental music across the Appalachian Divide, civic leaders in western towns reached back to the seaboard and to Europe for "proper" fare (Evanson, Stevens). The coal and iron industries brought workers from England, Scotland, and Ireland in the decades spanning the Civil War. Skilled Welsh and Cornish metal workers carried considerable cultural baggage: trade secrets, union loyalty, ethnic zeal, narrative art, time-tested music.

Folklorists often see culture through a geologist's eyes, alert to layered strata: elite, popular, folk, tribal. Social historians introduce other terms (*local, vernacular, plebeian*) to establish contrast with bourgeois culture. Francis Couvares helps us understand the Iron City's repertoire of venues and enactments: riverboat, circus ring, sports arena, singing society, art shop, brass band, freak show melodrama, temperance play, horse race, cock fight, baseball diamond, rowing club, fire company soirée. David Blyth's genre paintings illuminate Pittsburgh's plebeian culture as contemporaneous news accounts of Fourth of July parades detail the Iron City's expressive diversity.

Before the construction of the iron mills and glass factories that edged the Monongahela, the valley retained a bucolic flavor; a forest had blanketed the region for uncounted centuries. As late as 1879, Homestead held fewer than six hundred residents. In that year, several entrepreneurs incorporated the Pittsburgh Bessemer Steel Company; in 1880, mill executives secured a borough (municipal) charter; during 1883, Carnegie purchased the Homestead Works. Mill expansion turned Homestead into an industrial boomtown as it divided along ethnic and craft lines. Only in time of crisis did the necessary solidarity of the work force break the normal patterns of division.

The town's citizenry arrayed itself largely in terms of national origin: "Americans" (the majority) and "Hunkies" (the minority). Americans from the British Isles, Germany, and northern Europe further categorized themselves as either native born or immigrant. The Irish initially formed the major old-country group of greatest ethnic distinction. In time, Slavs took on this role, constituting a peripheral group. Work experience paralleled nationality in establishing Homestead's plural identities. Did the newcomer (Welsh or Cornish) arrive with a long and proud tradition of skill in metal work? Did he (Irish) arrive from the coal and lumber camps of Pennsylvania with some experience on the industrial front? Was he (American) fresh off the farm? Captain Jones, Carnegie's most dynamic mill superintendent, liked "buckwheat boys"—uncomplaining farm boys accustomed to hard labor and long hours and without trade union values.

Because many Homesteaders, native or foreign born, retained a strong rural outlook even while they toiled in America's major industry, they could accommodate both traditional music and the entertainment world's popular melodies. We have wonderful evidence from the pages of Pittsburgh's *National Labor Tribune* of topical ballads composed by millhands and set to a rainbow of tunes. On March 30, 1875, Reese Lewis called on Vulcan's sons to unite in the "March of the Rolling-Mill Men." Lewis saluted his fellow workers; a few lines suggest his style: "Hearts of oak and arms of metal, / Who by dint of skill and muscle, / Fashion bridge and iron vessel, / Ever true and brave."

Lewis set this song to the Welsh martial air "Men of Harlech," knowing that it was familiar to his companions. As we look back to his composition, do we label it *folk* or *plebeian*? We face a similar problem in poetic analysis and nomenclature with Richard Realf's "Hymn of Pittsburgh" (*National Labor Tribune*, February 23, 1878). We have no evidence that anyone set his poem to music, although it could have been sung to a standard sacred tune. Realf's rhetoric clearly points away from today's notions of workers' folk expression. One stanza makes the point:

My father was mighty Vulcan,
  I am Smith of the land and sea,
The cunning spirit of Tubal Cain

Came with my marrow to me;
I think great thoughts strong-winged with steel,
I coin vast iron acts,
And weld the impalpable dream of Seers
Into utile lyric facts.

By the mid-nineteenth century, commercial music publishers fed massive numbers of popular songs into America's mainstream. Heart songs (for gathering at the family piano) proved especially welcome. Certain titles mark his period: "After the Ball," "The Man That Broke the Bank at Monte Carlo," "A Bicycle Built for Two." Tin Pan Alley occasionally offered an occupational piece, for example, "Drill Ye Tarriers, Drill." Published in 1872, "Down in a Coal Mine" achieved popularity in New York's gas-lit variety houses before Hibernica, a traveling show, carried it throughout Pennsylvania to audiences of Irish miners, loggers, boatmen, and metal workers.

We can only speculate whether workers' bards of the 1880s and 1890s drew sharp lines between ballads from the "auld sod," topical poetry composed out of new work experience, and the comic and sentimental ditties that came to them ready-made from New York's saloons and sidewalks. Pittsburgh's musical fare in 1892 accordingly encompassed traditional ballads, sacred numbers, and show business hits. Homestead's two key strike songs actually stem from Manhattan. I suggest that "Father Was Killed by the Pinkerton Men" and "A Fight for Home and Honor" muddy clear pools of category—*folk, popular, plebeian.*

## Delaney's Song

William W. Delaney's niche is assured by his having bought or begged popular sheet music from publishers to reissue song texts in inexpensive booklets. These eighty-nine items include the incredible total of more than 15,000 songs. Many pieces contained this headnote: "Words and music of this song will be sent to any address, postpaid, on receipt of 40 cents, or this and any other two songs for One Dollar, by Wm. W. Delaney, 117 Park Row, New York. One-cent postage stamps taken same as cash."

The publisher Edward Marks recalled his pleasure when Delaney would buy something for reissue; it signaled that the latter had sensed a forthcoming hit. Research libraries and collectors of Americana prized Delaney's ephemera, but even students of popular music find his life obscure. Born in 1864 in New York's Irish Gas House district, Delaney began work as age fifteen as a printer's devil. He advanced to compositor on Charles Dana's *Sun* but gave up the trade in favor of Park Row songbook publishing.

In business from 1890 to 1924, Delaney supplied America with songs of dying firemen, brave policemen, maudlin drunks, and assorted Bowery waifs. Because of his previously required skill as a compositor, he could set type for his own songbooks. Never rising above his station as a printer, he impressed his peers by his gentility. In 1924 he closed his shop, unable to compete with new tastes in "canned music" and "dance-mad" jazz. For his final years, Delaney returned to the printing trades as a proofreader, but not before selling a huge stock of sheet music and songbooks to Buffalo's Grosvenor Library (Hayward).

Some months after Homestead details had drifted from newspaper front pages, Delaney composed "Father Was Killed by the Pinkerton Men," printing its text in sheet music and in *Delaney's Song Book—No. 2*. I do not know which came first; however, under the pseudonym Willie Wildwave, he submitted the sheet music to the Library of Congress Copyright Office (registered on December 15, 1892). The songbook text follows:

'Twas in a Pennsylvania town, not very long ago.
Men struck against reduction of their pay;
Their millionaire employer, with philanthropic show,
Had closed the works till starved they would obey.
They fought for home and right to live where they had toiled so long,
But ere the sun had set some were laid low;
There're hearts now sadly grieving by that sad and bitter wrong,
God help them! for it was a cruel blow.

Chorus:
God help them to-night in their hour of affliction,
Praying for him whom they'll ne'er see again;

Hear the poor orphans tell their sad story:
"Father was killed by the Pinkerton men!"

Ye prating politicians who boast protection creed,
Go to Homestead and stop the orphans' cry;
Protection for the rich man—ye pander to his greed,
His workmen they are cattle and may die.
The freedom of the city, in Scotland far away,
'Tis presented to the millionaire suave;
But here in free America, with protection in full sway,
His workmen get the freedom of the grave.

Accurate in its narrative core, Delaney's song shows the strike rising out of the mill's closing, and contrasts Carnegie's freedom during his overseas vacation with workers' deaths in Homestead. The reference to "protection creed" now seems dated, but Delaney's sentiments were intense in 1892, when the Democrat Grover Cleveland had campaigned against the Republican President Harrison. The high protective tariff championed by the party in power served as an inflammatory issue. Democrats successfully used Homestead in posters showing Pinkertons attacking workers, thus identifying Carnegie and Frick with the Republican White House.

Popular culture historians have commented on the topicality of "Father Was Killed by the Pinkerton Men." No one has offered evidence that Delaney's piece traveled widely. I have no knowledge that he sang it or that a star performer introduced it to New York audiences. Two accounts, however, indicate that "Father" had some slight oral circulation. Godfrey Irwin, an Englishman who had hoboed from Canada to Mexico, compiled a tramp dictionary (1931) that included a number of song texts encountered on the road. Irwin's "Daddy Was Killed by the Pinkerton Men" retained Delaney's first stanza and chorus. Unfortunately, Irwin cited no time, place, or circumstance of collection, hence lessening this variant's value as a traditional number.

During 1958, a stanza and the chorus of "Father" appeared once more in print in Olive Wooley Burt's *American Murder Ballads*. She identified the item correctly as coming from Delaney's hand, adding that she had heard it sung in 1922 at Embreeville, Pennsylvania. Questioning the song's life in tradition,

I wrote to her, only to learn that, though it had been sung by a schoolboy named Charles Patterson, he had also provided Burt with a worn, discolored copy of the sheet music from which she had copied the words.

To the Irwin and Burt partial texts, I add the important printing of full lyrics and music by Sigmund Spaeth in *Weep Some More My Lady*. Spaeth, unconcerned with living folksong, presented "Father" as a "relic." However, he did reprint the song without punctuation exactly as he found the sheet music. In 1942, Douglas Gilbert printed a full and punctuated text in *Lost Chords,* with the interesting comment that the rabble-rousing song seemed foreign to Delaney's gentle expression.

Spaeth, Gilbert, Irwin, and Burt did not target trade union audiences. However, in 1935, Edward Levinson's book on Pearl Bergoff, *I Break Strikes,* contained the first stanza and chorus of "Father," without citing source. To my knowledge, this partial text represented the first printing of Delaney's piece in a labor-oriented book. Levinson may have used the song about "murderous Pinkerton men—the scum of the earth" because previous writers had connected "Pinks" with the scurrilous term *fink* (discussed previously).

I doubt that any student can now discover the precise circumstance of Delaney's composition of a Homestead song. Did he have special affinity with trade unionism? Did he attempt to sell "Father" in Pittsburgh and other steel centers? Did the song retain any visibility between 1892 and 1927, when Spaeth brought it to light? Although current judgment fails to grant "Father" folksong status, it is a social document—a rank-and-file vignette of the industrialist dubbed "Baron Carnage-y" and a clue to emotions generated during America's most memorable labor war.

## Kelly's Song

John W. Kelly, an Irish-American comedian, composed the steel strike song that did enter tradition, "A Fight for Home and Honor at Homestead, Pa." Born in Philadelphia about 1858, Kelly moved to Chicago as a young man to seek employment in the raw city's new iron mills. He "acted" on the job for fellow workers, to their delight and his advance. Somehow, he met Lew Hawkins, a blackface minstrel performer who recognized Kelly's gift for fashioning rhymes and tunes, as well as for dancing and story telling. Hawkins took the millhand onto the entertainment circuit. By March 1881, the duo had reached Harry Miner's Bowery Theatre in New York, where the playbill identified Hawkins and Kelly as "dialect emperors, [with] banjo, and all sorts of musical instruments" (Odell, 11:349).

No biographical account fully details Kelly's show business career, although most books about Tin Pan Alley note some of his exploits (Geller, Gilbert, Marcuse, Marks, Witmark). In January 1891, the entertainment journal *Clipper* identified Kelly as "comparatively new on the Bowery stage—a Westerner and comes highly recommended" (Odell, 14:644). During 1892, he starred at Tony Pastor's, receiving billing as the Rolling Mill Man. The impresario Pastor (1837–1908), a circus and minstrel troupe veteran, had opened a Bowery "Opera House" in 1865. Moving to Fourteenth Street in 1881, he built Ameirca's leading variety show and vaudeville house (Zellers).

One song, "Maloney, the Rolling Mill Man," called up Kelly's craft experience. Maloney, in the mill, sends out for a can of draft ale; at church, he takes up the collection; on election day, he watches polls from morn to night. The Chicago publisher Will Rossiter kept this in print for years. As late as 1928, the Max Stein Publishing House, Chicago, included "Maloney" in *Comic Songs, Funny Stories and Recitations.* (Stein either purchased or appropriated Rossiter's lists.)

Stage historian George Odell commented on Kelly's achieving an astonishing Manhattan record; Edward Marks labeled him the greatest of Pastor's many artists; Douglas Gilbert described his act as follows: "[Kelly] worked without make-up of any sort. He appeared in a rather rusty Prince Albert coat, a silk hat, with old-fashioned spectacles dangling from the end of his nose. He based his monologues on human traits and peculiarities: The man who risks his life crossing the street and then turns 'round and watches the vehicles pass for ten minutes" (203).

Had Kelly stayed in the steel mills among Irish immigrants he would have remained an "ideal" anonymous folksinger and tale teller. But like many traditional performers, before and after, he parlayed his natural talent into full-scale professionalism. I see him as similar to Merle Travis, a Kentucky coal miner's son, tradition bearer, and Hollywood-Nashville performer-composer. Just as our memory of Travis hinges on "Sixteen Tons" and "Dark As a Dungeon," many accounts of American popular music identify Kelly with his best remembered comic sterotype, "Throw Him Down McCloskey" (1890), and his second-ranking hit, the baseball perennial "Slide, Kelly, Slide" (1889).

Edward Marks offered an anecdote named "The Corner Saloon with Three Doors on Two Street" that revealed Kelly's wit and foreshadowed his early death in 1896 from Bright's disease: "Kelly, according to his own story, went into a saloon and drank until the bartender refused him liquor—a prim, pre-Volstead custom. Kelly walked out, went around the corner, saw the other door and re-entered, thinking he had found another saloon. Again he was refused. Out went Kelly, only to re-enter by the third door. But the bartender ordered him out. 'Good God, man,' yelled the astonished Kelly, 'do you tend all the bars in the city?' " (131).

Despite much search, I have not learned the precise circumstances of Kelly's composition of his Homestead song. I assume that the Rolling Mill Man, while at Tony Pastor's, followed closely the Monongahela battle. Very likely, Kelly held strong sympathy for the Amalgamated Association of Iron and Steel Workers. As a young millhand, he may well have joined a Chicago AA lodge before Hawkins took him into minstrelsy. One of Kelly's earliest published songs, "The Land League Band" (1883), revealed his wish "to see old Ireland free," a sentiment shared by Erin's sons throughout American industry.

The Library of Congress registered Kelly's Homestead sheet music on July 16, 1892, indicating that he had composed it during the week of the strike's initial shock. The Chicago publisher Will Rossiter held the song's copyright. I do not know the elapsed time between the sheet music release date and the subsequent songbook printing of "A Fight." Rossiter had submitted the *J. W. Kelly Songster* to the Copyright Office, on April 25, 1892, a few months before Homestead erupted. However, after the strike, Rossiter placed the then-popular Homestead piece in the *New "Ali Baba" Song Book*, the *J. W. Kelly's Irish Song-Book No. 1*, and other collections.

I have not found the sheet music for "A Fight," but I have

obained a partial text in *"Ali Baba"* and a variant text in *Delaney's Song Book—No. 3.* It seems unlikely that Delaney secured Rossiter's permission to use Kelly's ballad. Possibly, Delaney had heard Kelly sing at Tony Pastor's and had noted the words directly from the Rolling Mill Man's rendition. This could account for textual variation in Kelly's song within Delaney's booklet.

Laborlore students face barriers of discontinuity—lost texts, questionable histories, faulty memories. I have been puzzled by the disappearance of all copies of the sheet music for Kelly's song despite the Homestead strike's prominence. The registration copy sent to the Library of Congress in 1892 has vanished. Seemingly, no one in Pittsburgh retained a copy in a family scrapbook or attic trunk. Nor have I found anyone who collected Rossiter's song publications.

Will Rossiter (1867–1954), Chicago's most successful popular music publisher, developed aggressive marketing techniques, issuing provocative booklets such as *"How to Write a Song" and Become Wealthy* (Geil). His *"Ali Baba"* dates to 1893. (I lack a date for Kelly's *Irish Song-Book.*) To my knowledge, Kelly's Homestead song circulated orally but remained hidden in ephemeral print until 1942, when Douglas Gilbert "rescued" it for *Lost Chords.* Sadly, Gilbert did not specify a source. I assume that he had located a copy of the original sheet music or one of the Rossiter songbooks. Gilbert's text follows:

We are asking one another as we pass the time of day,
Why men must have recourse to arms to get their proper pay,
And why their labor unions now must be recognized,
While the actions of a syndicate must not be criticised.
The trouble down at Homestead was brought about this way,
When a grasping corporation had the audacity to say,
You must all renounce your unions and forswear your liberty,
and we'll promise you a chance to live and die in slavery.

Chorus:
So the man that fights for honor, none can blame him,
May luck attend wherever he may roam,
And no son of his will ever live to shame him
While liberty and honor rule his home.

When a crowd of well armed ruffians came without authority,
Like thieves at night, while decent men were sleeping peacefully,
Can you wonder why all honest men with indignation burn,
Why the slimy worm that crawls the earth when trod upon will turn?
When the locked out men at Homestead saw they were face to face
With a lot of paid detectives, then they knew it was their place
To protect their homes and families and that was nobly done,
And the angels will applaud them for the victory they won.

See that sturdy band of working men start at break of day,
Determination in their eyes which surely meant to say,
No men shall drive us from our homes, for which we toiled so long,
No men shall take our places, No! for here's where we belong;
A woman with a rifle saw her husband in the crowd,
She handed him the weapon and they cheered her long and loud.
He kissed her and said Mary, you go home till we are through;
She answered "No! if you must fight, my place is here with you."

We expect variation when songs enter oral tradition; we know also that printers and editors make scribal errors. For whatever reasons, the Rossiter, Delaney, and Gilbert texts show differences. To compound such incongruities, these "prime" texts can be contrasted with a small, undated broadside on cheap newsprint found in the Harris Collection, Brown University Library.

This broadside, without author's credits, carries an altered but appropriate title, "Homestead Strike." Perhaps a labor partisan carried the text in printed form, or in memory, to a local printer after the song had been "lost" to Kelly. The International Typographical Union "bug"' (label) from Sharon, Pennsylvania, implies that his anonymous song belonged to those trade unionists who liked it enough to pay for its printing and distribution. The reader will note some word changes and jumbled lines in comparing the Rossiter and Delaney printing to the Sharon broadside.

I have already indicated that "A Fight for Home and Honor" became a folksong—in short, that individuals within occupational communities treasured Kelly's composition, altering it considerably as it moved away from time and place of origin. Ideally, a history of the Rolling Mill Man's ballad ought to begin with a precisely dated account of its appearance in Pittsburgh during 1892. However, I have failed to unearth such an immediate reference in diary or periodical.

Pittsburgh citizens sang "A Fight for Home and Honor" during 1892, but our knowledge of such performance is indirect. Some years ago, I corresponded with Mrs. Walter Willis at Lakemore, Ohio, who had looked for the Homestead song when her neighbor Robert Butler recalled a fragment from his father, a Carnegie worker during the strike. The elder Butler represented hundreds of "displaced" millhands who had carried strike lore away from the Monongahela.

In 1988, I shared my interest in Kelly's ballad with Doris Dyen, an ethnomusicologist and folklorist in Pittsburgh. Involved in efforts to conserve Homestead's industrial heritage, she joined in the search for song lore. Following a lead provided by the Pittsburgh historian George Swetnam, she reached John, Jr., and Ken Hubenthal, retired Jones & Laughlin steel workers, on July 25, 1990.

The brothers indicated that their father, John Fritz Hubenthal, had made a reel-to-reel tape recording in 1955 of "Homestead Strike" (subsequently duplicated on audio-cassette). One of his grandsons transcribed the text, presenting a typed sheet and cassette to Dyen. Significantly, the typed heading read "The Homestead Strike of 1892—J. W. Kelly." The elder Hubenthal's twenty-eight-line text held three stanzas and a chorus in the exact sequence as Kelly's piece (Rossiter/Gilbert printing) but displayed variation in particular lines.

Dyen learned that Hubenthal had been born in Germany in 1878, arriving with his parents at Pittsburgh in 1882. At age fourteen, he began work as a waterboy in the Jones & Laughlin South Side plant, retiring in 1953. He told his sons that a J & L union contingent had gone to Homestead to help oppose the Pinkertons in 1892, a bit of knowledge that reinforced his emotional attachment to the strike song. Dyen has treated the Hubenthal song elsewhere. Here, I note only that his stanza melody is unconnected to those previously collected for Kelly's piece, save that it is in 6/8 meter, holding stylistic characteristics of nineteenth-century Irish popular music.

John Fritz Hubenthal's fellow workers enjoyed his Homestead rendition in Pittsburgh's many taverns along Carson Street. During World War II's boom years, he put the song aside, asserting that young steel workers no longer understood the 1892 strike's importance. Nevertheless, his grandsons recall that he sang it at family gatherings until his death in 1966. However, they did not learn it. Dyen notes that unless we find another area singer who learned Kelly's song within a Monongahela Valley setting, we must assume that it no longer lives in direct oral tradition. Hence, I look elsewhere—print, sound recording, film tracks, "folksong revival circuit"—for other lines of transmission.

I am indebted to four collectors for printed variants of Kelly's song. On May 26, 1940, George Korson recorded a full version of Peter Haser's "Homestead Strike" at New Kensington, Pennsylvania. Throughout the 1930s, Haser, a representative of the United Mine Workers of America, had sung the ballad at Labor Day celebrations in the region. Transcribing the text alone for *Coal Dust on the Fiddle,* Korson noted the ballad's popularity among miners. Born in 1870, Haser had learned the song at about age twenty-two and had retained it in memory thereafter.

During 1947, Jacob Evanson also netted the "Homestead Strike" from John Schmitt, a retired Pittsburgh steel worker, who had learned it at age sixteen. Evanson transcribed the tune, splicing it to Haser's text in "Folk Songs of an Industrial City." Inasmuch as Kelly's sheet music had vanished, this transcription literally made the song's melody available to modern audiences. Ben Botkin, in *Sidewalks of America,* gave additional prominence to Evanson's find. In my visit with Mr. and Mrs. Evanson at home in Pittsburgh (1972), they shared their excitement in exploring the lore of blast furnace and rolling mill.

In 1946, Helene Stratman-Thomas recorded a number of Winfred Bundy's ballads for the Library of Congress Archive of Folk Song and the University of Wisconsin School of Music (Peters). Writing to the collector, I learned that Bundy had learned "The

Homestead Strike" from her older brother and had remarked: "I believe that was one of the first big strikes. It was something to sing about."

The recoveries noted above establish the traditionality of Kelly's composition, although he had been forgotten and his song altered well before any folksong enthusiast found it. If Haser, Schmitt, or Bundy knew anything of the song's genesis at Tony Pastor's or of printings by Will Rossiter, the singers did not convey such details to collectors.

By good fortune, an additional find surfaced in 1957. Ellen Stekert, then a Cornell student, met Ezra "Fuzzy" Barhight at Cohocton, New York, and taped many of his songs, including "The Trouble Down at Homestead." Subsequently, she recorded a selection of his ballads and shanties on a Folkways LP entitled *Songs of a New York Lumberjack.* Enjoying the LP, I shared my research with her. Following the album's release, Irwin Silber ran its Homestead text and tune in *Sing Out.* In 1966, Stekert included Kelly's ballad in an article on Barhight. Born in 1876, Fuzzy worked in lumber camps across Potter, McKean, and Cameron counties, Pennsylvania. He learned the Homestead song while strike troubles were current. He did not read music and did not report a visit to Pastor's. Hence, Stekert suggested that Barhight had "learned the song just one step from Irish music hall performance."

Because Hubenthal, Haser, Schmitt, and Barhight all gained their versions of the Homestead ballad while strike emotion resonated, I believe that itinerant workers carried Kelly's contribution from New York City stage to coal patch, lumber camp, and mill borough. A plausible alternative remains: a Pittsburgh entertainer learned the ballad from sheet music and performed it in union circles, picnics, conventions, or Homestead memorial meetings. Perhaps both forms of dissemination, work camp and union hall, intersected.

## Crossings

The geographic spread of a single topical piece reveals travel across skill boundaries. Such movement also displays a song's utility in providing statements of identity within separate labor disputes. Because Pennsylvania lumber camps and coal patches abutted Monongahela steel mills, we should not be surprised that woodsmen and miners shared Kelly's songs. We do not know precisely how "A Fight" reached Winifred Bundy in Wisconsin, but we can track the ballad's journey to Ohio, Kentucky, South Dakota, and Maryland.

For three decades before Homestead, Ohio's Hocking toilers attempted organization in the American Miners Association, Miners National Union, and Knights of Labor. Each made some advance only to be beaten back, until all the splinter groups coalesced into the United Mine Workers of America on January 25, 1890. The Hocking Valley Strike of 1873–74 had significant consequences—namely, the introduction of Negro strikebreakers. Eventually, these scabs became staunch UMWA members and participated in new organizational drives (Gutman).

A wage cut in 1884 led to protracted troubles. A few years later, economist Edward Bemis characterized this dispute as "the bitterest strike in the entire mining industry of America . . . when even presidential candidates feared to be thought involved" (27). On the night of August 30, unionists attacked strikebreakers, burning mine tipples, hoppers, and railroad bridges. At New Straitsville, Ohio, someone rolled several cars of blazing coal into mine shafts, setting rich veins on fire. The militia restored "order" and the strike ended in 1885, but for eight decades the underground mines continued to burn, destroying uncounted millions of tons of coal.

The New Deal's Works Progress Administration hired unemployed miners in an attempt to halt the fire, but in vain. In 1940, geologists estimated the damage from the subterranean blaze at fifty million dollars. Through the 1960s, new fissures let oxygen into the earth's crust, renewing the smoldering coal (Vincent, Wallace, Wright). Union partisans have denied that strikers started the fire, suggesting instead either that the inferno stemmed from a mine explosion or that hostile nonunion miners set it. These conflicting interpretations will not be resolved.

One folk account clearly blames the strikers for the underground fire. During 1953, Anne Laylin Grimes did extensive folksong collecting, a sample of which she recorded for her Folkways LP *Ohio State Ballads.* Some of Grimes's best pieces came from

Reuben Allen, a Zanesville Negro and former medicine-show performer, who gave her a number of unusual underground railway songs. To these he added a comment on "his" Homestead piece. Obviously, the Hocking Valley Strike preceded the Homestead strike by eight years, yet someone in Ohio had fused the two events and localized Kelly's song to New Straitsville.

Allen's text for "The Homestead Song" (transcribed by me from Grimes's tape copy of his material in the Library of Congress) follows:

A man who fights for his honor none can blame him,
May peace be with him wherever he will roam,
No child of his could ever go to condemn him,
A man who fights for his honor and his home.
It was a frosty morning when the fire was set,
The whole band was playing in the snow,
But nobody knowed 'cept the union leader,
That what was taking place in the hole.

When they heard the boom,
When they heard the boom,
And the [ . . . ] come blowing up,
Oh the man who fights for his honor,
None can blame him,
He fights for his honor and his home.

When the crowd was in the hall,
They were talking about their fame,
It was nobody know whatever it was to be,
Then the bomb it was exploded,
And they know not what it meant,
They all hurried on the way.

Although Allen's irregular rhetoric reflects both improvisatory talent and memory loss, his song states that unionists set the fire. Allen had no knowledge of Homestead to convey to collector Grimes, but he knew New Straitsville lore intimately because of Zanesville's proximity to the burning site. In my visit with Grimes (1960), she noted that Allen had learned the song well after the initial fire and that it had been sung by "heavy union people." He reinforced the piece's historicity by explaining that the "militia was down here" with guns at that time. Without additional variants, I cannot reconstruct the circumstances of a New Straitsville participant incorporating Kelly's words into a mine fire/explosion narrative. Again, Reuben Allen reminds us that much laborlore is either lost or fragmentary and distorted when found.

A year before the battle between Homesteaders and Pinkertons, an equally intense but prolonged conflict erupted in the hills of east Tennessee over the operation of the state's convict-lease system. The practice of leasing prisoners to industrial firms helped owners and, correspondingly, injured free labor. The Tennessee Coal, Iron, and Railroad Company (TCI) not only used prisoners in its mine but subleased them to others. In the spring of 1891, the TCI confronted miners at Briceville, Anderson County, with a denial of the right to their own checkweightmen and a demand for an "ironclad" or "yellow dog" contract (a pledge not to join a union and never to strike).

Previously, Tennessee miners had organized into Trades Assembly Number 135, a Knights of Labor branch. Some men had also joined the then-new United Mine Workers of America. Putting aside internal differences, well-armed miners at Briceville freed the convicts on Bastille Day, 1891. Governor John Buchanan responded by ordering the state militia to return prison workers to their stockades. On July 20, the "Free Men of the Mountains" again liberated the convicts, forcing the militia from the area. In August, the Tennessee General Assembly met in Nashville to consider redress for the miners' grievances, but TCI lobbyists dominated the session as legislators passed additional antilabor laws.

Rebuked by state power, the unionists prepared once more for direct action. Many had served in both Civil War camps; Union and Confederate veterans joined against the militia. In October and November, miners burned stockades in Anderson and distant Grundy counties. Guerrilla warfare continued through 1892. Together, state and industry finally routed workers, but public sentiment supported labor's cause. On January 1, 1896, Tennessee's convict-lease system ended with the expiration of the last TCI prison contract.

The rebellion's major ballad, "Coal Creek Troubles," took its name from a community later renamed Lake City (near the TVA's

Norris Dam); it entered tradition, as did several mine explosion songs. Uncle Dave Macon and the Allen Brothers preserved related convict work "blues" on hillbilly phonograph records. (I describe these man-made and natural disaster compositions in *Only a Miner.*)

"Coal Creek March," a banjo instrumental, complements the rebellion's various narratives and blues. In a provocative essay, folklorist Neil Rosenberg, brings this piece into present-day "revival" repertoires. Normally, it appears as a straight "chording piece," but at times, a performer adds effects to denote militia bugle calls, miners firing guns, dogs barking at prisoners, or closing funeral sounds. Some banjoists add a story text to these effects. Folklorist Ed Kahn collected several "March" versions, both straight and with added elements. In 1958, Forrest Lewis of Parksville, Kentucky, sang an unusual "Ballad of Coal Creek." He had learned this song from his father, and he gave Kahn a dramatic introduction:

> Well, you take about '97 or '96, they went down there, them fellows did—strikers—tryin' to break that Coal Creek stuff up there, an' them fellows did a lot of killin'. There's hundreds of 'em killed there before they got it settled. Teddy Roosevelt was President then, and he went down there and got it stopped with the soldiers, you see. The national guards over here tried to stop 'em and they went out like this: [banjo sounds a reveille, fingers make drum sound on banjo head.]

Sings:

It's hand me down my rifle, that cracks long and loud
And listen while I sing this little song.
Trouble down in Coal Creek come up all about this
A lot of disorganized men come to take away their work.

Chorus:

But the man who fights for honor, none can blame him
As long as old honor rules our home.
Now a woman in the crowd with rifle in her hand
She come bak all in fear,
He says you go home and take your place at home
For they'll never take old Coal Creek from here.

(instrumental break)

Now you can stand here, and you can wander here and there
And you may leave this State for another
But the State they love, and the State they died for
Was old Coal Creek, Tennessee.

(instrumental ending)

Kahn submitted Lewis's text and tune to *Sing Out* (1960), commenting on its obvious relationship to Homestead. Although Lewis advanced the time of both the Homestead and Coal Creek troubles to Theodore Roosevelt's presidency and exaggerated the death toll, he clearly used key lines from Kelly.

A question thrusts itself into all song lore study: how long does a given composition stay in the memories of folksingers? During the summer of 1971, I met Ernest Hodges at the Smithsonian Institution's Festival of American Folklife. He had come to Washington from his Fiddle Shop in Gainesville, Georgia, to demonstrate instrument repair and restoration. Born in North Carolina, Hodges had lived in Kentucky while performing with fiddle and banjo on barn dance radio programs. He played "Coal Creek March" for me as a sprightly banjo solo, ending it by singing a brief ballad related to Forrest Lewis's adaptation of Kelly's Homestead song.

After meeting Hodges, I learned something of his sources from John Garst, a University of Georgia chemist. Hodges reported that he had played with Frank Lewis and Bailey Briscoe, Kentucky banjoists who had toured with Dakota Jack's Medicine Show in the 1920s (Forrest Lewis, who had given a mine strike ballad to Kahn, was Frank's son). Garst noted that the banjo team "got up" "Trouble Down at Coal Creek" as a show piece, perhaps as early as the 1890s. Hodges, unaware that his father and Briscoe might have heard Kelly's Homestead song, believed that their brilliant piece originated in commentary on Coal Creek's trauma.

In 1976, Charles Wolfe pulled together previous research on the hybrid instrument/narrative "March." To construct a progress report, he looked back at influential recordings by Marion Underwood, Pete Steele, Dock Boggs, and Doc Hopkins, as well as a Georgia TV documentary, "From the Hands of Ernest Hodges." In interviews, Hodges affirmed that, indeed, Lewis and Briscoe had composed the "Coal Creek March."

Hodges performed the Lewis-Briscoe piece with all of its flourishes, for the Georgia film, but he did not offer the matching ballad. However, he did tape-record it for Wolfe in 1974, adding his personal transcription of the "Cole Creek March's" text:

The trouble down at Cole Creek
Came about this way,
A lot of distant men came
To take their jobs away.
No son will ever live to shame them
As long as old Coal Creek stands today

You'll see this honest miner
At the break of day
Standing with a rifle in his hand
And from the crowd a woman
Came by his side to stand
And she had a rifle in her hand

He looked at her with pride
And with an honest eye
And said, "You go take your place at home,
The children there are crying,
The old men stand and moan,
This trouble shouldn't take us very long."

Oh! The sweethearts and wives
Came to mourn o'er the dead,
As they carried them in the ambulance all the way
You can travel north or east or west
Or travel anywhere
But old "Cole Creek" stands there today.

The strike song collected by Anne Grimes at Zanesville, 1953, reported a nearby happening at New Straitsville, Ohio. Ed Kahn, in 1958, and Charles Wolfe, in 1974, found Kentuckians who sang about an event in neighboring Tennessee. By contrast, Wayland Hand, in Butte, Montana, unearthed another Homestead offshoot—one localized to distant Lead in the Black Hills of South Dakota, where the "richest one hundred square miles on earth" houses the Homestake Gold Mine. The largest gold producer in the Western Hemisphere, this mine also holds the longest record for continuous operation in the world (Cash, Fielding, Peattie).

During 1876, Mose Manuel prospected Gold Run Creek, unaware that it would become an American bonanza. Selling his claim to California entrepreneur George Hearst, the latter incorporated the Homestake Mining Company in San Francisco. While Hearst's engineers turned to technical problems of water supply and transportation, Lead miners organized a local labor union. Initial relations between the men and management proved excellent, but after George Hearst's death in 1891, his son William Randolph plowed Lead's wealth into his newspaper chain. As this Hearst turned to jingoistic politics and yellow journalism, his crews helped build the Western Federation of Miners, a militant and democratic industrial union. WFM president Charles Moyer started in the Lead local.

The Black Hills attracted a motley work force: returning Argonauts from California, coal miners lured west from anthracite and bituminous fields, European immigrants. At the turn of the century, Homestake included some twenty ethnic groups. In 1906, the WFM began a successful eight-hour-day drive within the nonferrous metal mining industry. Three years later, the union pressed for complete organization in the Black Hills. The Homestake Company refused to deal with its unionists; relations deteriorated until Thanksgiving eve, 1909, when a lockout and strike commenced.

Failing to bring the Hearst empire to terms, the WFM saw paternalism replace collective bargaining. In January 1913, the pioneer local of 1877 abandoned its union hall, Lead's largest building and its site for opera and concert. As blacklisted men dispersed, their best friend in town, Catholic Bishop Joseph Busch, also felt the company's power. With his flock facing a seven-day work week, he sought Sunday leisure for worship. This temerity led to his banishment. President Moyer summed up: "As a condition of earning daily bread [the company] has demanded that a man in consideration of employment must agree to give up his religion, his home, his society, his property" (Jensen, 252).

Fortunately, Homestake did not parallel Homestead in blood. In other regards, however, the strikes were similar, though seventeen years apart. Some time after 1909, a Lead miner, perhaps in the Black Hills or further west, recalled or learned "A Fight for Home and Honor." Similarity in place name may have reinforced the gold mine song's name, "The Homestake Strike." This piece fell into Wayland Hand's net in Butte on July 29, 1948. Copper miner John Dell Duffy sang it for Hand, who held it from publication until something of its antecedents could be established.

A child during the Homestake strike, Duffy did not tell Hand whether he had learned the song from a Black Hills Homestaker in Butte or from someone without a special Lead association. Nonferrous miners drifted about as notorious "ten-day stiffs" or "sundowners." Hence, anyone could have carried the gold song to copper country. During 1958, Hand presented "The Homestake Strike's" text to me; I shared with him my earliest tracings of "A Fight for Home and Honor." Duffy's text transcribed by Hand follows:

We've been asking one another
At the time and break of day,
When the miners had to resort to arms
To receive their proper pay.

Now the striking down at Homestake,
Was brought about this way,
When a grasping corporation
Had the audacity to say:

"You must not recognize your union
Nor foreswear your liberty;
But we'll give you all a chance to work,
And die in slavery."

So the man that fights for honor, none can blame him;
They look at him wherever he may roam;
And no son of his will ever live to shame him,
When liberty and honor stands OK.

Composers cannot anticipate fully all the adventures of their songs. J. W. Kelly died in 1896 knowing that two of his comic hits had achieved wide popularity. Could he have imagined that Reuben Allen, Ezra Barhight, Winifred Bundy, John Duffy, Peter Haser, Ernest Hodges, John Hubenthal, Forrest Lewis, and John

Schmitt would eventually gift collectors with folk variants of his Homestead ballad? These nine individuals—divided otherwise by discrete badges of identity—retained large or small segments of Kelly's song. There may well have been other fragments lost by virtue of the process of oral/aural circulation, transregional dispersal, and shifts in the fortunes of carriers of organized labor's creativity.

At times, folksongs surface without the benefits of meetings between performers and academic scholars. I cite one remarkable example. During 1900, a strike broke out at the Consolidation Coal Company's Hoffman Mine in George's Creek Valley, Allegany County, Maryland (Harvey). We find many reasons for job action in the history of the United Mine Workers of America, but few as unusual as that at Hoffman. A superintendent precipitated the dispute by disciplining ninety-five men who had left work (March 31) to hear Samuel Gompers speak at a national eight-hour-day meeting at Lonaconing. With a large strike underway in Maryland's Appalachian counties, unionists rallied on April 11 at Frostburg's opera house.

Robert Simpson, a coal miner, opened the evening rally with a rendition of his composition "The Hoffman Mine." Fortunately, a *Sun* correspondent at the meeting dispatched a strike report to Baltimore (April 12) including the full song. Surely, Simpson had seen either Kelly's sheet music or a songbook printing. Did the UMWA entertainer, who "received great applause," give the reporter hand-copied words or did the latter literally transcribe the text from Simpson's singing?

The Hoffman variant bears comparison with Kelly's original, in either Rossiter's, Delaney's, or Gilbert's representation, as well as with traditional forms recovered by Korson and Stekert. Kelly had composed a twenty-eight-line ballad—three stanzas with a four-line chorus. Simpson retained Kelly's narrative sequence but dropped the "slimy worm" half-stanza of four lines. By contrast, Fuzzy Barhight kept the "violet worm" image but dropped other portions to reduce his song to twenty lines, while Peter Haser remembered all twenty-eight lines but jumbled Kelly's squence. Such vagaries in individual taste and memory become engine levers that construct and deconstruct folksong.

Simpson's "Hoffman Mine" did not remain hidden in the *Bal-*

*timore Sun*. Some time after the strike, a student at the Lonaconing Valley High School cut it out of the newspaper for inclusion in a scrapbook. Subsequently, *Tableland Trails*, a Maryland regional magazine, reprinted this text and, in 1972, Richard Spottswood placed it in the Smithsonian Institution's Festival of American Folklife program booklet. I welcomed the new audience for Simpson's song, while noting that it recalled an obscure event at Hoffman rather than the shattering strike at Homestead. The Smithsonian printing served also to remind that other variants of Kelly's Homestead ballad may be hidden in newspaper files, scrapbooks, and correspondence.

## Tally

While tracing "A Fight for Home and Honor" and "Father Was Killed by the Pinkerton Men," I found scattered references to similar pieces. Professor Don Woodworth, Indiana University of Pennsylvania, has also uncovered such material. In a centennial anthology on Homestead's conflict, he notes the use of traditional imagery by strike sympathizers—resistance to tyrany and slavery. Many millhands were veterans of the Civil War, which provided a "reservoir of feeling" for worker-poets. I know of no inclusive tally of Homestead songs and poems. A partial list follows.

*1. "The Homestead Strike"*

Sometime in 1892, the New York publisher Henry J. Wehman issued an elephant-folio broadsheet in newspaper format holding twenty-six songs. He titled the entire broadsheet, "Homestead Strike Songster." This heading broke away from previous meanings for *songster*, a term generally restricted to describe material of booklet or music-folio size.

Wehman's lead item (at the top of the left-hand column), "The Homestead Strike," carried a note reading, "as sung by the National Trio." Because the song text made no reference to violence at Carnegie's mill, I assume that a Trio member or a Wehman employee wrote it before July 6. Seemingly, Wehman published Homestead's first strike song only a few days before events overshadowed his broadsheet's topicality. The National Trio's history is unknown. Philip Foner has reprinted its strike text (1975, 244).

*2. "Stand by the Workmen at Homestead"*

On July 15, 1892, the Library of Congress Copyright Office registered Stephe S. Bonbright's "Stand by the Workmen at Homestead." Composed after July 6 and rushed to Washington by the Home Music Company, Cincinnati, the sheet music came with a remarkable cover. A cartoonlike drawing catches the violence "seen" by readers across the continent who envisioned the Monongahela battle from telegraphed newspaper reports. In the absence of biographical data on the author, I assume that Bonbright lived in Cincinnati and relied on secondhand accounts of the fight at Homestead.

Those of us today who view news through the eyes of TV cameramen have difficulty in comprehending the problems faced by sheet music (and other popular print) illustrators who never saw the events they illuminated. Bonbright's lethal battlers fought on both north and south river banks. The major vessel in the foreground (north) resembled an excursion boat with an elevated cabin superstructure. The river's far shore revealed a distant pair of utilitarian barges or scows, appropriately at the foot of the huge mill.

The two barges carrying Pinkertons did land on the Monongahela's south shore at the mill's river entrance. Bonbright's artist added an imaginary northside encounter by the large boat's Pinkertons at the Swissvale shore, across the river from the Homestead Works. This detail, of no great present significance, helps unscramble the images that must have flashed into the minds of readers in 1892 as they pictured the strike scenes.

Apparently, no one has reprinted Bonbright's original piece. It reminds us that many more songs memorialized union disputes than entered tradition. Some defied appeal by their heavy rhetoric; some, by their failure to touch deep beliefs; others, by their awkward adjustment of lyrics to music. "Stand by the Workmen at Homestead" adds little to the historical record, but it does mark agrarian populism's link to labor. The first and third stanzas follow:

There are watchers who weep where the hearths dimly burn,
Where many a loved one is missing tonight;
Where capital's ruling what man's labor should earn,

With law of its own against reason and right:
The Iron King's stronghold with detectives to taunt,
With gunboats, and armor and rifles for fight,
In vain with their bluster did they working men daunt,
But in conflict surrender'd at Homestead that night.

Can not intrenchment by capitalists cease,
And labor be given the station it due?
Let loosen the fetters and manhood release,
Then old days of peace and goodwill shall renew:
The farmer whose bins are ladened with grain,
Must not sell to those who gamble in flour;
And toil of mechanics and workmen's vain,
When they're in jeopardy from hour, to hour.

3. *"The Strike at Homestead"*

On September 16, 1892, the Copyright Office registered W. B. Leonard's "The Strike at Homestead," dedicated to the Amalgamated Association of Iron and Steel Workers. Whether Leonard had been an AA member, I do not know. His song leaves no doubts about his sympathies with the Pinkertons' victims. Leonard submitted sheet music from his own publishing company in Cortland, New York. His song holds an unusual feature—a tribute to strike leader Hugh O'Donnell. Stanza three follows:

Hark! amidst the noise of battle, comes a voice so clear and strong,
From their savior Hugh O'Donnell, who had plead their cause so long.
List! he speaks! now all is silent, See! how quickly stops the fray,
May God bless their noble leader, ev'ry working man should pray.
Pause and think, ye toiling people, Who are honestly the slayers,
Of your happiness and loved ones, But these dreaded millionairs.
Rally men and strike for freedom, Let us battle with the foe,
We are marching on to vict'ry, See, oh see our banner go.

4. *"Homestead Strike, or, Homestead Down in Pennsylvania" (Will J. Hardman)*

5. *"Fight for Rights at Homestead, Pa." (M. E. Nibbe)*

6. *"Homestead Strike" (A. J. Blochinger)*

These three titles appear in Library of Congress Copyright Office entries; I have not located sheet music or printed texts for any of them in private or public archives, although William Rossiter published Hardman's composition in Chicago. Rossiter registered this piece on July 14, 1892. Nibbe, a Chicago resident, registered his song on August 26, 1892. Blochinger, a Homestead resident, registered his piece on September 2, 1892.

Blochinger has left a better trail than Hardman or Nibbe, thanks to efforts by historian George Swetnam. As former editor of the *Keystone Folklore Quarterly,* Swetnam wrote an excellent article entitled "Songs of a Strike" for the *Pittsburgh Press Family Magazine* (February 5, 1967), combining some of my early findings with his research, Russell Gibbons called additional attention to our investigations in an article for *Steel Labor* (March 1967), the newspaper of the United Steelworkers of America.

Swetnam's article brought to the surface important material from *Press* readers who sent him fresh leads. He shared letters with me from Hazel Durstine, Carl Kamphaus, Mrs. John Hubenthal, and others. Here, I summarize Swetnam's findings. About 1955, he had collected two stanzas of "The Battle of Homestead" from an eighty-four-year-old caretaker at Pittsburgh's North Side Elks Club. (This employee may have been the doorman "Schemer" Wiggin.) He told Swetnam that he had learned the ballad directly from its author, a Homestead blacksmith during the strike. With this lead, Swetnam reached Mrs. L. E. Bishop of Connellsville, the niece of August J. Blochinger. She reported that her uncle had been born in Bolivar, near Homestead, and that the family remembered him as a local singer. She was surprised to learn that he had composed a song and mailed it to the Copyright Office in Washington.

Speculating that Blochinger's "battle" song may have been the only locally composed Homestead strike ballad, Swetnam sought additional details. After the *Press* feature appeared, Hazel Durstine of Smithson sent him another stanza. She had heard it recited as a poem by her eighty-nine-year-old father, R. R. Lynn. He recalled that strikers' friends sold this poem printed on a wallet-sized card for twenty cents each and used the proceeds to buy groceries for destitute families. Homestead citizens carried the card in their vest pockets to indicate solidarity with the unionists. As a lad, Lynn had been taken to a Knights of Labor meeting where he recited the poem, earning for his efforts nineteen cents in pin money.

In 1967, Lynn asked his daughter to mail his stanza to Swetnam. Our record in gathering laborlore ephemera remains ragged. I know of no extant Blochinger card or broadside. Nor have I located the Library of Congress registration copy. After I enlisted help at the American Folklife Center, Joe Hickerson noted that A. J. Blochinger had also submitted two books, *Homestead Budget No. 1* and *Homestead Budget No. 2,* to the Copyright Office. I lack information on their format and am curious about Blochinger's use of the term *budget.*

Fortunately, we do have three stanzas of Blochinger's "Battle" ballad—two from the Elks Club employee Wiggin and one from R. R. Lynn. Their joined portions read:

> Say, comrades, did you hear about the towboat *Little Bill,*
> That caused so much excitement at Carnegie's Homestead mill?
> With model barges well equipped, Billy Rodgers, sly and slick,
> Brought Pinkerton assassins there, employed by H. C. Frick.
>
> 'Twas on the sixth, July, '92, just at the dawn of day,
> The Pinkerton marauders tried to land at Fort Frick Bay.
> But there they met their Waterloo, from Vulcan's brawny sons,
> Who repulsed them in a moment, and stifled all their guns.
>
> Some weeks before the tragic act, Carnegie went away
> To see the banks of Bonnie Dawn that Frick might have his say.
> 'Twas there he wired to Pinkerton, "I want five hundred strong,
> A five a day will be your pay so bring your thugs along."

These twelve lines whet my appetite for the full text. Surely, the blacksmith ended his composition with a comment on the battle's meaning or a message warning despots to avoid future assaults on working people. Who can add to Blochinger's story, his ballad, or his two *Budgets?*

### 7. *"Come All Ye Hearty Working Men"*

Swetnam's article elicited several Homestead fragments, one of which came from Carl Kamphaus of Ross Township, Pittsburgh. He recalled his father's singing thirteen lines, including "A woman with a rifle . . ." and Kelly's original chorus. Beyond revealing that the ballad had remained in the memories of Steel City citizens as late as 1967, Kamphaus contributed a fresh opening:

> Come all ye hearty working men of iron and of steel,
> And listen to these few words 'til I tell you how I feel.
> 'Tis about the Homestead strikers who so bravely fought and
>   fell
> To kill the dirty Pinkertons on the tugboat *Little Bill.*

I have found no other Homestead references to this "come-all-ye" opening. It could have come from a song, presently unknown, or from Kamphaus's father.

### 8. *"I Want to Die a Poor Man"*

A decade before Homestead erupted, Andrew Carnegie had turned to philanthropy, giving a library to Dunfermline, Scotland, in 1881 (Wall). He continued such bequests until his death, providing special endowments for buildings at three steel towns: Homestead, Braddock, and Duquesne. The historian Curtis Miner identifies Homestead's French Renaissance "cultural fortress" as a "Parthenon upon the hill" and notes its role as a "controversial symbol of corporate paternalism." Homesteaders constructed their library on the hill used by militiamen as a camp during the strike.

Carnegie's many libraries served positively to deflect attention from his misdeeds and negatively to allow critics to stain his reputation. Arthur Gordon Burgoyne, born in Ireland and for three decades a Pittsburgh journalist, wrote an early history of the strike, as well as considerable poetry. Touching on Carnegie's philanthropy, Burgoyne, in 1892, penned, "On public libraries he spent / Of shekels not a few" (1979, 316).

Harold Nason, in a letter to the *Boston Globe* (reprinted in *Sing Out* [1961]) revealed folk memory's longevity. He reported a mocking song, possibly of vaudeville origin. The text follows:

I want to die a poor man
I often have said so,
And the only way to do it
Is by spending all the dough.

But Andrew, Andrew,
Oh, why so reckless pray?
Just send a million to Homestead
And we'll add it to their pay.

Homestead, Homestead,
That's where you got it from
And we want the world to know it
For a hundred years to come.

Homestead Library's
The name that ought to be
On every public library
Built by Andrew Carnegie.

*9. "A Parody on the 'Blue Bells of Scotland' "*

On December 8, 1982, the *National Labor Tribune* printed the text of a song by Alfred Morton. He satirized Carnegie's travels in Scotland and his purchase of castles while his agents at home hired Pinkertons to open the Homestead mill. I do not know the extent of this parody's circulation after the strike, although Morton had used a memorable tune.

*10. "A Song"*

D. R. Lewis's contribution appeared in the *National Labor Tribune* on August 27, 1892, with the note "Tune—'The Land of My Fathers.' " I speculate that Lewis intended a song, but his awkward rhetoric discouraged singers. Clark Halker, in *For Democracy, Workers, and God,* introduces the useful category of "labor song-poetry" to describe a massive body of turgid Gilded

Age material similar to Lewis's offering—suspended between elite and folk verse, neither widely sung nor recited.

The ten pieces cited, when added to the ballads by Delaney and Kelly, form a core group of a dozen Homestead songs. Surely, others remain lost. Here, I turn to a few representative poems that hold no apparent ties to music. Early in this chapter, I reprinted "The Fort That Frick Built." Its tongue-in-cheek humor marked the confidence with which spirited artisans viewed "their mill's" physical barrier. No matter the grime or clatter, injury or death, as workers converted ore to steel they also transformed sweat into belief. Homestead poetry called for victory and made defeat bearable.

Michael McGovern (1848–1933), the most prolific steel bard, recited topical verse at union conventions and published a poetry book in 1899. At his death, he left more than a thousand poems in manuscript. Born in Ireland, he followed the iron trades to Ferndale, Pennsylvania, before moving to his final home at Youngstown, Ohio. In "The Homestead Struggle or Fort Frick's Defenders," McGovern, "The Puddler Poet," caught a mechanic's gritty image: "That Vulcan's sons 'gainst Pinkertons / were steel compared to cinders" (Foner 1975, 244).

In May 1902, the Western Federation of Miners printed a ten-stanza poem entitled "Andrew Carnegie's Library" (*Miners' Magazine*). The editor credited Alice T. Sorenson in the San Francisco *Advance,* a Socialist Labor party paper. She spoke for comrades who never forgave Carnegie. Stanzas one and eight follow:

> There's a scent on the books of dead men's bones,
>   And a splatter of blood over all;
> There's a rough ragged hole in each leaf you turn,
>   Like the wound from a rifleman's ball.
>
> And this is his gift, still reeking with blood.
>   The gift that he proffers with arrogant hand;
> And this is his penance for murder and lust—
>   This his jest to the slaves of the land!

I close this poetry sampling with reference to three items. D. T. Morgan from Newburg, Ohio, submitted "A Song for the Day" to the *National Labor Tribune* (October 8, 1892). It seems unlikely that anyone could have sung it; Don Woodworth notes that Morgan provided a shopping list of remedies for working-class ills.

"A Man Named Carnegie" appeared in the *National Labor Tribune* (July 30, 1892). The editor had received it from a contributor in Stockton, California, who dated it July 7. In a letter to me, Professor Woodworth suggests that it came from a poet of considerable talent who chose anonymity. As part of the Homestead strike centennial, David Demarest has edited a commemorative anthology entitled "*The River Ran Red.*" This dramatic title stems from a line in the Stockton poem compressing Carnegie's power and terror into a single metaphor. We can appreciate the complexity in laborlore study as we ponder the transcontinental journey of an anonymous poem from 1892 to an anthology book title from 1992.

Finally, the University of Pittsburgh Press holds a rare broadside dated July 6, 1892, "Lines on the Homestead Riots." It is sixty-four lines long and sold for three cents a copy at printing. We can read it in full in "*The River Ran Red*" (103). The anonymous author of "Lines" concluded prophetically that Homestead's deadly scenes "ne'er can be forgotten."

## Recycle

Shifts in global markets, corporate buyouts, chaotic deindustrialization, and civic neglect have combined to close Monongahela Valley libraries and mills alike. In this past decade, activists and academicians have scrambled to explain America's industrial decline. I cite one report: John Hoerr, a Braddock-born journalist, offered a microscopic account of steel's backward steps in the provocatively named *And the Wolf Finally Came* (1988). Like other natives, Hoerr would have preferred a happier metaphor for the title.

I have been intrigued by steel's saga: technical prowess, princely prerogative, turbulent labor. Such personal concern dates back to my school years, when I read Louis Adamic's *Dynamite*, a beacon leading me to Homestead, Gastonia, Wheatland, Butte, and Coal Creek. Reading about Homestead during the CIO's formative years in Samuel Yellen's *American Labor Struggles*, I identified closely with steel workers in their organizational drives. In 1971, I belatedly visited Homestead—as much a pilgrimage as an ethnographic field trip. There, I entered the noisy mill, Local 1397's hall, the Carnegie library, and Joe Chiodo's saloon. Nearby, I viewed the then-discolored memorial shaft erected by the CIO in 1941.

During 1941, I had begun work in heavy industry at South San Francisco's Western Pipe & Steel. Our whole shipyard (mold loft, plate shop, launching ways, outfitting dock) seemed immense to me, yet it could have been dropped into a forgotten corner of the Homestead Works. As a young shipwright, I did not know the term *automation,* then more a mystery than a threat. As the word seeped into our consciousness, we anticipated that it might eliminate some jobs but not entire factories. Yet today, we have come to accept the reality of giant mills reduced to scrap.

Our concern over scrap and rust extends beyond forge and furnace to matters of human pride, skill, and belief. Within the setting of "wolves" coming to Homestead and sister communities, I ponder industry's present-day strength in "A Fight for Home and Honor." We do well to marvel at its compass: Pinkertonism's evil, Carnegie's duplicity, plebeian dignity, workers' courage. J. W. Kelly scored with a brilliant ballad title; Homesteaders who repulsed armed strikebreakers at "Fort Frick" did defend home and honor.

The historian Linda Schneider has read Kelly's composition as "expressing a kind of class solidarity" (61). She helps us look back in wonder at one expression of family cohesion: "a woman with a rifle" offers to pit herself against Pinkerton Winchesters. With hindsight, we know that stock tickers and legislative hoppers have proved more powerful than rifles in present-day assaults on blue-collar towns. The historian Paul Krause places the Monongahela battle in the largest frame of communal rights versus individual privilege. This debate, built into the American psyche, stretches from Bunker Hill to Homestead to the ghettos of New York and Los Angeles in 1992.

Homestead's brass mementos and stone monuments seem destined to outlast its steel mills. Some of the early Carnegie strike songs did not live beyond their entry into the Library of Congress's files. In contrast, Kelly's ballad became memorable to Pittsburgh toilers and, beyond their hearths, to workers in other trades from Maryland to Wisconsin, Kentucky, and Montana.

Antiquarians and conservators face a delemma in finding cabinets for their laborlore relics, in conceptualizing the means for presenting workers' treasures. Environmentalists recycle scrap iron, aluminum cans, glass bottles, daily newspapers; who recycles the creative lore of factory hand, timber beast, coal digger, bobbin girl, and their myriad brothers and sisters?

"A Fight for Home and Honor" journeyed widely before reaching preservationists and performers. I recapitulate its road:

1892: Will Rossiter prints original sheet music
1942: Douglas Gilbert reprints text
1943: George Korson prints a folk text
1949: Jacob Evanson prints a folk tune
1958: Ellen Stekert records a song on an LP album.

Gilbert's book appealed to popular music fans; Korson, Evanson, and Stekert reached folksong enthusiasts. During 1970, Kelly's song moved back into union territory, when the United Steelworkers of America produced an educational film entitled *The Counting Starts with One*. For the sound track, a modern rock band (sons of Pueblo, Colorado, union members) provided a spirited version of the Homestead ballad. The band had received text and tune from John Powderly, a steelworkers' union staff member. He had access in the union's national office to Peter Haser's archival disc. Thus, we can follow Kelly's song from New Kensington to Pittsburgh to Pueblo and, via film, to union locals across the land.

In 1978, the United Steelworkers of America again re-presented Kelly's song, this time within *Songs of Steel & Struggle*, an LP by Joe Glazer and the Charlie Byrd trio. This unusual pairing brought together "labor's troubadour" and a modern jazz combo. The album held fifteen songs—a dozen internal to iron and steel and three of general labor appeal. Glazer included a full version of "The Homestead Song," crediting text and tune to Korson and Evanson. The union packaged its first LP in a handsomely illustrated jacket with a detailed insert brochure, placing the songs in their historical frames.

A third rendition comes through the voice of Pete Seeger. On

January 11, 1980, some eight hundred fans gathered in Harvard University's Sanders Theatre for a two-hour singalong concert. Folkways Records issued the performance, slightly edited, in a double-LP set with a sixteen-page explanatory brochure. The text and tune of the "Homestead Strike Song" also stemmed from Korson and Evanson (via Philip Foner's printing of the text). Seeger's presentation is especially welcome for its spoken introduction dealing with the song's background, as well as with his decision in choosing this particular piece. He states, "When I first saw this song in a book, I said well that's kind of a barroom Irish song. I don't think it's as good as some of the union songs I've heard, I didn't learn it. . . . I went back to Homestead to sing a couple of years ago and I figured I'd learn the song. Sonofagun, the song rang true, the whole audience knew it. They must have been singing it in the bars ever since 1892."

Seeger's reference to Homestead singing bears elaboration. In a "Johnny Appleseed" column (1977), he noted having learned the song to participate in an Ed Sadlowski campaign for the presidency of the United Steelworkers of America. Insurgent Sadlowski lost his bid to incumbent Lloyd McBride. However, their campaign gave *Rolling Stone* reporter Joe Klein (1977) the opening for a sharp look at the Homestead rally. As Seeger performed at the Leona Theater before a mural depicting 1892 events he seemed both pleased and stunned by his warm reception. He had enjoyed singing for unionists in Almanac Singers days; however, such audiences had fallen away during the Cold War years. Probing for large issues in the concert, Klein mentioned the controversies over communism that had touched Seeger for decades.

In 1971, Sadlowski helped Seeger regain a labor audience, but the singer alone could not guarantee the challenger success in his pitch for union office. Klein correctly sensed that the evening would be remembered. "Pete Seeger at Homestead" posters and live-concert tapes are sought-after memorabilia. The *Rolling Stone* reporter concluded with a query: would the concert "be remembered as the beginning of a new era of trade union activism, or just a momentary indulgence in nostalgia?" Clearly, recent union cultural activists have not arrested labor's decline. Nevertheless, we need not infer from Klein's dichotomy that song performance, however fleeting, is but nostalgic indulgence.

Songs function variously to entertain, educate, exhort, memorialize, pace work, or dissipate tension. Kelly's Homestead ballad remains useful as a social text recalling an 1892 crisis, as a capsule of emotion tugging at personal beliefs, and as a road sign for working people overwhelmed by scrap and rust. It has been recycled in film, sound album, union election meeting, and Harvard concert. Sound tracks or discs carry Kelly's song great distances from Pittsburgh. Meanwhile, in the Monongahela Valley, folksong fans and laborlore buffs continue to spread the version taught by Seeger. In 1989, he highlighted the ballad at the Pittsburgh Labor Arts Festival; students at the Philip Murray Labor Studies Institute have made the Kelly/Seeger song a local favorite.

We need not list every sighting of a painting on a gallery wall to prove its beauty. We do not denigrate Mother Jones because she lacks the present fame of Madonna. Similarly, I do not certify the value of Kelly's Homestead song by virtue of a census of appearance in print or stage performance. Kelly's composition holds promise wherever workers reflect on their past or seek psychic energy in community revitalization.

During October 1892, Hamlin Garland, populist and novelist, had visited Carnegie's Homestead Works. Reporting for *McClure's Magazine*, he found a "pandemoniac sight"—a figure from Hell's Capital in *Paradise Lost*. Garland saw a squalid town with sullen workers in perilous trades. He heard men call the converting mill "a death trap." His report opened by asserting Homestead as "infamously historic," and closed, "Its industries lay like a cancer on the breast of a human body." For a century since Garland's visit, Homesteaders, while fighting industrial ills, have joined unions, churches, and ethnic clubs to counter the forces of social cancer.

On Labor Day, 1988, *New York Times* reporter William Serrin penned a "Requiem for a Steel Town": "This summer, men with acetylene torches and earth- and equipment-moving machines came to tear down the [Homestead] mill." Observing efforts by Monongahela unionists, teachers, and ministers to save devastated towns, Serrin reflected, "I am not optimistic, for the nation has a wretched record in saving or rebuilding sick communities, particularly when the people . . . working-class people, are considered unimportant."

Garland viewed industry as a cancer; Serrin saw victims reduced to ciphers. In 1992, *Washington Post* reporter Dale Russakoff sketched mini-portraits of unemployed hands at the USX Fairless Works on the Delaware River. Built in 1951, this mill headed for obsolescence from its opening days. Austrian steel men had already perfected a "next-generation" basic-oxygen furnace that literally cut a six-hour process to forty minutes. By 1992, plant layoffs turned men and women without "whiskers" (seniority) into "scrap." Unlike scrap that can be melted down, the Fairless unemployed have not been recast as productive workers.

How do people from the Delaware to the Monongahela, and far beyond Pennsylvania's borders, extend their local traditions to assert individual and collective worth? I name five representatives, who, by example, make a difference at Homestead. Doris Dyen, public folklorist and musicologist, carries on the work of Jacob Evanson in gathering steel song lore. Russ Gibbons, editor and educator, reminds fellow unionists of cultural treasures. Randy Harris, journalist and preservationist, lobbies to save the Bost Building (1892 strike headquarters) and similar landmark sites. Steffi Domike and Nicole Fauteux, documentarians, gather graphics and stills for a film on the 1892 struggle.

These creative workers understand Homestead's century-long fight for home and honor. Together with their colleagues they participate in community regenerative efforts. In cooperation with the U.S. National Park Service and other public agencies, they seek to establish a museum on a portion of the old Homestead Works. This area will include the pumphouse and watertower, the two buildings remaining at the site of the Pinkerton landing, and will also take in the Carrie furnaces across the Monongahela River. If such plans materialize, Homestead will serve as a model industrial museum with steel workers and their children serving as guides and docents.

No museum, no treasured artifact, no union election concert, no anti-plant-closing rally, can singlehandedly save a mill community. Yet a town struggling to survive must fall back on those cultural traditions that light the path from past to future. In cataloging strategies for linking historical preservation, natural conservation, and cultural presentation, I have tried not to exaggerate the potency of any poetic or musical construct. By definition, creative expression holds limited utility in many settings.

Stripped to its essence, "A Fight for Home and Honor" speaks to the best impulses within the American labor movement. To recycle the ballad comments on present meaning for Kelly's song. We shall never fully learn his perception of the piece. We do not know whether he felt any personal statement about Homestead beyond this composition. We do not know where his body rests, or whether his grave holds an epitaph. Did he picture himself only as an entertainer? Did he appreciate his extended role as social critic? Would it have mattered to him that his Homestead ballad entered tradition as a folksong?

Regardless of the answers to such rhetorical questions, we know that puddlers, rollers, loggers, miners, and other workers across skill and regional boundaries cherished John W. Kelly's contribution. Carnage in the Monongahela Valley in 1892 stirred working people wherever telegraph wires carried news, wherever artistic depictions of the battle appeared. Deeply troubled by moral issues posed by Carnegie, Frick, O'Donnell, and Berkman, those unionists who heard the Homestead song sensed that it reaffirmed personal and collective values. This ballad, one of many strike narratives, holds an extra measure of meaning—it marks a site memorable to working people throughout America.

**"In the Mill"**

# 8

# A Southern Cotton Mill Rhyme

Textile workers' traditions in the United States have not received attention comparable to those of railroaders or coal miners. No millhand starred as the central character in a riding-into-the-sunset film. No "linthead" rivaled John Henry's power or Joe Hill's zeal. No bobbin girl ascended Mother Jones's pedestal. No mill novel matched the appeal of John Steinbeck's *Grapes of Wrath* or Upton Sinclair's *Jungle*. Not until the release of *Norma Rae* in 1979 did Hollywood celebrate mill workers' vitality.

In a lifetime of collecting, the eminent North Carolina ballad hunter Frank C. Brown amassed a magnificent folkloric cornucopia, but his seven volumes hold no textile songs. Seemingly, he requested no occupational lore from Tar Heel workers. The first article treating textiles in any major American folklore journal did not appear until 1972, when Betty Messenger dealt with Irish linen rather than Carolina cotton.

In my mind's eye, I see mill lore hidden in a crenelated red-brick factory, with singers and storytellers appropriately draped in fabrics of their own making: cotton, wool, worsted, linen, burlap, muslin, ticking, felt, flannel, denim, calico, gingham, corduroy, silk, brocade, rayon, nylon. These goods display the texture of many cloths and evoke the histories of their production and ultimate use. Could they have been woven or spun without their makers engaging in bantering wordplay or creating downhome music?

It may come as a surprise to learn that America's oldest industrial folksong with continuous life in tradition is a textile ballad, "The Factory Girl." Printed as a broadside about 1835 in or near Lowell, Massachusetts, itinerants carried it to Bangor, Maine, and Fort Worth, Texas, at the century's turn. I collected a variant in 1962 at East Rockingham, North Carolina, from Nancy Dixon, its last traditional singer. Testament Records issued it, with related material by Dixon's brothers Howard and Dorsey, on *Babies in the Mill.* Subsequently, Nancy's plaintive rendition reached Mike Seeger, Heddy West, and others. In Seeger's *Tipple, Loom & Rail* and West's *Songbook,* we hear and see work songs moving from mine and mill to campus and festival circuit (Tamburro).

In selecting a southern song for study, I turn away from New England's "Factory Girl" to an indigenous Carolina ballad. "A Southern Cotton Mill Rhyme" opens many windows, letting us view an occupational community and its traditions, the conscious use of folk material by radicals, and the diverse roads a song travels. This rhyme found disparate vehicles: poetry chapbook, proletarian fiction, agitprop drama, hillbilly record, folksong album.

Over the years, American readers have had access to textile labor histories and sociological observations. Southern millhands have constituted an enclaved occupational group in a particular region for more than a century, and, like other people set apart, their experience has been compressed into scholarly monographs. Books by Jacquelyn Hall, Doug DeNatale, and Allen Tullos break new ground in explicating the expressive culture of Piedmont millhands. My chapter fits their large canvas.

## Gastonia

Grace Lumpkin submitted "A Southern Cotton Mill Rhyme" to the *New Masses* (May, 1930). The poem read:

I lived in a town away down south
By the name of Buffalo
And worked in a mill with the rest of the trash
As we're often called you know.

You Factory Folks who read this rhyme
Will surely understand

The reason why I love you so
Is I'm a Factory Hand.

While standing here between my looms
You know I lose no time
To keep my shuttles in a whiz
And write this little rhyme.

We rise up early in the morn
And work all day real hard
To buy our little meal and bread
And sugar tea and lard.

We work from weeks end to weeks end
And never lose a day
And when that awful pay day comes
We draw our little pay.

We then go home on pay day night
And sit down in a chair
The merchant raps upon the door
He's come to get his share.

When all our little debts are paid
And nothing left behind
We turn our pockets wrong side out
But not a cent can find.

We rise up early in the morn
And toil from sun till late
We have no time to primp
And fix and dress right up to date.

Our children they grow up unlearned
No time to go to school
Almost before they've learned to walk
They learn to spin or spool.

The Boss men jerk them round and
Round and whistle very keen
I'll tell you what the Factory kids
Are really treated mean.

The folks in town who dress so fine
And spends their money free

Will hardly look at a factory hand
Who dresses like you and me.

As we go walking down the street
All wrapped in lint and strings
They call us fools and factory trash
And other low down names.

Just let them wear their watches fine
And golden chains and rings,
But when the great Revolution comes
They'll have to shed those things.

Since 1956, six performers have included a version of this poem on LP albums. With some alteration in text, they have titled their offerings "Let Them Wear Their Watches Fine," viewing the piece as past social commentary worth preserving. From various perspectives, these singers have directed their efforts to unionists or to folksong fans attuned to work problems. The artist's names follow in order of the year of release (1956–85): Pete Seeger, Kathy Kahn, Joe Glazer, Jon Sundell, Roy Berkeley, Anne Romaine.

In album notes or letters, the singers following Seeger acknowledged him as the source for the text and tune. Glazer and Berkeley had encountered the text alone in John Greenway's *American Folksongs of Protest*. None of the performers related the song to "A Southern Cotton Mill Rhyme." No one seemed aware that Grace Lumpkin's printing stood behind Seeger's recording.

Fortunately, when "Cotton Mill Rhyme" appeared in the *New Masses*, Lumpkin had provided the editors with a footnote ideal in its attention to setting. She wrote:

> To my knowledge this song has never appeared in print before I came upon it in this fashion: We were sitting in the National Textile Workers Union Hall in Charlotte, N.C., waiting for the meeting to begin. It was a cold night. Somebody started Solidarity and then we sang Ella May's "ballets." Almost everybody knew them since many of the workers in the Union Hall were strikers from Gastonia and Bessemer City. At the end of one of the songs, Daisy McDonald of Gastonia asked her husband to lead The Southern Cotton

> Mill Rhyme. Some of us had not heard this song before and Mr. McDonald explained that many years ago he had worked at the loom next to a man in a mill in Buffalo, South Carolina. He said this weaver had spoken out the words of the Rhyme under the noise of the looms, making them up as he worked. And the song had gone from one worker to another and now it is known to hundreds of cotton mill hands who sing it as the workers did that night in the hall in Charlotte.

The National Textile Workers Union, a Communist party satellite, had been established in September 1928 as a rival to the United Textile Workers of America, AFL. On April Fool's Day in 1929, the tiny dual union undertook a strike at the Manville-Jenckes Company (Loray Mill) in Gastonia, North Carolina. This tire cord fabric mill, owned by Rhode Island capitalists, used then-modern scientific management techniques, termed by millhands as *speed-up* and *stretch-out.* The Loray Mill's power stretched to Detroit auto and Akron rubber assembly lines.

Although substantial grievances marked shop-floor life in Gastonia, NTWU vanguardists did not view their strike solely in pragmatic terms. Rather, they judged it as the beginning of a fundamental revolutionary upsurge in the United States. Their vision came both from affiliation with the Red International of Labor Unions (Profintern) in Moscow and from Loray discontent.

When sectarian unionists employed Bolshevik strategies, Gastonia's civic leaders responded in kind. Violent street battles by company vigilantes, local police, and National Guardsmen brought wide attention to the strike. On June 7, someone fatally shot Police Chief Aderholt, and, on September 14, an armed band murdered the union's ballad composer, Ella May Wiggins. She had worked at the American Mills in Bessemer City, a few miles north of Gastonia. The deaths of Aderholt and Wiggins seemed made to order in a divided community whose leaders reveled in apocalyptic behavior.

Gastonia called national attention to the disproportion between radical challenge and civic reaction. The legal assault on the strikers paralleled the illegal street floggings and midnight raids that rained down outside the courthouse. At two trials, in the summer and in the early fall, the state charged and convicted

NTWU organizer Fred Beal and other defendants for both deeds and ideas—murder and heresy. With an appeal pending, the "class heroes" visited the Soviet Union. When the North Carolina Supreme Court denied appeal in March 1930, Beal and his comrades jumped bail, remaining in Moscow. After Beal's faith in the revolutionary utopia dissolved, he returned to America, hiding as a fugitive until 1938. Captured and imprisoned, he was freed in 1942. Until his death in 1954, communists reviled him as a class traitor.

In the mid-1930s, the National Textile Workers Union disappeared, undercut by the Communist International's change in line during Popular Front years. Not only did the dual union fall victim to Soviet Union policy shifts, but, more importantly, southern workers abandoned the NTWU. Essentially, Red cadres stood at such an extreme cultural distance from mill workers that fervor alone failed to bridge the gulf. One organizer, unburdening herself to Mary Heaton Vorse, tried to explain the dissonance felt by communists in the Piedmont: [Southern textile hands] "are Americans like we are and yet our foreign workers in the North are much more comprehensible to us" (Haessly, 68).

The literature about Gastonia dwarfs that of all other southern textile battles. From the beginning, the Communist party spokesmen Albert Weisbord, William Dunne, and Jack Johnson cheered the uprising as vindicating their respective views of world events. In an early reflection on Gastonia, W. J. Cash, seeking balance, placed the owners' defense of the mill economy within a web of regional values that included rooted patriotism, Calvinist religion, and white supremacy (343). Cash noted that most owners perceived themselves as "Saviors of the South," defending home against Yankee and subversive.

Liston Pope's summation of the doomed strike remains useful: "Gastonia became a symbol, far and wide, of the confluence of plantation feudalism and a new boisterous industrialism, of underfed, unkempt children and lank, mute mill workers, of sudden violence in the night and quick death on the public highways" (322). Theodore Draper, looking back in "Gastonia Revisited," observed that this textile strike—neither the first, largest, nor the most typical in the South—had become legendary, "less noteworthy as a strike than as a tragic drama."

In 1977, Vera Buch Weisbord, an NTWU firebrand, offered a troubled autobiography touching on long-suppressed feminist concerns. Intensely loyal to communism, she had been victimized by the movement's chauvinists. Countering negative interpretations by Buch and others who had "recanted" or "surrendered," Carl Reeve, an International Labor Defense functionary, offered a sanguine reflection on communist rectitude: he and his comrades had gone "forward with history" (1984, 31). Perhaps unwittingly, Buch and Reeve reveal our present-day difficulties in making coherent Gastonia's mix of corrosive exploitation, explosive injustice, radical omniscience, regional mores, and rank-and-file resistance to mill owner and outside commissar.

Between 1930 and 1934, six novelists (Mary Heaton Vorse, Myra Page, Grace Lumpkin, Fielding Burke, Sherwood Anderson, and William Rollins) magnified Gastonia's significance (Reilly; Urgo). Gastonia's first stage play, *Strike Song,* appeared while battle passions ran through the Piedmont (Carmer, 534). James O. Bailey taught English at the University of North Carolina; Loretto Carroll, his wife, acted in productions of the campus-housed Carolina Playmakers. Together, the Baileys wrote *Strike Song*. Sympathetic to labor, Carroll had visited mill villages and union meetings to authenticate the play's themes (Bailey 1977).

The Carolina Playmakers presented *Strike Song* on December 10–12, 1931, with some sixty student actors, among them three daughters of mill owners. Loretto Carroll Bailey portrayed Mammy King, a village crone. The play drew on then-memorable Gastonia events: the death of Lily May Brothers (Ella May Wiggins); the burning of the strikers' tent city; the interplay between textile executives, Black Mask vigilantes, and the law. The Baileys integrated traditional and union songs—at the time, an innovative mixture. Frederick Koch, the Playmakers' director, lauded *Strike Song* as a "mature folk drama," comparing it to previous plays about mountain people, fisher folk, and tenant farmers. Professor Koch was ahead of his time in awarding industrial workers the accolade *folk*.

I believe that the Baileys would have used "A Southern Cotton Mill Rhyme" within *Strike Song* had they encountered it. We lack evidence that "Cotton Mill Rhyme" reached teachers or writers beyond Grace Lumpkin. However, I can reconstruct something of the readers' response to her find. Few *New Masses* subscribers during 1930 could have been unmoved by Gastonia's indelible imprint. Some waited for a statement atoning for individual deaths; others sought a creative opus that reaffirmed their faith in revolution. A few readers wrote to the magazine seeking a tune for the text and questioning its last stanza.

In June, the *New Masses* printed Lumpkin's follow-up letter:

> The tune as I heard it is original, perhaps the blending of some old ballads. But I know that the Rhyme, with a little adaptation, has been sung to the tune "John Hardy," a mountain ballad that is on Columbia Record No. 167-D, sung by Eva Davis who lives in the Great Smokey Mountains near Proctor, North Carolina.
>
> As regards the last stanza of the Rhyme. On the evening when the folks sang the Rhyme in the Union Hall in Charlotte they told me that the weaver who made the words said:
>
> Just let them wear their watches fine.
> And rings and golden chains
> But when the day of Judgment come
> They'll have to shed those things.
>
> During the strike of April, 1929, the workers changed the next to last line to "When the great revolution comes." Doubtless in other sections people still sing the last line as originally composed. Folk songs are made and changed from the knowledge and needs of the people who sing them.

Where and when did Grace Lumpkin develop her knowledge of folksong? Although she had learned "A Southern Cotton Mill Rhyme" from Daisy McDonald's husband in Charlotte within a year after the Gastonia's strike beginning, she placed the song's origin "many years ago" in Buffalo (Union County, South Carolina). She marked the importance of variation by contrasting the conventional sacred ending with the NTWU political ending.

Interestingly, Lumpkin identified the tune "John Hardy" from a Columbia recording. This startling discographical citation came before the wide academic use of commercial recordings. Eva Davis (banjo) and Samantha Bumgarner (fiddle) pioneered among the phonograph's earliest folk artists, making their debut in the summer of 1924. Without offering a musical transcription of their "John Hardy," I can identify it as standard—similar to the ballad recorded by the Carter Family and used subsequently by Woody Guthrie for the music of his "Tom Joad."

Had Grace Lumpkin's "Cotton Mill Rhyme" not survived beyond its initial publication, we would have been in her favor for adding an item to textile tradition's cache. But the "Rhyme" lived after Gastonia's strike, if not in the minds and hearts of Piedmont millhands, then initially in the radical movement's press. Jack Conroy and Ralph Cheney liked the *New Masses* poem enough to reprint it in *Unrest*, a gathering of revolutionary verse. Subsequently, Granville Hicks also included it—"an old ballad discovered by Grace Lumpkin"—in *Proletarian Literature in the United States*. This anthology circulated widely in the 1930s, thereby helping to keep "Cotton Mill Rhyme" in left consciousness. However, a novel and a play rather than the anthology brought the factory trash piece into folksong revival circles.

## To Make My Bread

Grace Lumpkin's *To Make My Bread* appeared in 1932; it included the rhyme she had learned in Charlotte's NTWU hall. The novel's title evoked the ogre in "Jack and the Beanstalk" who ground his victims' bones. Readers in the Depression's pit could understand Gastonia's owners as capitalistic giants, larger than life. Critics such as Robert Cantwell reported favorably on Lumpkin's book. Translated into Russian, it won the Maxim Gorky award in Moscow for the year's best labor fiction.

The *New Masses* accorded *To Make My Bread* a surreal review by A. B. Magil that contrasted Lumpkin's objectivity (bourgeois realism) with the scientific (dialectical) view necessary to writers of proletarian literature. Essentially, he approved the Gastonia strike subject but questioned the author's skill in fashioning a novel useful to workers as a self-transformational instrument. An ideal revolutionary novel, Magil pontificated, not only critically described existing society but also served as a challenge and prophecy.

Today, I find it difficult to appreciate *To Make My Bread*. Although it retains its strength in delineating mill folk and remains a creative endeavor helping outsiders feel Gastonia's pain, I cannot reread it with ease. In carrying a mountain farming family from the Blue Ridge to a Carolina mill village, Lumpkin combined the cloying characterizations of Appalachian romanticists with the didactic tone then demanded in radical fiction. Beyond this internal rhetorical duality, Lumpkin faltered in the difficult task of intertwining her major themes, the physical movement from agrarian to industrial life, and the spiritual shift from individual to class consciousness.

I dwell on Lumpkin's novel because proletarian literature, however dated or weak in form, is a storehouse for considerable laborlore. Radical fiction has been well studied by Daniel Aaron, Deming Brown, Walter Rideout, and others; however, no folklorist has examined such writings as potential sources for specific aspects of industrial tradition.

Had Lumpkin not used "A Southern Cotton Mill Rhyme" in *To Make My Bread,* the song would not have appeared on LP discs recorded after 1956. By comparison, some of Ella May Wiggins's Gastonia-inspired compositions (for example, "Mill Mother's Lament") reached folksong revivalists from Margaret Larkin's early articles and, subsequently, from academic studies (Greenway, Haessly, Joiner, Wiley).

Within *To Make My Bread,* Lumpkin employed the full thirteen-stanza poem she had submitted previously to the *New Masses.* She altered but a few words, for example, changing *read* to *sing.* Most significantly, she reverted to the poem's prestrike, nonrevolutionary ending. No clues explain this switch. Did the author feel the original text to be more authentic than the radical revision? In the time lapse from strike loss to crafting the novel, had leftists begun to criticize Gastonia story distortions?

Labor historians have advanced varied explanations for both the failure of radical creeds and their limited appeal in America. Several textile songs suggest the frame within which most Piedmont millhands understand job exploitation. In "Cotton Mill Colic," David McCarn literally "bellyached" about wretched working conditions. Whoever wrote "A Southern Cotton Mill Rhyme" also "colicked," but in a descriptive manner. The unknown worker who switched "day of Judgment" to "great Revolution" made vocal the transformation of endemic discontent into a declaratory statement of Marxist identity.

Lumpkin's novel offered an imaginative setting for "Cotton Mill Rhyme" by portraying its composer, John Stevens, as a weaver both more skilled and radical than his fellows. Lumpkin wrote:

> While the looms pounded up and down John Stevens sang. His voice came clear under the sound of the looms. Most people shouted trying to make their voices heard above the grinding, but John Stevens knew how to make his clear under the sound, just as people standing on the outside of a waterfall might scream to be heard, but one who stood in a cave underneath could speak with a low voice. John Stevens stood in the cave underneath. He spoke to his looms, and knowing each part, spoke of them. He liked his machines. "It's what they do to people . . . that makes me sick at heart." (258)

Grace Lumpkin had listened to workers talk and sing on and off the job; she had heard mill machinery's deafening roar, as well as the hypnotic rhythm of the loom's rise and fall. She knew that it took more than relentless clatter to stamp out the vitality of mill people and to reduce them to automatons. Born about 1900 at Milledgeville, Georgia, she lived after her tenth year near Columbia, South Carolina.

Katherine Du Pre Lumpkin, Grace's sister, in *The Making of a Southerner,* wrote a classic study of a "good family" divided by complex loyalties. While young, Grace cast her lot with Piedmont plain folk by teaching rural school and working as an industrial secretary for the YWCA. About 1924, she moved to New York, took menial jobs, and enrolled in classes at Columbia University. Championing causes such as the defense of Sacco and Vanzetti, she absorbed creeds of dissent. The *New Masses,* in 1927, accepted her first polemical story, "White Man."

About 1929, Grace Lumpkin married Michael Intrator, a fur worker active in the Communist party's Lovestone faction. One of her closest friends, Esther Shemitz, a young veteran of the 1926 Passaic silk strike, married communist journalist Whittaker Chambers. Lumpkin remained close to "Whit" in the years of his work with Alger Hiss and subsequent break with the left.

During the 1930s, Lumpkin wrote three novels; by 1941 she had pulled away from communist activity. On April 2, 1952, she appeared before Senator Joseph McCarthy's committee (Permanent Subcommittee on Investigations of the Committee on Government Operations).

Lumpkin completed a fourth novel, *Full Circle* (1962), dealing with a woman's participation in and withdrawal from the Communist party. Despite the searing effects of her loss of political faith, this confessional novel failed as fiction. In reading it, I searched for autobiographical clues to her interest in folksong but found none. If she ever reflected on her role in adding a significant song to the body of textile lore, her views remain hidden. Whether or not Grace Lumpkin will receive future attention from folklorists, literary critics, and feminist historians, I do not know. To date, studies of her work have been fragmentary (Cook, Gilkes, C. M. Smith, *Twentieth Century Authors*).

Conventionally, ballad scholars marshal song variants in direct chronological/geographical sequence and arrange their reports with matching logic. We perceive songs as passengers on a long train or sea trip, rocketed and buffeted but emerging intact at some distant depot or harbor. This useful metaphor implies that the song becomes a conscious traveler equipped with a passport, cassette recorder, and camera. In reality, only humans chart folksong paths. Hence, my report on "A Southern Cotton Mill Rhyme" also comments on a personal journey.

Attracted to trade union belief when John L. Lewis launched the CIO, I looked forward to the university as a place where I might develop skills useful in the labor movement. Then, I enjoyed Samuel Yellen's vivid account of Gastonia in *American Labor Struggles*. I can recall no prior acquaintance with Piedmont workers's culture prior to reading his book.

Although a continent separated Berkeley from Gastonia, mill shadows darkened my college room. I visualized red-brick fortresses ringed by barbed wire before seeing Ben Shahn's paintings of such factories and before traveling from San Francisco to the Carolinas in pursuit of textile lore. In Berkeley, I had read one Gastonia novel by William Rollins, *The Shadow Before*. Also, I had read *Proletarian Literature in the United States*. This anthology included Lumpkin's "Cotton Mill Rhyme," but the poem made no impression on me during student days.

Not until 1954 did this textile piece impinge on my consciousness, and then only after I encountered it in *American Folksongs of Protest*. Although the poem appealed as a poignant document, Greenway's headnote for "Let Them Wear their Watches Fine" troubled me. He stated that Will Geer had transcribed "Let Them Wear" from its composer, a West Virginia mountain woman who had put it to the tune of "Warren Harding's Widow." I knew that West Virginia's mountains held no cotton mills. If the actor Geer had actually met the composer, her name and the circumstances of meeting should have been detailed. Further, I could not locate a text or tune for "Warren Harding's Widow."

Only after hearing Pete Seeger's LP recording (1956) of "Let Them Wear" did I frame appropriate questions. His traditional melody proved convincing, for he figuratively had dusted his banjo with lint for the Folkways studio rendition. Irwin Silber's notes for Seeger's *American Industrial Ballads*, and a similar headnote in *Sing Out* by Josh Dunson, paralleled Greenway's "explanation" for the song. For their Will Geer reference, all commentators drew on the same headnote in an undated typescript in the People's Songs library. An anonymous compiler had copied Lumpkin's text from *Proletarian Literature in the United States*, dropping her name and changing the song title to "Let Them Wear Their Watches Fine."

Several writers have plumbed the history of People's Songs, among them R. Serge Denisoff, David Dunaway, Joe Klein, Robbie Lieberman, Richard Reuss, and Doris Willens. Hence, I need mention only that People's Songs had been incorporated in New York on January 31, 1946. Caught up in Cold War tension, Henry Wallace's failed presidential bid, and Stalinist aesthetics, the organization died in the spring of 1949.

I do not know who made the title shift for the People's Songs typescript. In a 1977 letter to me, Irwin Silber recalled that "Let Them Wear" had come to the People's Song library within a manuscript collection of hard-hitting songs compiled by Alan Lomax about 1939. Was the typescript deletion of Grace Lumpkin's name coincidental, or had she been stricken for breaking ranks with former comrades?

Speculation aside, the People's Songs headnote contained an invaluable musical clue by identifying the tune of "Warren Harding's Widow" as "the same tune 'John Catchins' was put to." Initially, I found this musical reference as esoteric as the "Harding" citation, but a clue appeared in a Library of Congress field recording list: "The Ballad of John Catchings." Alan Lomax had collected this piece on November 13, 1937, in New York City from Mr. and Mrs. Joe Gelders of Alabama. Years intervened between my obtaining the "Let Them Wear" typescript and my resolution of the "Harding"-"Catchins" tune connection.

## Let Freedom Ring

My curiosity about "Let Them Wear Their Watches Fine," stimulated by John Greenway's book and the People's Songs typescript, followed no marked trail. Ballad scholars do misread signs, backtrack, and jump fences. We seek bread crumbs in the forest, strings in the labyrinth. Regardless of our grand strategies, luck plays a large role in results.

During 1964, I wrote to Will Geer about "Let Them Wear" but failed to reach him. Some years later, I shared my interest with Richard Reuss, whose unpublished thesis on left-wing attention to folklore remains a treasure chest. He generously supplied a key reference: "Paterson Strikers Get a Ballad" (*Daily Worker,* November 26, 1935) by Al Hayes. Knowing Hayes as the writer of the Joe Hill popular ballad, I turned to his report on a New Jersey textile union meeting at which Geer performed:

> The tall gent on the platform in Lazzara Hall, the union hall of the United Textile Workers Union, Paterson Local, whose weavers, loomfixers, spinners and twisters are out on strike, was the same Mr. Will Geer, minus make-up, who six nights a week these days is the ballad-singing Grandpap Kirland of Albert Bein's Southern folk play, "Let Freedom Ring."
>
> It was an early hour for a late-working actor to be up; the morning sun outside the windows was just beginning to lift the fog off the slow, yellow Passaic River. But Mr. Geer, upon the express invitation of Francis J. Gorman, national vice-president of the textile union, had already spent a half-

hour singing some half dozen ballads or "ballits" for the striking weavers of Paterson, N.J.

It wasn't the first time Mr. Geer had sung ballads, some of which he had written himself, for union men. Back in California, they still remember Mr. Geer's original contribution to the folk-songs of the nation, entitled "The Ballad of the Wives and Widows of Presidents and Dictators," of which the following verse is an adequate example.

Warren Hardin's widow to the burial ground went
All dressed in blue
She knelt down by his grave and said,
Warren, I'll be true to you.
Pore boy!

. . . Mr. Geer then followed with his ballad, "The Song of the Blue Eagle," the only description of which is a political folk-song with gestures. However, Mr. Gorman had requested that "The Ballad of the Mill Hand," the fine moving narrative of the life of mill workers which Mr. Geer sings in "Let Freedom Ring," should be sung for these Northern millhands.

When he had come to the end of the refrain:

Just let them wear their watches fine
And rings and pearly things
But when our day of judgement comes
We'll make them shed their pretty things.

Mr. Geer paused a moment and then said, smiling, "Now we're going to try to make up some ballads of our own about Paterson, New Jersey."

Despite notions of scholarship by patient accretion, on reading Hayes, I longed to obtain instantly a recording of Geer's singing his presidential piece, as well as "The Ballad of a Mill Hand." Other *Daily Worker* details caught my eye. The fact that Francis Gorman had invited Geer to the Paterson meeting indicated a softening of political line in 1935, both by the AFL and the Communist party. With the spread of European fascism, communists toned down their previous invective in favor of united fronts with socialists and trade unionists. The AFL had opposed the NTWU in the Gastonia strike, yet at Paterson, AFL textile workers enjoyed a Gastonia ballad.

Hayes pointed me to the Samuel French publication of *Let Freedom Ring* (1936) and a search for Grandpap Kirkland's "bal-lit." Albert Bein had adapted the play from Grace Lumpkin's *To Make My Bread,* offering it to the Theatre Union, a left-wing professional company. When the group rejected Bein's play, he raised funds, producing it with the Actor's Repertory Company. Opening uptown at the Broadhurst (November 6, 1935), Worthington Miner staged it with imaginative sets by Mordecai Gorelik. The designer had pioneered in modern "constructivist" sets; for Bein's play, he spent a month in Carolina mill towns, returning to place before Manhattan audiences the clustered poverty-stricken villages and overbearing factories seen in the Piedmont.

The Broadhurst production closed after twenty-nine performances, giving Margaret Larkin a chance to reconsider the Theatre Union's initial rejection. Larkin helped Bein transfer the cast and sets downtown to the Civic Repertory Theatre in January. There, it ran for seventy-nine performances. In retrospect, *Let Freedom Ring* did not prove a glowing success or an abject failure.

Adhering as the play did to the political stance within Lumpkin's novel, change plagued the drama at the end of 1935. The ultramilitant National Textile Workers Union had vanished; strike heroes had been jailed or exiled; and Gastonia's rank and file remained unorganized. Throughout the communist movement, proletarian themes faced challenge from Popular Front modes. In short, polemical shifts dated Bein's play on its debut. Although tens of millions of Americans in the 1930s saw unionism as an instrument of hope, only a vanguard viewed labor through the lens of communist culture.

Publicity announcements billed *Let Freedom Ring* as "a drama of the 'lintheads.' " This vernacular usage, then new to Broadway, referred pejoratively to Piedmont millhands, who ended their shifts covered with fine dust. Seeking to understand the frame within which Geer sang Lumpkin's ballad in Bein's play, I turned to reviews in *Time, Newsweek,* and the *New York Times* (Atkinson), as well as to partisan comments in *New Theatre* (Gassner, Kline). Bein, Miner, and Larkin used letters to the *Times* to reveal tensions while staging the play. Beyond consulting such contemporary material, I mined studies of social drama (Flanagan, Goldstein, Himmelstein, Mathews, Rabkin, Williams).

New York critics rated *Let Freedom Ring* politically: left, right, center. For example, *Theatre Arts Monthly* dismissed it as a "Broadway failure." James Farrell, then deeply involved in realistic fiction on Chicago's Irish, defended Bein from critical naysayers. Clifford Odets outdid his peers in extravagant praise for the play. Brooks Atkinson called *Let Freedom Ring* a "folk drama," paralleling Al Hayes's tag, "southern folk play." Previously, Frederick Koch had labeled *Strike Song* as a "mature folk drama."

Although most scholars have reserved the rubric *folk drama* to cover ritual and ceremony within folk society, literary and drama critics in the 1920s extended the term to cover plays set in American regions. Atkinson could have distinguished Bein's offering from traditional folk drama had the distinction then seemed significant to intellectuals. Hayes anticipated the appropriation by radicals of *folk* as a badge of merit.

When *Let Freedom Ring* closed in New York, it continued to reach new audiences in unusual settings far removed from the summer "straw hat" circuit. Encouraged by the UTWA's Francis Gorman, a group of young troupers—some from the original cast, some newcomers—took the play on an evangelical bus-and-suitcase tour of labor halls from Lawrence, Massachusetts, to Camden, New Jersey (Spitz, *Newsweek*).

The Let Freedom Ring Company opened a cut-down version of the drama at Camden's Convention Hall in July 1936 before thousands of RCA strikers. In Rhode Island, the Woolen and Worsted Federation charged twenty-five and fifty cents for seats at union hall showings. When the UTWA opened its thirty-fifth annual convention in New York (September 14, 1936), the road company presented the play at the Hotel Woodstock for cheering delegates, some from the Carolinas.

One of the young performers in the touring company caught Will Geer's eye. Herta Ware (the granddaughter of Ella Reeve "Mother" Bloor, a Communist party luminary) played the role of a mountain girl turned prostitute. On October 15, 1938, Will and Herta married in a Manhattan union hall. Another of the actors, John Lenthier of Boston, had volunteered to fight for Loyalist Spain. Following his death in Madrid, the group renamed itself the John Lenthier Troupe. During 1938 and 1939, this set of artists helped form the TAC (Theatre Arts Committee to Aid Spanish Democracy).

In the busy years of the late 1930s, Will Geer joined TAC performers in Popular Front causes. He was indefatigable as a radical minuteman delivering "folk" recitations and topical ballads. Whether he continued to sing "The Ballad of a Mill Hand" after his last touring performance of *Let Freedom Ring*, I do not know.

In addition to its New York run and subsequent union showings, the Detroit unit of the Federal Theatre, Works Progress Administration, also presented *Let Freedom Ring* (May 22–December 4, 1937). Hallie Flanagan, a shaper of New Deal artistic achievement and proponent of regional theater, cheered its reception by Michigan factory workers and college students. Eleanor Roosevelt joined Flanagan in lauding the play.

In Detroit, the WPA production bulletin held fascinating instructions on the conjunction of avant-garde and traditional music; this production used both Arthur Honegger's "Pacific 231" and Albert Bein's "Ballit of Kirk McClure" (another name for "Cotton Mill Rhyme"). The stage director placed the ballad at several scenes, including the last one in the union hall. Initially, Grandpap sang Kirk's ballad alone, but all the workers joined at the finale. The Detroit sound effects sheet noted, "When the entire company on stage took up [the ballad], building to a triumphant close, [the cast] gave the end of the play a magnificent lift."

*Let Freedom Ring* served as a vehicle for one textile song's meaning. Within the drama, Tom Stevens announced the "ballit's" new purpose as he addressed Grandpap: "It ain't playin' the fiddle fer dancin' ye should be, John Kirkland—but to lead voices in anger" (74). Albert Bein, of course, viewed the ballad as a militant weapon in struggle. Accordingly, he cut "Cotton Mill Rhyme" down to eight key stanzas, moving its site away from Buffalo to Sandersville, an imaginary village.

Some critics seized on the ballad to represent the play's essential meaning. For example, *Time* concluded its review: "When the best of his brood is finally pinked on the picket line, Grandpappy sings a hillbilly hymn of hate at the big funeral scene.

Let them wear their golden watches
And their pearly strings.
When our day of judgment comes
We'll take away their pearly things."

Ballad scholars place oral transmission and subsequent variation at folksong's heart. Grace Lumpkin had heard "golden chains and rings." Albert Bein had written "rings and pearly strings." The *Time* reviewer wrote both "pearly strings" and "pearly things." These details standing alone are insignificant; together, they mark the rapidity of change as a folksong moves into the popular domain.

Print, sound recording, and film, when added to old modes of dissemination, immensely widen and alter audiences. Obviously, Mr. McDonald, singing in the Charlotte union hall for his comrades in arms, made a statement fully accepted by them as it confirmed their existential experience. Lumpkin's printing of "Cotton Mill Rhyme" in the *New Masses* enlarged its circle but lost the immediacy conveyed by a living performance. Geer, singing on the New York stage, brought music's sway back to the poem. However, no theatrical presentation in Manhattan could restore the power generated in Gastonia.

The song's enactment within *Let Freedom Ring* might have ended its circulation had not Alan Lomax, or a colleague, typed out its full text for a manuscript that ended up in the People's Songs library. This "broadside"—languishing in files until Pete Seeger recorded "Let Them Wear Their Watches Fine"—reached folksong enthusiasts, many of whom held no memory of Gastonia, and only a vague sense of textile life.

We understand that a song's meaning alters when the audience grows beyond folk society's inherent limits. Seldom do we see this process with such clarity as in the movement from "Cotton Mill Rhyme" to "Let Them Wear." The *Time* critic who alliteratively labeled Geer's song as a "hillbilly hymn of hate" disdained *Let Freedom Ring*, viewing it as a curiously limited agitprop drama. Today, we can see agitprop's role as one contributor to and crystallizer for the laborlore corpus.

Contracted from the combination of agitation and propaganda, the term *agitprop* covered a variety of skits and plays of social commitment. During the 1920s, such productions had been influenced markedly by German and Russian stage experimentation: minimal or abstract sets, monochrome characters, declamatory musical chants, rapid-fire action, visible class struggle. In Popular Front years, the producers of agitprop softened modernity's visage as they turned to musical comedy and patriotic pageantry. Curiously, "A Southern Cotton Mill Rhyme" in *Let Freedom Ring* stood between deep tradition and agitprop's challenge.

Playwright Bein had moved from village tradition to Broadway. Born at Kishinev, Romania, in 1902, he moved with his parents to a Chicago slum at age two. Tenement life led to crucial teen years in a reformatory for incorrigible boys. Falling in with a rough gang at age twenty-two, he received a five-year jail term following an attempted bank robbery at Kansas City (Blitzstein).

In prison, Bein wrote poetry and stories, sending some to Clarence Darrow and Zona Gale, both of whom encouraged his interest. Out of prison and hoboing, Bein lost a leg in an encounter with a cruel brakeman; he then turned to Manhattan. Accepting radical values from new friends, he wrote three social dramas: *Little Ol' Boy* drew on reform school experiences; *Let Freedom Ring* derived from Lumpkin's novel; *Heavenly Express,* a fantasy, fell back on jungle-campfire images in the folksong "Big Rock Candy Mountains" (Atkinson 1940).

When Albert Bein's *Let Freedom Ring* reached the stage, *Daily Worker* writers Don West, Carl Reeve, and Al Hayes cheered it. However, Mike Gold engaged Bein in a harsh exchange that revealed the Communist party's hold on cultural workers. Defending himself from Gold's criticism, the playwright, in a 1935 *New York Times* article, offered a Marxist rationale for *Let Freedom Ring* by comparing the trek of Appalachian folk into Gastonia's factories to the enclosure movement that had forced English peasants into early industry.

Other playwrights had previously noted the mimetic possibilities within the shift from mountain subsistence farming to industrial economy. For example, Tom Tippett used this theme in *Mill Shadows* (1932), a play based on an AFL strike at Marion, North Carolina. During October 1929, in the midst of Gastonia's second trial, Marion deputies killed seven mill workers and wounded twenty-four others.

Tippett, an Illinois coal miner and teacher at the Brookwood Labor College, Katonah, New York, gave *Mill Shadows* an ideological cast different from the one Bein gave to *Let Freedom Ring*. Brookwood's students presented Tippett's play to receptive audiences, also taking it on the road. However, the play did not reach Broadway; hence, social drama historians ignored it. Despite their strong political differences, Tippett and Bein both wrote out of a belief in workers' destiny. Bein added to the mantle of heroism a medicinal dose of historical determinism: an inevitable force—the birth of the American working class—propelled its victims in their march to proletarianization's drum.

In retrospect, *Let Freedom Ring* seems mechanistic. If workers are buffeted by mysterious forces beyond their control, and of which they are but dimly conscious, how can they act? How could Gastonia's millhands have made a revolution? Can workers' energies ever be harnessed to alter their own lives? Where does their humanity hide? Albert Bein, lifting himself from prison and hobo bondage, had moved to playwrighting. Could not the victims of social catastrophe in the Piedmont have effected a similar transformation?

## The Crown

Having established the route "A Southern Cotton Mill Rhyme" took from magazine to novel, play, library document, and LP album, I returned to the question of the ballad's origin. In 1961, I attempted to trace its early history. Arthur Palmer Hudson, a Chapel Hill folklorist, then suggested that I write to Francis Bradley, a philologist and dean at the University of South Carolina; Bradley shared with me a sixty-year-old poem mailed to him by Mrs. M. P. Mitchum of Columbia. She had received it from her Tar Heel uncle, Henry Tucker. Bradley submitted the poem with comments to his local newspaper, the *State and Columbia Record*, as well as to *North Carolina Folklore* (December, 1961).

"A Factory Rhyme" held fourteen stanzas, some similar to and some different from those previously printed in the *New Masses*. I select stanzas 1, 3, 13, and 14 from Tucker-Mitchum:

Now while I have a leisure time
I'll try to write a factory rhyme.

I live in Greensboro, a lively town,
And work in a factory, by name, The Crown.

'Tis not the intent of my heart
To write anything that would start
Animosity between my employer and me;
But what I write let factory people see.

And now you've read this rhyme all through,
And know that what I've written is true;
I hope all Christians will never forget
To pray for the "ignorant factory set."

But in the end we hope to see
These people as happy as they can be,
And when the Judge on his throne will sit
We hope he'll say "Come in, happy factory set."

In hindsight, the link between Lumpkin's find, Pete Seeger's song, and the Tucker-Mitchum piece is clear, yet no one made the connection on Dean Bradley's printing of "A Factory Rhyme." In a 1974 Chapel Hill talk, I first noted parallels in imagery and structure between the variants. The Buffalo, South Carolina, ballad named no mill; the Greensboro, North Carolina, poem named The Crown. This lead suggested that the original author may have worked at The Crown. Could the poet's work days be traced?

The separate poems printed by Lumpkin and Bradley each revealed "bottom" perspectives of Piedmont factory hands, laboring under tags such as "factory trash" or "ignorant factory set." The variants separated widely in worldview. The Crown's hand did not wish animosity between workers and employers and believed in heavenly redemption. The Buffalo hand lacked faith in bosses and looked forward to revolutionary redemption.

Initially, I found no ready way to reconcile the contradictory messages in these two poems seemingly stemming from a single source. I assumed that Bradley's find preceded Lumpkin's, in that communist rhetoric did not reach Carolina mills until the late 1920s. It also can be argued that Lumpkin had found an autonomous piece, although I doubt it; the Buffalo poet surely had heard or read the Greensboro "Factory Rhyme."

In 1961, Dean Bradley had ventured that Mrs. Mitchum's contribution was sixty-years old. Larry Rogin, a former educational director for the Textile Workers Union of America, accepted this turn-of-the-century timing but quizzed me about a puzzle, namely, the references to merchants in each poem. In Greensboro, workers paid "high prices" while merchants "got our money . . . when pay day comes." In Buffalo, the "trash" drew its "little pay" while "the merchant raps upon the door."

Rogin suggested that early mills had built their own company stores and paid wages by scrip, as did coal operators. Hence, mill village merchants did not venture out or rap on doors. Rogin asked why neither poem reflected company store checkoff or credit practices. Such questions remind us of the difficulty in matching specific customs within songs with the actual practices in occupational communities. Ballads that ring true to their composers or auditors may fail as historical documents.

While I sought the birthplace for the Buffalo and Greensboro items, Frances Tamburro pointed me to another fork in the road: an obscure 78-rpm disc by Wilmer Watts and the Lonely Eagles entitled "Cotton Mill Blues" (Paramount 3254). Recorded in New York City on October 29, 1929, Paramount held it for release until November 1930. We can assume the most limited sales during Depression years—perhaps as few as 1,000 copies.

Two LP reissues hold Watts's "Cotton Mill Blues": *Paramount Old Time Tunes* (JEMF 103) and *Poor Man, Rich Man* (Rounder 1026). Norm Cohen and Mark Wilson, respectively, commented on Watts's song in album brochure notes. Malcom Blackard and Donald Lee Nelson had previously gathered the few known facts on Watts. I had transcribed his "Chain Gang," a prison labor song related to the coal mine convict-lease song "Roll Down the Line," in *Only a Miner.* In 1987, Old Homestead Records released Roy Harper's *I Like Mountain Music;* it included "Cotton Mill Blues." Harper, a railroad brakeman from Manchester, Tennessee, had obtained this blues from Sid Harkreader, an early Grand Ole Opry performer. In turn, Sid had learned the song directly from the Paramount record.

Born about 1892 in Columbus County, North Carolina, Wilmer Watts moved to Belmont in Gaston County seeking work after World War I. He spent his entire adult life in the mills, at times as a skilled loomfixer, but he left his mark as a spirited string-band musician rather than as a textile hand. Watts's "Cotton Mill Blues" follows:

I have a leisure time
Trying to sing a cotton mill rhyme.
Live in Belmont, a lousy town,
Work in the mill by the name of Crown.

Got the cotton mill blues,
Got the cotton mill blues,
Got the cotton mill blues,
On my mind.

Perhaps you'd like to know my name,
You never will, I don't sing for fame.
Sing so the well-off classes know
How a cotton mill man has to go.

Chorus

We have hard times you all well know,
To church we never get to go.
When the Sabbath comes we are tired down
Working hard the whole week round.

Chorus

Uptown people call us trash,
Say we never have no cash.
That is why the people fret,
Call us the ignorant factory set.

Chorus

Education we have none,
Papa, mama, daughter, or son.
That is why the people fret,
Call us the ignorant factory set.

Final Chorus

Wilmer Watts had certainly read or heard the Crown Mill "Factory Rhyme" or a close relative. A comparison of the poem printed by Bradley with the Paramount recording reveals that Watts drew all stanzas from the poem, garbling some words. He shortened his blues to fit the time limit of a 78-rpm record.

Presumably, Watts set the words to music and identified his song by the familiar denominator *blues*. Although this widespread term referred originally to a specific African-American musical form, southern white country composers, such as Jimmie Rodgers, had also accepted *blues* to accommodate a variety of Anglo-American complaints or laments. (The "unbluesy" tune for "Cotton Mill Blues" resembles that of Frank Hutchison's "Old Rachel," Okeh 4509.)

My inability to reconstruct the sequence leading from "A Factory Rhyme" to "Cotton Mill Blues" touches on a troublesome problem. With few exceptions, the creators and carriers of workers' traditions left no logbooks, memoirs, or similar documents. Worn down by work, worn out by obscurity, they had to struggle not only against powerful institutions but also against larger society's pressure to identify workers with the objects fashioned by their hands. What happened to the bolts of cloth Wilmer Watts teased into existence or to the looms he nursed into precision and punctuality?

During 1929, Margaret Larkin, a radical with a keen ear for authentic folksong, met Daisy MacDonald (Lumpkin spelled the name as "McDonald"; I do not know which is correct). Larkin reported: "[Daisy] 'reckoned to find a money tree' when she left the mountains as a bride. . . . 'I'm a good worker, too . . . I've worked in more'n thirty mills and I ain't never been fired yet. I can do a heap of things in a mill—sorting, warping, carding, spooling. My last job was untangling yarn' " (690).

Margaret Heaton Vorse had also met the McDonalds. Writing for a national audience in *Harper's*, Vorse noted the family's condition. Daisy spoke: "My husband lost his leg and has a tubercular bone. What do you think's left to feed my people on when I pay my weekly expenses?" Daisy told the sympathetic labor journalist that she supported her husband and seven children on $12.90 a week (705).

In my mind's eye, I see the McDonalds and Wilmer Watts crossing paths in a Piedmont textile mill, pausing at their tasks, exchanging songs. What fate brought gifted writers—Lumpkin, Vorse, Larkin—to the McDonald family but not to Watts? Larkin and Lumpkin had traveled from New York to Gastonia out of revolutionary dedication; Vorse, out of solidarity with labor. These writers ensured that a few cultural "mill ends" survived. Wilmer Watts, reversing the intellectual's journey, traveled from Gastonia to New York to seek recognition by making records. This trip gave permanence to a handful of his songs.

We can outline Watts's career largely from evidence frozen in phonograph discs. Today, only bare tantalizing fragments in a few articles mark the McDonalds' experience; Mr. McDonald's Christian name is unknown. For both Watts and the McDonalds, we shall never learn enough to recognize appropriately their gifts. Yet these Tar Heels have fared much better than many of their brothers and sisters who remain buried within statistical reports on textile production or histories marking a troubled industry's ebb and flow.

## Will Geer

Unable to resolve all the questions posed by "Cotton Mill Blues," I returned to the "John Catchins" ballad recorded by Mr. and Mrs. Joe Gelders at the Library of Congress. Two text transcriptions had been made, one by John Greenway in *American Folksongs of Protest* and the other by Alan Lomax, Woody Guthrie, and Pete Seeger in *Hard Hitting Songs for Hard Hit People.* Prior to the library's field recording, the Gelders had used their own ballad text and tune in an article for the ILD's *Labor Defender* (July 1937).

On listening to the record by the Gelders, I identified its music by aural association with Guthrie's coal-mining ballad, "The Ludlow Massacre," as well as with his ditty "Clean-O." Other listeners may place this music in a tune family that includes material such as "Cruel Father," "Butcher Boy," "Tavern in the Town," and "Died for Love."

In their narrative, Mr. and Mrs. Gelders described the "frame-up" of John Catchings following an organizational effort in the summer of 1933 at Republic Steel's Thomas Furnace in Birmingham. Republic's die-hard president, Tom Girdler, rejected unionism during this Blue Eagle drive (National Industrial Recovery Act). Republic's "red ore" (iron) miners and furnace men struck in Alabama in May 1934. The walkout dragged on for four years as the Thomas furnace recruited a new work force.

The ballad closed with Catchings's fellow workers promising to "be in the CIO when brother John is free again." Historically, this song presented an anomalous time contraction in that Republic furnace men had joined Local 137 of the International Union of Mine, Mill, and Smelter Workers, AFL. The Committee for Industrial Organization (CIO) had not been established when Thomas workers struck. This indicates, of course, that the composers wrote their piece several years after the jailing of Catchings, but before his release (Cayton; Huntley).

The ballad deserves separate attention as a memorable addition to steelworkers' lore. Here, I comment only on the People's Songs typescript of "Let Them Wear Their Watches Fine" that linked tunes of "Warren Harding's Widow" and "John Catchins." Writing to Pete Seeger in 1974, I asked him about the tune to "Let Them Wear." He replied that he had never heard Will Geer sing the mill ballad. This response heightened my curiosity; where had Seeger found the tune?

At this juncture, Richard Reuss again helped, for he had met Joe Gelders's daughter at Malvina Reyonlds's Berkeley home. Writing to Marge Gelders (Mrs. Laurent Frantz), I received an exciting letter (July 23, 1974). She recalled the origin of "John Catchins":

> My father was doing civil rights work in Birmingham, Alabama, beginning in 1936. The song was written . . . in an effort to publicize the case of Catchings, on which [Dad] was then working. Dad, mother, and the local Communist Party organizer, Rob F. Hall, sat around one night over a bottle of bourbon and wrote it. The tune Dad had heard in a Broadway play by Albert Bein, *Let Freedom Ring*, which I think we saw in 1935 in New York. As I recall, that was a play about textile workers' struggle in the South and I don't know where Bein got the tune. Anyway, after the [Catchings] song was written, [my parents] mimeographed words and lyrics and sent them out to all the local unions in Birmingham and generally circulated them. Somewhere I have a picture of John Catchings in prison garb. . . .
>
> I went to the American Youth Congress convention in the summer of 1939 with an Alabama delegation I had organized.

> One night walking along the shores of Lake Geneva [Wisconsin] I heard someone in a tent up the hill singing the song. I was amazed because I didn't know anyone outside of Birmingham knew the song, and I knew all the people there from Alabama and nobody played a banjo like [that]. So I went up to the tent from which the song was coming, sat down on the floor and joined the singer in the rest of the verses. He was equally amazed because he didn't know anybody else knew the song. When it was over, I asked him ("him" turned out to be Pete Seeger) where he had heard it, and he said it was on a Lomax recording. I didn't know at that time that [my parents] had recorded it (I had been off to college for the year). . . . Anyway, Pete was interested in discovering a connection with Alabama and later came down and lived with us while he picked up new songs.

Marge Frantz, in her letter and a subsequent visit, made rational the melodic relationship of her parents' steel mill piece to the textile "ballit" in *Let Freedom Ring* and offered a vivid snapshot of song swapping at an American Youth Congress late in the New Deal period. Also, she documented Seeger's early interest in labor song.

A word about Joseph Gelders supplements his daughter's account. Birmingham born, Gelders taught physics at the University of Alabama until 1935. Responding to Depression problems, he gave up teaching to become active in Communist party groups such as the National Committee for the Defense of Political Prisoners. In 1936, steel company goons kidnapped him and blackjacked him into unconsciousness. These injuries plagued him until his death in 1950; they did not diminish his faith (Krueger).

The matter of the People's Songs typescript continued to intrigue me. Alan Lomax seemed the most likely author of the headnote in that he had recorded "John Catchins" in New York on November 13, 1937, and Will Geer's "Ballad of the Wives and Widows of Presidents and Dictators" in Washington, D.C., on July 9, 1938. Both field recordings can be found in the Library of Congress. In an eight-month span, Lomax had heard two discrete labor narratives set to an identical tune.

Determined to follow the tune to its source, I questioned Joe

Hickerson at the Library of Congress. Why did Geer's presidential ballad seem unknown to folklorists? Hickerson revealed that Geer's recording had not been listed in the Folk Song Archive's public *Check-List* (1942) and hence had been virtually buried. This massive listing had excluded a "Delta" song category—largely bawdy or politically suspect.

Obtaining a tape of Will Geer's ballad, I was overjoyed to hear him close his 1938 recording with a reference to the *Let Freedom Ring* song. Upon concluding the session, he stated: ["Wives and Widows"] "comes from an old ballad I made up for *Let Freedom Ring,* Albert Bein's and Grace Lumpkin's play about the Gastonia textile strike."

Knowing that playwright Bein had found Grandpap Kirkland's "ballit" in Lumpkin's novel, I scoffed at Geer's bold assertion of song authorship. Even for a "free spirit," his claim seemed wild. What impelled him at the recording session to tell Alan Lomax about Bein's play and, seemingly, to tell others that he had learned the mill piece from a West Virginia mountain woman?

The People's Songs typescript for "Let Them Wear Their Watches Fine" referred back to West Virginia rather than the Gastonia novel and play. Who garbled the typescript headnote? Why did Geer, talking to Lomax, invert the chronology of textile and presidential ballads? Surely, Geer knew better than anyone else that he had penned his presidential humor in Los Angeles several years before *Let Freedom Ring*'s Broadway debut. Did he take deliberate pleasure in playing the trickster within comradely circles?

I could not resolve the ambiguities about "Warren Harding's Widow" without meeting its composer. On Sunday, March 22, 1977, I visited Will Geer at Topanga Canyon, an hour's drive from Hollywood, for a glorious get-acquainted session—more a drop-in at Grandpa Walton's than a scholarly interview. Previously, I had seen Geer on television portraying a wrinkled sage. Sitting on a hay bale and basking in sunshine, I found it difficult to relate Grandpap Kirkland to Grandpa Walton, to shift from Carolina textile mill to Virginia Blue Ridge farm, from proletarian fiction and agitprop drama to cheerful TV Americana.

During our visit, I attempted to obtain facts about Geer's own ballads, but my curiosity extended to the actor's long commitment to radical politics. I had prepared by extensive reading of journalistic articles about Geer (Ed Adams, Ben Compton, Mike Gold, Al Hayes, Louise Mitchell, Ed Robbin, Judy Stone, Ted Strauss, Herta Ware). Despite my preparation, I could not elicit a sequential account of Geer's life. Rather, my queries stimulated a set of droll anecdotes, each verging on a miniperformance. Geer was not averse to self-parody. Clearly, he favored drama over autobiography.

Born on March 9, 1902, at Frankfort, Indiana, William Aughe Ghere learned farm life as a child. When his father turned to railroading, Will began to travel in the rural South. During these years of family wandering, his schoolteacher mother kept him at his books. He graduated in botany from the University of Chicago in 1924, ambitious to be a forest ranger. Summer work in tent shows and riverboats led Geer instead to a stage career with long stints in cinema and television. For his New York professional debut at the Knickerbocker (March 19, 1928), he played Pistol in *The Merry Wives of Windsor.* Arriving on Broadway, he served with giants such as Otis Skinner and Minnie Maddern Fiske.

Recalling his theatrical apprenticeship, Geer told me that before reaching Manhattan he had played with the Stuart Walker Repertory Company at Huntington, West Virginia. There, a theater buff named Jack Frost took Geer in hand and "hauled him off" to hear a mountain woman from Parkersburg sing at a Huntington Baptist Church social. Edith Mackie made a deep impression on Geer because of her traditional Appalachian ballad style and because she knew a version of "The Graveyard Song" ("There was an old woman all skin and bones") similar to one of his grandmother Jessie Aughe's favorites.

Geer particularly liked Edith Mackie's "Poor Boy," so much, in fact, that it stamped itself in his memory. During 1933, he recalled its melody and stanzaic form as he shaped one of his earliest parodies, "The Ballad of the Wives and Widows of Presidents and Dictators" ("Warren Harding's Widow"). Trying out for *Let Freedom Ring* in the fall of 1935, he also set the Lumpkin-Bein "Cotton Mill Rhyme" to Mackie's "Poor Boy" tune.

It had taken me two decades to trace the melody for "Let Them Wear Their Watches Fine" to "Poor Boy" as heard by Geer at a Huntington church social. To confirm his account, I returned to the staging of *Let Freedom Ring.* Jay Williams, a workers' theater participant in the 1930s, described the casting of Bein's play:

> It was a hard show to cast, since it required among others seven actors to play the hillbilly McClure family, all of whom had to be large-framed, had to look like mountain people and speak with reasonably authentic accents, and one of whom, Pap, had to be able to sing ballads and play a wire-strung square dance fiddle. Rounding them up put gray hairs on Bein's youthful head. At lunch one day, in a restaurant frequented by actors, he spotted a tall young woman with a southern accent. He jumped up and went over to her, exclaiming "You're Ora McClure!" "You're wrong," she said. She was Norma Chambers, a Virginian who was working as general understudy in [Lillian Hellman's play] *The Children's Hour.* He was right, however, and she got the part. (186)

Williams, in *Stage Left,* also noted that Grandpap posed a special problem until Geer marched into Bein's office and stated: " 'I heard you're doing an uprising play. I like uprising plays. I'll sing you an uprising song.' He launched into one he had written himself, called, 'The Ballad of the Wives and Widows of Presidents and Dictators.' " Geer got the part; he did not seem daunted by the wire-strung fiddle.

In 1980, Sally Osborn Norton completed a drama thesis on Will Geer at the University of Southern California. Among Geer's friends whom she interviewed, Earl Robinson cleared up the fiddle mystery. After gaining Grandpap's part, Will came to Earl, a proficient musician who had pioneered in melding left themes and popular music. Will needed a teacher for the new instrument. Earl recalled the actor as a "tall stentorian-voiced foghorn man who looked old then" (185). Using an identical tune, Will sang the play's "ballit" and his own presidential parody for Earl. Robinson added "Warren Harding's Widow" to his personal songbag; Geer learned to fiddle.

In an interview with Rebecca Conard and a subsequent visit to my home, Robinson elaborated on his friendship with Geer. Because the latter needed to play a square dance tune in *Let*

*Freedom Ring*, Earl taught him "Bile Dem Cabbage Down"—"a five-note tune, fingers fall into place on D and E strings." Regarding the "Cotton Mill Rhyme," Earl had never accepted the attribution of "Let Them Wear" as a Geer composition or discovery. Put simply, Robinson discounted the oft-circulated headnote in the People's Songs typescript.

While visiting Geer at his Topanga Canyon home, I identified myself as a folklorist interested in radical causes as well as in ballad origins. Indicating that I did not see labor songs as instruments of salvation, had not been a People's Songs partisan, and had long criticized Stalinism, I asked if he would discuss his views on the connection of politics to folksong. This seemed to amuse Geer more than it challenged him.

Moving from overarching issues to specific details, I questioned Geer about his 1933 parody that satirized Harding, Coolidge, Hoover, Franklin and Eleanor Roosevelt, Hearst, and Hitler. From my perspective, the Roosevelts did not belong in this company. Perhaps the most charitable rationalization for Geer's presidential ballad is that of its time of composition. In early New Deal years, the Communist party had branded Roosevelt a capitalist demagogue and social fascist. Only after the Popular Front replaced previous lines did communists embrace the president. Did Geer ever voice qualms over Red shifts from hostility to acceptance and, again, to castigation of FDR? Surely, Geer had reflected on his long devotion to Communist party positions.

With extensive time, Geer and I might have touched on matters of self-doubt, revisionism, and moral reflection. However, within our visit, he clung to impressionistic anecdotes. In 1977, I saw Geer as a droll actor, both on and off stage—red socks, white carpenter overalls, blue sneakers. Trying to visualize him as a red-hot performer declaiming "Warren Harding's Widow," I expressed curiosity about his initial use of a folk melody for a polemical song.

Geer backed into an explanation with a bit of personal history. After the death of Minnie Maddern Fiske (February 17, 1932), Geer shipped out of New York on a Panama Pacific liner. Jumping ship in San Francisco, he fell in with members of the Marine Workers Industrial Union, then agitating on the docks. He entertained sailors and longshoremen at clandestine waterfront gatherings. Soon he moved to Los Angeles, joining the Hollywood branch of the John Reed Club, a communist-directed group of writers, artists, and actors. In the Depression years, Geer sang and acted on behalf of club causes: Harlan County miners, the Scottsboro Boys, Tom Mooney. With great relish, Geer related his visit to Tom at San Quentin. There, Geer also paid respects to John and James McNamara, imprisoned for life after the *Los Angeles Times* bombing.

Marcella Isgur Stack, a Young Communist League activist in Oakland's canneries, had traveled from San Francisco to Chicago late in April 1933 to attend a "Free Tom Mooney Congress." In an interview with me, she recalled the bus load with comrade Will leading in agitprop fund-raising skits. During a Salt Lake City stopover, Geer appealed to Mormon elders for Mooney defense funds with great bravado. En route, he entertained by reciting Vachel Lindsay's "Congo" and beating out pseudo-African rhythms on improvised drums. The Chicago "Congress" left Marcella, Will, and other participants exhilarated but exhausted. A "counterrevolutionary downpour" sent much of the assembly home before the main rally. Communist party sponsors faced a Coliseum rental deficit. Quarreling sectarians disagreed on plans to free Mooney (Frost, 443).

On Decoration Day (May 30, 1933), several Red-front groups held an antiwar, anti-imperialism rally near San Diego's naval base. Police, American Legionaires, and Marines attacked the demonstrators, sending some to hospitals and others to jail. At the June 14–28 trial, their defense attorney, Leo Gallagher, gained freedom for Geer and his co-defendants by showing an unusual newsreel of police beating the crowd.

In 1935, Geer directed Clifford Odets's *Til the Day I Die* at the Hollywood Playhouse. Four "Friends of New Germany" kidnapped and beat Geer, objecting to a scene where an actor tore Hitler's picture from the wall. Whether Geer viewed jailing and beating as "natural" consequences of class struggle, or whether he elaborated them into milestones of personal growth, I do not know (Campbell; Weales; *Western Worker*).

During his John Reed Club years, Geer had accepted a mix of messianic politics and social drama as his special creative arena. Folksong, then, served to advance his sectarian political commitment and his thespian calling. By the end of 1935, appearing in *Let Freedom Ring,* he had begun to feel the seductive appeal within New Deal politics and popular culture. With considerable humor, he accepted the task of making folk material palatable to large audiences.

In hindsight, I see the setting of the Lumpkin-Bein "Cotton Mill Rhyme" to a traditional tune, "Poor Boy," coupled with Geer's apparent inability to treat seriously the matter of sources, as a dual sign pointing to his humor, as well as to the left's contradictory embrace of folk culture. Clearly, an "uprising song" held intrinsic worth—values not always accorded by vanguardists to "uprisers" who lived at society's margins.

Geer's story of learning a mill song from a West Virginia mountain woman can be seen as emblematic of the cavalier attitude on the part of many radicals committed to people's culture but dismissive of the folk's right to its discrete creativity. Storks do not deliver lore! To respect folk culture demands attention to matters of provenance, as well as to style, spirit, and substance.

Attempting to gauge the depth of Geer's interest in folksong, I asked him to describe the circumstances of his first awareness of the discipline of folklore. Again, he credited Jack Frost for taking him to hear Edith Mackie in Huntington. This surprised me. I had assumed that Carl Sandburg had served Geer in this introductory capacity, for in the 1920s, the poet had crisscrossed our land with guitar and songbag. Sandburg acted as prophet and proselytizer.

Heightening Frost's significance, Geer impressed on me an analogy to the Huntington meeting. In Hollywood in 1939, while acting in Pare Lorentz's documentary film *The Fight for Life,* Geer met his old friend Ed Robbin, a *People's World* reporter. Robbin took him to meet a then-unknown radio hillbilly from Oklahoma. Returning to New York to play in *Tobacco Road,* Will invited Woody Guthrie to join him in Manhattan. Frost had "hauled" Geer to folksong; Will "helped haul" Woody to an audience waiting for a troubadour who could pull together Dust Bowl pathos and *Daily Worker* certitude.

Ending our Sunday visit (the sun had long gone down; the chaparral hills had turned blue), I asked Geer whether he would consider recording "The Ballad of a Mill Hand" just as he had performed it in *Let Freedom Ring*. Asserting that the song would continue to live among folksong fans and laborlore enthusiasts, I suggested that his version could be a benchmark.

Touched by my appraisal, Geer surprised me in responding that he had made a home recording of the textile ballad in the late 1930s for use by a Midwest student theatrical group. This cast had read Albert Bein's script but knew no melody for the "Cotton Mill Rhyme." Geer accommodated the students by sending a disc recording made with the help of Moses Asch. Is it possible that an archival copy can now be found?

Home in San Francisco, I mailed to Geer a cheerful progress report on my research, raising an additional question: could he specify his meeting with Jack Frost and Edith Mackie by date? Local newspapers confirmed that the Stuart Walker Repertory Company had played in Huntington in the winter season, 1926–27, and again in 1927–28. In a card to me, Geer noted that Jack and Edith "were gone when he next played West Virginia in 1966." Can anyone expand the story of the mountain woman who impressed Geer with her traditional songs and, ultimately, provided Pete Seeger and others with a durable melody for "Let Them Wear Their Watches Fine"?

Will Geer died on April 22, 1978 (Gupte). A week later, his friends memorialized him in the Topanga Canyon's Theatricum Botanicum—a stage bringing together Will's earliest interests in plant life and performance. At the service, Earl Robinson declaimed in high style "Warren Harding's Widow." Others offered familiar folksongs.

Some of Geer's friends lauded him as a master storyteller, crusty and sentimental; others, as an actor for all seasons, commanding a thousand roles; still others, as a brave fighter against reaction. Previously, in 1974, while joshing with a *TV Guide* reporter, Geer prepared an outrageous epitaph: "I'm a folklorist . . . which means I can't vouchsafe for every last picayunish detail of my stories. But they're mostly true. Mostly."

## Grace Lumpkin; G. D. Stutts

Ballad study remains an inexact craft. Creative souls endlessly spin songs; few enter tradition. By the time a scholar takes up a particular piece, age has obliterated its trail. I first read "A Southern Cotton Mill Rhyme" in 1938, but nearly two decades elapsed before I heard Pete Seeger sing it under an altered name, "Let Them Wear Their Watches Fine." John Greenway's note for the latter version led me to doubt Will Geer's source, yet I did not meet the actor to question him until 1977. Similarly, in the mid-1950s, I found Grace Lumpkin's 1930 printing of "Cotton Mill Rhyme" while checking back issues of the *New Masses.* I did not talk to Lumpkin until 1979—a sad visit, for her life energies had ebbed.

For decades, Grace Lumpkin dealt with the disaffection of her friends and family, with rootlessness and isolation. Former comrades branded her a traitor for rejecting communism; conservative relatives never forgave her for her fiction revealing peculiarities in Southern mores. Essentially, when radicalism no longer provided a haven, she turned to church work. After her New York years, she resided with Dr. William Glenn, a nephew at Yale University.

During 1952, searching for roots, Lumpkin found tranquillity at King & Queen Court House, Virginia, where a colonial ancestor had settled on the Mattaponi River. There, the historian Jacqueline Hall interviewed her, learning something of Grace's loneliness after the failure of her marriage and her break with communism (Hall also interviewed Grace's sister Katherine at Charlottesville). In 1974, she returned to Columbia, South Carolina, to work on an unpublished autobiographical novel, *God and a Garden.*

I visited Grace Lumpkin on August 23, 1979, just as she had moved to her last residence, a Columbia nursing home. I felt rewarded in meeting her but uncertain about bringing to the surface a song she had heard half a century before. I opened by expressing interest in "Cotton Mill Rhyme," its meaning to her, and the circumstance of discovery. Particularly, I sought to place this poem within the web of workers' tradition.

Lumpkin found it difficult to recall the piece until I read it aloud from *To Make My Bread.* Eyes brightening, she asked if she also could read it. Reading the text silently, she then recited it as if from memory, dwelling on colloquial usages. I asked why she had used this poem in her novel. Did it stand above other items of textile lore? Lumpkin responded that when she was a teenage girl, she had a Columbia teacher who had taken her class to a mill village to see how folks lived. In short, the "Cotton Mill Rhyme" affirmed Carolina reality. Textile hands had been seen as "fools and factory trash."

To certify the poem's truth, Lumpkin chanted a "tease" predating her hearing the mill ballad in Charlotte's NTWU hall. She had known this formulaic verse since early childhood, using it in her novel to reveal the thoughtlessness of city boys who harass young John McClure (229). During the visit, I jotted down Lumpkin's "tease":

Buzzard flying through the air,
Caught a mill hand by the hair.
When he'd eat and drunk his fill,
He dropped the trash into the mill.

Returning to "Cotton Mill Rhyme," I questioned Lumpkin for its melody. She read the poem again, slowly moving into a chant, and, then, into song. Recognizing the tune of "Barbara Allen," I asked for its source. Lumpkin told me that her mother had sung this sad ballad to her children. To make certain that I identified the proper tune, Lumpkin sang several stanzas of her mother's song, of which I noted the following:

I dreamed a dream one summer day
When flowers all were blooming.
Sweet William on his death bed lay
For the love of Barbara Allen.

Whether Grace Lumpkin recalled "Barbara Allen" because my questions about mill life elicited childhood memories, or whether the ballad's tune fit the meter of the textile poem, I do not know. Folklorists seek "original" forms. However, we are not always handed transparencies to unveil the past. Moving away from "Barbara Allen," I asked about "John Hardy," the tune Lumpkin had named in her *New Masses* printing of "Cotton Mill Rhyme." She seemed puzzled by my new questions about "John Hardy." Either I had pushed too far back into time's cave, or my reference to the radical magazine called up troubled feelings.

Trying another course, I asked the circumstances of her collecting the text from Daisy McDonald's husband. I failed again.

Previously, Lumpkin had told Jacqueline Hall that she had heard this textile ballad at Ella May Wiggins's funeral in Gastonia. Who can square this recollection with the *New Masses* note? Perhaps the McDonalds had attended the funeral and subsequent union gatherings in Charlotte; we lack biographical details to elaborate their life history.

Sadly, we also lack a published account of Grace Lumpkin's closing years: her return to Columbia, the break in inspiration for writing, her estrangement from her relatives, the difficulties in rejecting a political stance that demanded absolute loyalty by its followers. Grace Lumpkin died on March 23, 1980. The (Columbia) *State* printed a brief obituary; a full evaluation is yet to come.

With Grace Lumpkin and Will Geer both gone, I sensed that I had pursued "A Southern Cotton Mill Rhyme" to its end. Hence, I was most surprised to learn of another fork in the road. In 1987, Doug DeNatale telephoned and followed with a photocopied gift. At the University of North Carolina Library, he had stumbled onto a chapbook entitled *"Picked Up Here and There" and "Gleanings from the Gullies."* Author J. S. Stutts had published this little collection about 1919 at Haw River (Alamance County) as a memorial to his father, G. D. Stutts. The booklet's unusual double title reflected the father's initial collection and the son's subsequent addition. DeNatale's find led him to search for the original printing of *Picked Up Here and There* (1900) by Edwards & Broughton in Raleigh. Two reprintings followed; the last in 1907.

Miracle of miracles: both booklets by father and son contain "A Factory Rhyme," a fifteen-stanza poem—clearly the source for Lumpkin's "Cotton Mill Rhyme" (1930), Bradley's "Factory Rhyme" (1961), and Watts's "Cotton Mill Blues" (1930). Apart from the connection of these items, each chapbook deserves attention by students of Piedmont mill culture.

Born on March 22, 1842, in rural Moore County, George Dumas Stutts fought in the Civil War, moved to the Greensboro-Burlington area for mill employment, and died on April 30, 1918. John C. Stutts (1868–1952) lived in Alamance County. Both father and son, in their respective collections, interspersed mill poetry with traditional ballads, sentimental songs, and anecdotal humor.

Their chapbooks, overlooked by scholars, help us feel millhand creativity. G. D. Stutts's "A Factory Rhyme" of 1900 follows:

Now, while I have a leisure time,
I'll try to write a factory rhyme.
I live in Greensboro, a lively town,
And work in a factory, by name the Crown.

Perhaps you'd like to know my name,
But you never will—I don't write for fame.
But I write to let all classes know,
How cotton-mill hands have to go.

'Tis not the intent of my heart
To write anything that would start
Animosity between my employer and me,
But what I write let factory people see.

That while in factories we remain
We are looked upon as a set insane;
The upper tens who swell and fret
Call us the "ignorant factory set."

We were not bred in college walls,
Never played in theaters or danced in opera halls,
Nor eat ice cream, nor drank lemonade,
Nor smoked cigars, Havana made.

Nor went to picnics every other day,
Nor went on excursions without pay,
Nor wore fine clothes and derby hats,
Nor rode bicycles and played with ball and bats.

But now I'll tell you what we do,
And factory hands know it's true;
We rise up early with the lark
And work from dawn till after dark.

We have hard times you all well know,
To church we hardly get to go;
When the Sabbath comes we are tired down
From working hard the whole week round.

We are looked upon as the lowest grade
Of the whole creation God has made.

And I'll have you all to ne'er forget,
We are called the "poor, ignorant factory set."

We pay high prices for all we eat—
Molasses and coffee, bread and meat;
And should we fail our money to get,
We are the "lying factory set."

The merchants love to see us at work,
But our company on Sunday they will shirk;
But when pay-day comes our money to get,
Then we are the "paying factory set."

The darkies call us "white factory trash."
And say we never have a bit of cash;
But I'll have all colors ne'er forget
We are the "moneyed factory set."

Education we have none,
Father nor mother, daughter nor son,
And that is why the people fret
And call us the "ignorant factory set."

And now you've read this rhyme all through,
And know what I've written is true,
And I hope all Christians will ne'er forget
To pray for us, the "ignorant factory set."

But in the end we hope to see
These people as happy as they can be,
And when the judge on his throne shall sit;
We hope he will say, "come in, happy factory set."

When Stutts gathered a sheaf of poetry for printing at the last century's end, could he have imagined that "A Factory Rhyme," in various forms, would reappear in 1930 in a communist magazine and on phonograph disc? All writers dream that their work will live; few guide tradition's hand. Even if Stutts had selected but one poem for longevity, could be have seen its progression from a Raleigh chapbook to a Broadway play to an LP album?

Such rhetorical questions go beyond the intrinsic merit of "A Factory Rhyme." Literary critics are troubled by folk poetry, with its awkward construction, lack of subtlety, and maudlin imagery.

Stutts, of course, wrote for factory hands who knew in their bones his truths: "We rise up early with the lark / And work from dawn til after dark." Today, we have the luxury to dig under "truths" for messages. Stutts wanted no animosity between hands and bosses, a position unacceptable to confirmed radicals.

We can fault Stutts for acquiescing to raw exploitation or respect him for making time to publish "mill trash" experience. In employing verse as a survival tool, he spoke for many workers who suffered harsh conditions, supported populist remedies, and accepted the near-divine rights of owners to operate their mills. Carolina textile masters held powerful cards: a huge labor force moving from farm to factory; a fundamentalist clergy using Scripture to bless the status quo; New South doctrines of progress wrapped in Dixie's banners.

A significant difference between Stutts's original poem and its printing by Dean Bradley in 1961 demands attention. Stutts, in stanza twelve, wrote, "The darkies call us white factory trash." Someone deleted this stanza in the 1961 printing, surely out of sensitivity to an outmoded racial tag. Black sharecroppers in the South did struggle to advance into cotton mill employment. We do not know whether Stutts had encountered black workers in Greensboro's Crown mill.

Communist organizers at Gastonia faced a divisive issue in 1929: whether to trumpet black-white unity; to go along with "linthead" descriminatory norms; to opt for separate labor unions; to advocate a distinct sovereign state, a Black Belt Republic. Gastonia brought into focus the difficulties faced by radicals in squaring intersecting demands of class, region, and race.

The poem's "darkie" comment would not have appealed to Margaret Larkin or Grace Lumpkin in 1930. Today, it calls attention to pejorative language, past color bars, and barriers to be overcome. This stanza by Stutts also reminds outside scholars that their knowledge of workers' mentalities may be skewed by visionary belief.

## Ballad's End

No folksong report closes as long as its subject continues to move in tradition. I am aware that the few singers—activists and interpreters—who presently offer "Let Them Wear Their Watches Fine" at union rallies and college concerts constitute a revival set far removed from Gastonia's mills. Wilmer Watts and Mr. McDonald represent the last singers of whom we have knowledge for traditional versions of the ballad. Did other Tar Heels sing Stutts's "Factory Rhyme"?

I would have liked to enrich this study with additional material on Watts and McDonald. They lived and worked in the same community in 1929, embracing ideologies a world apart. Further, I am conscious that I have been unable to trace Jack Frost or Edith Mackie, the source for Will Geer's melody. Such gaps plague song study; we seek texture and tone only after dust covers their trails.

In looking back at the path of "A Factory Rhyme," I regret never having met Margaret Larkin (1899–1967). She had traveled to Gastonia with her husband, Liston Oak, to help in the strike. There, she met and wrote about Daisy McDonald. More sophisticated in folksong collecting and analysis than any of her radical peers, Larkin helped disseminate textile lore in articles and performance. While working on Theatre Union productions in New York, she expressed reservations about Albert Bein's *Let Freedom Ring*. I have long been curious to know her thoughts on Will Geer's rendition of the mill play's ballad.

To my knowledge, Larkin was the first musician in the communist orbit to deflate the polemics of Marxist critics who had called American folk melodies "arrested" or "immature"—debased by capitalist exploitation (1933). Ahead of her time in appreciating intrinsic integrity within the Appalachian style, in the *New Masses* and other forums, she championed Ella May Wiggins and sister performers from the mountains. Lynn Haessly's unpublished thesis at Chapel Hill holds the best assessment of Larkin's contribution.

We employ various metaphors to describe ballad study: journey, mosaic, family tree, pebble in pool. Regardless of what figure of speech we use, ballad movement hinges on exchanges between creative individuals and community-shaped meaning. Under separate titles, "A Southern Cotton Mill Rhyme" moved from poem to ballad and blues; from chapbook to novel, drama, and LP album. "Let Them Wear Their Watches fine" now rests within a handful of technologically dated LPs.

In performance, whether in sound studio or on festival platform, "Let Them Wear" poses future questions. It holds an intrinsic provocative challenge to Marxist aesthetic formulas. In the years between the Gastonia strike and Eleanor Roosevelt's endorsement of *Let Freedom Ring*, Communist party cultural arbiters had debated matters of revolutionary purpose for artists who faced polarizing discourse: formalism/realism, complexity/simplicity, elites/masses.

Looking back at the 1930s, critic R. G. Davis presently pairs Charles Seeger (folk) and Hans Eisler (experimental) as key figures who disagreed on proletarian music. By this formula, Davis rejects "Let Them Wear" as inappropriate to a revolutionary play. Grace Lumpkin had heard calls from Eisler and Seeger. Because *To Make My Bread* carried a mountain family to a mill village, she turned to Appalachian expression. In retrospect, her choice seems "natural"; yet, in 1932, most of her comrades had not embraced either traditional or sanitized folksong.

In correspondence with Bein, I questioned whether he or Lumpkin might have requested Geer to seek the mill ballad's original Carolina tune. In 1935, Lumpkin or Larkin probably could have found Daisy McDonald's husband. Apparently, no one involved in staging *Let Freedom Ring* felt such a musical quest to be important. Bein wrote to me that "Geer delighted us all by singing it ["Poor Boy"] during rehearsal. It was the first time I heard the tune." Fortunately, Geer had intuitively selected a traditional melody—now glued forever to "Let Them Wear Their Watches Fine" by virtue of Seeger's LP recording.

At this juncture, I flash back from music to visual art with reference to Mordecai Gorelik's stage sets for *Let Freedom Ring*. The designer had rejected picture-frame realism in favor of truncated interiors and stark abstractions to heighten the play's agitprop message. Should Geer have selected a dissonant tune for the mill ballad to complement the play's sets and struggle theme? Previously, I called attention to the Detroit WPA production in which the director juxtaposed Honegger's avant-garde "Pacific 231" with Geer's Appalachian "ballit" tune. Clearly, the Detroit director sought the best of dual cultural realms.

In the New York staging of *Let Freedom Ring*, Geer's fiddling for "Bile Dem Cabbage Down" anticipated a shift away from leftist infatuation with Brechtian drama, Shoenbergian music, and

Joycean literature. Geer's "Poor Boy" tune worked on Broadway in 1935, adding a tone of down-home authenticity to mill life's depiction. Folksong, stark or contrived, has been used on the stage for decades. It remains to be seen whether folksong tied to traditional communities will continue to serve union activists in years ahead.

Grace Lumpkin had submitted "A Southern Cotton Mill Rhyme" to the *New Masses* because she wanted the poem to help readers condemn exploitation and join in a revolutionary movement. Within *To Make My Bread,* Lumpkin touched on a mill hand's feeling for the ballad when John Stevens asserted "I feel good sometimes to think I've spoken to folks . . . when they feel the sorrow of working without much recompense" (260). Lumpkin knew that mill folk, like the weaver Stevens, were despised, but she also believed in their potential for growth. Gastonia's lost strike did not initially change her conviction that loom fixers and bobbin girls could alter their conditions—that they could touch history.

I believe that the singers who recorded "Let Them Wear Their Watches Fine" between 1956 and 1985 perceived it in moral terms, if not in sectarian formulas, similar to those held earlier by Grace Lumpkin. Until the song is taken up by a new generation of performers, if indeed it is, we cannot predict the politics of those who may embrace it. To comprehend continuity in blue-collar tradition, one must also deal with discontinuity. Will "Let Them Wear" continue to appeal to radicals? Will this ballad's social base hold fast?

The emotion engendered on a folksong revival platform functions at a different level of intensity than the passion generated long ago by hope in Gastonia. This goes to the heart of the matter in current presentation. Should "Let Them Wear" be a call to arms or a historical portrait? Can this 1900 rhyme acquire a fresh lease on life, a dynamic cluster of values? My queries lead to large matters of bonds within occupational communities, the relationship of expressive culture to social change, and laborlore's deepest meaning.

To delve further into "A Factory Rhyme" and its offspring will help in the exploration of workers' traditions throughout America: craft-centered, community-oriented, right, center, left, liberal, socialist, syndicalist, anarchist, old left, new left, nonleft. George Stutts, in his poem, and Pete Seeger, in folksong performance, intended the poem's/song's text to educate. It holds no muted voice; it eschews metaphor. This ballad's significance today goes beyond that of a lost strike or a close description of textile conditions.

Performed on the revival platform for an audience familiar with unionism, the song connotes labor militance and idealism. Some listeners hear "Let Them Wear" as a paradise lost, an idealized revolutionary moment; others hear and see it as a viable pragmatic necessity—work conditions calling for remedy. Despite such contrasting interpretations, the song affirms a special identification with working people.

In opening this chapter, I indicated that the Carolina collector Frank C. Brown had found no mill songs. It is our loss that he did not meet his contemporaries—J. C. Stutts, Wilmer Watts, Daisy McDonald. We are fortunate that extant chapbooks, strike novels, and LP albums complement Brown's volumes. We can but hope that some of *Norma Rae*'s fans will find their way to "Let Them Wear Their Watches Fine."

By exploring "Cotton Mill Rhyme's" progression, we can sense again work's importance and its promises. Terror, economic and political, stubbornly persists on many jobs. Workers survive by seeking meaning for their endeavors. All people dream special endings for their lives—Judgment Day, Great Revolution, Mystical Ecstasy. Whatever ending we claim as our own, we draw one moral from an obscure textile song. Millhands, factory bosses, mandarins, politicos, commissars, executioners, festival singers, labor historians, and ballad scholars in the end must shed their fine watches and pearly strings.

Al Tura retires

# 9

# Our Ritual Grabbag

The word *ritual* conjures an endless variety of ceremonial acts: sacred, profane, communal, personal. We both broaden and diminish our key's resonance by applying it to red-white-and-blue convention balloons, cowgirls at football rallies, starlets at Oscar award nights. Should not the rites of passage marked by baptism and wake or the calendric customs signaling the planet's turns take precedence over popular hype? Should not the eloquent belief in work's sanctity or in job justice, when enacted and repeated, be understood as a form of occupational ritual?

Mythologists and literary critics are not alone in treating arcane ceremony or habitual rite. Ironworkers who top out an erected skyscraper with a little fir tree or who leave their building site when a buddy falls "do the right thing" without invoking academic nomenclature. Office workers, gossiping at the watercooler or coffee bar, enhance their talk "by the numbers"—employing repetition, stereotyping, allusion. Such internal office patter, a shared mumbo jumbo, constitutes an elegant brew.

My opening chapters on John Henry and Joe Hill touched on memorial enactments. We treasure ballads that mark the steel driller's death; we affirm solidarity in voicing "I dreamed I saw Joe Hill last night." Singing and hearing flow into memory and rite. My studies on *Wobbly* and *fink* dealt mainly with verbal texts, either single words or those gathered in story and song. Here, I select language used descriptively to encompass acts of special significance on the job and at the union hall. Such behavior ranges widely from individual resistance at work to elaborate ceremonies away from job sites.

Rather than developing a detailed case study for each item or event, I pull shreds and patches from a grabbag of memory, supplemented by reading. Others can take up the systematic gathering and analysis of occupational ritual. I offer bits and pieces of play and pretence, humor and color, joy and stress. I move about from Labor Day parade to sabotage talk. Rhetoric and action converge to mitigate job tension, to herald radical change, and to reiterate needs for social cohesion.

## Rough Music

We pelt newlyweds with rice and tie clattering tin cans to their getaway cars. Noisemakers salute the first night. Gifts of fertility and longevity shower the happy couple. An occasional present hides signs of vulgarity or hostility. These practices, intermingling affection and anxiety, come together in the charivari (shivaree), a boisterous mock serenade. This custom has long served to bless joyous pairs, as well as to harass ill-conceived marriages such as those of widows or widowers who remarried hastily. Couples who displayed great age disparity or who broke domestic rules invited shivarees of disapproval.

The shivaree custom itself is part of a widespread ritual long used to enforce folk community codes and define moral boundaries. Operating outside the formal judicial system, village or town dwellers might beat pots, shoot guns, blow horns, ring bells, inflate pig bladders, carry effigies, and parade as grotesques to punish sexual deviants, adulterers, unwed mothers, cheating merchants, or lazy workers. We appreciate the custom's spread by its many labels: *charivari, whitecapping, bald knobbing, skimmington, skimmety, riding the stang, donkey riding, scampanate, cencerrada, ceffye pren, katzenmusik, rough music.*

The literature on these forms is extensive; Bryan Palmer's article in 1978, "Discordant Music," opens the subject to labor historians. Palmer treats the culture clash between the plebeian world and constitutional authority, offering examples from work's domain. At this juncture, I turn to two examples of ritualistic job control in the United States.

The historian Richard Morris, drawing on Massachusetts court records, noted the transatlantic crossing of medieval regulations protecting guild workers from interlopers. Craftsmen sought exclusivity in restricting their jurisdiction to local inhabitants. With the changes from medieval to mercantile and industrial economies, civil law weakened the "inherent" rights of craft workers to guard their codes. Morris wrote:

> In 1675 a group of ship carpenters who had ridden an interloper out of Boston on a rail because he had worked in the yard without having served his full seven years' apprenticehsip were fined five shillings apiece payable to the government and a like amount to the victim. John Roberts and the eight other defendants admitted the charge of having forcibly carried John Langworthy "upon a pole and by violence" from the north end of Boston to the town dock. This "occasioned a great tumult of people meeting there with the Constable who did rescue him." The defendants justified their conduct on the ground that "hee was an interloper and had never served his time to the trade of a Ship carpenter and now came to work in theire yard and they understood such things were usuall in England." (147)

Some readers may object to linking a report of workers' violence with the marriage shivaree, a happy event, but there is a connection. I prefer *rough music* as the generic term for stylized acts of social control by the "lower orders." In societies with elaborate legal systems, those at the bottom seek the means to invert state-imposed relationships. Boston's colonial shipwrights defended themselves by asserting that their conduct had been "usuall" (traditional) in England. Although the court records in the conflict between Roberts and Langworthy reported no music, I assume that the interloper's ride on the pole called for discordant tones.

I shall not detail other examples of riding a malefactor on a rail, whether rule-breaking artisans, errant husbands, or scolding wives. Villagers resorted to many forms of punishment such as pond ducking, branking, hobby-horse riding, or parading a wretch tied to a ladder or seated backward on a donkey. Using a ritual of similar form, the Boston workers understood that their notions of craft autonomy and self-regulation clashed with the state's duty to protect its residents. We can look back at the Boston constable of 1675 as tipping the balance of power from skilled shipwrights to ascendant employers.

W. C. "Billy" Webb served as the first president of District 19, United Mine Workers of America, at Jellico, Tennessee. Previously, he had led Appalachian coal diggers in District 5, Knights of Labor. On the eve of the Bastille Day uprising by Coal Creek miners in 1891, Webb reported to the then-new *UMWA Journal*. At Coal Creek, in August, he saw a group of trapper lads in action. They opened and shut heavy ventilation doors in mine passageways to permit mule drivers' entry and exit. Lonely work in total darkness, frequently in water and muck, functioned as part of apprenticeship. Trappers whose strength developed in time become skilled miners. Webb noted:

> About one dozen boy trappers at Coal Creek mine received notice of 10 cents reduction per day (they were getting 50 cents per day). The result was the boys stopped at once and the mine stood idle one day after the boy trappers ceased to work. A young man went and took one of the doors to trap. At that juncture the whole crowd of striking trappers seized the scab and took him to the creek nearby and ducked him in the hole of water prepared to wash mules. They told him if he would not blackleg anymore they [the boys] would take him to the company "pluck me" [store] and treat him. The scab agreed not to blackleg anymore and went on his way terribly dilapidated.

I find instructive the contrast between the circumstance of the Boston shipwrights in 1675 and the Tennessee trapper boys in 1891. Colonial law punished the mechanics who invoked the pole-riding ritual against an interloper. Seemingly, no sheriff in Anderson County observed or caught the striking trappers in their cool-staffing action. Might not a Coal Creek lawman have rationalized the trapper lads' episode as but a prank? We lack a full study of rough music happenings on the American work scene explaining differential response to a time-honored ritual.

The social historian E. P. Thompson has offered a succinct definition for *rough music:* "The generic term applied to a widespread and variegated group of customs, all of them ritualized, all of them expressive of controlled community hostility towards individuals who have in some way offended against community practices and sanctions" (1968; 1972). The *Oxford English Dictionary* gives 1708 as the first printed usage for *rough music*. This word combination denoting a noisy uproar also served to cover action in 1847: He "had been more than once rough-musicked by his neighbors."

In 1865, the antiquarian Thomas Wright described the connection of charivari to English trade objects and tools, mentioning "the music of marrow-bones and cleavers, with which the marriages of butchers are popularly celebrated" (85). William Walsh similarly noted the role of Parisian charcoal burners in a 1751 charivari. Adorning donkeys with trade implements and sounding a musical fanfare, they formed a procession to punish "such of their fellows as had married aged widows" (211). When the charcoalers extended their mummers' humor across jurisdictional lines to a cobbler's home, the latter informed "the syndic of the guild." With the tables turned, the cobblers then mobbed the charcoal burners. Although the workers in leather had precipitated the violence, two donkey-riding charcoalers were imprisoned for inciting to riot.

Other such cases can be cited in which craft custom, guild status, and law court reaction came together. Leaving readers to make their own further discoveries, I round out these notes on rough music with a little-known Wobbly colloquialism, *battleship building*. This word combination holds overtones of ritual devoid of elaborate ceremony.

In 1884, a Pittsburgh court prevented three women from "tin-horning" coal mine strikebreakers. A correspondent to *John Swinton's Paper* reported that the miners' wives had harassed scabs by noise making and name calling. Defying the law, the women resorted to mouth organs (Gutman, 64). In 1912, Louisiana lumber employers broke up union meetings by "tin-panning"—beating circular saws to drown out speakers. Unionists also turned this practice against bosses (Fred Thompson 1976, 68). In Louisiana, we hear of tin utensils used in pro- and antilabor settings.

During the years 1908–12, members of the Industrial Workers of the World used jail-house cups, plates, and spoons to "raise hell" in free speech fights. Austin Lewis (1914) commented on the San Diego jailing: "The Industrial Workers . . . followed the tactics of passive resistance, went to jail, sang songs in jail, 'made battleships' (which means that they beat upon the bars of their cells with tin cups), and in many ways made themselves a nuisance to the authorities" (461). The biographers of labor attorney George Vanderveer described the Spokane jail "battleship" as "producing a din that would test the walls of Jericho" (Hawley and Potts, 176).

Ralph Chaplin, in his autobiography, reported the 1917 jailing of IWW members in Chicago for opposition to the government's compelling their participation in the war. In response to the hanging of an inmate, signaled by the entrance of a priest and undertaker, an emotional explosion occurred. "We rattled our cups against the bars, beat with our stools against the walls, and added to the pandemonium with screams and curses. It was a real I.W.W. 'battleship' " (234). While in the Cook County jail, Chaplin and his fellow workers received news of the Russian Bolshevik Revolution. They cheered, sang, and made a tumult with tin cups. "With this I.W.W. 'battleship' we celebrated the birth of the New Society, the end of war, social injustice, and exploitation—the dawn of industrial democracy!" (235).

"Tiger" Thompson worked as an electrician in Butte's copper mines, where he held cards in the Industrial Workers of the World and the International Brotherhood of Electrical Workers. He balanced the idealism and pragmatism of the two organizations, calling himself a "double header." While Wallace Stegner at Stanford University gathered material for a novel about Joe Hill, Tiger shared his union adventures with the author's teenage son, Page.

In Butte, the "town clowns" (lawmen) had thrown Wobbly soapboxers and copper mine militants in jail; these rebels resorted to lusty singing and "building battleships." Anyone who has ever heard shipyard riveters in action will appreciate this IWW locution. Thompson placed *building a battleship* in a humorous frame by noting that it served as a satiric pun on wartime patriotism (Stegner 1960).

*Rough music* encompasses such complex ritual acts as those of Parisian charcoal burners carousing and parading and Boston shipwrights riding an interloper out of town on a rail. I have extended this rubric to include Wobbly *battleships* built with jailhouse tin utensils. Readers may question whether any particular enactment fits into the *rough music* lexicon. This matter of placement remain open while we construct our categorical bins. In short, one is free to link or separate such practices as pond ducking and tin panning. Workers, with skill to erect landscape barriers, do not always fence off physical blow from aural clatter. Regardless of such differences, we continue to hear dulcet and discordant chords on every work site.

## Small Shovel

In efforts to alter directly conditions on the job, as well as to organize unions of their own choice, working people have dodged sticks, stones, and verbal assault. Within courtrooms, press columns, and public forums, as well as on picket lines, antagonists have hurled charges of revolution, monopoly, greed, discrimination, jacobinism, bolshevism, and sabotage. All such lances have penetrated workers' hides; the word *sabotage,* more than others, continues to precipitate fear.

Whether understood as deed or creed—literally throwing sabots into machinery or relishing tales about pretended action—sabotage has generated an immense body of commentary. Writers on the Industrial Workers of the World such as Joseph Conlin, Melvyn Dubofsky, Philip Foner, Dan Georgakis, and Salvatore Salerno have displayed wide differences in treating the subject. Their books hold bibliographic leads for further reading.

In these pages, I do not cast a ritual net over disparate sabotage beliefs. Rather, I gather a set of related anecdotes, sparse or embroidered, that illustrate the alleged practice. These brief narratives constitute verbal enactments—essentially, a substitute for action. A dozen examples range from joke to minitale; most, but not all, center on the shovel, a tool long signifying hard work.

The reports found in print have jumped over job fences, crossed the Atlantic, and spread through America. Within two settings, logging and cotton stowing, the shovel itself has disappeared while the lesson remains. Below, I arrange the texts in an arbitary sequence reflecting the time assigned by various storytellers to validate their respective accounts. Where the anecdote holds no internal date, I fall back on its time of publication, paraphrasing some accounts to combine narrative setting and theme. Each item holds a source citation. Full references follow at book's end.

*1. From ca. 1875*

"Chinese workers on the old Central Pacific are reported to have cut six inches from their shovel handles to equalize things when their wages were cut" (Hand 1942b, 144).

*2. From 1896*

John Spargo (1876–1966), a granite cutter/stone mason in Cornwall, became an early champion of federation among Britain's disparate craft, local, and sectional unions. Emigrating to America in 1901 and serving as a publicist and lecturer for the Socialist party, he spoke and wrote against syndicalism in party debates, 1912. Within a reminiscent etymological passage, he related the Scottish colloquialism *ca' canny* (to go wisely, cautiously, slowly) and English *soldiering* (job malingering) to the then-recent French *sabotage* (to work clumsily or destructively).

Spargo placed the formalization of the clandestine ca' canny policy in a failed British maritime strike in 1896. Unable to win on the waterfront or at the ballot box, dockers and seamen sought a new tactic. Leslie Johnson and other leaders urged the men to "strike by stealth while keeping on the pay roll"—essentially substituting guerrilla warfare for open battle. To "strike the employers' pocketbooks, their real souls," one of Spargo's peers (perhaps Johnson) offered an illustration drawn from the past and further distanced by invoking Celestial agents: "A familiar story told was of some Chinese coolies who, when refused an increase of wages, promptly cut off a large part of their spades, saying, 'small pay, small work' " (Spargo, 153).

*3. From 1908*

Emile Pouget (1860–1931), a French anarchist, receives credit for coining *sabotage* as used in labor and radical circles. I shall return to his contribution, but at this juncture, I note only that Arturo Giovannitti translated *Le Sabotage* (1910) as *Sabotage (1913)*. Pouget, too, had used the shovel incident to comment on "instinctive and primordial" sabotage: "It is just this that in 1908 at Bedford, Ind., U.S.A., was deliberated upon by some hundred workers who had been notified of a forthcoming reduction of wages. Without saying a word these workers went to a neighboring machine shop and had their shovels cut smaller—whereupon they returned to their work and answered to their bosses: 'Small wages, small shovels' " (Pouget, 76).

*4. From 1908*

Louis Adamic, a Slovenian immigrant in Chicago's "slave market" in the 1920s, encountered Wobbly "gospel." On a pick-and-shovel job near Joliet, a "sabotage evangelist" admonished Louis: "Take it easy, kid. Don't try to build the road in a day. Put the brakes on, kid. Go take a sip of water. Tomorrow's another day." The mentor continued such instructions for "striking on the job." "Don't take so much on the shovel, kid. Don't break your back."

Continuing his pitch, the Wob reminisced: "Which reminds me of what a bunch of stiffs did down in Bedford, Indiana, back in 1908, when the boss told 'em their wages were cut. They went to a machine shop and had their shovels shortened, and said to the boss, 'Small pay, small shovel.' They had the right dope" (Adamic, 378).

*5. From 1909*

In an IWW pamphlet entitled *Industrial Unionism: New Methods and New Forms,* William Trautmann described European syndicalist tactics applied in the United States. When workers could not overcome police, injunction judges, or jailers, he urged them to consider direct action. Trautman offered an example: "In Harvey, Ill., where contractors of railway construction work announced a reduction of 50 cents per day for the Italian workers, the latter, having learned enough of the principles of industrial unionism, decided at once to cut their shovels half an inch, and work with these cut shovels, which they did; and, with the protestation, 'Short pay, short shovels,' they forced the contractors to restore the former wages" (Salerno, 135).

*6. From 1909*

In his pamphlet *Revolutionary Unionism,* E. J. B. Allen, an English syndicalist, cited the case of a gang of navvies (construction laborers working on canals and railways in Britain) faced with a wage reduction: "They had promptly cut a strip about an inch to an inch and a half wide, off their shovels, saying, 'Short pay, short shovels' " (Brown 1977, 53).

*7. From ca. 1910*

At a Birmingham museum gathering on February 28, 1986, Allen Bales, a University of Alabama professor, told me a family anecdote. I shared it with folklorist Joey Brackner, who subsequently obtained its text from Dr. Bales. He noted having heard it at home about 1935:

> In the very early 1900s, my maternal grandfather worked for one of the blast furnaces in Ensley, Alabama [possibly Tennessee Coal and Iron Company—TCI]. At that time, a sizable immigration of Italians and other East Europeans provided cheap labor for the mines and furnaces of the growing metal industries in the Birmingham area.
>
> One day my grandfather, working as a master carpenter/draftsman for the mill, came across one of the laborers busily working on the end of his shovel with a file. My grandfather asked him what he was doing and the laborer replied, "De cutta de pay, I cutta de shovel." (Brackner letter, April 16, 1990)

*8. From 1914*

Double header Tom Bogard (a member of the International Association of Bridge, Structural and Ornamental Iron Workers and of the Industrial Workers of the World) told me a graphic story in which he switched from "straight talk" to Irish brogue to mock-Italian dialect. Tom had first heard it in 1914 at Portland, Oregon, from IWW soapboxer "Windy" Wright. The latter had also used various tongues to mark ethnic difference. Tom recalled:

> The King Snipe, a railroad section boss, was Irish. One day he brought his gang their cash pay in separate envelopes. Each held a letter from the superintendent announcing a cut of one-fifth in pay. The next morning, the section boss went down to the tool house where he saw his gang of laborers

using big chisels to cut one-fifth off their shovel blades on the edge of the steel rail.

The boss cried out, "Oh, Jasus Christ, and what are ye men doin'?"

The Italian track workers replied, "Da bigga de boss cutta da pay a one-a da fifth, we cutta da shov a one-a da fifth." (Bogard visit, San Francisco, August 16, 1960)

*9. From 1920*

Stewart Holbrook found "derby hat" employment in 1920 as a bookkeeper in a Fraser River lumber camp in British Columbia. Subsequently, he turned his work experience into short stories, novels, and popular histories. Describing a Jenson Camp crew of Chinese fallers and buckers, Holbrook noted that the "China boys . . . knew more than the white loggers when it came to the scientific application of pure, unadulterated Marxism."

As prosperity took a postwar dive, lumber operators slashed wages to the bone. Many of the loggers, partisan to One Big Union, protested and found themselves in Vancouver's Salvation Army soup lines. Meanwhile the Chinese continued to harvest the Douglas fir. The "bull bucker" (crew leader), Washington Duck, "had been on the West Coast since before the anti-Chinese riots early in the century." He understood the rise and fall in wages without resorting to the usual "no savvee" business.

When the bookkeeper Holbrook notified Old Duck of a 10 percent cut in wages, the latter said cheerfully:

> "All right, . . . China boy no care; we catch log all same."
>
> They did. They catched the log, all right, but their output was uncannily exactly 10 percent less than it had been before the 10 percent wage cut. I [Holbrook] complained, officially, about the falling off in the log scale.
>
> "Timber get awful tough," Duck explained to me carefully, "She hard for China boy. Never see so hard timber."
>
> Such fellows needed no Marx or Big Bill Haywood. (Holbrook, 1931, 351)

*10. From ca. 1931*

Martin Ward, international president of the United Association of Journeymen and Apprentices of the Plumbing and Pipefitting Industry of the United States and Canada, served in 1971 on the tripartite Construction Industry Stabilization committee. As an AFL craft leader, Ward emphasized high productivity correlated with freedom in collective bargaining. In commenting on wage guidelines limiting advances to six percent, Ward recalled a moralistic story his father had told him about Depression days: "Because [the elder Ward] couldn't get a job at his craft, for a while he became a digger, a day laborer. In those days, you had to provide your own shovel. And the employer would often take advantage of the situation, and cut the hourly wage. When they did that, [Marty's] father said, 'We just went ahead and cut the size of the shovel!' " (Herling, [p. 2]).

*11. From 1933*

Gilbert Mers learned to stow cotton bales by hand in Corpus Christi, Texas, during 1929. After forty years on the docks as a rank-and-file member of the International Longshoremen's Association, he retired holding to democratic ideals. In a fascinating memoir entitled *Working the Waterfront*, he recounted a Gulf strike that collapsed in 1933. Undaunted, Paul Cecil, a class-conscious rebel, advised his fellows to stave off total defeat: "They've cut your wage from eighty to seventy cents. Work just seven-eighths as fast as you did before" (Mers 42).

*12. From 1946*

Describing the skill of Cousin Jack (Cornish) hard rock miners in the West, Wayland Hand reported several beliefs associated with singlejack hammers. The folklorist "had heard that a shortening of hammer handles resulted every time there was a reduction in wages. This is most likely only a story" (Hand 1946b, 176).

Choice anecdotes invite elaboration. These twelve linked items can whet our appetite for predecessors or analogues. Scholars look for variants to demonstrate a text's traditionality; historians seek contextual evidence to prove authenticity; storytellers relish parallels to expand their repertoires. Despite an individual narrator's wish to ground fiction in reality, no empirical proof has surfaced demonstrating a worker literally cutting off a portion of his shovel blade or handle to reduce its productive capacity. Has any such altered shovel been displayed in a museum case with a neat card reading "sabotage symbol"?

Wayland Hand stated wisely that a hammer handle anecdote was "likely only a story." In 1913, a socialist polemicist had placed the shovel reminiscence in a British port, 1896. In 1920, a "sabotage evangelist," while educating a young immigrant, placed the same account in Indiana's limestone quarries, 1908. Allen Bales heard his variant within a family setting; Tom Bogard learned his from a Wobbly soapboxer. William Trautmann, IWW activist, and Martin Ward, AFL craft leader, both adopted the same story to support their respective ideologies.

I leave it to readers to make other comparisons, assign meanings, or search for origins and parallels. I assume that a spread from Great Britain to California and from Alabama to British Columbia indicates additions in print or memory. No reference handbook surveys this laborlore treasury. No finding list indexes "Small Shovel" narratives.

I have chosen to place this set of anecdotes within a ritual frame rather than one of tale or jest. Here, I stress that the rubric *ritual* need not be confined to celebratory, mystical, mythic, or sacred enactments. Complaining about an abusive boss, joking about payday, relating a dismal story after a job accident, or recalling a pretended sabotage scene are patterned oral forms elevated to ritual status. Workers caress everyday talk until it emerges as sacramental wine or wafer.

Ritual combines narrative and enactment, colorful banter and exaggerated jive. The same shovel anecdote can bind a narrator and audience into a conspiracy of shared cause or dissolve a different audience into terror. Some hear a shovel story from a distance, absorbing it with a grain of salt without challenging its authenticity. Folklorists invite fishnet weavers to festivals to display their occupational skills away from the sea. Does not the "play" net acquire ritual meaning?

How does the festival visitor distinguish a net at sea from the net woven under the public awning? Is one artifact more "real" than the other? Why does the listener separate a shovel jest from an act of physical sabotage? Essentially, hearers and viewers assign special meanings to actions or objects linked to deep belief systems. Ultimately, anecdotes about shortened shovel blades function symbolically to reinforce notions of fair compensation for toil, job justice, and equity within the economic domain. The briefest shovel story points to time-tested human values.

A few details complement my assertions of grand meaning for shovel ritual. For example, miners greased shovel blades to bedevil novices. A Civil War shovel earned the tag "Irish spoon." California building tradesmen denigrated laborers in the act of shoveling by referring to them as "operating a Mexican dragline." After the dragline—a self-propelled dredging machine with rotating buckets—reached construction sites, its proud operators demeaned those men still digging by pick or shovel. The *Industrial Worker* (May 25, 1911) ran a sardonic filler, "A Few Thoughts By a Lumber Jack." In it, two aphorisms implied knowledge of steel mill ownership, as well as of railroad tycoon James J. Hill and the shovels used by Great Northern track crews: "A steel worker's delight—Andy Carnegie shoveling slag"; "A mucker's delight—J. J. Hill on the busy end of a No. 2."

Shovel stories point in many directions: moral judgments of botched work, ethnic rankings within laboring crews, transference of sabotage from job action to rhetorical performance to ritual act. Discrete expressive forms do serve as multifaceted tools; no inherent element within the "Small Shovel" set demands a single explication. I liken these gathered stories to the tool itself used variously in deep mines, slag heaps, and peat bogs. Laborers test their shovels as they shift about in ore, rock, sand, gravel, clay, gumbo, and guano.

My gathered shovel anecdotes, apart from their intrinsic meaning and capacity to reveal traditionality, hold historical clues that help demystify origins for the word *sabotage*. Accordingly, at this juncture, I look back to John Spargo's reflections on *ca' canny, soldiering,* and *sabotage* as they supported his "familiar" shovel anecdote. Currently known beyond union folds, the S word surfaces among Wall Street inside traders, Washington dirty trick operatives, and San Francisco Earth Firsters. Individuals in the latter group also use the terms *ecotage* and *monkey wrenching.*

During 1896, British seamen and dockers had established a

short-lived International Federation of Ship, Dock and River Workers seeking worldwide maritime unity. Spargo caught their spirit: "The capitalist crocodile snaps its jaws in Hamburg when you step on its tail in London, Liverpool, or New York" (150). Plans to organize all ocean ports faded as IFSDRW strikes failed in England. In this climate of despair, Leslie Johnson urged ca' cannyism—less on the shovel blade, less on each barrel load, poor work for poor pay.

Spargo continued by noting that news of the Scottish tactic had crossed the channel to France, where two anarchists sought a French equivalent for *ca' canny.* Emile Pouget and Paul Delesalle (at the 1897 Toulouse Congress of the Confédération Générale du Travail) hit on a dramatic locution, *sabotage.* Behind their novel usage lurked the centuries-old noun *sabot* (wooden shoe), the verb *saboter* (connoting variously to *blow, bump, jog, jar, jolt, jostle, shake, strike*), and *sabotage* (fabricating wooden shoes). A particular saying tied these objects to work scenes, "travailler à coups de sabots"—to clump about in wooden clogs, to work clumsily. With *sabotage* firmed in French syndicalist speech, it moved to Britain and America, appearing in print in anglicized form in 1910.

IWW members have long had to defend, deny, or explain direct action calls with elaborate notions such as the "conscientious withdrawal of efficiency" or with Joe Hill's jingle "A Rebel's Toast":

> If Freedom's road seems rough and hard,
> And strewn with rocks and thorns,
> Then put your wooden shoes on, pard,
> And you won't hurt your corns. (Gibbs Smith, 255)

Fred Thompson, borrowing from Thorstein Veblen, pushed the etymology to note that French peasants continued to wear sabots after urban workers could afford leather shoes (1976, 81). Hence, clumsy peasants used as strikebreakers became saboteurs or job bunglers. Thompson likened them to hayseeds; some workers continually use *hayseed, hick, clod,* and *hillbilly* to denominate the unskilled.

Why did *sabotage* drive *ca' canny* from American speech? The latter term seems to have had little labor circulation in the United

States. Perhaps the metaphor of kicking a clog into a loom proved more exciting than the Scottish colloquialism. Certainly, Wobbly printed stickers—little silent agitators—reinforced the wooden shoe's appeal with pictures of sabots crushing the snake of exploitation or stopping time clocks.

In 1913, John Spargo helped popularize the ca' canny/sabotage connection. Actually, Emile Pouget, anticipating this explanation, had offered an earlier date than 1896 for ca' cannyism's acceptance by British unionists and had pointed away from Spargo's memory of Leslie Johnson as the natal figure. French readers of the pamphlet *Le Sabotage* and American readers of Giovannitti's translation learned Pouget's account of the word's extension.

Pouget did not claim coinage for *sabotage*. He knew it in active form, making wooden shoes, and in a vernacular figure of speech, "to work clumsily as if by sabot blows" (37). Following the CGT meeting, he strengthened his account of the word's "christening" in union circles with reference to the practice, yet unnamed, in Balzac's description of Lyon's silk workers' riots in 1831. Further, Pouget cited the experience of Glasgow dock strikers who had invoked a go-slow or ca' canny policy in 1889. In his view, they had inspired the need for an equivalent French term.

Significantly, Pouget cited *The Social Museum* (*Le Musée Social*) to reveal that farmers had scabbed on longshoremen in Scotland, breaking their dock strike. Unionists scorned the scabs who "could not even keep their balance on the bridges . . . and dropped in the sea half the cargo they loaded and unloaded" (42). The dockers' secretary urged them to "Work then just like the farm hands did." Unionists, returning to work and practicing ca' canny, scrupulously imitated clumsy farmers, but not to the point of falling overboard.

The historian Frederick Ridley noted that Paul Delesalle (Pouget's partner in the CGT report on boycott and sabotage) had described the Scottish ca' canny tactic to French unionists at their 1897 congress. Delesalle, too, fell back on the Glasgow dockers' experience, advising CGT members to follow their example (120).

Fortunately, Geoff Brown, in a series of English Workers' Educational Association talks and in a book entitled *Sabotage* (1977), elaborated the Glasgow-Toulouse journey. His findings confirm the linguistic elasticity of *sabotage,* a construct ranging from the rhetoric of machine smashing to the everyday practice of the slow down. With great industry, Brown unearthed the ephemeral publications that detailed ca' canny's French connection. I summarize his documentation.

When the National Union of Dock Labourers struck in Glasgow during June 1889, employers brought in blacklegs (scabs) from farms. In trouble, NUDL president Richard McGhee and secretary Edward McHugh articulated a ca' canny policy. McHugh, born in Ireland, had lived in Scotland since childhood. A gifted printing-trades compositor and enthusiastic follower of Henry George's land reform schemes, McHugh threw himself into the dockers' cause. He and McGhee were familiar with the canonical arguments of the day; these officers countered the employers' positions by asserting that those who offered "jerry buildings, coffin ships, and watered milk" and refused to pay for genuine workmanship deserved "veneer and shoddy" labor (Brown, 6–7).

The Glasgow go-slow innovation spread to other ports, challenging conservative leaders but appealing to the advocates of "New Unionism." Tom Mann, Havelock Wilson, Ben Tillett, James Sexton, and Leslie Johnson worked closely with McGhee and McHugh to form the International Federation of Ship, Dock and River Workers. Johnson edited the *Seamen's Chronicle* for the National Sailors' and Firemen's Union. This newspaper, which also served IFSDRW members, found its way to ports remote from London.

During parts of 1894–95, the years in which maritime unionists envisioned their international federation, Emile Pouget had been exiled to London. Questioning the isolation of French anarchists, he turned to a policy of entering and transforming existing syndicats (unions). In a setting that tied revolutionary anarchism to trade unionism, Pouget argued analogically from the usage *ca' canny* to *sabotage*.

A few citations underscore this cross-channel word migration. Leslie Johnson formulated a sophisticated and prescient slogan, "Value for Value," in the *Seamen's Chronicle*. On September 19, 1896, the paper reported enthusiastically on the "famous" ca' canny weapon—then seven years old. If employers ignored maritime demands, workers would not strike but would "hurry up or ease down according to the pay received" (Brown, 13).

On October 2, the international federation issued two circulars. The first asked "What is 'ca'canny'?" The second announced a three-choice ballot: immediate strike, more time to organize, "don't sweat yourself at work." The *London Times* reported fully on these ca' canny documents while shipping-trade journals, alarmed, reprinted them to displace the threat employers faced. Within its month of publication, the original circular appeared in a French translation published by *Le Musée Social.* Pouget leaned on it, giving added legitimacy in radical circles to Glasgow's innovative action.

During 1904, Carroll D. Wright, the United States commissioner of labor, prepared a massive report to Congress entitled *Regulation and Restriction of Output.* Explaining ca' canny's origin, Wright reprinted both London circulars (725–26). He quoted extensively from speeches by Britain's maritime union leaders, and, overlooking Edward McHugh's role, named Richard McGhee as ca' canny's "inventor."

Recently, in *The Dockers' Union,* the historian Eric Taplin sketched background facts for McHugh's urging of Glasgow longshoremen to work as inefficiently as blacklegs (30). The *North British Daily Mail* (June 22, 1889) reported that a scab had drowned, falling into the river while wheeling a hand truck up a plank (Brown, 4). I believe that stories about McHugh's admonition to the dockers to work cautiously and to stay dry must have circulated orally following this drowning. However, I have not found any firsthand printed account firming McHugh's articulation of the labor term *ca'canny* in 1889.

The historian Frederick Ridley, commenting on Delesalle's CGT's committee report at Toulouse (1897), noted that after the loss of the Glasgow strike, the dockers' secretary had told the men: "The farm boys dropped their load now and then and two of them couldn't do as much as one of us; so do the same kind of work, ca canny, take it easy; only those fellows used to fall into the water, you needn't go as far as that" (121). Previously, Ridley had noted Pouget's variant of this story in *Le Sabotage* (1910).

As the National Union of Dock Labourers grew, Edward McHugh moved its headquarters to Liverpool, England's second largest port. There, he elaborated the Glasgow go-slow policy in a manifesto on February 14, 1891. I quote a portion: "Fellow-Workmen—be on your guard; Ca-canny. . . . But be of good cheer. Ca-canny is of endless application; it is very economical of hooks (Hooks OUGHT NOT TO BE WORN instead of Buttons). You know what Ca-canny means" (Taplin, 41).

McHugh invoked this Scottish colloquialism to uphold morale on the Mersey River docks. His tricky wordplay on hooks/buttons appealed to longshoremen never without their indispensable tool, a hand-held iron hook joined to a wooden handle. Hook in hand, a docker manipulated sacks, boxes, crates, bundles, and barrels. In effect, McHugh encouraged dockmen, "Hooks down, Buttons up!" He referred, of course, to union buttons to be worn openly while each man decreased the cargo hook's productivity.

In 1896, London's dock leader, Ben Tillett, also played on the criticism of the union's "skulker's button." When the shipowners had tagged ca' cannyism as "a policy of skulking," Tillet retorted, "good luck to the skulker . . . [our aim] is to skulk from drudgery . . . to skulk from being pitted against each other" (Wright, 727). The *Seamen's Chronicle* (October 17) turned union buttons into highly charged emblems: "It is not intended to be the sign of a man who will only give a half a day's work for a full day's pay, but it is the badge of a man who refuses to give a whole day's work for a quarter day's pay" (Wright, 728).

Tillett's inversion of skulking's negative valence followed McHugh's Liverpool manifesto. The latter illustrated work humor linked to survival strategy, at the same time as it contributed to lexicography. The *OED* glosses *canny* to 1637, *ca' canny* to 1814, and the latter, in its labor setting, to 1896. With the Liverpool document at hand, we can move the *OED* citation back to 1891.

Eric Taplin and Geoff Brown, in their respective studies, clarify the early reports to American readers by Carroll Wright and John Spargo that had credited Richard McGhee and Leslie Johnson for carrying ca' cannyism to unions. Edward McHugh deserves this honor, and his fellow maritime unionists helped disseminate the term and the practice. Together, the dockers' secretary from Glasgow and the seamen's editor from London contributed strategy, rhetoric, and rationale to Paul Delesalle and Emile Pouget.

Conscious that he had participated in the Toulouse "syndical baptism" of *sabotage*, Pouget noted in 1910 that it had "secured its rights of citizenship in the Larousse [dictionary] and there is no doubt that the Academy (unless it is itself 'saboted' before arriving at the letter S of its dictionary) will have to bow to the word SABOTAGE its most ceremonious curtsey and open to it the pages of its offical sanctum" (38).

Emile Pouget's humor sparkled in 1910, for the compilers of France's official dictionary, *Tresor de la Langue Francaise,* have not yet reached the letter S. Eventually, academicians will move *sabotage* from past to present. I leave this word's further exploration to others, noting that Edward McHugh, Richard McGhee, Leslie Johnson, and Emile Pouget, from their respective vantage points on the battlefield, used traditional metaphor to advance labor's cause. Like other visionaries, before and after the heady days of syndicalism, they treated words as tools and weapons.

Certain doctrines, such as nihilism, terrorism, and syndicalism, seem destined to be fingerprinted and photographed for mug books. Pouget closed *Le Sabotage* by contrasting bourgeois and proletarian morality, boss exploitation and worker defense. Conscious that French rivals disputed his convictions, he took note of criticism by Jean Leon Jaures in 1907. The socialist leader made a telling point oft repeated in debates: "Sabotage is loathsome to the technical skill of the worker, which skill represents his real wealth" (69).

In part, evangelists for sabotage ritualized their narratives precisely to counter the hostility of those who found both word and deed repugnant. To illustrate: E. J. B. Allen, an English gas (utility) worker from Huddersfield and a tireless advocate of industrial unionism, had reported in 1909 a story of navvies cutting a strip off their shovels. While parliamentarians and revolutionists contested for the loyalty of Britain's trade unionists, W. S. Jerman (in *The Socialist,* January 1911), disputed Allen's bold message with fact and philosophy.

Jerman noted that "navvies' shovels were of various sizes, owing to constant use. As it was the custom for workers to buy their own shovels, the behavior Allen reported, and appeared to recommend, was senseless." Not only did the pragmatist strive to rebut Allen, but Jerman also took a swipe at syndicalism: "The socialist aim was not the destruction of the means of production but their capture" (Challinor, 96).

I am reluctant to leave polemicist Jerman, with his socialist creed, holding the last word. His faith in the proletariat capturing the means of production needs reexamination. Today's workers have not yet captured the world's pick and shovels, let alone modern technology. Even those states that profess workers' control keep shovels, actual and symbolic, in political hands.

Controlling the industries that destroy the earth's resources and poison life—today's Augean stables—will require super shovels. In this sense, environmentalists, the new rebels, have become "muck-stick artists." Do they decrease the size of polluters' spades or do they enlarge their own tools of reconstruction? In linking past to future, and by moving from barricade to meadowland, I speculate that shovel stiffs in decades ahead will continue to cut blades rhetorically and ritualistically.

## Labor Day

For four decades, Harold Rosenberg (1906–78) served as one of America's most formidable art critics, seeking always to place particular artistic works in complex settings. He helped explain the school of abstract impressionism as he commented perceptively on realism's limitations. Here, I bypass such theoretical considerations in favor of an appealing anecdote.

In a delightful essay entitled "Reverence Is All" (1970), Rosenberg presented a memory of his childhood discoveries at the Metropolitan Museum of Art. After his sixth year, he viewed medieval armor, Japanese swords, and pharoahs' tombs in filtered light. Glass cases, marble columns, and polished floors conspired to proclaim the sacredness of past time, the timelessness of objects isolated and venerated. To illuminate the museum's ambience, he fell back on a parallel childhood memory:

> In those years the trade unions used to parade on Labor Day, carrying objects representing their crafts. I remember a parade on upper Fifth Avenue in which the Bakers' Union bore aloft a twist-bread that was a whole block long—a magnificent creation; in today's terms, a work of art. But the aura of this edible sculpture was entirely different from that which surrounded objects at the Metropolitan, and it did not occur to anyone to deliver the bread there. The Union's

> product inspired such practical speculation as, Where did they find an oven big enough to bake it? How are they going to cut it up? Who's going to eat it? In an Egyptian frieze, baking had nothing to do with matters of this sort: it belonged to the realm of the fox-headed god and the dead Pharoah's voyage around the sun.

The art critic closed his parable on twist-bread and the Metropolitan by asserting the difference "between crafts and cosmic systems and between breads and breads" (135). Without quarreling with Rosenberg's contrast, I suggest that the Metropolitan Museum of Art might well have acquired a bakers' union twist-bread, as well as the craft's banners, buttons, labels, and minute books. Much of labor's ephemera has become as remote as the fox-headed deity in a museum frieze. Today, such ephemera does mark the cosmic voyages of working people.

Folklorists and historians share an interest in origins, whether of museum antiquities or union parades. Labor dates its first big parade to New York City, September 5, 1882. Not until 1894 did President Grover Cleveland sign the law formalizing labor's holiday to the first Monday in September. During 1972, Jonathan Grossman brought to the surface rival claims to the fatherhood of Labor Day by the International Association of Machinists and the United Brotherhood of Carpenters and Joiners of America.

The IAM favored Matthew Maguire; the UBCJA, Peter J. McGuire. I have no wish to enter this dispute. Rather, I return to Rosenberg's Labor Day memory of a block-long twist-bread. Other unionists will recall similar marvels: an ironworkers' model of the Golden Gate Bridge, a teamsters' horse-drawn wagon mounted atop a modern rig, a steamfitters' Rube Goldbergian gleaming contraption of pipes and joints, a Chinese New Year's dragon prancing among culinary and needle trades floats.

Seeing a displayed twist-bread through an art critic's eyes, I ask questions of ethnicity and faith. Could the bakers who marched on Fifth Avenue during 1912–16 have been Jewish? Could they have shown New York viewers a block-long challah (the Friday night ceremonial bread of the orthodox)? When did the young Rosenberg first juxtapose a Labor Day twist-bread with a pharaoh's tomb? Should not the Egyptian tyrant have invoked unleavened bread or matzoh? Why didn't the union bakers prepare a block-long matzoh for their holiday parade?

In our agnostic family, my mother constantly purchased Jewish bread, rye and pumpernickel regularly, and challah for special occasions. She had the power to secularize twist-bread. These loaves all came from Brooklyn Avenue bakeries in Boyle Heights. Los Angeles in the 1920s was an open-shop town with organized labor at its lowest ebb. Old-timers then looked back at the McNamara brothers case—the bombing of the *Times*—as unionism's Waterloo. Somehow, despite this bitter defeat, a few craftsmen paid dues and stubbornly kept alive labor's traditions.

Jewish immigrant bakers argued unionism, socialism, communism, and anarchism with a fervor mysterious to their fellow workers in "American Plan" Los Angeles. I heard echoes of these debates by virtue of my childhood in Boyle Heights. Political discourse came with the territory as union symbolism entered my family experience. I first saw union labels at home when my mother brought rye and pumpernickel from the bakery (challahs carried no labels). These little postage-stamp-sized paper labels, printed in red and black, held lions rampant. Whenever I could, to my mother's distress, I ate the paper lions. I felt that eating them brought good luck.

As a child, Harold Rosenberg must have seen similar labels on breads that graced his family's table. Further, viewing bakers marching on Fifth Avenue with their giant twist-bread, he might also have noticed their banners holding heraldic lions. Were Harold's parents trade unionists? Did they know that (in the very years they had introduced their son to museum splendor) many Jewish members of the Bakery and Confectionary Workers International Union of America had advocated industrial organization? Some dissidents eventually seceded from the BCWIUA. Did young Harold hear any radical workers in polemical debate? Did he wonder at the union's rampant lions?

The *BC&T News* (February, 1986) explained its former BCWIUA label, now designated the union's seal:

> The bakers' label reaches back to 1529 when workers in underground bakeries in Vienna detected barbarian hordes trying to tunnel beneath the city's walls. Their endeavors

> saved the city and a grateful King Ferdinand honored them by awarding the Bakers Guild its own coat of arms. As they emigrated to America in the 19th century, the Austrian bakers used the same coat of arms as a label—affixed directly to bread since it was hand-made in those days—to demonstrate their pride of craftsmanship and as a symbol of quality.

I would have been mystified by this story in childhood, not knowing anything about the siege of Vienna. I suspect that Harold Rosenberg, too, might have been intrigued by this account. However, I must turn back from the bakers' heroic coat of arms to bread, sacred and profane. The New York Labor Day paraders who baked a twist-bread that seemed a block long in a child's imagination were brothers in sister locals to those Los Angeles bakers who provided union-labeled rye and pumpernickel for our family.

I speculate on why Boyle Heights challah held no union lions. Proletarian bread for everyday use could carry union symbols. However, challah, although baked in union shops, connoted sacred systems separate from unionism. Clearly, some radicals elevated their cause over that of the synagogue. Regardless of such heresy, even the most rebellious baker could not affix his label onto challah. Whether my wild speculation can be verified, I do not know, but I remain confident that Jewish locals of the Bakery and Confectionary Workers International Union of America debated hotly and codified talmudically this weighty matter.

Unionists, whether devout or skeptical, could not have ignored the ritual meaning of challah turned into a Labor Day icon, a secular grail. Young Harold Rosenberg in New York saw a gigantic bread loaf as a work of art— a visual and ornamental text holding rich subtexts of pageantry and ideology. Such thoughts carry me far from an art critic's recollection of cosmic bread entombed with a pharoah and reentombed in the Metropolitan Museum of Art. Probably, the critic deliberately joined his childhood museum experience with a Labor Day picture of twist-bread to contrast sacred and secular domains. Perhaps, he unconsciously sensed the need to treat Labor Day ritual as touching on the bedrock of workers' beliefs. For me, a reader of Rosenberg's essays, his anecdote evoked challah's symbolism, rye bread's aroma, lions rampant on label and banner, and, ultimately, unionism's cause.

Beginning shipwright work in January 1941, I looked forward to my first San Francisco Labor Day parade. We marched from the Embarcadero to City Hall, buoyed up by the still-vibrant spirit of the 1934 maritime strike. That September, I knew no one who anticipated Pearl Harbor or could sense the contours of postwar changes in the labor movement. Holding to their early symbols, shipwrights marched under a banner displaying a wooden vessel on its launching ways. Other participants carried streamers: "Labor Creates All Wealth," "An Injury To One Is An Injury to All."

In recent years, Labor Day has marked summer's end or a last vaction fling. Activists lament our holiday's demise and call for a revival of tradition, the reenactment of ritual. Such calls restate the symbolic role of the bakers' carrying challah on Fifth Avenue and the shipwrights' representing antique wooden vessels on Market Street. Three decades ago, I became aware of yet another icon marking the dignity of labor.

Working in 1958 on an "uptown" carpentry crew engaged in enlarging St. Elizabeth's Infant Shelter in San Francisco, I met Merle Croy, a former coal miner from Muskogee, Oklahoma. Knowing of my interest in laborlore, he regaled me at lunchtime with his family traditions. His father had mined coal in Ohio when his fellows first organized the United Mine Workers of America. Blacklisted in Ohio, the elder Croy migrated to the Indian Territory to resume his trade. Merle grew up believing the *UMWA Journal* to be a second Bible. He attained the rank of fireboss—an inspector for gas who makes his lonely rounds undergound before the miners begin work.

During the "Grapes of Wrath" migration to California, Croy arrived in the Bay Area, where he switched to the building trades and the Carpenters Local 2164. On our lumberpile lunch site at St. Elizabeth's, I learned as much about Oklahoma coal as I did about the physical details of the maternity hospital under construction. Merle recalled that fellow miners had looked forward each year to their Labor Day celebrations.

While working underground, the miners looked out for unusual formations—an especially large chunk of unbroken coal, a fossil tree-trunk butt with extended roots snaking through the seam. Carboniferous age boulders bore visual tags: *bellmound, horse-*

*back, spider, niggerhead, washtub, kettlebottom.* Good fortune led the diggers to coal chunks of unusual size or fantastic shape. Miners did not break such finds for surface loading but guarded them in a chamber until the last week in August. Foremen and superintendents knew of this practice, overlooking the extra time lost in the effort.

Merle described for me the step-by-step skill and sweat necessary to bring the prize piece to the cage (vertical shaft) for hoisting to the surface. In his mind's eye, he saw again each fossil tree, each monstrous chunk of coal. He had helped in hauling such "lumps of coal" through underground "avenues" and "cross streets." The mine's main vertical shaft, together with the cage apparatus structure, determined the dimensions of the largest piece that could be lifted out for the Labor Day parade.

At the surface, the miners in their respective local unions mounted their finds on trucks borrowed from various employers. The men marched on foot carrying their UMWA banners. A committee of elders awarded holiday honors to the largest "lump." Croy assured me that he had seen pictures of such prizewinners. Who has retained a photo, or a newspaper clipping describing this practice?

Merle Croy and I worked again on the Town School for Boys in San Francisco's fashionable Pacific Heights district. He and other building trades buddies encouraged me to leave carpentry and to get on with my commitment to explore workers' traditions. Following their advice, I found myself at the University of Illinois, Urbana, and making new friends in Chicago, among them, Jack Conroy.

Conroy (1899–1990) had contributed an early proletarian novel, *The Disinherited,* based on his father's work in the "Monkey Nest Mine," at Moberly, Missouri (Wixson). I met Jack at a Wobbly gathering in Chicago, and we shared anecdotes. He mentioned that an Illinois coal local had shipped a Labor Day fossil to a Chicago Northside fuel yard, where the dealer kept it on the sidewalk for years. Jack visited this talisman from time to time, for it reminded him of his childhood, when his father's mates in Randolph County had used an enormous lump of coal in their parades. As an apprentice in the Wabash Railroad car shops, Jack joined the Brotherhood of Railway Carmen and proudly helped pull a freight car down Moberly's streets on Labor Day.

An "exile" in Chicago, Conroy saw its coal lump as a memorial to his father's beliefs. Jack urged me to make this pilgrimage with him to the fuel yard. We live with many regrets for tasks undone, projects unfinished: Jack retired to Moberly; I, to San Francisco; I never walked with him to view the iconic chunk of coal. Is it still extant in Chicago, or did someone pulverize it, unaware that it had served as a ritual object?

No matter our distance from hand labor, we know that twist-bread or a coal lump can be invested with special meaning. An art critic who looked at a pharoah's tomb in the Metropolitan Museum of Art related it to challah baked for a Labor Day parade. A novelist who viewed a Labor Day coal fossil related it to this father's sacrifice in a primitive mine.

I have not yet witnessed a parade in which an assembly line robot or an antiseptic computer is revered. Perhaps the day will come when such objects also will signal antiquity. I suggest that working people committed to modernity will continue to elevate particular products of their skill as they ritualize work experience. Parading by the numbers, unfurling old banners, declaiming tested slogans—all contribute to humanity's control over the workplace.

## Winding Down

Only during modern times and within highly industrial societies has retirement ritual marked the formal shift from work to leisure, from gainful employment to senior citizenship. Before the Industrial Revolution, death and disability weeded old workers from mine and mill. With the triumph of early capitalism, the notion that aged factory hands might have value beyond their working years seemed utopian if not insane. Changes came haltingly in practices that relegated "old hands" to society's scrap heap.

During 1810, the English Parliament legislated a noncontributory pension plan for civil servants. In the 1800s, Chancellor Bismarck extended social legislation to German citizens beyond the age of sixty-five. In 1875, the American Express Company (the predecessor of Railway Express) initiated a system of gratuities for its retired workers. It became "good business" to replace slow with active employees. I shall not address further the legislative pension web or its role in the welfare state. Rather, I turn to a few retirement ceremonies, long incognito in folklore studies.

Robert McCarl (1984) described a specific roast staged by Washington, D.C., fire fighters. *Roast* translates metaphorically to good food well prepared and lavishly served, to gifts serious and satiric, and finally, to an extended poetic rap roasting a retiree. When Jerry, completing his required years, "put in his papers," his peers planned his "last supper" and selected a playful emcee to preside. Most firehouses—indeed, nearly all occupational groups—hold talkers ready with improvisation, verbal dart throwers able to roast buddies as readily as a suckling pig or trussed turkey.

McCarl not only described the dinner ceremony but also transcribed an actual roast: 436 lines of text ranging from "pure corn" to scatology. One bit of esoterica holds topical reference to the District of Columbia's black fire chief sending a gift of grape Kool-Aid to a white fireman. We can decode such generosity by recalling the mass suicide tragedy that befell Jim Jones's followers in Guyana.

The Kool-Aid detail points to a large area of tension over race relations within many locals of the International Association of Fire Fighters. Just as the retirement emcee's recitation included firehouse work knowledge and commentary on world events, McCarl combined ethnographic description with interpretation. His article serves as a model for those who wish to explore the nature and symbolism of retirement ritual.

No one has counted the number of Americans honored in formal retirement during this century, or how much has been expended to purchase plaques, pins, watches, or other tokens of longevity. Occasionally, a country and western song emerges to invert the cheerful formula: a worker uses his farewell party to "punch out" a boss, or at least to express a hidden desire to do so. Cynical or negative commentary only highlights the usual positive reporting of retirement events.

I have been impressed by the attention of journalists to "human interest" retirement reports. Hundreds of such accounts can be culled from everyday print. These stories, scattered in local and national newspapers, combine to portray the mixture of pain and pleasure most Americans experience on winding down their working days.

On April 13, 1988, the *New York Times* carried a feature on Govan Brown: "Praised Bus Driver, 53, to Get a Rare Farewell." A New York City Transit Authority publicist noted that Brown's party would be the first retirement event held in the bus depot at 100th Street and Lexington Avenue. The transit officials planned to give him a plaque and a model bus inscribed with his name on the destination signs. His fellow workers anticipated six-foot hero sandwiches and an emotional speech by Brown. The honored driver, in twenty years, had racked up enough Manhattan miles to reach the moon.

Reporter Douglas Martin, interviewing the star driver before the party, learned that Brown, anticipating his leisure, had already enrolled in an acting class to prepare for TV commercials. As one of Brown's first exercises, he had to improvise a *Honeymooners* episode playing Jackie Gleason's Ralph Kramden, the surly, forever frustrated bus driver. (Life does mimic art!) The *Times* photo of a smiling Brown at the wheel of his own bus revealed a union button on his neat collar. However, the reporter Martin failed to mention Brown's affiliation with the Transport Workers Union of America. Do we infer that New York's readers are unaware of transit unionism?

A continent removed, San Francisco columnist Herb Caen also offered a retirement report (April 6, 1988): "Some sight at the Nordstrom dept. store [construction] site at Fifth and Market: 35 electricians holding their pipe benders aloft in an arch under which Al Tura walked as he departed the job for the last time; retiring after 40 yrs., 'born and raised' [in San Francisco] Al then went outside to find his wife waiting in a stretch limo for a tour of his favorite spots."

As in the case of New York, Caen did not mention Al Tura's long membership in the International Brotherhood of Electrical Workers Local 6. Nor did the columnist identify Al's employer, Rosendin Electric. Caen used language deftly to magnify a visual "sightem"—hard hats holding pipe benders aloft as if they were flashing sabres. Electricians use EMT (electric metallic tubing) benders or hickies, respectively, to shape angles in thin wall or rigid pipe conduit. Mike Tompkins, a navy veteran and Local 6 member on the Nordstrom job, in casting about for a way to honor Tura, recalled pictures of martial ceremonies. It seemed "natural" to substitute benders for sabers.

I had never observed a ceremony in which workers held tools aloft as in a military wedding; I did know that work tools could serve as ritual props. Hence, the *Chronicle* "gossip" item heightened my curiosity about "homemade" job farewells. The *Progress*, a neighborhood throw-away paper, serviced San Francisco districts with local color stories. On February 17, 1988, the paper ran a photo by Jim Kelly—ritual captured visually—with an extended caption capturing an unusual retirement act:

> SO LONG JOE—Who says the waterfront is dead? You couldn't prove it by this mob, especially Joe Jones, the guy shown being patted down by . . . could that be a cop? The action happened Friday at Pier 30, on the bulkhead fronting Red's Java House. To explain. It was a nice day, see, too good to waste indoors. So, as they've been doing off and on for years, the work crew from Lera Electric Co. on lower Brannan Street dropped by Red's for a beer or two, a tradition observed on special occasions like the World Series and Joe's last day on the job. An electrician for 40 years, the last 10 with Lera, the Pacifica resident was retiring. Big Mike Voss bought the Bud, and more or less everyone chipped in to bring Lisa to the scene, Lisa Kay—her working name—model, dancer and, on days like Friday, an all-in-fun impersonator. Scene Two moved inside where with Tom "Red" McGarvey presiding, Jones was favored with, among other things, a plaque framing his last Lera paycheck. Then everyone but Joe went back to work. Or more beer'n'burgers. She has life in her yet. San Francisco, that is.

We know the photographer Jim Kelly's name; we lack the name of the *Progress* caption writer who caught the spirit of Joe Jones's retirement. Did Kelly just happen to be at Red's Java House in time to photograph Lisa Kay "patting down" the retiring journeyman? Who on Lera's electrical crew hired Lisa and alerted the *Progress* to this merry happening?

Some present-day observers will view the Jones retirement photo as representing a sexist scene. Clearly, it holds suggestive tones. Lera workers found humor in its inversion: model/dancer Lisa impersonating a tough cop checking out a working stiff not for carrying a weapon but for retiring. Other viewers will see the same photo as documenting a ritual that closed out four decades of constructive labor. Joe's fellow workers honored him with beer and burgers, as they likened his last day to a World Series celebration.

Curiously, the *Progress* caption writer overlooked Jones's membership in IBEW Local 6. Do we infer from the three newspaper reports cited here that unionism holds no significance in retirement ceremonies? We do learn that Jones's last Lera paycheck had been "plaqued." Did the electrician cash it before framing, or did he retain it, uncashed, as a symbol of his long years of wire pulling and conduit bending?

Folklorist McCarl's report of fireman Jerry's retirement roast fits the confines and style of an academic journal. Kelly's photo of Lisa Kay "patting down" Joe Jones caught one aspect of retirement. Similarly, Caen's squib noting the essentials of Al Tura's choreographed ceremony and Martin's feature detailing Govan Brown's final bus drive reported unusual finales. Perhaps scholars, photographers, journalists, and film makers should join in fully documenting retirement rituals symbolized by toy buses, raised benders, or framed checks.

During my waterfront apprenticeship days, I never witnessed a retirment ceremony similar to those described above. President Roosevelt signed the Social Security Act on August 4, 1935; initial payroll deductions by employers dated to January 31, 1937; three years later, the legal secretary Ida Fuller became the first New Deal retiree. It took some years for the shipwrights union to develop its own ceremonies for post–Social Security retirees.

In the years prior to the New Deal, our Local 1149 had continued a traditional security arrangement for widows and children of deceased members. Shipwrights, marine joiners, boatbuilders, caulkers, and drydockers formed some of San Francisco's pioneer trade unions. These artisans, in addition to their regular work on docks and ways, dismantled ships for the finished and metal parts valued in building construction during Gold Rush years. Highly skilled Bay Area shipwrights, operating under various union designations, organized local units prior to the formation of the United Brotherhood of Carpenters and Joiners of America.

The knowledge that the local had a long history—older than the national union—guided new members in respect for traditional customs. Although Local 1149 included members who clashed on ideological grounds, they agreed substantially on the need to preserve craft custom, to maintain solidarity, and to honor the dead. When an old-timer died, fellow workers carried his tool box to the union hall. Huge and heavy chests, frequently ornate, held handmade tools. We believed that rosewood planes or chisels with long hickory handles would float if dropped overboard. We tried not to test such beliefs.

At the conclusion of the meeting following an old-timer's death, our local's president auctioned the tools one by one, gathering a purse for the departed member's family. The auction provided a primitive form of security for the widow, but it also held further significance. Before Pearl Harbor, Local 1149 had been a small organization; all the members worked together from time to time. When one member purchased a deceased colleagues's tools, he kept some of his brother's spirit alive. More importantly, he kept the tools out of skid road pawn shops and out of the hands of strangers.

This tool auction memory carries me back to the period before my navy service in World War II. Returning home, I found that the ritual had been terminated in favor of a newly won fringe benefit: employers now bought the tools, turning them into pieces of hardware. Collective bargaining gains, Social Security legislation, and elaborate welfare plans, despite their value, combined to rob unions of time-tested folkways. The destruction of a tool auction ritual broke the continuity of a tradition that evoked elements of sympathetic magic much older than labor organization.

I have seen the shipwrights' tool auction as both a ritual and a memorial act. It can also be viewed as a chronological statement—the end of a particular practice. Marcus Rediker, while treating the cultural life of Anglo-American seamen in the early eighteenth century, noted touching rituals of ocean burial. Sailors knew the price of death on the water, for bodies could not be preserved for the long voyage home. The sailmaker would sew up the corpse in a piece of old canvas, perhaps ballasting it with a cannonball. As crew members heaved the body overboard, the captain or a mate might offer a prayer for the departed.

Conscious that sea predators mutilated and ate the corpse, thus denying the soul its rest, seamen tried to soften the starkness in ocean burials. Rediker observed: "One of the most touching rituals of death took place several days after a man had passed away. The dead man's goods—his chest, bedding, clothes, and the few other items he possessed, perhaps a book or two, cards, or a musical instrument—were auctioned off as everyone gathered round the mainmast. Seeking to honor the dead and to provide for his family, seamen purchased all of the goods at an 'extreme dear rate' " (197).

Richard Simson, in his journal documenting a voyage through the Straits of Magellan in 1689, noted that the dead man's effects "were sold at the Mast according to Custome." Richard Field of Dalhousie University has elaborated on the auction by attention to material culture, the concrete representations of life at sea:

> [Chests] held private belongings and keepsakes of a sailor's land-based life and family, and these wooden sea chests were often decorated on the inside, the outside, or both, with drawings and paintings of sailing vessels or decorative motifs of the sailor's world, including compass stars or hearts. They often held implements and artifacts of the mariner's own making: carved scrimshaw, needle cases, jagging wheels, valentines, painted ditty bags, fancy rope work, busks, and flutes, to name only a few items. There was a rich material life that seamen created, and the artifacts embody beliefs, values, assumptions, and ideals that sailors had about their world. (77)

A ritual enactment seemingly as simple as a tool auction in 1941 can take us back hundreds of years as it invokes the memory of past ocean burials. Initially, I related Local 1149's ceremony to the then-current interest in Social Security legislation. Upon reflection, I turned to notions of sympathetic magic, because we kept tools within our fraternity. With the passage of decades, I see an auction event, in which I was privileged to participate, as continuous with rituals lost in time.

It will require assembly lines of antiquarians and ethnographers to compile an encyclopedia of occupational ritual. The examples cited stem from my memory and reading. New as I was to waterfront work in 1941, the solemnity of our shipwrights' tool auction etched this event in mind. Then, I felt no need to log such happenings. Two decades later, Tom Bogard's shovel story impressed me to the point of writing it down.

Local 1149's tool ceremony afforded members the chance to participate within a parting ritual by purchasing old tools. I have retained an auctioned brass-bound mahogany bevel square; its present function is ceremonial. My fellow worker Bogard, reconstructing a soapbox spiel, helped me sense the transition from verbal art to ritual act. Reading art criticism by Harold Rosenberg in the mid-1970s, I stumbled on his delightful vignette of Labor Day parade twist-bread. The interconnection of one's personal experience with that of others—observed, heard, read—opens laborlore paths.

Anticipating that partisans of workers' culture will decipher rituals they have encountered, I suggest a range of comparative and conceptual strategies: particular case reports, analysis that questions shibboleths. Does it not seem strange that we lack a folklorist's account of Labor Day events? On October 17, 1866, the *Glasgow Herald* noted a Reform League procession that cries for comparison to American parades:

> Flags were flying in all directions and men were mustering in every quiet street, covered with medals, rosettes of all colours, aprons and silk sashes, and attended by instrumental bands. . . . I saw stalwart stonemasons and bricklayers, plasterers and slaters, plumbers and painters by the hundreds . . . bearing splendid banners, miniature houses and monster chimney stalks. Blacksmiths, joiners, ship carpenters, and cabinetmakers were also there carrying model ships, model machinery, anvils, vises, chests of drawers, wardrobes, pulpits, tester beds, sections of ship fittings and other articles of similar description. . . .
>
> But the letter press printers, the lithographic ditto, the pipemakers and the nail makers took the shine out of the representative models displayed by the other trades. They

> had large lorries or wagons where their trades were carried on as the procession moved along and people by the way had the opportunity of seeing the work done and of getting printed bills, pictures, tobacco pipes or horse nails hot from the hammer, the hand and the printing machine. (King, 146)

Many building-trades mechanics have marched in parades displaying their skills. In addition, they have heard and told lumber pile and tool shed tales, humorous or grim. Dangerous work demands talk. Lunchtime and coffee break on many jobs become traditionalizing circles—settings in which artisans generate and perpetuate lore. Some folklorists have labeled Paul Bunyan and Joe Magarac as "fake" or "synthetic," beginning life in print. Attention to such points of origin intrigues scholars but often neglects lore's multiple meanings.

In my trade, I heard Bunyan- and Magarac-like fragments after industrial accidents. A construction wall collapse, an elevator shaft fall, or a crane boom touching a high-voltage line would precipitate a functionally therapeutic talk-fest. Anecdotes likened the specific injury or death to previous hazards, as well as to lucky or fantastic escapes. It hardly mattered whether the narrator had actually seen the described accident, had heard about it from others, or had indulged in imaginative projection. Absorbed in such horror stories, we dissolved our fears within a comrade's tragedy. Essentially, we turned story sessions into ritual, helping us borrow courage from previous job victims.

A skeptic may question whether accident accounts related by construction stiffs constitute ritual. Some observers will relegate such tales to the narrative bin. Regardless of the placement for particular anecdotes, I come back to the ritualistic aspect of mechanics touching fear by elevating former mates to heroic status. Only the living honor the dead, whether by tool auction or by tales of demons lurking in evey crane's shadow.

Labor history and fiction have impressed me with the overwhelming variety of job rites awaiting exploration. For example, economists and employers often decry restriction of output by workers. In turn, employees try variously for fair conditions established contractually or by informal practices that set production norms. One who gives all on the job leaves little for family or community.

Over the years, artisans have named code violators: *hog, rooter, chaser, pacer, pusher, rusher, runner, speeder, leader, bell horse, swift, pet, suck, brown nose, popsicle man.* Beyond seeking nuances of differences in such tags, we must consider the encoding of routines to enforce conditions of employment. To illustrate: in the era before power tools, stone cutters held to a custom restricting a quarryman's heavy pick in place of point and hammer. They appealed for use of the small tools against the brute-force large pick. Did they enforce this rule by branding the pick as unlucky, surrounding it with narratives of misfortune, or by ritualizing point and hammer techniques?

In most trades, old workers taught apprentices defensive norms—to work by the rule, to guard energy, to spread employment, to hold decision making close to the shop floor. Floaters, ten-day stiffs, sundowners, and boomers carried such rules from site to site as they struggled to educate home guards. Conservative craftsmen affiliated with AFL unions, decrying IWW calls for sabotage, nevertheless employed tactics of surreptitious slowdowns. The strike weapon served as the ultimate arbiter, whether choreographed strikes sanctioned by formal union vote or unauthorized quickies or wildcats.

Richard Boyden, in a dissertation on San Francisco's machinists, reported a little-noted outlaw ritual, "dragging the string." One of the boomers walked through the shop trailing a long knotted string. "As he passed by, each worker shut off his machine, grabbed hold of a knot and followed along, until the whole shop filed out on strike" (73). Who knows this act's age, background, or spread? Questions about knotted strings, of course, can represent our curiosity about the totality of work custom.

Not all quickie strikes leave a formal record. Not all daily conversation channels into a traditional tale. Not all oak-splint baskets end as museum pieces. Not all pick-and-shovel work leads to ceremonial recitation. Hence, scholars and curators, using such tools as they can muster, look for ritual acts of great significance, for artistic expression patterned by repetition.

Warren Roberts, an Indiana University folklorist, called attention in 1978 to the customary practice by stone carvers of carving tools on local tombstones, thus memorializing themselves and fellow craftsmen. A few miles from his campus, he could look into a hole in the ground from which all the limestone had been quarried for the Empire State Building. In the Bedford Cemetery, he found a remarkable monument to Louis Baker, who had died from a lightning bolt at age twenty-three (August 29, 1917). Roberts described Baker's footstone:

> His fellow carvers made an exact replica of his workbench, or "banker" as stone carvers call it. On the banker is the piece of architectural stone, unfinished, exactly as he left it. . . . Atop this stone appear his tools; a mallet, a hammer, a pitching tool, chisels, a square, a head of a broom, and his apron. The fidelity of this work is amazing; the wood grain of the bench is clearly shown as are the bent-over nails holding the bench together and the straw in the broom. . . . These stone carvers, who normally executed the designs of architects, draughtsmen, and others, produced a striking and poignant memorial of their own design—one that speaks to a craftsman far more movingly than a classical urn or some similar ornament.

During January 1984, San Francisco Bay Area newspapers reported a strike by refinery workers at the Rodeo Union Oil Company plant. Members of Local 1-326 of the Oil, Chemical and Atomic Workers Union objected to a two-tiered wage system allowing low pay for new hires. Such technical labor news, common in the Bay Area, does not merit wide coverage. However, on January 19, an independent driver of an eighteen-wheel rig killed a plant gate picketer, Greg Goobic, age twenty.

Goobic's fellow workers staged a subdued protest march from the local's hall to the death scene. Hank Miller, president, addressing the ranks, "held up a Union Oil belt buckle presented to him for his outstanding safety record, then vowed never to wear it again, saying it would be melted down with others to create a memorial plaque for Goobic" (Diringer). A year later, Rodeo Local 1-326 dedicated the plaque to mark Greg's sacrifice.

These sparse facts do not plumb the depth of the oil workers' ritual. Who initiated the meltdown for company safety awards? Did anyone in Rodeo articulate this ceremony's antiquity? Vulcan's sons knew that good spirits pass through the forge into new armor. Medieval masons had placed silver coins in cathedral mortar to ward off evil. Long before the word *recycle* connoted responsible citizenship, the aphorism "to beat swords into plowshares" marked a transformation of metallic substance and a spiritual command.

Those who treasure laborlore will find significance in Hank Miller's act of turning his belt buckle into a plaque for Greg Goobic. Occupational rites include hand-me-downs from the earliest days of metal, stone, and wood fabrication to everyday ceremonies reported by public press and television newscast. We need not assume that exotic folk alone practice magic.

In this chapter, I have walked through a museum of antiquity and modernity, pausing to reflect on shivaree, rough music, small shovels, ca' cannyism, challah, coal chunk, tool auctions, a gravestone, and a belt-buckle plaque. I view my book as a museum entrance invitation. Our password *ritual* ties disparate action and rhetoric together. Workers' rites don rainbow cloaks, speak in strange tongues, and tower above the plain.

"PILEBUTT"
STORIES AND PHOTOGRAPHS
ABOUT PILE DRIVING
COLLECTED BY
MICHAEL S. MUNOZ
PATRI

"Pilebutt"

# 10

# Pile Butt Pennants

### *Antoine Barada, Hurry-up Man*

Antoine Barada was a hurry-up man, always rushing, rushing, can't wait for anything. One time he got tired of watching a pile driver working along the Missouri with the hammer making the up-down, up-down, the driver yelling "Git up! Git-up! Whoa! Back! Back! Whoa!" and then all of it over again and the piling going down maybe a half inch. So Antoine he picked up the damned thing in his bare hand, throws it high and far so it lights clear over the Missouri where it bounce and bounce leaving ground tore up for miles and miles and making what the greenhorns call "Breaks of the Missouri." But at last it stop and if you dig down in them high ridges you find it is the damned pile driver with grass growing over him, a little poor soil, you understand. . . . When Antoine had disposed of the Johny Jumper hammer he sees that the piling that is left stands a mile higher than the rest, so he gives it a lick with his fist and it pop down into the ground so deep it strike buried lake, the water flying out like from bung hole fifty feet high and like to drown out the whole country if Antoine he did not sit on the hole first. (Pound 1943, 141)

### *Ray Sparrow, Pile Monkey*

I climbed the ladder to a little platform aloft. After the donkeyman hauled up the pile, I used a spud—a tool made out of a 2″ × 4″ board with a short line attached. When the pile danced in the air, I whipped the spud around the pile to pull it into the leads. With both hands full, I used a mouth whistle to signal: Ready. You had to step back fast before the hammer came down. Then, I dropped to the deck on the monkey line. Sometimes, the pile monkey had to jump for the line if it dangled out of reach. Some of the ex-loggers also called me a punk, or whistle punk. If someone seemed reluctant to go aloft, an old timer snorted, "Get your ass up there, punk, come down with the hammer. We don't care how you drop!" (Interview, April 12, 1983)

These brief narratives—far apart in time, place, purpose—illustrate the wide range of expressive material available to workers who treasure job traditions or who probe laborlore's meanings. Louise Pound, while searching during the 1930s for tall tales about Nebraska strong men, visited Marie Sandoz, a Midwest regional novelist. Sandoz recalled stories she had heard in childhood told by "half-breeds" around Pine Ridge (the southeast corner of the state). Some anecdotes featured a local strong man, Antoine Barada (1807–86), who picked up huge boulders or pulled stranded boats from sandbars.

Pound's retelling in 1943 of the Sandoz story extolled Barada's physical strength; she could, as well, have accented an etiological purpose—explaining a natural feature's original cause. Native Americans along the Missouri used myth and legend to treat the river's power and course. French voyageurs, Spanish explorers, and Yankee settlers adapted Indian legendry as they contributed their own accounts to explain the Missouri River's passage through hill country.

Seemingly, neither Sandoz nor Pound were especially conscious that they had brought to print an early folk account of a horse-powered pile-driving machine. More importantly, the Johny Jumper hammer drove pilings but a half inch at a time, whereas Barada drove one a mile deep with a single blow. Allowing for some exaggeration, we can speculate whether pile-driving men beyond the Missouri Breaks had ever heard this tale. Could it have been told only by Barada's admiring neighbors without deep reference to occupational setting?

Like the John Henry ballads, ambiguity marked the "boast" about Barada. In a contest between man and machine, John Henry gained victory at the cost of his life. Barada destroyed the horse-powered machine only to drive the last timber by hand. Who, then, emerged victorious? Barada's ultimate role—altering nature's landscape—does seem appropriate to the present self-image of many construction workers. Such gigantic changes normally flow from machine use, from technology, not from old-fashioned sinew. What did the "original" storytellers signify in the creation of the Breaks of the Missouri by a man throwing away a machine? Do we lack an ending where Barada, the natural man, dies of battered muscle and broken heart?

In her childhood, Sandoz heard tales about Barada from Omaha "half-breeds"; I heard Ray Sparrow's pile monkey anecdote during a long visit in his California "redwood modern" Mill Valley home. In 1983, he dated the happening back to 1939 on a Pescadero concrete bridge job at the Pacific's edge (San Mateo County). Because of his agility, and perhaps cockiness, he had been sent high on the rig's leads "to monkey"—to physically position piles under a pulsing hammer. In contrast to Barada's storytellers, Sparrow, in self-description, had no need to exaggerate. Descriptive narrative served to explain his work to an outside folklorist.

If the "moral" in Barada's story is now obscure or lost, it seems clear enough in Sparrow's account, where an old-timer commanded: "Come down with the hammer. We don't care how you drop!" Such gallows humor (a pile-driving rig's leads can resemble a gallows frame) referred to the pile monkey's potential death under the hammer. Sparrow's reminiscence offered no hint to his acquisition of skill over the years, his "graduation" from "whistle punk" to "super" (superintendent) on New York's Guggenheim Museum job. Instead, his report clued listeners to the stylized verbal patter, the constant exchange by which seasoned hands educated newcomers.

I have accented the differences between two work accounts, traditional tall tale and personal reminiscence. A common element in each demands of listeners a minimum knowledge of pile-driving technology. Born in 1807, Barada would have been involved with horse-powered equipment as a young man. His "pile driver" referred to the whole machine; his "driver yelling" referred only to the crew member teaming the horses. Sparrow's reference to a "donkeyman" in 1939 keys us not to an animal but to a craftsman/engineer and his gear, a steam-propelled hammer raised by a donkey engine mounted on a barge or scow. Sparrow pulls listeners away from Barada's slow world of limited power to the present complex of booming change in construction techniques.

How can readers visualize machines in which horses were harnessed to a hammer—not a hand-held tool used to drive nails, but a massive cast-iron weight dropped onto a wooden pile head? How can anyone who has neither seen or heard a modern rig in action "see" a pile monkey on his monkey board (platform)? Does the loggers' term *whistle punk* (the individual who passes signals from the rigging slinger to the donkey engineer when yarding logs) offend or amuse? Whether or not we seek a relationship between the accounts of Barada and Sparrow or place them at their respective ends of an array, each leads to the arcane world of pile-driving crews, tools, and lore.

All crafts—skilled and unskilled, as well as those judged demeaning in contrast to those prized—hold dramatic elements. However, not all work is blessed with compelling novels or memorable films. Countless tasks remain hidden to the writer, artist, or documentarian. Pile-driving crews, which construct waterfront docks, shore freeway bridges, or underpin city skyscrapers, are neither subjects within popular fiction nor screen heroes; they have also eluded labor economists and social historians. Clearly, pile work is as significant as that of the seafaring whaler or steamboat pilot. Perhaps a Melville or a Twain will yet emerge to discover the pile rig; meanwhile, its toilers (*pile butt, pile buck,* or *pile doe* in their vernacular) continue to craft legends and treasure lore.

Pile drivers, who have established a considerable coherence as a work group over centuries, shaped their names and tales in a manner parallel to that of speakers within other occupational communities. Workers do not haphazardly acquire special traditions or terminology. Rather, they favor a bright phrase or anecdote that comments pungently on technological continuity, job anxiety, work reward, or labor solidarity. New speech must ring to the ear as it comes to life in settings of shared values. The best job narratives help workers gain control over demanding conditions and complex social relationships.

Pile drivers, like brothers and sisters across the land in diverse occupations, contribute both to lore that is known to all Americans (e.g., "John Henry") and that known to but an infinitesimal section of the citizenry (e.g., "Hurry-up Man" or "Pile Monkey"). The tale about Barada and the remembrance by Sparrow, then, can be shared inside and outside the pile community.

No matter how we distinguish the categories of occupational folklife, we can sense in the opening tale and reminiscence a further distinction between broad traditions (American boastfulness) and narrow accounts (an individual's specific experience). Ultimately, if novelists, film makers, or historians approach the pile rig, they must listen to and absorb the locutions of various children of Antoine Barada and Ray Sparrow; those who could throw whole machines across rivers and those who have come down to deck safely with the monkey line.

## Charter of Deeds

Where pride and skill join on a job, workers turn to the rhetoric of jurisdiction, often understood as a charter for good deeds. Before the rise of modern labor unions, artisans combined in guilds, lodges, friendly societies, or worshipful companies. Such associations—civic, celebratory, quasi-religious—asserted their members' special roles in written ordinances, covenants, and constitutions. Unions, today, claiming jurisdiction in a variety of documents including by-laws and collective-bargaining agreements, continue to lend strength to workers' consciousness of their worth and place.

Medieval craftsmen who built pile wharves and bridges mainly handled timber; at times, they used iron devices fashioned by blacksmiths (shoes, ties, rods, bolts, straps, plates). However, masons laying below-ground stone foundations also drove wood piles for building supports and for bridge footings. A master mason who could conceive, design, and erect an arched bridge felt no qualms in beginning at the bottom with timber piles.

As wood-working pile men sought to demark their particular craft, they had to distinguish it from that of rival workers with stone and mortar. While some pile drivers set themselves apart from stone masons, other pile men drew guild lines between themselves and fellow woodworkers (carpenters, shipwrights, millwrights) and from watermen (inland boatmen) on barge, scow, and lighter. We deal here with codifying rule books over centuries, not decades.

With the construction in 1779 of England's first major cast-iron bridge on the Severn River, its builders extended their reach from traditional wood and stone to metal. An entrepreneurial ironmaster then set up a blast furnace at the water's edge to cast ribs on site. With some imagination, we can look back at the flow of techniques from the furnace or foundry to bridge carpenters and iron and steel erectors. About 1800, an English engineer introduced cast-iron piles at Bridlington Harbor, and for the following century, pile drivers slowly increased their mastery over metal.

The perfection of the Bessemer steel-making process in 1856 led, two decades later, to steel bridge construction. When rolling mills fabricated piles of steel, pile men added the riveting gun and acetylene torch to their hammers and saws. In 1892, the French engineer François Hennebique patented a reinforced concrete beam. Despite initial resistance, European and American crews accepted concrete as a "natural" material similar to wood or iron.

We can grasp the enlargement of each pile driver's competence by observing today's crews at work. For example, we may see an auger-cast pile "grow" within the earth by grout pumped under pressure into a continuously bored hole. This pile forms itself underground without the driving machine pulsing or booming overhead. We see pile crew "supers" struggle with computer printouts supplementing "old-fashioned" blueprints. We marvel at the power bottled within new science-fiction-like machines.

Today's pile workers become conscious of their craft's continuity (through centuries of time and above the demands of technological change) when they dismantle docks or bridges and discover pilings in place long after their drivers have vanished. Perhaps the best instance of such continuity dates from Venice: The St. Mark's campanile fell in 1902; its preservationists found good foundation piles more than a thousand years old and still serviceable. To unearth an ancient pile becomes an archeological adventure. To find such a relic is not unusual; to search for and find an aged document on pile driving is.

In the years of rebuilding after San Francisco's earthquake-fire of 1906, eager craftsmen from the world's corners flocked to the Golden Gate. These "earthquake mechanics" carried tools and templates, codes and loyalties. About 1911, in their then-new Local 77 hall, a pile union committee drafted working rules for the entire state. At least one printed copy has survived in the University of California's Bancroft Library. The local's brochure asserted extremely broad jurisdiction, based on work actually performed as well as ambitions articulated by a craft conscious membership. At this juncture, I present the 1911 claim, breaking it down into discrete units:

> Construction, reconstruction, repairing, removing, and wrecking of wharves, piers, docks, bridges, viaducts, towers, masts;
> Coal, rock or other bunkers;
> Hoists, "A" frames, derricks, trestles, hoppers, travelers' false work, pile drivers, structural steel or iron work;
> Building and placing cylinders, caissons, cofferdams, retaining walls, jetties, weirs, timber and concrete dry-docks;
> Pile driving in all its branches;
> Cutting off and capping of piles, abutments, foundations, submarine or other work in connection therewith;
> All light iron or steel used in any of the above work—riveting, cutting, or bending of same;
> Operation of all derricks, tools or machinery necessary in performing any of the aforesaid work;
> All work in sewers and tunnels where any of the above said machinery is used.

A few terms such as *therewith* and *aforesaid* obviously came from the legal fraternity, stretching back ultimately to ecclesiastical law. Behind this canonical language, the ontological tone of proud tough craftsmen resonates: I am a pile driver because I hammer, cut, cap, lift, place, climb, crawl, bend, burrow, dig, dive. My command of work shouts identity. My daring deeds contribute to the human endeavor. I am that which I do!

The San Francisco committee charged with composing these work rules in 1911 assumed that all its clauses were understood by peers. It never entered the minds of compilers to explain to outsiders such terms as *"A" frame, travelers' false work, caissons,* or *jetties.* Often, a pile man's safety depended on certainty that his fellows shared familiarity with the relevant techniques and tools, that they had internalized these jurisdictional claims. To work by the rule signaled leaving the job alive.

Job jurisdiction translated itself into identity, authority, competence, and safety; for ideologues, it also conveyed conflict. Occasionally, a correspondent offered a vignette illuminating the tension packed into by-law brochures. For example, the *Industrial Worker* (October 10, 1912) carried a San Francisco report entitled "Craft Unionism Fails on the Waterfront." This pronouncement concerned Pile Drivers Local 77, affiliated with the International Association of Bridge, Structural and Ornamental Iron Workers.

Local 77's members worked constantly with timber (piles, caps, braces, bents, planks), hence overlapping the traditional jurisdiction of carpenters. With the shift from wood to concrete in dock building, iron workers also "infringed" on wood form builders, common laborers who spread concrete, and cement finishers. One IWW activist characterized AFL dock work as a "moving picture show" where rival craftsmen shifted props from scene to scene. Stepping into the "show," the IWW organized concrete laborers who worked side-by-side with skilled AFL pile drivers.

Essentially, alert IWW members in this century's opening decades had responded to a technological transformation, to "progress." The *Industrial Worker* correspondent touched an underlying chord separating craft from industrial proponents: "The labor skates [AFL business agents] are stampeded and . . . clustered around the bars in the waterfront saloons devising ways and means of keeping hold of their jobs, while the I.W.W. members are busier than ever agitating on the job."

To delve into any trade's lore demands knowledge of job techniques, work rules, and craft rhetoric. When IWWs called union rivalry a "moving picture show," AFL officers fell back on constitutional language. No set of activists held a linguistic patent on work description. In treating union claims, I have been helped by an unpublished research paper (1968) prepared by John Rogers for the United Brotherhood of Carpenters and Joiners of America. It traces jurisdictional difference between ironworkers and carpenters, much of it centered on pile driving.

These two international unions faced transitions from wood to iron and steel in setting false work and scaffolding for bridges and skyscrapers. Erectors complained justly of death and disability when "other men, be they mechanics or laborers," put up scaffolds or false work (temporary timbers to hold steel in place during construction). In a Chicago meeting of the Structural Trades Alliance, 1906, both unions sought awards based on material handled, wood or steel. No written "no-raiding" agreements or legal formulas hold forever; jurisdictional battles respond to technical advances and political power. We need to ferret out lore that echoes workers' fears of others who encroach on their livelihoods.

Young artisans absorb extensive on-the-job vocabularies without sensing how foreign these words sound to outsiders. At building sites across the continent, observers see hard-hatted pile men mired in muck at the foot of towering machines. Few opportunities arise for crew members to explain themselves to those beyond the fence—those who peer in amazement into the excavation pit and see or hear machines in action.

Dialogue hardly exists across "keep-out" and "hard-hat zone" fences. Imagine an encounter between a pile driver and a sidewalk superintendent in which the former tries to explain his essential gear: the pile is like a peg hammered into the ground; our crane lifts each pile to place it between leads or guides under the hammer; these leads look like tracks or cages or pogo sticks; some leads are fixed while others swing; that telescoping brace at the crane's bottom pushes the leads to the right place, just where we need to drive each pile; some of the gang call this bottom brace a *spotter,* but others name it *spider, kicker, stinger,* or *apron.* Enough! Do onlookers focus on the brace's mechanical function, its funny "handles," or the purposes served when workers give their tools insider's names?

All of us are outsiders when facing the work of others. We glimpse their job routines in talk and text, or by pictures in the press and on the screen. To fathom the complexity within strange tasks we begin, in one instance, by asking pile drivers to make their work known. It then becomes our choice whether we wish to decipher their occupational lore. We help ourselves in self-identification by using the job anecdotes and narratives of others to frame their humanity as well as our own.

Whether or not we can talk to pile crews, we continue to see their work and sense their charter claims at the water's edge (dock, pier, wharf, weir) and on the land (bridge, overpass, causeway, trestle). Even when piles are invisible under foundations, we feel their presence if only by aural memory. Who has not heard a pile driver's clatter? Where contemporary workers drive piles on city jobs, idle watchers congregate to observe the forcing of a creosoted timber, prestressed concrete casting, or sleek steel column into muck or rock. This act seems inherently mysterious to outsiders. Do we believe that the roaring hammer drives care away?

This chapter explores lore's meaning within an obscure occupational community. I believe that discrete items of job wisdom become pennants figuratively hoisted over rigs. Although I associate pile rigs primarily with maritime sites, long travel has persuaded me that many pile men favor foundation work far from shoreline. In "inland" tasks, pile driving seems fascinating to urban onlookers whether at a Manhattan skyscraper excavation or a New Orleans levee edge. Indeed, some workers and watchers place no stock in the distinction of pile work on water and land.

Previous chapters focused on individual heroes or items of lore. Here, I combine genres into a craft mosaic by pursuing artistry and enactment wherever floating or mobile rigs pause. Engineering, business, and labor history illuminate the platform on which pile lore lives. In the pages ahead, I draw on varied published materials (the full citations appear in the bibliography): Carson, Chellis, eM-Kayen, Healey Tibbitts, Jacoby, Little, MacKinnon, Mackley, McKiernan-Terry, Morken, Munoz, Quinn, Riedel, Stephens, Young.

## Metaphor

Working people constantly jump craft speech boundaries, even while clinging to jurisdictional rules to protect income and identity. Terms such as *hot wire* or *highball* no longer belong exclusively to electricians or railroaders. At times, metaphoric usages become so common that speakers are unaware of the shifts in setting. To illustrate, we voice "the ship that plows the sea" or "Jack Tar plows the waves" without consciousness of movement from agrarian to nautical action.

I suspect that *pile drive/driver/driving* belong in as many figurative vocabularies as in those of the construction trades workplace. During the nineteenth century, writers found it useful to extend *pile driver* to varied spheres. The earliest example in the United States, to my knowledge, dates to 1855 from the pen of political humorist Mortimer Neal Thomson. In *Doesticks,* an antihero applies for a police job in Manhattan, where he meets a powerful rival—"a six foot Welshman, a rod and a half across the shoulders, with a fist like a pile-driver" (285). A few years later in Britain, Augustus Mayhew used the same term in an "unfashionable novel" set in London; in *Paved with Gold* he penned: "After some sparring, Jack threw out his 'pile-drivers' and caught Ned on the 'sniffer' " (189).

Sportswriters—whether focusing on boxing, wrestling, soccer, or football—relished *pile* figures to designate jabbing hits, wrenching falls, forceful kicks, and plunging attacks. Professional wrestlers in the age of television have twisted this usage to describe a combatant who lifts an opponent, turns him upside down, and slams his head to the ring floor (Fromer). Novelists who deal in spy intrigue (such as Dan Lees) relish accounts of "big boys . . . dishing out pile-drivers and body-slams, cracking heads and snapping spines" (33). Such treatment parallels cowboy talk of *pile-driving broncos,* which jolt riders by coming down on all fours, hooves closely grouped with their legs as stiff as ramrods (Adams).

Sailors have borrowed the same term to describe the action of a vessel heading into a heavy sea (Bowen). In 1898, the *Nautical Magazine* reported on the *Natuna*'s 225-day passage from London to San Francisco: "After pile-driving off Cape Horn for some days, she squared away" (355). In this vein during 1940s, I heard longshoremen use *pile driver* disparagingly to name a careless winch operator who set down loads too heavily. Such job analogies often circulated without the benefit of print.

In my study of *fink,* I noted its utility in political discourse. *Pile drive,* too, has long served in this arena. A 1982 example from Austin makes the point: Billy Clayton "a genuine unreconstructed good ol' boy . . . has 'suspended' more rules with his pile-driving speaker's gavel than any man in Texas history" (McNeely). One can literally follow pile idioms from field to field. Mitford Mathews cites *pile driver* in 1857 to name a small gray heron, "the homeliest creature in these [New York] woods" (1241). Finally, some bartenders, using bodily humor, liken screwdriver and pile driver drinks—vodka with orange juice, vodka with prune juice.

These brief citations from diverse realms do not exhaust the list. In an oral reminiscence (similar to Ray Sparrow's account of pile monkeys), ironworker "Peanuts" Coble described his years on the Golden Gate Bridge. Talking to Stephen Cassady, Coble recalled his north-tower work. Steel units fabricated by Bethlehem in the east came by ship via the Panama Canal, then by barge to Bethlehem's Alameda yard for drilling rivet points, and finally by barge again to the bridge's work site. As the tower arose, an enormous two-headed traveler (like a giant spider) crawled up and down the steel uprights. The traveler, a derrick crane, lifted each huge tower member into position, dropping it into place for temporary bolting and permanent riveting. Coble explained:

> Sometimes, we'd be up there with a sixty-five-ton piece of steel in the clear and ready to go down. I'd tell the boss to lower it, and the operator would literally drop it from the boom the last six or eight inches. And it might not go down. Sixty-five ton of steel, and it wouldn't budge an inch, it fit that tight. So we would take a twenty-five-ton—or maybe it was twelve and a half, I don't recall—airhammer and piledrive that sonofabitch into place. Still, it might be two inches off. Then, it was just a matter of putting more and more weight into them to force those girders down. Let's say you have a sixty-five-ton piece and six pieces on top: six times sixty-five is 390, almost 400 ton of weight before those holes would align close enough so's you could drive a rivet in them. (68)

Throughout this century, construction work in the United States attracted immigrants from many lands; no single dialect, no overarching lexicon, marks the building trades. Coble's account typifies much construction talk: concrete rather than abstract, generally free from allusion, and with few ambiguities in thought. Only in Coble's phrase "piledrive that sonofabitch into place" do we hear the colloquial voice and sense a release of tension—bringing a sixty-five-ton girder into alignment for rivet holes an inch in diameter. I never met Peanuts Coble to question him; his recollection illuminates how one "raising gang" bridgeman combined metaphor (a girder is not a pile to be driven) and profanity to modify a remembrance aimed beyond his fraternity of work.

To listen to construction chatter is to know ubiquitous erotic and scatological imagery. No one has traced the earliest use of *pile drive* extended to sexual prowess. John S. Farmer, the indefatigable searcher for "heterodox speech of all classes of society," noted such borrowing in Victorian England. We find also a Mississippi Valley usage in 1930. Guitarist Joe McCoy recorded "Pile Drivin' Blues" on a 78-rpm disc, Vocalion 1612. By way of opening, he boasted: "I drove so many piles, my hammer's all worn out, / When I do my drivin', they begin to jump and shout."

McCoy may have heard such lines sung by levee hands in his Hinds County home or in his travels from Vicksburg to Memphis. He may have slotted the pile-driving metaphor into a previous bawdy song known to other bluesmen; he may have made up an entirely new song. Without speculating on origin, many construction stiffs will attest to the aptness of his song.

"Pile Drivin' Blues" pulls us to a mystery. Collectors of African-American music appreciate a very rich shanty tradition—Sea Island rowers, Caribbean launching gangs, Mobile Bay cotton stowers, Mississippi River roustabouts, Chesapeake Bay boat caulkers. Has anyone in the United States found references to similar pile-driving chants? Surely, a black pile man in Charleston, Savannah, Biloxi, or Galveston used song to pace his crew's line hauling and hammer driving.

Publication in 1984 of J. H. Kruizinga's *Haal Op Die Hei! (Pull Up That Ram)* calls attention to Dutch pile shantying. Three partial selections—lines not "too scabrous for our twentieth-century ears"—follow (34). In sequence, they celebrate the sound-of-heart pile tree, Anne-Marie's grinding, and Amsterdam built on batons (*palen, paal, paaltje*).

One, two, three,
Pull up that tree;
It is grown
In the month of May,
Deep in the ground,
Safe and Sound.
Fresh and round;
Sound of heart.

* * *

One, two, three, pull up that tree, perfect bliss!
For Ann-Marie, that dear young miss,
That has accepted a sailor's kiss.
I've gained more money in only one night
Than you with grinding in a fortnight.

* * *

Pull up that ram
It is cut
In the mud
And Amsterdam that glorious town
That is all built on batons
Hololodree, Hololodree Hurree, hurrah.

## Butt/Buck/Doe

My first day-to-day meetings with pile drivers occurred as a shipwright's helper during 1941 at Western Pipe & Steel (South San Francisco). Previously, this firm had contracted with Healy Tibbitts for a pair of unusual side-launching ways. When their work ended, a few pile men stayed on at "The Pipe" by switching from ways building to marine carpentry. Jimmy Allan, a journeyman who had made this transition, patiently described for me his boyhood in Scotland, service in a United Fruit banana boat "black gang," and education at the pile driver's and shipwright's trade. His constant encouragement told me that I, too, might comprehend the mysterious connections of ship's stem to stern.

After Pearl Harbor, to double its production goals, Western Pipe & Steel needed a second pair of ways; Healy Tibbitts again undertook the construction. While shipwrights continued to labor on existing hulls, two giant pile-driving barges and their crews worked across the narrow inlet. In addition to these floating rigs, a trim red tugboat guided pile rafts from the bay into our launching channel.

Healy Tibbitts's workers familiarly called each other *pile butt*. To my beginner's eyes, shipwrights—whether handling timber shores and cribs for the hull above or fairing steel plates and structural members for the emerging vessel—seemed strangely ancient and wise. By contrast, pile butts seemed young and vigorous, almost arrogant in their competence and indifference to danger.

Curious about the meaning of an occupational nickname then new to me, I asked an old-timer to explain *pile butt*. He obliged, telling me that his fellow workers drove pilings above their intended grade, later cutting off each butt end to bring the piles to a designated elevation. This constant and necessary butt cutting somehow led to a verbal shorthand. The old-timer was explicit in detailing the work process but not in the matter of linguistic invention. Stimulated, I watched the work closely and speculated on the term's beginning.

The men used crosscut handsaws to behead each pile, figuratively turning heads into tails. At times, an ax man trimmed off the tip (tapered end) of an especially long timber before the pile, butt up, could be positioned aloft in the vertical leads under the hammer. In such instances, a pile man initially trimmed a horizontal timber by ax and eventually cut the vertical piling by handsaw. The discarded pile head, technically identified as a *butt*, resembled a tree stump. When crew members sounded *pile butt* as their name, they transformed a stumpy object (hard, rooted, ancient) into a symbol of skill and stamina. By imaginative extension, the physical butt came to personify a brawny worker.

Joe Ploium, a pile man for thirty-five years, had marched up through the ranks: crew member, foreman, field superintendent, and finally, area manager for Reidel International, Western-Pacific Foundations Company, at Portland, Oregon. Hearing work talk for decades, he recalled a "hearsay" account for *pile butt*'s naming. In letters to me he observed that years ago, there were no guides or leads to hold each pile in position under the drop hammer. Hence, to keep a pile erect, pile butts would support it for a time with their bodies.

Ploium's fine explanation geared to time ("before I started to do this type of work") reveals how job speech gains vitality when certified by antiquity. In the timeless past, stout men stood tall while supporting huge timbers. Figuratively, a tree's spirit flowed from nature's butt into individual worker's backbones, helping each in strength and elan.

I assume a direct, but inverted, connection between the actual butt at the bottom of a tree and the butt or discarded top of a cut-off piling. This can be visualized best by contrasting a telephone pole with its heavy end mudded in the ground (butt down), and a pile with its tapered end driven into the ground (butt up). Pile drivers today who handle steel and concrete continue to cut butts—steel with burning torches, concrete with diamond-wheel scoring saws. Whether the pile end is timber, metal, or precast concrete, its butt is everpresent in job talk. Pile drivers, as well, know the word *butt* in its numerous work-associated forms.

*Butt* familiarized itself to woods workers by its reference to the first portion of a log cut above the stump. Generally, butt logs reached the sawmill (hauled, skidded, floated) with one end still shaped by the axe's starting kerf or jagged notch. Each such log had to be placed in the carriage of a butting saw to square off its rough end for safety and utility. In such work, "to butt a log" carried a most positive charge. Strong words and phrases from one workplace thus served to reinforce speech in other settings.

Building and metal tradesmen continue to use the word *butt* for item and action. Shipwrights butt plates together; riveters join plates with butt straps; welders fashion butt joints; trim carpenters and ship joiners hang doors with butt hinges. Some construction hands know *abutment* as an engineering term for a bridge cable anchorage or as a structural unit receiving the thrust of an arch. In nontechnical speech, "stiffs" hear danger warnings "Keep your butt down"—a sharp command that does not imply a cigar's end.

Some British colliers had long worked together in a butty-gang system, dividing their pay (Gresley). American miners altered *butty* to *buddy* to signify a pair of coal diggers inseparably joined—partners working head-to-head, back-to-back, butt-to-butt. Teamsters now use "good buddy" as a friendly signature in CB talk; we hear such repartee within TV over-the-road dramas. In *Thelma and Louise,* we see a women's "buddy movie."

I do not know precisely when or where a pile driver first labeled himself or his buddy a *pile butt,* or when such occupational speech entered print. This utterance, fully understood by working crews, may have circulated orally for several decades before reaching anyone in written form. The engineer Richard Vlach, in 1982, recalled for me an anecdote illustrating the distance between insiders and outsiders. During World War II, a timekeeper for the Bay area contractor Ben C. Gerwick wrote *pile butt* on a government job's pay slips. The Washington federal auditor refused payment, objecting that he knew nothing of such a job classification.

If the initial usage of *pile butt* becomes established, we may learn of its association with an initiation prank, exuberant gesture, or joking horseplay. Possibly, such conduct will be linked to a worker's memory of having heard *butt* tied previously to an individual of unusual strength or to a salty character on the crew. We can appreciate the reach to fresh occupational speech by seeing such jests enacted.

As early as 1813, friends of the Alabama congressman Dixon H. Lewis, viewing his 450-pound bulk, familiarly called him "the But-cut." John Quincy Adams unkindly styled Lewis, "a Falstaff, without his wit and good humour" (Thornton; Jack). In 1844, members of a rowdy political club in New York tagged themselves "Butt-End Coon-Hunter" (Mathews). Does the name hint that such blowhards hunted only "on their butts" in saloons and ward halls?

During the decades before the Civil War, several American humorists created a gallery of grotesque heroes and rogues. Johnson Jones Hooper, in the *Adventures of Captain Simon Suggs*, portrayed a frontier trickster given to vernacular wordplay. Suggs, preparing to cheat a Tallapoosa land speculator, described the stranger's horse: "In two hours more [it] wont be able to step over the butt cut of a broom straw" (34).

At this point, readers may object that the proper locution under consideration is not *pile butt* but rather *pile buck*. Because standard dictionaries have overlooked entries for both terms, we lack dates that set priorities; nevertheless, I assume one preceded the other. I have speculated that someone either misheard *buck* for *butt* or else considered the noble stag to be more dignified than human buttocks. Americans have applied widely the name for a male deer in contrasting positive and negative sense to Indians, African slaves, and soldiers. We may recall Vachel Lindsay's line from his appealing and troubling poem of 1914, "The Congo": "Fat black bucks in a wine-barrel room."

The verb *buck* surfaced among woodsmen who felled trees and then bucked or sawed them into sections prior to floating or hauling the logs to the mill. A bucko mate at sea proved an especially hard taskmaster, while a buckaroo (cowboy) tried to master his bucking horse. Heater, catcher, bucker, and driver composed riveting gangs in high steel.

Many workers of rural origin could drive a buckboard wagon or dance a buck-and-wing—springing about, flinging legs, clicking heels. How many piledrivers experienced buck fever when first hunting in the woods? Any of these varied usages for *buck* and its relatives could have suggested the nickname *pile buck* or served to lend it resonance.

*Collier's* (September 12, 1942) included a short story by John Hawkins entitled "Man Working," in which young Jeff Stone proves his competence as a donkyman (engineer) on a dam trestle job. He is a pile buck and new union member who has picked up a bit of experience while "punching donkey" in high-line logging. Hawkins sets his story at the time of American losses at Wake Island; Jeff works on "the number one defense project in the Northwest."

Jeff's rig sits and advances on the trestle top; his crew drives piles and hangs braces to stiffen the spidery structure. In time this trestle will support a gantry crane to handle concrete and steel for the dam's power house to be built in the river bottom. Hawkins's familiarity with construction details suggests that he, or a family member, had worked on the Grand Coulee or the Bonneville dams. On one of these jobs or at a similar site, Hawkins had heard someone voice *pile buck*. To my knowledge, his short story represents this nickname's first printing.

During the weeks of April 10–May 22, 1943, the *Saturday Evening Post* featured a seven-part serial entitled "The Saboteurs," by John and Ward Hawkins. Simultaneously, E. P. Dutton published this serial in a mystery novel retitled *Pilebuck*. Strangely, no lexicographer then noted *pile buck* either from the *Post*, the Dutton book, or the previous story in *Collier's*. The Hawkins brothers centered their novel on a Gestapo sabotage gang in an American shipyard during World War II. Sam Gallagher, former newspaper correspondent and intrepid federal agent, takes a blue-collar job to unmask Hitler's henchmen. (Incidentally, the pile buck Sam wins the hand of fellow-agent Jill McCann.)

Accepting the convention that reviewers of thrillers do not

reveal plot details, I focus instead on a laborlore mystery. Did John or Ward Hawkins first encounter a pile-driving crew on a dam or a shipyard job? Where? Did they hear anyone voice *pile butt* parallel to *buck?* The authors dedicated their book to Jack, "one of the better pilebucks." Who was Jack? Could he have been a Hawkins family member? Where did he work? Did he seek out the writers, or did they look for him after deciding on a wartime melodrama?

Despite weaving an implausible plot, John and Ward Hawkins carefully described a platonic shipyard—fifty thousand workers; two aircraft carriers, two cruisers, two mine-layers, tankers, freighters, and Liberty ships under construction; twenty-five shipways, outfitting docks—a city of toil. Although they named no river or harbor, Jack must have worked either on the Puget Sound or at the junction of the Columbia and Willamette rivers.

In the novel, Sam's brother, foreman Jeff Gallagher, explains his trade's scope: "We build the yards. We move in where there is nothing but a stretch of shore and some timber. We build the shipways, the outfitting docks, the drydocks, the Whirley trestles. The boys who build the ships follow us. Most of the time they're stepping on our heels. They are laying keel before we finish a shipway. . . . The old Hog Island yard wouldn't be a patch on the seat of the pants of this one" (19).

*Pilebuck* did not make a stir in 1943. Its Fifth Columnists were as contrived as Sam Gallagher, the government's undercover hero. By contrast, the realistic working stiffs surrendered their roles to fictive characters. However, the novel's word pictures retain considerable value in portraying the vernacular speech of American war workers.

A few examples penned by the Hawkins brothers follow: "A good pilebuck is part carpenter, part steel-man, part rigger, part mill-wright, with a liberal shot of plain mule" (20). A pile buck describes the contents of his square whiskey flask as "anti-freeze for my radiator" (29). A tough foreman runs down a new worker as a "Joe McGee, this Sunday pilebuck" (108). When the shipyard's floating crane (called a Chinook) is sabotaged, Sam Gallagher takes an icy bath. Rescuing him from the water, his buddies throw a blanket around his shoulders. A company official observes to Sam, "With that blanket, you look like an Indian buck" (177).

John and Ward Hawkins's *Pilebuck* appeared as a "who-done-it" story, yet its greatest mystery resides in its source for pile-driving culture. John was born in 1910, and Ward in 1912. While still in their teens at Oregon City, south of Portland, they began writing for pulp magazines. Their talent accelerated graduation to the "slicks." In 1942, Ward broke in as a pile buck on the Bonneville Dam (two decades later, he sketched this experience in "Talk Big and Walk Tall"). In 1943, he and John enlisted in the Army Signal Corps. During and after the war, they collaborated on Pacific Northwest fiction: *Broken River* treats "gyppo" loggers; *The Devil on His Trail* portrays merchant seamen.

In 1958 John left Portland for Los Angeles to take up television writing and production; a few years later, Ward joined him. We continue to see their work in reruns of *Bonanza* and *Little House on the Prairie* (Murphy). We no longer see *Secret Command,* the 1944 Columbia picture based on *Pilebuck.* Pat O'Brien and Carole Landis starred as Naval Intelligence officers unmasking shipyard saboteurs. Critic Bosley Crowther found the film too muscular even for a wartime drama—O'Brien brawled with fellow workers as he stalked Nazis. To my knowledge, *Secret Command* is the first, if not only, Hollywood film depicting the pile-driving craft in full dimension.

In 1958, the Oregon Historical Society published *Woods Words,* a comprehensive dictionary of loggers' terms by Dean Walter McCulloch of the Oregon State School College of Forestry. His book reveals close job connections: loggers who cut trees selected for piling; sailors, longshoremen, railroaders, and teamsters who handle such cargo; pile drivers who work with the products of the woods. McCulloch included *pile buck* (a pile driver engineer); does anyone know when he encountered this usage?

On a visit to New Orleans Local 2436 during 1982, I met hall custodian Russell Alney, age sixty-nine and Texas born. Having driven piles for forty years from Houston to Norfolk, he gave me a "logical" explanation for *pile buck.* In the south, after a crew member had hooked a pile by chain or cable to lift and place it in the leads, he tied it off in the middle with a buck line (rope). This snubbing action—similar to restraining a bucking bronco—prevented the pile's flopping about or snapping in two while pounded by the hammer. In short, Alney asserted that the technical term *buck line* preceded the slang *pile buck*. For emphasis, he scornfully rejected any suggestion that *pile buck* might have derived from "a he-deer."

I heard *pile butt* voiced in 1941, thus, favoring it over *pile buck*. Like other workers, I assumed that the vernacular first known to me took precedence over secondary hearings or sightings. By the same token, another mechanic constantly hearing *pile buck* would believe "his" word to be proper. Would John and Ward Hawkins have titled their novel *Pilebuck* if they had encountered the trade in San Francisco?

Paul Hauter of Local 1957, Toledo, prepared a forty-question quiz on pile driving for the *Carpenter* (August 1954). He defined *pile butt* technically as the waste after the pile is cut to grade and as a nickname for pile drivers. Hauter may well have been the first carpenter to use *pile butt* in print in his union's national journal.

To my knowledge, T. G. Lish became the first scholar to link *pile butt* and *buck* in a formal linguistic setting. After working as a carpenter in the western states and Alaska for twelve years, he compiled a construction list for the American Dialect Society (1961). Within the category of jargon, he included *pile butt* and *pile buck*, defining them together as a man who works primarily with piling, either timber, concrete, or steel, but whose area of work overlaps that of carpenters in many localities. In response to my query, Professor Lish noted that he had encountered both "old" terms about 1953 on a Cowlitz River job near Longview, Washington.

During 1981, the Deep Foundation Institute published an excellent *Glossary of Foundation Terms* edited by Alan G. MacKinnon and Hal W. Hunt, both professional engineers and construction firm executives. In correspondence with me, Hunt stressed that none of the fifty contributors to the glossary used *pile butt* in responding to a DFI survey. Accordingly, he entered the "correct" *pile buck*, defining it as a proper term for a member of a pile crew. Complementing this respect for prescriptive language, two officers in Local 2436, New Orleans, indicated to me that they knew the paired "slang" terms *butt/buck* but rejected both in favor of the formal *pile driver* in Louisiana jurisdiction.

On a stimulating visit with Richard Smith, the president of

Healy Tibbitts, San Francisco's oldest marine engineering construction firm, he offered this experiential evaluation of the twin terms: *Pile buck* echoes positively because the buck saw (together with the practice of bucking logs) was long familiar to woodsmen, who literally followed timber from the forest slope to the ship hold to the construction site. To the contrary, *pile butt* gathered to itself negative and derogatory overtones. After cutting the pile to its designated grade, the crew literally cast butts adrift. At times, if clean (without creosote), the butt might be split into fuel and reduced to ash in the donkey's (boiler) firebox. Would any worker desire to be likened to a discarded object or to industrial waste?

Clearly, *pile butt* and *buck*, together or singly, gather conflicting charges. One worker feels strength in the tree's spirit; another sees waste in the discarded butt. One sees nobility in the stag's posture; another feels degraded by an animal comparison. Despite these questions about propriety and priority, we know that *pile butt* and *pile buck* are no less dignified than *sandhog, timberbeast, rodbuster, pearldiver, snake, toad, dockwalloper, shovelrunner, baggagesmasher, bollweevil, muleskinner,* or *greasemonkey*—all of which have long tagged American occupations.

The term *pile doe* helps account for contemporary shifts in language as it accommodates to social change. In July 1983, *Carpenter* editor Roger Sheldon wrote a feature article, "The Pounding World of Pile Bucks and Does." In February 1982, he had pictured Kathy Cookson as our "first pile doe." Writing to her, I learned that she began as an apprentice member of St. Louis Local 47 and worked on the Alton (Mississippi River) lock and dam site. There, she helped construct a deep cofferdam of interlocking sheet-steel piling.

The union journal report on Cookson troubled Seattle business representative William Sullivan (Local 2396), who, disputing the St. Louis claim, noted that Puget Sound provided a home base for many pile does, including Billie Jean Chaney. A look back at the *Carpenter* reinforced *pile doe*'s novelty. In April 1981, cover girl Chaney had been identified only as "a lady piledriver." Previously, the journal had featured the progress of three women members, picturing Laurie O'Gara, a welder and diver, as New

York Local 1456's "first full-book, card-carrying female dock-builder."

Someone dissatisfied with *lady piledriver* and *female dock-builder* had good reason to search for a fresh nickname. Sherwood Kerker, the editor of joint union newspapers in the St. Louis area, must be credited for his sensitivity to fair employment practices and receptivity to colorful speech. On interviewing Cookson during October 1981, he wrote a perceptive account of her achievements, heading the story: "A 'Pile Doe' on the New Lock and Dam: Platinum Nails, an Arc Torch and a Hard Hat."

Kerker included essential news elements about Kathy: age thirty-two, mother of two boys, now "on her own," an office worker who wanted to be "outside." She waited eight years for her move into heavy construction, assisted during the 1970s by fresh breezes in the women's movement. George Pierson, the pile-driving foreman for the Alberici Company, noted that, after thirty years at the trade, the task of supervising a woman was a "new experience." General foreman Tom Reimert, Local 2119, explained *pile doe*'s genesis. Someone at the river job site had started calling Cookson a pile doe instead of the customary pile buck, in use "for years."

Kerker picked up another unusual bit of work parlance in describing one of Cookson's new responsibilities. Within the cofferdam's huge steel cells, she engaged in "pimping"—standing safety watch for a welder whose helmet reduced vision. Clearly, this work locution holds considerable irony as it places a pioneering woman in a position analogous to that of a street pimp watching over his "stables."

Sherwood Kerker's story about Kathy Cookson makes dramatic a woman's entry into a dangerous trade while catching the nuances of workers' emerging speech. Cookson revealed her own sense of pride in an ancient calling by grasping a rung on tradition's ladder, "Someday my boys can point to the dam and tell their children, 'Your grandma worked on that!' "

Linguists and lexicographers label terms such as *pile doe* "neologisms"—literally, new words. Mississippi River crews found it far easier to alter the gender of *buck* than to attempt turning *butt* into *buttess*. Through long familiarity, we are comfortable with *waiter/waitress* or *steward/stewardess*, but we are not likely to be comfortable with *buttess* if applied to a journeywoman pile driver. Only time will tell whether *pile doe,* the novel term, circulates widely within occupational speech.

Paths through cultural forests do not always lead to clear meadows; sojourners do lose themselves in dismal swamps and at cliff edge. Blazed trails fall prey to weather's decay. I have pursued expressive practices or beliefs often to find cold trails and overgrown paths. Thus, I feel rewarded to have traced *pile doe* in print to St. Louis, October 1981.

Many laborlore items will always remain hidden. We talk to peers, ask endless questions, and ultimately return to the library. For pile references used in this chapter, I have benefited from lexical works by Berrey, Cassidy, Cohen, Craigie, Flexner, Mathews, Mencken, and Read. Books and articles on building-trade culture have provided backdrops for my studies. Abell, Alford, Applebaum, Erlich, Hewett, Salzman, and Singer represent different approaches, ethnographic and historical, to ancient and current construction scenes. The journey from pile rig to library shelf provides its own gifts.

## Rig/Ram/Monkey

Young workers, regardless of their status, ethnicity, gender, region, language, or craft, face similar problems in job entry. How does one learn the mass of rules, formal and informal, governing each trade, assembly line, sales counter, or office module? Some green hands, thrown into the water, survive by observation and imitation; others benefit from long-codified apprenticeship procedures; still others thrash about and move by trial and error until "luck" lands them in the hands of a congenial old-timer, a friendly teacher.

We develop personal competence by acquiring mechanical skill, as well as by adapting to a complex of social norms. Job training remains far from a passive process, especially when certain traditional codes involve resistance to a domineering boss, overly demanding production quota, or inhumane workplace. Newcomers who reflect on their entrance into trades often comment initially on their growth in command of the trade's lingo. A vessel has more than a thousand parts from keel to crow's nest. Office keyboarders, today, face a lexical jungle in computer terminology. The mastery of nomenclature signifies the first control over job demons.

As do other workers, new pile drivers strive to identify their tools and equipment. A crew that can handle conventional tasks (carry a building's load, wall off earth or water) can also pioneer. Challenging "specs" (plans, blueprints, specifications) face pile butts on preservation sites and in calls to stabilize loose soil, burn metal under water, and use sonar or laser devices in precision surveying. Each fresh technique demands names; no pile butt on the job had to know *sonar* before 1950 or *laser* before 1960.

Three ancient terms that have retained their utility over the centuries (*rig/ram/monkey*) enter a young pile worker's vocabulary almost immediately. These words emerged in the past to describe pile-driving equipment, whether mounted on a matt, skid, scow, barge, crawler tread, railroad car, or mobile crane. In the United States, present-day crews use *rig* most widely to name diverse pile machines. Viking invaders carried the hoary locution to Scottish and English shores. In its new land, *rigge* came to mean variously a hilly ridge, an animal's back, the elevation between plow furrows, a roof top, a storm, a wanton girl, or a prank. It stood for action as well: to dress, fit out, banter, cheat, hoax.

Although the precise interchange of Norse and English terminology remains unclear, the *Oxford English Dictionary* reports that as early as 1489 *rig* had a nautical usage that stems from "wrapping" or "binding" sails—making a ship ready for sea. In time, this verb became a noun describing a vessel's gear. An 1822 citation reads, "I could distinguish by a telescope every sail, the general rig of the ship." Seamen carried this handy three-letter word ashore to name mechanical devices that resembled or held masts, booms, and spars.

During 1845, a passenger on the propeller ship *Massachusetts* reported to *Niles National Register* the vessel's initial seventeen-day trip from New York to Liverpool: "The new rig works to a charm." This observer, who saw steam supplying auxiliary power to traditionally rigged sails, caught *rig* in its earliest-known application to a working engine.

By 1868, an Iowa reporter had called a cane syrup mill a rig;

by 1872, Pennsylvania oil well drillers accepted it for combined platform and derrick. Apparently, after the Civil War, crews followed oil drillers in applying *rig* to pile-driving apparatus. I have been unable to find an early date for *pile rig* (combining derrick, donkey engine, leads, hammer, and platform).

Men drove piles by hand for countless years before the development of primitive machine contrivances. Essentially, the early devices held hoisting frames of sheer-legs and rope pulleys to raise heavy hammers of wood or metal. Just as seamen raised sails, pile men hauled up gravity hammers to be dropped onto pile heads. A cagelike set of guides (leads) kept the pile erect as the drop hammer fell. Although such hand labor sanctioned by tradition seemed changeless, pile-driving technology did change slowly over the centuries.

Before 1800, inventors had perfected steam engines to pump water out of mines, propel locomotives, and operate factory equipment. Generally, building-construction engineers and their skilled workers resisted steam's appeal. However, in 1838, Smithe Cram patented a steam-powered combined double pile driver/cut-off saw for the Syracuse & Utica Railroad. Cram's machine used steam power to complete the tasks of men and horses, that is, to lift the hammer (Vogel, 123). W. T. Brande, in his scientific dictionary of 1842, accounted for the pile driver's energy source: "It may be worked by men or horses, or by a steam engine."

The steam-activated pile hammer dates to July 3, 1845. James Nasmyth, a Scottish mechanical engineer, had invented a steam hammer for iron forge work in 1839, thus preparing the way for his efficient steam-hammer pile driver. Introduced at the Royal Navy Devonport Docks, his machine revolutionized pile construction technology.

Before Nasmyth, energy in various forms powered the necessary equipment, but initially, it was human energy: muscle for direct pounding with a hand maul on a pile head; muscle for lifting and dropping a hand-held ram; muscle for lifting an iron hammer by windlass or treadmill. These latter winding and turning tools depended entirely on strong bodies. In time, horses harnessed to lifting lines and waterwheels rigged to similar gear supplemented human labor.

With the initial application of steam to pile driving, a mechanical hoisting engine fitted with a friction clutch raised and dropped the hammer. Seamen, loggers, and pile men generally named such engines *donkeys*. But steam could do more than raise a weight by turning a winch drum; it could feed into and propel the hammer itself. Symbolically, James Nasmyth strengthened the ravenous hammer by giving it a diet of steam, as he gave his crew members the mythic power not of plodding donkeys but of countless herds of wild horses.

About 1900, diesel hammers followed steam, using an oil-derived fuel to generate internal power within the hammer, thus propelling its downward blows. In recent decades, gravity, steam, and diesel have all been complemented, but not replaced, by compressed air, electricity, vibrators, hydraulic jacks, and water jets. Laymen who observe modern pile-driving apparatus can demystify such gear by asking questions. What raises the pile, guides its descent, and drives it into the earth?

The word *rig* took more than four centuries to journey from mariners making a ship ready for sea to oil well drillers accepting a short name for their platform/derrick/drill. Two other old words, *ram* and *monkey*, have been tied to pile-driving gear; each opens doors to considerable lore: jest, prank, boast, tale.

Aries, the first zodiac sign, has long signified butting and striking power. Hellenic bards claimed that Greek soldiers invented the battering ram to breach walls during the siege of Troy. Greek sailors at Salamis (480 B.C.) turned bow spars into deadly rams to destroy Persian ships. Did a soldier or sailor, home from the wars, carry the military ram into construction tasks?

English tenth-century chronicles record workmen beating the ground with "frequent blows of rams" to prepare for erecting a stone tower at Ramsey. About the year 1200, Neckam described an earth rammer as a "chelindro" (cylinder) used to prepare the ground prior to driving piles into "the bowels of the earth." In 1256, a Woodstock carpenter built "sliddreies and rammes," referring to the uprights or leads used to slide the driver's ram (drop hammer) onto the pile head (Salzman, 83–88).

The *OED*, in a citation from 1440, noted a "great Gebet-ram," a pile driver resembling a huge gibbet or gallows frame. Not only did *ram* continue to identify a very heavy machine, but it also fit the specific action of driving pile as heard in the sentence "A quavery or maris [marshy] and unstable foundacion, must be hople with great pylys of alder, rammed downe" (1519), and the phrase "workmen ramme in pyles" (1530). Going beyond iron hammers, Westminster workers, in 1532, used a "gynne with a Rammer of brasse" (OED; Salzman, 83–88).

Contemporary crews will find familiar objects but strange language in a London Bridge wardens' inventory (in Norman French) of stores prepared during the reign of Edward III: timber fully wrought for immediate building, elm piles, Portelond hand-worked and squared stone, barrels of pitch, large drawbridge nails, assorted small nails such as plaunchenails (plank), new cord, iron shoes for piles, grapes of iron (prongs), schuyt (a barge to carry timber), cauldrons for melting pitch, "two engines with three rammes, for ramming the piles of the said bridge" (Riley, 216).

Building-trades historians have found descriptions of early engines to be invaluable in looking back at technology's constancy, as well as its development. Entries by Martin John de Hurland on the building of a pile driver during 1329 list hemp rope, brass fittings for the driver's beam, seal skin ("selyskyn") for the beam, leather straps, ale to temper the skin, herring oil to grease the skin, iron hooks to control the ram's descent, brass rods for these hooks, a winding tool (winch or windlass), pulleys, grease, and nails ("spykes"). The artisans who built this machine "for fixing piles in the water" were familiar with its many parts from previous observation (Salzman, 328).

Functionally, in modern times, *ram* has generally meant the actual iron weight dropped on pile heads. We recall, here, the opening line in the Dutch pile shanties, "Haal Op Die Hei!" (pull up that ram). To this day, pile men have not surrendered the word *ram,* which continues to designate the moving or driving part (piston) of an air, steam, or diesel hammer. In short, Aries still watches over those who use his sign as an everyday tool.

Curiously, pile men also tagged the ram weight with the word *monkey,* referring both to the hammer and the snatch hook used in its raising. We find this *OED* definition for *monkey* in 1750: an iron block, with a catch, used in ginns (engine) for driving piles. *Monkey* has maintained its long association with pile driving. Compiling his monumental *American Mechanical Dictionary*

(1872), Edward Knight noted that the piles extending the great quay at Rouen were driven by a monkey of 1,200 pounds falling twenty feet to deliver a blow equal to pressure of 300,000 pounds.

Over the years, *monkey* has moved from designating the physical object to naming the worker; the man who climbs the leads to position a pile under the hammer has become a *pile monkey.* Ray Sparrow used this term during work in 1939. Technically, monkeys are loftsmen engaged in lofting or raising piles. Today, monkeymen may also perch upon a sheet-piling wall, threading together individual interlocking units. The pile monkey riding on sheet steel becomes a man in a saddlelike seat or yoke, often with his feet in stirrups, like a cowboy. Inexplicably, on some jobs the loftsman is tagged *pile rabbit,* presumably because he leaps about with great agility (MacKinnon).

A snorting billy goat (ram) and a pile-driving machine offer a graphic analogy. However, the original allusion to a monkey as a hammer has proved difficult to fathom. By speculating on how a key piece of gear might have turned into a monkey, we can sense something of mystery in language. Perhaps an artisan pulled an iron weight high like a climbing monkey. Perhaps an iron founder marked a casting with a seal that resembled a monkey. Perhaps a master who cast cannons called "brasse monkeys" also supplied pile drivers with weights or hammers called iron monkeys.

The past usage of *monkey* for a hammer weight and the present usage of *pile monkey* for a worker aloft come together in the term *monkey stick,* used to represent a crane's spud-lead system. This expression also reveals the extension of words across craft lines. Oil field gangs include a derrickman, who is often called a *monkey, monkeyman, pipestabber,* or *skyhooker.* He stands on a combination crow's nest and tiny platform from which he positions the hoisted drill pipe sections preparatory to coupling below (Boone). He tags this perch the *monkey board.* Pile-driving loftsmen and oilfield derrickmen perform similar tasks; not surprisingly, they accept the same moniker *monkey.*

In addition to using *monkey stick* to describe guides, pile men identify a single lead as a *pogo stick:* a long steel pipe rather than a latticed and braced boxlike or horseshoe-shaped structure

(MacKinnon). While we hear or read the combined words *pogo stick,* we see in our minds' eyes a child's jumping toy and sense the incongruity in a giant pile-driving tool becoming a plaything.

By penetrating meaning in language, we can understand that workers use wordplay to reduce huge machines to human scale. When a pile driver turns the technical name for a piece of heavy equipment into that for a toy, he gains a degree of mastery over his circumstance. The joke lore built into linguistic conversion—leads into pogo stick, man into monkey, hammer into ram—serves to neutralize the machine's looming danger. The imaginative individual who leads words as easily as vertical leads guide piles lightens an entire crew's load.

## Machine-men and Tidemen

Drawings of neolithic houses built on piles along the shores of Switzerland's Lake Lucerne have intrigued generations of schoolchildren. During World War II in the Philippine Islands, I marveled at similar thatched-roof dwellings built on piles. These two pictures now juxtapose in my mind's eye as I explore pile traditions. Curiosity has prompted me to ask when anyone first linked *pile* as an object's name with the verb *to drive.* Without formally studying archaeology, we know that Lucerne's lake dwellers drove piles. How did they articulate the connection of object to action, and in what now-lost tongue?

The *OED* cites the combination *pile* and *driver* from 1772, applied only to a machine. These same words identifying a human operator do not appear until 1882. Charles Annandale, in revising John Ogilvie's dictionary, noted for *pile driver* the following definition: "A workman whose occupation is to drive piles." Annandale did not indicate whether he had heard this term in speech or read it in a technical report. His date seems late. Who can find a previous usage?

Crew members before 1882—dock builders, bridgemen, wharf carpenters—held names now long forgotten. For example, James Nasmyth called his pioneers of 1845 "pile-driving machine men." Apart from emphasizing the word *machine* during the age of steam, Nasmyth related an excellent story that anticipated a John

Henry theme. The engineer, of course, accepted mechanical progress as destined, never questioning its triumphant march.

In his autobiography, Nasmyth described his innovative steam hammer at Devon:

> There was a great deal of curiosity in the dockyard as to the action of the new machine. The pile-driving machinemen gave me a good-natured challenge to vie with them in driving down a pile. They adopted the old method, while I adopted the new one. The resident managers sought out two great pile logs of equal size and length—70 feet long and 18 inches square. At a given signal we started together. I let in the steam, and the hammer at once began to work. The four-ton block showered down blows at the rate of eighty a minute; and in the course of four and a half minutes my pile was driven down to the required depth. The men working at the ordinary machine had only begun to drive. It took them upwards of twelve hours to complete the driving of their pile!
>
> Such a saving of time in the performance of similar work—by steam versus manual labour—had never been witnessed. The energetic action of the steam hammer, sitting on the shoulders of the pile high up aloft, and following it suddenly down, the rapidly hammered blows at the end of each stroke, was indeed a remarkable sight. When my pile was driven, the hammer-block and guide case were speedily re-hoisted by the small engine that did all the labouring and locomotive work of the machine; the steam hammer portion of which was then lowered on to the shoulders of the next pile in succession. Again it set to work. At this the spectators, crowding about in boats, pronounced their approval in the usual British style of "three cheers!" (265)

To learn some of the now-lost terms for pile workers before James Nasmyth altered their age-long routines, I turn to medieval construction accounts. For example: the wardens of the Old London Bridge kept records in Latin on parchment rolls. During 1382, the wardens noted in their employ various trades including carpenters, masons, sawyers, and a mariner, as well as twenty-one tidemen (also spelled tidesmen) working at the ram for six-hour shifts.

Supervised by the tide carpenter, this crew maintained the starlings that protected the bridge's stone piers and arches against river scouring, ice floes, and constant maritime traffic. Tidemen on barges could repair or replace piles only at low tide, often working at night by torch and lantern. The tide's ebb and flow itself determined the crew's short shift, whereas other workers labored from dawn to dusk (Home, 143).

L. F. Salzman's *Building in England Down to 1540* offers a fascinating overview of medieval structures: churches, castles, houses, shops, inns, walls, bridges, wharves, water-powered mills. He includes more than a hundred contracts in Latin, French, or English, some of which held technical terms in use before the occurrences cited for them in the *OED*. His book is especially valuable in reinforcing attention to the growth of craft competence and in demarking jurisdiction.

I select from Salzman three passages on pile driving by carpenter, mason, and millwright. In 1335, the parishioners of St. Martin, York, contracted with Robert Giles, carpenter, to build a row of houses. The lengthy agreement between the parties included this detail: the foundations to be made firm with piles and stones ("Grundes ecian brunt pilati" 430). In 1389, King Richard, bargaining with three masons to build a wharf, specified the ground to be firmed with piles at the King's expense: "Le Roi le ferra fosser ou pyler" (469).

During 1467, the Sussex millwright Nicholas Wyleford agreed to rebuild a mill (malt and corn)—to pull down the old mill, saw new oak timbers, prepare the mill stones, divert water, and ram banks—in six months time. Although the "endentur" (contract) did not mention piling, it specified repair work to pile-based structures: "Shall new make well and sufficiently the Tymber bridge of the Northmille." This timber bridge was integral to millpond dam and water race; hence, I infer millwright Wyleford's familiarity with pile construction (Salzman, 536).

I round out these citations by returning to the word *tidemen* with a note on the construction of the Rochester Bridge, 1382–93. Its builders drove more than 10,000 elm piles, twenty feet in length, into the river bed. An eight-inch platform of Kentish ragstone covered each pile-enclosed starling. One Sunday after vespers during 1409, a great tempest of wind and rain arose, causing eight "tydemen" doing repair work to fall into the water. After nearly drowning, they received extra pay in the form of bread, wine, and verjuice—sour green juice of crab apples or other unripe fruit (Salzman, 87).

The need to compensate for work accidents has deep roots, and the actual fees have changed but slowly. Verjuice in modern decanters still ushers special occasions; pile drivers, like other workers, are not strangers to fruit and barley extracts in all their guises. During a Tacoma visit, Percy Watkins told me something of his many construction jobs: the Grand Coulee Dam, the Shasta Dam, Seattle's Boeing Plant (thousands of piles in marshy ground), the Todd-Pacific Shipyard, the Tacoma Narrows Bridge. Severe tides plagued the bridge caisson crews. Those who fell into the water had to bring a fifth of whiskey to work the next morning. Did any Puget Sound pile men know this custom's longevity? By linking sour crab apple verjuice at the Rochester Bridge to whiskey fifths at the Tacoma Narrows Bridge, we can sense continuities and discontinuities in work tradition.

## Antiquity's Scroll

I have talked to pile men intermittently since 1941, never accepting the caricature that working under the hammer diminishes an individual's capacity for fruitful curiosity and creative thought. Pile drivers, whether working at the water's edge or in "uptown" excavations, find archaeological treasures—"pickled" piles, sailing-ship hulls, jugs, coins, bottles, fossils. The jump from past to present is palpable when one pulls an artifact out of rock. Crews also sense antiquity, but indirectly, when they use relic words such as *ram* or *monkey*. From time to time, a pile man, his curiosity stimulated, turns to the library seeking an engineering text or a literary classic.

In 1986, Local 34's Michael Munoz published *"Pilebutt": Stories and Photographs about Pile Driving,* an attractive fifty-page book holding pictures and historical texts. He ranged from Caesar's Rhine Bridge, to Local 77 pile men posed with riveting forge and catching bucket, to a giant Lorain crane in desert country at Lovelock, Nevada, 1977. The graphic artist Sandra Cate provided the layout design for *"Pilebutt,"* thus signaling a creative collaboration in the blue- and white-collar fields.

Munoz gave his book's cover an added dimension by using a Giacomo Patri print from 1943, invoking the visual appeal in romantic realism: five heroic workers in unison canting an immense timber. Munoz's book, now at the Library of Congress and Smithsonian Institution, serves to inspire brothers and sisters in parallel trades to recapture their particular traditions.

Workers in wood continue to pride themselves on the timelessness of their trades. Wherever forests were plentiful, prehistoric builders used wood to fashion dwellings or implements and carve ceremonial trinkets or religious icons. Timber piles remain among the best preserved wooden relics known to scholars. Pile crews also know time's toll by barnacles, worms, and rot.

The Roman Pons Sublicius, the first bridge at the Tiber River, lives only in mythological memory. Its name in translation, a bridge supported on wooden piles, stems from *sublica,* a Latin derivation of *sub* (under) and *ligo* (to bind or fasten)—thus, a bridge's underpinning, a pile. Reputedly built of oak by Ancus Martius in 621 B.C., this famed Tiber structure gathered to itself sacred beliefs. Because humans angered river gods by obstructing their paths, bridge builders sought to propitiate Father Tiber with human sacrifices thrown from Pons Sublicius (Middleton). Latinists have explained the sacred titles Pontifex and Pontifices by reference to the bridge-building guardian priests who conducted rites at the Tiber. To turn from sacred to secular themes, Macauley's poem of brave Horatio at the Tiber defending Rome from its Etruscan enemies stands for a hero's willingness to sacrifice himself for country.

Rome may have been built on seven hills, but its myths include homage to pile-driving builders. Before Rome's rise to glory, Greek empire builders extended their power using the skill of nameless soldier-engineers. Alexander the Great, marching into Asia Minor, built a pile mole (causeway) during the destruction of the island city of Tyre (332 B.C.). His engineers cut cedars in Lebanon for piling as they plundered Old Tyre stone on the mainland for the mole's fill (Fox). (Such pile-perimeter/rock-fill construction persisted in New York's harbor through the 1830s.)

Romans hauled elaborate pile-driving machines throughout their realm and left records of a most famous "boss," Julius Caesar. Conquering Gaul, he strove to impress Germanic tribes beyond the Rhine with his invincibility. Erecting "a firm bridge of piles, buttressed to withstand the force of the flood," he marched into their land (Holmes 1911, 100). In this maneuver, his soldiers took ten days to complete the trestle pile structure. We know about Caesar's feat from his account in *The Gallic War,* a classic text serving students for centuries (Wiseman).

Construction of the Old London Bridge, beloved in nursery rhyme by generations of children and endlessly falling down, took place between 1176 and 1209. Previously, I noted that its builders drove elm piles into the Thames in lieu of temporary coffer dams. Tidemen then filled these dew-shaped artificial enclosures (starlings) with rubble stone. Each elm-bound "island" held closely driven pitch-coated larch piles. Oak sleepers capped these piles, serving to seat the stone piers for the nineteen huge masonry arches of the bridge (Home, 35–37).

Throughout Europe, from the Baltic to Mediterranean, Renaissance artisans labored in marshy coastal areas with complicated engines to drive foundation piles, a few inches a blow. Generally, workmen cut piles below groundwater level and decked them with timber and masonry caps on which palaces or cathedrals rose. A few such ornate monuments still stand as reminders of human constancy. In looking back at construction chronicles, the act of driving a pile, moving it scant inches per hammer blow, symbolizes the immense time span for these memorable buildings, decades in completion.

Comprehending the generational time devoted to cathedral building or bridge maintenance, we can attune to a key construction word's chronology. *Pile* as used to describe a sharpened timber driven vertically dates to English-language beginnings. The modern noun *pile* (a wood, steel, or concrete column in earth or water) stems from a distant interchange between several Latin terms: *subicio,* underlying part, place under, support; *sublica* and *sudis,* pointed stick, stake, spike; *palus,* length of unsplit wood, post, stake; *pila,* squared pillar, column, pier; *pilum,* a throwing spear or javelin used by Roman legions (OLD; Latham).

Classicists know *subicio/sublica/sudis,* terms unknown today to

English-speaking construction hands. However, the Latin words *palus/palis/pila/pilum* echo in modern objects such as pile, post, pillar, pilaster, pylon, palisade, and in metaphors such as "beyond the pale." When wooden stakes marked territorial boundaries, English conquerors in Ireland ventured at their own risk outside Dublin's safety—beyond the pale.

The transformation of related Latin words into the English-language building-construction *pile* did not occur in a day. As speakers shifted about, altering familiar speech or experimenting with novel usages, old and new expressions coexisted. Philologists have used many explanations to reveal change over time and across frontiers. My focus on the singular *pile* requires attention to language growth.

We return to the predecessors of *palus/palis/pila/pilum*. Caesar, in his Rhine Bridge report, seemed fascinated by its challenge, as evidenced by the engineering details he left to posterity. Among the technical terms subsequently translated as *pile* he used *tigna bina sesquipedalia* (balks), *sublicae* (buttress piles), and *defensores* (fender piles) (Edwards, 200).

During the rule of Emperor Augustus (27 B.C.–A.D. 14), Vitruvius wrote an enduring treatise, *De Architectura*. Acquainted with the Latin of "mason's yard and carpenter's bench," he made several references to piles, employing the vernacular of those artificers he had observed or overheard: alder piles resist moisture; temple foundations require piles of alder, olive, or charred oak—driven closely together by machinery; for harbor work, prefabricated cofferdams of oak piles chained together are let into the water; hoisting machines can be guyed by cables to sloping piles—these to be secured by ramming the ground around each pile (Granger, xiv).

In all his instructions, Vitruvius used terms such as *palo, pali, palum, palationibus*. He avoided the older and more formal names stemming from *subicio*. In short, between the years of Caesar and Vitruvius, Roman workmen had dropped unfashionable words in favor of the familiar terms related to *palus*. We are not surprised to learn that pile crews have always used vernacular speech bonded to their experience.

When Rome's sovereignty waned in Europe, native tongues replaced Latin. Nonetheless, learned writers retained the latter in describing building projects as local workers modified officially received language. While editing the *Oxford English Dictionary,* James Murray and his colleagues addressed such modification in arriving at their initial etymology for *pile:* "The Latin *pilum* was no doubt adopted by the Germans in the Latin sense 'javelin,' which passed on the continent into that of 'dart,' and hence 'arrow,' in which latter sense it superseded the native word. In Old English the sense 'javelin' passed into those of 'dart' and 'pointed stake' (= Latin *sudis*)."

Such formal philological reasoning assumed travel for *pilum* from Rome north to Germanic speakers, perhaps between the third and fifth centuries A.D., and west to England with the Teutonic invasion. We need to be open to alternatives to the "javelin" conjecture, for Roman speakers had carried various forms of *palus* (meaning pole or post driven into the ground), throughout the empire. Post-Vitruvian construction terms served in Roman Britain at least until A.D. 449, when Teutonic tribes began their invasion.

A building-trades historian especially versed in linguistics may well ask how Britain's Celtic speakers described a timber pile before the Romans brought their language to Albion's shores. A parallel question concerns the retention by Anglo-Saxon artisans of work vernacular after the Norman (French speakers) invasion at the Battle of Hastings, 1066. For five centuries, Celtic, Latin, Anglo-Saxon, and French terms for *pile* coexisted. To sort out such overlap is a formidable task, if indeed it can ever be accomplished.

A long-lived literary account highlights the *pilum/pile* transition. During the Roman invasion of Britain, 54 B.C., Caesar led his legions to the site of present-day London. According to his account, Celtic defenders under Caswallan (Cassivellaunus) drove lines of pointed stakes (a palisade) on their bank as well as underwater to impede the approaching enemy at a Thames River ford. This pile structure did not slow the Roman advance, but it embedded itself in British tradition (Holmes 1907, 692).

Caesar himself described the sharp stakes technically as "acutis sudibus," an obstruction to be overridden or overcome in battle. During the early Christian era, historians repeated Caesar's account without making significant changes. However, in 739, Bede completed *Ecclesiastical History of the English People.* Writing in Latin, he stated that an immense multitude (the Britons of Cassobellaunus) blocked the Thames with sharp stakes, "acutissium sudibus praestruxerat."

Bede noted that traces of the stakes were still visible in his day, adding their dimension: "About the thickness of a man's thigh encased in lead and fixed immovably in the river bed" (Colgrave, 23). Scholars have asserted that Bede simply made up the matter of lead-cased stakes and their visibility. We can interpret his improbable references either to Celtic tradition or to a patriotic need to enhance an act of guerrilla resistance to foreign power.

Following Bede, another embroiderer of Brittanic history, Nennius, also writing in Latin, converted the lead-encased stakes to iron pikes ("sudes ferreas"): "For the same consul [Belinus] had placed iron pikes in the shallow part of the river, and this having been effected with so much skill and secrecy as to escape the notice of the Roman soldiers, did them considerable injury; thus Caesar was once more compelled to return home without peace or victory" (Giles 1848, 392).

Writing in the *Historia Regum Britanniae,* ca. 1140, Geoffrey of Monmouth also expanded the account to include stakes of iron and lead ("palis ferreis atque plumbatis"). Originally, the stakes may have blocked the Romans temporarily in fording the Thames. However, according to Geoffrey, Celtic pile men, following a strategy of native opposition to the invaders, constructed a defense so powerful that it sank Caesar's ships.

In retrospect, we can marvel at Geoffrey's imagination as we read Griscom's translation: "And when Kassawllawn heard this he ordered iron stakes of the thickness of a man's thigh along the middle of the Temys in the course of Ilkassar's [Caesar] ships and without warning, they ran upon the stakes and the ships were pierced and thousands of his men were drowned" (312).

In moving from Bede and Nennius to Geoffrey, we witness a legend's growth by slow accretion and sheer exaggeration. Also, we follow a particular word's alternate Latin forms: *sudibus, sudes, palis.* I have pursued the matter of the Thames stakes for intrinsic narrative interest, as well as to trace shifts for *pile* from Latin to Old English, and beyond, to French and Anglo-Norman texts.

Arthurian scholars know the works of Robert Wace and Layamon, twelfth-century poets. Wace's *Roman de Brut (Chronicles of Britain)* led to Layamon's *Brut,* a semi-Saxon paraphrase from Wace's French. The former had identified the Thames stakes as "peus ferres" (iron stakes). Other poets used *peuz* or *pel,* the latter term approaching the modern *pile* (Bell, 192). Subsequently, Layamon turned *peus* into *raftres* ("nomen longen raeftres, stronge and rihte"). Madden explained that these long rafters (strong, straight, and shod with iron) destroyed Caesar's ships, drowning his troops (334). Today, we associate rafters with roofs, not with underwater warfare.

Writers of English who encountered and extended the Thames legend also needed to name piles within a series of histories (seven manuscripts) titled either *The Old English Chronicle* or *The Anglo-Saxon Chronicle.* These cumulative records, each built on predecessor versions, cover the years from Julius Caesar to the coronation of Henry II in 1154. From many translations, I draw on a few representative texts (Earle, Garmonsway, Giles, Rositzke, Savage, Thorpe, Whitelock).

The matter of the Celtic defenders at the Thames and their river palisades concerns students of pile lore. The *Worcester Chronicle,* one of the seven manuscripts, observes: "Ða genamon þa Walas and adrifon sumre ea ford ealne mid scearpum staengum greatum innan þam waetere. Seo eu hatte Taemese" (Thorpe, 5). In a move significant to those tracing *pile*'s journey, the *Peterborough Chronicle*'s scribe, about the year 1122, altered *staengum* to *pilum.*

Three modern renditions reveal differences in treating this word switch: "Then the Welsh took and drove great sharp stakes in the water right across the ford of a certain river—the river was called the Thames" (Rositzke, 28). "Then went the British and staked all the ford of a certain river with great sharp piles under the water" (Garmonsway, 5). "Then the Britons held the ford of a certain river and staked it all with stout sharp posts below water" (Whitelock, 6). We see here three terms (*stake, pile, post*) used to describe the identical object.

For centuries, *The Old English Chronicle* inspired dramatists and historians. About 1339, Robert Manning wrote the *Story of England,* drawn largely from the poet Wace. Manning, in the English of his era, offered: "Long pyles & grete did they [Britons] make" (Furnivall, 161). Manning's vernacular *pyle* also appeared in work contracts and state documents of the thirteenth and fourteenth centuries. I do not treat *pyle* beyond Manning's use of the Thames stake legend.

I return to the *OED* explanation for *pyle* rooted in the Latin *javelin*. Note the centrality of a switch by a scribe from *staengum* to *pilum*. What might have transpired had he selected alternate Anglo-Saxon words such as *steng, stang,* or *sting* rather than the Latin-based *pilum*? The Germanic terms associated with *staengum* translate as *stake, stick,* or *staff,* as well as with the verb *to pierce* (Bosworth). Although we cannot move language backward, we marvel that in present-day construction terminology long piles support huge structures while surveyors drive small stakes in laying out building sites.

A century after the Peterborough monk chose *pilum* to describe the Thames stakes, Alexander Neckham, in a treatise on nature, explained how workers tested a foundation's solidity with driven piles: "Nunc palis in viscera terrae missis soliditas fundamenti exploratur" (Wright, 282). In short, Neckham's learned Latin *palis* coexisted with the Old English *staengum* in the very years when native speakers replaced both with the Latin-into-English *pilum*.

Language study offers one passport to the past. Working people pursue many paths in decoding antique messages tied to skills. A millright apprentice setting a cable car sheave in a San Francisco "barn" may ask his journeyman about the word *millwright,* work in a horseless barn, or the connection between a giant cable sheave and a grist mill water wheel.

A pile driver visiting a museum may marvel at a model of Caesar's Rhine Bridge—especially, how it resembles present structures. Antiquarians, working with literature and artifact, explore the symbolism in both a Rhine and Thames pile crossing. I cite such instances to underscore the necessity to listen always to work talk, to seek its roots, to read widely enough to place it in the fullest setting of remembrance and experience.

*"Pilebutt"* by Michael Munoz holds illustrations spanning a millennium, 55 B.C. through A.D. 1977. Similarly, in unrolling antiquity's scroll, I have "pictured" priestly bridge builders at the Tiber River's Pons Sublicius, 621 B.C., and verjuice drinkers in 1409 at England's Rochester Bridge. Such depictions stretching

to mythological eras reveal how long pile-driving tradition has thrived.

To continue to treasure tradition and to comprehend its re-emergence in fresh guise, crews must inscribe their speech and stories on scrolls handed them by predecessors. My curiosity about the nickname *pile butt* dates to 1941. Michael Munoz, in the 1980s, felt this term to be important enough to select it to title an innovative local history.

We expect a scholar to find *The Old English Chronicle* on library shelf and a pile man to recognize a relic in a foundation ditch. Literary explication, archeological digging, and folkloric exploration share energies. Hence, I have visited pile drivers' union halls, Boston to San Pedro, to gather material for this book, and to urge pile butts to jump jurisdictional fences. Academic provinces guarded by ethnographers, classicists, and historians need apprentices from work's domain.

## Boston, New York

On a visit to Boston's Local 56 (pile drivers, bridge, wharf, dock carpenters, burners, welders, and divers), I became acutely conscious of the lack of attention scholars have given to pile work. On the rainy mornings of April 19–20, 1983, I talked to more than a dozen men seeking work at their hall, as well as to Jerome MacDonald, business manager/financial secretary, Stewart Watkins, state business representative, and Henry Riley, recording secretary. All were friendly as they offered anecdotes or recollections and suggested names of old-timers known as good storytellers.

While at the Boston hall, I observed the framed charter granted on November 26, 1919, by the United Brotherhood of Carpenters and Joiners of America to Local 56 in a merger of locals 1393 and 1671. No one present seemed to know the circumstances of this chartering. It does not surprise me that rank-and-file unionists separate formal history from their day-to-day experience, or from their formulations of identity: nationality, family, religion, residence.

One Local 56 member noted that pile drivers had worked endlessly on a subway excavation at Harvard's gates, yet no one on campus saw the work in terms other than dirt and detours. Seemingly, pile-driving history is opaque both at Harvard and at Local 56. Nothing in the schooling of the men in the hall impressed on them the knowledge that their distant predecessors literally had built Boston into a world seaport before 1776.

When the Massachusetts Bay Colony stretched north to include present-day Maine, fishermen and ship carpenters during 1636 "fell into a mutany" (an embryonic strike) at Richmond Island (Morris). Fishermen needed docks, piers, and wharves. Further, shipwrights built their own stocks and launching ways before they could lay keels for new vessels. Accordingly, we look to the earliest colonial documents for pile-driving history. For example, in 1667, Massachusetts ship carpenters who had built a repair dock petitioned the General Court for assurance that others would not build a rival facility in their vicinity.

Similar references occur in colonial accounts of bridge building. In 1634, Israel Stoughton secured a grant from the General Court to bridge Neponset River, connecting Dorchester and Milton. Carpenters erected a wooden footbridge over the Charles at Watertown in 1641; seven years later they rebuilt it as the first horse bridge in Massachusetts. These pioneer structures often rested on sapling-sized tree trunks (piles) driven by hand maul into the stream's edge.

When Major Samuel Sewall designed a 270-foot pile-trestle bridge at York, Maine, in 1761, he called for thirteen bents of four piles each. At still tide, workers floated these substructural units into place, guying them temporarily. Ingeniously, they raised heavy oak logs by tackle above the bent's cap. Releasing the lines, they let the "hammers" fall with great force, driving the bent to the desired depth into the river bed. Fortunately, Sewall left bridge plans and descriptions of his unusual oak log pile driver (Edwards).

While New England was still an agrarian colony, with its inhabitants alternating between subsistence farming and domestic handicrafts, shipbuilding evolved into an advanced labor-intensive industry. Specialized work led, in turn, to early guilds, friendly societies, and labor unions (Baker, Nellis). We honor Boston's militant ship caulkers for their role in the Revolution. If gathered, Local 56 history will prove equally as fascinating as that of the caulkers.

Locals 1393 and 1671, two predecessors of Local 56, had been chartered in 1904 at East Boston and in 1908 at Boston, respectively. Local 1671 held ship carpentry jurisdiction. Each of these turn-of-the-century locals had grown out of previous associations stretching back for two centuries. Whether a labor historian will look into Boston's maritime record remains to be seen. Charter dates calibrate history; workers' experience brings life to written chronicles.

Local 56 members to whom I talked expressed two key elements in placing their lives in meaningful frames, danger and ethnicity. Several noted (as had Ray Sparrow), "We're always under the hammer. We have to be alert and stick together to survive." Workers sitting out the rainy day touched on such physical survival humorously: One day, a pile driver who could not swim fell into deep water. Instead of drowning, he just walked ashore. Another joke followed: A guy had his ear torn off by a jagged splinter. The foreman rushed to the bleeding man, asking "Are you hurt?" The injured worker replied, "No, it was just a glancing blow."

In response to my query about the terms *pile butt/buck*, the men remained vague. One had worked briefly in California following his navy duty and knew *pile butt*. Another, who had worked on a Boston subway excavation for Morrison-Knudsen, a Boise contractor, reported that the Idaho superintendent labeled all his crew *pile bucks*. However, Bostonians seemed to prefer *dockworker* and *lighterman*. This latter word derived, of course, from lighter barges that held pile-driving rigs.

In asking about *pile butt* as a nickname, I heard a trickster anecdote that ringed the object butt with humor at the expense of innocent outsiders. In Boston's cold clime, timber scraps are prized by firewood scavengers. One day an elderly man asked if he might take a load of (creosoted) butts. The lighterman replied, "Sure, just help yourself, you won't need to chop kindling. Just put a match to the butts and step way back."

Stories about toughness or cunning led to accounts of Newfoundlanders, formerly the ethnic majority in Local 56. Several of the men in the hall identified themselves as third-generation "screech drinkers" (dregs at the bottom of the rum barrel) or as "herring chokers" (fishermen/fish eaters). This latter locution stemmed from the fact that "Newfie" grandfathers had come originally to Boston fish markets to peddle their catch. A few lingered ashore to repair boats, to work on harbor dredges or tugs, and to do odd jobs on the docks.

In the early years of this century, Newfies took over nearly all "offshore" pile-driving work. Accustomed to wresting a living from the environment, they accepted as natural the hardships in pile employment. When maritime work declined, they fanned "uptown" by following building-foundation and underpinning work. Although Newfoundlanders continued to hear *Newfie* as a pejorative, its meaning alters in Local 56. Within this craft community, the label signifies the values of hard work and the discipline engendered by traditional practices.

The oldest workers in the Boston hall seemed especially sensitive to generational differences attributed to greenhorns. Members, commenting on conditions and heritage, told me that youngsters would "go into deep mud without boots on. They're only looking at sixteen dollars an hour, not the mud. They'll come on the job without wearing union-made bib overalls. They dress like hippies. They use Jim Dandy hammers."

This reference to "Jim Dandy" tags nonstandard brand-name tools. A hall man elaborated on the linkage between using cheap tools and lack of respect for tools and workmanship with a traditional anecdote about an on-the-job prank. One day an apprentice choked his hammer high on the handle, cutting down his control over the tool, and, of course, skill and efficiency. The foreman cut off the handle and gave back the metal claw head. When the lad protested bitterly, the foreman snapped, "You never use the handle anyways."

Several pile men capped the matter of personal competence by asking whether I had ever heard of a gopher knot. I recalled that electrical linemen named their assistants on the ground *grunts* or *gophers*. Also, feminists in the work force have deprecated gopher work—flunkies going for others' coffee, or secretaries running personal errands for the boss. I knew of no connection between such gophers and gopher knots.

My education proceeded: when an inexperienced apprentice tied a "useless" knot (one that either slipped or tightened too much under the load's strain), he was told to go for the ax. "Go for the ax, that line won't come back." In short, a gopher knot represented both stupidity and waste. Too many manila lines "untied" (slashed) by an ax, and the youngster would find himself hiking down the road alone on payday.

This Boston excursion to Local 56 suggests that colonial records and modern charters tell one story, whereas anecdotes about Newfie hands and gopher knots tell another. Ultimately, both dates and anecdotes intersect as pile drivers recapture their past. Boston crews master new tools to underpin modern structures, as well as to safeguard historic buildings. Pile men and women have yet to devise mechanisms to preserve and present rich traditions, to underpin and safeguard their special histories.

No where is the need to recapture pile lore greater than in New York City. Its dock builders figuratively sit on a treasure chest of undocumented tradition. The port's sheer age, territory, accumulated wealth, ethnic mix of work force, union battles, political clout, and saints and sinners in command together have generated an expressive life that awaits a historian's pen and a folklorist's log. It is no coincidence that *On the Waterfront* remains among the handful of memorable films touching on the experience of American workers. The task of collecting and interpreting Gotham's pile lore belongs to others; here, I offer but a bare-bones report, a glimpse into the treasure chest.

Soon after Dutch colonists settled Manhattan Island in 1609, New Amsterdam's fur traders built an East River dock of wood. During 1647, they added a stable pier made of rock fill within timber cribbing. In the years of British rule after 1664, traders with the West Indies slowly extended the needed pier construction, which continued through the Republic's early decades (Condit). On the eve of the port's rise to world status, James Fenimore Cooper wrote (in 1824), "The time has not yet come for the formation of massive permanent [stone] quays in the harbor of New York. Wood is still too cheap, and labor to dear, for so heavy an investment of capital. All the wharves of New York are of very simple construction—a frame-work of hewn logs is filled with loose stone, and covered with a surface of trodden earth" (Albion, 220).

I seek accounts by Cooper's contemporaries to reveal the ethos of those wharf builders he observed. Did any of the Jacksonian societies of the 1830s include log hewers, stone carters, earth trodders? Do references exist to waterfront construction union organizers in the midnineteenth century? Who knows the history of the Bay Labor Club, a post–Civil War union in which dock workers gathered? What success did the Knights of Labor have with port artisans?

Between 1890 and 1920, three powerful international unions and their local affiliates in longshore, carpentry, and iron trades fought over New York's dock-building and maintenance work. At times, these unionists "played chess," moving locals across jurisdictional boards; on occasion, the "chessmen" resorted to clubs and guns. In 1907, Samuel Gompers granted a direct AFL federal charter to the Independent Dock Builders Union (IDBU). Following an internal split in this local, Gompers also chartered the rival Municipal Dock Builders Union (MDBU).

About 1905, a semiliterate Canadian laborer named Robert Brindell joined the IBDU'S predecessor. Amassing power in New building-trades circles, and as a Tammany Hall ally, he turned to extortion, bribery, and violence. During 1915, William Hutcheson, the United Brotherhood of Carpenters and Joiners of America president, aligned with Brindell to merge the IBDU and MBDU, rechartering it as Dock and Pier Carpenters Local 1456. To counter this move, the International Association of Bridge, Structural and Ornamental Iron Workers then sheltered "unreconstructed" men in Local 177 (New York) and, later, Sub-Local 189-A (Jersey City). In a bitter dispute running through three AFL conventions (1915, 1916, and 1917) the UBCJA prevailed over the IABSOIW. Meanwhile, Brindell's path led to Sing Sing; he died in 1927, unrepentant and unmourned (Galenson, Hutchinson, Seidman).

At the century's turn, a strong unit of Scandinavian immigrants, generally social democratic, took root in New York's pile-driving trade. Charles Johnson then emerged as the leader of this Nordic bloc of dock builders in the independent union and, subsequently, in Local 1456. He remained active in the brotherhood until 1946, passing the mantle to his son Charles. On my Manhattan visit in 1990 with Frederick Devine, president, he noted that 1456 was a "father and son local." This generational stability kept skill "in the family" and shored the union's pragmatic politics.

Local 1456 activists today look back to the Johnsons as their pioneers and to a balance of leaders from various ethnic groups as the guarantor of strength within New York's politically charged building trades. The union maintains extensive claims over dock building, pile driving, steel and wood sheeting, bridge and building foundations, trestles, overpasses, underpinnings, caissons, cofferdams, diving, tending, concrete forms, shoring, and house moving. Such jurisdiction defines itself verbally by the self-evident assertion, "our work." In turn, members have backed words with waterfront mores as they have moved uptown to bed world-famous skyscrapers in Manhattan rock.

In a profile of dock builder Arthur Langenegger, Joe Doyle compresses six decades at the trade: days in sewers and caissons, years of timbering and blasting. The son of Swiss immigrants, Langenegger dates his apprenticeship to 1927. After a variety of jobs, he secured a coveted card in Local 1456. A project in 1934 building a Harlem River walkway (126th to 128th streets) left grisly memories of Prohibition era crime. When dredging, the crane men pulled up autos holding decayed bodies—gangsters' tolls. The crew placed the death cars on scows to be towed past the Ambrose Light and dumped again in unceremonious burial.

In retirement, Langenegger has turned his garage into a craft museum: massive cant hooks, a razor-sharp adze, chisels galore, a four-man lug hook to tote giant timbers. The old-timer is especially proud that his two grandsons have followed him into Local 1456. Recently, grandson Robert helped moor the South Street pilot house at the Fulton Street pier. Four centuries of engineering feat, job tension, ethnic rivalry, labor dispute, and recollections comparable to that of dredging water-logged death cars in the Harlem River await the compiler of Gotham's fascinating pile story.

Rather than selecting a choice anecdote to close out this New York pile excursion, I offer an unsigned obituary from the *Carpenter* (January 1883). Had he toiled in anthracite coal, Daniel Hurley would have been memorialized by an elegiac ballad; had he worked at a Butte copper mine, by a Celtic tale. From Brooklyn's piers, however, we find an eloquent yet formal obituary—one that points to but is not built with the language of oral literature:

> The labor movement has suffered a severe blow in the

> loss of one of its purest, noblest and most devoted men. On Dec. 9th last, Daniel Hurley, aged 37, died in Brooklyn, N.Y., from a compound fracture of the skull, received while at his work of dock-building. He lingered three days from the date of the injuries. His remains were escorted to the grave by the Knights of Labor, the New York Central Labor Union, the Dock Builders' Union, Post Mansfield No. 35, G.A.R. and other organizations of which he was a member.
>
> His sad and untimely end deprives us of a cherished friend, and one whose whole life was wrapped up in the work of doing good for his fellow man. It leaves a gap that will not be easily filled. For years he served the cause of labor. Many a night after toiling hard all day at his trade of dock building, he would leave his home and travel to encourage some meeting of workingmen. Not only were his time and talents given to this work, but his means also. This is but a poor tribute to DANIEL HURLEY!
>
> Had he devoted his ability and eloquence to men opposed to our interests, he could have placed himself and family beyond the reach of want. But he was too honest and too honorable for that. He has left a widow and five small children unprovided for. The working people of America owe it to themselves and to Daniel Hurley, to place this widow and the five small children beyond danger of want. And for this purpose a *Daniel Hurley Fund Association* has been organized and subscriptions are requested from every man, who desires to show that Labor is not so ungrateful as to forget those who devoted their lives to our welfare.

This farewell, along with the appeal for family aid, has pulled at my emotions as it has raised a thousand questions about labor's forgotten heroes. Does not G.A.R. membership suggest Civil War activity? On what industrial battlefield did Hurley sustain his fatal injury? Was the Dock Builders' Union an independent local or an affiliate with the Knights of Labor? What connection did Hurley have with the AFL United Brotherhood of Carpenters and Joiners of America? Did Peter J. McGuire, the brotherhood's devoted founder, write his journal's obituary for Hurley?

I shared these concerns with the folklorist Tom Walker in

Brooklyn; in turn, he searched microfilm copies of the *Irish World and American Industrial Liberator* for the months surrounding Hurley's death. Patrick Ford founded this influential newspaper in 1870 to champion Land League, Greenback, temperance, and labor causes. The *Irish World* addressed immigrants poised at crossroads of many issues: Eire nationalism, American patriotism; revolution, reform (Rodechko; Foner).

On December 23, 1882, the *Irish World*'s editor eulogized Hurley:

> How uncertain is the tenure of our mortal existence. A few days ago DANIEL HURLEY stood forth in the prime of manhood, a foremost champion and leader in the ranks of Reform. . . . We knew him closely and well. His force of character, his brave efficiency in arduous, heavy work for his "daily bread," and his zealous, untiring war against the giant wrongs that are settling down on the men who labor, stand side by side.
>
> Never did his day's toil flinch him from the evening's work in the Ranks of Reform. Always foremost, always forceful, always dealing a blow at the wrongs before him, always pointing to the Land as the secure refuge. He wished to go upon that land and hard did he strive to save and carry out that will. But the wants of his children were too imperative. He has now gone with his stainless record wither we all must follow.

The *Irish World*'s poignant tribute coupled with the *Carpenter*'s obituary clue readers to Hurley's devotion to the Land League dedicated to agrarian reform in Ireland. Daniel Hurley "wished to go upon the land"—a dream of refuge shared by countless workers from the Industrial Revolution's dawn. Even some of those who accepted "scientific socialism" and concomitant "progress" as historically inevitable felt that a plot of land might mitigate the factory's terror.

A few facts from the *Irish World* add to Hurley's compelling story:

> (December 30, 1882) Dock Builders' Union meets Sunday at Rose Hill Hall to consider case of late and lamented

Brother Hurley. . . . James Mulhane, James Allan, and Stephen Ellsworth form Daniel Hurley Fund Association.

(January 6, 1893) Mulhane reports initial individual Fund receipts from 50¢ to $15.00.

(January 13 through April 28) Fund continues to grow with contributions across the land from the Cotton-yardmen's Benevolent Association of New Orleans, Cigarmakers Union of Jacksonville, Florida, and other locals.

Readers are free to ask additional questions about Daniel Hurley and his brothers and sisters across the land, victims of industrial death. We have come to accept job carnage as a "natural" cost in raising office towers and burrowing for earth's treasures. We know more about Hurley than fellow pile drivers, not for his everyday toil, but for his devotion to "the Ranks of Reform." Articulate editors such as Patrick Ford and Peter J. McGuire could salute their comrade in elegiac language. Certainly, Dan Hurley's fellow dock builders also memorialized him in their vernacular. Probing for such expression enlarges our respect for industrial heroism.

## Rock Slingers and Orange Peelers

On December 10, 1990, I journeyed to San Pedro and Wilmington for a pile-driving exhibit at the Los Angeles Maritime Museum and a visit with seven retired pile butts in Local 2375. In turn, these old-timers reminded me again of the wealth of tradition in all American workplaces and the need for a host of explorers within the ranks. It is inappropriate for a visiting folklorist, airplane ticket in hand, to attempt to do justice to one elder's story without long hours of careful interviews and previous preparation. Nevertheless, I plunged ahead.

With but a day at the Los Angeles harbor, I welcomed the chance to talk to a few of its builders and to hear them articulate their history. Early in 1990, a few members in Local 2375 had planned a seventieth birthday, for their carpenter's charter dated to November 1920. Business agent Bill Myers suggested a celebratory display at the Maritime Museum in San Pedro.

The museum rested on piles driven by 2375's crews in the year before the attack on Pearl Harbor. The building had served as a ferry station connecting the mainland to Terminal Island. After the completion of the Vincent Thomas Bridge in 1963, the San Pedro ferry terminal took on its museum function, housing thousands of artifacts: oars, anchors, figureheads, sea paintings, dugout canoes, ships in bottles, launching photographs, harpoons, brass fittings, travel logs.

San Pedro ties to Los Angeles by an eighteen-mile "annexation shoestring." The Maritime Museum connects to Hollywood by displayed models built for films such as *The Poseidon Adventure* and *Mutiny on the Bounty.* On the day of my visit, the *Ever General,* in from Kingston, Jamaica, unloaded huge red and green containers at the modern dock directly across the channel from the museum. I found it stimulating to observe cultural displays overshadowed by ongoing seafaring and waterfront work.

Bill Myers introduced me to the museum's director, "Pete" Lee, and to its curator, Sheli Smith. They had given the pile show the ambitious title of "Building America, Yesterday, Today and Tomorrow." Specifically, Sheli and Bill shared their respective technical and curatorial skills. I have already noted that Michael Munoz had used one of Giacomo Patri's black-and-white drawings in woodcut style on the cover of *"Pilebutt."* This 1943 cut also appealed to Myers, who enlarged it to form an inviting photo mural at the museum's outside entrance. Critics who delve into matters of workers' aesthetic codes might well question Munoz and Myers about the continued appeal in Patri's romantic/realistic depictions of craftsmen.

For the interior exhibit, Myers built a dolphin—not the sea mammal but rather a clustered set of slanted piles bound together at a centered king pile, a pile structure used to moor, anchor, breast, or turn a vessel. In a superb touch of humor, Myers secured a taxidermist's seagull, placing it atop the dolphin. The creosoted structure itself held a circular iron emblem three feet in diameter mounted at eye level. This metal assemblage combined features of a religious medallion and an enlarged union button.

Its creator, Gerry Berg, a working bridge builder and metalsmith, shaped a set of silhouetted craftsmen from several time periods with their respective tools and dress. Local 2375's full roster includes pile drivers, bridge, wharf and dock carpenters, welders, rig builders, drillers and rotary helpers, and marine divers and tenders. Berg used some of these designations to rim his emblem and placed a cutout of the Los Angeles City Hall behind the various figures to signify their sprawling jurisdiction. Members skilled with welding and acetylene tools appreciated Berg's creativity without questioning the artistic categories of abstraction and realism.

Among the many photographs and artifacts on display, a 1920 Western Union telegram caught my eye, for it focused on a set of difficult labor history questions. Previously, I touched on the alliance in New York during 1915 between Robert Brindell (Local 1456) and William Hutcheson, president of the United Brotherhood of Carpenters and Joiners of America. Brindell's violence and greed led him to Sing Sing; Hutcheson used the Manhattan dock local as a pry bar to transfer pile drivers out of the International Association of Bridge, Structural and Ornamental Iron Workers.

I reiterate this esoteric detail because it is central to the matter of Local 2375's age. In May 1920, Hutcheson had rechartered San Francisco Local 77 (IABSOIW) as Local 34 (UBCJA). A few months later, Don Cameron, Local 77's last president, became an international representative for the brotherhood. In one of his first tasks, he traveled to Los Angeles to shift Pile Drivers Local 51 (IABSOIW) to carpenter's union affiliation. On November 28, Cameron telegraphed headquarters reporting on his successful maneuver and requesting a low number for Local 51 in its reincarnation. Hutcheson granted the charter but, strangely, awarded a high number, 2375, to Los Angeles pile drivers.

Local 51 should not be forgotten. Its number suggested that it dated to the opening years of the century. Located at the Los Angeles harbor, its members would have defended John McNamara, the ironworkers' international secretary-treasurer, and his brother James when they were tried and sentenced to prison for the bombing of the *Los Angeles Times* in 1910. These details "hide" in a yellowed telegram. Telegraph operators decode messages tapped out on their keys. Who demystifies the layers of meaning hidden in a coded telegram mounted in a museum case? How do we bring Local 51's narrative to light?

Local 2375 planned its museum exhibit during 1990 to celebrate a seventieth birthday. Had its members known Local 51's story, they could well have asserted eighty-five to ninety years with the legitimate claim that 51 and 2375 held continuous existence; indeed, they were one and the same organization. It is not my sole purpose to add decades to the life of a local; rather, I wish to alert members to continuities within their association, to disputes and rivalries built into their behavior.

This digression on the 51/2375 transition points to a puzzle touched on throughout my book. Civil-engineering students in college classes learn more about pile technology than young pile drivers in apprenticeship classes learn about their trade's history. How do workers, organized or unorganized, recapture their origins? I have chipped away at this question by putting laborlore to work, by extracting meaning from job artistry and group traditions, and by placing verbal art and crafted artifact along paper trails.

Don Cameron's 1920 telegram is a wedge driven into hard strata. Bill Myers had obtained a facsimile from UBCJA headquarters and mounted it in the museum exhibit. Its number, 51, jumped at me; I surmised that San Pedro pile drivers had obtained their IABSOIW charter about 1904. With a starting date in mind, Myers turned to library newspaper microfilms, uncovering paydirt with "Pinhead's Game Spoilt" (*Los Angeles Times,* March 14, 1904).

This curious head referred to Patrick Henry McCarthy (the powerful head of the San Francisco Building Trades Council) and his team of "Frisco agitators" who had come south to stir up trouble. "Pinhead"—with J. P. Jones and J. S. Parry, pile union leaders—talked to men on the Long Beach steel double-deck pleasure pier, urging them to organize. The *Times,* hostile to labor, stressed failure by the San Francisco trio. However, on March 8, the *Los Angeles Examiner* had reported a "rousing meeting" in San Pedro among pile drivers, bridge, and structural ironworkers. Frank Buchanan, IABSOIW president, addressed the men, after which they voted to apply for a charter.

These bare facts hint at a large story. Buchanan came from Chicago, indicating an organizational drive planned well before a charter vote. Local 51 had actually started life "uptown" in Los Angeles about 1902–3 and had not taken root. Hence, the IABSOIW switched its charter to San Pedro in March 1904. These dates, gleaned from microfilm, come to life in the beliefs of workers like Bill Myers who cherish familial and organizational traditions. Myers's father, a coal miner, had migrated to California from Spadra, Arkansas, during World War II, joining Local 2375. Bill displayed his father's toolbox within the Maritime Museum exhibit.

The elder Myers represented both history and honor for his son. However, no one now living could carry young Myers back to the turbulent years before his father and fellow "Grapes of Wrath" newcomers entered Local 2375. In talking to Bill about his family toolbox, creosoted dolphin, metal emblem, photographs, and Don Cameron's telegram, I accepted the task of extending 2375's timeline back to 1904, and perhaps earlier, to the very construction of a modern world-class port miles from the old Los Angeles plaza.

The literature on Los Angeles's harbor is extensive and dramatic (Ludwig; Queenan; Silka; Thompson). Here, I cite a few chronological markers to help in telling 2375's full story:

1542: Juan Cabrillo, Portuguese explorer, sights San Pedro's marshes.
1771: Mission San Gabriel established; Franciscan padres receive supplies by ships from San Blas.
1840: Richard Henry Dana in *Two Years before the Mast* describes hide and tallow trade on Southern California's coast.
1855: Phineas Banning builds a 700-foot wharf; subsequently, he names Wilmington after his Delaware home.
1893: Southern Pacific (Collis Huntington and others) builds the longest pier in the world at Santa Monica (5,084-feet; 90-foot piles).
1896: Congress appropriates federal funds to build a breakwater at San Pedro; construction begins in 1899.
1910: Breakwater completed.

Seldom have historians looked at the muscle needed in constructing a massive port. Initially, Gabrielino Indians lifted cargo from Spanish galleons to small boats to mule backs or ox carts. Who built the docks for Banning and Huntington? Who quarried the mountain granite above San Bernardino for rail transfer to the harbor? Who dumped rock into tideland, thus dividing ocean currents from safe berths?

The first San Pedro stone barrier, 1871–80, stretched from Rattlesnake Island to Deadman's Island. Army engineers employed steam-powered drivers to set parallel pile rows. Crews then dumped sand between the pilings to form an artificial shoal. They covered this core with rubble stone barged from Catalina Island. Pile men made the necessary transitions from wood to stone on breakwaters, jetties, revetments, and sea walls.

Builders of giant breakwaters at the century's end took advantage of railroad-borne heavy machinery. After pile crews built a temporary rail trestle either at the breakwater position or alongside it, an engine pushed hoppers or flatcars onto the tracks. Laborers dumped run-of-the-quarry rock directly out of cars into the water. Cranes lifted huge stone blocks from flatcars for placement at the barrier's slopes and cap. Trestles in breakwater position would literally be encased in stone; trestles alongside the breakwater would be dismantled.

At San Pedro's outer breakwater, built 1899–1910, some granite rocks weighed more than ten tons each. Bulk and weight required chain or wire-rope slings that might snap like exploding bombs. Crews also handled quarried blocks transported by barge or scow. Steam derricks afloat proved far less steady than railroad cranes. In rough water, riggers needed considerable skill and stamina to move irregularly shaped stones without damaging gear or threatening lives.

No one knows when a now-forgotten rigger or deckhand voiced *rock slinger,* a tag that has escaped lexicographers, although *slinger* (rigger) has been used in Britain for more than a century. In the 1930s, several unions claimed jurisdiction over water-based rock slinging: the International Union of Operating Engineers (derrick barge operators and riggers); Inland Boatmen's Union of the Pacific (barge and scow deckhands); United Brotherhood of Carpenters and Joiners of America (breakwater workers in all categories).

Among Local 2375's back files, a significant memo from M. Freeman, Atkinson & Pollock's personnel manager, to Tom Randall names "all [90] pile butts and rock slingers now employed." Though the typewritten document is undated, Freeman penned in "64 men working Jan 24–41." This memo preceded an April petition signed by fifty-nine of the A & P men requesting the pile union to negotiate on their behalf. I infer that before 1941, San Pedro harbor workers had accepted, as informal terms in job classification, *pile butt* and *rock slinger.* Freeman's list is the earliest I have found "in print" for either term.

Over five decades, breakwater engineers have perfected crane-suspended rock grapples with lobsterlike tines or claws to grasp huge stone blocks. Bill Myers, standing before a museum photo of a three-tine, four-yard grapple, called it an "orange peel." Alonzo Quinn offers a wartime (ca. 1944) citation from Coco Solo, Canal Zone: "The traveler [crane] placed the lower 4-ton rock armor from railroad cars with an orange-peel bucket" (181).

An unknown imaginative worker first compared heavy equipment to a peeled orange on a table plate or to a hand-held kitchen utensil. Myers identified the Connolly Pacific rigger who placed the granite as an "orange peeler." Bill Gomary, in the exhibit photo, seemed casual in command of the crane load and rock. I saw him protected, literally, by working knowledge and, magically, by a naming triad: *pile butt, rock slinger, orange peeler.*

In leaving this breakwater work behind, I emphasize that no one has pulled together a coherent history of Los Angeles's port from the perspective of a pile butt "up to his ass in water, rock dust in his craw." Union activists complain that the mass media ignore or inaccurately portray working people. What can we say about a rich and powerful port without a cultural history of its own builders?

With this rhetorical question, I turn to a visit with several old-timers in Local 2375's hall at Wilmington. Before my arrival, Myers had invited seven veterans to the hall. I asked the men to identify themselves by "home" place and year of entrance into the trade. Their names follow:

Kenny De Walsche, Moline, Illinois, 1946
Bob Davis, Alva, Oklahoma, 1944
George Swart, Cherryvale, Kansas, 1941
Jasper Perkins, Pocatello, Idaho, 1938
Slim Yarbrough, Coos Bay, Oregon, 1935
Otto Maier, Worland, Wyoming, 1929
Johnny Moreno, San Diego, California, 1917

No sooner had I jotted this information on a pad than I noticed that six had migrated to California. I asked Joel Harzan, the local's recording secretary, about his union's ethnic cast. Joel replied, "Just everyday redneck." I had met Newfies in Boston, Cajuns in New Orleans, and Squareheads (Scandinavians) in Manhattan. Clearly, if Local 2375 discovers its history, someone will have to treat the intersection of the union's economic power with its members' sense of identity.

Together, my new friends in the hall commented on nicknames, pranks, escapes from danger, and the universal Joe McGee in all his guises. In this regard, 2375's members shared general traditions with fellow pile butts, blue-collar building tradesmen, and waterfront salts. I queried the old-timers about their entrance into the trade. Some had constructed shipyards during World War II; others had started on Imperial Valley irrigation canals or offshore oil-drilling platforms. Kenny De Walsche had worked for the contractor Guy Atkinson for twenty-five years; others, more restless, had switched jobs like birds in flight. Joel Harzan noted that recent members frequently "broke in" on L.A.'s dominating freeway network.

A self-described "splinter picker" gave me a fine anecdote on "taming" a tough foreman at Long Beach. The pile job could be reached only by a long, floating, wooden catwalk. The boss, not content to lay out work in the morning and leave his crew alone, constantly jogged from land to water site, hectoring the men. One morning, as a pile butt diverted the boss, a brave soul sawed the catwalk's supporting beams nearly through. As the boss bounded out on the walk, hollering ahead, he broke the beams and plunged into the brine. No one threw him a lifeline. Soaking wet, he waded ashore and kept on going, never to return. Does this story describe a rite of passage?

The old-timers differed on the best way to educate a tyrant. One worker simply asserted that he would pick up his tools, doff his overalls, and quit—the most individual form of direct action. Others insisted on the need for multiple skills; a worker had to prepare for shifts from wood, to rock, to metal. Some stressed their wide jurisdiction—the ability to work as a marine diver, a foundation carpenter, or an oilfield rig builder. Otto Maier quietly touched on matters of skill and affiliation. A star welder, he had supported the unsuccessful drive of welders and burners to break away from the many craft unions they had to join. Ultimately, Local 2375's members found ways to balance collective action with personal independence.

Although I promised not to highlight a single old-timer, George Swart startled me with a recollection. He had worked at Calship during the war when a Hollywood studio sent a screenwriter to gather background material for a film involving pile drivers. Lloyd Darrell, "an old pile butt," took this writer in hand, supplying authenticity by the ream. I have touched on *Secret Command* in previous comments on *Pilebuck*. Here, I note that John and Ward Hawkins had modeled their novel on Portland's shipyards, but Columbia Pictures camera crews shot Calship location scenes in San Pedro.

A constant element in accounts of workers' traditions is that of interaction between radicals and conservatives in the hall and on the job. For decades, political tension and its resolution marked San Francisco's Local 34. Did Los Angeles dock builders and rock slingers escape such heated dispute? Mexican miners—singlejackers, doublejackers, dynamiters—helped quarry and transport San Pedro's breakwater granite. Some of these miners were Magonistas, libertarian partisans of the Mexican Revolution. Did any hardrockers switch jobs from quarrying granite to placing it in the breakwater? Could any of them have helped organize Local 51 or predecessor associations?

Joe Hill worked as a San Pedro longshoreman in 1910 while penning IWW songs "to fan the flames of discontent." In treating *Wobbly* and *fink*, I have noted Upton Sinclair's brush with authority on Liberty Hill in 1923. The Big Strike of 1934 found two early San Pedro martyrs when goons killed ILA (International Longshoremen's Association) pickets Dick Parker and John Knudsen. Bosun's mate Joe Curran led a sit-down strike on the *California* while docked at San Pedro. This 1936 "mutiny" stands as a birth rite for the National Maritime Union. Chester Himes, a black writer and wartime shipfitter at San Pedro in 1943, placed the experience of bigotry in a biting novel, *If He Hollers Let Him Go*.

The names Magon, Hill, Sinclair, Parker, Knudsen, Curran, and Himes suggest points of entry in filling out Local 2375's narrative.

Did no Angeleno pile butt report the politics of class and race? In my visit to Wilmington, Jasper Perkins mentioned that he had worked at Boulder Dam when the IWW organized in the Depression's pit. He had seen the police chief club a Wobbly to the ground, blood streaming down the agitator's face. Did San Pedro pile men experience such terror? Perhaps the answers to these questions become muted when a visitor talks to veterans, to survivors for whom pride itself contributes to survival.

On my asking the men to contrast their best and worst jobs, Slim Yarbrough noted laconically that he had tried to forget weary scenes. We expect pollyannas to gloss over difficult jobs, to avoid radical analysis. However, Slim, who learned his trade building trestle bridges in Oregon logging country, had made it through many cold Decembers by attention to each day's challenge. He exemplified those workers who outlast hard times by sheer grit.

Bob Davis summed up the cardinal virtue in treasuring bright memories. He had helped convert the old sailing ship *Glendale* into the *Point Loma,* a huge derrick and salvage barge. The refitted vessel, newly clad with armor-steel bottom plates, retained its sleek hull design; thus, the barge could maneuver in tight channels and make exceedingly heavy lifts. Davis's voice lifted as he described the *Point Loma*'s prowess.

I leave to other students the task of balancing Local 2375's scales: skill, strength, militancy, pragmatism. These attributes—individual and collective—have reinforced Los Angeles's civic thrust to build a booming harbor. My southland report closes with respect to Johnny Moreno, age ninety-three. At the hall, I had noticed his silver and turquoise bolo and belt buckle, as well as an intricate walking stick topped by a carved blue sea dolphin.

As a Chumash Indian, Johnny knew Southern California's coastal waters from childhood. He had taken up pile driving before Don Cameron merged Local 51 into 2375. From the storehouse of memory granted by his impressive longevity, he treated me to a slow drag "yo-ho, heave" that he and his mates had used to slide big timbers. Never before had I heard any pile butt voice such a traditional work chant.

Moreno reported an experience at Port Hueneme, where he had worked as a spoolman on a floating rig. When an emergency demanded extra exertion, the crew completed "a year's work in a day." The men followed Johnny's every move, "they never missed a lick." Moreno's mates dubbed him "the fastest hands in the West," a tribute to more than skill. As our session ended, I met his daughter, who had accompanied him to the hall. Georgiana Valoyce Sanchez teaches Native American studies at California State University, Long Beach. I urged her to write her father's story: Chumash youngster, tribal elder, shantyman, spoolman, amulet carver, former president of Local 2375.

Johnny Moreno died on August 15, 1991. He represents one pile driver among many across the land who have bound together strands of personal belief, job competence, and union solidarity. I have named others elsewhere in this chapter, and for related trades throughout by book. After visiting the Los Angeles Maritime Museum and Local 2375's hall, I returned home confident that the pile butt Bill Myers—aided by fellow workers, curators, and teachers—would ably portray peers and honor elders.

## Hard Hats and Red Hots

I first heard *pile butt* voiced in 1941 by Healy Tibbitts crews at Western Pipe & Steel. Becoming active in Shipwrights Local 1149, I observed a few pile men vocal in labor politics as delegates from their Local 34 to the San Francisco Bay District Council of Carpenters. The council functioned as forum for minute contract "beefs," as well as for world-shaking issues. Even as a young mechanic, I understood the divisions within our brotherhood, locally and nationally: a craft-conscious Republican party leadership, a majority membership mainly loyal to President Roosevelt's New Deal, a class-conscious minority pledged to industrial unionism but split internally over rival left causes. Local 34 included followers from all these camps.

Retiring from teaching in 1982, I visited several old-time pile drivers, requesting aid in laborlore exploration. Frank Gallegos helped me unearth typed and printed citations, 1942–46, for *pile butt*. Here, I sketch something of Frank's story, full of contradictions in experience between high skill and "low" status as an immigrant.

Gallegos (born at Granada, Spain, March 7, 1900) migrated to California seeking farmwork employment. Moving to heavy construction on PG&E power plants in the Sierras, he met a few pile men. He joined Local 34 on September 15, 1924, dropped out in 1926, and rejoined "for good," in 1928. On the Duncanson-Harrelson job at San Francisco Bay's Carquinez Straits Bridge, he met a few Wobblies as well as many Local 77 stalwarts. Fraternizing with Wobs and 77's "rusteaters" proved significant for Gallegos.

Before 1920, all San Francisco pile men had belonged to the International Association of Bridge, Structural and Ornamental Iron Workers, Local 77. Around 1911, its members had compiled the jurisdictional by-laws to which I alluded early in this chapter. When the ironworker's union lost jurisdiction to the carpenters' in 1920, president William Hutcheson rechartered IABSOIW Local 77 as a new UBCJA Local 34 (Morin).

Arcane matters of affiliation puzzle outsiders but serve as road markers for labor activists. A tiny union button becomes a blazing neon sign or a looming billboard trumpeting the wearer's value positions. During the 1920s, some of Local 77's pile men, unreconciled to "woodbutcher" rule, simply refused to switch from 77 to 34. Instead, they transferred to other IA units, chiefly in high-steel construction.

Other pile men from Local 77, accepting "Big Bill" Hutcheson's power, maintained a quasi-independent stance within Local 34. Gallegos traced his personal commitment to workers' power to his immigrant status and education by Local 77 diehards. Selecting high goals, he set about to master English speech, mechanical skill, and union principles. In 1927, Gallegos and Jack Wagner, a young casual laborer, batched together on an ark at Antioch, California. A decade later, Frank, a partisan of Spain's embattled republican government, supported his friend Wagner in election as business agent for Local 34.

Jack Wagner (born at Crowley, Louisiana, July 10, 1903) served in the navy during World War I and, following that, began work on a San Francisco rigging crew in 1924. While assembling steel circular sectional forms for the Alameda Tube, Jack learned the rudiments of pile driving. He joined Local 34, but wanderlust drove him east for a stint of "boxcarring" and factory jobs. Returning to San Francisco, he rejoined Local 34, working on both the Golden Gate and Bay bridges. During 1936, he and two fellow workers became "gunny sack" contractors; this venture proved unsuccessful. Wagner found less interest in business enterprise than in New Deal and leftist politics as he embraced Communist party Popular Front programs.

During 1935, workers in sea and shore unions formed the Maritime Federation of the Pacific, bringing together an unstable alliance: Stalinist cadres, syndicalists, ex-Wobblies, social democrats, New Deal liberals, Catholic activists. For a few short years of unity, need compelled these antagonists to make common cause (Lampman). As San Francisco's four waterfront carpentry unions (Pile Drivers 34, Shipwrights 1149, Caulkers 554, Lumber Handlers 2559) affiliated with the MFP, they challenged the carpenters brotherhood's commitment to craft unionism and the Republican party.

Following the creation of the Committee for Industrial Organization in 1935, longshore leader Harry Bridges remained loyal to the AFL. However, when industrial organizers captured the attention of mass-production workers, and when communists abandoned their dual unions in favor of the CIO, Bridges switched positions. In 1937, John L. Lewis appointed him to head the CIO's Pacific Coast efforts. As Bridges and the Maritime Federation offered support to loggers and sawmill workers in the Northwest, Hutcheson ordered San Francisco's waterfront carpentry locals to withdraw from the CIO-tainted MFP. After much conflict and some violence Hutcheson prevailed, but not before Wagner and a rank-and-file slate gained office in the pile drivers local during June 1938.

Under various "progressive" banners, Jack Wagner held office for decades, opposing the conservative local secretary Dan Campbell while maintaining peace with Hutcheson's national leadership in Indianapolis. Although Wagner defined himself as a radical, he relished the give-and-take of machine politics, drawing particular pride in his ability to work within UBCJA structures.

For many years, Local 34, defying convention, brought together right-wing building tradesmen and red-hot leftists, U.S. Navy Seabees and Spanish Civil War vets, pork-chop pragmatists, and sectarian ideologues. This union's fascinating history demands attention. Until a student turns to Local 34, we can gain a sense of its setting in books on the maritime and building trades in California by Frederick Ryan, Michael Kazin, and Bruce Nelson. Here, I have focused on two pile drivers, Frank Gallegos and Jack Wagner, as representatives of others who integrated craft skill and class formula to build a union's strength.

Essentially, an active band—left, right, center—creates or appropriates a set of distinctive expressions to laud deeds, energize tasks, and mark values. Often, a rank-and-file worker, attracted to labor history (read or heard), unconsciously assumes the role of tradition bearer for his peers. We err in asserting that only workers on the left shape labor tradition.

Political culture and occupational expression do not always intersect. Indeed, these forces may well compete for workers' loyalties. Radical unionists frequently assert large claims in representing "the people," whereas craft unionists generally limit their rhetoric by excluding others from "their territory." Yet both camps defy "logic" to champion the same line when appropriate.

On the eve of World War II, Local 34 grew tremendously with the expansion of Bay Area shipyards and military sites. At that time, many "defense members" became pile drivers without previous experience or immersion in union politics. These newcomers—johnny-come-latelies—quickly adopted the term *pile butt* to enhance their status in a rugged fraternity. I well recall "refugees" from professional and artistic realms turning to war work and seeking "native speakers" to help in the mastery of labor lingo. In this circumstance, an inside name holding both pejorative and ameliorative elements became a bright badge worn proudly within Local 34's several caucuses.

Gallegos recalled a meeting in 1942 when members discussed their nickname *pile butt*. He felt the term to be undignified but could not stem novel influences. The new war workers had a need for blue-collar identity. Wagner discounted this stress on wartime innovation by placing the locution back to the turn of the century. Both proved to be wrong: Jack's hunch, too early; Frank's, too late.

By 1942, *pile butt* had circulated orally for at least a decade and had been accepted throughout Local 34's ranks. This finding flows from evidence in typed minutes of pile stewards' meetings.

In responding to defense growth, 34 had established a stewards' network to extend contractual conditions throughout Northern California, Nevada, and Utah.

For its stewards, the union published and distributed a pocket-sized booklet, *How to Organize the Job,* placing special emphasis on training, safety, political education, and the battle for home-front production. A second booklet, *Victory through Unionism,* integrated labor history with a patriotic anti-Axis message. These booklets, illustrated by Giacomo Patri, helped introduce pile drivers as responsible citizens within wartime America.

During the war years, stewards' meetings occurred regularly and frequently. Two select passages from minutes of such meetings follow:

> August 13, 1942: Brother Tom Waggoner discusses safety. *Pile Butts* maximum of 236 accidents [time period unspecified]. Chief cause of accidents aside from faulty rigging is lack of instruction to green men.
>
> September 3, 1942: Steward Phil White, from Army Base, reports argument about Laborers carrying 6″ × 6″ 's [heavy timbers]. *Pile Butts* sent [by steward to replace interlopers].

I have underscored the term *pile butts* to call attention to actual usages by stewards in their 1942 meetings. These passages complement the previous *pile butt/rock slinger* citation in San Pedro, January 1941. Local 34's reports mark concerns: untrained workers, jurisdictional rivalry. Further, the stewards' minutes indicate that, by 1942, *pile butt* had become acceptable to the full membership, left and right. If the term had ever held special political resonance, this aura disappeared after Pearl Harbor.

On June 7, 1944, several members endorsed Bruce Anderson while he campaigned for office in Local 34. Printed broadsides on his behalf bore the salutation "Brother Pile Butts." Early in 1946, the union issued a series of attractive mimeographed newsletters with a printed masthead reading "PILE BUTT SPECIAL." Whereas stewards' meeting minutes had little circulation, the newsletter reached 34's entire membership, as well as other unionists in the West.

Perhaps written or printed citations for *pile butt* before 1941 will surface. Presently, I trace it in print:

1941: San Pedro contractor's personnel list
1942: Local 34 stewards' minutes
1944: Local 34 election broadside
1946: Local 34 mimeographed newsletter
1954: *Carpenter,* nationally circulated magazine
1961: *Publications of the American Dialect Society*

Unless another natal site appears, we can assume that California construction crews extended *pile butt* into the Rockies, north to Alaska, west to Pacific Islands, and around the world to Arabian and Indonesian principalities. Ben C. Gerwick, Jr., a civil engineering professor at the University of California, Berkeley, in an exciting interview, alerted me to the geographic sweep of Bay Area pile men.

Gerwick came of age in his father's firm doing wharf, bridge, aqueduct, freeway, and high-rise office construction. As a teenager in the 1930s, he learned to cut metal and weld before his father's superintendent, Howard Harris, allowed him on a pile rig. Harris commanded the beginner, who eagerly sought crew status: "If you're going to learn it at all, learn it right the first time"—pragmatic advice familiar to all building-trades workers.

In memory, Gerwick placed *pile butt* back to 1932, indicating that it had always denoted pride and power. What is more important, he had observed San Francisco pile men as they "ran work" from the Bering Sea to the Persian Gulf. In his view, their productivity resulted from previous decades of hand labor with "undersized" equipment and their willingness to tackle "impossible" assignments.

San Francisco crew men had learned to use personal energy at its most efficient level. Gerwick had seen them improvise on every site, pushing each old machine to its last rattle. He speculated that Local 34's particular mix of hard hats and activists contributed to the temper in which they tackled overseas jobs. Having combined rig labor and college teaching, Gerwick stood at a choice vantage point to plumb pile spirit.

Retired engineer Richard Vlach, who had run pile work for five decades, helped me see large concerns behind his jobs: defense strategies, minority employment, environmental needs. Starting in 1939 as a Sierra's goldmine surveyor, he closed out work in

1985 as Morrison-Knudson project manager on San Francisco's massive outfall sewer at Ocean Beach. This 4½-mile-long concrete pipeline crossed the San Andreas Fault, necessitating stout earthquake-resistant pipe sections with articulating joints. Vlach explained the sewer's progression to me as we walked above the surf on a giant steel trestle. After talking to pile butts lowering a 12-foot diameter pipe section, he described the outfall's function in our city's clean-water program (eM-Kayan).

In a Berkeley visit (1991) with Dick Vlach, he showed me a home movie he had made in 1948 on the Kahului Breakwater at Maui Island. His crew was mainly Hawaiian; I marveled at the action of riggers setting huge basalt rocks on the breakwater's slopes, diving underwater to nest each boulder and to release its slings. These Maui pile men must have been born in Neptune's caves.

I left the Vlach home with a memorable line, "The pile grub is the pile butt's best friend." Dick attributed this to Ben Gerwick's "super," Harris. Waterfront hands use the word *grub* broadly to include teredoes, shipworms, beetles, borers, termites, or other pests that feast on wooden pilings. Before the building of the Golden Gate and Bay bridges, San Francisco ferryboats required hundreds of piers and slips—choice fare for pile grubs. Harris and Vlach knew that millions of grubs conspired to make work for pile crews.

I am unable to date the pile grub aphorism; it would help firm *pile butt* in colloquial speech. Word sleuths never tire. We live like gold miners seeking precious nuggets in drab placer sand. Could I find other recollections placing *pile butt* before 1941? Who might help in my quest?

Retired pile man Jack Fitch, in a personal San Francisco "gallery"—a flat filled with his own oil paintings—shared memories with me. Born in 1899 in Minnesota, Fitch drifted west at age seventeen, seeking work in lumber camps and ice camps (cutting lake ice for storage and use in railroad "reefer" cars). Working as a bridgeman during 1928, Jack drove piles on the Western Pacific's Feather River route out of Gerlach, Nevada. At that time, he knew no special nickname for railroad pile-driving crews. After a stint at Boulder Dam, he made his way to San Francisco as a framing carpenter on the Bay Bridge. Joining Local 34 in 1933, he picked up the term *pile butt,* continuing to use it in self-description until retirement in 1966.

Fitch, Vlach, and Gerwick—from different perspectives—placed *pile butt* back in memory before Pearl Harbor Day. A fourth, serendipitously discovered usage helped me affirm this time frame. Al Zampa (born in 1905) had started work at Crockett's California & Hawaii sugar mill while a teenager. In 1926, he shifted outside to rigging and pile driving for the Carquinez Straits Bridge foundations. In the mid-1930s, Zampa worked on both the Golden Gate and Bay bridges. On the Golden Gate span, as a "raising gang" ironworker, he joined the Half-Way-to-Hell Club—the bridgemen's name for those who survived falls. Zampa spent twelve weeks in the hospital after his plunge on Columbus Day, 1936 (Berson, Blakey).

I met Zampa when the San Francisco Tale Spinners presented *The Ace,* an experimental drama based on his oral history. At opening night, July 22, 1986, Al took a curtain call and on stage supplemented the actors' presentation of his life story. In detailing his life's time sequence, Zampa mentioned that he had "gone down to the pile butt's hall, 34 in 1934, for a caisson job on the Bay Bridge. We built the deepest pier in the world, 242 feet."

In the presence of sophisticated little-theater devotees, Zampa assumed that his auditors would know the term *pile butt,* as well as his reference to 34, the local union. He knew that his life story needed no special amplification, for his fall of 740 feet and his work at the bay's bedrock proved more dramatic than a staged play. Sitting in the audience, I felt pleased to hear him recall a colloquialism I had pursued for years.

The verbal usages for *pile butt* by Gerwick, Vlach, Fitch, and Zampa can be corroborated by a fifth example within a taped interview (1969) Brooks Penney conducted with James Dean Osborn. Osborn's words serve also as a useful window to the concerns addressed by the cadre of class-conscious workers within San Francisco's Local 34.

Born on November 4, 1901, in Latour, Missouri, Osborn grew up on an Idaho frontier farm. At age seventeen, he broke in on a Montana railroad bridge construction gang; in 1924, he joined the Seattle Structural Ironworkers Local 72 as an erector on high steel. Lured to San Francisco by Bay Bridge work (twenty-two months as a rigger on the main anchorage caisson), Jim "got into the pile butts" when he joined Local 34 (November 3, 1933).

During World War II, Osborn switched from private employment to the State Board of Harbor Commissioners, retiring in 1963 as a "spoolman" (manning the winch drums and lines used to move the barge). He died on July 20, 1981. I have reconstructed his experience from visits with his widow, Frances, and with his close friends Carl Anderson and Marshall Uran, a pile driver and a stationary engineer, respectively.

Osborn's work sequence—farm chores, railroad bridge, high steel, deep caisson, waterfront rig—is not unusual for construction hands. However, Jim added to this journey a long commitment to socialism, going back to his association with dissident unionists in Seattle. Within 34, he concerned himself mainly with bread-and-butter issues and "Jimmie Higgins' " tasks.

In my chapter on the word *fink*, I indicated that *Jimmie Higgins* personified the radical movement's quiet member who stacked chairs, passed out leaflets, and served on innumerable committees. Osborn had read Upton Sinclair's novel honoring the rank-and-filer who accepted responsibility for such work. Perhaps this willingness helped Jim avoid the isolation of many sectarians within unions. All who recalled him lauded his calm demeanor and cogent analysis.

Osborn left no written record of his animating ideology, but he did comment on technological change and social exchange: hand labor decline and skill loss balanced by wage gains. He recalled early jobs when horse-drawn lines lifted the pile hammer, and when gangs riveted by hand: "Two on the mauls and another guy holding the die." Using a hand drill, Jim bored twelve-by-twelve-inch timbers while cribbing bridge falsework (Penney tape).

Brooks Penney, a pile driver and ironworker, understood Osborn's work descriptions. Jim and his buddies had moved skid rigs by hand, constantly reblocking (leveling) the rig by carrying heavy, greasy timbers fore and aft. He raised stiff-leg derricks on bridge footings to stay ahead of the Columbia River's icy spring tides. He expressed his initial encounter with a pneumatic saw for cutting pile heads pungently: "They were heavy bastards and didn't work too damn good either."

Countless workers cursed their tools, bosses, weather, and fate. Jim differed only in connecting his toil to a vision of justice framed within Marxist precepts. Like many radicals, he welcomed the diminution in backbreaking labor. Technology liberated; Osborn opposed Luddites who discounted modernity's blessings. In the decades of his retirement, a few young pile drivers, touched by ecological causes, questioned the assumptions of "progress" firmly held by previous generations of building tradesmen. Whether Jim lived long enough to meet "green" Reds, I do not know.

It is our loss that Osborn confined his personal experience tape to technical matters. As he entered the iron trades in 1924, an outlaw "white card" faction took over the Seattle erectors' local (IABSOIW). Puget Sound syndicalists and secessionists then battled IA loyalists on the job and in court for four years before returning to the "fold" (Local 401).

In San Francisco's Local 34, Osborn experienced internal union disputes when the pile drivers broke ranks with the UCBJA over issues of CIO industrial form and Pacific Coast maritime unity. Despite his participation in opposition ranks in Seattle and San Francisco locals, Osborn closed out his working years on a State of California crew. His reflections on dual unionism, internal democracy, public employment, and present-day ecology would have composed a valued legacy.

The labels *hard hat* and *red hot* represent wide polarities, as well as the interpenetration of discrete workplace roles. My years in Shipwrights Local 1149 and other venues have suggested to me no clear demarcation of dominant values governing labor. Rather, I have encountered a bewildering mix of conflict and convergence, accommodation and intransigence, in key positions on the job and at the hall. The few preceding vignettes of Local 34 members but hint at deep complexities required for laborlore analysis.

Frank Gallegos spent a lifetime with his tools, putting them away only for a few years as a "pie card" (official). Sensing no great conflict between job skill and union loyalty, he assumed their mutuality. Looking back with pleasure at his stint as a business agent, he treated the office as an interlude in a worker's life. Gallegos's friend, Jack Wagner, thrived on arcane labor politics and Communist party intrigue. Once elected to office in Local 34, he placed his tools in storage and remained a battling activist, a true believer until his death (July 15, 1984).

Jim Osborn, a long-time follower of Leon Trotsky, "survived" in Local 34 through many years of opposition both to Stalinist dogma and right-wing maneuvers by UBCJA representatives. One of Jim's close friends, Jack Fitch, paid no attention to left or right positions. Instead, he used his handsome earnings as a pile man to purchase oils and canvas, to create a personal studio/gallery. His job pay translated into landscape, still life, and visual dream. Fitch and I had worked together on a Furniture Mart expansion site in the 1950s. I did not know then of Jack's artistry; he did not know of my turn to folklore. Like too many workers, we kept our hobbies private.

What will become of Fitch's paintings, Gallegos's tools, Wagner's politics, and Osborn's idealism? These four individuals may or may not have typified Local 34's membership. In highlighting this quartet, I am conscious of having selected but a few details out of their rich stories. In the pages ahead, I turn to Herb Edwards and Frank Wilkinson, Puget Sound workers. In my book's afterword, I recall Spokane Tom, a wrinkled shipwright and pile butt who held membership in locals 77, 34, and 1149. All these toilers, and their nameless companions, deserve better memorials than a few pages in a folklorist's study.

## Herb Edwards and Frank Wilkinson

Pictures of pile crews in Boston, New York, San Pedro, and San Francisco remain impressionistic when seen through the lens of language. I am conscious that pile butts have left few written records or memorable literature. In this regard, they differ from cowhands, sailors, and coal miners who have used diary, log book, poetry, and fiction to narrate their experience.

Fortunately, Northwest woodsman and boilermaker Herb Edwards left a lengthy, unpublished autobiography containing insightful pages on pile-driving work. Edwards (1894–1976), a Norwegian immigrant, had been christened Hagbart Marius Edvartsen. In New World forests, he became a confirmed Wobbly and, in 1923, a class-war prisoner (criminal syndicalism) at San Quentin.

Like Fred Thompson and other IWW inmates, Herb did not waste subsequent years in bitter recollection of the prison jute mill or license-stamping shop.

Recalling his early work, Edwards noted that in 1916, the Clearlake Lumber Company had built a new logging road in Skagit County, Washington. As "stiffs" moved freely from camp to camp, a pile foreman offered Edwards a "niggerhead" job on a makeshift pile driver, putting in bridges over gullies. Looking back at this initiation, Herb combined physical description of the tasks, portraits of his fellows, and criticism of craft consciousness from an IWW perspective.

Edwards's superb synthesis, flavored with Wobbly salt and pepper, reveals hard-earned beliefs born in backbreaking toil. I extract his comments on pile driving:

> That job consisted of adjusting the lines [cables] around the power-driven "spool" or shaft which pulled the driver [rig] in any direction we wanted to go.
>
> "Big Ed," the engineer or "hammer man," had . . . made arrangements to get me released from the [Clearlake] job as a rigging slinger without having to quit. He was an impressive giant with steady blue eyes, a face that was used to smiling and good laughter, and with the physical appearance of a super-trained athlete—a kindly, tolerant man who was in no danger of being challenged off or on the job. He was also a member of the Pile Drivers Union of the A.F. of L., then affiliated with a different International Union [Iron Workers] than it is now [Carpenters]. As we got better acquainted, he asked me to join that union, and he offered to help me to get in.
>
> With a few elementary instructions, it did not take me long to "get on to the ropes." But though I got along well enough from the start with the boomer foreman, who had encouraged me to take the job, I soon became annoyed by his confusing signals. No matter what direction we were going, he had only one signal for it, and his stentorian voice could probably be heard across the Skagit county; it was "skin'er back" from beginning to end of the shift. . . .
>
> The foreman had the good Irish name of O'Connor, but

aside from that there was nothing in his physiognomy which was a credit to the human race. Powder-marked features which added color to his Bourbon complexion, week-old wire-brush whiskers with blue-black base through which his small eyes peered as black diamonds, a thin slit of mouth exposing snaggly teeth; and in the middle of this gargoyle was the wreck of a nose which had been broken and scarred so many times that it showed no indication of its original shape—a perfect model for a pirate, or a hangover nightmare. In an argument over signals, I quit the job and went to Seattle. . . .

Shortly after New Year, 1917, I was back in Seattle, and there I contacted Big Ed to get his assistance to get me into the [Pile] Union. He had his home and family in Tacoma but, as far as I can remember, he was a member of the Seattle Local. At their first meeting of the season I was voted in to be a member.

My first job was on a pile driver at Tacoma, where Big Ed was the engineer. Though I had gained some experience with the work at Clearlake, this was a much bigger driver, and I required more knowledge of the work than I had learned on the other simple operation. . . . [The job] consisted of driving sheath piling for a coffer dam where land was being reclaimed from the Sound to make room for a shipyard. This became one of the Todd Corporation yards which became famous during World War II as a builder of "baby flattops."

For both mental and physical reasons, work on pile drivers did not agree with me. Not only did the constant hammering and shaking make me feel as if I was getting punch drunk, but the general scandalizing clannishness of some of the crews affected me even worse. Generally they were rugged and able men who knew their work from A to Z, and they certainly earned every cent they were paid, but their insufferable vocational snobbery was a strain to endure. Interest and pride in accomplishment, or what Veblen called "the instinct of workmanship," may be necessary for doing good work, but when men get the notion that their craft is the only important one and all other crafts are inferior and parasitic, then the narrowminded prejudice of craft-union members become insufferable and a daily bore. . . .

Not that these fellows—"pile butt," as they are now referring to themselves—lacked fellowship among themselves; indeed, they were mostly generous splendid fellows who worked, drank, and fought well together. Besides, an excessive condition of clannishness has been a general trend of all craft-union members who work a long time or all their lives in one industry. In fact, there are indications of it being encouraged by class-conscious employers to prevent industrial solidarity.

Fortunately, I overcame such prejudice before I was "hooked" by a "steady job" in one industry. My last job and experience as a "pile butt" was on a water or floating pile driver near Port Orchard, where we drove pilings at a dock. I got in with a crew that had worked together a long time and their experience was coordinated into a clocklike unit. I was a stranger with little experience—unable to join in their shop-talk during lunch period, which dealt mostly with previous jobs and the ignorance and uselessness of people not present. A few days of that was enough for me, and I quit. (223–27)

During a lifetime of unrelenting labor, Edwards worked a year as a pile man. Dismissed many times for Wobbly organizational efforts in lumber camps, he remembered being "fired once for lack of workmanship" at the age of sixteen (222). He could well have followed pile driving for decades: he had the strength for rugged work; he understood the scatological "skin'er back"; he could quote Thorstein Veblen's theories. Above all, he quickly learned "the ropes" on each job.

Although Edwards as a Wobbly decried "vocational snobbery," he shared the pride in work of his AFL crew mates. Essentially, he faulted craft unionists for lacking consciousness of class. With a brief service under the hammer, Herb Edwards held the ability to balance clashing words and colliding worlds. I believe that other pile men made similar conjunctions, and I have urged folklorists and historians to record the narratives of such individuals.

On November 13, 1990, Tacoma folklorist Phyllis Harrison visited Frank Wilkinson at his home in Everett. She has shared with me transcripts of her taped interview. Wilkinson was born in 1906; his parents moved to Seattle from Arkansas in 1908, where Frank's father found employment as a saw filer in the Erlich & Harrison hardwood mill. While still in his teens, Frank started as a logging-camp "whistle punk," going on to choking and loading logs. Observing that pile drivers made more money than woodsmen, he entered a pile crew for Monroe Logging and joined Seattle Local 2396 in 1928. During the Depression years, he fell behind in dues, but he rejoined in 1934 and held continuous membership until his retirement in 1971.

Wilkinson broke in on building logging-train bridges. He liked "big jobs" and over the years worked on the Grand Coulee Dam, the Weyerhauser Pulp Mill, Seattle's Alaska Way Viaduct, the University of Washington's service tunnels, and the original Tacoma Narrows Bridge. Puget Sound residents recall the last as "Galloping Gertie," a reference to the wind-induced disaster of 1940. Frank joked: "We built a bridge up in Tacoma in about a year and a half, and we wore it out in four months."

There are interesting similarities and differences between Edwards and Wilkinson. The former worked as a pile man for a year; the latter, a lifetime. One oriented himself by Wobbly philosophy; the other revealed no political stance. Herb rejected craft clannishness; Frank took craft consciousness in stride.

Not all job survivors retain colorful anecdotes or are comfortable in embroidering their life stories. On showing Phyllis Harrison a crew photograph, Wilkinson stated laconically that he was "the only one left out of the seven." Without dwelling on his longevity, he chuckled as he noted that his mates had called him "Sonny Boy"—"I was young, just a kid." We can sense Wilkinson's matter-of-fact verbal style in his description of pile work's divisions, as he pointed out his fellow workers in the photo:

> Well, there's an engineer. He used to be a pile driver, but he belongs to the engineers now. And they have a fireman, he belongs to the engineers [International Union of Operating Engineers]. It wasn't that way, though, for a long time. Then they have what they call a niggerhead man. The spools—

two spools coming off of the drum—that's how you move the thing, with ropes, you wrap the ropes around the spools and you move the thing [rig] sideways, forward and back. I was a niggerhead man . . . I took care of the ropes.

And then there's two men on the front end. They called them front-end men. They guide the pile, put a rope around it and guide it in the leads before they strike the hammer. Then they have to set the rigging off to pick it up or move it sideways, one of the two. And on the ground is what they call a ground man. He sets a pile where it's supposed to go at the bottom, and goes out and hooks the pile on, too, with a chain.

Then there's one other man. What the dickens did they call him? He's the one who fresh-headed the piles, cut them to the right length and all that stuff. And that's about the size of it.

Frank Wilkinson's wrap-up phrase, "the size of it," seems understated for a veteran of the Grand Coulee Dam and Tacoma Narrows Bridge. He employed sparse language in descriptions of brushes with death on several jobs and of jurisdictional disputes with rival unions. Responding to his visitor's question about the Northwest usage of *pile buck* or *pile butt*, Frank chose the latter. When she asked whether there were other nicknames, he responded, "Oh, probably some that you wouldn't want to hear."

The suggestion that a folklorist might not want to hear a pile driver's off-color nicknames implies multiple hidden themes of alternation: insider/outsider, male/female, old/young, blue collar/white collar. Phyllis Harrison presented herself as representing Life on the Sound, affiliated with the Institute of the North American West. Frank Wilkinson identified himself as having worked over the decades for "old man" Rumsy, a Seattle contractor. Before Harrison and Wilkinson's meeting, Life on the Sound and Rumsy might as well have inhabited the North and South Poles rather than the shores of Puget Sound.

In the Harrison-Wilkinson interview, both addressed questions requisite to demystifying work narratives. In my placing in sequence the experiences of Herb Edwards and Frank Wilkinson, I begin to decode the internal rules that bring workers together and hold them apart. We are fortunate to know something of these two pile butts, for they speak to workers far beyond the Northwest woods and waterfront.

### New Tools

In this book's preceding case studies, I shifted vertically from term to tale, ballad, and ritual. In this chapter, I move horizontally to reveal a single trade's dimensions, what pile drivers do and how they express their identity in creative form. We find folkloric precedent for attention to John Henry and Joe Hill; no pile butt has emerged to become a similar occupational or labor union hero. Lacking a defining demigod or memorable ballad, pile crews, instead, have built a mosaic of tradition—thousands of verbal fragments and artistic enactments.

From my former shipyard vantage point and present peephole in construction keep-out fences, I have heard and continue to hear pile-driving speech and story. Figuratively, each spoken gem becomes a ceramic chip in our pile inlay. In this manner, we can see and hear single tiles as well as grand mosaics. Realists divide visual from aural sensation; workers on many jobs survive only by integrating eye and ear messages.

In reading and listening, I have called on Caesar's classic prose, London Bridge ledgers, Boston Newfie jokes, Johnny Moreno's memories, Michael Munoz's story picture book, and Bill Myers's searches to help outsiders view pile rigs and hear pulsing hammers. I am confident that young workers and academic allies will continue this cultural exploration, thereby breaking down their respective invisibilities. I caution seekers with tape recorders or video cameras to remain alert to wide differences in occupational expression, definitional formula, and philosophic stance.

Some workers are as laconic as Spartan warriors; others, as colorful as TV talk-show hosts. This distinction in rhetorical style seems obvious, yet it must be deciphered in our search. How does one separate incessant job talk from traditional gifts, daily routines from those practices that comment reflexively on work itself? I touch on a puzzle here. Many workers acquire craft skill and technique traditionally; some individuals heighten their work's meaning by imagery, verbal or tactile. I select contrasting examples to serve as guides.

In 1973, Captain Sidney Sprague, a lobster smack skipper at Isle Au Haut, Maine, told folklorist David Taylor how he built a dolphin for the *William McLoon:* "The boat was 81 feet long and I put a dolphin off from his [owner] wharf 60 feet. That would be one center piling driven in the mud and then I drove five around it and then hauled them all together at the top and bolted them through and wired them, and left the one in the center sticking up above the rest. So, when the *William McLoon* went in there, well, they'd go in alongside this dolphin, tie the stern, make the bow fast, and load."

As a youth, George Hayward worked in the Wichita, Kansas, city dump. He moved to California and became, in sequence, a fish cannery hand, ship joinery shop "sawdust boy," shipyard unionist, and pile butt. We met in 1941 and remained friends until his death in 1984. After five decades, one of George's anecdotes about his brother Stack (a Local 34 member) still sticks in my mind:

> Stack hired out on a Treasure Island job, a raftsman—bringing in pile brails [logs boomed together by manila lines or chains]. One day, he got into a beef with the super. Maybe by accident—its hard to tell—Stack lost the raft. When the super saw his Oregon fir floating out to the Golden Gate, he cursed Stack. The big Swede tore off his hard hat, threw it to the ground, stomped it flat as a Dixie cup at a Klan rally. Would've flattened Stack, too, but, luckily, he was in a motor launch and got away. Turned up at the hall for another job.

Captain Sprague built a dolphin traditionally—without blueprints. Knowing the length of lobster smack, location of dock, and Maine channel currents, he proceeded economically. We do not have to see his dolphin at Isle Au Haut to appreciate its functional lines. We compare his verbal description to his pile work: sparse, clean, undecorated.

George and Stack Hayward both heard Southwestern and Midwestern tall tales in childhood. They enjoyed comic exaggeration, "windies," and "roarers." I cannot verify the Treasure Island story that Stack told to George, but I marvel at its hard hat allusion.

Are discarded paper cups flatter at KKK rallies than at ordinary picnics? Did George mask a hidden metaphor linking violence in Dixie with a super's urge to stomp his brother Stack?

This pairing of technical and verbal anecdotes by a smack skipper and a raftsman suggests analytic concerns in language and literature. Pile butts may disclaim skill in such areas. It is my book's purpose to encourage workers to move into academic realms regardless of boundary markers. We can move ahead by looking back at the Sprague and Hayward accounts. One unionist might ask why a skipper infringes on "our work." A skeptic may believe that Stack "lost" the pile boom in the spirit of job resistance. In short, we approach laborlore with tools sharpened at diverse grindstones.

I suspect that pile drivers seeking their trade's cultural strength will begin with matters of jurisdiction and skill—"I am that which I do." Recall that Bill Myers built a dolphin for his union's anniversary at San Pedro's Maritime Museum. Why do I fall back on a lobster smack skipper's description of such a task? My reply is indirect.

On a Tacoma visit in 1991, Fred Dessin told me how he became a pile man. At age seventeen (1928), he started work at the Bellingham Canning Company setting salmon traps in icy waters and treacherous currents. "We drove piles one hundred feet long, ten feet above high tide; wove heavy-duty chicken wire between the piles. No one really fished, the scow-derrick man just scooped the salmon out of the water. In 1934, voters outlawed traps."

Also in Tacoma, I met Gordon McConnaughey, the manager of McFarland Cascade, a forest products company in wood preservation—piling, railroad ties, decking, utility poles, industrial timber. Although his crews did not drive piles, they were members of Seattle Pile Local 2396. In command of a lathe 110 feet long and thirty-four inches in diameter, McConnaughey noted a series of unusual jobs in which he had participated: providing a replacement mast for *Old Ironsides* and a new mast for the sloop *Providence,* a replica of America's first naval vessel, and then transporting these especially crafted masts cross continent to Boston and Newport.

I juxtapose these vignettes of Sprague, Hayward, Dessin, and

McConnaughey to underscore the kaleidoscope of pile experience and concomitant interpretive strategies. A Maine skipper drives piles; a Puget Sound pile buck builds fish traps; a San Francisco trickster loses a fir pile raft to Pacific tides; an Atlantic shipwright awaits Douglas fir masts turned by pile unionists. I believe that workers who handle dolphins, fish traps, pile rafts, and timber shaped for historic preservation projects can also construct and inhabit towers of cultural exploration.

I turn from workers' accounts of self to a job-centered challenge. In the 1970s, construction hands flocked to Alaska like steel filings to a magnet. At Prudhoe Bay, crews drove "refrigerated" piles to keep the tundra from melting (McPhee, 86). What were the thoughts of men handling these science-fiction-like devices? Did Prudhoe pile butts see their engineering feat as but a "normal" conquest of nature? Did any reflect on the hidden costs in altering Alaska's environment? How many returned to the "lower 48" sensitive to hills and hollows at home?

We can only speculate whether lunch-bucket pragmatists and Sierra Club idealists will utilize their combined heritage of craft skill and social activism to keep tundras and similar terrains inviolate. This is the most explosive issue challenging present-day building-trades workers. Must ecology and economics always clash, or can these polar fields find their equatorial mean? Pile drivers do not remain immune from ecological pressures.

In preceding pages, I have offered a few cameos of pile work, past and present. Workers constantly externalize their pain and pleasure in job talk, some of which makes its way to print in chronicle, contract, rules brochure, technical treatise, museum placard, formal history, fiction, autobiography, or folk narrative. Not all occupational speech moves beyond job site, however. Hence, we must combine oral and published sources to comprehend a craft's full dimension.

We can learn about Antoine Barada's legendary strength from a folklorist's academic article; we can learn of Daniel Hurley's devotion to fellow dock builders by searching for his obituary in fragile newsprint. We can then speculate about lost Barada accounts and seek clues to Hurley's warmth and style. In my visit to Boston's pile-driving union hall, I learned gopher knot jokes directly, not having heard them previously or found them in print. This go-for-the-ax jest suggests, once more, the indispensable complementarity of reading and hearing.

In this chapter's opening, I observed that no major novelist or filmmaker has been attracted to pile driving. However, I did find the forgotten mystery novel *Pilebuck* by John and Ward Hawkins. In San Pedro, I learned that a Hollywood studio had pictured shipyard pile work. Seemingly, some labor remains obscure by destiny. If pile work is to become familiar beyond the keep-out fence, we shall have to see a widely shown film about such construction. We need such occupation-centered films, as well as fact and fiction, to follow pile lore from initial site to union hall, parlor, archive, and cinema palace.

I end with curiosity about a naming term I first heard in 1941. An Alabama politician in 1830 had become a "but-cut." A century later, Californians accepted *pile butt* at San Francisco and San Pedro. During the same years, Northwest crews became familiar with *pile buck*. In 1941, Local 2375 received a list of pile butts and rock slingers; a year later, *Collier's* printed Jack Hawkins's "Man Working," a story about a young donkeyman pile buck. I am impressed and puzzled by the fact that I have found no printed citations for these dual nicknames before 1941.

We still do not know the exact time, place, or sequence of interchange from *pile butt* to *buck*, or the reverse. Perhaps my findings will jog memories and bring fresh material to light. Essentially, I wish to encourage present-day crew members to seek elders, listen to their stories, and assist in celebrating traditions at outdoor festivals and within museum walls. My book asks workers far beyond the pile hammer's roar to piece together and cherish their own mosaics of lore.

My journey from early reading of stories about Swiss lake dwellings to work on San Francisco's waterfront has been rewarding. Friendly lexicographers and historians, as well as patient old-timers, loyal union members, and experienced engineers, have assisted me. Pile drivers continue to cut timber, concrete, and steel butts. Their nickname holds a long pedigree. Those who sound *buck* rather than *butt* move away from the tree stump as a sign of strength. However, *buck* standing alone holds powerful work associations. Essentially, *butt* and *buck* run together in sound and meaning as each expresses object and action.

Floating barges and mobile cranes that hold pile-driving gear seldom fly pennants. I believe that men and women who sound *pile butt* or *pile buck* hoist symbolic pennants above their towering machines. Workers who cut butts and buck piles daily will continue to cut corners in language, fashioning new tools from old terms while reaching for vivid expressions that match demanding brawn and wisdom.

Part Three

# Afterword

"Tug Boat Captain"

# Spokane Tom: Memory and Monument

Among thousands of other young men who joined the Civilian Conservation Corps during the New Deal period, I trekked to a Klamath River camp in California's Siskiyou Mountains. There, our raw crews mastered fire fighting and road building while learning to use dynamite tampers and timber saws, surveyor's transits and double-bitted axes. Best of all, our Karuk foreman Lawrence Roberts introduced raw city kids to his native beliefs. Preaching and teaching by example only, he taught "3-C boys" reverence for salmon and fir, serpentine and owl. We honored Roberts's values as we strove to comprehend his traditional creed.

At the end of 1940, I left the Siskiyous to seek work in heavy industry. Sheer luck led me to a waterfront carpentry union—the Shipwrights, Joiners & Boatbuilders Local 1149. Beginning at Western Pipe & Steel between Oyster and Sierra Points, South San Francisco, I saw several Maritime Commission C-1 and C-3 freighters "grow" on their launching ways. Nothing in my previous experience had prepared me for keel block or bilge shore, loft template or Plimsoll mark. I was innocent of ship construction and seafaring practices.

However college years at Berkeley before my CCC enrollment had prepared me to see waterfront experience through a wide lens. On campus, I had been caught up by President Franklin Delano Roosevelt's enthusiastic politics, as well as by John L.

Lewis's commitment to industrial unionism. Following their visions, I imagined the University of California as a stereopticon show. Slides from popular picture magazines and newsreels dissolved marble-and-granite-clad buildings. I saw Gastonia mill villages and Detroit assembly lines where Wheeler Hall and the Doe Library stood. Mainly, I transformed "Cal" into Harlan County: our campanile became a coal tipple; our university president doubled as a coal operator.

Had I completed my CCC term in Kentucky, I would have sought mine employment gladly, but a continent's span kept me from an Appalachian UMWA local. Instead, I found myself in California joining an ancient craft local affiliated with the United Brotherhood of Carpenters & Joiners of America. San Francisco shipwrights had begun to organize after the 1849 Gold Rush, establishing a series of short-lived associations prior to the formation of the UBCJA in the East.

My mentors at Western Pipe had served demanding apprenticeships in Scotland's Clyde River shipyards. A few had sailed on coal-fired steamers in "black gangs"; others had voyaged around the globe as ship carpenters. They knew the texture of lignum vitae and alloy steel, the varnish of builder's half-model and wheelroom grate. Nothing seemed beyond the capability of a Clydesider in mastering a vessel's structure and spirit.

In 1941, I stood in awe of Ben Carwardine, Art Ross, Billy Dean, Jimmy Allan, Jock McIvor, and their peers. They seemed as crafty as Merlin, as canny as Solomon. Bringing a keen sense of reality to the ever-present abstract blueprints guiding their work, they knew that a ship demanded buoyancy and grace. I viewed shipwrights as magicians and felt that I had stumbled into a sorcerer's apprenticeship. To plumb a bow peak, to erect a towering mast, and to shape a deck's camber implied a very close bargain with Father Neptune.

Two decades after helping Carwardine and Allan set a pair of hawsepipes on a hull's forepeak, I entered my respect for their "magic" in a study on *dutchman* submitted to *American Speech.* The journeymen who instructed me in the care of maul and adze combined mechanical skill, remarkable literacy, and union loyalty. They observed safety codes, guarded jurisdictional territory, and wore union buttons as badges of honor; they taught me that other workers would operate the ships we had fashioned. Shipwrights translated skill into life itself for mariners.

A youngster's climb from helper or apprentice to mechanic's status involved considerable growth in personal maturity as well as in social consciousness. Before Henry Kaiser cut production time on Liberty ships in his new Richmond yards, hulls grew slowly on the ways. At Western Pipe, Bethlehem, or Moore's Drydock, you could work a year—plate by plate, seam by seam—waiting for launching day, and then a second year on this same vessel at its outfitting dock. The careful steps necessary to handcraft such pulsing giants helped young workers marshal their energies and acquire patience.

Pearl Harbor marked a sharp turning point for new shipwrights. Many of us advanced quickly by leapfrogging to positions as leadmen and foremen. In normal times, we would have marched for decades before being trusted to "run work." Along with other waterfronters during war years, I joined the navy, serving in ship repair units across the Pacific to China's Huangpu River.

Returning to San Francisco, I resumed my trade. For a few postwar years, maritime work held steady with port "turnaround" repair and ship reconversion. By 1950, however, the decline in waterfront work, as well as responsibility for a growing family, combined to send me "uptown" as a building-trades carpenter. Eventually, I left high-rise construction behind for a scholar's calling in folklore. In 1982, I retired from teaching in Texas and turned to shaping this book on workers' culture under the rubric *laborlore*.

Among my multiple quests, I sought the origin of the nickname *pile butt* (a worker on a pile-driving crew). As a shipwright, I had been familiar with sister Local 34's crews on and off their rigs. Also, I had read something of this craft's fascinating chronology (see chapter 10). In this concluding vignette, I delve only into a mystery—the identity of Spokane Tom, an old pile butt who touched my life briefly after I joined Local 1149.

During the turbulent 1930s, San Francisco waterfront unions clustered above and below Market Street near the Ferry Building. On Bloody Thursday (July 5, 1934), during the Big Strike, police shot two men at the corner of Mission and Steuart. The location of Shipwrights Hall at 123 Steuart, a stone's throw from the killing site, reminded us constantly of labor's struggles. Not only did 123 Steuart convey a vibrant sense of history, it also spoke to the ethnic composition of San Francisco's port. Old-timers had named Steuart Street "Finn Alley" to mark past days when Scandinavian and Baltic seamen manned California's coastal lumber schooners.

New to Local 1149 and the Embarcadero, I explored the neighborhood—stevedore firms, ship chandleries, marine machine or boiler shops, lumber yards, and rooming houses for sailors, longshoremen, and fellow blue-collar hands. Workers who lived in decaying Rincon Hill flats or Third Street flophouses could walk to their respective union halls for job waits and continue on foot after dispatching to nearby docks and shops. At that time, not all members owned autos; fortunately, streetcar fares held fast at a nickel. Often insensitive to the implications of our rough humor, we joked about the trolley-ride price: "skinning the buffalo," we called it, or "scalping the Indian."

The shipwrights hall functioned variously: a tiny dispatch office filled one corner; endless racks held huge wooden toolchests; a potbellied stove warmed loungers waiting for work. Members read, played cards, sharpened tools, joked, gossiped, or swapped stories. We might have been enclaved in a Himalayan village. Although the daily papers brought terrible news from the war fronts, something within our unostentatious hall internalized our discourse.

Many years elapsed before I understood fully the significance of the banter in Local 1149's hall—that it followed traditional patterns of coal miners digging fantastic tonnage in saloons or grogshop sailors yarning about "pierhead jumps" onto good luck ships. No shipwright used formal language to describe the function of a "traditionalizing circle." New to the trade, I found the constant talk about work's scope overwhelming. In their anecdotal form, jobs could be only dazzling or dismal, nothing in between the two.

One member lounging in the hall described in blissful detail a gang lining a Matson sugar boat's holds with clean, dry, sweet-smelling pine. Since raw Hawaiian sugar, if wet, could eat through the hull's steel plates, Matson hired shipwrights to protect the inner surfaces of the sugar carriers. The men cut, shaped, and fit a pine "ceiling" to mask all steel surfaces against the sugar's corrosive power.

Another member recalled with horror a job at the Anderson & Cristofani yard in India Basin near Hunter's Point. An innocent crew had been hired to replace the sodden, slimy planking that sheathed the underside of a harbor scow. Every brine-pickled plank had to be dislodged, one at a time, from the scow's bottom. The gang labored for weeks in a barnacled purgatory. The old planks were wet and heavy, the new planks just heavy.

In such yarning sessions joining tall talk and memory of past tasks, Local 1149's warriors launched and outfitted enough vessels to rescue a dozen Helens of Troy. During 1942, in this dilapidated and warm setting, I met Spokane Tom. The map of Ireland lined Tom's wrinkled face; early in life he had kissed the Blarney Stone. Grizzled and garrulous, he regaled listeners with accounts of the maritime strike in 1934.

One of Tom's narratives looked back a few years to his strike actions in setting up a soup kitchen and in sending fellow workers out to scavenge for meat and vegetables. Produce warehouses and cold storage plants shared Embarcadero space a few blocks north of Market Street. From time to time, a teamster dropped a gunny sack or wooden crate. Tom's scouts could pick up potatoes, carrots, onions, cabbages, and other necessities; occasionally, exotic fruit came to hand.

Tom also sent joiners to gather scraps of firewood for the hall's stove. At each pier head, the men picked up armloads of broken dunnage—rough lumber battens and mill strips used in stowing cargo. I have long remembered Tom's firewood detail and relished its irony: superbly skilled tradesmen, who could turn a wood surface into a mirror and who knew teak or ebony as friends, hauling timber scraps for the hall's stove. Tom kept a stew pot on the iron monster, feeding strikers after picket duty on raw, foggy days. He drew no line between shipwrights and other craftsmen. The halls of the Sailors Union of the Pacific, the International Longshoremen's Association, and the Caulkers Union abutted ours. Hungry men must have followed their noses to Tom's mulligan.

I enjoyed Tom's arcane stories and his willingness to instruct youngsters. Here, I must confess that in the months before and after Pearl Harbor I did not anticipate a folklorist's career. Cassette recorders were unknown; I kept no diary; I failed to log union events as they engulfed me. As a teenager, I had read John Lomax's *Cowboy Songs* and had treasured 78-rpm folksong discs. Nevertheless, I was slow to place my own experience within academic frames. Only in retrospect and after the passage of decades did I recognize Spokane Tom as a Celtic shanachie, a master tale teller, a keeper of his people's spirit.

Literary critics know the power in Proust's novel of *la recherche du temps perdu*. We invoke memory for solace and certainty; we use it as armor for everyday battles. With the passage of five decades, I now see and hear Spokane Tom through memory's mist. My recollections of him, as well as the mysteries he invoked that I can no longer resolve, raise large issues of meaning reflected variously throughout my book's separate chapter studies.

Until I met Tom, I had never heard a distinct Irish brogue, although Local 1149 drew artisans from the world's ports: Frank Falzon had mastered English in Malta's Royal Navy dockyard; Pete Koenig favored Dutch colloquialisms; Lars Anderson might have been a Viking sailing through the Golden Gate; Ben Carwardine carried Clyde murmurs to Frisco Bay. Together, they and Tom contributed to the coruscating texture in American speech.

Regretfully, I cannot now reconstruct Tom's politics. In 1942 I viewed him as a Wobbly, a red-card member of the Industrial Workers of the World. Assuming simply that his nickname reflected his tramping days, I likened it to boxcar door monikers such as Topeka Slim. During adolescent years, I had been impressed by IWW soapboxers. At Western Pipe I met a few former Wobs: seamen, hard rock miners, lumberjacks. Tom seemed to fit into this favored fraternity.

Coincidentally, in his physical features and his brogue, Tom resembled Harry "Haywire Mac" McClintock, a former Wobbly and radio songster who had popularized classic hobo and cowboy ballads. (Mac's copper tale, "Marcus Daly Enters Heaven," appears in chapter 5.) I knew McClintock only through radio broadcasts and phonograph records. However, I could sit with Spokane Tom in our hall and absorb his "old country" inflections, observe his gestures, and savor his presence.

Spokane Tom's narrative of Local 1149's soup kitchen reached me as an example of Wobbly camaraderie carried into a craft union. Those IWW members I had met previously impressed me deeply with their left-libertarian philosophy, puritanical morality, job bravery, and devotion to rank-and-file unionism. Tom's account of transforming a potbellied stove into a hobo jungle campfire fueled my imagination. Presiding at the stove, he provided loaves and fishes for the hungry as his anecdotal gifts bonded "hall cats" into a purposeful association.

As a neophyte unionist, I had the good fortune to join a local spanning an ideological rainbow. In 1934, Harry Bridges had emerged as a radical longshore leader and, for many workers, a champion of class struggle. Ever dissident, the Clydeside immigrants in Local 1149 viewed Bridges not as a hero but rather as a misguided Muscovite. Carwardine and McIvor, particularly, linked Scottish nationalism, independent socialism, and radical Calvinism into a coherent whole. At that time, with my limited knowledge of international labor history, I assumed that Spokane Tom shared some of these perspectives, perhaps derived from James Connolly.

From the first union meetings I attended, I sensed equal suspicion of communist functionaries and of craft leaders on the right. Our shipwrights identified Reds by their Aesopian jargon and AFL politicos by their natty "duds." Scornful Clydesiders branded craft tycoons as "labor fakirs," "corrupt pie cards," and "sell-out artists." Following the 1934 maritime strike, Ben Carwardine, along with other metal tradesmen, had organized a fledgling Local 7 of the Industrial Union of Marine & Shipbuilding Workers. These rebels fought craft privilege and Stalinist dogma as twin evils.

Crushed by the yard owners, AFL leaders, and the rising power of communist cadres, industrial unionists in Bay Area shipyards failed, but Ben's vision animated Local 1149 for a decade. Within our local, young shipwrights became conscious of his role in articulating the call for a broad union for all shipbuilders. We mourned the CIO's lost effort to spark a horizontal base in our shipyards; nevertheless, our local remained a democratic bastion. No singular tenet, no totalitarian line dominated our assembly.

After joining the navy, I never again saw Spokane Tom. Returning to waterfront work at the war's end, I found that Local 1149 had abandoned its Steuart Street hall in favor of a then-splendid building at the foot of California Street. Old-timers, uncomfortable in the posh headquarters, drifted away. Death also thinned our ranks. The decline in postwar shipbuilding and repairs decimated membership. Nothing in our cosmos had prepared us for the devastating shift in U.S. ship construction from domestic to Asian ports. I have already noted my personal move from maritime work to laborlore exploration.

Within the pursuit of workers' vernacularity, I immersed myself in stories, songs, and speech that had come to me on learning my trade. Seeking examples of *pile butt,* I canvassed old friends. During 1983, Frank Gallegos gave me a small collection of Local 34 ephemera: election slate cards, by-laws, contracts, stewards' manuals, meeting minutes. Among these treasures, I found several copies of *Pile Butt Special,* a one-page mimeographed bulletin. The issue for June 6, 1946, carried an obituary: "Brother Tom Cain, a member of Local #1149 but for many years of Local #34, passed away in the San Francisco Hospital, Tuesday June 4th. Funeral announcement later. Brother Cain was a member of old #77 and was intimately familiar with the history of #77 and #34 and delighted in recounting incidents and strange characters that came and went."

This brief paragraph—read thirty-seven years after its printing—startled me, pulling Spokane Tom out of my memory's long shadows. I could not recall that anyone in Local 1149 had commented on his death. Most disturbing, I found no precise way to verify that the Spokane Tom in my memory was the same Tom Cain whose obituary appeared in *Pile Butt Special.* This perfect tribute, that [he] "delighted in recounting incidents and strange characters that came and went," memorialized a carrier of labor tradition.

Pile Drivers Local 34's mimeographed bulletin also carried a burden, impelling me to fill out Tom's story. A first chance came on April 24, 1987, when I delivered the Archer Taylor Memorial Lecture at UCLA. Recounting one of Tom's trickster tales set in the Sierra Nevada's Mother Lode country, I urged students to seek their own workplace teachers, their respective Spokane Toms. (My initial comments on Tom appeared in *Western Folklore* [1987].)

How does one reconstruct a worker's life without a paper trail? Strangely, the minutes for the shipwrights local held no memorial for Cain. Our membership cards for the years prior to contractual benefit plans had carelessly been discarded. To add concern, I could locate no death notice for Tom Cain at the San Francisco Board of Public Health.

Had Cain died a pauper? Had his remains been carted to potter's field? Could Tom have been hospitalized under a different name? Sharing these concerns with Michael Munoz, activist and historian in Pile Local 34, I appealed for help. On checking the minutes for June 7, 1946, Mike found: "The meeting stood in silence for one minute in respect to the memories of our late Brother R. M. (Dick) Elton and Brother Wm. Cain, a member of #1149, but a longtime member of old #77 and #34."

Local 34's official minutes provided the vital clue. Wm. Cain's nickname must have been Spokane Tom. The unsigned obituary in the mimeographed bulletin had referred to Tom familiarly, while Local 34's secretary preparing the meeting minutes fell back upon William, the given name. Returning to the public health office where I had previously failed to find Tom Cain's death certificate, I obtained one for William Henry Cain dated June 4, 1946.

The certificate confirmed the notice in *Pile Butt Special* and added details: born in Ontario, Canada, December 7, 1870; father, Patrick Cain, born in Ireland; mother, Catherine Lyons, born in Canada; W. H. Cain's wife Myrtle survived him at 145 Henry Street; Cain had lived in San Francisco for fifty years; Cain's occupation, carpenter; place of work, the San Francisco waterfront; social security number 561–01–3042.

At the Washington, D.C., headquarters of the United Brotherhood of Carpenters & Joiners of America, John Rogers and his staff unearthed other details. In the decades between 1870 and 1900, San Francisco pile drivers had formed various independent associations. On May Day, 1901, Samuel Gompers granted a direct AFL charter to the Pile Drivers Local 9078. On May 21, 1904, this unit affiliated with the International Association of Bridge, Structural and Ornamental Iron Workers Local 77. In 1920, the UBCJA asserted jurisdiction over pile men, rechartering "old 77" as Local 34.

Rogers also found an early roster that included W. H. Cain's initiation in January, 1904, carrying his membership back some months before Local 77 replaced its independent predecessor. A few other facts emerged from UBCJA files. After 1920, Cain briefly cleared into and out of various "uptown" locals, probably pursuing "wood-butcher" jobs as waterfront work ebbed, always returning home to Local 34. In the slough of hard times, he fell into dues arrears; Local 34 suspended Cain from membership in September 1933. I can only speculate at this lapse: illness, joblessness, a dispute with someone in the pile trade, the depressing sense that his working life had ended.

As Depression clouds lifted, Cain, then nearly sixty-six years of age, reaffiliated on October 20, 1936, as an honorary member in San Francisco's Carpenters Local 22. I do not know whether he actually worked under 22's jurisdiction or whether sentiment alone had pulled him back to unionism. His application in 1936 indicated that he was unmarried and living at 165 Third Street, an area then known as "skid road." Apparently, waterfront leprechauns tugged at Cain's heart, for, after a short time in Local 22, he transferred to Local 1149.

These dates and local numbers must seem esoteric, if not incomprehensible, to outsiders. Nevertheless, they are the only blazes I have found on Spokane Tom's trail, 1870–1946. With such factual material at hand in 1989, I rephrased a set of questions that might transform this detail into insight. When and where did Cain learn his trade? Did his nickname imply residence in Spokane en route from Ontario to San Francisco? What led him to unionism in 1904? What was his very last job? Unmarried in 1936, when did he leave bachelorhood behind?

Such questions are endless. Perhaps Clio will yet provide a few answers. Cain's death certificate listed Duggan's Funeral Parlor and the Cypress Lawn Memorial Park. My trip to Duggan's, near Mission Dolores, proved rewarding. In 1946, Cain's widow, Myrtle, had called for no church service; Cypress Lawn is not a Catholic cemetery. Could Cain have been Protestant, or, more likely, a freethinker? Duggan's had prepared a newspaper notice for Cain that confirmed his final membership in Local 1149. It also listed six brothers and sisters: James C., John P., Frank, Sarah Card, Mary Keating, Catherine Doyle. New questions surfaced.

Did Cain's siblings live in Canada, California, or points between? Where do their children now reside? Do any nieces or nephews hold memories of their waterfront uncle?

I return to my first impressions of Spokane Tom, those formed in 1942. Then, I had assumed his Wobbly membership; I knew him to be a superb tale taller. In retrospect, I have found no evidence of his participation in the IWW. Nevertheless, I remain unshaken in my recollection of his creativity. I know of only one other shipwright still alive, Don Jeffrey, the son of a Clydesider, who also remembers Tom as our craft's storyteller. Is there anyone else alive who fell under Tom's spell?

Jeffrey, whose years in our trade go back to 1938, helped me pose a Chinese-box puzzle. When I met Tom, his stew pot anecdote had impressed me as an act of quintessential brotherhood. His narrative towers in my memory. I did not read it; no one else related it. Yet stubborn facts intrude. To begin: during the months of the 1934 Big Strike, William Henry Cain had let his union membership lapse. If indeed he presided at Local 1149's soup kitchen, I must assume that he remained loyal to labor throughout tough times and "hung out" in the hall with other hand-to-mouth members then barely meeting dues requirements.

Shipwrights had not moved to their Steuart Street hall until 1939. However, our sister Caulkers Local 554 had occupied 113 Steuart throughout the '34 strike. Tom could have cooked stew in the caulkers hall. Whether I misheard or conflated his story elements, I do not know. Clearly, no one can now demonstrate that Tom actually fed hungry workers anyplace on the waterfront. Still, I take no pleasure in casting doubt on an account that functioned so strongly in shaping my sense of workers' tradition.

Spokane Tom personified union values, and ultimately, he helped lead me to laborlore study. After all these years, his brogue still resonates. I continue to picture him dishing out stew on Steuart Street. He lives for me as emblematic of the many rank-and-filers who gave spirit to the Big Strike. Tom never boasted of leadership on a local committee; he planned no grand strategy; he brought no brilliant political credo to his fellows.

Folklorists know that many narratives hold intense meaning regardless of their historicity. Tom may have exaggerated his presence in the Big Strike; unconsciously, I may have enlarged his account. Regardless, he lives for me poised at the union hall stove—with free dunnage firewood—ladling stew fixings for the asking. Within this frame of retrieval, he served as one of my teachers alongside the Klamath River's Lawrence Roberts, the Clyde's Ben Carwardine, and Berkeley's distinguished professors.

Tom had passed his seventy-first birthday when we met. I pen these recollections at the age of seventy-four. As a folklorist, I am conscious that I help bridge time. Cain, frozen in iconic time, can represent the unsung advocates found within every American union, as well as on jobs where organizations either have not taken root or have decayed.

Perhaps Brother Cain belongs to the legion of anonymous builders of monuments for mighty rulers. However, I refuse to accept his anonymity. Rather, I assert that he personifies all workers who tie craft history to job mystery, who fashion toil into expressive delight. Surely, the bard memorialized in an ephemeral union bulletin—"recounting incidents and strange characters that came and went"—lives in the piles he drove, piers he capped, docks he decked, boats he patched, and ships he launched. Where else can he live? As if to defy both biography and history, Cain's Cypress Lawn grave lacks a stone marker. Grass is his final cover.

I feel it important to honor a long-forgotten pile driver–shipwright born in 1870. Many workers today grip dead-end tasks in the economy's tombs: shuttered mills, stagnant mines, padlocked plants. Others face toxic danger carried by wind and water. Some are deskilled and dehumanized by the very forces from which they wring a living. Some cling to old slogans that promised pots of gold. A few workers continue to envision bright futures.

Although no powerful elixir spilled from Spokane Tom's stew pot of 1934, the recollection of his feeding-the-hungry story surfaces as I close my book's cultural explorations. William Henry Cain provides a metaphor for problems integral to laborlore study. Most traces of his adventures have disappeared. A serendipitous find and helpful friends have combined to unearth a few shards but not to suggest finality. I think Tom would have enjoyed commenting on the elusive and fragmentary nature of folkloric explication. He served dually as a carrier of oral traditions and as a figurative beam in the heritage manse erected by his waterfront companions.

I would like my book's recollections and research to aid young workers who will eventually cast their own identities in timber, metal, glass, and stone. In this sense, techniques and tools merge into essential humanity. Torch and chisel, saw and hammer, and pick and shovel give way to laser beam and computer chip, but unending toil continues. The freshest apprentices at present ship-launching ways or rocket pads need only to look over their shoulders to encounter friendly bards casting spells.

My past work in Siskiyou road building and San Francisco ship building helps me inscribe a few letters, not in Cain's headstone, but in this personal essay. Pulling his story from my memory's recesses serves both as a substitute monument for him and as a marker for the unseen roads of others. Workers will continue to encrust experience, to externalize belief, and to create vernacular texts while building docks, spinning cotton, mucking ore, and performing endless varied tasks. Under the term *laborlore* or parallel rubrics, Spokane Tom's successors will take up their burdens in deciphering work's meaning and in affirming workers' affinities.

**A folk carver's John Henry**

# References

This reference list holds citations to material quoted directly or paraphrased throughout my book. The list brings together books, journals, sound recordings, films, correspondence, interviews, and ephemera. Notwithstanding such breadth, I do not reference every item alluded to in the preceding pages. For example, *Moby Dick* appears in the text but is not cited among the references.

Although the dividing line between the material included and that excluded is arbitrary, I have provided readers with checks to specific sources. We lack, and need, a comprehensive bibliography covering the intertwined areas of laborlore, occupational folklife, and workers' culture. Perhaps my book will stimulate the compilation of such a listing. Finally, I reiterate a point made in the acknowledgments: my reference list serves also as this compiler's "thank you" to those who walked before.


Aaron, Daniel. 1952. *America in Crisis.* New York: Knopf.

———. 1961. *Writers on the Left.* New York: Harcourt, Brace & World.

Abell, Westcott. 1948. *The Shipwright's Trade.* Cambridge: Cambridge University Press.

Abrahams, Roger, et al. 1985. *By Land and by Sea.* Hatboro, Pa.: Legacy.

Adamic, Louis. 1931. *Dynamite.* New York: Viking.

Adams, Ed. 1978. "Grandpa Walton Laughs Last." New Albany, Ind. Unpublished memorial in author's file.

Adams, Ramon. 1968. *Western Words.* Rev. ed. Norman: University of Oklahoma Press.

Ade, George. 1894. [" 'Stumpy' and Other Interesting People."] *Chicago Record,* March 17. First printing of Ade's original sketch appeared untitled in his daily column. The newspaper reprinted it, April 1, in a paperback, *Stories of the Streets and the Town* (first series).

Franklin J. Meine, 1941, titled the sketch when he reprinted it in Ade's *Chicago Stories* (Chicago: Caxton Club). Book reprinted, 1963. Chicago: Regnery.

———. 1902. "What Father Bumped Into at the Culture Factory." *Indianapolis Journal,* October 19. Fable reprinted, 1903, in Ade's book *People You Know.* New York: Russell.

Adler, Nathan. 1992. Interview with author, San Francisco, March 3.

Albion, Robert. 1939. *The Rise of New York Port.* New York: Scribner's.

Alford, B. W. E., and T. C. Barker. 1969. *History of the Carpenters Company.* London: Allen and Unwin.

Allan, James. 1941–43. Conversations with author, San Francisco.

Allen, E. J. B. 1909. *Revolutionary Unionism.* London: Industrialist League.

Allen, Reuben. 1953. "The Homestead Song." Collected by Anne Grimes. Tape at Library of Congress.

Allsop, Kenneth. 1967. *Hard Travelin'.* London: Hodder & Stoughton.

Alney, Russell. 1982. Interview with author, New Orleans, June 7.

"A Man Named Carnegie." 1892. *National Labor Tribune,* July 30.

Ancelet, Barry Jean. 1990. Letter to author, December 4.

Anderson, Carl. 1983. Interview with author, San Francisco, February 27.

Anderson, Henry. 1991. Letter to author, May 1.

Anderson, Nels. [Dean Stiff, pseud.] 1931. *The Milk and Honey Route.* New York: Vanguard.

*Anglo-Saxon Chronicle. See* Earle, Garmonsway, Giles, Rositzke, Savage, Thorpe, Whitelock.

Annandale, Charles. 1882–83. *The Imperial Dictionary of the English Language.* Augmented four-volume edition drawn from John Ogilvie's *Comprehensive English Dictionary.* London: Blackie & Son.

Appel, Benjamin. 1939. *The Power-House.* New York: Dutton.

Applebaum, Herbert. 1981. *Royal Blue: The Culture of Construction Workers.* New York: Holt, Rinehart & Winston.

Arbolino, Jack. 1942. "Navy Yard Talk." *American Speech* 17: 279–80.

Archibald, Katherine. 1947. *Wartime Shipyard.* Berkeley: University of California Press.

Ardery, Julia. 1983. "Editor's Introduction." In Garland, *Welcome the Traveler Home,* xxxi–xxxvii.

Atkinson, Brooks. 1935. "The Play: 'Let Freedom Ring,' Being a Magic Drama about the Fortunes of Labor in Cotton Mills." *New York Times,* November 7.

———. 1940a. "The Play: John Garfield and Aline MacMahon Appearing in Albert Bein's 'Heavenly Express.'" *New York Times,* April 19.

———. 1940b. "Hobo Heaven: Albert Bein's Fantasy Is Acted with Enthusiasm and Originality." *New York Times,* April 28.

Auerbach, Jerold. 1966. *Labor and Liberty.* Indianapolis: Bobbs-Merrill.

Averich, Paul. 1984. *The Haymarket Tragedy.* Princeton: Princeton University Press.

Bacon, Emory. 1959. Interview with author, Madison, Wis., November 18.

Bailey, James. 1977. Letter to author, May 31.

Bailey, Loretto C., and James Bailey. 1931. "Strike Song: A Play of Southern Mill People." Unpublished typescript in University of North Carolina Library.

Bain, Robert, et al. 1979. *Southern Writers: A Biographical Dictionary.* Baton Rouge: Louisiana State University Press.

Baker, Mary Roys. 1973. "Anglo-Massachusetts Trade Union Roots, 1130–1790." *Labor History* 14: 352–96.

Bales, Allen. 1990. Letter to Joey Brackner, April 9.

*Baltimore Sun.* 1900. "Coal Miners' Strike." April 12.

Banc, C., and A. Dundes. 1986. *First Prize: Fifteen Years! An Annotated Collection of Romanian Political Jokes.* Rutherford, N.J.: Fairleigh Dickinson University Press.

Bancroft, Caroline. 1945. "Folklore of the Central City District, Colorado." *California Folklore Quarterly* 4: 315–42.

Banik, Joseph. 1957. "The Homestead Steel Strike of 1892." Five-part series. *Homestead Daily Messenger,* August 6–10.

Banks, Ann. 1980. *First Person America.* New York: Knopf.

Barnes, Charles. 1915. *The Longshoremen.* New York: Survey.

Barnett, Eugene. 1961. Interview with author, Spokane, June 5.

Barry, John D. 1914. "Ways of the World: In Marysville." *San Francisco Bulletin,* February 3, 4.

*BC&T News.* 1986. "Look for the BCT Label." February.

Beal, Fred. 1937. *Proletarian Journey.* New York: Hillman-Curl.

Becker, Fred. 1978–79. Telephone interviews with author, November 27, January 29, June 5.

———. 1979. Interview with Barry O'Connell, Amherst, Mass. July 9. Tapes in author's possession.

Bede. *See* Colgrave, Giles, Stevenson.

Bein, Albert. 1935. "Of 'Let Freedom Ring.'" *New York Times,* December 1.

———. 1936a. *Let Freedom Ring.* New York: Samuel French.

———. 1936b. "From the Drama Mailbag." [Response to Larkin and Miner on *Let Freedom Ring.*] *New York Times,* November 29.

———. 1977. Letter to author, July 4.

Bell, Alexander. 1969. *An Anglo-Norman Brut.* Oxford: Blackwell.

Bell, George. 1914. "The Wheatland Hop-Fields Riot." *Outlook* 107 (May 16): 118–23.

Bemis, Edward. 1888. "Mine Labor in the Hocking Valley." *Publications of the American Economic Association* 3: 27–42.

———. 1894. "The Homestead Strike." *Journal of Political Economy* 2: 369–96.

Benjamin, Steven, and Renate Benjamin. 1980. "Origin of American English Fink." *Comments on Etymology* 9 (15): 10–11.

Berkeley, Roy. 1977a. *Roy Berkeley with Tim Woodbridge.* Innisfree/Green Linnet Records 1007 (New Canaan, Conn.).

———. 1977b. Letter to author, April 4.

Berrey, Lester, and Melvin Van Den Bark. 1953. *The American Thesaurus of Slang.* 2d ed. New York: Crowell.

Berson, Misha. 1987. "Fingerprints on Steel." *San Francisco Examiner, Image,* May 10.

*Billy Moore, Chesapeake Boatbuilder.* 1980. [30-minute, 16-mm color film.] Newport News: Mariners' Museum.

Bimba, Anthony. 1927. *The History of the American Working Class.* New York: International.

Bird, Stewart, et al. 1985. *Solidarity Forever: An Oral History of the IWW.* Chicago: Lakeview.

Bishop, Mrs. L. E. *See* Swetnam.

Biskind, Peter. "The Politics of Power in 'On the Waterfront.'" *Film Quarterly* 29 (Fall): 25–38.

Blackard, Malcolm. 1969. "Wilmer Watts and the Lonely Eagles." *JEMF Quarterly* 5: 126–39.

Blakely, Scott. 1986. "He Built Them All, Large and Small." *San Francisco Chronicle,* November 4.

Blitzstein, Madelin. 1936. "Sketches from Life: The Playwright Who Served an Apprenticeship in the Penitentiary." *St. Louis Post Dispatch, Sunday Magazine,* February 16.

Blochinger, A. J. 1892a. "Homestead Strike." [Sheet music (location unknown).] Homestead: Author. Composite text in Swetnam, 1967, and letter to Swetnam from Hazel Durstine, in author's files.

———. 1892b. *Homestead Budget No. 1.* Homestead: Author.

———. 1892c. *Homestead Budget No. 2.* Homestead: Author.

Bogard, Tom. 1960. Interview with author, San Francisco, August 16.

Bolinger, D. W. 1939. Item on fink. In Tamony files, Western Historical Manuscript Collection, University of Missouri.

Bonbright, Stephe. 1892. "Stand by the Workmen at Homestead." [Sheet music.] Cincinnati: Home Music.

Boone, Lalia. 1952. *The Petroleum Dictionary.* Norman: University of Oklahoma Press.

Boroff, David. 1962. "Showdown on Fraternity Row." *New York Times Magazine,* November 11.

Bosworth, Joseph. 1898. *An Anglo-Saxon Dictionary.* Edited and enlarged by T. N. Toller. London: Milford.

Botkin, Benjamin. 1944. *A Treasury of American Folklore.* New York: Crown.

———. 1949. "Industrial Lore." In Leach, *Standard Dictionary,* 521–22.

———. 1954. *Sidewalks of America.* Indianapolis: Bobbs-Merrill.

Bowen, Frank. 1929. *Sea Slang.* London: Sampson Low, Marston.

Boyden, Richard. 1988. "The San Francisco Machinists from Depression to Cold War, 1930–1950." Ph.D. diss., University of California, Berkeley.

Brackner, Joey. 1990. Letter to author, April 16.

Bradford, Roark. 1931. *John Henry.* New York: Harper.

———. 1939. *John Henry* [play]. New York: Harper.

Bradley, Francis. 1961a. "Carolina Folklore." [South Carolina] *State and Columbia Record,* February 19.

———. 1961b. "A North Carolina Factory Rhyme." *North Carolina Folklore* 9 (December): 29–31.

Brande, W. T. 1842. *A Dictionary of Science, Literature and Art.* London: Longman.

Braun, Emily. 1985. *Thomas Hart Benton: The America Today Murals.* New York: Equitable.

Brazier, Richard. 1960. Interview with author, New York, December 31.

Bridge, James. 1903. *The Inside History of the Carnegie Company.* New York: Aldine.

Brier, Stephen. 1988. "A History Film without Much History." *Radical History* 41: 120–28.

Brissenden, Paul. 1913. *The Launching of the Industrial Workers of the World.* Berkeley: University of California Publications in Economics.

———. 1919. *The I.W.W.: A Study in American Syndicalism.* New York: Columbia University Studies in History, Economics and Public Law.

———. 1920. "The Butte Miners and the Rustling Card." *American Economic Review* 10: 755–75.

———. 1960. Letter to author, January 12.

Brody, David. 1960. *Steelworkers in America*. Cambridge: Harvard University Press.

Broven, John. 1983. *South to Louisiana: The Music of the Cajun Bayous*. Gretna, La.: Pelican.

Brown, Deming. 1962. *Soviet Attitudes toward American Writing*. Princeton: Princeton University Press.

Brown, Elizabeth, et al. 1980. *Benton's Benton*. Lawrence: University of Kansas, Spencer Museum of Art.

Brown, Frank C. 1952–64. *The Frank C. Brown Collection of North Carolina Folklore*. 7 vols. Durham, N.C.: Duke University Press.

Brown, Geoff. 1977. *Sabotage: A Study in Industrial Conflict*. Nottingham: Spokesman.

Brown, Ronald. 1979. *Hard-Rock Miners*. College Station: Texas A & M University Press.

Browne, Waldo. 1921. *What's What in the Labor Movement*. New York: Huebsch.

Bubka, Tony. 1965–68. Correspondence with author.

———. 1965–69. Correspondence with Peter Tamony.

———. 1966. "Jack London's Definition of a Scab." *American Book Collector* 17 (November): 23–26.

———. 1968. "Time to Organize!: The IWW Stickerettes." *American West* 5 (January): 21–26.

Buhle, Mari Jo, et al. 1990. *The Encyclopedia of the American Left*. New York: Garland.

Bulmer, Martin. 1975. *Working Class Images of Society*. London: Routledge & Kegan Paul.

Burgoyne, Arthur. 1893. *Homestead*. Pittsburgh: Rawsthorne Engraving. Reprinted in 1979 as *The Homestead Strike of 1892*. Afterword by David Demarest. Pittsburgh: University of Pittsburgh Press.

Burke, William Allen. 1943. *See* WPA Writers' Program, *Copper Camp*.

———. 1964. *Rhymes of the Mines*. Vancouver, Wash.: Lowden.

Burt, Olive Wooley. 1958a. *American Murder Ballads*. New York: Oxford University Press.

———. 1958b. Letter to author, November 14.

*Butte Evening News*. *See* WPA Writers' Program, *Copper Camp*.

Caen, Herb. 1986. "Sunday Shortline." *San Francisco Chronicle, Sunday Punch*, September 14.

———. 1988. "Hello Out There." *San Francisco Chronicle*, April 6.

Caesar. *See* Edwards, Holmes, Wiseman.

Cage, R. A. 1987. *The Working Class in Glasgow 1750–1914*. London: Croom Helm.

Calagione, John, et al. 1992. *Workers Expressions*. Ithaca: State University of New York Press.

"California *v.* Richard Ford." 1914. [Unpublished trial typescript bound in four volumes.] Marysville, Calif. Held in Bancroft Library, University of California, Berkeley.

Calkins, Clinch. 1937. *Spy Overhead*. New York: Harcourt, Brace.

Calmer, Alan. 1934. "The Wobbly in American Literature." *New Masses* 12 (September 18): 21–22.

Calvert, Jerry. 1988. *The Gibralter: Socialism and Labor in Butte, Montana, 1895–1920*. Helena: Montana Historical Society Press.

Camp, Charles. 1989. *Time and Temperature*. Washington, D.C.: American Folklore Society.

Camp, William. 1947. *San Francisco, Port of Gold*. Garden City, N.Y.: Doubleday.

Campbell, Mary, et al. 1987. *Harlem Renaissance Art of Black America*. New York. Abrams.

Campbell, Russell, and Tony Safford. 1977. "Radical Cinema in the 30s: Film and Photo League." *Jump Cut* 14 (March 30): 23–33.

Cannon, Hal. 1989. "Folklorists and Cowboy Poetry." In Camp, *Time & Temperature*, 69–71.

Cantwell, Robert. 1932. "Effective Propaganda." *Nation* 135 (October 19): 372–73.

Carmer, Carl. 1932. "Adventures in Playmaking." *Theatre Arts Monthly* 16 (July): 529–45.

*Carpenter*. 1883. "Daniel Hurley." January 3.

———. *See also* Sheldon.

Carson, Arthur. 1965. *Foundation Construction*. New York: McGraw-Hill.

Cash, Joseph. 1973. *Working the Homestake*. Ames: Iowa State University Press.

Cash, Wilbur J. 1941. *The Mind of the South*. New York: Knopf.

Cassady, Stephen. 1979. *Spanning the Gate*. Mill Valley, Calif.: Squarebooks.

Cassidy, Frederick. 1983. "Fink." *Comments on Etymology* 12 (15): 15–6.

———. 1985. *A Dictionary of American Regional English*. Vol. 1. Cambridge: Belknap. Others forthcoming.

Cayton, Horace, and George Mitchell. 1939. *Black Workers and the New Unions*. Chapel Hill: University of North Carolina Press.

Challinor, Raymond. 1977. *The Origins of British Bolshevism*. London: Croom Helm.

Chambers, Whittaker. 1952. *Witness*. New York: Random House.

Chaplin, Ralph. 1948. *Wobbly*. Chicago: University of Chicago Press.

Chappell, Louis. 1933. *John Henry: A Folk-Lore Study.* Jena: Frommannsche Verlag.

Chellis, Robert. 1951. *Pile Foundations.* New York: McGraw-Hill.

Churchill, Thomas. 1980. *Centralia Dead March.* Willimantic, Conn.: Curbstone.

Clarke, John, et al. 1980. *Working-Class Culture.* New York: St. Martin's Press.

[Cochran, Bert]. 1954. "Founding of the Socialist Union." *American Socialist* 1 (January): 3.

Coe, Robert. 1974. *The History of Wheatland.* Wheatland, Calif.: Wheatland Historical Society.

Coffin, Tristram P. 1965. Interview with author, Philadelphia, November 10.

Cohen, Gerald. 1979. "Fink." *Comments on Etymology* 9 (1): 4–5.

———. 1988. "Comments on Fink." *Comments on Etymology* 18 (3): 1–2.

Cohen, Norm. 1974. Brochure notes for *Paramount Old Time Tunes.* JEMF Records 103 (Los Angeles).

———. 1981. *Long Steel Rail.* Urbana: University of Illinois Press.

———. 1965–92. Correspondence and conversations with author.

Cohen, Steven. 1981. "Steelworkers Rethink the Homestead Strike of 1892." *Pennsylvania History* 48: 155–77.

Coleman, McAlister. 1943. *Men and Coal.* New York: Farrar & Rhinehart.

Colgrave, Bertram, and R. Mynors. 1969. *Bede's Ecclesiastical History of the English People.* Oxford: Clarendon.

*Columbia State.* 1980. "Miss Grace Lumpkin, Southern Author, Dies." March 24.

Commons, John, et al. 1918–35. *History of Labour in the United States.* New York: Macmillan.

Compton, Ben. 1938. " 'Grandpap' Takes a Bride." *Daily Worker,* October 14.

Condit, Carl. 1980. *Port of New York.* Chicago: University of Chicago Press.

Conlin, Joseph. 1969. *Bread and Roses, Too.* Westport, Conn.: Greenwood.

———. 1981. *At the Point of Production.* Westport, Conn.: Greenwood.

Conroy, Jack. 1933. *The Disinherited.* New York: Covici, Friede. Reprinted, 1991. Columbia: University of Missouri Press. Introduction by Douglas Wixson.

———. 1961. Conversations with author, Chicago.

———. 1985. *The Weed King and Other Stories.* Westport, Conn.: Lawrence Hill. Introduction by Douglas Wixson.

Conroy, Jack, and Ralph Cheyney. 1931. *Unrest.* New York: Harrison.

Cook, Sylvia. 1981. "Grace Lumpkin." In Mainiero, *American Women Writers,* vol. 4.

Cookson, Kathy. 1983. Letter to author, April 1.

Cooper, Patricia. 1987. *Once a Cigar Maker.* Urbana: University of Illinois Press.

Copland, Aaron, and Vivian Perlis. 1984. *Copland: 1909 through 1942.* New York: St. Martin's Press.

Cortez, Carlos. 1985. *Wobbly: 80 Years of Rebel Art.* Chicago: Gato Negro Press.

*The Counting Starts with One.* 1970. [Film.] Pittsburgh: United Steelworkers of America.

Couvares, Francis. 1984. *The Remaking of Pittsburgh.* Albany: State University of New York Press.

Cowley, Malcolm. 1980. *The Dream of the Golden Mountain.* New York: Viking.

Craigie, John. 1910. "The Professional Strike-Breaker." *Collier's* 46 (December 3): 20.

———. 1911. "The Violent Act of Strike-Breaking." *Collier's* 46 (January 7): 22.

Craigie, William. 1938–44. *A Dictionary of American English on Historical Principles.* 4 vols. Chicago: University of Chicago Press.

Crowther, Bosley. 1944. "The Screen: Biff! Bang!" *New York Times,* June 14.

Croy, Merle. 1958. Conversations with author, San Francisco.

Crump, Irving. 1917. *The Boy's Book of Mounted Police.* New York: Dodd, Mead.

Cuniberti, Betty. 1987. "Hot Flash." *Los Angeles Times,* September 23.

Cushman, Karen. 1983. "Jane Addams and the Labor Museum at Hull House." *Museum Studies Journal* 1 (Spring): 20–25.

D'Addesa, Frank. 1989. "Fink for Hire." [Minneapolis] *Twin Cities Reader,* August.

Daniel, Cletus. 1978. "In Defense of the Wheatland Wobblies." *Labor History* 19: 485–509.

Daugherty, James. 1936. *Their Weight in Wildcats: Tales of the Frontier.* Boston: Houghton Mifflin.

David, Henry. 1936. *The History of the Haymarket Affair.* New York: Farrar & Rhinehart.

———. 1952. "Upheaval at Homestead." In Aaron, *America in Crisis,* 133–70.

———. 1964. "Problems of Labor." In Lorant, *Pittsburgh,* 207–18.

Davis, Bob. 1990. Interview with author, Wilmington, Calif., December 10.

Davis, R. G. 1988. "Music from the Left." *Rethinking Marxism* 1 (winter): 7–25.

Delaney, William W. 1892a. "Father Was Killed by the Pinkerton Men." [Sheet music.] New York: Delaney.

———. 1892b. *Delaney's Song Book—No. 2.* New York: Delaney.

———. 1892c. *Delaney's Song Book—No. 3.* New York: Delaney.

Demarest, David. 1992. *"The River Ran Red": Homestead 1892.* Pittsburgh: University of Pittsburgh Press.

———. *See also* Burgoyne.

DeNatale, Doug. 1987. Letter to author, July 17.

———. 1993. *The Origins of Southern Mill Culture.* Chapel Hill: University of North Carolina Press.

Denisoff, R. Serge. 1971. *Great Day Coming.* Urbana: University of Illinois Press.

Desin, Fred. 1991. Interview with author, Tacoma, Wash., April 13.

[Detroit Federal Theatre]. 1937. *Production Bulletin, Let Freedom Ring* [Mimeograph.] Detroit: Federal Theatre.

Devine, Frederick. 1990. Interview with author, New York, February 28.

De Walsche, Kenny. 1990. Interview with author, Wilmington, Calif., December 10.

Dewhurst, Kurt, and Marsha MacDowell. 1980. *Cast in Clay.* East Lansing: The Museum, Michigan State University.

DiGirolamo, Vincent. 1988. "Families in the Field." Unpublished paper on Wheatland in author's file.

Diringer, Elliot. 1984. "A Dozen Unions March in Rodeo for Dead Striker." *San Francisco Chronicle,* January 26.

Dixon, Dorsey. 1964. *Babies in the Mill.* Testament Records 3301 (Chicago). With Howard Dixon and Nancy Dixon.

Dolker, Helmut. 1955. *Festschrift für Will-Erich Peuckert.* Berlin: Erich Schmidt.

Doree, E. F. 1915. "Gathering the Grain." *International Socialist Review* 15 (June): 740–43.

Dorson, Richard. 1948. "Dialect Stories of the Upper Peninsula." *Journal of American Folklore* 61: 113–50.

Dos Passos, John. 1930–36. *U.S.A. (The 42 Parallel; Nineteen Nineteen; The Big Money).* Boston: Houghton Mifflin.

———. 1961. *Mid-century.* Boston: Houghton Mifflin.

Downing, Mortimer. 1913. "The Case of the Hop Pickers." *International Socialist Review* 14 (October): 210–13.

———. 1914. "Bloody Wheatland." *Solidarity,* January 3.

———. 1923. "How 'Wobbly' Originated." *Nation* 117 (September 5): 242.

Doyle, Joe. 1993. "Arthur Max Langenegger, Dockworker." Forthcoming.

Dozema, Marianne. 1980. *American Realism and the Industrial Age.* Cleveland: Cleveland Museum of Art.

Draper, Theodore. 1971. "Gastonia Revisited." *Social Research* 38: 3–29.

Drew, John. 1985. *UAW Local 72: The First 50 Years.* Kenosha, Wis.: The Local.

Dubofsky, Melvyn. 1969. *We Shall Be All.* Chicago: Quadrangle.

[Duden]. 1963. *Der Grosse Duden: Etymologie.* Vol. 7. Manheim: Bibliographisches Institut.

Dueto, Reynosa. 1967. "Rinches de Texas." Oro 230 (45-rpm disc). Reissued on *Chulas Fronteras,* Arhoolie Records 3005 (El Cerrito, Calif.).

Duffy, John Dell. 1948. "The Homestake Strike." Collected by Wayland Hand. Tape at Library of Congress.

Duffy, Joseph H. 1937. "Poems." Helena: Montana Historical Society. Typescript collection gathered by Elizabeth MacDonald for the society.

———. 1941. *Butte Was Like That.* Butte, Mont.: Greenfield.

Dunaway, David. 1980. "Charles Seeger and Carl Sands: The Composers' Collective Years." *Ethnomusicology* 24: 159–68.

———. 1981. *How Can I Keep from Singing: Pete Seeger.* New York: McGraw-Hill.

Dunson, Josh. 1977. Headnote, "Let Them Wear Their Watches Fine." *Sing Out* 26 (July/August): 27.

Duranty, Walter. 1935. *I Write As I Please.* New York: Simon & Schuster.

Durstine, Hazel. *See* Blochinger.

Dyen, Doris. 1988–92. Correspondence and conversations with author.

Earle, John. 1865. *Two of the Saxon Chronicles Parallel.* Oxford: Clarendon.

Eastman, Phineas. 1913a. "Rosepine Rebels in Action." *Industrial Worker,* January 23.

———. 1913b. "The General Strike and the I.W.W. Convention." *Industrial Worker,* June 12.

Edwards, Herb. 1965. "Slowly We Learn: A Norwegian Wobbly in America's Northwest." Unpublished typescript at Charles Kerr Publisher, Chicago.

Edwards, H. J. 1917. *Caesar: The Gallic War.* Cambridge: Harvard University Press.

Edwards, Llewellyn. 1933. "The Evolution of Early American Bridges." *Transactions of the Newcomen Society* 13: 95–116.

Ellington, Richard. 1987. *"Wobbly"—80 Years of Rebel Art.* San Francisco: Labor Archives & Research Center, San Francisco State University.

*eM-Kayan* [Morrison-Knudsen Company magazine]. 1982. "Trestle Strides Seaward as Initial 'Platform' for Laying Big Outfall Pipe." (June): 10–13.

Emmons, David. 1989. *The Butte Irish.* Urbana: University of Illinois Press.

Emrich, Duncan. 1942. "Songs of the Western Miners." *California Folklore Quarterly* 1: 213–32.

Erikson, Kai, and Steven Vallas. 1990. *The Nature of Work: Sociological Perspectives.* New Haven: Yale University Press.

Erlich, Mark. 1986. *With Our Hands.* Philadelphia: Temple University Press.

Evanson, Jacob. 1949. "Folk Songs of an Industrial City." In Korson, *Pennsylvania Songs and Legends,* 423–66.

———. 1972. Interview with author, Pittsburgh, January 11.

Farmer, J. S., and W. E. Henley. 1890–1904. *Slang and Its Analogues.* 6 vols. London: Various printers. One-volume reprint, 1970. New York: Arno.

Farrell, James. 1935. "The Theater: 'Let Freedom Ring.' " *New Masses* 17 (November 19): 27–28.

Faulconer, J. E. 1969. "Hinton Around" *Hinton Daily News,* July 16.

———. 1972a. "The Long-Awaited John Henry Statue Is Finally Erected." *Hinton Daily News,* December 28.

———. 1972b. "Hinton Around" *Hinton Daily News,* December 29. See also front-page photos of statue on railroad flat car.

———. 1978. Telephone interview with author, June 13.

Feintuch, Bert. 1988. *The Conservation of Culture.* Lexington: University Press of Kentucky.

Ferrell, Geoffrey. 1982. "The Brotherhood of Timber Workers and the Southern Lumber Trust, 1910–1914." Ph.D. diss., University of Texas, Austin.

Fickle, James. 1981. "Race, Class, and Radicalism: The Wobblies in the Southern Lumber Industry, 1900–1916." In Conlin, *At the Point of Production,* 97–113.

Field, Richard. 1990. "Review of Marcus Rediker's *Between the Devil and the Deep Blue Sea.*" *Winterthur Portfolio* 25: 76–77.

Fielding, Mildred. 1970. *The Treasure of Homestake Gold.* Aberdeen, S.D.: North Plains.

Filigno, C. L. 1913a. "May Day As It May Be." *Industrial Worker,* May 1.

———. 1913b. "Philadelphia M.T.W. Still Winning." *Voice of the People,* October 16.

Fisher, Arthur. 1923. "Montana: Land of the Copper Collar." *Nation* 117 (September): 290–92.

Fitch, Jack. 1983. Interview with author, San Francisco, April 9.

Flanagan, Hallie. 1940. *Arena.* New York: Duell, Sloan and Pearce.

Flexner, Stuart Berg. 1982. *Listening to America.* New York: Simon & Schuster.

Flower, B. O. 1892. "The Menace of Plutocracy." *Arena* 6: 508–16.

Folkart, Burt. 1991. "Earl Robinson; Ballads Chronicled Labor Movement." *Los Angeles Times,* July 23.

Foner, Eric. 1978. "Class, Ethnicity, and Radicalism in the Gilded Age: The Land League and Irish-America." *Marxist Perspectives* 1: 6–55.

Foner, Philip. 1965. *History of the Labor Movement in the United States.* Vol. 4. New York: International.

———. 1975. *American Labor Songs of the Nineteenth Century.* Urbana: University of Illinois Press.

———. 1981. *Fellow Workers and Friends.* Westport, Conn.: Greenwood.

Fox, Robin Lane. 1973. *Alexander the Great.* London: A. Lane.

Frantz, Marge. 1974. Letter to author, July 23.

———. 1977. Interview with author, Santa Cruz, Calif., February 24.

Fraser, Douglas. 1985. Interview with Joe Glazer, Kenosha, Wis., May 11.

Fredericks, B. T. 1905. "James Farley, Strike-Breaker." *Leslie's Monthly Magazine* 60 (May 5): 106–10.

Friedman, Morris. 1907. *The Pinkerton Labor Spy.* New York: Wilshire.

Frommer, Harvey. 1979. *Sports Lingo.* New York: Atheneum.

Frost, Richard. 1968. *The Mooney Case.* Palo Alto: Stanford University Press.

Furnivall, Frederick. 1887. *The Story of England by Robert Manning of Brunne,* A.D. *1338.* London: Eyre & Spottiswoode.

Galenson, Walter. 1983. *The United Brotherhood of Carpenters.* Cambridge: Harvard University Press.

Gallegos, Frank. 1937–47. Ephemera from Pile Drivers Local 34. Held by Local 34, Oakland, Calif.

———. 1982. Interview with author, San Francisco, December 16.

Garland, Hamlin. 1894. "Homestead and Its Perilous Trades." *McClure's* 3 (June): 3–20.

Garland, Jim. 1983. *Welcome the Traveler Home.* Lexington: University Press of Kentucky.

Garmonsway, G. N. 1953. *The Anglo-Saxon Chronicle.* London: Dent.

Garst, John. 1973. Letter to author, March 9.

Gassner, John. 1935. "The Play's the Thing: Let Freedom Ring." *New Theatre* 2 (December): 11–13.

Geer, Will. 1938. "The Ballad of Wives and Widows of Presidents and Dictators." Library of Congress, Archive of Folk Song AFS 1769 A. Recorded by Alan Lomax and Kay Dealey, July 9, Washington, D.C.

———. 1977a. Interview with author, Topanga Canyon, Calif., March 27.

———. 1977b. Letter to author, June 13.

Geil, Jean. 1986. "Rossiter, Will." In *The New Grove Dictionary of American Music,* 97.

Gelders, Joseph. 1937. "Tom Girdler in Alabama." *Labor Defender* 11 (July): 8–9.

Gelders, Mr. and Mrs. Joe. 1937. "The Ballad of John Catchings." Library of Congress, Archive of Folk Song AFS 1947 B. Recorded by Alan Lomax, November 13, Washington, D.C.

Geller, James. 1931. *Famous Songs and Their Stories.* New York: Macaulay.

Geoffrey. *See* Griscom.

Georgakas, Dan. 1985. "The IWW Reconsidered." In Bird, *Solidarity Forever,* 1–18.

Georgakas, Dan, and Lenny Rubenstein. 1983. *The Cineaste Interviews.* Chicago: Lakeview Press.

Gerwick, Ben C., Jr. 1983. Interview with author, San Francisco, April 6.

Gianni, Gary. 1988. *John Henry.* New York: Kipling Press.

[Gibbons, Russell]. 1967. "Songs of a Strike." *Steel Labor* (March): 12.

Gilbert, Douglas. 1942. *Lost Chords.* New York: Doubleday.

Giles, J. A. 1848. *Six Old English Chronicles.* London. Bohn.

———. 1849. *The Venerable Bede's Ecclesiastical History of England: Also the Anglo-Saxon Chronicle.* 2d ed. London: Bohn.

Gilkes, Lillian. 1976. "Afterword." In Lumpkin, *The Wedding.*

Gill, Peter, [and Ottilie Markholt]. 1942. "The Sailors' Union of the Pacific from 1885 to 1929." Unpublished typescript. Held at Bancroft Library, University of California, Berkeley.

Gillmore, Inez Hayes. 1914. "The Marysville Strike." *Harper's Weekly* 59 (April 4): 18–20.

Ginger, Ray. 1949. *The Bending Cross.* New Brunswick, N.J.: Rutgers University Press.

Giovannitti, Arturo. *See* Pouget.

Giroux, Henry. 1980. "Norma Rae: Character, Culture and Class." *Jump Cut* 22 (May): 1, 7.

Glazer, Joe. 1955–92. Correspondence and conversations with author.

———. 1974. *Textile Voices.* Collector Records 1922 (Washington, D.C.).

———. 1978. *Songs of Steel & Struggle.* Collector Records 1930 (Washington, D.C.).

Glinn, Lillian. 1929. "Wobble It a Little, Daddy." Columbia 14617-D (78-rpm disc). Reissued on *Lillian Glinn,* Vintage Jazz Mart Records 31 (London).

Gold, David. 1983. "Preliminary Remarks on the Origin of the English Slangism Fink." *Comments on Etymology* 12 (9–10): 38–40.

Gold, Michael. 1933. "What a World." *Daily Worker,* October 19.

———. 1935. "Change the World." *Daily Worker,* November 12, December 5, December 10. Columns on Albert Bein's play.

———. 1938. "Change the World." *Daily Worker,* May 17. Column on Will Geer and Burl Ives.

Goldberg, Joseph. 1958. *The Maritime Story.* Cambridge: Harvard University Press.

Golden, Hyman. 1950. *Dictionary of American Underworld Lingo.* New York: Twayne.

Goldstein, Kenneth, and Robert Byington. 1966. *Two Penny Ballads and Four Dollar Whiskey.* Hatboro, Pa.: Folklore Associates.

Goldstein, Malcolm. 1974. *The Political Stage.* New York: Oxford University Press.

Gompers, Samuel. 1905. "Editorial: The Trade Unions to Be Smashed Again." *American Federationist* 12 (March): 139–41.

Gordon, Allan. 1988. *Echoes of Our Past: The Narrative Artistry of Palmer C. Hayden.* Los Angeles: Museum of African American Art.

Gorelik, Mordecai. 1935. [Scenes from *Let Freedom Ring;* photos from designer's models.] *New Theatre* 2 (October): 16–21.

Granger, Frank. 1931. *Vitruvius on Architecture.* Cambridge: Harvard University Press.

Grant, Jess. 1990a. "Western Workers Labor Heritage Festival." *Bay Branch Bulletin* [IWW, San Francisco], January.

———. 1990b. "Joe Hill Is Dead! Long Live the IWW! *Industrial Worker,* March.

Graves, Bennie. 1974. "Conflict and Work Force Stability in Pipeline Construction." *Urban Life and Culture* 2: 415–31.

———. 1988. Letter to author, September 16.

Green, Archie. 1960a. "John Neuhaus: Wobbly Folklorist." *Journal of American Folklore* 73: 189–217.

———. 1960b. "Dutchman: An on-the-Job Etymology." *American Speech* 35: 270–4.

———. 1965. "American Labor Lore: Its Meanings and Uses." *Industrial Relations* 4 (February): 51–68.

———. 1972. *Only a Miner.* Urbana: University of Illinois Press.
———. 1976. "Peter Tamony's Words." *JEMF Quarterly* 12: 202–11.
———. 1978a. "Industrial Lore: A Bibliographic-Semantic Query." *Western Folklore* 37: 213–44.
———. 1978b. "John Henry Depicted." *JEMF Quarterly* 14: 126–43.
———. 1979a. "Fred Becker's John Henry." *JEMF Quarterly* 15: 30–37.
———. 1979b. "A Folklorist's Creed and a Folksinger's Gift." *Appalachian Journal* 7: 37–45.
———. 1979c. "Charles Louis Seeger (1886–1979)." *Journal of American Folklore* 92: 391–99.
———. 1980. "Palmer Hayden's John Henry Series." *JEMF Quarterly* 16: 199–213.
———. 1983a. "John Henry Revisited." *JEMF Quarterly* 19: 12–31.
———. 1983b. "Afterword." In Reuss, *Songs of American Labor,* 95–107.
———. 1985. "Singlejack/Doublejack: Craft and Celebration." In Abrahams, *By Land and by Sea,* 95–111.
———. 1987. "At the Hall, in the Stope: Who Treasures Tales of Work." *Western Folklore* 46: 153–70.
———. 1988. "Fink, the Labor Connection." *Comments on Etymology* 17 (15): 1–28.
———. 1989. "Working with Laborlore." *Labor's Heritage* 1 (July): 66–75.
———. 1993. *Songs about Work: Papers for Richard A. Reuss* (forthcoming).
Green, James. 1973. "The Brotherhood of Timber Workers." *Past and Present* 60: 161–200.
Greenway, John. 1953. *American Folksongs of Protest.* Philadelphia: University of Pennsylvania Press.
Gresley, William. 1883. *A Glossary of Terms Used in Coal Mining.* London: Spon.
Grimes, Anne. 1957. *Ohio State Ballads.* Folkways Records 5217 (New York).
———. 1960. Interview with author, Columbus, Ohio, February 25.
Griscom, Acton. 1929. *The Historia Regum Britanniae of Geoffrey of Monmouth.* London: Longmans, Green.
Gronow, Pekka, et al. 1982. *Ethnic Recordings in America: A Neglected Heritage.* Washington, D.C.: Library of Congress, American Folklife Center.
Grossman, Jonathan. 1972. "Who Is the Father of Labor Day?" *Monthly Labor Review* 95 (September): 3–6.
Gunderson, Gwen. Transcription of Hayes interview at the Library for Social Studies and Research, Los Angeles.

Gupte, Pranay. 1978. "Will Geer Dies at 76 after Career as Character Actor for Six Decades." *New York Times,* April 24.

Gutman, Herbert. 1962. "Reconstruction in Ohio." *Labor History* 3: 243–64.

———. 1976. *Work, Culture and Society in Industrializing America.* New York: Knopf.

Haessly, Lynn. 1987. " 'Mill Mother's Lament': Ella May, Working Women's Militancy and the 1929 Gastonia County Strike." M.A. thesis, University of North Carolina, Chapel Hill.

Halker, Clark. 1991. *For Democracy, Workers, and God.* Urbana: University of Illinois Press.

Hall, Covington. 1912a. "Revolt of the Southern Timber Workers." *International Socialist Review* 13: 51–52.

———. 1912b. "I Am Here for Labor." *International Socialist Review* 13: 223–26.

———. 1912c. "Louisiana—A Rival to Despotic Russia." *Industrial Worker,* November 28.

———. 1912d. "The Victory of the Lumber Jacks." *International Socialist Review* 13: 470–71.

———. 1913. "With the Southern Timber Workers." *International Socialist Review* 14: 805–6.

———. 1923. "Why Is a Wobblie?" *Industrial Worker,* March 21.

Hall, Jacqueline. 1987. *Like a Family: The Making of a Southern Cotton Mill World.* Chapel Hill: University of North Carolina Press.

Halper, Albert. 1970. *Good-bye, Union Square.* Chicago: Quadrangle.

Hand, Wayland D. 1941. "Folklore from Utah's Silver Mining Camps." *Journal of American Folklore* 54: 132–61.

———. 1942a. "California Miners' Folklore: Above Ground." *California Folklore Quarterly* 1: 24–46.

———. 1942b. "California Miners' Folklore: Below Ground." *California Folklore Quarterly* 1: 127–53.

———. 1946a. "The Folklore, Customs, and Traditions of the Butte Miner." *California Folklore Quarterly* 5: 1–25.

———. 1946b. "The Folklore, Customs, and Traditions of the Butte Miner, Concluded." *California Folklore Quarterly* 5: 153–78.

———. 1950. "Songs of the Butte Miners." *Western Folklore* 9: 1–49.

———. 1957–86. Correspondence and conversations with author.

Harper, Roy. 1987. *I Like Mountain Music.* Old Homestead Records 80081 (Brighton, Mich.).

Harris, Leon. 1925. "The Steel-Driving Man." *Messenger* 7 (December): 386–87. Reprinted, 1957. *Phylon* 18: 402–6.

Harris, Randolph. 1988. "Homestead's Historic Landmarks: Are They History?" *Mill Hunk Herald* 20 (September): 44–45.

Harrison, Phyllis. 1989–92. Correspondence and conversations with author.

Harvey, Katherine. 1969. *The Best-Dressed Miners.* Ithaca, N.Y.: Cornell University Press.

Harzan, Joel. 1990. Interview with author, Wilmington, Calif., December 10.

Hauter, Paul. 1954. "The Locker." *Carpenter* 74 (August): 17–18.

Hawkins, John. 1942. "Man Working." *Collier's* 110 (September 12): 50–56.

Hawkins, John, and Ward Hawkins. 1943. *Pilebuck.* New York: E. P. Dutton. Also printed as "The Saboteurs." *Saturday Evening Post,* April 10 through May 22.

Hawkins, Ward. 1960. "Talk Big and Walk Tall." *Reader's Digest* 77 (November): 43–47.

Hawley, Lowell, and Ralph Potts. 1953. *Counsel for the Damned.* Philadelphia: Lippincott.

Hayden, Miriam. 1980. Letter to author, November 13.

Hayden, Palmer. 1947. "Foreword." In catalog, *The Ballad of John Henry.* New York: Argent Galleries.

Hayes, Alfred. 1934a. "In a Coffee Pot." *Partisan Review* 1 (February–March): 12–15; "To Otto Bauer." *Partisan Review* 1 (April–May): 10–11. Both poems reprinted in Hicks, *Proletarian Literature.*

———. 1934b. "Into the Streets May First." *New Masses* 11 (May 1): cover and 15–16.

———. 1935a. "Mother Bloor Cheers a Play." *Daily Worker,* November 5.

———. 1935b. "Paterson Strikers Get a Ballad." *Daily Worker,* November 26.

———. 1947. *Shadow of Heaven.* New York: Howell, Soskin.

———. 1982. Interview with Gwen Gunderson, Culver City, Calif., May 30.

Hayes, Gertrude. 1992. Letter to author, January 16.

Hayward, George. 1941–84. Conversations with author, San Francisco.

Hayward, Walter. 1924. "Songs of Their Day." [Buffalo, N.Y.] *Grosvenor Library Bulletin* 6 (June): 1–5.

Haywood, William D. 1912. "Timber Workers and Timber Wolves." *International Socialist Review* 13: 105–10.

———. 1929. *Bill Haywood's Book.* New York: International.

Healy Tibbitts. 1980. *Healy Tibbitts Construction Company.* [Illustrated booklet.] San Francisco: The company.

Heisley, Michael. 1983. "*Corridistas de la huelga:* Songmaking and Singing in the Lives of Two Individuals." Ph.D. diss., University of California, Los Angeles.

Hemmersam, Flemming. 1988. "Workers' Folklore and Worker Culture." *ARV: Scandinavian Yearbook of Folklore* 44: 50–102.

Hensen, Curt. 1970. "Sartori, August Anton Heinrich." In *Schleswig-Holsteinischen Biografischen Lexikon.*

Herling, John. 1971. *John Herling's Labor Letter.* May 1.

Hewett, Cecil. 1978. "Anglo-Saxon Carpentry." *Anglo-Saxon England* 7: 205–29.

HFR. 1987. "Zum Start brauchte er noch einen 'Strohmann.'" *Kieler Nachrichten,* June 6.

Hickerson, Joe. 1960–92. Correspondence and conversations with author.

Hicks, Granville, et al. 1935. *Proletarian Literature in the United States: An Anthology.* New York: International.

Hicks, Robert. 1930. "Doin' the Scraunch." Columbia 14591-D (78-rpm disc). Reissued on *Barbecue Bob,* Collector's Classics Records 36 (Sweden).

Hill, Richard. 1987. *Skywalkers: A History of Indian Ironworkers.* Brantford, Ontario: Woodland Indian Cultural Educational Centre.

Hills, Patricia. 1979. *The Working American.* Washington, D.C.: Smithsonian Institution.

Himelstein, Morgan. 1963. *Drama Was a Weapon.* New Brunswick, N.J.: Rutgers University Press.

Himes, Chester. 1945. *If He Hollers Let Him Go.* Garden City, N.J.: Doubleday, Doran.

Hinton, Sam. 1974. "Sam Eskin (1898–1974)." *Sing Out* 23 (September/October): 26.

Hirsch, Jerrold. 1988. "Cultural Pluralism and Applied Folklore: The New Deal Precedent." In Feintuch, *The Conservation of Culture,* 46–67.

Hodges, Ernest. 1971. Interview with author, Washington, D.C., July 3.

———. 1974. "Cole Creek March." Taped for Charles Wolfe. Text in Wolfe, *JEMF Quarterly.*

Hoerr, John. 1988. *And the Wolf Finally Came.* Pittsburgh: University of Pittsburgh Press.

Hogg, J. Bernard. 1943. "The Homestead Strike of 1892." Ph.D. diss., University of Chicago.

Hogue, Richard. *See* Downing 1923.

Holbrook, Stewart. 1926a. "Wobbly Talk." *American Mercury* 7 (January): 62–65.

———. 1926b. "Editorial Notes: Response to Lance." *American Mercury* 8 (June): xviii–xx.

———. 1931. "Bughouse Camp." *American Mercury* 22 (March): 347–52. Reprinted in 1948 in *Little Annie Oakley and Other Rugged People.* New York: Macmillan.

Hollander, Lee. 1962. *The Poetic Edda.* Austin: University of Texas Press.

Holliday, Walt (Rags). 1924. *Mining Camp Melodies.* Butte, Mont.: Author.

———. 1927. *Mining Camp Yarns.* Butte, Mont.: Author.

Holmes, T. Rice. 1907. *Ancient Britain and the Invasion of Julius Caesar.* Oxford: Clarendon.

———. 1911. *Caesar's Conquest of Gaul.* Oxford: Clarendon.

Holt, Alfred. 1936. *Phrase Origins.* New York: Crowell.

Holtzberg-Call, Maggie. 1992 *The Lost World of the Craft Printer.* Urbana: University of Illinois Press.

Home, Gordon. 1931. *Old London Bridge.* London: John Lane.

"Homestead Strike." Ca. 1893. Undated broadside from Sharon, Pa. Held at Brown University Library, Harris Collection.

Hooper, Johnson J. 1969. *Adventures of Captain Simon Suggs.* Chapel Hill: University of North Carolina Press. Facsimile reprint of 1845 edition.

Hoover, W. H. 1950. *Marcus Daly (1841–1900)—and His Contributions to Anaconda.* New York: Newcomen Society.

Hoppe, Arthur. 1986. "A New Fad—Democracy." *San Francisco Chronicle,* February 26.

Howard, Sidney. 1924. *The Labor Spy.* New York: New Republic.

Hubenthal, John, Jr., and Ken Hubenthal. 1990. Interview with Doris Dyen, Pittsburgh, July 25.

Hubenthal, Mrs. John, Jr. 1967. Letter to George Swetnam, February 7. In author's files.

Hugill, Stan. 1985. Interview with author, San Francisco, June 15.

Hunt, Hal W. 1982. Letter to author, June 21.

Huntley, Horace. 1977. "Iron Ore Miners and Mine Mill in Alabama: 1933–1952." Ph.D. diss., University of Pittsburgh.

Hurley. See *Irish World,* and *Carpenter.*

Hustvedt, Lloyd. 1985. "O. A. Tveitmoe: Labor Leader." *Norwegian-American Studies* 30: 3–54.

Hutchinson, John. 1970. *The Imperfect Union.* New York: Dutton.

Hyland, Douglas. 1980. "Benton's Images of American Labor." In Brown, *Benton's Benton,* 23–31.

*Independent.* 1916. "Sleeping fink." [Picture caption.] Vol. 87 (September 25): 454.

*Industrial Pioneer.* 1926. "Wobbles." [Humor page head.] April.

*Industrial Worker.* 1911. "A Few Thoughts by a Lumber Jack." May 25.

———. 1912a. "Craft Unionism Fails on Waterfront." October 10.

———. 1912b. "Doings of the Locals." October 10.

*International Socialist Review.* 1909a. "Free Speech Fight. Missoula, Mont., Oct. 3." Vol. 10: 466–67.

———. 1909b. "The Free Speech Fight at Spokane." Vol. 10: 483–89.

*Irish World.* 1882. "Daniel Hurley." December 23.

———. 1882–83. "News from All Parts of the United States." Various pages for items on Daniel Hurley Fund Association.

*Ironworker.* 1971. "Iron Workers Perform at Smithsonian Institution." Vol. 71 (August): 14–15.

Irwin, Godfrey. 1931. *American Tramp and Underworld Slang.* London: Partridge.

Ives, Edward. 1985. " 'The Teamster in Jack MacDonald's Crew.' " In Jabbour and Hardin, *Folklife Annual,* 74–85.

Jabbour, Alan, and James Hardin. 1985. *Folklife Annual 1985.* Washington, D.C.: Library of Congress, American Folklife Center.

Jack, T. A. 1937. "Dixon Hall Lewis." In *Dictionary of American Biography,* 11: 209–10.

Jackson, Louis. 1914. *A Vocabulary of Criminal Slang.* Portland, Ore.: Modern.

Jacob, Mary Jane, and Linda Downs. 1978. *The Rouge: The Image of Industry in the Art of Charles Sheeler and Diego Rivera.* Detroit: Detroit Institute of Arts.

Jacoby, Henry, and R. P. Davis. 1941. *Foundations of Bridges and Buildings.* New York: McGraw-Hill.

James, William. 1899. *Talks to Teachers on Psychology.* [First book printing of 1892 lecture, "What Makes a Life Significant." New York: Holt.

Jeffrey, Don. 1990. Interview with author, San Francisco, March 29.

Jensen, Vernon. 1950. *Heritage of Conflict.* Ithaca, N.Y.: Cornell University Press.

"Joe Hill." 1936. [Text and music.] *Daily Worker,* September 4.

*Joe Hill.* 1971. [Feature film edited and produced by Bo Widerberg.] Sagittarius Productions.

Johns, Orrick. 1934. "The John Reed Club Meets." *New Masses* 13 (October 30): 25–26.

Johnson, Alvin. 1916. "Andrew Furuseth." *New Republic* 9 (November 11): 40–42.

Johnson, Charles. 1927. *Ebony and Topaz.* New York: National Urban League.

Johnson, Guy. 1927. "John Henry—A Negro Legend." In Johnson, C. *Ebony and Topaz,* 47–51.

———. 1929. *John Henry: Tracking Down a Negro Legend.* Chapel Hill: University of North Carolina Press.

Johnson, Guy, and Guion Johnson. 1980. *Research in Service to Society.* Chapel Hill, University of North Carolina Press.

Johnson, Paula. 1988. *Working the Water.* Charlottesville. University Press of Virginia.

Jones, Michael Owen. 1984. "Introduction—Works of Art, Art as Work, and the Arts of Working." *Western Folklore* 43: 172–78.

Jordan, Cecil. 1984a. "The Agony and the Ecstacy." Unpublished paper on construction work in author's file.

———. 1984b. Letter to author, July 17.

Joyce, Rosemary. 1989. *A Bearer of Tradition: Dwight Stump, Basketmaker.* Athens: University of Georgia Press.

Joyner, Charles. 1964. "Up in Old Loray." *North Carolina Folklore* 12 (December): 20–24.

Juravich, Tom. 1990. Letter to author, December 21.

Kahn, Ed. 1960. "The Ballad of Coal Creek." *Sing Out* 10 (April): 18.

Kahn, Kathy. 1972. *The Working Girl.* Voyager Records 305 (Seattle).

Kamphaus, Carl. 1967. "Come All Ye Hearty Working Men." Text submitted to Swetnam. Letter in author's files.

*Kansas City Star* and *Kansas City Times. See* Levinson.

Kazin, Alfred. 1965. *Starting Out in the Thirties.* Boston: Little, Brown.

Kazin, Michael. 1987. *Barons of Labor.* Urbana: University of Illinois Press.

Keats, Ezra Jack. 1965. *John Henry: An American Legend.* New York: Pantheon.

Kellogg, Paul. 1909. "The Pittsburgh Survey," *Charities and the Commons* 21 (January 2): 517–26.

Kelly, Jim. 1988. "So Long, Joe." [Photo and caption.] *San Francisco Progress,* February 7.

Kelly, John W. 1883. "The Land League Band." [Sheet music.] Boston: Oliver Ditson.

———. 1892a. *J. W. Kelly Songster.* Chicago: Rossiter.

———. 1892b. "A Fight for Home and Honor at Homestead, Pa." [Sheet music (location unknown).] Chicago: Rossiter.

———. 1892c. "A Fight" In *Delaney's Song Book—No. 3.*

———. 1893. "A Fight" In Rossiter, *New "Ali Baba."*

———. Ca. 1894. "A Fight" In *J. W. Kelly's Irish Song-Book No. 1.* Chicago: Rossiter.

———. 1928. "Maloney, the Rolling Mill Man." In Stein, *Gems of Inspiration.*

Kemble, John. 1957. *San Francisco Bay: A Pictorial Maritime History.* Cambridge, Md.: Cornell Maritime Press.

Kerker, Sherwood. 1981. "A 'Pile Doe' on the New Lock and Dam" *St. Louis Labor Tribune,* October 22. Printed also in *Southern Illinois Labor Tribune,* same date.

King, Elspeth. 1987. "Popular Culture in Glasgow." In Cage, *Working Class in Glasgow,* 142–87.

Kiplinger, W. M. 1942. *Washington Is Like That*. New York: Harper.

Kizer, Benjamin. 1966. "Elizabeth Gurley Flynn." *Pacific Northwest Quarterly* 57: 110–12.

Klein, Frederick. 1971. "Ironworker Tom West Wrestles Steel Beams High above Ground." *Wall Street Journal*, March 4.

Klein, Joe. 1977. "Pete Seeger's Steelyard Benefit." *Rolling Stone*, March 10.

———. 1980. *Woody Guthrie: A Life*. New York: Knopf.

[Kline, Herbert]. 1935. "Editorial." *New Theatre* 2 (December): 3.

Knight, Edward. 1872–76. *Knight's American Mechanical Dictionary*. 3 vols. Boston: Hurd and Houghton.

Koch, Frederick. 1932. " 'Strike Song': A New Play of Southern Mill People." *The Carolina Play-Book*, June.

Kodish, Debora. 1986. *Good Friends and Bad Enemies*. Urbana: University of Illinois Press.

Kornbluh, Joyce. 1964. *Rebel Voices*. Ann Arbor: University of Michigan Press. Rev. ed., 1988. Chicago: Kerr.

———. 1960–92. Correspondence and conversations with author.

Korson, George. 1938. *Minstrels of the Mine Patch*. Philadelphia: University of Pennsylvania Press.

———. 1943. *Coal Dust on the Fiddle*. Philadelphia: University of Pennsylvania Press.

———. 1949. *Pennsylvania Songs and Legends*. Philadelphia: University of Pennsylvania Press.

———. 1958. *Songs and Ballads of the Anthracite Miners*. Library of Congress AFS L16 (Washington, D.C.). LP remastered from field disks of 1946; released 1948 on 78-rpm set.

———. 1965. *Songs and Ballads of the Bituminous Miners*. Library of Congress AFS L60 (Washington, D.C.). LP remastered from field disks of 1935–40.

———. 1955–67. Correspondence and conversations with author.

Kortum, Karl. 1960—90. "Annals of the Steam Schooners." [Transcribed oral histories.] Held at San Francisco National Maritime Museum.

Kraft, Joseph. 1973. "Cox's Claim to the Tapes." *Washington Post*, July 24.

Krause, Paul. 1987. *The Battle for Homestead, 1880–1892: Politics, Culture and Steel*. Pittsburgh: University of Pittsburgh Press.

Krueger, Thomas. 1967. *And Promises to Keep*. Nashville: Vanderbilt University Press.

Kruizinga, J. H. 1984. *Haal Op Die Hei!* Almere: International Construction Equipment; Amsterdam: Buijten & Schipperheijn.

*Lake Charles American Press*. 1912. "For Tampering with Witnesses." October 23.

Lampman, Robert. 1951. "The Rise and Fall of the Maritime Federation of the Pacific, 1935–1941." In Wallace, *Proceedings,* 64–68.

Lance, James. 1926. "Editorial Notes: Response to Holbrook." *American Mercury* 7 (April): xxx–ii.

Lang, Frederick. 1943. *Maritime.* New York: Pioneer Publishers.

Larkin, Margaret. 1929a. "Ella May's Songs." *Nation* 129 (October 9): 382–83.

———. 1929b. "The Story of Ella May." *New Masses* 5 (November): 2–4.

———. 1929c. "Tragedy in North Carolina." *North American Review* 228 (December): 686–90.

———. 1933. "Revolutionary Music." *New Masses* 8 (February): 27.

———. 1936. "From the Drama Mailbag." [Comments on *Let Freedom Ring.*] *New York Times,* November 22.

Larrowe, Charles. 1955. *Shape-up and Hiring Hall.* Berkeley: University of California Press.

Latham, R. E. 1965. *Revised Medieval Latin Word List.* London: British Academy.

Layamon. *See* Bell, Madden.

Leach, Maria. 1949. *Standard Dictionary of Folklore, Mythology and Legend.* New York: Funk and Wagnalls.

Leadbitter, Mike. 1971. Liner notes for *Nothing but the Blues.* CBS Records 66278 (London).

Leary, James. 1990. Letter to author, February 24.

———. 1991. *Midwestern Folk Humor.* Little Rock, Ark.: August House.

Lees, Dan. 1973. *Rape of a Quiet Town.* New York: Walker.

Legman, Gershon. 1968. *Rationale of the Dirty Joke.* New York: Grove.

Lemisch, Jesse. 1986. "I Dreamed I Saw MTV Last Night." *Nation* 243 (October 18): 361, 374–76. *See also* letters to Lemish in *Nation,* December 13 (658, 672), and his response, December 20 (700, 702–4).

Leonard, W. B. 1892. "The Strike at Homestead." [Sheet music.] Cortland, N.Y.: Author.

"Let Them Wear Their Watches Fine." 1939. New York: People's Song Library. Typescript copy in author's files.

Levinson, Edward. 1935. *I Break Strikes.* New York: McBride.

Lewis, Austin. 1914. "Movements of Migratory Unskilled Labor in California." *New Review* 2 (August): 458–65.

Lewis, D. R. 1892. "A Song." *National Labor Tribune,* August 27.

Lewis, Forrest. 1958. "Ballad of Coal Creek." Collected by Ed Kahn. Text and music in Kahn, *Sing Out.*

Lewis, Reese. 1875. "March of the Rolling Mill Men." *National Labor Tribune,* March 30.

[Library of Congress]. 1942. *Check-list of Recorded Songs in the English Language in the Archive of American Folk Song to July, 1940.* Washington: The Archive.

Lieberman, Robbie. 1989. *"My Song Is My Weapon."* Urbana: University of Illinois Press.

*Lightning over Braddock.* 1988. [Film by Tony Buba.] Pittsburgh.

Lindsay, Vachel. 1914. *The Congo and Other Poems.* New York: Macmillan.

"Lines on the Homestead Strike." 1892. [Broadside.] In the collection of the University of Pittsburgh Press.

Lingenfelter, Richard. 1974. *The Hardrock Miners.* Berkeley: University of California Press.

"L'Internationale." In Seeger and Reiser, *Carry It On!* 95–98.

Lish, T. G. 1961. "Word List of Construction Terms." *Publication of the American Dialect Society* 36: 25–31.

———. 1982. Telephone interview with author, July 7.

Little, Alan. 1961. *Foundations.* London: Arnold.

Local 34. 1943a. *How to Organize the Job: A Handbook for Stewards.* San Francisco: Pile Drivers Local 34.

———. 1943b. *Victory through Unionism.* San Francisco: Pile Drivers Local 34.

———. 1946. *Pile Butt Special.* [Mimeographed newsletter.] San Francisco: Pile Drivers Local 34.

Local 77. Ca. 1911. *Working Rules.* San Francisco: Pile Drivers Bridge and Structural Iron Workers Union Local 77. Copy in Bancroft Library, University of California, Berkeley.

[Local 401.] 1971. "An Informal History of the Iron Workers." Philadelphia: Local 401, International Association of Bridge, Structural and Ornamental Ironworkers. Written initially by a Local 401 member. First printed, 1971, in six issues of the *Ironworker:* February, April, June, August, October, and January, 1972. Subsequently reproduced by photocopy; also reprinted in various pamphlet formats.

Lockwood, Yvonne. 1984. "The Joy of Labor." *Western Folklore* 43: 202–11.

Logsdon, Guy. 1989. *"The Whorehouse Bells Were Ringing" and Other Songs Cowboys Sing.* Urbana: University of Illinois Press.

Lokasenna. *See* Hollander.

Lomax, Alan, et al. 1967. *Hard Hitting Songs for Hard-Hit People.* New York: Oak.

Lomax, John. 1910. *Cowboy Songs and Other Frontier Ballads.* New York: Sturgis and Walton.

Long, Haniel. 1935. *Pittsburgh Memoranda.* Santa Fe: Rydal.

Lorant, Stefan. 1964. *Pittsburgh.* Garden City, N.Y.: Doubleday.

*Los Angeles Examiner.* 1904. "San Pedro Starts a New Local Union." March 8.

*Los Angeles Times.* 1904. "Pinhead's Game Spoilt." March 14.

Ludwig, Ella. [1927.] *History of the Harbor District of Los Angeles.* [Los Angeles]: Historic Record Company.

Lumpkin, Grace. 1927. "White Man." *New Masses* 3 (September): 7–8.

———. 1930a. "A Southern Cotton Mill Rhyme." *New Masses* 5 (May): 8.

———. 1930b. "Letters from Readers: 'The Cotton Mill Rhyme.' " *New Masses* 6 (June): 22.

———. 1932. *To Make My Bread.* New York: Macaulay.

———. 1939. *The Wedding.* New York: Lee Furman. Reprinted, 1976. Carbondale: Southern Illinois University Press.

———. 1962. *Full Circle.* Boston: Western Islands.

———. 1974. Interview with Jacquelyn Hall, King and Queen Court House, Va., August 6.

———. 1979. Interview with author, Columbia, S.C., August 23.

Lumpkin, Katharine Du Pre. 1947. *The Making of a Southerner.* New York: Knopf.

———. 1974. Interview with Jacquelyn Hall, Charlottesville, Va., August 4.

Lundeberg, Harry. 1955. "Statement." *In Hearings of House Committee on Merchant Marine and Fisheries. Labor-Management Problems of the American Merchant Marine* 3: 441–536. 84th Congress, first Session.

Luster, Michael. 1990. "The Return of the Menhaden Chanteymen." *NC Arts* (spring): 1–3.

MacDonald, Jerome. 1983. Interview with author, Boston, April 19.

MacDowell, Marcia. 1984. "Visual Descriptions of the Work Experience." *Western Folklore* 43: 178–92.

MacKinnon, Alan, and Hal Hunt. 1981. *Glossary of Foundation Terms.* Springfield, N.J.: Deep Foundation Institute.

Mackley, F. R. 1981. "The History and Development of Sheet Piling." In Young, *Piles and Foundations,* 100–188.

Madden, Frederic. 1847. *Layamon's Brut, or Chronicle of Britain.* London: Society of Antiquaries.

Magden, Ronald. 1991. *The Working Longshoreman.* Tacoma, Wash.: R-4 Typographers.

Magden, Ronald, and A. D. Martinson. 1982. *The Working Waterfront.* Tacoma, Wash.: ILWU Local 23.

Magil, A. B. 1933. "To Make My Bread." *New Masses* 8 (February): 19–20.

———. 1939. "Trotsky Admits It." *New Masses* 32 (August 1): 15–16.

Maher, J. Peter. 1984. "German Fink in American Slang." *Comments on Etymology* 13 (15): 3–4.

Maier, Otto. 1990. Interview with author, Wilmington, Calif., December 10.

Mainiero, Lina. 1981. *American Women Writers.* 4 vols. New York: Ungar.

Mally, Lynn. 1990. *Culture of the Future.* Berkeley: University of California Press.

Malone, Michael. 1981. *The Battle for Butte.* Seattle: University of Washington Press.

Manning. *See* Furnivall.

Marcus, Charles. 1963. Interview with Patricia Wilson and author, Detroit, October 5.

Marcuse, Maxwell. 1959. *Tin Pan Alley in Gaslight.* Watkins Glen, N.Y.: Century House.

Markholt, Ottilie. 1961. Interview with author, Tacoma, June 2.

———. 1987. Letters to author, September 28 and November 24.

———. 1993. *Maritime Solidarity: The 1934 Strike* (forthcoming).

———. 1993. *Maritime Solidarity: The Federation, 1935–38* (forthcoming).

———. *See also* Gill.

Marks, Edward. 1935. *They All Sang.* New York: Viking.

Martin, Douglas. 1988. "Praised Bus Driver, 53, to Get a Rare Farewell." *New York Times,* April 13.

Martin, James. 1895. *Which Way, Sirs, the Better? A Story of Our Toilers.* Boston: Arena.

*The Masses and the Millionaires — The Homestead Strike.* [Educational film.] 1973. New York: Robert Saudek Associates.

Mathews, Jane De Hart. 1967. *The Federal Theatre, 1935–1939.* Princeton: Princeton University Press.

Mathews, Mitford. 1951. *A Dictionary of Americanisms on Historical Principles.* 2 vols. Chicago: University of Chicago Press.

———. 1959. Letter to author, October 29.

Matson, Art. 1977. Interview with Karl Kortum, San Francisco, April 18.

Mayhew, Augustus. 1858. *Paved with Gold.* Rev. ed., 1971. London: Cass.

Mayo, Elton. 1933. *Human Problems of an Industrial Civilization.* Cambridge: Harvard University Press.

McCallum, Brenda. 1988. "Songs of Work and Songs of Worship." *New York Folklore* 14: 9–33.

McCarl, Robert. 1974. "The Production Welder: Product, Process and the Industrial Craftsman." *Western Folklore* 30: 243–53.

———. 1984. " 'You've Come a Long Way—And Now This Is Your Retirement.' " *Journal of American Folklore* 97: 393–422.

———. 1988. "Occupational Folklife in the Public Sector: A Case Study." In Feintuch, *The Conservation of Culture,* 132–53.

———. 1970–92. Correspondence and conversations with author.

McCarn, David. 1930. "Cotton Mill Colic." Victor 40274 (78-rpm disc). Reissued on *Singers of the Piedmont,* Folk Variety Records 12505 (Bremen).

McCarthy, Charles. 1975. "1915 Trolley Strike Was Bitterly Fought." *Wilkes-Barre Sunday Independent,* May 11.

McClintock, Harry K. 1957. Interview with Sam Eskin, San Pedro, Calif., November 17.

———. 1972. *Harry K. McClintock "Haywire Mac."* Folkways Records 5272 (New York).

———. 1981. *Hallelujah! I'm a Bum.* Rounder Records 1009 (Somerville, Mass.).

McClymer, John. 1974. "The Pittsburgh Survey, 1907–1914." *Pennsylvania History* 41: 169–86.

McConnaughey, Gordon. 1991. Interview with author, Tacoma, Wash., April 12.

McCoy, Joe. 1930. "Pile Drivin' Blues." Vocalion 1612 (78-rpm disc). Reissued on *10 Years in Memphis 1927–1937,* Yazoo Records 1002 (New York).

McCulloch, Walter. 1958. *Woods Words.* Portland: Oregon Historical Society.

McDavid. *See* Mencken.

McGovern, Michael. 1899. *Labor Lyrics, and Other Poems.* Youngstown, Ohio: Vindicator.

McKay, Ian. 1981/82. "Historians, Anthropology, and the Concept of Culture." *Labour/Le Travailleur* 8/9: 185–241.

McKenney, Ruth. 1939. *Industrial Valley.* New York: Harcourt.

McKiernan-Terry. 1949. *Pile Driving Equipment.* [120-page illustrated catalog.] New York: The company.

McLain, Marjorie. 1986. *Peter Tamony: Word Man of San Francisco's Mission.* Folsom, Calif.: Wellman.

McNeely, Dave. 1982. "Era Passes as Clayton Goes Home." *Austin American-Statesman,* May 31.

McPhee, John. 1977. *Coming into the Country.* New York: Farrar, Straus, and Giroux.

McQuiston, F. B. 1901. "The Strike Breakers." *Independent* 53 (October 17): 2456–58.

Meloney, William. 1905. "Strikebreaking as a Profession." *Public Opinion* 38 (March 25): 440–41.

Mencken, Henry. 1936. *The American Language.* 4th ed. *Supplement One,* 1945; *Supplement Two,* 1948. New York: Knopf.

———. 1963. *The American Language. Abridged with Annotations and New Material.* ed. Raven McDavid. New York: Knopf.

Mers, Gilbert. 1988. *Working the Waterfront.* Austin: University of Texas Press.

Messenger, Betty. 1972. "Picking Up the Linen Threads." *Journal of the Folklore Institute* 9 (June): 18–27.

Mezzrow, Milton. 1946. *Really the Blues.* New York: Random House.

Middleton, J. H. 1891. "Pons." In Smith, *Dictionary,* 456–60.

Milburn, George. 1930. *The Hobo's Hornbook.* New York: Washburn.

———. 1931. "Circus Words." *American Speech* 24: 351–54.

Miles, Dione. 1986. *Something in Common: An IWW Bibliography.* Detroit: Wayne State University Press.

Miner, Curtis. 1989. *Homestead: The Story of a Steel Town.* Pittsburgh: Historical Society of Western Pennsylvania.

Miner, Worthington. 1936. "Actors' Repertory Company." *New York Times,* November 15.

Mitchell, Joseph. 1949. "Mohawks in High Steel." *New Yorker,* September 17. Reprinted in 1960 in Wilson, *Apologies to the Iroquois.*

Mitchell, Louise, 1946. "Will Geer Rounds Corner of 25 Years in the Theatre." *Daily Worker,* June 4.

Mitgang, Herbert. 1985. "Alfred Hayes, 74, a Novelist, Poet and Screenplay Writer." *New York Times,* August 15.

Mlotek, Eleanor, and Joseph Mlotek. 1988. *Pearls of Yiddish Song.* New York: Workmen's Circle, Education Department.

Moise, Lionel C. 1910. "The Workin' Stiff." *Industrial Worker,* November 17.

*Montana Standard.* 1938. "Old-time Butte Man Succumbs." [Matt Kiely obituary.] September 14.

Monteleone, Vincent. 1945. *Criminal Slang.* Boston: Christopher.

Montgomery, David. 1987. *The Fall of the House of Labor.* Cambridge: Cambridge University Press.

Moreno, Johnny. 1990. Interview with author, Wilmington, Calif., December 10.

Morgan, D. T. 1892. "A Song for the Day." *National Labor Tribune,* October 8.

Morin, Paul. 1920. "Report of President." *Bridgemen's Magazine* 20 (May): 212–13.

Morken, Paul. 1964. "58 Fruitful Years of Construction: The Story of Ben C. Gerwick, Inc." *American Builders* 8 (May): 1–13.

Morris, Richard. 1946. *Government and Labor in Early America*. New York: Columbia University Press.

Morton, Alfred. 1892. "A Parody on the 'Blue Bells of Scotland.'" *National Labor Tribune*, December 8.

Munoz, Michael. 1986. *"Pilebutt": Stories and Photographs about Pile Driving*. San Leandro, Calif.: Pilebutt Press.

———. 1982–92. Conversations with author.

Murphy, Francis. 1978. "TV Writer-Producer, ex-Portlander Dies." *Oregonian*, August 31.

Myers, Bill. 1990–92. Conversations and correspondence with author.

Nash, June. 1989. *From Tank Town to High Tech*. Ithaca: State University of New York Press.

[Nasmyth]. 1885. *James Nasmyth: Engineer, An Autobiography*. Ed. Samuel Smiles. London: Murray.

Nason, Harold. 1961. Letter to editor [includes text of "I Want to Die a Poor Man"]. *Sing Out* 11 (February): 66. Reprinted from *Boston Globe*.

*Nautical Magazine*. 1898. "Speculative Underwriting." Vol. 67 (May): 355.

Neckam. *See* Wright.

Nellis, Eric. 1977. "Labor and Community in Massachusetts Bay, 1630–1666." *Labor History* 18: 525–44.

Nelson, Bruce. 1988. *Workers on the Waterfront*. Urbana: University of Illinois Press.

Nelson, Donald Lee. 1973. "'Walk Right in Belmont': The Wilmer Watts Story." *JEMF Quarterly* 9:91–6.

Nelson, Raymond. 1984. *Kenneth Patchen and American Mysticism*. Chapel Hill: University of North Carolina Press.

Nennius. *See* Giles, Stevenson.

*New Songs for Butte Mining Camp*. 1918. Butte, Mont.: Century.

*Newsweek*. 1935. "Labor." Vol.. 6 (November 16): 19–20.

———. 1936. "Propaganda." Vol. 8 (July 25): 21.

*Niles National Register*. 1845. "The Propeller 'Massachusetts.'" October 25.

Norton, Sally Osborn. 1980. "A Historical Study of Actor Will Geer, His Life and Work in the Context of Twentieth-Century American Social, Political, and Theatrical History." Ph.D. diss., University of Southern California.

O'Bang, "Patsy." 1913. "Its Rip Roaring Revolution." [Los Angeles] *Citizen*, April 11. Reprinted in *Miners' Magazine* 13 (April 24): 5.

Odell, George. 1927–49. *Annals of the New York Stage.* 15 vols. New York: Columbia University Press.

Odets, Clifford. 1935. "Letter, Praise from Mr. Odets." *New York Times,* November 17.

Odum, Howard, and Guy Johnson. 1916. *Negro Workaday Songs.* Chapel Hill: University of North Carolina Press.

[OED]. 1884–1928. *Oxford English Dictionary.* 10 vols. Oxford: Clarendon. Supplements 1933, 1972, 1976, 1982, 1986. 2d ed., 20 vols., 1989.

Ohrlin, Glenn. 1974. *The Hell-Bound Train.* Urbana: University of Illinois Press.

[OLD]. 1968. *Oxford Latin Dictionary.* Oxford: Clarendon.

*Old English Chronicle. See* Earle, Garmonsway, Giles, Rositzke, Savage, Thorpe, Whitelock.

Oliver, Robert. 1932. "Junglese." *American Speech* 7: 339–41.

Olmsted, Roger. 1972. *C. A. Thayer and the Pacific Coast Lumber Schooner.* Los Angeles: Ward Ritchie.

O'Neill, Eugene. 1922. *The Hairy Ape.* New York: Boni and Liveright.

Ord, John. 1930. *The Bothy Songs and Ballads of Aberdeen, Banff and Moray, Angus and the Mearns.* Paisley: Gardner.

Osborn, James Dean. 1969. Interview with Brooks Penney, San Francisco. Transcript in author's file.

Osborn, Mrs. J. D. (Frances). 1983. Interview with author, Redwood City, Calif., April 7.

*Outlook.* 1915. "The Strike at Wilkes-Barre." Vol. 111: 825–26.

*Out of Darkness.* 1990. [Film.] Washington, D.C.: United Mine Workers of America.

"Overalls and Snuff." 1914. [Cleveland] *Solidarity,* August 1; [San Francisco] *Organized Labor,* August 1.

Owen, William. 1912. "Editorial." [Los Angeles] *Regeneracion,* April 27. Reprinted as "Wobbly Gene" in *Industrial Worker,* May 9.

Palmer, Bryan. 1978. "Discordant Music." *Labour/Le Travailleur* 3: 5–62.

———. 1981/82. "Classifying Culture." *Labour/Le Travailleur* 8/9: 153–83.

Parker, Carleton. 1920. *The Casual Laborer and Other Essays.* New York: Harcourt, Brace and Howe.

Partridge, Eric. 1949. *A Dictionary of the Underworld.* London: Routledge.

Patchen, Kenneth. 1934. "Joe Hill Listens to the Praying." *New Masses* 13 (November 20): 8–9.

Patri, Giacomo. *See* Local 34, two booklets, 1943.

Patterson, Daniel. 1991. *Sounds of the South.* Chapel Hill: Southern Folklife Collection, University of North Carolina Library.

Peattie, Roderick. 1952. *The Black Hills.* New York: Vanguard.

Peña, Manuel. 1985. *The Texas-Mexican Conjunto.* Austin: Center for Mexican-American Studies, University of Texas.

Penney, Brooks. 1969. Transcript of interview with James Dean Osborn in author's files.

Perkins, Jasper. 1990. Interview with author, Wilmington, Calif., December 10.

Pesotta, Rose. 1944. *Bread upon the Waters.* New York: Dodd, Mead.

Peters, Harry. 1977. *Folk Songs out of Wisconsin.* Madison: State Historical Society.

Peterson, Charles. 1976. *Building Early America.* Radnor, Pa.: Chilton.

Pettis, Ashley. 1934. "Marching with a Song." *New Masses* 11 (May 1): 15.

Phillips, Utah. 1981. *We Have Fed You All for a Thousand Years.* Aural Tradition Records 103 (Vancouver, B.C.); Philo Records 1076 (Cambridge, Mass.).

Pilcher, William. 1972. *The Portland Longshoremen.* New York: Holt, Rhinehart & Winston.

*Pile Butt Special. See* Local 34.

*The Pittsburgh Survey.* 1910–14. 6 vols., Ed. Paul Kellogg. Authors: Elizabeth Butler, Margaret Byington, Crystal Eastman, John Fitch. New York: Charities Publication Committee for the Russell Sage Foundation.

Ploium, Joe. 1984. Letters to author, October 18 and 31.

Pohl, Frances. 1989. *Ben Shahn: New Deal Artist in a Cold War Climate, 1947–1954.* Austin: University of Texas Press.

Pollock, Theodora. 1914. "The Tragedy of the Hop Fields." *Everyman* 8 (April–May): 2–13.

Poole, David. 1977. *Land and Liberty: Anarchist Influences in the Mexican Revolution.* Montreal: Black Rose.

Pope, Liston. 1942. *Millhands and Preachers.* New Haven, Conn.: Yale University Press.

Pound, Louise. 1943. "Nebraska Strong Men." *Southern Folklore Quarterly* 7: 133–43.

———. 1949. "Nebraska's Antoine Barada Again." *Nebraska History* 30: 286–94.

Pouget, Emile. 1913. *Sabotage.* Chicago: Kerr. Translated by Arturo Giovannitti from *Le Sabotage,* Paris, 1910.

Powderly, John. 1971. Interview with author, Homestead, Pa., May 24.

Powers, Charlene. 1978. *The New Uff-Da.* Crosby, N.D.: Journal.

Prescott, Kenneth. 1973. *The Complete Graphic Works of Ben Shahn.* New York: Quadrangle.

Preston, William. 1971. "Shall This Be All?" *Labor History* 12: 434–53.

Quam-Wickham, Nancy. 1990. Interview with author, Albany, Calif., September 9.

Queenan, Charles. 1983. *The Port of Los Angeles.* Los Angeles: Harbor Department.

Quinn, Alonzo. 1961. *Design and Construction of Ports and Marine Structures.* New York: McGraw-Hill.

Quint, Howard. 1953. *The Forging of American Socialism.* Columbia: University of South Carolina Press.

Rabkin, Gerald. 1964. *Drama and Commitment.* Bloomington: Indiana University Press.

Rammel, Hal. 1990. *Nowhere in America.* Urbana: University of Illinois Press.

[Random House]. 1966. *Random House Dictionary of the English Language.* New York: Random House. 2d ed., 1987.

Ranke, Kurt. 1955. "Schwank und Witz als Schwundstufe." In Dolker, *Festschrift für Will-Erich Peuckert,* 41–59.

Read, Allen Walker. *See* Stacey.

Realf, Richard. 1878. "Hymn of Pittsburgh." *National Labor Tribune,* February 23.

Reaney, P. H. 1977. *A Dictionary of British Surnames.* 2d ed. London: Routledge & Kegan Paul.

Redfield, Robert. 1947. "The Folk Society." *American Journal of Sociology* 52: 298–308.

Rediker, Marcus. 1987. *Between the Devil and the Deep Blue Sea.* Cambridge: Cambridge University Press.

Reed, Merl. 1971. "Lumberjacks and Longshoremen: The I.W.W. in Louisiana." *Labor History* 13: 41–59.

Reeve, Carl. 1935. "Southern Mill Hands in a Vivid Play." *Daily Worker,* November 11.

———. 1984a. "The Great Gastonia Strike." *Political Affairs* 63 (March): 37–40.

———. 1984b. "Gastonia: The Strike, the Frameup, the Heritage." *Political Affairs* 63 (April): 23–31.

Reid, John. 1914. "Reid's Confession as Contained in the Following Affidavit." With unsigned news report, "Spies Control I.W.W. in Akron." *Solidarity,* January 17.

Reilly, John. 1974. "Images of Gastonia." *Georgia Review* 28: 498–517.

Rengo, Oscar. 1910. "Hiring a Pink." *Industrial Worker,* December 29.

Renshaw, Patrick. 1978. *The Wobblies.* New York: Doubleday.

Renwick, Roger. 1990. Letter to author, April 2.

Resner, Herbert. 1936. *The Law in Action During the San Francisco Longshore and Maritime Strike of 1934.* Berkeley: Works Progress Administration, Alameda County.

Reuss, Richard. 1960–86. Correspondence and conversations with author.

———. 1967. "The Ballad of 'Joe Hill' Revisited." *Western Folklore* 26: 187–88.

———. 1971. "American Folklore and Left-Wing Politics: 1927–1957." Ph.D. diss., Indiana University.

———. 1979. "Folk Music and Social Conscience: The Musical Odyssey of Charles Seeger." *Western Folklore* 38: 221–38.

———. 1983. *Songs of American Labor, Industrialization and the Urban Work Experience: A Discography.* Ann Arbor: Labor Studies Center, University of Michigan.

Reynolds, Gary, and Beryl Wright. 1989. *Against the Odds.* Newark: Newark Museum.

Richards, Sam. 1993. "The Joe Hill Legend in Britain." In Green, *Songs about Work.*

Richmond, Al. 1973. *A Long View from the Left.* Boston: Houghton Mifflin.

Rideout, Walter. 1956. *The Radical Novel in the United States.* Cambridge: Harvard University Press.

Ridley, Frederick. 1970. *Revolutionary Syndicalism in France.* Cambridge: Cambridge University Press.

Riedel International. 1983. *Imagineering a Better World.* [64-page illustrated booklet.] Portland, Ore.: The company.

Riley, Henry. 1868. *Memorials of London and London Life in the Thirteenth, Fourteenth, and Fifteenth Centuries.* London: Longmans, Green.

Riley, Henry. 1983. Interview with author, Boston, April 20.

Robbin, Ed. 1939. "Will Geer Comes Home." *People's World,* July 6.

Roberts, Harold. 1944. *The Rubber Workers.* New York: Harper.

Roberts, Randy. 1985. "Words Enough to Fill a Life." *Writing Words* 2 (May/June): 5–10.

Roberts, Warren. 1978. "Tools on Tombstones." *Pioneer America* 10: 107–11.

Robinson, Earl. 1986a. Interview with Rebecca Conard, Santa Barbara, October 15.

———. 1986b. Interview with author, San Francisco, October 29.

———. 1986c. "I Dreamed I Saw Joe Hill Last Night." *Talkin' Union* 14: 13.

Robinson, Jesse. 1920. *The Amalgamated Association of Iron, Steel and Tin Workers.* Baltimore: Johns Hopkins.

Rodechko, James. 1976. *Patrick Ford and His Search for America*. New York: Arno Press.

Roediger, David. 1989. Interview with author, Columbia, Mo., October 15.

Roediger, David, and Franklin Rosemont. 1986. *Haymarket Scrapbook*. Chicago: Kerr.

Rogers, John. 1968. "Research Paper over the Jurisdiction of Dock Building and Pile Driving." [Photocopy.] Washington, D.C.: United Brotherhood of Carpenters & Joiners of America.

———. 1989. Letter to author, July 6.

Rogin, Larry. 1977. Letter to author, March 24.

*Rolling Stone*. 1969. "Random Notes." June 28.

Romaine, Anne. 1985. *Take a Stand*. Flying Fish Records 323 (Chicago).

Roosevelt, Eleanor. 1937. "Letter on Let Freedom Ring." In Detroit Federal Theatre, *Production Bulletin*.

Rosemont, Franklin. 1985. Letter to author, March 17.

———. 1988. "A Short Treatise on Wobbly Cartoons." In Kornbluh, *Rebel Voices*, rev. ed. 425–43.

———. 1989. Letter to author, September 17.

Rosenack, Charles. 1982. " 'A Person Has to Have Some Work to Do' S. L. Jones, Woodcarver." *Goldenseal* 8 (spring): 47–53.

Rosenberg, Harold. 1970. "Reverence Is All." *Art News* 68 (January): 27–29. Reprinted in 1973 in *Discovering the Present*. Chicago: University of Chicago Press.

Rosenberg, Neil. 1993. "An Icy Mountain Brook." In Green, *Songs about Work*.

Rositzke, Harry. 1951. *The Peterborough Chronicle*. New York: Columbia University Press.

Rossiter, Will. 1893. *New "Ali Baba" Song Book*. Chicago: Rossiter.

———. 1898. *"How to Write a Song" and Become Wealthy*. Chicago: Rossiter.

Rovere, Richard. 1964. "A Reporter at Large—The Campaign: Goldwater." *New Yorker* 60 (October 3): 201–17.

Royko, Mike. 1988. "Speakes the Fink Trips on Tongue." *Chicago Tribune*, April 18.

Rubens, Lisa. 1985. *The Big Strike*. Virginia City, Nev.: Silver Dollar.

Rubenstein, Harry. 1989. "Symbols and Images of American Labor." *Labor's Heritage* 1 (April): 36–51 and (July): 344–49.

Russakoff, Dale. 1992. "The Final Shift: When Workers Become Obsolete." Four-part series. *Washington Post*, April 12–15.

Russell, Phillips [Union Man]. 1912. "The Newspaper War in Chicago." *International Socialist Review* 13 (July): 7–11. "The Strike on Chicago Papers." (July): 12–15.

Ryan, Frederick. 1936. *Industrial Relations in the San Francisco Building Trades.* Norman: University of Oklahoma Press.

Safire, William. 1987. "On Language: Goons and Ginks and Company Finks." *New York Times Magazine,* November 1.

Salerno, Salvatore. 1989. *Red November, Black November.* Albany: State University Press of New York.

Salvatore, Nick. 1989. " 'Lest We Forget': The Paintings of Ralph Fasanella." *Labor's Heritage,* October 24–31.

Salzman, L. F. 1967. *Building in England down to 1540.* Oxford: Clarendon.

Sandburg, Carl. 1927. *The American Songbag.* New York: Harcourt, Brace.

*San Diego Evening Tribune.* 1912. "Editorial: Raising Vagrants to the Dignity of Great Criminals." March 4.

Sandoz, Marie. *See* Pound, Louise.

Sanfield, Steve. 1986. *A Natural Man: The True Story of John Henry.* Boston: Godine.

*San Francisco Chronicle.* 1980. "A Fink in the Gang of Four." November 25.

———. 1988. "Why the Earth Wobbles Like a Clothes Washer." July 14.

———. 1990a. "Choreographers: Ballet's Wobbly Future." February 4.

———. 1990b. "Hubble's Wobble Stops." May 5.

*San Francisco Examiner.* 1966. "Old 'Wobblie,' Pal Now Non-Students." February 9.

Sapoznik, Henry. 1981. Brochure notes for *Kapelye: Future & Past.* Flying Fish Records 249 (Chicago).

———. 1991. "Motl der Opreyter." In *Pearls of Yiddish Song.* [Audiocassette recording.] New York: Workmen's Circle.

Savage, Anne. 1982. *The Anglo-Saxon Chronicles.* London: Phoebe Phillips/Heinemann.

Sayles, John. 1987. *Thinking in Pictures: The Making of the Movie "Matewan."* Boston: Houghton Mifflin.

Schneider, Linda. 1982. "The Citizen Striker: Workers' Ideology in the Homestead Strike of 1892." *Labor History* 23: 47–66.

Scholl, Eric. 1991. *The Return of Joe Hill.* [Video-cassette.] Chicago: Prairie Grass Productions.

Schrader, Paul. 1983. Interview with Gary Crowdus and Dan Georgakas on *Blue Collar.* In Georgakas, *The Cineaste Interviews,* 205–15.

Schwartz, Stephen. *Brotherhood of the Sea.* New Brunswick: Transaction Books.

Schwendinger, Robert. 1989. *Maritime Arts and Crafts.* San Francisco: San Francisco Craft and Folk Museum.

Scott, Jack. 1975. *Plunderbund and Proletariat*. Vancouver, B.C.: New Star.

Scott, Leroy. 1905. " 'Strike-Breaking' as a New Occupation." *World's Work* 10: 6199–204.

Seeger, Charles. 1984. Interview with Vivian Perlis. In *Copland*, 225.

Seeger, Mike. 1965. *Tipple, Loom & Rail*. Folkways Records 5273 (New York).

Seeger, Pete. 1956. *American Industrial Ballads*. Folkways Records 5251 (New York).

———. 1974. Letter to author, May 1.

———. 1977. "Johnny Appleseed Jr." [Includes text and music for "The Homestead Strike."] *Sing Out* 25 (January): 38–9.

———. 1980. *Pete Seeger: Singalong*. Folkways Records 36055 (New York).

Seeger, Pete, and Bob Reiser. 1985. *Carry It On!* New York: Simon & Schuster.

Seidman, Harold. *Labor Czars*. New York: Liveright.

Semien, Sidney. 1971. "Keep on Pushin'." In *Nothing but the Blues*. CBS Records 66278 (London).

Seroff, Doug. 1986. *Birmingham Quartet Anthology*. Clanka Lanka Records 144001/002 (Sweden).

Serrin, William. 1988. "Requiem for a Steel Town." *New York Times*, September 5.

Shapiro, Irwin. 1945. *John Henry and the Double Jointed Steam-Drill*. New York: Messner.

Shattuck, Roger. 1989. "The Redding of America." *New York Review of Books*, March 30.

Shay, Frank. 1930. *Here's Audacity*. New York: Macaulay.

[Sheldon, Roger.] 1981a. "Hard Work, 'Folded' Feelings Mark Progress of Three Women Members of the Union." *Carpenter* 101 (January): 21.

———. 1981b. [Cover photo collage.] *Carpenter* 101 (April).

———. 1982a. "First 'Pile Doe' in Missouri." *Carpenter* 102 (February): 27.

———. 1982b. " 'Pile Does' Abound in Seattle Area." *Carpenter* 102 (May): 21.

———. 1983. "The Pounding World of Pile Bucks and Does." *Carpenter* 103 (July): 8–9, 38.

Shulman, David. 1988. "Follow-Up on Fink." *Comments on Etymology* 18 (3): 3–4.

Silber, Irwin. 1956. Brochure notes for *American Industrial Ballads*. Folkways Records 5251 (New York).

———. 1959. "Trouble Down at Homestead." *Sing Out* 9 (winter): 18–9.

———. 1977. Letter to author, April 14.

Silka, Henry. 1984. *San Pedro: A Pictorial History.* San Pedro, Calif.: San Pedro Bay Historical Society.

Simpson, Robert. 1900. "The Hoffman Mine Song." Text in *Baltimore Sun,* April 12. Reprinted in *Tablelands Trails* (fall 1953) and *Festival of American Folklife,* Smithsonian Institution, 1972.

Sinclair, Upton. 1919a. *The Brass Check.* Pasadena, Calif.: Author.

———. 1919b. *Jimmie Higgins: A Story.* New York: Boni and Liveright.

———. 1924. *Singing Jailbirds.* Pasadena, Calif.: Author.

———. 1959. Letter to author, November 9.

Singal, Daniel. 1982. *The War Within.* Chapel Hill: University of North Carolina Press.

Singer, Charles. 1954–58. *A History of Technology.* 5 vols. Oxford: Clarendon.

Smiles. *See* Nasmyth.

Smith, C. Michael. 1979. "Grace Lumpkin." In Bain, *Southern Writers,* 287–88.

Smith, Gary. 1990. Letter to author, October 30.

Smith, Gibbs. 1969. *Joe Hill.* Salt Lake City: University of Utah Press. Reprint, 1984. Layton, Utah: Peregrine Smith.

Smith, Richard. 1982. Interview with author, San Francisco, November 16.

Smith, William. 1891. *A Dictionary of Greek and Roman Antiquities.* London: Murray.

Sorenson, Alice. 1902. "Andrew Carnegie's Library." *Miners' Magazine* 2 (May): 22–23. Poem reprinted from *San Francisco Advance.*

Spaeth, Sigmund. 1927. *Weep Some More My Lady.* Garden City, N.Y.: Doubleday, Page.

Spargo, John. 1913. *Syndicalism, Industrial Unionism and Socialism.* New York: Huebsch.

Sparrow, Ray. 1983. Interview with author, Mill Valley, Calif.: April 12.

Spiegelman, Judith. 1982. "Hayes, Alfred." In *Contemporary Authors,* 106: 232–34.

Spielman, Jean. 1923. *The Stool-Pigeon and the Open Shop Movement.* Minneapolis: American.

Spitz, Laurence. 1936. " 'Let Freedom Ring' on Tour." *New Theatre* 3 (November): 24–25.

Spottswood, Richard. 1975. *Songs of Labor & Livelihood.* Vol. 8 of *Folk Music in America.* 15 vols. Library of Congress, Music Division, Recording Laboratory (Washington, D.C.).

———. 1990. *Ethnic Music on Records.* 7 vols. Urbana: University of Illinois Press.

Sprague, Sidney. 1973. Interview with David Taylor, Rockland, Maine, July 12.

Stacey, Michelle. 1989. "Profiles—At Play in the Language." *New Yorker* 65 (September 4): 51–74.

Stack, Marcella Isgur. 1977. Interview with author, San Francisco, May 14.

Stangland, E. C. 1982. *Grandson of Norwegian Jokes*. Sioux Falls, S.D.: Norse.

[Stanwood, Mrs. Edward]. 1914. "Scrapbook of Clippings on the Wheatland Hopfield Riot." Presented to Bancroft Library, University of California, Berkeley.

Stearns, Marshall, and Jean Stearns. 1968. *Jazz Dance*. New York: Macmillan.

Steele, George. 1972. "John Henry Tall on Park Pedestal." *Charleston Gazette*, December 29. With Steele photo of statue on railroad flatbed car.

Stegner, Page. 1960. "Labor History in Fact and Song." *Caravan*, November 20.

———. 1967. "Protest Songs from the Butte Mines." *Western Folklore* 26: 157–67.

Stegner, Wallace. 1950. *The Preacher and the Slave*. New York: Houghton Mifflin.

Stein, Max. 1928. *Gems of Inspiration*. Chicago: Max Stein.

Stekert, Ellen. 1958a. *Songs of a New York Lumberjack*. Folkways Records 2254 (New York).

———. 1958b. Letters to author, September 20 and November 29.

———. 1966. "Four Pennsylvania Songs Learned before 1900, from the Repertoire of Ezra V. Barhigh." In Goldstein, *Two Penny Ballads and Four Dollar Whiskey*, 15–31.

Stephens, John. 1976. *Towers, Bridges and other Structures*. New York: Sterling.

Sterling Jubilee Singers. 1952. "Spirit of Philip Murray." Tiger 100 (78-rpm disc). Reissued on three LPs; *see* Glazer, Seroff, Spottswood. Original release under group name, CIO Singers at Bessemer, Ala.

Stevens, Henry. 1948. "Folk Music on the Midwestern Frontier, 1788–1825." *Ohio Archaelogical and Historical Quarterly* 57: 126–46.

Stevens, James. 1925. "Logger Talk." *American Speech* 1 (December): 135–40.

———. 1926. "Editorial Notes: Response to Lance." *American Mercury* 8 (July): xviii–xx.

Stevenson, Josephus. 1838a. *Nennii Historia Britonum*. London: Sumptibus Societatis.

———. 1838b. *Venerabilis Bedae Historia Ecclesiastica Gentis Anglorum*. London: Sumptibus Societatis.

Stewart, Jon. 1989. "The Enforcer." *San Francisco Chronicle,* July 7.

Stiff, Dean (pseudonym). *See* Anderson, Nels.

Stolberg, Benjamin. 1938. *The Story of the CIO.* New York: Viking.

Stone, Judy. 1972. "To the Devil and Back with Will Geer." *New York Times,* December 17.

Stowell, Myron. 1893. *"Fort Frick"; or, The Siege of Homestead.* Pittsburgh: Pittsburgh Printing.

Strachwitz, Chris. 1976. Brochure notes for *Chulas Fronteras.* Arhoolie Records 3005 (El Cerrito, Calif.).

Stratman-Thomas, Helene. 1966. Letter to author, May 14.

———. *See* Peters.

Strauss, Theodore. 1940. "Road Presents W. Geer." *New York Times,* January 21.

Strigalev, Anatoli, et al. 1990. *Art into Life: Russian Constructivism 1914–1932.* New York: Rizzoli.

Stutts, George Dumas. 1900. *Picked Up Here and There.* Raleigh, N.C.: Edwards & Broughton.

Stutts, John S. 1919. *"Picked Up Here and There" and "Gleanings from the Gullies."* Haw River, N.C.: Author.

Sundell, Jon, et al. 1975. *Brown Lung Cotton Mill Blues.* June Appal Records 006 (Whitesburg, Ky.).

Swart, George. 1990. Interview with author, Wilmington, Calif., December 10.

Swetnam, George. 1967a. "Songs of a Strike." *Pittsburgh Press, Sunday,* February 5.

———. 1967b. Correspondence with author.

Taft, Philip. 1978. "The Limits of Labor Unity: The Chicago Newspaper Strike of 1912." *Labor History* 19: 100–29.

Tamburro, Frances. 1974. "The Factory Girl Song." *Southern Exposure* 2 (spring): 42–51.

Tamony, Peter. 1948. "Fink." *American Notes & Queries* 8 (May): 29–30.

———. 1959. "Bessie: Vocumentary." *Jazz* 4: 281–85.

———. 1966. "Shanghai." *Western Folklore* 25: 41–45.

———. 1971. "The Wobblies." *Western Folklore* 30: 49–54.

———. 1980. "Material from Peter Tamony on Fink." *Comments on Etymology* 9 (15): 11–26.

———. 1954–85. Correspondence and conversations with author.

———. See also McLain.

Taplin, Eric. 1985. *The Dockers' Union.* Leicester: Leicester University Press.

Tauber, Chaim. Ca 1947. "Motl der Operator." Asch 6018 (78-rpm disc). Song appeared previously in sheet music, 1934, and in film, *Motel the Operator,* 1939.

Taylor, Archer. 1951. *English Riddles from Oral Tradition.* Berkeley: University of California Press.

Taylor, David. 1990. Letter to author, January 3.

Taylor, Joshua. 1976. *America as Art.* Washington, D.C.: Smithsonian Institution Press.

Taylor, Lori Elaine. 1990. Brochure notes for *Don't Mourn—Organize.* Smithsonian/Folkways Records 40026 (Washington, D.C.).

*Theatre Arts Monthly.* 1936. Photo and caption for *Let Freedom Ring.* Vol. 20 (January): 31.

Thompson, E. P. 1968. "English Trade Unionism and Other Labour Movements before 1790." *Bulletin of the Society for the Study of Labour History* 17 (autumn): 19–24.

———. 1972. " 'Rough Music': Le Charivari Anglais." *Annales ESC* 27: 285–312.

Thompson, Fred. 1955. *The I.W.W.: Its First Fifty Years.* Chicago: Industrial Workers of the World. Reprinted and updated, 1976.

———. 1960. "Wobbly Folklore: Thompson Reviews Article about John Neuhaus." *Industrial Worker,* November 30.

———. 1964. Letter to Tony Bubka, February 5.

———. 1988. "Introduction: What Is This IWW?" In Kornbluh, *Rebel Voices.*

———. 1959–85. Correspondence and conversations with author.

Thompson, Merry. 1980. *The Miracle of a Muddy Tide Flat.* Wilmington, Calif.: General Phineas Banning Residence Museum.

Thomson, Mortimer Neal. 1855. *Doesticks: What He Says.* New York: Livermore.

Thornton, Richard. 1912. *An American Glossary.* London: Francis.

Thorp, N. Howard "Jack." 1966. *Songs of the Cowboys.* Revised by Austin and Alta Fife from editions of 1908 and 1921. New York: Potter.

Thorpe, Benjamin. 1861. *The Anglo-Saxon Chronicle, According to the Several Original Authorities.* 2 vols. London: Longman.

*Time.* 1935. "Let Freedom Ring." Vol. 26 (November 18): 40.

Tippett, Tom. 1932. *Mill Shadows.* Katonah, N.Y.: Brookwood Labor College.

Trautmann, William. 1909. *Industrial Unionism: New Methods and New Forms.* Chicago: Kerr.

Troyen, Carol. 1987. *Charles Sheeler.* Boston: Little, Brown.

Tullos, Allen. 1989. *The Habits of Industry.* Chapel Hill: University of North Carolina Press.

*Turnaround.* 1976. [Documentary film, 28 minutes.] University Park, Pa.: WPSX-TV, Pennsylvania State University.

Turner, George. 1913. "The Puzzle of the Underworld." *McClure's* 41 (July): 99–111.

*TV Guide.* 1974. "The World's Oldest Hippie." Vol. 22 (October 26): 21–24.

Tveitmoe, Olaf. 1914. "The Wobley's Warning." [San Francisco] *Organized Labor,* August, 4.

*Twentieth Century Authors.* 1942. "Grace Lumpkin." New York: Wilson. *First Supplement,* 604.

Union Man. *See* Russell.

Uran, Marshall. 1983. Interview with author, San Francisco, April 8.

Urgo, Joseph. 1985. "Proletarian Literature and Feminism." *Minnesota Review* 24: 64–85.

[Vancouver, Wash.] *Columbian.* 1969. "William 'Pop' Burke Dies Following Illness." November 28.

Van Kleek, Mary. 1913a. *Women in the Bookbinding Trade.* New York: Survey Associates.

———. 1913b. *Artificial Flower Makers.* New York: Survey Associates.

Van Valen, Nelson. 1984. "Cleaning up the Harbor." *Southern California Quarterly* 66: 147–72.

Vincent, Robert. 1960. "Mine Fires." *Columbus Dispatch Magazine,* February 21.

Vitruvius. *See* Granger.

Vlach, John Michael. 1981. *Charleston Blacksmith: The Work of Philip Simmons.* Athens: University of Georgia Press.

Vlach, Richard. 1982. Interview with author, San Francisco, November 16.

———. 1991. Interview with author, Berkeley, August 3.

Vogel, Robert. 1976. "Building in the Age of Steam." In Peterson, *Building Early America,* 119–34.

Vorse, Mary Heaton. 1929. "Gastonia." *Harper's* 159: 700–710.

Wace. *See* Bell, Madden.

Wagner, Jack. 1978. Interview with Harold Rossman. Typescript by Harry Sheer for Radical Elders Oral History Project, Berkeley.

———. 1982–83. Interviews with author, San Francisco, December 10 and 16; May 16 and 20.

Wald, Alan. 1981. "Remembering the Answers." *Nation* 233 (December 26): 708–11.

Walker, Thomas. 1989–92. Correspondence and conversations with author.

Wallace, Mrs. Owen. 1966. Letter to author, March 7. Includes her undated newspaper story "World Famous Mine Fire at New Straitsville Breaking into the Open Again."

Wallace, Robert. 1951. *Proceedings of the Twenty-fifth Annual Conference of the Pacific Coast Economic Association.* [Pullman, Wash.]: The association.

Wall, Joseph. 1970. *Andrew Carnegie.* New York: Oxford University Press.

Wallin, "Dust." 1919. "Stoolpigeon." [Drawing] *One Big Union Monthly,* April.

Walsh, William. 1896. *Curiosities of Popular Customs.* London: Lippincott.

Ward, Donald. 1972. "The Fiddler and the Beast." *Fabula* 13: 108–21.

———. 1987. Letter to author, May 7.

Ward, Martin. *See* Herling.

Ware, Herta. 1938. "Through the South with a Drama Group." *Sunday Worker,* August 14.

Watkins, Percy. 1991. Interview with author, Tacoma, April 14.

Watkins, Stewart. 1983. Interview with author, Boston, April 19.

Watts, Wilmer. 1929. "Cotton Mill Blues." Paramount 3254 (78-rpm disc). Reissued on *Paramount Old Time Tunes,* JEMF Records 103 (Los Angeles), and *Poor Man, Rich Man,* Rounder Records 1026 (Somerville, Mass.).

Weales, Gerald. 1971. *Clifford Odets: Playwright.* New York: Pegasus.

Webb, W. C. 1891. "Strike of Boy Trappers at Coal Creek." *United Mine Workers Journal,* September 3.

[Webster's]. 1934. *Webster's New International Dictionary of the English Language.* 2d ed. Springfield: Merriam.

———. 1988. *Webster's New World Dictionary of American English.* 3d college ed. New York: Webster's.

Wehman, Henry. 1892. *Homestead Strike Songster.* Elephant folio broadsheet.

Weisbord, Vera Buch. 1977. *A Radical Life.* Bloomington: Indiana University Press.

Wentworth, Harold, and Stuart Berg Flexner. 1960. *Dictionary of American Slang.* New York: Crowell.

West, Don. 1935. "Southern Organizer on 'Let Freedom Ring.'" *Daily Worker,* November 18.

West, George. 1921. "Andrew Furuseth and the Radicals." *Survey* 47 (November 5): 207–9.

———. 1923. "Andrew Furuseth Stands Pat." *Survey* 51 (October 15): 86–90.

West, Hedy. 1969. *Hedy West Songbook.* Erlangen: Gekeler.

*Western Worker.* 1933. "15 at Southern California Youth Day; Battle Cops." June 12.

———. 1935. "Play Director Kidnapped and Beaten by Nazis." June 3.

White, Earl. 1981. "The United States *v.* C. W. Anderson et al.: The Wichita Case, 1917–1919." In Conlin, *At the Point of Production,* 143–64.

Whitelock, Dorothy. 1961. *The Anglo-Saxon Chronicle.* London: Eyre & Spottiswoode.

Whitten, Woodrow. 1948. "The Wheatland Episode." *Pacific Historical Review* 17: 37–42.

Widner, Ronna Lee. 1986. "Lore for the Folk." *New York Folklore* 12: 1–21.

Wiley, Stephen. 1982. "Songs of the Gastonia Textile Strike of 1929." *North Carolina Folklore* 30 (Winter): 87–98.

*Wilkes-Barre Record.* 1916. "Rioting in Many Parts of Valley." March 27.

Wilkinson, Frank. 1990. Interview with Phyllis Harrison, Everett, Wash., November 13. Tape at Life on the Sound, Tacoma.

Willens, Doris. 1988. *Lonesome Traveler: The Life of Lee Hays.* New York: Norton.

Williams, Ben. 1963a. "American Labor in the Jungle: Saga of One Big Union." Unpublished typescript in Labadie Collection, University of Michigan Library.

———. 1963b. Interview with Joyce Kornbluh, Lorain, Ohio.

———. 1963c. Letter to author, October 16.

Williams, Brett. 1983. *John Henry: A Bio-Bibliography.* Westport, Conn.: Greenwood.

Williams, Jay. 1974. *Stage Left.* New York: Scribner's.

Willis, Mrs. Walter. 1959. Letter to author, April 9.

Wilson, Edmund. 1960. *Apologies to the Iroquois.* New York: Farrar, Strauss and Cudahy.

Wilson, Mark. 1980. Brochure notes for *Rich Man, Poor Man.* Rounder Records 1026 (Somerville, Mass.).

Wilson, Patricia. 1963. Typescript summary of interview with Charles Marcus, Detroit, October 5. In author's files.

Wilson, William. 1976. "The Study of Mormon Folklore." *Utah Historical Quarterly* 44: 317–28.

Wiseman, Anne, and Peter Wiseman. 1980. *Julius Caesar: The Battle for Gaul.* New translation. Boston: Godine.

Witmark, Isadore, and Isaac Goldberg. 1939. *From Ragtime to Swingtime.* New York: Lee Furman.

Wixson, Douglas. 1985. "Introduction." In Conroy, *The Weed King and Other Stories,* xi–xxxi.

———. 1991. "Introduction." In Conroy, *The Disinherited,* 1–24.

———. 1993. *Worker-Writer in America: Jack Conroy and the Tradition of Midwestern Literary Radicalism, 1898–1990.* Urbana: University of Illinois Press.

Wolfe, Charles. 1976. "New Light on 'The Coal Creek March.' " *JEMF Quarterly* 12: 1–8.

Wolfe, Leon. 1965. *Lockout.* New York: Harper & Row.

Woodworth, Don. 1991. Letter to author, July 15.

———. 1992. "The Homestead Poets Recall the Civil War." In Demarest, *"The River Ran Red,"* 124–25.

Wortman, Roy. 1985. *From Syndicalism to Trade Unionism.* New York: Garland.

WPA Writers' Program. 1943. *Copper Camp.* New York: Hastings House.

Wright, Carroll. 1904. *Regulation and Restriction of Output.* Washington, D.C.: Government Printing Office. Includes "Origin of Ca' Canny," 721–36.

Wright, M. R. 1972. "The Underground Inferno in Ohio." *United Mine Workers Journal* (June 15): 25–26.

Wright, Thomas. 1863. *Alexandri Neckham: De Naturis Rerum.* London: Longman.

———. 1865. *A History of Caricature and Grotesque in Literature and Art.* London: Virtue Brothers. Reprinted, 1968. New York: Ungar.

Wyman, Mark. 1979. *Hard Rock Epic.* Berkeley: University of California Press.

Yarbrough, Slim. 1990. Interview with author, Wilmington, Calif., December 10.

Yellen, Samuel. 1936. *American Labor Struggles.* New York: Harcourt, Brace.

Young, Art. 1936. *The Best of Art Young.* New York: Vanguard.

Young, F. E. 1981. *Piles and Foundations.* London: Telford.

Young, Henry. 1981. *Haywire Mac and the Big Rock Candy Mountain.* Temple, Tex.: Stillhouse Hollow.

Young, Otis. 1970. *Western Mining.* Norman: University of Oklahoma Press.

Zampa, Al. 1986. Interview with author, San Francisco, July 22.

Zanger, Martin. 1969. "Politics of Confrontation." *Pacific Historical Review* 38: 383–406.

Zellers, Parker. 1971. *Tony Pastor: Dean of the Vaudeville Stage.* Ypsilanti: Eastern Michigan University Press.

Ziebarth, Marilyn. 1975. "R. D. Ginther, Workingman Artist and Historian of Skid Road." *California Historical Quarterly* 54: 263–71.

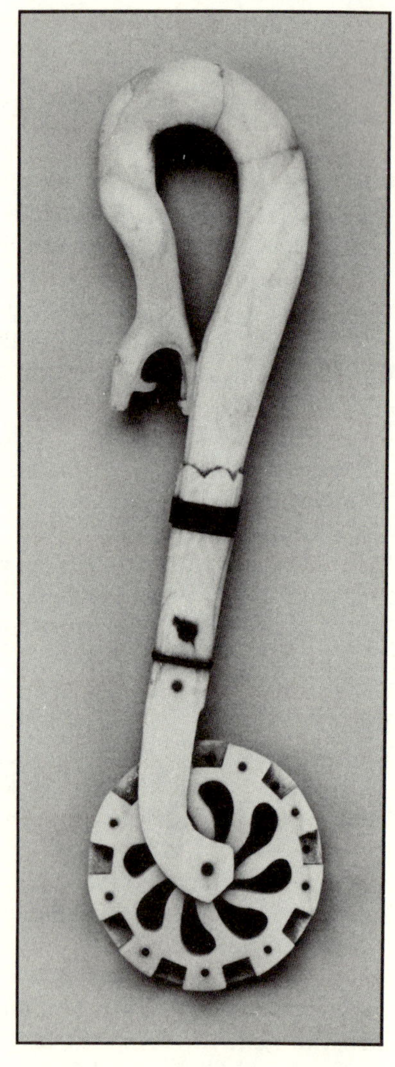

Scrimshaw jagging wheel

# Illustrations

# Index

**Folklore and Society**

George Magoon and the Down East Game War:
History, Folklore, and the Law
*Edward D. Ives*

Diversities of Gifts: Field Studies in Southern Religion
*Edited by Ruel W. Tyson, Jr., James L. Peacock,*
*and Daniel W. Patterson*

Days from a Dream Almanac
*Dennis Tedlock*

Nowhere in America: The Big Rock Candy Mountain
and Other Comic Utopias
*Hal Rammel*

The Lost World of the Craft Printer
*Maggie Holtzberg-Call*

Listening to Old Voices: Folklore in the Lives
of Nine Elderly People
*Patrick B. Mullen*

Wobblies, Pile Butts, and Other Heroes:
Laborlore Explorations
*Archie Green*